Model–Driven Software Development:
Integrating Quality Assurance

Jörg Rech
Fraunhofer Institute for Experimental Software Engineering, Germany

Christian Bunse
International University in Germany, Germany

 **INFORMATION SCIENCE REFERENCE**

Hershey · New York

Director of Editorial Content:	Kristin Klinger
Senior Managing Editor:	Jennifer Neidig
Managing Editor:	Jamie Snavely
Assistant Managing Editor:	Carole Coulson
Typesetter:	Jennifer Neidig
Cover Design:	Lisa Tosheff
Printed at:	Yurchak Printing Inc.

Published in the United States of America by
Information Science Reference (an imprint of IGI Global)
701 E. Chocolate Avenue, Suite 200
Hershey PA 17033
Tel: 717-533-8845
Fax: 717-533-8661
E-mail: cust@igi-global.com
Web site: http://www.igi-global.com

and in the United Kingdom by
Information Science Reference (an imprint of IGI Global)
3 Henrietta Street
Covent Garden
London WC2E 8LU
Tel: 44 20 7240 0856
Fax: 44 20 7379 0609
Web site: http://www.eurospanbookstore.com

Library of Congress Cataloging-in-Publication Data

Model-driven software development : integrating quality assurance / Jörg Rech and Christian Bunse, editor.

    p. cm.

  Summary: "This book provides in-depth coverage of important concepts, issues, trends, methodologies, and technologies in quality assurance for model-driven software development"--Provided by publisher.

  Includes bibliographical references and index.

  ISBN 978-1-60566-006-6 (hardcover) -- ISBN 978-1-60566-007-3 (ebook)

  1. Computer software--Development. 2. Model driven architecture (Computer science) I. Rech, Jörg. II. Bunse, Christian.

  QA76.76.D47M624 2009

  005.1--dc22

                         2008009115

British Cataloguing in Publication Data
A Cataloguing in Publication record for this book is available from the British Library.

All work contributed to this book set is original material. The views expressed in this book are those of the authors, but not necessarily of the publisher.

Table of Contents

Section I
Introduction: MDSD and Quality

Ariadi Nugroho, Leiden University, The Netherlands
Michel Chaudron, Leiden University, The Netherlands

Teade Punter, Embedded Systems Institute, The Netherlands
Jeroen Voeten, Embedded Systems Institute, The Netherlands & Eindhoven University
of Technology, The Netherlands
Jinfeng Huang, Eindhoven University of Technology, The Netherlands

Sowmya Karunakaran, MDA Research Initiative, Chennai, India

Anna E. Bobkowska, Gdańsk University of Technology, Poland

Section IV
QA for MDSD in Specific Domains

Detailed Table of Contents

Section I
Introduction: MDSD and Quality

Ariadi Nugroho, Leiden University, The Netherlands
Michel Chaudron, Technische Universiteit Eindhoven, The Netherlands

The quality of a model can be considered from many different perspectives. This chapter considers the following perspectives: First, is the model complete in the sense that it describes the information that developers need to know about a system? Second, to which degree does a model of a system corresponds with its implementation.

Teade Punter, Embedded Systems Institute, The Netherlands
Jeroen Voeten, Embedded Systems Institute, The Netherlands & Eindhoven University
of Technology, The Netherlands
Jinfeng Huang, Eindhoven University of Technology, The Netherlands

Model Driven Engineering looks like a promising approach to addressing the late integration and the difference in development productivity between disciplines in embedded systems design. This chapter provides a conceptual framework for understanding the possibilities and the flaws in quality assurance in the MDE design flow.

Chapter III

This chapter aims at highlighting the increased development productivity and quality that can be achieved by Model Driven Software Development (MDSD). The above statement is substantiated by discussing many experiments and case studies in the field of Model Driven development. The main emphasis lies on case studies for the measurement of the quality of the models.

Chapter IV

Successful realization of the model-driven software development visions in practice requires high-quality models. This chapter focuses on the quality of the models themselves and discusses context-free and context-dependent quality criteria for models. It then moves on to methods of evaluation that facilitate checking whether a model is good enough.

Section II
Evaluating the Model Quality

Chapter V

Techniques from model-driven software development are useful for analyzing the performance of a software architecture during early development stages. This chapter provides an overview of the Palladio Component Model (PCM), a special modeling language targeted at model-driven performance predictions. Software architects can use the results of the analytical models to evaluate the feasibility of performance requirements, identify performance bottlenecks, and support architectural design decisions quantitatively.

Chapter VI

This chapter describes work to facilitate the task of integrating measurement and redesign tools in modeling environments for Domain Specific Visual Languages (DSVLs). The developed DSVL called

SLAMMER includes generalizations of some of the more commonly used types of product metrics and frequent model manipulations, which rely on visual patterns for the specification of the elements that should be measured in each metric type.

One way of assessing quality in a given domain is to define domain metrics. This chapter presents the S metric, which is generic across metamodels and allows the easy specification of an open-ended, wide range of model metrics.

Section III
Improving the Model Quality

This chapter explores the emerging research domain of model-driven software refactoring that raises many new challenges. Based on a concrete case study with a state-of-the-art model-driven software development tool, AndroMDA, some of these challenges are explored in more detail. Furthermore, it proposes solutions to some of the encountered problems by relying on well-understood techniques of meta-modeling, model transformation, and graph transformation.

Class models are typically specified at a high level of abstraction and subsequently refined with textual constraints requiring significant expertise and effort. In this chapter, typical refinement problems for class models are identified and it is shown how a list of refinement tasks can be automatically compiled from a given model.

This chapter presents empirical data on several issues related to transitioning from code-centric (CC) to MDSD projects in industry. It first presents results from a set of experiments that evaluate how a domain-specific notation affects the effectiveness and efficiency of reading techniques used for inspecting models. Second, it presents a comparison of productivity increase when changing to MDSD projects from one of the large Swedish companies. Finally, it presents a short survey on the prioritization of products, projects, and resource metrics in MDSD projects.

Patrizio Pelliccione, University of L'Aquila, Italy
Davide Di Ruscio, University of L'Aquila, Italy
Henry Muccini, University of L'Aquila, Italy
Antonio Bucchiarone, IMT of Lucca, Italy

Model-based specifications of a component-based system permit to explicitly model the structure and behavior of components as well as their integration. This chapter proposes an architecture-centric model-driven approach to validate required properties and generate the system code. Requirements are elicited and used for identifying expected properties the architecture shall express. The architectural compliance to the properties is formally demonstrated, and the produced architectural model is used to automatically generate the Java code.

Silvia Abrahão, Valencia University of Technology, Spain
Marcela Genero, University of Castilla-La-Mancha, Spain
Emilio Insfran, Valencia University of Technology, Spain
José Ángel Carsí, Valencia University of Technology, Spain
Isidro Ramos, Valencia University of Technology, Spain

Usually, there are several ways to transform a source model into a target model. Alternative target models may have the same functionality but may differ in their quality attributes (e.g., understandability, modifiability). This chapter presents an approach to dealing with quality-driven model transformations. Specifically, it focuses on a specific set of transformations to obtain UML class diagrams from a requirements model.

Pankaj Kamthan, Concordia University, Canada

In this chapter, a semiotic framework for understanding and systematically addressing the quality of use case models is proposed. The quality concerns at each semiotic level are discussed and process- and product-oriented means to address them in a feasible manner are presented.

Section IV
QA for MDSD in Specific Domains

The automotive industry has already applied model-driven approaches for some time (usually in the form of Matlab/Simulink) and proves to be a fertile ground for advancing assurance methods for the maintainability of model-based systems. This chapter describes a two-dimensional quality metamodel and presents an instance that defines maintainability for MDSD with Matlab/Simulink and TargetLink. It exemplifies how such a model serves as the basis of all quality assurance activities and reports on experiences made in an industrial case study.

In the domain of automotive software engineering, there is a lack of automated checking for standard conformance. In this chapter, the model-based design of automotive vehicle functions is taken as an example to show how textual rules describing development standards to be met can be transformed into a formal notation using the open standards Meta Object Facility and Object Constraint Language.

Service-oriented architecture is a recent approach to software systems integration where quality aspects ranging from interoperability to maintainability and performance are of central importance for the integration of heterogeneous, distributed, service-based systems. This chapter presents an approach for addressing the quality of services and service-based systems at the model level in the context of model-driven service engineering.

This chapter introduces model-driven integration in complex information systems by giving two practical examples from the public utilities domain. The purpose of the first project (MINT) was to provide an integration approach allowing interoperability among several different legacy systems. Hence, the project itself only acted as a "bridge" between the systems. The second project (DER) was built from scratch and approached the challenge of integrating several existing third-party systems into the newly designed system. In this project, the main system is a core element and only needed to integrate existing legacy systems for specific tasks.

This chapter examines model-based design in the context of development of critical software in NASA's James Web Space Telescope. The chapter discusses the context and nature of this software development effort, and why they motivated the choice of model-based development approach. Illustrations are provided of the elements of model-based design that are proving to be beneficial. The chapter also considers how software assurance practices are being adapted to work with this approach.

Foreword

Modern model-driven development in its current, widely recognized form was born 10 years ago when the UML 1.0 proposal was submitted to the OMG. As a unification of the leading object-oriented methods existent at that time, UML 1.0 set aside trivial notation debates and galvanized the software engineering community into exploring the true potential of modeling. In the early years, models were primarily seen as an aid to analysis and design activities. By providing compact and easy-to-understand depictions of system properties, models were found to be useful for communicating ideas to customers and fellow developers, and for exploring design ideas. However, they were not regarded as central artifacts in the development process, but rather as imprecise, auxiliary visualizations of the "true" product – the code. As a result, there was little point in worrying about the quality of models – it was the quality of the code that mattered.

With the advent of true model-driven development during the last few years, however, all this has changed. Not only has the UML gone through several revisions, giving it a much more precise and well-documented abstract syntax and semantics, but a new generation of tools and transformation languages have emerged, which largely automate the translation of models into code. UML models therefore have a much tighter and well-defined relationship to code and are no longer regarded as unimportant, supplemental artifacts. Indeed, the day is not far off when models will become the primary development artifacts and traditional source code will be regarded as supplemental. But as the role of models becomes more central and more important, so does their impact on the overall quality of the software product. This means that instead of being of marginal interest, in the years to come the quality of models will play an ever more central role for the success of software projects and products.

Assuring quality in model-driven development is much more challenging and multi-faceted than quality assurance at the code level, however. First, model-driven development involves a lot more views and diagram types than code-level representations of software, and keeping all these different views consistent and optimized is much more difficult than maintaining a single, textual view of a software product. Second, since model-driven development regards the definition of model transformations as a normal part of software engineering, these are primary development artifacts in their own right, and must be subject to the same defect detection and quality assurance activities as other human-defined documents. Third, since the abstraction gap between primary (i.e., human-developed) artifacts and execution platforms is much greater when models are used to describe software rather than source code, the relationships between model properties and product properties is much more tenuous and ill-defined. A whole new genre of quality metrics therefore needs to be defined and their value as quality indictors needs to be established and experimentally confirmed. And last but not least, there is the issue of the expressive power and representation fidelity of the modeling notations themselves. Although the UML was a significant step forward over previous notations, it is certainly not the last word in visual representation languages, and a great deal of work still needs to be done to evaluate which notations best convey different types of information and are the least prone to errors.

Although the field is in its infancy, this book demonstrates that a lot of work has already been done and there is an active and vibrant research community studying the quality aspects of model-driven development. With the creation of this book, the editors and authors have compiled one of the most comprehensive and authoritative overviews of the state of the art in model-driven quality assurance available to date. The book therefore represents an important step in the evolution of model-driven development and helps turn it into a mature engineering discipline. There is currently no better or more extensive body of knowledge on quality assurance in model-driven development, and I hope you will be able to learn from the book as I have.

Colin Atkinson
University of Mannheim
May 2008

Preface

The success of the Unified Modeling Language (UML) reflects a growing consensus in the software industry that modeling is a key ingredient in the development of large and ultra-large software systems. Recent developments to industrialize the software development process are also using technologies such as components, model-driven architectures (MDA), and product lines. These technologies drastically alter the software development process, which is characterized by a high degree of innovation and productivity. MDA and model-driven software development (MDSD) focus on the idea of constructing software systems not by programming in a specific programming language but by designing models that are translated into executable software systems by generators. These characteristics enable designers to deliver product releases within much shorter periods of time compared to the traditional methods. In theory, this process makes it unnecessary to worry about for an executable system's quality, as it is "optimized" by the generators.

However, proponents of MDSD must provide convincing answers to questions such as "What is the quality of the models and software produced?" The designed models are a work product that requires a minimal set of quality aspects (e.g., the maintainability of models over a longer life-time). Furthermore, models created in the earlier phases of development (e.g. analysis and design) are often only used as an abstract template for the software and typically are of little value, unless they can be readily mapped to correct and efficient executable forms, which means high-level object-oriented programming languages. Any problem in the transformation path from requirements via models to code not only has a negative impact on the quality of the delivered software system, but also obstructs its future maintenance and/or reuse.

Quality assurance techniques such as testing, inspections, software analysis, model checking, or software measurement are well researched for programming languages, but their application in the domain of software models and model-driven software development is still in an embryonic phase. In general, quality assurance is related to all phases of the software lifecycle, is needed within all application domains, and comes in many different flavors, ranging from reviews and inspections via metrics and quality models to holistic approaches for the quality-driven development of software systems. The goals of quality assurance for model-driven software development are diverse and include the improvement of quality aspects such as maintainability, reusability, security, or performance. Quality assurance for model-driven software development will play an important role for the future wide-spread usage of model-driven architectures in general, as well as in specific application domains.

In order to foster the development of quality assurance research in MDSD and to give a solid overview of the field, we have brought together research and practice in this book.

MODEL-DRIVEN SOFTWARE DEVELOPMENT

Model-driven software development methods aim at supporting software engineers in producing large and ultra-large software systems that are very flexible, portable, and of high value to their customers. Basically, programmers are freed from the burden of tedious standard tasks, which are also a source of errors. It is envisioned that by systematically applying MDSD, the quality of software systems, the degree of reuse and thus, implicitly, the development efficiency will improve.

The core idea of MDSD is that models are becoming the "source code" of a system from which the executables are simply generated. Thus, models cover different abstraction layers, ranging from conceptual diagrams in the problem space to detailed low-level models adapted to a specific platform. In general, model-driven software development is the process of generating executable software systems from formal models, starting with computational independent models (CIMs) that are extended to platform independent models (PIMs) to be adapted into platform specific models (PSMs) and finally result in source code (e.g., Java). In other words, models now bridge the traditional gap between, human-readable requirements and source code. Contemporary approaches of MDSD also create platform specific skeletons (PSS), which have to be completed by programmers.

Typically, models have had a long tradition in software engineering and are used in many software projects. However, there is not one commonly used language for models used in software development. Software models may range from sketches on a whiteboard via UML diagrams to mathematical specifications.

In order to enable the automatic generation of executable models, these models have to follow a precisely defined syntax and semantic. One widespread language for depicting such models is the Unified Modeling Language (UML), but model-driven development is not necessarily bound to the UML. Other modeling languages (e.g., Petri-nets, MathLab, Modelica, etc.) are successfully applied and have their value. And while the UML provides a large selection of diagram types and a more formal specification language (e.g., OCL), the information contained within a model is often not sufficiently concise and precise (i.e., UML models often have to be enriched by textual specifications).

Nevertheless, by using the full power of the UML diagrams on different abstraction layers with accompanying textual specifications, we can model complete systems today. However, as with other work products such as source code, this opens the question of how to assure quality within model-driven development. Quality assurance in MDSD has to address quality issues at different abstraction levels and has to face the challenge of the very richness (and complexity) of the UML. Today, quality assurance is often used as a synonym for testing, but in reality it is a much wider discipline – it includes other techniques such as inspections or metrics. Even though model-based testing is a well-known way to use models for quality assurance, modeling has much more potential in this regard: Models can be verified before code is generated, requirements can be modeled and checked against design models, etc.

OVERALL OBJECTIVE OF THE BOOK

This book aims at providing an in-depth coverage of important concepts, issues, trends, methodologies, and technologies in quality assurance for MDSD. It focuses on non-testing approaches for quality assurance and discusses quality in the context of MDSD. This premier reference source presents original academic work and experience reports from industry that can be used for developing and implementing high-quality model-based software.

It is a comprehensive guide that helps researchers and practitioners in the model-driven software development area to avoid risks and project failures that are frequently encountered in traditional and agile software projects. The whole development process and the developed products (i.e., CIMs, PIMs, PSM, etc.) must be analyzed, measured, and validated from the quality point of view.

TARGET AUDIENCE

The topic of integrating quality assurance into model-driven software development is broad and comes in many different flavors. However, when applying model-driven development and quality assurance, the basic principles and concepts have to be known to all participants of such a project. This book provides a comprehensive overview to those who are interested in studying the field of quality assurance for model-driven software development. However, this book is not meant to be a textbook that supports lectures or self-studies for novices. This book is aimed at researchers, project managers, and developers who are interested in promoting quality assurance for model-driven software development, in further educating themselves, and in getting insights into the latest achievements.

VOLUME OVERVIEW

The following chapters provide significant details about the topics outlined in this introduction. All chapters describe innovative research and, where possible, experience collected in industrial settings. Therefore, this book provides significant contributions to both the research and practice of assuring quality in model-based development. Several case studies are presented as a means for illustrating approaches, methods, and techniques in order to provide evidence. Most authors use or refer to the Unified Modeling Language (UML) in their chapters as a means for modeling the problem or solution domain. However, it appears that the latest version of the UML (version 2.1.1) is not used consistently. Thus, it is important to note that all references to the UML cover versions 1.x to 2.x. In summary, the book is organized as follows:

- Section I gives an introduction to quality in model-driven software development, which is presented in four chapter (Chapters I to IV). The chapters cover quality in general, quality aspects, and quality models for quality assurance in model-driven software development.
- Section II presents three chapters (Chapters V to VII) that are concerned with the evaluation of software models. They cover techniques for obtaining objective information from models that support the measurement, evaluation, and assessment of the model's quality.
- Section III covers the improvement of a model's quality. Six chapters (Chapters VIII to XIII) present different techniques such as refactoring, inspections, and constraint checking that help to improve the quality of a model. The chapters address approaches from the viewpoint of quality criteria and describe how model-driven development might become quality-driven model-based development.
- Section IV presents four chapters (Chapters XIV to XVIII) on using quality assurance techniques for model-driven development in specific application domains. Most papers are devoted to the domain of embedded systems (esp. in the automotive domain) and report about experience collected in specific industrial environments.

In summary, this book provides an overview of state of the art approaches to quality assurance in model-driven software development and presents the main challenges surrounding the subject. Each of the following chapters presents a set of issues and problems commonly encountered when performing research on or applying model-driven development. All authors share their vision about the importance of quality issues and agree that quality has a strong impact on system development and deployment. We hope that the insights and experiences described in this book will provide readers with new research directions and valuable guidelines.

Jörg Rech and Christian Bunse
Editors

Acknowledgment

Our vision for this book was to gather information about methods, techniques, and applications for quality assurance in MDSD that does not focus on testing, but on other quality assurance techniques. This important field will see more attention in the future, and we wanted to collect and share this information with the community. Furthermore, we hope that this book will foster the distribution and exchange of ideas, experiences, and evidence across projects and organizational boundaries.

This vision has become a reality only because of the hard work of the chapter authors, and we want to thank them for their contributions. Many of the authors also served as reviewers for chapters written by other authors. Thanks go to all those who provided constructive and comprehensive reviews.

Furthermore, we want to thank the publishing team at IGI Global for their continuing support throughout the whole publication process. Deep appreciation and gratitude is due to Jessica Thompson, editorial assistant at IGI Global, and Julia Mosemann, editorial assistant at IGI Global, who supported us and kept the project on schedule.

Jörg Rech and Christian Bunse
The Editors
May 2008

Section I
Introduction:
MDSD and Quality

This introductory section presents several chapters that provide an overview of quality in general, its management, and its evaluation in the context of model-driven software development.

Chapter I
Managing the Quality of UML Models in Practice

Ariadi Nugroho
Leiden University, The Netherlands

Michael R. V. Chaudron
Leiden University, The Netherlands

ABSTRACT

Many studies have been carried out to investigate what makes up good quality software. Some of the early models that define the quality of software come from Boehm (1976) and McCall (1977). Works in this field of quality models have traditionally focused on quality of the final software product. Since the 1970's models of software have been used and this has recently attracted much attention through the popularity of model-driven software development (MDSD). However, quality of software models has rarely been considered (Lange & Chaudron, 2005). In the software development life cycle, the ability to assure software quality long before the testing phase may save a lot of money since less defects found in the testing phase will mean less effort to be allocated for rework. Currently, the importance of model quality is starting to gain attention from computer scientists. Work in this area has since focused on developing tools, metrics, and frameworks to improve the quality of models that guide implementation, particularly in the context of UML modeling which has become the de facto standard for building object oriented software. Quality of models can be considered from many different perspectives. In this chapter, we will consider the following perspectives: Firstly, is the model complete in the sense that it describes the information that developers need to know about a system? Secondly, we look at the degree in which a model of a system and an implementation correspond. This degree of correspondence indicates to what extent analyses of—or predictions based on the model are valid for the implementation. We present the main findings from case studies into quality of modeling in the software industry as well as findings from a survey amongst professional software developers. We also provide a discussion on the contemporary methods for design quality assessments.

INTRODUCTION

Despite the fact that the notions of good quality software have been around since four decades ago, many software companies are still struggling to get their software product into production without numerous defects. Defects can be interpreted as deviation from specification or expectation (Fenton & Neil, 1999).

Since defects will eventually affect the operation of software as the final product, the discussion on defects cannot neglect the notion of software quality. In general terms, the notion of quality is the absence of defects. Thus, if defect means deviations from specification or expectation, we can perceive quality as a conformance to specification and requirements/expectations.

In their search of qualifying aspects in software quality, computer scientists have come up with quality models that are generally constructed by quantitative approaches. Two of the most renowned quality models came from the work of Boehm, Brown, and Lipow (1976) and McCall, Richards, and Walters (1977). Boehm's quality model is shown in Figure 1.

While quality models are generally more focused on the quality characteristics of the final software product, many efforts have been devoted to prescribe standard procedures and processes so that eventually software will have the quality attributes as have been defined in many quality models. In this regard, SEI (Software Engineering Institute) has come up with the Capability Maturity Model (CMM) that is currently becoming the

Figure 1. Boehm's quality model (©2007 Ariadi Nugroho. Used with permission)

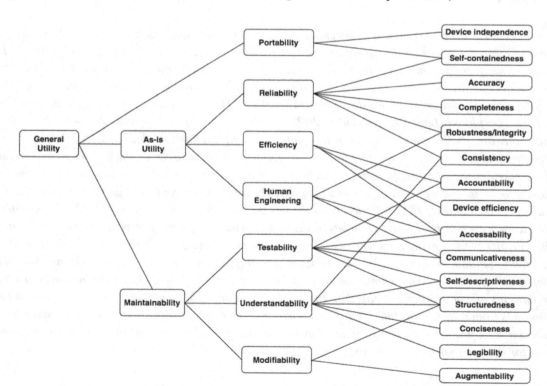

Figure 2. The ISO 9126 (©2007 Ariadi Nugroho. Used with permission)

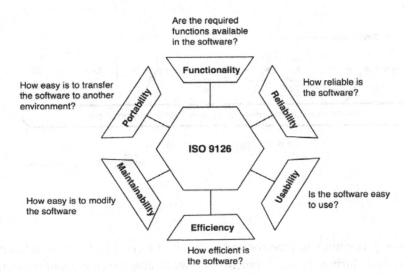

de facto standard in the area of software process improvement to achieve good quality software (Runeson & Isacsson, 1998).

The CMM prescribes five evolutionary stages, i.e. Initial, Repeatable, Defined, Managed, and Optimizing, which indicate the maturity level of an organization's software process. The CMM is particularly important to mention here because it defines software quality assurance as one of the key process areas in CMM level 2. The key components of the CMM's quality assurance is the presence of review and audit to assess the compliance of software process and the resulted products to a defined standards and procedures from which manager can react upon.

Another quality model that deserves attention is the ISO 9126. This quality model is based on McCall's model. Figure 2 illustrates the ISO 9126 quality model.

Below are the main two concepts that are important in concluding our discussion on soft-

ware quality. Figure 3 visualizes how these two concepts are put into the perspective of software development:

1. Software quality model is a set of software quality characteristics and their associations. These characteristics are generally quantifiable so that eventually a quality model can be a basis for assessing the quality of software products. Consequently, the nature of quality models is more product-oriented, i.e. in the form of final software product or transitional products of certain phases in the software development lifecycle.

2. The effort to assure that software will have certain quality attributes have led to the emergence of the so-called Software Quality Assurance. Instead of focusing merely on the products, SQA also put emphasis on the procedures and activities to assure the quality of the final products. It defines sets

Figure 3. SQA and software quality assessment in software development (©2007 Ariadi Nugroho. Used with permission)

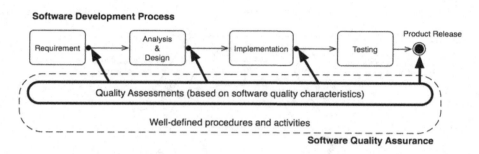

of activities or procedures to monitor and control a product during its development lifecycle so that at the end it will possess the expected quality attributes.

Figure 3 shows a software development lifecycle where each phase delivers a milestone that can be assessed in terms of its quality. These assessments can be quantitative in nature (e.g. using metrics) or qualitative through informal assessments such as peer review though the former is generally more preferable since it provides more objective and measurable results. Nevertheless, in order to be effective, these methods or techniques have to be organized into a well defined procedures and activities. These procedures and activities for instance, may prescribe guidelines in reviewing or auditing products, reporting the results, and following-up the recommendations. The quality assessments together with the procedures of how they must be done, reported, and followed up are essentially the very notion of software quality assurance.

Having discussed all the above notions, the main purpose of this chapter is to provide a discussion on how the efforts on managing software quality vary in theory and practice. However, special attention is given particularly on the effort in managing the quality of UML models. The structure of this chapter is as follows. In Section 2 we discuss the contemporary methods for design quality assessments. In Section 3 we discuss a case study of quality assurance in UML modeling. Subsequently, future trends, conclusion, and future research direction will be discussed in Section 4, 5, and 6 respectively.

CONTEMPORARY METHODS FOR DESIGN QUALITY ASSESSMENTS

As the focus of this chapter is on design quality assurance, i.e. the activity to monitor and control design's conformance to requirements and specifications, in this section we will discuss the methods and techniques for maintaining the quality of software design. From our observation in the literature, we identified three mainstreams in design quality assessment: design measurements, design inspections, and the use of formal methods. Thus, in the following passages we will further explore these approaches in terms of methods, characteristics, and how they can improve the quality of software designs.

Figure 4. Lange's framework for quality of UML models (©2007 Ariadi Nugroho. Used with permission)

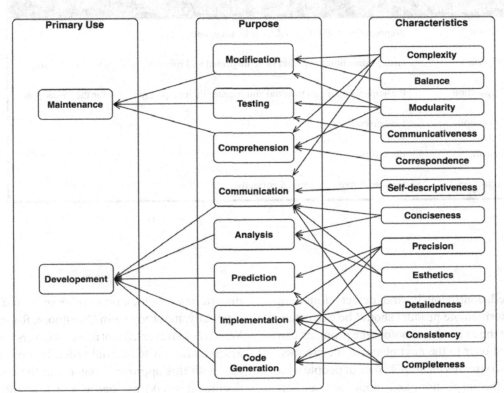

Quality Models for UML Models

A framework for quality of UML models was proposed by Lange and Chaudron (2005). This quality model differs from the traditional models of Boehm, McCall and the ISO 9126 in that it considers UML models as an intermediate product of software development that derives it quality from the degree by which it supports other software engineering activities. Figure 4 depicts Lange's quality framework of UML models.

A related, but more general approach to defining the quality of software models is the approach proposed by Lindland, Sindre, and Sølvberg (1994). Their approach distinguishes three categories: syntactic, semantic and pragmatic. As such these criteria are not directly related to any specific goal, nor to any specific modeling notation. Leung and Bolloju (2005) have specialized this framework to evaluate UML models produced by novice software engineers.

Design Inspection

Fagan's seminal work (Fagan, 1976) laid the very foundations of current software inspection methodologies. Inspection was defined as a formal, efficient, and economical method of findings errors in design and code, and which main aim is to detect and correct defects as close as possible to the point where they were created. He proposed that software inspection must be

Table 1. Summary of Fagan's inspection process

Operations	Objectives
Planning	Preparing the right material, people, time, and place.
Overview	Group education over what to be inspected and role assignments to participants.
Preparation	Participants learn the material and prepare their respective roles for the inspection.
Inspection	Find errors.
Rework	Fix errors.
Follow-up	Ensure all fixes are applied correctly.

performed continuously and defects found in every intermediate product should be corrected, and meet the exit criteria before the products can be handed over to the next phase of the process. Fagan also stresses the importance of people who perform the inspection, i.e., moderator, author, reader, and tester, and the process of the inspection. Table 1 provides a summary of the phases in Fagan's inspection process and their main objectives (Fagan, 1986).

Additionally, it is worth noting other quality assurance method, namely walkthrough. Walkthrough is very similar to inspection except that it does not practice repeatable process and data collection (Fagan, 1986). Thus, walkthrough can be considered as an informal inspection.

The Development of Inspection Methods

One of the problems with inspection is that the defects found are often trivial or cosmetics in nature (Laitenberger, 2002). This might be due to inexperienced reviewers or the absence of clear guidelines in the inspection process (e.g.,

uncertainty of which types of error to find). Additionally, the study from Dunsmore, Roper, and Wood (2001) revealed that most reviewers perform assessment in a sequential order. It is presumed that with this approach contents at the end of a document would not get as much attention as those at the beginning of the document.

Nowadays there exist variances of inspection methods that were proposed to improve the effectiveness of inspection in finding defects. Table 2 provides a comparison of six well-known inspection methods and Fagan's, based on the study of Aurum, Petersson, and Wohlin (2002). The black bars (except that of Fagan) indicate the phases in which the listed methods have proposed improvement from Fagan's inspection. For instance, Active Design Review (Parnas & Weiss, 1985) proposed different approach in the preparation and the inspection meeting.

Reading Techniques

This section focuses on reading techniques that aid reviewers to effectively inspect and find defects in software artifacts.

Table 2. Well-known inspection methods and their processes

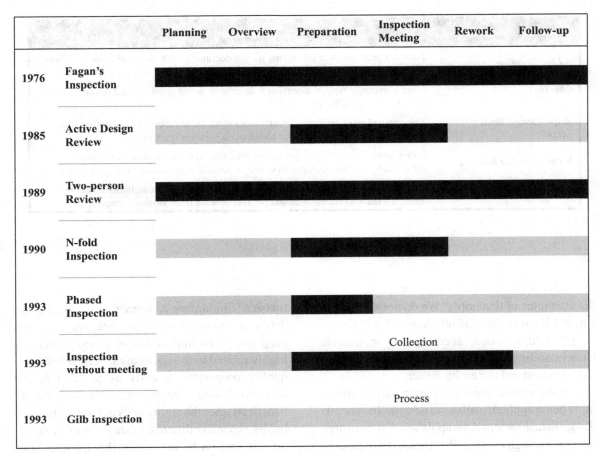

	Planning	Overview	Preparation	Inspection Meeting	Rework	Follow-up
1976 Fagan's Inspection						
1985 Active Design Review						
1989 Two-person Review						
1990 N-fold Inspection						
1993 Phased Inspection						
1993 Inspection without meeting			Collection			
1993 Gilb inspection			Process			

Reading technique is "a series of steps or procedure which purpose is to guide an inspector in acquiring a deep understanding of the inspected software product" (Laitenberger, 2002). As noted previously, the way a reviewer reads a document is influential to the effectiveness in finding defects. Recalling the previous example, when a document is read sequentially it might be that the contents inspected later will get less attention as the attention level of a reviewer is degrading over time. Table 3 lists five well-known reading techniques for inspecting software artifacts.

Design Measurement

Fenton (1999) provides a formal definition of measurement:

Measurement is the process by which numbers or symbols are assigned to attributes of entities in the real world in such a way as to describe them according clearly defined rules (p. 20).

With the above definition, Fenton suggests that when we measure an entity, we actually measure

Table 3. A summary of reading techniques

Reading Technique	Description
Ad-hoc Reading	Informal procedures of inspecting design documents. No clear guideline is defined for the process.
Checklist	More systematic way of assessing a document. Some questions are formulated and must be answered by reviewers.
Active Design Review (ADR)	This method requires active involvement from the reviewers (e.g., writing code fragment of models) in addition to answering review questions.
Scenario-based Reading	Using scenario to guide inspectors in detecting defects. Each reviewer uses different, systematic techniques to search for different, specific classes of faults.
Perspective-based Reading	Focus on the point of view or needs of the customers or consumers of a document. Thus this method encourages quality assessments from various perspectives.

the attributes of that entity. We do not measure a car, but we measure the attributes of a car, e.g., height, width, speed, acceleration, or weight. Understanding the attributes of an entity helps us to understand the entity better.

For the same reason, measurement is increasingly being applied to software designs. In general, design measurement is the application of measurement to a design artifact. By employing measurement to a design we can characterize and describe certain aspects of the design in quantitative terms. However, design artifacts, e.g., UML models, are only intermediate products of a software system. Therefore, the application of design measurement is primarily aimed at understanding, predicting, controlling, or improving the quality attributes of the final software product.

The emphasis of this chapter is on quality assurance of UML designs. Therefore, for the rest of this section we restrict our discussion to object-oriented design measurement.

Object-Oriented Design Metrics

The practices of measurement in software design have been primarily revolving around the use of

metrics (Chidamber & Kemerer, 1994). We can define design metrics as some measures of design properties. The importance of design metrics is highly related to the necessity to assess software quality properties as early as possible in the software development process. This is primarily beneficial since the ability to fix defects earlier will be less expensive than to fix them later in the development process. By measuring the characteristics of an object-oriented design, it is expected that the quality attributes of the final software product can be predicted and/or improved. In this respect, previous study by Briand, Wüst, Daly, and Porter (2000) and Abreu and Melo (1996) investigated the relationships and impacts of object-oriented design metrics on software quality.

The most renowned design metrics to date originate from the work of Chidamber and Kemerer (1994). They developed six object-oriented design metrics that are still widely used in various design measurement activities nowadays. Table 2.4 provides brief definition of these metrics.

Many of these metrics have been the subjects of further investigation to reveal their relations with system quality attributes such as reliability, maintainability, and understandability. The work

Table 4. Chidamber and Kemerer's metrics suite for object-oriented design

Metrics	Definition
Weighted Method per Class (WMC)	The sum of weighted methods in a class. Each method is weighted based on its complexity value.
Depth of Inheritance Tree (DIT)	The length of inheritance tree of a class.
Number of Children (NOC)	The number of immediate subclasses of a class in the inheritance hierarchy
Coupling between Object Classes (CBO)	The number of other classes to which it is coupled.
Response for a Class (RFC)	The number of methods that can be potentially executed in response to a message received by an object of that class.
Lack of Cohesion in Methods (LCOM)	The degree of similarity between methods in a class. The similarity is determined by the use of common instance variables.

of Briand, Daly, Porter and Wüst (1998) investigated the relation of object-oriented metrics with the probability of fault detection in system classes. Likewise, the work of Basili, Briand, and Melo (1996) validated Chidamber and Kemerer's metrics as predictors of error-prone classes. El-Emam, Melo and Machado (2001) proposed a prediction model of faulty classes using object-oriented metrics. Harrison, Counsell, and Nithi (2000) specifically investigated the impact of inheritance to the maintainability of object-oriented systems.

Although the above previous works confirmed the usefulness of metrics in predicting quality attributes such as maintainability and reliability, there are some well-known cautions for using them. Metrics seldom provide a complete explanation of a quality property. As stated by Harrison, et al. (2000) for instance, DIT metric does not provide us with a complete view of the inheritance hierarchy of a system—thus, DIT metric *alone* does not provide clear explanations of system quality attributes such as maintainability or understandability. Additionally, researchers regularly find a correlation between a metric and

a quality property, but this does not necessarily provide a causal explanation. See the work of Fenton and Neil (1999) for further observation in this particular issue.

With the potential of metrics for predicting some quality aspects of object-oriented systems, employing them for monitoring and controlling design quality will be beneficial. However, this activity will be quite time-consuming if performed manually. Although there exist many tools that support metrics evaluation from code, few have been developed to analyze design metrics, e.g., SDMetrics (www.sdmetrics.com) and MetricView (www.win.tue.nl/empanada/metricview). These tools can read XMI files produced by UML CASE tool in order to calculate metrics values of UML design documents. With the metrics data of the designs, further design quality analysis can subsequently be performed.

The Use of Formal Methods for Design Quality Assessment

In the previous sections we have discussed design inspection and design measurements as methods to assess the quality attributes of design documents. In this section we discuss the application of mathematically rigorous approach to assure design quality.

The term formal methods refer to the use of mathematically based techniques for describing system properties. Using formal methods, people can specify, develop, and verify systems in a systematic, rather than ad hoc, manner (Wing, 1990). One of the features formal methods have to offer is preciseness in design specifications. It is argued that the imprecise semantics of most current object-oriented methodologies and graphical techniques often leads user and analysts to ambiguous interpretation, which at the end results in the introduction of defects (Aleman & Alvarez, 2000). In this particular respect, many works, e.g., from France, Evans, Lano, and Rumpe, (1998) and from McUmber and Cheng (2001), have been devoted to formalizing object-oriented design notations, to increase their preciseness. It is promised that with a formalized modeling notation, UML models become amenable to rigorous analysis, e.g., consistency check within and across models (France et al., 1998).

A study that proposed a method and techniques for checking the consistency of UML model comes from the work of Engels, Kuster, Heckel, and Groenewegen (2001). He proposed a method for specifying and analyzing consistency of object-oriented models, particularly with respect to their behavioral aspects. For this purpose a tool called Consistency Workbench (Engels, Heckel, & Kuster, 2003) has been developed. The consistency checking is performed using partial translations of models into a formal method, through which the formulation and verification of semantic consistency conditions are possible.

Another attempt to create more precise UML models was performed using the OCL (Object Constraint Language). The OCL is part of the UML standard and was introduced to enforce the creation of more precise and unambiguous models. An experimental investigation conducted by Briand, Labiche, Penta, and Yan-Bondoc (2005) reported that OCL could significantly improve engineer's ability to understand, inspect, and improve UML models. Provided that the use of OCL requires intensive user training, it has become a consideration as to what degree the benefits of using OCL can offset the efforts and costs for the necessary training.

Another use of formal methods with regard to quality assessment is verification. Two well-established approaches to verification are model checking and theorem proving (Clarke & Wing, 1996). Model checking has been primarily used in hardware, protocol verification, and, also, to analyze software specifications. Theorem proving, on the other hand, is increasingly used in the mechanical verification of safety-critical properties of hardware and software designs (Clarke & Wing, 1996). With regard to object-oriented design, the study from David, Moller, and Yi (2002) proposed a formal verification of UML state charts. The work of Traore and Aredo (2004) proposed to include model-based verification into structured review.

Although the use of formal methods to specify and verify design artifact offers high precision and correctness, there seems to be few works have been devoted to examine its effectiveness and benefits in the industry. For instance, the work of Pfleeger and Hatton (1997) revealed that there is no compelling quantitative evidence that formal design techniques *alone* produce a higher quality of code than informal design techniques. Additionally, they also learnt that formal specification and design are effective under some but not necessarily all circumstances.

To improve the practicality of formal methods, some important developments have been done, which include the introduction of more user-friendly notations and more comprehensible feedbacks of the model analysis results (Heitmeyer, 1998). The advance of formal methods into this direction is very beneficial because the existence of methods and tools that can encapsulate the complexity of formal methods will improve its practicality and acceptance in the industry.

Modeling Conventions

Another approach to enforce a good quality design is the use of modeling conventions. As with programming conventions, modeling conventions provide some rules or guidelines to guide designers in creating models of a system. Although this approach is not as popular and mature as programming conventions, an empirical study of the effectiveness of UML modeling conventions conducted by Lange, DuBois, Chaudron, Demeyer (2005) shows that the use of modeling conventions might potentially reduce defects in UML models. Ambler (2005) also provides thorough guidelines of how to create more effective UML diagrams.

Some pitfalls of using modeling conventions exist. As with other types of conventions, the commitment from people who use them is vital. In order to assure user commitment, it was also proposed that conventions must be tailored to a particular context and created by those who

will use them. Additionally, an overly specified modeling convention may distract designers from addressing the main solution in the first place. Thus, modeling conventions must be concise yet effective to avoid common mistakes and inefficiencies in modeling.

Table 5 provides a summary of design quality assessment methods that we have discussed in this section.

A CASE STUDY ON QUALITY ASSURANCE IN UML MODELING

Research Context and Scopes

The findings discussed in this paper come from case studies and a survey. The case studies were conducted in two IT organizations in the Netherlands, whereas the survey was performed online and includes several IT organizations from the Netherlands as well as from other countries. For confidentiality purpose, in this paper we will not

Table 5. Summary of contemporary methods in design quality assessment

Design Quality Assessments	Descriptions
Quality Models for Software Models	Describe important model quality attributes and their relations with the quality of the final software product.
Design Inspection	Design inspection includes methods and techniques to detect and remove defects in software models.
Design Measurements	Focus on the attempts to measure and quantify some measurable attributes of model entities. It is believed that by doing so will allow better control and prediction over the quality of the final software product.
Formal Methods	Formal methods provide more rigorous approach of assessing model quality. It uses mathematical techniques to verify the quality of models.
Modeling Conventions	Modeling conventions focus on the enforcement of conventions and rules in modeling. Having these rules or conventions, designers are expected to develop more consistent and complete software models.

mention the names of those organizations. One of the two companies within which the case studies were conducted has diverse application domains that include finance, insurance, e-government, and space. The other company mainly focuses on e-government systems.

As we have mentioned earlier, the main purpose of this chapter is to investigate how software developers manage the quality of UML designs. To this aim, we examined four software projects from the above two organizations. These software projects vary in size, status, and their engagement with off-shoring activities. Nevertheless, all of the projects were using UML in specifying the software design. Table 3.1 provides an overview of the project's characteristics.

The projects were chosen based on three main criteria. First, those projects to a large degree were using UML in specifying the design. Second, the projects were chosen because of the availability of information sources—for instance, many of the project members are still working in the company, thus information and clarifications can be obtained relatively easy. Finally, the projects used UML

CASE tool to create the design. Many CASE tools now support UML data exchange through XMI. Given this support, it was possible to export the UML data to other tools for further analysis.

Although none of the four projects has fully adopted a full-fledged model-driven development approach, one project was, to a certain degree, using automatic code generation from UML models. The rest of the projects mainly used UML models to communicate system designs to software developers.

Research Questions and Research Methods

The main research question we wanted to answer in this case study is as follows:

"How do software developers manage the quality of UML models?"

To answer this question, we started by investigating how UML is used in software development. The investigation involves exploring issues and

Table 6. Project characteristics

Characteristics	Project 1	Project 2	Project 3	Project 4
Project size (man-years)	20	10	10	50
Approx. number of staff	25	20	30	30
(Expected) duration (years)	2.3	3	1	6.5
Off-shored	Yes	Yes	Yes	No
Status	Finished	Finished	Finished	Development
Model Size (in use case)	104	10	100	More than 80
UML tools used	XDE	XDE	XDE	RSA

problems related to the use of UML in software projects, particularly with regard the management of design quality. We provide further discussions over the issues in the sections that follow.

In this study we conducted three types of data collection, namely interview, survey, and UML design artifacts collection. The interview was mainly intended for designers, although in fact we also performed interviews with developers and project managers. The interview was semi-structured, wherein the same set of questions were asked to all interviewees. The questions were grouped into four categories: 1) project context, 2) the use of UML in the project, 3) design quality assurance in the project and, 4) the use of UML tooling. All of the interviews were tape-recorded, and subsequently transcribed. In total we interviewed fifteen people from all the projects.

The survey was primarily aimed at software developers. It was conducted online and the participants were not limited to the two organizations studied in this case study. At the end we received 65 participants from various IT organizations originated from 10 countries.

The collection of project artifacts was focused on UML design documents and inspection documents. Although the interviews involved designers and developers from all the projects, because of confidentiality reasons we could not have access to the UML design artifacts of Project 4. This has prevented us from conducting further design analysis for this particular project. Nevertheless, we decided to use the results of the interviews with the project members when necessary and relevant.

Issues and Challenges in Managing UML Design Quality

The essence of model-driven development lies on two fundamental aspects—that is, raising the level of abstraction and raising the level of automation in developing software (Selic, 2006). Higher level of abstraction allows more focus on problem domains

rather than on implementation domains. On the other hand, code generation enables automatic model translation into code. Nevertheless, the practice of model-driven development varies. In the most pragmatic approach, models are used to generate code; once the code has been generated the models are seldom concerned. More rigorous approach not only uses models to generate code, but also keep the models updated as the code changes. In the fully automated approach developers only work with models and never directly deal with the implementation code (Selic, 2006).

The issues discussed in this paper primarily relevant to the practice of model-driven development where not all of the implementation code is automatically generated; hence software developers still have the role in writing some portions of the code or solving code integration issues. In fact, to the best of our knowledge this practice is the most commonly observed in the industry.

From our investigation, many software designers regard UML design quality as important. In bringing up the issue of design quality in the discussions with software designers, we introduce two aspects that we believe pertain to the quality of a UML design:

* The proportion and completeness of UML designs
* The design – code correspondence

The Proportion and Completeness of UML Designs

Design completeness is related to the decisions taken by software designers in modeling a software system—that is, the degree to which a design specifies the required elements of a system being developed. For example, designers might choose to model certain parts of a system while hiding others. This is sometimes done proportionally, which takes into account certain aspects of those parts. This practice is very common because exhaustively modeling all parts of a system takes considerable time and modeling effort.

The notion of design proportion emphasizes the presence of conscious decisions with regard to completeness in modeling. Use cases, for instance, are one of the units of analysis to determine proportionality. In this respect, designers might decide not to model CRUD (create, retrieve, update, delete) use cases in their design. When there is no particular reason that can explain the absence or existence of some system parts, it is very likely that design proportion is not taken into account in the modeling process.

According to Lange's framework in Figure 2.1, maintaining design completeness is primarily related to the purposes of prediction, implementation, and code generation. As the framework suggests, design completeness influences predic-

tion, implementation, and code generation. These three concepts are part of the use of models in development phase. In other words, in development phase design completeness is particularly important for the purpose of quality prediction, basis for (manual) implementation, and code generation.

One aspect of design completeness concerns the consistency between diagrams. In capturing a design it is common to use multiple diagram types. Each diagram type captures the same design from different angle or perspective. For instance, in describing how the functionality of a use case is realized in an object-oriented design, we can use a sequence diagram to depict the interaction between objects, and a class diagram to capture the structure and relationships of the object's classes. The use of multiple diagrams leads to

Figure 5. An illustration of UML design completeness (©2007 Ariadi Nugroho. Used with permission)

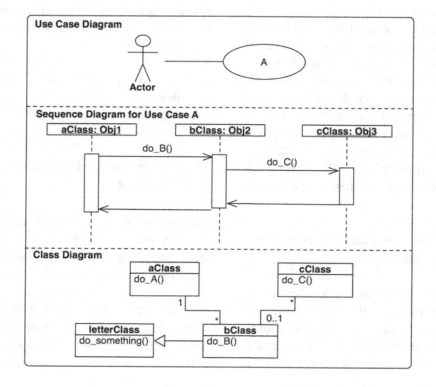

overlapping design elements, e.g., a method that exists as a message in a sequence diagram also appears as a method of a class in a class diagram. These overlapping elements, if properly specified, increase the consistency amongst diagrams and add to the clarity and preciseness of the concept or design construct being specified. Figure 5 provides an illustration of the above description.

As Figure 5 illustrates, a use case that is present in a use case diagram must have a corresponding sequence diagram(s) describing its dynamics. Likewise, classes that are mentioned in a sequence diagram must also be present in the corresponding class diagram. A higher degree of completeness can be achieved by modeling additional diagrams to add clarity to a design construct. In elaborating a use case for instance, instead of only modeling sequence diagrams, which show only the ordering of messages, a designer can also model collaboration diagrams to show the links and interactions between objects.

As there can be many factors that influence the decisions of design proportion and completeness, our main question in this respect is:

"What is the main rationale behind the practice of creating proportionate and complete UML designs?"

Additionally, we also sought to answer the following question:

"How do developers experience the degree of design completeness in their projects, and how do they prefer proportion and completeness realized in a design?"

The Rationale Behind Design Proportion and Completeness

From the interviews that we have performed, all designers agreed that they should not model all parts of a system in an equal level of detail. To give an overview of what designers regard as the main rationale behind their decisions to design a system in particular level of details, in Figure 3.2 we illustrate the main factors and their influences to the design decision-making process.

In Figure 6 we point out three main factors behind the decision toward design proportion and completeness: *comprehensiveness*, *simplicity*, and *time constraint*. Comprehensiveness is the drive to design a software system as clear as possible. A client for instance, may require a system documentation that covers all main functionalities in great details. Additionally, implementers of a design might also ask for more extensive designs.

Figure 6. Rationale behind design proportion and completeness (©2007 Ariadi Nugroho. Used with permission)

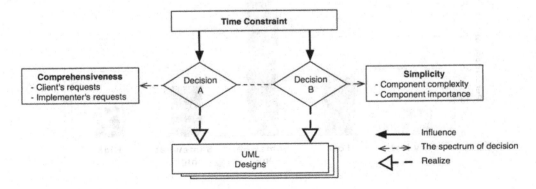

In this respect, designers are encouraged to create more complete and comprehensive designs.

The second factor is simplicity. In designing a system designers generally try to be as concise and simple as possible and yet try to capture the essence of the solution. In this regard, we identified two qualifications that are commonly used by designers in justifying their decisions to model certain parts of a system:

- **Component complexity:** Complexity reflects the level of difficulty of certain parts to be understood and, later, implemented. Hence, the need to focus on more complex parts of a system is to make sure that other parties (e.g., implementers) can easily understand difficult design constructs.

- **Component importance:** Designers model certain system elements because of its criticality to the functioning of a system. Designers want to make sure that these important elements are understood and implemented correctly to avoid system failures.

The last factor is time constraint. As with any other phases in software development process, design activities must be performed within a certain time frame. Thus, designers must make economical choices in order to assure that designs have an appropriate degree of completeness and are delivered within the scheduled time.

As illustrated in Figure 6, designer's design decisions can be somewhere within the design decision spectrum, which consists of two extremes: comprehensiveness and simplicity. These two factors have influence on the design decision as if pulling it to be leaning toward their respective sides. It is generally the case that designers will create a design as concise and simple as possible. On the contrary, other parties, e.g., implementers, may ask for more extensive designs. Here, designers must accommodate the requests by increasing the level of detail. Nevertheless, in doing so designers must also take the third factor, time constraint, into account. Figure 6 illustrates two decisions: one leaning toward comprehensiveness and the other leaning toward simplicity. This suggests that

Figure 7. The average degree of design completeness in UML projects (©2007 Ariadi Nugroho. Used with permission)

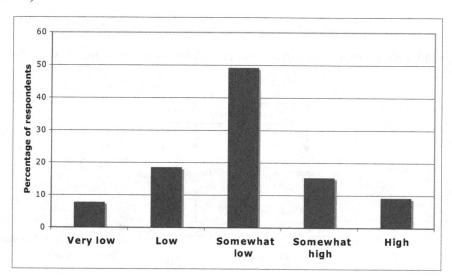

designer's design decisions are polarized between being comprehensive and concise at the same time; and time constraint seems to be the determining factor in justifying the right balance.

Developer's Experience on UML Design Proportion and Completeness

In order to understand developer's experience with regard to UML designs completeness, we present the findings from a survey that we have conducted. In analyzing the data, we decided to also include responses originated from sources outside the companies being studied in order to increase the representation of the results to a broader population.

The first finding concerns the degree of completeness of UML designs. We asked developers to rate (on average) the degree of design completeness in their projects. The results in Figure 3.3 reveal that nearly half of the respondents, 49 percent, rate the degree of UML design completeness in their UML projects as *somewhat low*. Further, 18 percent of the respondents rate the degree of completeness as *low*; and only 15 percent and 9 percent of the respondents regard the degree of completeness as *somewhat high* and *high* respectively. Finally, only 7 percent of the respondents opted *low* for the degree of completeness of UML designs in their projects.

The next finding is especially related to design proportion. While in the previous section we investigated designer's design decisions with regard to design proportion and completeness, here we present developer's preference over the level of details in UML designs. We asked developers to indicate their agreements over four statements that reflect different approaches of designing a software system as shown in Table 3.2 For each statement, we asked developers to indicate their agreement: disagree – somewhat disagree – neutral – somewhat agree – agree. The results are given in Figure 8.

The results in Figure 8 show that the majority of the respondents agree that complexity and criticality of system components should be the basis of determining the level of detail, i.e., more complex or critical parts should be given more emphasis. This is shown by the fact that 55 percent and 63 percent of the respondents *agree* on the second and third statements respectively (See table 7). For the last statement, which suggests freedom for developer to determine implementation details, 35 percent of the respondents *agree*, whereas slightly lower, 33 percent, express *somewhat agree*. Although in total these figures account for 68 percent of the respondents leaning toward an agreement, the high percentage of those opted for *somewhat agree* may indicate that there is uncertainty amongst developers as to what extent the freedom can be exercised. Lastly, the first statement, which suggests equality of details for all system parts, is not very popular amongst developers. Forty percent of the respondents *disagree* and 26 percent *somewhat disagree* on the idea to specifying all system parts in an equal amount of detail.

The above findings show that in principle developers believe that a UML design must concentrate on certain design elements, which are selected based on their characteristics of complexity and importance. This is obviously consistent with designer's perspective on design proportion and completeness discussed earlier. Yet, the finding in Figure 7 also reveals that 49 percent of the developers participated in our survey still consider the degree of completeness of UML designs in their project as somewhat low. Thus, this again confirms the importance of designer's role in finding the right design decisions, which include paying attention to feedback from other parties such as developers.

The Model: Code Correspondence

In the previous section, we have discussed how software designers and developers thought and dealt with the issue of design proportion and completeness. In this section the issue of design

Table 7. List of statements on design proportion

Labels	Statements
Equal details for all parts	All parts of a system should be specified in an equal amount of detail.
Focus on complex parts	Different parts of a system should be specified in a level of detail that is proportional to the complexity of the parts being modeled.
Focus on critical parts	Parts that are more critical for the functioning of the system should be specified in more detail.
Programmers determine details	A model should explain how the system works, but allow programmers freedom to determine implementation details.

Figure 8. Developer's agreement over approaches in design proportion (©2007 Ariadi Nugroho. Used with permission)

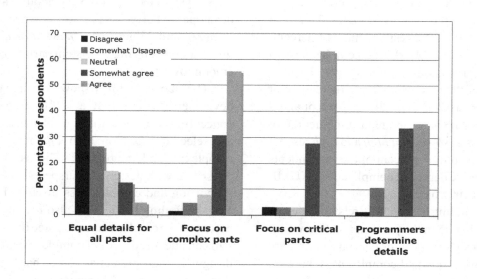

– code correspondence will be discussed. We first introduce the notion of correspondence and subsequently address the issue in practice.

At the level of classes we say that a class or group of classes in an implementation corresponds to a class in the model if the former class(es) implement(s) the latter. There is a high degree of correspondence between a UML model and an implementation if a large percentage of the elements of the model, in particular classes and associations, corresponds to elements of the implementation. There are several reasons for maintaining model – code correspondence. First, a software design is often a representation of the intended solution to address a certain set of requirements. When an implementation deviates from its designs, there is a risk that the implementation will not satisfy the requirements. Second, the model is a roadmap for understanding the implementation. A model provides a high level overview from which it is easier to understand the big picture. This information is chiefly beneficial for understanding systems in their maintenance phase, e.g., for adding or changing functionality. If there is low correspondence, then the model cannot serve this purpose. Hence, if there are good reasons to change an implementation, then these changes must be reflected back into the model —otherwise it becomes obsolete.

Lange's framework in Figure 2.1 also depicts correspondence as a characteristic that influences comprehension of a system. When a model is obsolete—no longer corresponds to the code, we lose the main benefit of model as a source of architectural information.

Figure 9 gives an illustration of model – code correspondence between model and implementation classes. It shows how three classes from the model, i.e., letterClass, aClass, and bClass are exactly mapped into their implementation classes. The correspondence can be recognized from their similarity in properties such as name, operation set, attribute set, or relations. Nevertheless, there is a class in the model without a clear corresponding class in the implementation, i.e., cClass. Likewise, there are three implementation classes that have no corresponding classes in the model. Considering its association to bClass, it may be the case that cClass has evolved or changed into the zClass in the implementation. Class bb1Class and bb2Class, however, seem to be introduced in the implementation.

Until now, only few methods and techniques have been proposed to maintain correspondence. One of the latest works we can find in the literature proposed the use of a metric based on inter-module couplings (CMB) to assess software design (Tvedt, Costa, & Lindvall, 2002). Earlier works in this subject include the works from Sefika, Sane and Campbell (1996), Antoniol, Caprile, Potrich, and Tonella (2000), and Murphy, Notkin, and Sullivan (2001). However, despite the scarcity of methods that aid software engineers, present UML CASE tools, such as IBM Rational (XDE and Rational Software Architect) and Poseidon, have introduced an automated round-trip engineering feature that promises to maintain the design (i.e., UML models) in sync with the implementation code. As we

Figure 9. An illustration of model – code correspondence (©2007 Ariadi Nugroho. Used with permission)

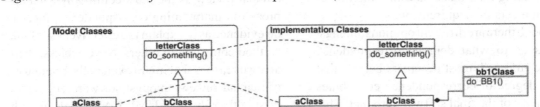

will see later, the presence of these features does not solve correspondence problems.

Our main concerns with regard to model – code correspondence can be expressed as:

"How important is this model – code correspondence in the eyes of software engineers?"

"What methods are used in practice to maintain correspondence, if any?"

"Do developers think correspondence should be different for different elements of the model?"

Designer's Attitude towards Correspondence

When we asked software designers about design – code correspondence, most of them confirmed its importance. From the designer's point of view, we identified two main perspectives with regard to correspondence. The first perspective views correspondence as applicable only for some significant elements of a system. Here, too, we encountered the notion of disproportion, which is considered in maintaining correspondence. The second perspective views correspondence as another form of traceability. It suggests that a correspondence is satisfied as long as elements in an implementation can be traced back to the models.

Nevertheless, there is an opinion against the practice of maintaining correspondence. The main argument was that maintaining correspondence is time consuming. It was argued that the most important thing is to make sure that the implementation meets the requirements.

Although there are different opinions amongst designers as to what degree correspondence should be enforced, most designers believe that a higher degree of correspondence contributes to the quality of the final software product. This is particularly shown by developer's opinion: by maintaining model – code correspondence, design decisions are consistently conveyed down to the implementation. At the end, this will result in a software system that reflects the decisions taken during the analysis and design phase.

Method Used in Maintaining Correspondence

From all the projects we studied, there is no special method used in maintaining model – code correspondence. Most designers mention manual review, i.e., manually inspect the actual implementation code and update the UML model when there are changes, as an approach to maintain correspondence. Some also mention that they requested developers to inform any changes in the implementation so that necessary modification to the corresponding models can be performed. In project 4 we identified a practice of using naming convention to ease correspondence checking. For instance, the names of classes in the implementation must remain the same as in the model.

The use of manual review to check model – code correspondence is in fact popular amongst software engineers. From our survey, as shown in Figure 10, 46 percent of the responses indicate the use of manual review. This figure is still higher compared to the use of reverse engineering and roundtrip engineering together (38 percent). This shows that the use of systematic methods to maintain correspondence is still less common than the use of manual review. The result also shows that a small number of responses, 14 percent, indicate the absence of activity to maintain correspondence.

Although the result of our survey also confirms manual review as the most commonly used approach in maintaining correspondence, there is no evidence as to explain the effectiveness of this method compared to others. Nevertheless, there are two reasons that might explain the popularity of manual review amongst software engineers. First, although some UML CASE tools already support the round-trip engineering features, we recognized that many designers are reluctant to use them because of their immaturity. Second, manually checking the correspondence between

Figure 10. Methods used in maintaining correspondence (©2007 Ariadi Nugroho. Used with permission)

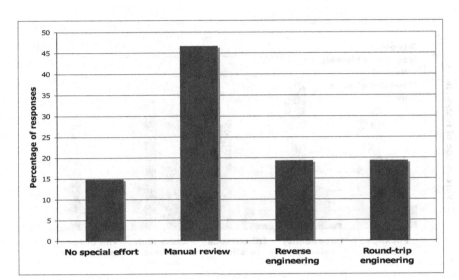

source models (reverse-engineered code) of a large system and its models is a delicate and tedious activity. More advanced tools are required in order to perform the activity effectively and efficiently.

Strictness in Correspondence for Different Constructs

To investigate the extent to which developers value correspondence, we asked developers to indicate how strict certain UML design constructs should be implemented. We asked software developers to indicate how strictly they thought the following statements should be applied:

- The package structure in an implementation should correspond to the package structure in the design.
- The dependencies between classes in an implementation should correspond to the dependencies between classes in the design.

- The inheritance relations in an implementation should correspond to the inheritance relations in the design.
- The names of classes and methods in an implementation should correspond to names in the design.
- The order of method calls in an implementation should correspond to the order of messages in the design.

The results of this questionnaire are shown in Figure 11. These results show that maintaining correspondence of inheritance relations is often regarded important to be strictly applied—that is, 46 percent of the respondents confirmed. Somewhat less, 27 percent of the respondents chose *somewhat strict* for this statement. However, in total (73 percent), the percentage is slightly lower than that of maintaining dependency relations, which accounts for 78 percent—that is, 38 percent and 40 percent for *strictly* and *somewhat strict* respectively. The correspondence of class and

Figure 11. The strictness in implementing UML design constructs (©2007 Ariadi Nugroho. Used with permission)

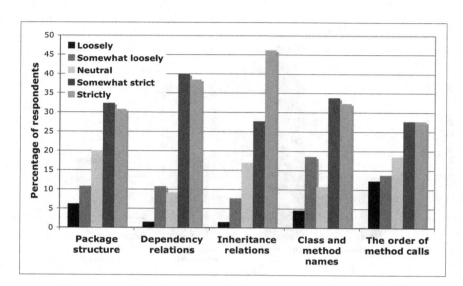

method names follows in the third place with 32 percent for *strictly* and 33 percent for *somewhat strict*. Next, the correspondence of package structure with 30 percent for *strict* and 32 percent for *somewhat strict*. Finally, the correspondence of method-call order accounts for 27 percent for both *strict* and *somewhat strict*. Also note that this statement has the highest percentage (25 percent) for somewhat loosely or loosely applied.

The above findings show that developers regard inheritance and dependency relations as should be followed more rigorously than the other UML design constructs. For instance, developer's conformance to these constructs surpasses the conformance of class and method names. This is especially interesting because class and method names are the most obvious elements to trace model—code correspondence. Although prioritizing inheritance and dependency relations is understandable—misapplying both concepts in an implementation can cause high coupling between objects, there has to be similar awareness

that lack of class name correspondence might also damage system maintainability.

Further, our study of the project's UML design artifacts revealed that the level of detail used in modeling might be a factor that contributes to the strictness of implementing it. Models with a low level of detail leave more freedom for developers to implement. This, for instance, applies to trivial classes and methods such as getters and setters. Additionally, in models with a low level of detail package structures are often either not taken into account or not organized according to implementation considerations. This is particularly the case with Project 2 in which models are packaged according to their use case associations.

The Relation between Design Completeness and the Degree of Strictness in Maintaining Model – Code Correspondence

As with level of detail, we believe that the degree of model completeness also has consequences on developer's strictness in implementing design

Table 8. Pearson correlation between strictness and model completeness

	Package structure	Dependency relations	Inheritance relations	The order of method calls	Class and method names
Design Completeness	0.090	0.266**	0.329**	0.363**	0.411**
R-square	0.81	0.07	0.108	0.131	0.169

*** Indicates significance at p = 0.01*

constructs—that is, the higher the degree of completeness of a model, the higher developer's conformance is to a design. To explore this assumption, we performed a correlation analysis between the strictness of implementing design constructs and the average degree of UML design completeness (shown previously in Figure 8).

Table 8 indicates the correlation between the average degrees of UML design completeness in software projects and developer's strictness in implementing various design constructs. We can see from the table that, except for the package structure, the strictness in implementing all of the design constructs is significantly correlated with the degree of UML design completeness. The table reveals that the strongest correlation exists between design completeness and the strictness of implementing class and method names. Yet, this only accounts for 16.9 percent (R square = 0.169) of the variability in the strictness of implementing class and method names—hence other factors account for 83.1 percent of the variability. Although the correlation coefficient does not indicate the direction of causality, we believe that model completeness affects developer's strictness in implementing modeling constructs.

Although the above findings seem to confirm our assumption, please note that design completeness is only one of the factors that might drive developer's strictness in implementing a design. It contributes for 16 percent, 13 percent, 10 percent, and 7 percent for the strictness in implementing

class and method names, the order of method calls, inheritance relations, and dependency relations respectively. Other factors may include the level of detail used, developer's experience, tool support, and so forth. Nevertheless, this is an indication of how design quality affects developer's conformance to a design.

Techniques and Methods in Design Quality Assurance

In this section we discuss the methods and techniques that are used in practice to assess the quality of the UML models. In this respect, we especially focus on the methods used to assure design completeness and proportion as well as model – code correspondence.

Peer Review as an Assessment Method for UML Design Documents

Of the four projects being studied, all have a 'formal' approach to inspect UML design documents. In assessing the quality of the models these projects used review checklists. This review process is normally performed by architects or other experienced designers—this is why the process is also called peer review. Nevertheless, having reviewed the checklists, only the ones from Project 1 are proven to have comprehensively assessed the quality properties of the designs documents. Apart from these checklists, we did not see any well-defined inspection process. The process seems to be informal wherein checklists are created and given to some inspectors who later come up with feedbacks about the model.

From Project 1's design review documents, we identified some interesting checkpoints that are related to model completeness and proportion. These checkpoints were drawn from three design checklists, i.e., design model, design subsystem, and design class, out of seven design checklists that were available (we found that these checklists

were adopted from the RUP – the Rational Unified Process – design review checklists).

Table 9 shows a selection of design checkpoints that are relevant to the issue of model proportion/completeness and design – code correspondence. In the design model, i.e., checkpoint 1 – 4, the checkpoints are somewhat in a high level. They suggest how in general the modeling practice must be performed. Recalling the rationale behind model proportion and completeness discussed

Table 9. A selection of Project 1's peer review checklists

Design Model	
1.	The model is at an appropriate level of detail given the model objectives.
2.	The model's use of modeling constructs is appropriate to the problem at hand.
3.	The model is as simple as possible while still achieving the goals of the model.
4.	The design is appropriate to the task at hand (neither too complex nor too advanced).
Design Subsystem	
5.	Each operation on an interface realized by the subsystem is utilized in some collaboration.
6.	Each operation on an interface realized by the subsystem is realized by a model element (or a collaboration of model elements) within the subsystem.
Design Class	
7.	The class satisfies the behavioral requirements established by the use-case realizations.
8.	The demands on the class (as reflected in the class description and by the objects in sequence diagrams) are consistent with the class's state machine.
9.	Class names follow the naming conventions specified in project design guidelines.
10.	The state machine and operations completely describe the behavior of the class.
11.	Each operation is used by at least one use-case realization.
12.	All relationships of the class are required to support some operation of the class.
13.	The role names of aggregations and associations describe the relationship between the associating and associated classes.

earlier, the checkpoints in the design model really reflect designer's opinion to be selective in modeling. For instance, checkpoint 1 and 2 are very relevant to the notion of proportion in modeling, i.e., appropriately using amount of detail and modeling constructs by taking into account the objectives and problems being addressed by the model.

The remaining checkpoints, except for checkpoint 9, are related to model completeness at the diagram level. They generally suggest that certain design elements in a diagram must have corresponding elements in the other relevant diagrams, e.g., checkpoint 7: a class must satisfy the behaviors of its instances in use case realizations (sequence diagrams). Further, checkpoint 10 suggests completeness in a class level by introducing state chart diagram to describe the behaviors of a class. Nonetheless, of all the review checkpoints observed, only checkpoint 9 that is somewhat relevant to the notion of correspondence. It suggests the use of class naming convention in the model. This is particularly true because without introducing class-naming conventions early in the design phase, the risk of having poor model – code correspondence might be higher.

The review checklists we discovered from the other projects are basically focusing at the same themes: simplicity, understandability, and completeness. However, an interesting practice that we encountered in Project 4 is to maintain code traceability by enforcing the use of use case references in the implementation code. In this project, this practice is assessed and required as an exit criterion for the code unit review. This kind of practice is claimed by one interviewee to be common in identifying the links between designs and implementation.

Tool Supports in Design Quality Assurance
All the projects we studied used UML CASE tools from IBM, i.e., IBM Rational XDE and IBM Rational Software Architect (RSA). In terms of model completeness, these tools offer some basic checking features. For instance, Rational XDE prevents designers to manually add or edit the class reference of an instance in a sequence diagram. For this purpose, the tool provides an automatic referencing mechanism to the existing classes, thus preventing designers from creating inconsistent models. We believe that this kind of features also present in other UML CASE tools like Rational Rose, Power Designer, and so forth. Moreover, as with other tools, Rational XDE and RSA also provide model validation features that will warn designers when certain UML models are incomplete, e.g., operations in a sequence diagram that do not exist in the corresponding class diagrams.

In terms of model – code correspondence, both Rational XDE and RSA offer a round-trip engineering feature. With this feature designers can create UML models of a system and subsequently generate the code elements. Developers can then add implementation details and modify the code elements as necessary. Eventually, to get the actual picture of the implementation code, designers can reverse engineer the code back to the model. With this feature, model – code correspondence can be improved and maintained.

Despite the above features that are available in most present UML CASE tools, we were interested to understand the extent to which the tools/features help in maintaining model quality. Surprisingly, when asked about how the tools help in assuring the quality of UML designs, most designers expressed their disappointments. Most of the disappointments, however, are not related to the role of the tool in maintaining model quality, e.g., the usability and stability of the tools. Nonetheless, some designers stated that they had difficulties to use the round-trip engineering feature. It was not easy for them to have it set up and running. At the end, the feature was never used.

In spite of the above facts, few designers indeed mentioned that the tools do help because they can validate the UML models they have created. One designer who was using Rational

XDE to develop a .NET application, especially liked the integration of the tool with Visual Studio .NET. It gave him an integrated development environment for both designing and coding the application. This also implies that it was easier for the designers and developers to keep the code and model consistent.

Although many UML CASE tools like the ones from IBM Rational have provided useful features to assure the quality of the UML models, there is no clear evidence that explains how effective those features are in practice. This is especially true if we consider some designer's experience in setting up the round-trip engineering features. Moreover, as far as model completeness is concerned, the use of model validation or verification will not be effective if the UML designs are in low level of detail where many details are hidden for simplicity reason. Running the validation tool in this particular situation will only result in hundreds of meaningless errors and warnings.

Some Reflections over the Issues

In the previous sections we have discussed the issues of design proportion and completeness as well as model code – correspondence and how software designers and developers thought them and dealt with them. In this section we highlight what we have learnt from these studies.

Realizing Complete and Proportional Designs

We have learnt that time constraint is almost always a determining factor in any software development activities. Thus, creating exhaustive models of a software system might be at odds with the schedule. Nevertheless, this should not be a justification of being over-simplistic in modeling. The fact that most developers still regard the degree of model completeness as *somewhat low* also supports this argument. Thus, software designs must be proportionally complete, meaning that designers must strategically choose which

aspects to be modeled more extensively in order to capture the most appropriate level of abstraction. To our knowledge, the design inspections performed have addressed little, if any, issues of completeness and proportion. In fact, of all the projects we studied, only one project found to be quite aware of these issues.

The above evidence has led us to the following recommendations. First, the level of completeness and proportion targeted in a project should be established in dialogue between the creators and users of the model. This dialogue must be established early enough in order to help designers estimating and targeting the most appropriate level of abstraction that meet the identified constraints, such as time schedule and developer requests. Second, design inspection must be applied in a way that it will assure design completeness and proportion. The use of checklist for instance, can be improved in such a way that it also captures multiple perspectives in a particular project, e.g., implementer's-, tester's-, and maintainer's perspectives. By understanding the needs of the users of the models, inspection checklists can then be tailored to address the required aspects.

More Rigorous Approaches toward Correspondence

In this study, we found that designers and developers agree on the importance of model – code correspondence. In spite of this fact, we did not see any well-defined activities or procedures to enforce correspondence in the projects we studied. We learnt that this might due to the following reasons. First, most designers and developers put more emphasis on more general types of correspondence, e.g., correspondence to requirements, than a specific, low-level type of correspondence, such class or method names. Second, it is often the case that developers receive models in a low level of detail. This encourages developers to conform only on modeling constructs that are more resilient or less likely to change, e.g., inheritance and dependency relations. Finally, the features in current UML CASE tools that might help maintaining correspondence, e.g., reverse engineering and round-trip engineering, are not yet mature. This tends to discourage designers and developers to spend their time and effort to set up and use them.

Considering the above factors, we recommend the following approaches. First, maintaining correspondence is not necessarily time consuming and tedious activity. By introducing class-naming convention early in the design phase for instance, the correspondence of model and code can be improved. Second, integrating correspondence checking with code inspection activities might give more insights to designers and/or architects over deviations in an implementation. Inspectors can perform this activity relatively cheaply and easily by comparing model and code metrics with tools like SDMetrics and DICTool (Opzeeland, 2005). Finally, given its importance, the notions of maintaining correspondence should be transformed into a well-defined activity, which later can be integrated with the software development process.

In summary, techniques for assessing model quality and model – code correspondence are immature. Also, activities for quality assurance of models are generally not or poorly integrated in development processes.

FUTURE TRENDS

We identify the following future trends in quality assurance of models. The first trend concerns broader application of formal methods in model quality assessments. Formal methods allow more rigorous assessment of quality checking of models. As noted earlier in this paper, the advance of formal methods has enabled assessments of models to be executed by people without advanced mathematical knowledge, which is mainly attributable to the presence of more user-friendly tools

that can automate the process and encapsulate the complexity of analysis in formal methods. Therefore, future trend in this direction would be toward the integration of formal methods into CASE tools, which will also foster the application of more formal quality assessments of models in software development process.

Other trend in the area of quality assurance of models is the use comprehensive model testing. While many model validation approaches generally focus only on behavioral aspects of models, comprehensive model testing provides better assessments by taking into account other views of models (e.g., static structure). This is particularly important since the behavior of a system will be constrained by its static structure, which in the UML is specified in class diagrams. The work of Pilskalns et al. (Pilskalns, 2007) for instance, proposed a method that integrates multiple UML views, generates an integrated model from it, generates test cases of the model, and finally executes the model on the test cases. Thus, future quality assessments of models with model testing will not only take into account the behavioral aspects of models (e.g., behavioral consistency), but also involve broader aspects of models such as their static structure.

Additionally, we underline the importance of the findings of this study for quality assurance of models. The notion of design proportion is very practical for selecting the candidates for automatic generation. Automatic code generation requires design elements to be more formally and precisely modeled. However, not every design element deserves low-level of abstractions. Only those that can be beneficial for automation are eligible for comprehensive modeling (Mellor, Clark, Futagami, 2003). In this chapter we have discussed two of the candidates: 1) complex design elements and, 2) critical design elements. The benefit of focusing on complex and critical design elements for code generation is two-fold. First, automating the generation of complex design elements can reduce the complexity for implementing them.

Second, automatic generation of critical design elements can assure that the implementation is addressed correctly, hence mitigating the risk of system failures. These will consequently result in increased productivity and improved software quality.

One of the challenges in model-driven development is the traceability of design artifacts (Aizenbud-Reshef, Nolan, Rubin, & Shaham-Gafni, 2006). With immense design documents created during development, manually maintaining and tracking changes amongst related design documents can be tricky and tedious, especially when models are created with different CASE tools. The practice of checking correspondence with tool support can somewhat reduces this traceability problem. As with checking model – code correspondence, checking the links amongst models can be performed by comparing some design element properties, such as classifier names or metric profiles. These data can be exported from CASE tools in XMI format (currently available in most UML CASE tools). By linking design artifacts based on their similarities, we can track changes that occur in models as well as compare different versions of models.

CONCLUSION

In this chapter we reported the main findings from our case study into quality assurance of model-based software development. The results are based on four UML projects from two IT organizations in the Netherlands. Additionally, we also reported the findings from an online survey we have performed. Both the case study and survey were aimed at investigating issues related to the management of model quality. Further, this chapter also provides a discussion on contemporary design quality assessments methods. We explored the use of design inspections, design measurements, and formal methods for the purpose of inspecting quality attributes of design documents.

From the case studies we identify the following findings:

- Both designers and developers agree that a model must be proportional and complete—that is, design elements that are important and complex must be modeled more extensively than the trivial ones. Furthermore, we learnt that modeling decisions are influenced by three factors: 1) the drive for being simplistic, 2) the drive for being comprehensive, 3) time pressure. The decision concerning proportion and completeness is eventually a compromise between these three factors.

- Although most designers agreed that model – code correspondence is important, few attempts have been performed to maintain it.

- Despite the fact that most designers agreed on the importance of model quality, few considerations have been given to develop well-defined design inspection processes to assess model quality. So far we only see the use of checklists to inspect design documents without clear procedures or guidelines that guide the activity.

- We discovered that the level of detail and the degree of completeness of models might affect developer's strictness in implementing them. Both a low level of detail and a low degree of completeness tend to result in low conformance in implementing modeling constructs. Additionally, we suspect that these also contribute to the ineffectiveness of UML CASE tools used to perform model validation.

FUTURE RESEARCH DIRECTIONS

For future works, we encourage more research to be directed toward the development of frameworks that will aid designers in justifying their modeling decisions. Particularly with regard to the issue of design proportion and completeness, we have not seen any clear guidance that can be used to effectively address the issues. Relevant checklists that were found merely cope with the issue in a general way. Hence, frameworks that provide well-defined guidelines and measurements of model proportion and completeness will contribute to the practice of maintaining the quality of software designs.

With regard to the issue of model – code correspondence, we particularly underline the absence of well-established and effective methods to maintain model – code correspondence. In this respect, it is well known that current methods and tools to maintain correspondence often suffer from their delicacy and ineffectiveness. Thus, future work in this area is required to define which types of correspondence need to be preserved, their implications, and ways to measure them. Having addressed these questions, further work should be carried out to develop correspondence assessments methods and techniques accordingly.

Finally, further investigations must be carried out to disclose the factors that can improve developer's conformance to a model. We have discovered that the level of detail and the degree of model completeness are two of the potential factors that influence developer's strictness in implementing modeling constructs.

REFERENCES

Abreu, B. F., & Melo, W. (1996). Evaluating the impact of object-oriented design on software quality. *Third International Software Metrics Symposium (METRICS '96)*, 90-99.

Aizenbud-Reshef, N., Nolan, B.T., Rubin, J., & Shaham-Gafni, Y. (2006). Model traceability. *IBM Systems Journal, 45(3)*, 515-526.

Aleman, J.L.F., & Alvarez, A.T. (2000). Can intuition become rigorous? Foundations for UML model verification tools. *Proceedings of the 11th International Symposium on Software Reliability Engineering*, 344-345.

Ambler, S.W. (2005). *The elements of UML 2.0 style*. New York: Cambridge University Press.

Antoniol, G., Caprile, B., Potrich, A., & Tonella, P. (2000). Design-code traceability for object-oriented system. *Annals for Software Engineering, 9*, 35-58

Aurum, A., Petersson, H., & Wohlin, C. (2002). State-of-the-art: software inspection after 25 years. *Software Testing Verification and Reliability, 12(3)*, 133-154.

Basili, V.R., Green, S., laitenberger, O., Lanubile,F., Shull, F., Sørumgård, S., et al. (1996). The empirical investigation of perspective-based reading, *Empirical Software Engineering, 1(2)*, 133-164.

Boehm, B.W., Brown, J.R., & Lipow, M. (1976). Quantitative evaluation of software quality, *Proceedings of the 2nd international conference on Software Engineering*, 592-605.

Bowen, J.P., & Hinchey, M.G. (1995) Ten commandments of formal methods. *IEEE Computer, 28(4)*, 56-63.

Briand, L.C., Daly, J., Porter, V., & Wüst, J. (1998). A comprehensive empirical validation of design measures for object oriented system. Proceedings of the 5th International Software Metrics Symposium, 246-257.

Briand, L.C., Wüst, J., Daly, J.W., & Porter, D.V. (2000). Exploring the relationships between design measures and software quality in object-oriented systems, *The Journal of Systems and Software, 51(3)*, 245-273.

Briand, L.C., Labiche, Y., Penta, M.D., Yan-Bondoc, H.D. (2005). An experimental investigation of formality in UML-based development. *IEEE Transactions on Software Engineering, 31(10)*, 833-849

Chidamber, S.R., & Kemerer, C.F. (1994). A metrics suite for object oriented design. *IEEE Transaction on Software Engineering, 20(6)*, 476-493. .

Clarke, E.M., & Wing, J.M. (1996). Formal methods: State of the art and future directions, *ACM Computing Survey, 28(4)*, 626-643.

David, A., Möller, M.O., & Yi, W. (2002). Formal verification of UML statecharts with real-Time extensions, *Lecture Notes in Computer Science, 2306*, 208-241.

Dunsmore, A., Roper, M., & Wood, M. (2001).. Systematic object-oriented inspection—an empirical study. *Proceedings of the 23rd International Conference on Software Engineering*, 135-144.

El-Emam, K., Melo, W., & Machado, J.C. (2001). The prediction of faulty classes using object-oriented design metrics. *Journal of Systems and Software, 56(1)*, 63-75.

Engels, G., Küster, J.M, Heckel, R., & Groenewegen, L. (2001). A methodology for specifying and analyzing consistency of object-oriented behavioral models. *ACM SIGSOFT Software Engineering Notes, 26(5)*, 186-195.

Engels, G., Heckel, R., & Küster, J.M. (2003). The consistency workbench: A tool for consistency management in UML-based development. *Lecture Notes in Computer Sciences, 2893*, 356-359.

Fagan, M. (1976). Design and code inspection to reduce errors in program development. *IBM Systems Journal, 15(3)*, 182-211.

Fagan, M. (1986). Advances in software inspections. *IEEE Transactions on Software Engineering, 12(7)*, 744-751.

Fenton, N.E. (1999). *Software metrics, a rigorous approach*. London: Chapman & Hall.

Fenton, N.E., & Neil, M. (1999). Software metrics: Successes, failures, and new directions. *Journal of Systems and Software, 47(2-3)*, 149-157.

France, R., Evans, A., Lano, K., & Rumpe, B. (1998). The UML as a formal modeling notation. *Computer Standards & Interfaces, 19(7)*, 325-334.

Harrison, R., Counsell, S., & Nithi, R. (2000). Experimental assessment of the effect of inheritance on the maintainability of object-oriented systems. *Journal of Systems and Software, 2(3)*, 173-179.

Heitmeyer, C. L. (1998). On the need for practical formal methods. In *FTRTFT '98: Proceedings of the 5th International Symposium on Formal Techniques in Real-Time and Fault-Tolerant Systems*, pages 18–26, London, UK. Springer-Verlag.

Lange, C.F.J., & Chaudron, M.R.V. (2005). Managing model quality in UML-based software development, *Proceedings of IEEE Conference on Software Technology and Engineering Practice 2005 (STEP)*, 7-16.

Lange, C.F. J., DuBois, B., & Chaudron, M.R.V. (2005). Experimentally investigating the effectiveness and effort of modeling conventions for the UML. *Lecture Notes in Computer Science*, 4364, 91-100.

Laitenberger, O. (2002). *A survey of software inspection technologies*. In Handbook on Software Engineering and Knowledge Engineering. World Scientific Publishing.

Laitenberger, O., Beil, T., & Schwinn, T. (2002). An industrial case study to examine a non traditional inspection implementation for requirements specifications. *Empirical Software Engineering, 7(4)*, 345-374.

Leung, F., & Bolloju, N. (2005). Analyzing the quality of domain models developed by novice systems analysts. *Proceedings of the 38th Hawaii International Conference on System Sciences*, 188b-188b.

Lindland, O. I., Sindre, G., & Sølvberg, A. (1994). Understanding quality in conceptual modeling. *IEEE Software, 11(2)*, 42-49.

McCall, J.A., Richards, P.K., & Walters, G.F. (1977). *Factors in software quality*, vol. 1-3 of AD/A-049-015/055. Springfield.

McUmber, W.E., & Cheng, B. (2001). A general framework for formalizing UML with formal languages. *Proceedings of the 23rd International Conference on Software Engineering (ICSE '01)*, 433-442.

Mellor, S.J., Clark, A.N., & Futagami, T. (2003). Model-driven development – Guest editor's introduction. *IEEE Software, 20(5)*, 14-18.

Murphy, G.C., Notkin, D., & Sullivan, K.J. (2001). Software reflexion models: Bridging the gap between design and implementation. *IEEE Transactions on Software Engineering, 27(4)*, 364-380.

Opzeeland, D.J.A. (2005). *Automated techniques for reconstructing and assessing correspondence between UML designs and implementations*. Unpublished master thesis, Technische Universiteit Eindhoven, Eindhoven, The Netherlands.

Parnas, D.L., & Weiss, D.M. (1985). Active design review: Principles and practices. *Proceedings of the 8th international conference on Software engineering*, 132-136.

Pfleeger, S.L., & Hatton, L. (1997). Investigating the influence of formal methods. *IEEE Computer, 30(2)*, 33-43.

Pilskalns, O., Andrews, A., Knight, A., Ghosh, S., and France, R. (2007). Testing uml designs. *Information and Software Technology*, 49(8):892–912.

Porter, A.A., Siy, H.P., Toman, C.A., Votta, L.G. (1997). An Experiment to assess the cost-benefits of code inspections in large scale software development. *IEEE Transactions on Software Engineering, 23(6)*, 329-346.

Runeson, P., & Isacsson, P. (1998). Software quality assurance – concept and misconception. *Proceedings of the 24th. EUROMICRO Conference (EUROMICRO'98), 2*, 853-859.

Sefika, M., Sane, A., & Campbell, R. H. (1996). Monitoring compliance of a software system with its high-level design models. *Proceedings of the 18th International Conference on Software Engineering*, 387–396.

Traore, L., & Aredo, D.B. (2004). Enhancing structured review with model-based verification. *IEEE Transactions on Software Engineering, 30(11)*, 736-753.

Tvedt, R.T., Costa, P., & Lindvall, M. (2002). Does the code match the design? *Proceedings of the International Conference on Software Maintenance (ICSM)*, 393-401.

Wing, J.M. (1990). A specifier's introduction to formal methods. *IEEE Computer, 23(9)*, 8-24.

ADDITIONAL READINGS

This paper reports on a controlled experiment (consisting of two parts at different institutes) that investigates the impact of UML documentation on software maintenance. The results show that for complex tasks and past a certain learning curve, the availability of UML documentation may result in significant improvements in the functional correctness of changes as well as the quality of the design. There seems not be a savings in time.

Arisholm, E., Briand, L.C., Hove, S.E., & Labiche, Y. (2006). The impact of UML documentation on software maintenance: An experimental evaluation, *IEEE Transactions on Software Engineering*, 32(6), 365-381.

This paper describes techniques for analyzing large UML models. It describes heuristics and processes gathered from industrial projects for creating semantically correct UML analysis- and design models. One of its findings is that just evaluating UML models provides important lessons that are invaluable for improving the modeling process.

Berenbach, B. (2004). The evaluation of large, complex uml analysis and design models. *Proceedings of the 26th International Conference on Software Engineering* (pp. 232–241). IEEE Computer Society

This is a workshop paper that presents preliminary results on the measured benefits of following guidelines for style and design of software. Early results indicate that style guidelines are often violated and that - in contrast with common claims- one the use of design patterns - can lead to more change prone classes.

Bieman, J.M., Alexander, R., Munger III, P.W., & Meunier, E. (2001). Software design quality: Style and substance. *Proceedings of the Workshop on Software Quality (WoSQ)*. ACM, 2001.

This is one of the earliest papers that proposes a quality model for software based on a iterative decomposition of the notion of quality into factors and metrics. The resulting tree-structure is common to most software quality models.

Boehm, B.W., Brown, J.R., Kaspar, H., Lipow, M., Macleod, G.J., & Merrit, M.J. (1978). *Characteristics of software quality*, volume 1 of TRW Series of Software Technology. Amsterdam: North-Holland Publishing Company.

This paper provides an overview of the state-of-the-art (d.d. 1999) in empirical knowledge on object-oriented software development methods and processes and suggests research directions.

Briand, L.C., Arisholm, E., Counsell, S., Houdek, F., & Thevenod-Fosse, P. (1999). Empirical studies of object-oriented artifacts, methods, and processes: State of the art and future directions. *Empirical Software Engineering*, 4(4), 387–404.

This paper presents an experiment that studies the effect of design guidelines (such as cohesion, coupling, clarity of design, depth-of-inheritance, simplicity) on the maintainability of OO designs. Within the limits of the experiment, the paper reports a positive impact.

Briand, L.C., Bunse, C., & Daly. J.W. (2001). A controlled experiment for evaluating quality guidelines on the maintainability of object-oriented designs. *IEEE Transactions on Software Engineering, 27(6)*, 513–530.

This paper formalizes the structure of UML models using OCL-predicates (a bit like a meta-model approach). If a change is performed to one diagram of a model, predicates may become false which points to places that also need to be adapted in order to maintain correct structure of the UML model. This is presented as an impact analysis method.

Briand, L.C., Labiche, Y., O'Sullivan, L., & S 'owka, M.M. (2006). Automated impact analysis of UML models. *Journal of Systems and Software, 79(3)*, 339–352.

This paper applies model-checking techniques to detecting errors in behavioral descriptions.

Campbell, L.A., Cheng, B.H.C., McCumber, W.E., & Stirewalt, R. E. K. (2002). Automatically detecting and visualising errors in UML diagrams. *Requirements Engineering, 7,* 264–287.

This paper compares different reading techniques that are tailored to UML models.

Cantone, G., Colasanti, L., Abdulnabi, Z.A., Lomartire, A., & Calavaro, G. (2003). Evaluating checklist-based and use-case driven reading techniques as applied to software analysis and design UML artifacts, *LNCS, 2765,* 142–165.

This paper examines the expressiveness of OCL as a language for defining queries over UML models. It concludes that OCL has enough expressivity.

Chimiak-Opoka, J., & Lenz, C. (2006). Use of OCL in a model assessment framework: An experience report. *Proceedings of OCLApps workshop,* 53-67.

The paper describes an experiment performed at Ericsson in Norway to evaluate the cost-efficiency of tailored OORTs in a large-scale software project. The results showed that the OORTs fit well into an incremental development process, and managed to detect defects not found by the existing reading techniques.

Conradi, R., Mohagheghi, P., Arif, T., Hedge, L.C., Bunde, G.A., & Pedersen, A. (2003) Object-oriented reading techniques for inspection of UML models – an industrial experiment. *Proceedings of the European Conference on Object-Oriented Programming ECOOP'03, LNCS, 2749,* 483–501. Springer.

The next two papers address approaches for analyzing extra-functional quality properties of systems described at an architecture level by UML diagrams. The approaches have in common that they add annotations to commonly used UML

diagrams, and then provide a systematic translation from the annotated UML design to a model for performance or reliability.

Balsamo, S., Marco, A.D., Inverardi, P., & Simeoni, M. (2004). Model-based performance prediction in software development: A survey. IEEE Transactions on Software Engineering, 30(5), 295-310.

Cortellessa, V., Singh, H., & Cukic, B. (2002). Early reliability assessment of UML based software models. *Proceedings of the 3rd international workshop on Software and performance,* pages 302–309, New York: ACM Press.

This paper describes result from a survey under industrial software engineers as to the manner in which the UML is used.

Dobing, B., & Parsons, J. (2005). Current practices in the use of UML. *Proceedings of the 1st Workshop on the Best Practices of UML, LNCS.* Springer.

This paper describes a technique and a supporting tool that automatically performs a number of consistency checks on a UML model. It emphasizes the performance of the proposed implementation. It claims interactive checking is possible during the creating of the design.

Egyed, A. (2006). Instant consistency checking for the UML. *Proceedings of the 28th International Conference on Software Engineering (ICSE '06),* 381–390. ACM.

This paper presents an approach to check the compliance of OO design with respect to source code. The process works on design artifacts expressed in (the pre-UML) OMT notation and accepts C++ source code. It recovers an "as is" design from the code, compares recovered design with the actual design and points out regions of code which do not match with design. The recovery process exploits regular expression and edit distance to bridge the gap between code and design.

Fiutem, R., & Antoniol, G. (1998). Identifying design-code inconsistencies in object-oriented software: A case study. *Proceedings of the International Conference on Software Maintenance*, 94-102.

Classic paper that discusses different views on product quality.

Garvin, D. (1984). What does 'product quality' really mean? *Sloan Management Review, 26(1)*, 25–45.

The paper explores - based on a controlled experiment - how early metrics which measure internal attributes, such as structural complexity and size of UML class diagrams, can be used as early class diagram maintainability indicators. The experiment has a small sample size. The conclude that early indicators for maintainability can be based on UML metrics, but are careful to generalize based on the small sample size of the experiment.

Genero, M., Piattini, M., Manso, E., & Cantone, G. (2003). Building UML class diagram maintainability prediction models based on early metrics. *Proceedings of the Ninth International Software Metrics Symposium (METRICS 2003)*, 263–275. IEEE.

This book has over the years remained an popolar reference for professional software engineers because it provides practical guidelines for performing software inspections.

Gilb, T., & Graham, D. (1993). *Software Inspection*. Addison Wesley Publishing.

This paper provides quantitative approach to determine the cost effectiveness of quality assurance in software (i.e., when to stop testing). It gives insights to answer questions related to quality in modeling.

Huang, L., & Boehm, B. (2005). Determining how much software assurance is enough? A value-based approach. *International Symposium on Empirical Software Engineering*, p. 10.

This book attempts to provide full coverage on metrics and models in software quality engineering. A recommended reading for both academics and practitioners who are interested in software measurements.

Kan, S.H. (2002). Metrics and models in software quality engineering. Addison Wesley Professional.

This is a classic paper that provides sound discussion on the term of "software quality" and why its definition must be targeted toward a specific goal.

Kitchenham, B., & Pfleeger, S.L. (1996). Software quality: The elusive target. *IEEE Software, 13(1)*, 12–21.

This paper provides a good overview of software inspection methods and come up with a taxonomy that can help practitioners identify inspection experience directly related to a particular life-cycle stage.

Laitenberger, O., & DeBaud, J. (2000). An encompassing life-cycle centric survey of software inspection. *Journal of Systems and Software, 50(1)*, 5-31.

This paper discusses the notion of completeness in UML designs; a very useful reference to start with model quality assessments.

Lange, C.F.J., & Chaudron, M.R.V. (2004). An empirical assessment of completeness in UML designs. *Proceedings of the 8th International Conference on Empirical Assessment in Software Engineering (EASE '04)*, 111–121.

A paper based on an experiment that reveals the effects of syntactic defects in UML models. It also provide a ranking of the defects based on their impacts.

Lange, C.F.J., & Chaudron, M.R.V. (2006). Effects of defects in UML models - an experimental investigation. *In Proceedings of the 28th International Conference on Software Engineering (ICSE '06)*, 401–411. ACM.

Based a survey and industrial case study, this paper uncovers common problems in UML models and techniques for controlling their quality.

Lange, C.F.J., Chaudron, M.R.V., & Muskens, J. (2006). In practice: UML software architecture and design description. *IEEE Software, 23(2)*, 40–46.

This paper proposed some techniques to analyze UML models, particularly related to inconsistency and incompleteness issues.

Lange, C.F.J., Chaudron, M.R.V., & Muskens, J., Somers, L.J., & Dortmans, H.M. (2003). An empirical investigation in quantifying inconsistency and incompleteness of UML designs. *Proceedings of the 2nd Workshop on Consistency Problems in UML-based Software Development*, 26–34.

This paper discusses the result of an experiment that investigated the effect of using modeling conventions in creating UML models. The factors measured were syntactic quality and the effort spent in modeling.

Lange, C.F.J., DuBois, B., Chaudron, M.R.V., & Demeyer, S. (2006). An experimental investigation of UML modeling conventions. In Oscar Nierstrasz, Jon Whittle, David Harel, and Gianna Reggio (Ed.), *Proceedings of the 9th International Conference on Model Driven Engineering Languages and Systems (MoDELS 2006), LNCS 4199*, 27–41, Heidelberg: Springer.

This paper discusses a replicated experiment that investigated the impact of complexity metrics in state charts on their understandability—another useful reference that justifies model quality assurance.

Miranda, D., Genero, M., & Piattini, M. (2003). Empirical validation of metrics for UML statechart diagrams. *Proceedings of the Fifth International Conference on Enterprise Information Systems (ICEIS '03)*, 87–95

A very relevant paper with respect to design-code correspondence. It reports on design-code correspondence analysis of industrial case studies using a correspondence tool.

van Opzeeland, D.J.A., Lange, C.F.J., & Chaudron, M.R.V. (2005). Quantitative techniques for the assessment of correspondence between UML designs and implementation. In Houari A. Sahraoui, Coral Calero, Michele Lanza, Geert Poels, and Vernando Brito e Abreu (Ed.), *Proceedings of the 9th ECOOP Workshop on Quantitative Approaches in Object-Oriented Software Engineering (QAOOSE '05)*, 1–18

This paper is one of the classic papers that initiated discussion on model-based measurements. It is a good reference for readers who are interested in early ideas and practices in design measurements.

Rombach, H.D. (1990). Design measurements: Some lessons learnt. *IEEE Software, 7(2)*, 17-25

This paper evaluates the cost of software quality by proposing some metrics to measure its benefits. The report was based on a real case study of software quality improvement initiative.

Slaughter, S.A., Harter, D.E., & Krishnan, M.S. (1998). Evaluating the cost of software quality. *Communications of the ACM, 41(8)*, 67–73.

From a survey amongst software developers, this paper reported 30 problems in using the UML 1.3, which categories include inconsistency and ambiguity.

Simons, A.J.H., & Graham, I. (1999). 30 things that go wrong in object modeling with UML 1.3. In H. Kilov, Bernhard Rumpe, and I. Simmonds (Ed.), *Behavioral Specifications of Business and Systems*, chapter 17, pages 237–257. Kluwer Academic Publishers.

This paper provides a good introduction to Model-driven Engineering (MDE), its future, and challenges.

Schmidt, D.C. (2006). Model-driven engineering. *Computer, 39(2)*, 25–31.

This paper reports on the result of an experiment that assesses the qualitative efficacy of UML diagrams in aiding program understanding.

Tilley, S.R., & Huang, S. (2003). A qualitative assessment of the efficacy of UML diagrams as a form of graphical documentation in aiding program understanding. *Proceedings of the 21st International Conference on Systems Documentation (SIGDOC 2003)*, 184–191. ACM.

This paper discusses the results of an experiment that suggests how models with higher level of abstraction are more resilient toward some types of changes.

Verelst, J. (2005). The influence of the level of abstraction on the evolvability of conceptual models of information systems. *Empirical Software Engineering, 10(4)*, 467– 494.

This paper is related to the notion of design-code correspondence. It proposed an approach to analyze the evolution of software from its logical design.

Xing, Z., & Stroulia, E. (2005). Analyzing the evolutionary history of the logical design of object-oriented software. *IEEE Transactions on Software Engineering, 31(10)*, 850–868.

Chapter II
Quality in Model Driven Engineering

Teade Punter
Embedded Systems Institute, The Netherlands

Jeroen Voeten
Embedded Systems Institute, The Netherlands & Eindhoven University of Technology,
The Netherlands

Jinfeng Huang
Eindhoven University of Technology, The Netherlands

ABSTRACT

This chapter argues that embedded systems design faces several challenges of which late integration and the difference in development productivity between disciplines are major ones. Model driven engineering (MDE) looks a promising approach to address these challenges. However, MDE is a new approach which has to be defined and implemented in close interaction by academia and industry the near future. We therefore provide a conceptual framework to understand the possibilities and the flaws in quality assurance in the MDE design flow.

INTRODUCTION TO EMBEDDED SYSTEM'S DESIGN

A. Embedded Systems

Model Driven Engineering as we deal with it in this chapter is related to embedded systems design. An embedded system is the information processing and controlling part that is embedded in another (the embedding) systems, e.g., a copier or MRI scanner. The embedded system plays a controlling or monitoring role in the embedding (or hosting) system. Typically, embedded systems communicate to their embedding systems by actuators and sensors, not by human communication. This makes embedded systems different from information systems. Nowadays, embedded systems can be found everywhere. For example in cars, copiers, cameras, cell phones.

Embedded systems are *complex,* because of for example, but not constrained to, their heterogeneity, concurrency and power constraints. One reason that they are complex is simply that they are big systems, e.g.,: the effort to develop them is huge, they contain many lines of code. Embedded systems are *heterogeneous* because they are built out of various components, including software processes, processors, accelerators, memories, busses and networks. To design a component, assumptions have to be made about other (heterogeneous) components in the system. Since embedded systems observe and control many parts of their embedding system, multiple processes have to run in parallel. This requires *concurrent* handling. Many embedded systems have limited power supplies such as batteries. Battery use stresses the importance of energy constraints in embedded systems. For example, because they are portable (like cell phones), are implanted in humans (like medical devices) or are used in isolated areas (like wireless detection devices).

Characterizing Embedded Systems Design

Embedded systems design aims at the design of complex information processing (sub)systems that will meet their requirements (functional as well as non-functional). The design should be done in a cost-effective way and should deliver the product in time (time-to-market). An embedded system design will therefore be judged by three main criteria: quality, effort and time. Because of the growing system complexity, a methodological approach or design flow is needed to meet these criteria. The *design flow* is the set of design activities (cf. method or development process, like Rational Unified Process (RUP)) needed to develop the system. An example of a design flow is the ordered set of activities: requirements definition, design and development, integration & testing and releasing, as shown in figure 1.a. Other appearances of a design flow exist. For example, because of the experience that phases are not strictly separated but are intertwined (figure 1.b) or because of that other terminology is used for defining the phases (figure 1.c). Software tools are used to support the implementation of a design flow.

Embedded system design is often characterized as *co-design* of hardware and software (Wolf, 2003). For example, computer architecture provides designers with information about performance and energy consumption of processors. Knowledge about hardware components, and their cost, is needed to design software in a

Figure 1. Examples of design flows (©2007 Teade Punter, Jeroen Voeten, and Jinfeng Huang. Used with permission)

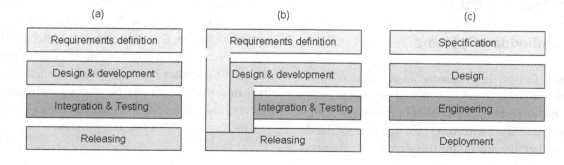

way that a cost-efficient system results that will meet its requirements. The embedding system might include involvement of other disciplines as well. Often disciplines are involved such as control engineering, electrical engineering and mechanical engineering. Taking more disciplines into account than software and hardware is denoted as *multidisciplinary approach* (Heemels & Muller, 2006). Each of these disciplines uses its own terminology, models of computation and tools. Knowledge about each of the disciplines and its interaction with other disciplines is needed to design embedding systems, such as a printer.

In this chapter, we focus on the design flow of embedded systems, more specifically: hardware and software co-design. This design flow will often be part of the development process of an embedding system. Therefore there will be an interaction of the design flow with multidisciplinary development. After having specified the (high-level and low-level) system requirements, the design phase starts which involves disciplines such as mechanical engineering, electrical engineering and software engineering. Although these disciplines are tightly coupled in the final system, their development is traditionally carried out in a rather mono-disciplinary and independent fashion, and the engineering results are delivered in a sequential way. Conventionally, first the mechanical subsystem is designed, then the hardware and finally the software.

Challenges for Embedded Systems Design

The need for Model Driven Engineering is often advocated by the problems that embedded systems design faces. Many problems can be distinguished. We focus on two of them in particular, namely: *late* integration and productivity.

Late integration – Working with several disciplines requires tuning. Choices made in one discipline, concerning for instance control rates and the position of sensors and actuators, have an impact on the required functionality and might increase system's complexity. Problems arising from this complexity often become visible during integration and testing, when the components/subsystems have to work together. So, while testing the subsystems in the separated disciplines proceeds without severe problems, the integration phase results in major problems that have to be solved, which take time that might cause project delays (Punter et al, 2002).

System design follows the design flow as indicated in figure 1, where system integration is performed inevitably in a late design stage. Due to the heterogeneity of the systems, many (design) errors are detected during integration. This might lead to substantial design iterations. In addition, the later an error is detected, the more costly it is to solve it (Boehm, 1989; Liggesmeyer et al, 1998). Further, during integration, verification and quality assessment is mainly performed by testing the physical realization or prototype. This is difficult because of uncontrollability and unobservability and because of the Heisenberg principle in testing (Vranken, 1998; Huang et al, 2002). Therefore, late integration is a challenge in embedded system design.

Differences in productivity amongst disciplines – another challenge is the difference in productivity amongst the disciplines, see e.g. (Corporaal, 2006a). This trend is seen by industry as a problem. For example, at ASML -world's largest producer of wafer steppers- the technologies for servo's and lenses is considered to be cutting edge, in the leading group. Meanwhile software is considered as being in the rear. These differences in technology productivity will have a negative impact on quality, time and effort: decreasing quality, increasing effort and time-to-market. "For each new generation of a waferstepper the number of software developers is doubled" (Roos, 2006). The following figure shows that also hardware productivity does not pace up with the total pro-

Figure 2. Differences in software and hardware productivity compared to general process productivity. Taken from (Corporaal, 2006b).

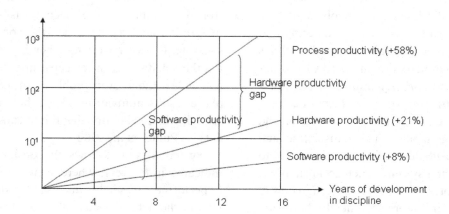

cess productivity. However, software productivity grows slower than hardware productivity; see also (Genuchten, 1991; 2007).

The problems of late integration and low productivity are only two examples to advocate Model Driven Engineering (MDE). With MDE, the abstraction level of systems and software development is raised meanwhile making important implicit structures more explicit. This enables architects and engineers in having a better system overview, which is also available more early in the development process.

Others argue that MDE is promising to address platform complexity and the inability of third-generation languages to alleviate this complexity (Schmidt, 2006). We perceive the benefits of MDE in its assumption of yielding significantly shorter design times. We are aware of the danger of advocating a "silver bullet", like software reuse has been advertised in the past as being the solution for low software productivity. Little empirical data about the impact and added-value of Model Driven Engineering exist. At this moment MDE is more a belief. In this chapter we do not advocate that MDE is the ultimate solution. Instead we focus on how to organize MDE

to assure its process quality as well as the quality of the resulting system. The following section introduces Model Driven Engineering.

MODEL DRIVEN ENGINEERING (MDE)

Model Driven Engineering (MDE) refers to the systematic use of models as primary engineering artifacts throughout the engineering lifecycle[1]. Modeling a system might focus on its behavior (any event or action that the system performs), its structure or system functionality. To *model* we need a particular language (formalism as well as notation) to express the domain concepts of a discipline effectively.

A model transformation takes as input a (source) model and produces as output a (target) model. Both models might be restricted by the requirement that they conform to a source or target meta-model. The *transformation* might be conducted to refine the model into a model of a lower abstraction level or from a lower abstraction level to a higher one, e.g. reverse engineering. Even the abstraction level might not change during the

Figure 3. Possible directions for model transformations (©2007 Teade Punter, Jeroen Voeten, and Jin-feng Huang. Used with permission)

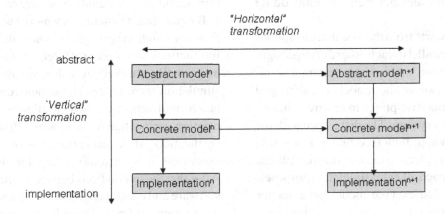

transformation, e.g., if the model is re-factored. The transformation from higher level models to lower level models is often addressed as vertical transformation. For example the transformations from platform independent models (PIM) to platform specific models (PSM) in software discipline, e.g., (Gool et al, 2006). The transformation on the same or similar abstraction level is than addressed as horizontal transformation, e.g., the migration of an architecture (with its related platform), e.g., (Nieuwelaar, 2004; Graaf et al, 2005).

A transformation takes a source model as input and transforms it into target model or other artefact, which means often that source and target are different. However, in case of a model redesign the source and target model are the same. (Software) synthesis is a particular form of model transformation during which a model is transformed into an implementation, e.g., code.

A third element of MDE is *view,* which is a graphical representation that provides a perspective on the system. Views are related or derived from particular paradigms or models of computation. They are a set of "laws" that govern the interaction of components in a system. Several

models of computation exist, e.g., (Hylands et al, 2003). In the software discipline behavior and structure of software can be modeled by different paradigms, like input output processes and finite state automata.

A fourth element of MDE is executable models, which enable the execution of a behavioral model by a simulator (a tool that simulates the model). Executable models are especially important to deal with concurrent and timed behavior in an embedded system.

The way how MDE is used within a design flow is determined by the way how models are used by the involved disciplines. We think that two basic strategies for applying MDE exist.

Strategy 1 starts by defining an integrated system model, at a manageable abstraction level. From this (unique) model, incremental transformation to less abstract and more detailed models should be possible. These detailed models are the starting points for code generation and synthesis as well as for modeling in other disciplines. This strategy requires a modeling language that can cope with abstract system modeling in a systematically refined way until synthesizable models can be generated. This is a feasible approach for (digital) hardware development, but not for multidisciplinary development of embedding systems yet.

Strategy 2 starts from the idea that disciplines will remain in parallel to each other during design. Models are defined within these separate disciplines. Information of the models is exchanged to models in other disciplines to ensure coherent development of a system. The difference with the conventional design flow (see figure 1.a) is that early feedback is given to each of the disciplines. Disciplines use each other for simulation purposes. So, simulators that execute model behavior for other disciplines, e.g., "hardware-in-the-loop", are necessary. This approach of MDE is advocated by the Ptolemy project (Ptolemy, 2007). This is also addressed as co-simulation in which the interfaces between different domain-specific modeling languages are defined, e.g., of Matlab Simulink to Rose Real Time (Hooman et al, 2004). Strategy 2 is not only used for multi-disciplinary development. See for example in UML, where a software system is specified by using different models (e.g. class diagrams, sequence diagrams, etc.), and mechanisms should be provided in order to guarantee their consistency.

An example of MDE is the design of the software part of a mechatronic system: a complex production cell system (Huang et al, 2007a). The design consisted of two major parts: systematic modeling and correctness-preserving synthesis. On the one hand, the design has to provide solutions to deal with concurrency and timeliness issues of the system. On the other hand, it has to glue different disciplines (such as software, control and mechanics) of the system as a whole. The modeling stage was divided into four steps, which focused on different aspects (such as concurrency, multiple disciplines and timeliness) of the system respectively. The modeling process started from an informal description (called handshake diagrams) of the system, where the system was considered to be a set of concurrent components (called players). Based on the proposed guidelines, the players could be intuitively identified and their interaction patterns could be easily constructed. Following that, a concurrency model was derived from the handshake diagram, where the un timed interactions between different players could be formally checked by using verification and simulation techniques. The concurrency model has formal semantics, which allowed us to use existing verification tools such as SPIN to do the verification. At the same time, the model is also executable it is naturally ready for simulation. After that the interactions between especially the software and control engineers were investigated in a refinement (multi-disciplinary model) of the concurrency model. In the end, the quantitative properties (real-time properties) were analyzed in the refinement of the multi-disciplinary model. Furthermore, the consistency between the models at the different abstraction levels could be maintained so that properties that were analyzed at a higher level model were still valid in the models at lower abstraction level.

After the specification of the important system aspects and an analysis (of the unified model) a software implementation was automatically synthesized from the model, which correctness was ensured by construction. The synthesis is formally proven in (Huang et al, 2007b). The approach was perceived as effective because it divides the system behavior into different aspects which can be modeled easily while the consistency between the different models is maintained. The development of the production cell system shows that the 75% design time could be reduced using this MDE approach.

Having defined the principles of MDE we now look back at the two problems expressed in section 2 for which MDE promises to be the answer. MDE's answer to the problem of late integration is by providing models that facilitate a better understanding of the design problem. These models provide possible solutions for design which enables simulation earlier than waiting untill the implementation is available. This advances the integration and test phase of the design flow.

MDE's answer to increase software productivity is by its increasing of the levels of abstraction which avoids implementation of platform specific details. This will yield significantly shorter design times. An illustration is the "documentation problem" that we noticed in some embedding system projects. Following a waterfall-like way of designing a system (see figure 1.a) the technical software documents that will be produced will be hard to verify at once. Because the system requirements will change over time as well as because integration and testing will give new insights to improve design, it will be likely that the technical documentation will be not up-to-date soon. This has a negative impact on the software productivity. By documenting design as a set of models, and generating (or synthesizing) code from them, it will be likely that the design can be maintained up-to-date.

Model Driven Engineering looks a promising approach to address particular problems in embedded systems design. This chapter further focuses on the question how to establish quality in an MDE design flow. We believe this has an impact on system quality, although we are aware that the relation between process and product quality is still not completely understood.

QUALITY ASSURANCE IN THE MDE DESIGN FLOW

The MDE design flow is a process. We therefore want to apply concepts about the quality of processes to the design flow. We do not look at the maturity of processes and process improvement as expressed in, e.g., the Capability Maturity Model (SEI, 2007). Instead we look at more fundamental principles of processes as applied in system's theory that was elaborated for the software engineering domain by (Punter, 2001; Punter et al, 2004).

System theory considers a process as a system with an input and an output. Executing a process means that an input is transformed into an output. Key in this approach is the control of processes. Control is needed to generate an output that meets expectations. In terms of the design flow: a design that meets customer expectations, passing verification and validation phases. From this theory we formulated a framework of thinking to analyse design flow by looking at four elements.

1. Goal formulation – controlling a process means that the process aims at achieving particular goals. For example, in process approaches like done with CMMi (SEI, 2007) and ISO15504/Spice this principle is effectuated by the idea that a process should be conformant to baseline- or key practices. To be able to achieve goals, they should be well-formulated to be able to steer the process in the right direction. Well-formulated means e.g., that the goals are specific and measurable, see e.g., (Park et al, 1996) as well as (Mannion and Keepence, 1995). We know that goals will by principle change over time. Goal formulations that once were mentioned by stakeholders as being important might have less weight after a while, and vice versa. Also new goal formulations might appear. This is especially an issue for processes that last for longer periods. Changing of goals has an impact on the iterations in a design process. Each iteration starts from a goal formulation. When the goal formulation has changed, a new iteration starts.

2. Integrated activities – a process in control means also that the activities are related to each other. This implies that outputs of activities are input for its successor activity or activities. Unclear or non-existing relationships between activities cause activities that are conducted in isolation; meanwhile uncertainty exists about whether activity outputs will be applied by successor activi-

ties. Managing such a process is not possible, because the relations between goals and activities are not specified explicitly. Therefore a controlled process requires integrated activities.

3. Trade-off between goals and resources – resources are needed to perform activities. The appropriate resources should be chosen to achieve the goals. People as well as techniques are the main categories of process resources. The trade-off between goals and resources is about setting the right goals with the available resources or to acquire additional resources to achieve the stated goals. It might be necessary to reformulate goals if the appropriate resources are not available. The trade-off mechanism is necessary to find the right balance between goals and resources. To achieve quality assurance in a process, this mechanism should be active continuously. When goal formulations are available and the supportive resources are known, the trade-off should start. But when the trade-off is set for a process, disturbances in the process, e.g., changes in goals or lack of resources might imply a mismatch, which requires the setting of a new trade-off.

4. Feedback – quality assurance of processes implies also the monitoring of processes. This is needed to determine if the process moves into the right direction and will (probably) achieve the defined goals. Monitoring requires feedback information about the process. If deviations are discovered, then steering actions are required to achieve the desired result(s) after all.

In the following sections we explain what these factors imply for the MDE design flow.

GOAL FORMULATION

Goal formulation is essentially the specification of why a design flow is conducted. In section 5

we will see that activities in a design flow can be of two types: analysis and design activities. Design activities are part of the design flow in the way that they result in the blue print of the system. Analysis (or aspect) models are about an aspect of the design, e.g., performance. The goals for the respective activities are therefore different by their type. The goal formulation of the analysis activities for the design flow will be related to what is commonly addressed as the specification of quality characteristics, like reliability. In the software discipline non-functional requirements, e.g., (Chung et al, 2000) or the ISO-standard for software product quality (ISO 9126, 2001) applied. For systems engineering other properties are required, e.g., addressing evolvability and dependability; see for an example proposal (Muller, 2004). Goal formulation that applies to design activities is about the phases in the design process, such as synthesis and verification.

The goals for a design flow should be derived from or should be related to business goals, such as time-to-market, quality and effort. Guidelines for refining business goals into sub goals are provided by (Park et al, 1996) and (Punter et al, 2004). Goals cannot be formulated right while not looking at the information about the system and design context. A framework that will help to define goals for multidisciplinary development is the CAFCR-method for embedded systems architecting (Muller, 2004). Key views of this method that help goal setting are: customer objectives, application and functional areas.

In embedded systems design – focusing on the hardware and software discipline – we distinguish analysis activities in a design flow; see next section. To define the goals for analysis activities explicitly, a template might be helpful, just like the goal measurement template in the Goal Question Metric (GQM) approach (Basili and Weiss, 1984). We therefore propose to formulate goals by applying this GQM template as expressed in table 1. The template consists of 4 topics: object, quality focus, purpose and viewpoint. The object

Table 1. Proposal to formulate analysis goals in a design flow

Object	`<design, synthesis, etcetera>`
Quality focus	`<reliability, performance, dependability, evolvability>`
Purpose	`<understanding, improving, verification & validation, synthezise (an implementation out of models)>`
Viewpoint	`<project leader, engineer, architect>`

specifies the activities in the design flow upon which the analysis will focus. Quality focus is about the type of analysis that will be conducted. Purpose expresses the ambition of the analysis in the design flow. It is just to understand the design or if analysis is needed e.g., to verify or to synthesize an implementation. Viewpoint expresses the stakeholder(s) that will use the analysis results.

INTEGRATED ACTIVITIES

The main purpose of models is to help engineers understand the interesting aspects of the future system. Models are therefore widespread used by engineers in a variety of disciplines. For example, hardware engineering apply models in notations/ languages like VHDL

Integration of activities in an MDE design flow deals with models at different abstraction levels and the transformation(s) between them. We distinguish here two types of models: aspect (or analysis) models and design models, which are related to two types of activities in the design flow, namely analysis and design activities respectively. These are mutually inverse activities that are continuously performed during the design flow. Design activities aim at refinement, which try to add more implementation details to the design models, thereby reducing the gap between the implementation (e.g., code) and design model.

Analysis activities try to remove (or hide) as much as possible irrelevant information by abstracting from the design models. This improves the comprehensibility of the existing design models and facilitates the evaluation of different design solutions. Where design models are characterized as being *the core* of the design flow, analysis models provide additional information to the design models that enables the analysis of the design. Design models are the "first class citizens" of the design flow, see figure 4. The aspect models are abstracted from the design models. This enables designers to look at particular aspects, such as concurrency and performance, which provide a feedback to the design.

This distinction impacts the organization of the models. Design models are organized and categorized according to different levels of abstraction. Aspect (or analysis) models apply information from different design models and therefore have to cope with information that is related to different levels of abstraction.

Guidelines for Integrating Activities

An MDE design process can be carried out in a *stepwise* or/and *piecewise* manner in multi-stages. During a stepwise design stage, a series of design decisions is made at different abstraction levels. At each abstraction level, only a subset of the desired properties of the system is investigated.

Figure 4. Two types of activities in a design flow: analysis and design activities (©2007 Teade Punter, Jeroen Voeten, and Jinfeng Huang. Used with permission)

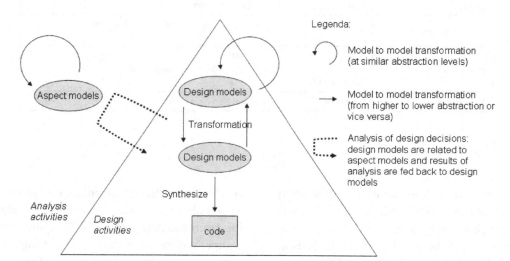

To make such a design process smoother, it is crucial for MDE to support *predictability*, allowing desired properties to carry over between different abstraction levels of the system. As a consequence, the properties of interest verified at one level of abstraction can be preserved into another level in a stepwise manner. During a piecewise design stage, the system is constructed by the recursive composition of separately exploited components.

Each component only contains a part of the total functionality of the system. To ensure that design decisions made in a component are still valid in the integrated system, *compositionality* is considered as a key feature of the MDE emphasizing semantic independency of components. As a consequence, the behavior of each component remains unchanged during the integration, and properties of the integrated system can be derived from those of the components. Design of a complex system can involve both stepwise and piecewise design processes.

The transformation of a system from one abstraction level to another can be achieved by a set of independent transformations of its components. Compositionality ensures that the transformation of each component can be carried out independently. On the other hand, the integration of components is usually reasoned about on the basis of the integration of their abstractions, which is ensured by predictability. Therefore, *compositionality* and *predictability* are two interdependent and indispensable features of MDE.

Executability is an important characteristic of the model during system design, because in the executable model, different aspects (such as interaction diagrams, class diagrams and state diagrams of UML) of the system can be naturally integrated, where inconsistency between different aspects can then be located (Huang et al, 2004). As a result, many design errors can be corrected in an early development stage, avoiding costly and time-consuming iterations.

Experiences with Transformation in the Software Discipline

MDE requires transformation. In this subsection we present our experiences with a "vertical" transformation (see section 2) in the software discipline. We focused on modeling coordination of the machine by software functionality. Input for this is a definition of high-level services (abstract behaviors) of a waferstepper in terms of low-level services (resources behaviors) and the machine parts (resources) that are needed to execute them. In the existing situation the platform runs C-code, while a higher level specification was written in Word documents without using specific modeling techniques (Punter et al, 2007).

The model transformation case study was conducted to define the lower level specification on a higher level of abstract, but also more precise than it is done in the word documents. We started with specifying the high-level specification of coordination as a set of UML2.0 Activity diagrams and Class diagrams. Next step was to specify the system at concrete level of abstraction as a set of UML2.0 Activity– and Class diagrams. Third step was to define the transformation itself. We have chosen the Query View Transformation (QVT) as a set of rules to define the transformation and using Borland Together ® for modeling as well as transformation purposes.

The structure (class) models could be relatively easily transformed from higher level of abstraction to concrete models. It was more difficult to transform the behavioral (activity) diagrams when using QVT. The arbitrary concepts have to be detailed to a level that can unambiguously be interpreted by the platform. Therefore language constructs were specified that helps to decompose behavioral description of higher level into lower level. This language is a compositional subset of UML 2.0 activity diagrams and consists of any activity that can be built with the patterns `proc, seq, assign, guard, if` and `call` (van Gool et al, 2006). It was possible to

define abstract behavior in their platform-specific form that was offered to a scheduling component, which tries to execute them in an optimal manner. For each abstract behavior, the scheduling component determines the set of resources that are needed for its execution and when they are needed. Although this is a first step in determining timing of behaviors, the timing itself is still outside of the scope of the implemented model. Appropriate timing is the responsibility of the scheduling component.

The approach of using a compositional subset of a standardized language (UML) turned out beneficial. Company's architects were quickly able to understand the language and discuss details of a coordination instance that was considered very complex. Furthermore, the language's compositionality guided the definition of the model transformation.

Integrated Activities and Multiple Disciplines

In a multidisciplinary approach the exchange of models is required. Software development might benefit from simulation of hardware (hardware-in-the-loop) and vice versa. Therefore we will try to understand models in the disciplines as expressed to abstraction level, the degree of complexity and heterogeneity (or variety) in the design space. The general trend to deal with system complexity is to make abstractions from reality. Abstractions are made to maintain the overview of the system. However, abstraction increases also the number of possible decisions in the design space, because the number of concepts increases. This is denoted as heterogeneity of modeling. As such the increase in heterogeneity is a good thing, because of the variety of modeling concepts that can be applied. However, much more interpretation is required because of multiple concepts. For example, a hardware design that is specified on transistor level is easier to interpret because the definition is more deterministic than a hardware design

Figure 5. Relation of abstraction level and heterogeneity within a discipline expressed; plus an example of abstraction levels for hardware discipline (©2007 Teade Punter, Jeroen Voeten, and Jinfeng Huang. Used with permission)

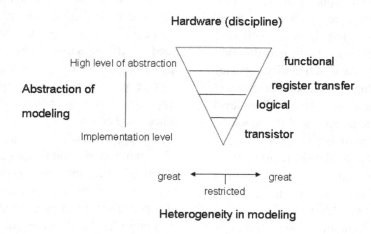

specified on functional level that containing, e.g., different processors, various memories and specific interfaces. The price of abstraction is the harder effort to define specified behavior: "there is no free lunch".

Figure 5 visualizes the trade-off between abstraction and heterogeneity in the design space. The consequence of this trade-off for multidisciplinary system development is the need of compatibility between models. For example, imagine the situation that hardware is modelled by specifying with VHDL targeting an FPGA. Can we also use this model to simulate software models that are expressed in Activity diagrams? To achieve our goals we might need parts of different models to make a thorough analysis.

One possibility is to define integrated models and derive the models of the individual disciplines (hardware, software) out of it. For example, (Huang et al, 2007b) presents a model specified in the POOSL modeling language on a high level abstraction, that covers hardware and software concepts.

A second option is to define interfaces between models in a way that models can use each other, e.g., for "hard-in-the-loop" simulation. We are aware that it is still difficult to determine the similarity of abstraction levels between models of different disciplines; the shaded part in figure 7 implies modeling at a particular level of abstraction. However, a logical scenario for model compatibility is to start with models of the discipline of physics. Latter discipline will deal with the most detailed behavior, continuous control (mechanics discipline) requires low level of control but can be specified at a higher abstraction than in physics. Discrete event control (high-level software control) will have the least detailed level of abstraction. Knowing the dependencies between the disciplines concerning the levels of abstraction helps us to understand that situation (a), expressed in figure 6, will be an unlikely situation to integrate models, because the physical model is defined at a high level of abstraction, compared to other models, while for example the software is specified at a lower level

Figure 6. Two situations of model at different levels of abstraction in multiple disciplines: (a) unlikely situation, (b) more likely situation for model compatibility (©2007 Teade Punter, Jeroen Voeten, and Jinfeng Huang. Used with permission)

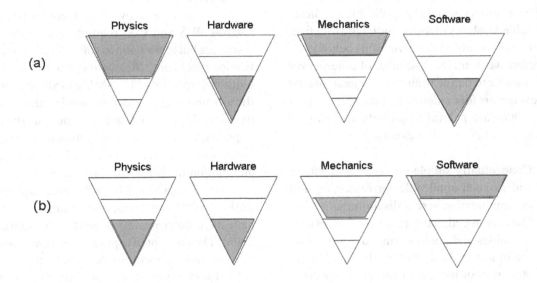

of abstraction. In situation (b) also different levels of abstraction are due, however here the order in levels of abstraction from physics to software enables compatibility.

In this section we have distinguished analysis and design activities in a design flow. Design activities determine product quality while design decisions are made. Analysis activities pay attention to particular aspects (with defining aspect models). Although both types of activities impact product quality of MDE, we focus on analysis activities further in the remainder of this chapter.

TRADE-OFF GOALS AND RESOURCES

Trade-off is a control mechanism to match appropriate resources to the stated goals. The appropriateness of resources will be mainly, but

perhaps not completely, determined by three factors, namely: effort, accuracy and usability.

Effort – Resources in a design flow are the engineers, architects and other people that are involved in system design as well as the techniques –like model checking or synthesis tools– that they use for (designing and) analyzing the system. Applying resources take effort (time, person years), which has to be estimated when choosing a technique.

Accuracy – Resources in an MDE design flow that are especially meant here are the techniques, applied to modeling. Models should be build and they should be reasonably accurate. The main concern here is that the model is a good abstraction of reality. This implies that an accurate model addresses an up-to-date design problem as well as that there is a common agreement amongst the users of the model that the model represents what it has to represent.

Usability – Resources, especially meant here are the techniques, should be applicable and therefore usable. Usability of technique is hard to define, because it depends on the "eyes of its beholders". Therefore we think that a number of criteria may be applicable to define usability. For example the success factors for modeling in industry (Beckers et al, 2006) are helpful to identify usability of modeling techniques. For example:

- Conceptually simple – easy to understand and as such applicable for reasoning and communication across disciplines.
- Use of conventional paradigms – e.g., of timing tables and position-time diagrams that are in use in the company already. Hence, outcomes of the model can be easily communicated.

In case we are able to express effort, accuracy and usability of MDE- resources we expect to be able to match the resources to goals, more specifically: the purpose of goals, see table 1. However, little empirical evidence about MDE resources exists today. Most information is scattered and incomplete. An exception is an overview of formal methods presented by (Vaandrager, 2006), that provides an overview of formal methods, see figure 7.

This overview shows that theorem provers, such as PVS and Coq require great skills and resources but allows one to solve very hard (verification) problems. Meanwhile, Model checking (with tooling like mCRL, SMV and SPIN) provide the advantage over theorem proving that once a model and a property are specified, analysis is in principle fully automatic. This saves some effort. Automated abstraction can be perceived as an addition to model checking to cope with the problem of scalability (the problem of state-space explosion). Abstractions, like symmetries, data-path have been proven powerful (Vaandrager, 2006). The concept of types and the development of automatic algorithms for establishing type correctness are examples of "invisible" formal methods. They are completely invisible to the user, but still have a good return on investment, being able to find a lot of bugs. This overview shows that techniques will be chosen depending on the required accuracy and the amount of available effort that those who want to verify want to spend. These criteria apply to other goal ambitions, like understanding a system, as well.

Figure 7. An example of expressing accuracy and effort of resources. Taken from Vaandrager, 2006.

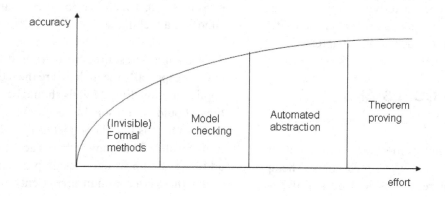

FEEDBACK

Feedback is a control mechanism that should monitor if the design flow is behaving right. More specifically: feedback is the identification of the most important conflicts in a design as well as the structuring of design options in situation of incomplete information (uncertainty). Another way of saying is to use feedback to determine system's (intermediate) quality , e.g., expressing this as performance or dependability: the "quality focus" in table 1.

Feedback information will be generated for all of the goal purposes as defined in the goal template in table 1, but applies to the verification and validation. Feedback information can be provided in many different ways. It can be the simulation information that is provided by e.g., "hardware-in-the-loop" models to find the constraints for the software discipline. Feedback information will be not restricted to the end of the design process. Especially in testing or verification processes, feedback information is required during all stages. An approach is to conduct model inspections, e.g., by checking model conventions, see e.g., (Lange et al, 2006a&b). This will generate design information of draft UML-models.

Also model checking might be an option. For example, by constructing a model in a particular process algebra language and check whether system meets its requirements, see e.g., (Ploeger & Somers, 2006). This approach enables early verification and synthesizes an implementation from the generated model[2].

A common approach in quality assurance would be to apply the feedback information to interpret the quality of the resulting system by using a quality model or set of quality characteristics, the "-ilities" mentioned before. However, it will be often hard to define applicable criteria to evaluate non-functional requirements of embedded software systems (Punter et al, 2002). Meanwhile the restriction in available design time (related to time-to-market and available man power)

implies that in-depth and often time-consuming modeling and analysis should be performed only for the essential and critical issues (Sandee et al, 2006). An alternative approach –so-called *threads of reasoning*- has been applied at Océ Technologies (Heemels, Muller, 2006). It is a graph-based iterative technique to identify the most important conflicts in the design problem and possible solutions. The system architect uses the information implicitly to integrate various views in a consistent and balanced way, in order to design valuable usable and feasible products. In fact the threads makes explicit what is already available implicit. Details of the method and guidelines to apply the method are provided by (Sandee et al, 2006). We remark that the "thread of reasoning"-method, as well as other ways to conduct feedback, depend much on the experience of the people involved.

In addition to the feedback mechanism we also want to address the importance of a *feed forward mechanism* in a design flow. This applies especially to the transformations of higher level models into more detailed models, resulting into synthesis of code. Dealing with feed forward we are interested in the reliability or predictability of the transformation. How sure are we that the specified model-to-model or model-to-code transformation provides the right result? When we look at the software discipline we perceive that a lot initiatives to transform UML-models with a model to code generation purpose focus on the syntax of the transformation. However, such syntactical transformation cannot always guarantee the consistency between the model and the implementation. To ensure the correctness by construction, the semantics of the implementation should respect to the semantics of the model. For instance, a synthesis approach in which this applies is proposed for concurrent real-time systems in (Huang et al, 2007a). The execution of the implementation follows the timing semantics of the model by synchronizing the time in the physical world and the time in the model.

FUTURE TRENDS

We see three main trends that will be relevant for successful implementation of model driven engineering (MDE), namely: predictability of the transformation, heterogeneity of modeling languages and getting empirical results.

Predictability of transformations - synthesizing implementations from models in a predictable way is still a challenging research topic. The challenge is to preserve the properties of a model transformation for a next transformation, so that no information will be lost during the transformation(s). In section 7 we already addressed the importance of a property preserving transformation approach for concurrent real-time systems. There are still many research challenges in this area. For instance, in a distributed system, the software components are distributed over a multiple-processor platform instead of a single processor platform assumed in (Huang et al 2007b). It is still an open issue to ensure the correctness consistency for distributed systems during code generation.

Heterogeneity of modeling languages – in our chapter we have referred to heterogeneity of modeling. Some modeling languages and techniques for communicating (or parallel) processes are CSP, Uppaal, SDL and POOSL. Understanding these languages is important to implement model driven engineering in the future. For example, some companies will not use off-the-shelf solutions because of high demands on their platforms. Instead they still want to use well-supported easy-to-learn design languages with a feasible approach to generation of code for all kinds of different platforms that are used in different versions of their products.

The trade-offs to use a language depends on domain, accuracy and scalability. We should be able to understand these languages as good as our community understands functional or procedural programming languages. We also think that this discussion on languages applies to the discussion between domain specific languages (DSL) and a unified modeling language (i.e. UML) in the software community, see e.g., (Staron & Wohlin, 2006).

A hierarchy of communicating languages is needed for this purpose. This will organize languages according to their expressiveness as well as their efficiency (timing). Abstract languages will than be ranked as good on their expressiveness, while they will likely to be worse for their efficiency and synthesis capabilities. Finding the trade-offs between expressiveness and efficiency can be enriched by taking accuracy, effort and usability of resources (section 6) into account as well. An interesting initiative to characterize some languages is provided by (Verhoef and Hooman, 2006).

Getting empirical results – model based engineering (MDE) like model based architecture (MDA) are approaches that address the increasing complexity of today's systems. However, modeling and dealing with abstraction requires developers and engineers that are open-minded to the approach. Training people to work with models and providing tools that are easy to use will than be key factors. In addition there is a need for empirical results of application MDE techniques in practice, as already noted in section 7. This insight is needed to determine when to use what technique. With this chapter we aim at providing a quality framework to interpret those results.

CONCLUSION

Model Driven Engineering (MDE) is the systematic use of models as primary means for the hardware and software discipline. We think that Model Driven Engineering addresses challenges in embedded systems design, such as late integration and the difference in development productivity. We remark that MDE should be done in interaction with a multidisciplinary approach -incorporating other disciplines- if applicable.

In this chapter we have recognized that MDE is immature and that there might be the danger of advocating a silver bullet. Therefore we have provided a framework to think about quality in the MDE design flow. The framework applies to the process of a design flow. We assume that organizing this process properly will be beneficial for system (product) quality as well.

The starting point of our framework is the need for control in a way that generated output of the design flow will meet expectations. Key elements of control are: goal formulation, integrated activities, trade-off between goals and resources and feedback. MDE terminology and concepts were defined for each of these elements. Successful quality assurance requires paying attention to each of the four elements.

Concerning activities in an MDE design flow we distinguish between design and analysis activities. To formulate goals for analysis activities a goal template was presented. Integration of activities in an MDE design flow deals with models at different abstraction levels and the transformation(s) between them. Based on our experiences we found that that compositionality and predictability are indispensable features of MDE.

To establish the right trade-off between goals and resources it will be necessary to identify effort, accuracy and usability of resources. Unfortunately, little empirical evidence about MDE resources exists. The feedback information that is generated during a design flow should be particularly be fed by data about the system (or product) quality. The opposite of feedback -but aiming at the same need to control- is feed forward. We think that MDE should be facilitated by predictable transformation means to enable feed forward.

Today, MDE is still in a kind of research phase. It's future success depends on its technical feasibility and how to introduce it into organisations. Our framework is meant as a means to discuss before -and to steer during- introduction of MDE.

REFERENCES

Basili, V.R., & Weiss, D.M. (1984). A methodology for collecting valid software engineering data. *IEEE Transactions on Software Engineering*, 10(6), 728-738.

Beckers, J.B.C., & Heemels, W.P.M.H., & Bukkems, B.H.M. (2006). Effective industrial modeling: The example of Happy Flow. In Heemels, W.P.M.H., & Muller, G.J. (Eds.) *Model-based design of high-tech systems*, (pp. 77-88). Eindhoven: Embedded Systems Institute.

Boehm, B. (1989). *Software Risk Management*. Los Alamos: IEEE.

Chung, L., & Nixon, B.A., & Yu, E. (2000). *Non-functional requirements in software engineering*. Boston: Kluwer.

Corporaal, H. (2006a). Embedded System Design. In *Progress White Papers 2006* (pp. 7-25). Utrecht: STW Progress.

Corporaal, H. (2006b), Embedded System Design. STW Progress presentation, May 10, 2006. Retrieved 4 March 2007, from: www.ics.ele.nl/~heco.

Genuchten, M. van. (1991). Why is Software Late? An Empirical Study of Reasons for Delay in Software Development. *IEEE Transactions on Software Engineering,* 17 (6), 582-590.

Genuchten, M. van. (2007), The Impact of Software Growth on the Electronics Industry. *IEEE Computer*, 40(1), 106-108.

Gool, L. van, & Punter, T., & Hamilton, M. (2006). Compositional MDA. In O. Nierstrasz et al (Ed.),

Proceedings of Models 2006 LNCS 4199, (pp. 126-139). Berlin: Springer.

Graaf, B., & Weber, S., & Deursen, A. van. (2006), Migrating Supervisory Control Architectures Using Model Transformations. In *Proceedings of 10th European Conference on Software Maintenance and Reengineering CSMR 2006* (pp.153-164). Los Alamos: IEEE Computer Society.

Heemels, W.P.M.H., & Muller, G.J. (Eds.) (2006). *Model-based design of high-tech systems*, Eindhoven, Embedded Systems Institute.

Hooman, J. & Mulyar, N., & Posta, L. (2004). Coupling Simulink and UML models. In Schnieder, B., & Tarnai, G. (Eds), *Proceedings Symposium FORMS/FORMATS 2004*, 304-311. Retrieved 29 October 2007, from http://www.ita.cs.ru.nl/publications/papers/ hooman/FORMS04.pdf.

Huang, J., & Voeten, J.P.M., & Putten, P. van der (2002). Performance Evaluation of Complex Real-time Systems: A Case Study. In *Proceedings of PROGRESS 2002*, (pp. 77-82). Utrecht: STW Progress.

Huang, J., & Voeten J.P.M., & Ventevogel, A. (2004). Predictability in Real-Time System Development - (1) Semantics Support for Development Languages. In Vachoux, A. (Ed.), *The Forum on Specification and Design Languages (FDL'04)*, (pp. 123-140). Gières: ECSI.

Huang, J. (2005). *Predictability in real-time software design* (PhD thesis). Eindhoven: Eindhoven University of the Technology.

Huang J., & Voeten J.P.M., & Groothuis M., (2007a). A Model Driven Approach for Mechatronic Systems. In *Proceedings of IEEE International Conference on Application of Concurrency to System Design (ACSD)* (pp.127-136). Los Alamos: IEEE Computer Society.

Huang, J., & Voeten, J.P.M., & Corporaal, H. (2007b). Predictable real-time software synthesis. *Journal of Real-time Systems*, 36 (3), 159-198.

Hylands, C., & Lee, E., & Liu, J. (2003). *Overview of the Ptolemy project*, Technical Memorandum UCB/ERL M03/05. Retrieved 21 November 2006, from http://ptolemy.eecs.berkeley.edu/.

ISO 9126 (2001). Information technology - *Software product evaluation, Quality characteristics and guidelines for their use*. Geneve: ISO/IEC.

Lange, C.F.J., & DuBois, B., & Chaudron, M.R.V. (2006a). An Experimental Investigation of UML Modeling Conventions. In O. Nierstrasz et al (Ed), *Proceedings of Models 2006 LNCS 4199*, (pp. 27-41). Berlin: Springer.

Lange, C.F.J., & Chaudron, M.R.V., & Muskens, J. (2006b). UML Software Architecture and Design Description. *IEEE Software*, 23(2), 40-46.

Liggesmeyer, P., & Rothfelder, M, & Rettelbach, M. (1998). Quality assurance of software-based systems (in German). *Informatik-Spektrum*, 21(5), 249-258.

Mannion, M. & Keepence, B. (1995). SMART Requirements. *ACM SIGSOFT Software Engineering Notes*, 20(2), 42-47.

Muller, G.J. (2004). *CAFCR: A Multi-view Method for Embedded Systems Architecting; Balancing Genericity and Specificity* (PhD-Thesis). Delft: Delft University of Technology.

Nieuwelaar, B. van den (2004), *Supervisory Machine Control by Predictive-Reactive Scheduling* (PhD thesis). Eindhoven: Eindhoven University of Technology.

Park, R, & Goethert, W., & Florac, W. (1996). *Goal-driven software measurement - a guidebook* (SEI report CMU/SEI-96-HB-002). Pittsburg: Carnegie Mellon University/Software Engineering Institute.

Ploeger, S.C.W., & Somers, L. (2006), *Analysis and Verification of an Automatic Document Feeder* (CS-Report 06-25). Eindhoven: University of Technology.

Ptolemy (2007). Ptolemy project site, University of California at Berkely. Retrieved October 22, 2007, from http://ptolemy.eecs.berkeley.edu/.

Punter, T. (2001). *Goal-oriented evaluation of software* (in Dutch) (PhD-Thesis). Eindhoven: Eindhoven University of Technology.

Punter, T., & Trendowicz, A., & Kaiser, P. (2002). Evaluating Evolutionary Software Systems. In M. Oivu, & S. Komi Sirviö (Eds), *Proceedings of the 4th International Conference PROFES 2002 LCNS 2559*. Berlin: Springer.

Punter, T., & Kusters, R., & Trienekens. J.J.M. (2004). The W-Process for Software Product Evaluation: A method for goal-oriented implementation of the ISO 14598 standard. *Software Quality Journal*, 12(2), 137-158.

Punter, T., & Hamilton, M., & Gurzhiy, T. (2007). Modeling the coordination idiom. In: Voeten, J.P.M. & Engelen, R. van, (Ed), IDEALS: evolvability in high-tech systems (pp.69-79). Eindhoven: Embedded Systems Institute.

Roos, N. (2006), No to requirements (in Dutch). In *Bits & Chips magazine*, Vol. 9. (pp. 24-26). Nijmegen: Techwatch.

Sandee, J.H., & Heemels, W.P.M.H., & Muller, G.J. (2006). Threads of reasoning. In: Heemels, W.P.M.H., & Muller, G.J. (Eds.), *Model-based design of high-tech systems*, (pp. 43-57). Eindhoven: Embedded Systems Institute.

Schmidt, D. (2006). Cover feature – Model Driven Engineering. *IEEE Computer*, 39(2), 25-31.

SEI (2007), Software Engineering Institute, Carnegie Mellon University, CMMi site. Retrieved October 22, 2007, from: http://www.sei.cmu.edu/cmmi/.

Staron, M., & Wohlin, C. (2006). An Industrial Case Study on the Choice Between Language Customization Mechanisms. In Münch, J., & Vierima, M. (Eds.), *Proceedings of 7th Interna-tional Conference on Product-Focused Software Process Improvement (PROFES 2006) LNCS 4034*, (pp. 177-191). Berlin: Springer.

Vaandrager, F. (2006), Does it pay-off? Model-based verification and validation of embedded systems! In *Progress White Papers 2006* (pp. 43-66). Utrecht: STW Progress.

Verhoef, M.H.G., & Hooman, J.J.M. (2006). Evaluating embedded system architectures. In Heemels, W.P.M.H., & Muller, G.J. (Eds.) *Model-based design of high-tech systems*, (pp. 151-159). Eindhoven: Embedded Systems Institute.

Vranken, H. (1998). *Design for test and debug in hardware/software systems* (PhD thesis). Eindhoven: Eindhoven University of Technology.

Wolf, W. (2003). A decade of hardware / software co-design. *IEEE Computer*, 36 (4), 38 – 43.

ADDITIONAL READING

Broy, M., Jonsson, B., Katoen, J.-P (Eds.) (2005), *Model-based Testing of Reactive Systems* LNCS 3472. Berlin: Springer.

This book provides a set of lectures on several topics that are related to model-based testing. Model-based testing will become increasingly important when MDE emerges. Topics vary from testing of finite state machines and labelled transition systems to test case generation, tools and test notation.

Czarnecki, K., & Helsen, S. (2006). *Feature-based survey of model transformation approaches*. IBM Systems Journal, 45(3), 621-645.

This paper provides a framework for model transformations (especially about the software discipline). Model transformations play a key role in model driven development.

Delnooz, C., Dohmen, L.A.J., Hee, J. van de, (2007). *The future of embedded real-time systems for high volume printing.* White paper Océ Technologies, (pp. 1-20), Retrieved October 31, from http://www3.oce.com/jobs/downloads/oce_embedded_systems.pdf

This white paper presents model driven development as one of the pillars for improving development at Océ Technologies (producer of printers and copiers). Other improvement pillars were reference architecture and software reuse.

Heemels, W.P.M.H., & Muller, G.J. (Eds.) *Model-based design of high-tech systems.* Eindhoven: Embedded Systems Institute.

Presents the results of an applied research project on model-driven technologies. This Boderc-project was conducted at Océ Technologies. It shows different examples of modelling and shows the need for multidisciplinary development (see section 2).

Kopetz, H. (1997), *Real-Time Systems: Design Principles for Distributed Embedded Applications.* Berlin: Springer.

This book provides an introduction to embedded (real-time) systems design.

Tretmans, J. (Ed.), *Tangram: Model-based integration and testing of complex high-tech systems.* Eindhoven: Embedded Systems Institute.

Presents the results of an applied research project on integration and testing (Tangram-project) that was conducted at ASML (producer of wafersteppers). This is interesting from a perspective of model driven engineering as well as its testing.

Pretschner, A., & Slotosch, O., & Aiglstorfer, E. (2004). Model-based testing for real – The inhouse card case study. *International Journal on Software Tools Technology Transfer*, 5 (2), 140-157.

This article provides experiences with model-based testing.

Chapter III
Examples and Evidence

Sowmya Karunakaran
MDA Research Initiative, Chennai, India

ABSTRACT

This chapter aims at highlighting the increased development productivity and quality that can be achieved by Model Driven Software Development (MDSD). The above statement is substantiated by discussing many experiments and case studies in the field of Model Driven development. The chapter will contain the study of various cases in which the Object Management Group's (OMG) Model Driven Architecture (MDA) has been used as a framework to build different applications. The reader will be provided with an overview of how the MDA paradigm greatly expedites application development with the proper tool support. The main emphasis will be on providing case studies for the measurement of the quality of the models.

INTRODUCTION

The software industry remains reliant on the craftsmanship of skilled individuals engaged in labor intensive manual tasks. However, growing pressure to reduce cost and time to market, and to improve software quality, may catalyze a transition to more automated methods. Evaluation of these methods will require more experiments and practical experience. Establishing of a comprehensive collection of benchmark problems would be a valuable next step in that direction. This chapter will serve as:

- A practical guide for software architects and developers as it is peppered with practical examples and extensive case studies.
- An Enchiridion for Model driven software quality assurance
- A rich resource, containing prominent examples for constructive Quality Assurance (QA) of MDSD
- A handbook of various techniques that can be employed for identifying the quality of models and model transformations.
- A trend analyzer, as it will give a broad overview on the tools and methods used by various researchers and professionals

BACKGROUND

MDA has enjoyed high visibility since its formal announcement by the OMG in March 2001. In three short years, well over 40 companies have come forward with software products said to implement MDA; while a smaller, but signifi- cant, number of success stories demonstrate that there really is something to this striking new concept.

It is no exaggeration to say that MDA has the potential to revolutionize the way we create and maintain software. Since MDA is becoming so popular, it is important to understand clearly what it is—and what it is not, but more importantly it is necessary to analyze the quality benefits it offers.

Let us see what the industry experts have to say about MDA:

MDA offers organizations several distinct advantages ... One of them which is, Interoperability and portability. The platform independence of the first stages of MDA development makes it easier to interoperate with, or even move to, different middleware. Given that the middleware space is crowded with Enterprise Java Beans, CORBA, Web Services, SOAP, C#, .NET and others, this represents a huge savings in time and cost. (Grady Booch)

Customer projects that previously took six months to complete are taking four using MDA. (PFPC Inc. in Wilmington, Del.)

Sophisticated organizations see the benefits of a model-driven approach, which is the future of effective software design. (Peter Young, Vice President, SUN ONE Studio Tools, Sun Micro- systems)

MDA is not about generating complete applica- tions from diagrams; it's about generating all the linkages to integrate applications from Unified

Modeling Language (UML) diagrams. It's also about having a common, high-level UML model of integration that can generate whatever proxies, bridges, and protocols are required to integrate a new application with those already in existence. (Wells Fargo Bank; IBM)

In the context of MDSD, the creation of mod- els and model transformations is a central task that requires a mature development environment based on the best practices of software engineer- ing principles. In a comprehensive approach to MDSD, models and model transformations must be designed, analyzed, synthesized, tested, main- tained and subjected to configuration management to ensure their quality. Working with multiple, in- terrelated models that describe a software system require significant effort to ensure their overall consistency. It follows that automating the task of model consistency checking and synchroniza- tion would greatly improve the productivity of developers and the quality of the models.

This chapter will give the reader an insight on how model driven architecture has been used to build different kind of applications that run on disparate platforms. It will also highlight the benefits like increased productivity, improved software quality and reduced complexity that were obtained by means of following a MDA approach.

The software industry is often ready to profess that MDA methodology and tools can produce code more quickly than manual hand-coding (the traditional way of software development) can. But unfortunately the industry is less ready to accept that these code generators can produce good quality code. The biggest concern is that these generators will turn out to be tumescent, one-size-fits all and on the whole produce im- practical code.

Interestingly, the concerns that the software industry currently has parallel those that program- mers/ software developers had years ago when "third generation languages" (3GLs) such as CO-

BOL started to replace assembly level languages. Programmers did not believe that compilers, which translated COBOL programs into lower-level assembly language, could produce assembly code of the same quality that humans can. In the early days of 3GLs, these concerns were rationalized. Eventually, though, compilers improved and the productivity boost that 3GLs provided over assembly language was so large as to overwhelm any lingering concerns about code quality. To a programmer using a modern 3GL such as .NET, the idea of programming a business application in assembly language would seem ludicrous since it would require ten times as many lines of code. The reasonable question, then, is: *"How far have the MDA methods and tools advanced in producing quality code / models?"*

Though there is no prescribed or defined way of determining the quality of models and model transformations, the various techniques used in different experiments and case studies will be presented in this chapter, which can be used to understand the quality of MDA models and tools.

MDA CASE STUDIES

In this following section we will discuss two case studies in detail. The first one deals with applying MDA for a Student Loan Origination System (LOS) and the second one is about adopting MDA for an Air traffic control system. Let us discuss them in more detail.

Adopting MDA for a Student LOS

Background

Introduction
The Model-Driven Architecture is a development paradigm that aims to insulate business and application logic from technology evolution. It helps to build code quickly, in a middleware-independent, well architected, consistent and maintainable fashion. When fully baked, MDA promises to revolutionize software development. It could bring greater productivity, quality and flexibility – all at the same time. However, the industry has to undergo the usual teething pains. Thus, this case study aims at ironing out some of the impracticalities of adopting MDA.

The LOS
The most essential feature of LOS is its Loan Application Processing Workflow. Each loan application is monitored from the time it is entered into the system, and tracked through the various work steps of review and approval process. LOS allows these work steps to be performed in different locations while maintaining control of the flow and making sure no required steps are being missed.

The Loan Origination System consists of the following modules.

*   Application Initiation
*   Decision
*   Product Configuration
*   Pricing
*   Application Completeness
*   Disbursement
*   Workflow
*   Customer Services

The MDA Pilot

Based on the domain information, business rules and expressions, a LOS domain model has been built. We have used UML as a key ingredient to underpin the models that we developed at various stages. As a first step, the MDA pilot team concentrated on just a set of modules which includes retrieving, displaying and validating loan application information.

Our preliminary results show that using MDA as the core element of software composition, leads to reduced development complexity, improved system maintainability, and increased developer productivity. The qualitative and quantitative results will be analyzed by comparing the efficiencies of the MDA approach with that of the traditional Software Development Lifecycle (SDLC) approach.(Sowmya, 2005)

The Build 0 Module

Constituents

The build 0 module (the initial phase of the project, that would consist of the very first build) consists of the document retrieval and review processes. The basic steps involved in this process are illustrated by Figure 1. Initially the supervisor enters into the Review documents phase were the promissory note verification is done. Based on the outcome of this verification process the user updates the document status after which the system checks whether the document under review should be accepted or rejected.

Pre-Conditions Assumed

The following conditions were assumed before the document review process began:

1. Application is completed and data is available
2. Documents are received from the applicant
3. Document reviewer has logged in to the system
4. Documents are loaded for reviewing

Retrieve and Display

Actor initiates document verification by entering the document verification section. System loads the documents based on the criterion chosen by the user. The document status is changed to In Review. System logs the status change. Document verification will be performed based on main document type and these will have individual check lists.

Figure 1. Major steps involved in Build 0 Module (©2007 Sowmya Karunakaran. Used with permission)

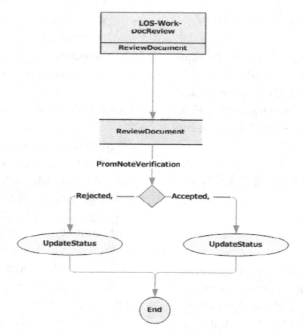

Document Verification

The actor initiates the review of documents. The content of document is compared against application data in the system. Once the checklist items are complete the actor submits the checklist .The system identifies the minimum requirements to pass the document verification based on check list items and calculates the status. A notification is sent to the borrower based on the outcome of the above event.

Traditional Strategy

The traditional strategy team followed the usual SDLC lifecycle and more importance was given to the technical, platform-specific design rather than to building perfect domain specific models. They arrived at a high level business process diagram (see Figure 2).

Once this was done the team came out with an architecture blueprint. They aimed at an architecture that could provide scalability, flexibility and maintainability. The business rules were decoupled from the application code. As per the traditional strategy flow diagrams were used to represent the various steps in that module. Figure 3.3 depicts one of the flow diagrams used in this approach.

MDA Strategy

Modeling

The traditional approach captured all the necessary details but flow diagrams are tools of structured programming era, as a solution the MDA strategy uses Business Process Modeling Language (BPML)—to represent business related information and UML—to provide appropriate

Figure 2. Architectural components (©2007 Sowmya Karunakaran. Used with permission)

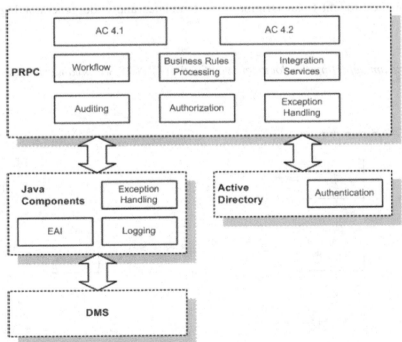

object oriented visual representations. Figure 4 represents a model of the student loan origination retrieval and verification process.

Code Generation

The MDA team created a UML Platform-Independent Model (PIM) as well as Platform-Specific Model (PSM) using their MDA tool. They auto-generated more of their code than the traditional team due to the UML code generation capabilities of the MDA approach. The team used a popular MDA tool called Arcstyler for this purpose (Sowmya, 2005).

There are, of course, parts of an application which cannot be generated because they either cannot be expressed appropriately in a UML model or are much easier to express in other ways. The user must therefore supply the custom layout for the front-end's user interface elements and implement appropriate reactions for certain events (actions).

EJB Tier

Figure 5 represents the model developed by the MDA team for the Student Loan Origina-

tion System. The R's in the diagram represent the resources (modeled as Entity bean classes). LOS-Data-Document contains details relevant to document like document id which maps to the scanned image stored in the DMS. The LOS-CheckList class contains the list of all checklist items which are of Boolean type (e.g.: IsBorrowerSignatureValid). The loan details and the client details are contained in their respective classes. The P's in the diagram represent the processes. The LOSRetreiver and LOSVerification processes are Session beans which perform the retrieving and verification operations. The complete details bean holds both the Loan details and the client details for retrieval process to happen.

Web Tier

The Accessor framework of the tool was used for developing a web application and the corresponding front end. It supports UML modeling of external interfaces of a software system by adding design assistants, wizards, property sheets and model generators.

Arcstyler Accessor MDA-Cartridges contain templates and code generator logic which can

Figure 3. Flow diagram depicting the document verification (©2007 Sowmya Karunakaran. Used with permission)

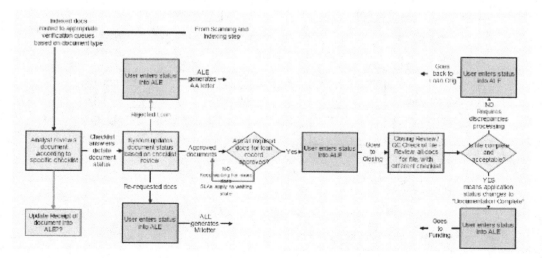

Figure 4. Business process model of retrieve and verify documents (©2007 Sowmya Karunakaran. Used with permission)

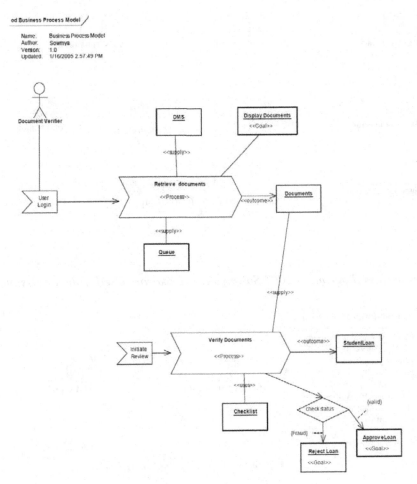

produce an almost complete application front-end from an Accessor model, including all the functionality for dispatching events, switching between windows in response to certain events and mapping resources.

Results of Case Study

Various inferences can be derived at from this case study. These give a holistic view of applying MDA to a real time project scenario.

- In case of the traditional method maximum amount of the project lifecycle was spent on coding, whereas in the MDA approach most of the code was auto-generated and only the code relevant to business logic had to be written by the programmer.

- Though the time taken for developing a domain model was slightly more, it was compensated to a great extent by the considerable saving in time during the implementation phase. The MDA approach took about 1/9th

Figure 5. EJB class diagram

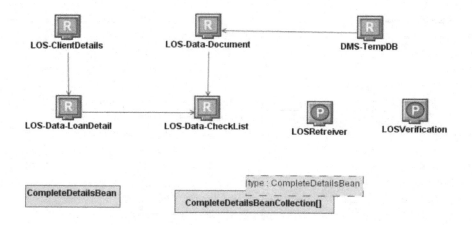

Figure 6. Accessor class diagram (©2007 Sowmya Karunakaran. Used with permission)

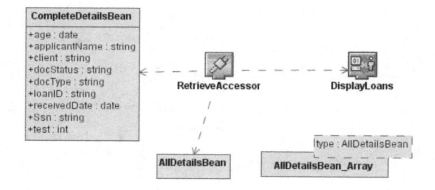

of the time required to develop using the traditional approach.

- The number of developers involved in the MDA approach was just 3, which is very small when compared to a regular project team size which was approximately 22.

- Initially the team faced technical difficulties due to lack of expertise on the tool, but it was not an impediment for long.

- The percentage purity of MDA in this approach entirely depends on the tool used. The tool ArcStyler was used which followed the MDA standards and principles to a great extent.

- Tools ought to be more comprehensive and MDA specific

- Maximum effort was spent on building the domain model; hence it would serve as a platform for use in another project of the same domain.

- Since the domain model had to be changed to reflect every small modification, the design was in sync with the implementation at all times. Addition of new features/deletion of unwanted features can be done by just making the corresponding changes to the design without messing up with the code. This means more flexibility and more maintainability.

Conclusion

Based on the results of this case study, the MDA team was impressed by the productivity gains experienced during this approach. The domain models (Platform Independent) have very long life span as it survives technology and lasts for many years. For more than 2.5 years since the generation of models there were only minimal changes made to the models and the code. This was possible because of the careful design of the models. All new requirements were incorporated by extending the existing models. Apart from the obvious speed advantages from model based code generation, the strong emphasis that this approach places on modeling and therefore on architecture is a huge benefit. The MDA team owes that any demerits arousing out of this approach might be because of the insufficiencies in the MDA tools that were available in 2005 like lack of in built compilers for modeling languages. With more evolution of the MDA tools, its true flavor can be relished.

Applying MDA to an Air Traffic Control System

In this case study we will be considering a prototype model the data sharing mesh (DSM). The DSM explores new methods for providing reliable data connections in heterogeneous networks. The DSM delivers the middleware to connect business applications that provide and consume data with defined quality levels. The software engineering process that comes with the DSM has to allow the measurement and feedback of relevant quality aspects at every step during development, test, and operation. In this section we will see the use of MDA in the development of the system and how software quality can be measured and improved.

The Air Traffic Control System

The Air Traffic Control System is shown in Figure 7; it presents a set of business applications and the DSM➜mesh network. The DSM➜Mesh network consists of nodes and margins. There are two types of nodes: circular nodes and triangular nodes. Circular nodes handle highly secure connections only, while triangular nodes do not provide specific security mechanisms. A margin refers to a network connection with specific characteristics, e.g. bandwidth. Business applications are listed on the left and on the right hand sides indicating that they are loosely coupled, i.e., they do not know anything of each other apart from data providing and consuming contracts. Each application is connected to at least one network node. In our simplified example a business application is a sink service that requires a specific type of data to work properly; or a source service that produces data needed by sink services.

The real-world scenario describes source services, like Detector I, Detector II and Meteorological tower; and sink services like the Air master or the Crash Detection Mechanism (CDM). The CDM needs data updates every three seconds. This data is provided by reliable detectors that react to conditions out of predefined limits. These limits are configurable. The Air Master requires reliable detector data on demand that must not be older than 0.59 seconds, to update the traffic situation overview and to coordinate the aircrafts flying around the airport. Based on the real-time data requirements a new version of the DSM➜mesh is generated, tested, and deployed whenever needed; changes are expected on a weekly basis. The range of application data demands is very wide, but all applications have requirements on reliability, timeliness, safety, service quality, failover, performance, maintainability, and flexibility.

Development of the DSM➜mesh focuses on models to define the business application requirements (see Figure 8)

- *Agreement* defines the communication needs of business application systems in the DSM➜mesh. An agreement has to identify the application in the network, provide syntax of attributes for each message type of the system, and specify the way how the system handles) and the attributes of the agreement (accuracy, confidentiality, urgency, priority).

- *System capabilities* describe the topology of the network, connection capabilities like capacity and type of connections, and useful information on lower-level middleware

such as protocols used of the systems that contribute to DSM➜mesh.

- *Plan-of-action (POA)* reflects interests of the organizations contributing to DSM and DSM-based applications; these specify the guidelines the model transformation process has to follow when building the system configuration plan. Such guidelines involve parameters concerning global settings (e.g., route secure message over specific secure nodes and margins only, the number of backup routes for failover), optimization criteria (e.g. favor low cost over speed), and operator restrictions (e.g. detector data has to be routed via a certain node).

- Fail-safe parameters define the failover mechanism behavior (automatic or user active) of the DSM➜mesh to adjust to failures (e.g., node or margin failure) as well-defined graceful performance degradation to the business applications and stakeholders.

Figure 7. Air traffic control system

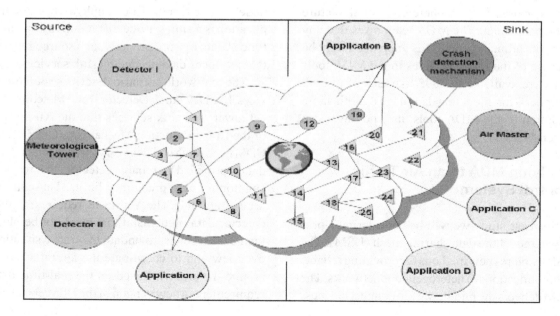

Figure 8. MDA software development life cycle with QA steps (©2007 Sowmya Karunakaran. Used with permission)

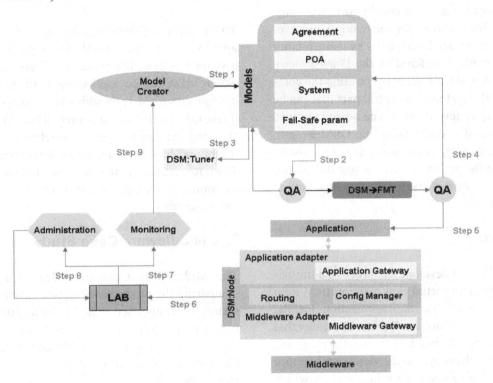

MDA Quality Assurance

A major issue in safety-critical systems is quality measurement, quality assurance, and auditing. We describe the key steps in the DSM life cycle that deal with QA. Before the models are used as input for the DSM➔FMT they have to pass the first QA checkpoint where type checks and semantic validation tests ensure formal consistency and validity of the models. If the QA finds contradictions, the errors are reported and the result of the process is fed back to the model descriptions. The configuration plan created by the DSM➔FMT is checked by another QA checkpoint. Here the intermediate models have to pass a static validity test, i.e., checking whether there is at least one contract matching source for each sink or whether there is a route between two services. Errors are reported, which can be used for correction in the models. The set of nodes that builds the DSM➔mesh can be tested in several scenarios in a lab environment before rolled out into field operation. Status and performance values are sent to the administrator, who may change configuration settings of DSM➔nodes directly. The values gained from monitoring the DSM➔mesh are valuable contributions to the work done by the DSM➔Tuner and Model Developer. Both roles may perform changes based on the results from previous calculations in the hope to improve the quality of the entire DSM➔mesh and starting from step 1 again.(Sowmya, 2007)

First of all the DSM➜FMT life cycle has been designed in a way that allows the installation of several quality assurance checkpoints, the usage of monitoring components and making improvements in the model descriptions by using quality feedback methods offered by the DSM➜mesh. The DSM➜FMT allows concentrating the complexity of the system at a central part that can be maintained by few experts. The advantage is in the number of systems using the DSM➜mesh. The result of corrected problems appearing in one system configuration affects not just the quality of the DSM➜mesh itself but also any system based on DSM.

Conclusion

In the traditional development process, administrators have just a partial view of the entire system and may try to optimize their applications locally. This may result in an overall system behavior that maybe was not intended. However, the proposed MDA approach always has the view over the entire system trying to optimize it in a way by which each of the participating systems can benefit.

Second, the models themselves may contain errors, but similar to specifications in traditional engineering these errors could be found with appropriate verification.

An advantage is the fact that those models support role-oriented abstraction; thus the system models are easier to understand and errors are easier to detect. Although the life cycle contains several QA checkpoints, the DSM life cycle itself may contain errors as well. As these get detected and eliminated, the corrected life cycle will have a positive impact on all those projects using the DSM life cycle.

HIGH QUALITY SOFTWARE MODELS

This section will introduce the reader to various applications in which MDA was applied. It will give the reader an insight on the diverse fields in which MDA can be applied and its benefits can be enjoyed successfully without any compromise on the QA. The Results section will help in understanding the various quality benefits that MDA offers and how they are utilized appropriately. The implementation specific details have not been elaborated as the emphasis is on QA benefits and measurements.

The Middleware Case Study

The Middleware Company released a study comparing the productivity of two development teams, where one used an MDA tool and the other used a more traditional Integrated Development Environment (IDE). The study concluded that the team using the MDA tool was significantly more productive.

The Middleware Company case study highlights the increased productivity (nearly 35% increase) benefits of MDA for Enterprise Application Development Projects. The study compared the productivity of two development teams. One team used a traditional IDE and the other used an MDA tool: Compuware OptimalJ. The organizers gave each team an identical specification for a distributed application, where upon the teams started building the application.(Frankel, 2003)

Productivity Results
Table 1 shows the overall productivity results. The MDA team finished the application in considerably less time than the traditional team. Furthermore, it bested its own hours estimate by a substantial margin. This can be attributed to the fact that the capabilities of the MDA tool used were underestimated.

Table 1. Productivity results

	Estimated Hours	Actual Hours
Traditional IDE Team	499	507.5
MDA Team	442	330

Quality Results

Although this was primarily a productivity study, the study's expert organizers inspected the code the two teams produced for general quality and found the two results were of good and roughly comparable quality. An automated check for acyclic dependencies, a common indicator of code quality, also produced favorable and similar results for the two teams. Furthermore, some bugs were found in the code produced via the traditional approach whereas none were found in the MDA team's code. This can be attributed to the fact that the code was generated by the tool with the input as the PIMs and PSMs which required very less manual intervention (coding).

Automation with MDA Framework

Wisconsin is part of a small but committed group of organizations that is turning to Model Driven Architecture. Wisconsin is replacing its collection of disparate mainframe- and client/server based unemployment insurance benefits applications with a Web based system with a MDA approach.

The following are the features that were noted by and highlighted in the MDA implementer's workshop 2003 (which was an outcome of the Wisconsin project case study):

- Ease of transition from one platform to another

- Ease of Integration with existing legacy applications
- Apply domain specific reference business
- Providing framework for vendor –specific transformation mappings
- Extended useful lifetime of system models
- Support for specialized computing environments

Applying MDA to Large Scale Distributed Systems

There are many challenges in the large-scale distributed systems like,

(i) Increasingly demanding end user requirements for quality and functionality
(ii) Complexities associated with integrating large-scale distributed systems composed of modular components.

This case study dealt with addressing those challenges by means of MDA. The motivation to the use of an integrated Model Driven Architecture (MDA) and component middleware approach to enhance the level of abstraction at which distributed systems are developed is to improve quality. The purpose of the study was to extend their current MDA modeling tools so they can perform a two step mapping from the domain specific model.

Result

The platform-independent component based architecture presented the platform- independent model to a component-specific implementation. This resulted in a marked increase in software quality and developer productivity and at the same time reduced the complexity of component integration.

Inventory Tracking System

Siemens Corporate Technology and Vanderbilt University applied MDA and component middleware software techniques to develop an Inventory Tracking System (ITS) that monitors and controls the flow of goods and assets in warehouses. Warehouse modeling, which simplifies the warehouse configuration aspect of the ITS system according to the equipment available in certain warehouses, including moving conveyor belts and various types of cranes. These modeling tools can synthesize the ITS database configuration and population. Modeling and synthesizing the deployment and configuration (D&C) aspects of the components that implement the ITS functionality were performed. These modeling tools use MDA technology along with CORBA Component Model (CCM) (Nechypurenko, Lu, Deng, Douglas & Anirudha , 2003).

Result

The MDA paradigm greatly expedites application development with the proper tool support. In the ITS project, if the warehouse model is the only missing or changing aspect in the system (which is typical for end users), little new application code must be written. The preliminary results show that using MDA tools and component middleware as the core elements of software composition leads to reduced development complexity, improved system maintainability, and increased developer productivity.

Enterprise Application Integration

Wells Fargo had large number of mainframe based Systems of Record(SOR's) which are based on CICS, COBOL, DB/2, IMS, etc and Client applications were Win/NT or UNIX based systems using object technology. They used CORBA middleware to bridge the two processing environments while meeting the service requirements. The structure of their major operations were to define the application in a platform independent model in UML, generate the appropriate UML platform specific models needed by the application, augment the model with any additional code needed by the application that completes the business logic functionality and generate the application programs

Result

An object based framework that normalizes the disparate SOR's present in the enterprise into a consistent, standard environment or logical system was achieved. It also provided a single interface to the client application business analyst and programmer. The framework was both platform and language neutral.

Model Driven Software Development and Offshore Outsourcing

Faced with a limited budget and a short time-to-market requirement, M1 Global chose the following solution for the software development project. First, they would employ Model Driven Architecture during the design phase of the project. M1 Global rightly identified that MDA would help them organize and manage enterprise architectures supported by automated tools and services for both defining the models and facilitating transformations between different model types. This enabled the M1 Global process experts to encapsulate their intellectual property into a PIM of the application. The model represented exactly what the software application would do regardless of the complexity of the application architecture. The model provided a high degree of confidence for both the development organization and the "business experts" that the application would be built exactly to the requirements defined by the team and expressed in the model. Additionally, based on the platform independence of the model, the intellectual property is not tied to a given technology but rather to the business logic. Thus, the application behavior captured in the model outlasts rapid changes in application architecture (OMG, 2004).

Result

M1 Global built an application using MDA, Model-Driven Development environment (MDE) and offshore development resources with impressive results. The R&D expense for the software project was $1,007,354. M1 Global was able to realize a cost saving of $7,500 per month per offshore development resource. Given that this was a large scale project, M1 had an average team size of 20 offshore resources over the 12 month period. The low cost of the offshore resources resulted in a net savings of over $1,200,000 over the life of the project. That was just the resource cost, the MDA approach brought about another significant benefit illustrated in Table 2.

The MDA approach and the MDE tool increased developer productivity by over 50 percent. The team's final productivity for the period was 177,963 optimized quality source lines of code (LOC) for an application that totaled 161 unique screens and 45 tables. With an iterative development process the team had actually produced over 3x that number of LOC throughout the project.

Using MDE, the team generated 112,506 LOC or just over 63 percent of the final implementation. This meant the hand written LOC in the final version were 65,457 and at a cost of $5.66 per hand written LOC, the benefits of model driven development where clear. Without it, it would have taken the same team over 32 months to complete the same work that was accomplished in 12 months. The total cost would have exceeded $6 million. The combination of MDA, MDE and offshore resources saved M1 over $5 million in development costs and reduced time to market by over 62%.

Inter-Enterprise Integration

Government computer based patient record system (GCPR) project was a joint effort of the DoD, US and Louisiana Medical center to maintain medical records on patient care. The key to gathering

Table 2. Comparison of results

	HAND WRITTEN LOC	COST/ LOC	TIME	TOTAL COST	PERCENT SAVINGS
Traditional U.S. Based Development	177,963	$ 34.83	32 Months	$ 6,198,812	N/A
With MDE	65,457	$ 34.83	12 Months	$ 2,280,000	272%
With MDE and Offshore	65,457	$ 5.66	12 Months	$ 1,007,354	615%

all the information on a single patient is to have a standard format into which information can be organized which was previously maintained on different computer platforms and have diverse ways of organizing, naming and coding .

The GCPR framework involves transforming data from various formats into a common one. In effect, Litton collaborated with the government to ensure that the UML reference model that described patient information could be incorporated and processed by the framework.

Thus this MDA based framework was useful in developing a powerful, generic solution to the transformation problem. The GCPR system is in the pilot testing phase. It will be ready for general use after security and privacy designs are implemented.

Total Business Integration

IONA is on the forefront of the move to MDA .IONA Global Services uses MDA principles to create flexible software solutions for customers. This involved isolating information and processing logic from technology specifics for building platform independent models. UML is independent of CORBA, COM, EJB, XML, etc., and thus is well-suited as a language for describing these models like mapping these models to specific platforms, maintaining the separation at the implementation level.

Result
IONA's Total Business Integration (TBI) requires the flexibility for the evolving environment. MDA has been important for building such solutions that can be flexibly applied in this kind of environment.

MDA Applied to Web Services and Federated Systems

Metanology is working on codifying architectural frameworks for web services and federated sys-

tems. Federated systems are loosely connected systems from different enterprises performing portions of the same application.

It involved Applications PIM loaded into the MDA tool (Application), Codified Architecture loaded into MDA tool (Platform), an MDA tool that generates 90% of application's implementation (Application on platform) and customize 10% of application

Result
The architectural cost was fixed, the code generation capability was over 90%, and there was a complete elimination of training developers on architecture. The complexity was also reduced. There were more economic benefits and increased adherence to corporate standards.

Implementation of Web Services, Simplified

Sun Microsystems has contributed a series of modules supporting MDA to the Net Beans open source project. This makes Netbeans platform first of its kind to support the MDA.

MDA protects the organizations software investments by capturing business logic -- business processes and their appropriate interactions -- in re-usable models. MDA can help significantly simplify the implementation of Web services, as the architecture insulates models from changes in the deployment infrastructure for the services. Models use a set of metadata -- the data describing the structure and characteristics of program elements or data.

Result
The MDA represents an advanced approach to software design based on models created using languages such as the UML. As business requirements change or evolve components of model-driven applications can easily be replaced, as long as they are standards based.

A Model-Based Architecture for Data Warehouse

The Component Warehouse Model (CWM) specification recently adopted by the OMG is an important milestone on the way to fully model-based architectures supporting data warehouse interchange.

The diversity of operational data sources and target data warehouse engines has made the construction and maintenance of data warehouses challenging. In these type of configurations, data warehouse deployment and maintenance tools interface with a shared store containing metadata about the structure of various operational data sources and target data warehouses as well as descriptions of the transformations required to move data between them (Tolbert, 2000).

Results
There were substantial savings even when the number of operational data sources and warehouse targets was as low as 3. There was considerable reduction in the number of semantic connections with which data warehousing tools must contend data warehouse applications by making them more compliant with a "Component/Connector" architecture in which the tools are the components and the shared model store serves as the connector.

MDA in Wireless (2.5 G)

Verizon used MDA for Code Division Multiple Access (CDMA) wireless switching, billing and activation with the help of Kabira technologies. Migration from Advanced Mobile Phone Service (AMPS) to CDMA wireless switching for 1.7 million customers involves changes to service packages, payment process etc.

France telecom mobile has a Short Message Directory Service (SMDS) in which name & number information is sent to phone via Short Message Service (SMS). All message manage-

ment is fully transactional, fully deployed, design & development in 9 weeks from UML Models and MDA.

Results
There was a considerable reduction in activation period from 3 days to 90 minutes and nearly 1600 hours per day in labor reduction. The support was increased to more than 12 million stubs and 6,000 operators on 6 servers. It is worthwhile to mention that it was the world's first SMS push based directory service implementation.

FUTURE RESEARCH DIRECTIONS

The following section will give you guidelines on interesting research topics in the MDA space.

Compilers for Modeling Languages. Model-driven software development has numerous advantages over manually developed software. The most important are: higher level of abstraction, facilitated maintainability, less erroneous code and higher re-usability. The higher level of abstraction allows the developer to concentrate on the important parts of the system and to leave the details to a compiler. This increases productivity because the developer does not need to deal with details, creates consistent implementations of designs and facilitates to deploy one design to several implementation technologies and/or platforms. The advantages of modeling languages compared to programming languages are the same as the advantages of high-level programming languages compared to assembly languages. Therefore the availability of compilers for modeling languages would lead to the replacement of high-level programming languages by modeling languages similar to the replacement of assembly languages by high-level programming languages.

Systematic empirical studies. Next steps after developing the core functionality of the MDA approach are systematic empirical studies to ensure the correctness and sufficient performance of the resulting system configurations.(Kan, 2002) An important aspect is early modeling for reliability design to consistently carry dependability concerns from the early to the late stages of software engineering.

Creating perfect models. Since only models drive the development they need to be very consistent and accurate. A misinterpretation done at a PIM level could affect the subsequent PSM's and the generated code. Hence more work has to be done in the field of creating perfect models. (Miller, Mukerji , 2007)

Introducing MDA within the organization. For organizations that use a traditional systems development approach a major question is when it is worthwhile to introduce a new development approach, such as MDA, which are expected to bring benefits to software development like faster or more efficient development. Again, empirical studies are needed to get evidence on the actual benefits and risks in comparable settings.

With all the business benefits and advantages that MDA offers it is vital that we understand to which type of projects that MDA will be most useful. Here are some general considerations to keep in mind when making such a decision.

- MDA is adopted mostly if there is a significant amount of experience with UML or for a new project.
- MDA may not be best suited for an intermediate stage of a development.
- Organizations that want the agility to change with the evolving technologies would find MDA beneficial.

This list is not exhaustive; there are many more instances of projects to which MDA can be applied. Identifying all these instances would be very interesting research area in the MDA space.

The transition plan. A transition plan should cover staff development, team organization, and updates to the way that IT relates to the business. The plan should outline a strategy for a gradual transition to MDA that coordinates groundwork on all of these tracks.

The plan should also plot a pilot project that serves as a mechanism to shake out bugs in the new approach and that, when complete, provides functionality that the business needs but that is of relatively low visibility. The plan should include an organized post-mortem to learn from mistakes and make corrections along the various tracks of the transition.

Importance of domain models. The most emphasized advantage that MDA offers is the ability to reduce the risk of technology lock-in. Since the development is based upon Domain models, which are technology independent it is possible to derive application models and code models based on any technology. This gives a considerable amount of versatility in meeting with changing business needs and technology. Hence progress in development of good and perfect domain models would certainly be a good step towards future.

Interesting and useful findings in the above mentioned research areas will contribute to improve the Quality Assurance of MDA based systems to a great extent.

INFERENCES

The high quality models and case studies discussed above give us the idea of the business advantages that MDA offered. The following points consolidate these advantages:

1. **Preservation of investment in application development.** As mentioned earlier, MDA ensures that rapid changes in technology do not render application useless.

2. **Increased productivity.** MDA emphasizes on the use of patterns. The use of patterns in turn assists the developer in automating the repetitive tasks hence reducing the time spent on writing code and allows focusing on the business perspective.

3. **Increased business agility.** MDA gives the ability to respond to changing business needs by changing the application model and the business framework.

4. **Reduced Development Cost and Time to Market.** MDA simplifies the tasks of maintaining the software. Since a good number of the development tasks are automated the development process time is much less.

5. **Improvement in the quality of product.** Since the use of patterns promotes best practices in coding. This in turn reflects upon the software as well.

The later a software error is discovered during the development process, the more expensive it is to fix and the more jeopardized a delivery date becomes. MDA model automation and testing has helped developers test their applications— at the model level, before coding begins. As a result, design flaws and application logic errors are uncovered much further upstream in the development process. In addition, many tools allow automation and testing of models on the target hardware to help uncover platform-specific problems earlier in the process. The fundamental simplicity of PIMs brings substantially improved system quality. We have also seen from this chapter that modeling has helped in improving communication between team members and facilitates early elimination of defects. Thus, it is apt to say that MDA adds lots of quality benefits to the resulting product.

CONCLUSION

To ensure that MDA gives the above said quality benefits certain issues should be dealt with properly. The transformations of PIM to PSM and then PSM to Code have to be consistent as well. Although the PSM to Code transformation is common the PIM to PSM is not. It is MDA's initiative to build a methodology that creates code from a PIM level. Hence the core of MDA lies in the patterns used in these transformations and should be the focal point in the MDA development scenario. The lack of standards for domain patterns can also be a concern.

On the whole, the MDA approach promises a number of benefits including improved portability due to separating the application knowledge from the mapping to a specific implementation technology, increased productivity due to automating the mapping, improved quality due to reuse of well proven patterns and best practices in the mapping, and improved maintainability due to better separation of concerns and better consistency and traceability between models and code.

REFERENCES

[1].De Miguel, M., Jourdan, J., Salicki, S.:(2002) *Practical Experiences in the Application of MDA.* In: Stevens, P., Whittle, J., Booch, G. (eds.): The 6th Int. Conf. on UML, Vol. 2460, Springer-Verlag (2002) 128-139.

[2].D'Souza, D., "Model-Driven Architecture and Integration: Opportunities and Challenges", Version 1.1. http://www.catalysis.org/publications/papers/2001mda-reqs-desmond-6.pdf

[3].Frankel,D.S, *Model Driven Architecture. Applying MDA to Enterprise Computing.* Indianapolis, Indiana. Wiley. 2003.

[4].Kan, S.,(2002) *Metrics and Models in Software Quality Engineering.* 2nd Edition; Addison Wesley.

[5].Kleppe, A., Warmer, J., & W. Bast (2003) , *MDA Explained. The Practice and Promise of the Model Driven Architecture.* Addison-Wesley, 2003.

[6].Miller, J., & Mukerji, J (January 2007), *Model Driven Architecture (MDA)*, http://www.omg.org/docs/ormsc/01-07-01.pdf

[7].Nechypurenko, A., Tao lu., Gan deng. , Douglas,C & Anirudha Gokhule (2003) Applying MDA and Component Middleware to Large Scale Distributed Systems, Vanderbilt University, Nashville,TN,USA

[8].[Online document] May 2007, Available at http://www.complang.tuwien.ac.at/richard/SW

[9].Sowmya, K.,(2005) *Reflections on MDA Case studies, MDA Research Initiative (MRI), Chennai, India*

[10].Sowmya, K.,(2007) Improving Air traffic control management system by adopting the MDA strategy, MDA Research Initiative, Chennai, India

[11].Tolbert, D., *CWM: A Model-Based Architecture for Data Warehouse Interchange*, Workshop on Evaluating Software Architectural Solutions 2000, University of California at Irvine, May, 2000. http://www.cwmforum.org/uciwesas2000.htm

ADDITIONAL READING

[1].   Stephen J. Mellor & Marc J. Balcer , *Executable UML: A Foundation for Model-Driven Architecture* , Addison Wesley Professional May 2002 .

This book prescribes the engineering process to follow while modeling a software system, and thoughtfully walks the reader through this process and the various UML models with numerous examples and real-world experiences. It provides complete executable semantics for an implementation independent interpretation of how models execute on any arbitrary implementation. This book uses a specific product and so it is most useful to BridgePoint tool users or those who are evaluating this tool set.

[2].   Evans,E., Domain-Driven Design: Tackling Complexity in the Heart of Software Addison Wesley Professional August 2003

This book announces to the world the ability of models and shows how the modeling processes scale up to very complicated domains. This book covers the problem domain space and the abstraction skills that free programmers to "break out of the box" of the implementation domain and solution objects into the critical area the business domain and corresponding domain objects. This is a great book for developers, business analysts, project managers, and anyone in the software business.

[3].   Warmer,J., & Kleppe,A., The Object Constraint Language: Getting Your Models Ready for MDA, second edition. Addison Wesley, 2003.

This book focuses on the Business Rules implementation in MDA, and brings the details needed. Step by step the book explains the OCL language and provides the reader with the knowledge to use OCL from a MDA point of view using transformation examples translating OCL to Java business rules. This book through explanations, clear and concrete examples and a concise case study shows the reader how to take your software engineering skills to the next level. It is a boon to students and new programmers.

[4].   Larman,C., Applying UML and Patterns: An Introduction to Object-Oriented Analysis and Design and Iterative Development, Third Edition Prentice Hall October 2004

The author argues convincingly that Unified Process is best implemented in an iterative process that looks more like Extreme Programming than the cumbersome waterfall process one typically associates with UP. Along the way of learning OOA/D, the unified process and design theory, you also learn how to create the most common UML diagrams. This includes use cases, domain model, interaction, class diagrams and others. This book will be beneficial to researchers as it also touches upon OOAD along with models and UML.

[5]. Kontio,M., Softera, Architectural manifesto: Choosing MDA tools, Developer Works IBM, Sep 2005 http://www.ibm.com/developerworks/library/wi-arch18.html?ca=drs-

This article not just gives an overview of selected tools it also categorizes the kinds of tools available and explain their usefulness in different parts of the MDA process. This enables the reader to comparatively evaluate tools of the same type, as well as let them look at such issues as productivity, efficiency, and ease of use. This is a must read article before deciding on the MDA tool to use for any project or case study.

[6]. Van Gorp, P.; Janssens, D.; Gardner, T. Write once, deploy N: a performance oriented MDA case study , Enterprise Distributed Object Computing Conference, 2004. EDOC 2004. Proceedings. Eighth IEEE International Volume , Issue , 20-24 Sept. 2004 Page(s): 123 – 134

This paper shows that Model Driven Architecture can become a successful standard for model based code generation by offering a set of high quality code generation languages. To focus the comparison of such languages on criteria that matter in practical development, there is an urgent need for more, and more realistic, case studies. This paper presents a complex middleware performance. From this case study the requirements for model refinement and code generation languages can be derived.

[7]. Conallen,J., Tropeano,D., & Brown,A,W., Practical Insights into MDA: Lessons from the Design and Use of an MDA Toolkit, in Model-Driven Software Development, pages 403-432, S. Beydeda, M. Book, V. Gruhn (Eds.), Springer Verlag, 2005.

This paper provides a set of practical lessons derived from the design and use of an MDA toolkit. It describes the MDA Toolkit and its use, and highlights the key lessons in the use of an MDA approach from these experiences. It concludes with some good observations on the MDA approach.

Chapter IV
Integrating Quality Criteria and Methods of Evaluation for Software Models

Anna E. Bobkowska
Gdańsk University of Technology, Poland

ABSTRACT

Successful realization of the model-driven software development visions in practice requires high quality models. This chapter focuses on the quality of models themselves. It discusses context-free and context-dependent quality criteria for models and then moves on to methods of evaluation which facilitate checking whether a model is good enough. We use linguistic theories to understand groups of criteria and their impact on other models, software product and the process of software development. We propose a strict distinction of the impacts of visual modeling languages, models of the system and tools for quality criteria. This distinction is helpful when designing the methods of evaluation and making decision about the point in time, scope and personnel responsible for quality assessment. As the quality criteria and several methods of evaluation has usually been considered separately we propose a methodology which integrates them. Such an integrated approach provides the following benefits. It allows for designing methods of evaluation based on quality criteria and elements of the model (or modeling language) in the context of specific needs. It can be applied for management of the scope of evaluation with quality criteria as well as configuration of the method to a specific situation. It allows for flexible and efficient conduct of the evaluation with selection of the methods of evaluation. Finally, this chapter presents case studies which illustrate the approach.

INTRODUCTION

Models play the central role in model-driven software development approaches. However, only good models really support work of analysts, managers and developers. Only good models have the potential to facilitate dealing with complexity, direct micro-process of software development, enable more efficient performance of the difficult tasks, facilitate management and increase satisfaction at work. On the opposite, "bad" models may cause mistake, waste time and be annoying in use. Despite that, much research has been done in the area of technology of model transformations and tools supporting this task. We argue that there is a need to focus on the quality of visual modeling languages (VML), which are used for creating the models as well as quality of models themselves.

This chapter takes a practical perspective to quality in modeling. In order to improve the quality of models one needs to understand quality criteria for models, know efficient methods for conducting evaluation and understand relations between them for effective configuration and management. The level of maturity of the technology is not satisfactory nowadays and one can observe several problems from the point of view of project and general knowledge.

From the point of view of the software project, there are several unrelated methods with limited scope of application. It is unclear what could be benefits of using them and how they could be integrated. Perhaps the most popular method for improving model quality are inspections or reviews with checklists. However, one often needs to customize the checklist provided with methodologies for a specific project. It is easy to remove unnecessary checkpoints, but the problem remains when deciding which checkpoints need to added. The problem of inflexible methods of evaluation appears even more clearly in the perspective of the current trend of software process configuration. It assumes that companies do not choose a process but rather they make a configuration of roles, artifacts and tasks for a given type of project within a framework. It means that model artifacts, modeling activities and model checking activities are objects of configuration. Thus, we need objective criteria to make decisions about the scope of modeling as well as methods of evaluation for software models.

From the point of view of maturity of modeling technology, some objective criteria and practical methods of evaluation are needed in order to provide frameworks for customization of the concrete software projects. There is a need to understand criteria why modeling languages should have such elements, diagrams, visualizations, etc. The methods of evaluation are useful for making efficient evaluation and quality criteria behind such decision allow for trade-offs when compromises are necessary. They could be applied by Object Management Group (OMG) members working on modeling standards, e.g., Unified Modeling Language (UML) and its profiles or Business Process Modeling Notation (BPMN). As these standards influence advances in practice, the increase of the maturity of modeling technology should result in better perception of this technology and more successful application in practice. This approach could be useful also for committees which work on application-type modeling languages, e.g., internet applications; special type of models, e.g., task models for user behavior modeling; and models for emerging technology, e.g., aspect-oriented technology. Finally, they could be applied in the area of domain specific modeling. The tasks of designing and evaluating modeling languages in this case are performed in software companies which means a universal application of the methods of visual modeling language evaluation.

The objective of this chapter is to present an approach to dealing with model quality in a way which integrates quality criteria and methods of evaluation. The quality criteria are useful for understanding which aspects are evaluated and for managing the scope of evaluation. The methods of evaluation are necessary for efficient conduct of evaluation. The integrated approach should provide the following benefits. It should allow for designing methods of evaluation based on quality criteria and elements of the model (or modeling language) in the context of specific needs. It should be applicable for management the scope of evaluation with quality criteria as well as configuration of the method to a specific situation. It should allow for flexible and efficient conduct of the evaluation with selection of the methods of evaluation. The most important features of the solution include:

- Improved understanding of the quality of models in the perspective of selected linguistic theories and separating impacts modeling language, model and modeling tools for the quality criteria;
- Proposition of a methodology for designing methods of evaluation based on quality criteria and elements of the model (or modeling language).

BACKGROUND

Although several quality criteria and some methods for evaluating models have been already proposed, the practical integrated approach is still missing. They solve one kind of problems but fail to satisfy other requirements. This section discusses related work in the area of identifying quality criteria for both models and visual modelling languages, and then available methods of evaluation.

Traditionally, software engineering researchers proposed technical quality criteria for models and visual modeling languages (VML). It was typical, that they were related to modeling technology in general. It can be illustrated with the following examples. Models should be expressive enough to allow developers to capture all interesting

strategic and tactical decision (Booch, 1994) and notation should allow to create complete, correct and consistent models (McGregor, 1998). The diagrams should be executable (Martin, 1993). A set of characteristics of a good notation include: clear and uniform mapping of concepts to symbols, ease to draw by hand, good look when printed, faxed and copied using monochrome images, consistency with past practice and self-consistency, simplicity of common case modeling, not-to-subtle distinctions, no overloading of symbols and suppressible details (Rumbaugh, 1999). More attempts to answer the question of the quality of models can be found (Firesmith et al. 1996; Hong, 1993). The set of desirable criteria for models also include: precision, constructability, expressiveness, executability, traceability, inspectability, and usability. A more recent research proposes the following key characteristics of engineering models (Selic 2003):

- Abstraction – possibility to remove or hide details irrelevant for a given viewpoint, it constitutes the means for coping with complexity;
- Understandability – presenting in a form that directly appeals to our intuition and thus reduces intellectual effort;
- Accuracy – true-to-life representation of the system;
- Predictiveness – possibility to predict system's features;
- Small cost – models should be significantly cheaper to construct and analyze than modeled system.

Analysis of the proposed criteria suggests that, in general, models should be easy to understand for software developers, integrators and maintainers, and on the other hand, they should be precise enough to allow for automatic transformations by the tools. However, it is not clear how these criteria could be satisfied. Separating impacts of visual modeling language, model and tools can be helpful in the analysis and allow for higher level of precision and more practical application. Not much work on systematic approaches has been done. The only exception was an attempt to distinguish between goals and means in conceptual modeling and to define syntactic, semantic and pragmatic quality (Lindland et al. 1994).

Many factors have impact on the models. The process of creating them, education and experience of designers, their purpose of use, and developer's subjective decisions are just a few examples. However, models quality depends, first of all, on the quality of visual modelling languages, which define syntax of correct models, their semantics and notation. In the area of VML evaluation, several methods of evaluation or just evaluations has been described in the literature, e.g. a method based on cognitive dimensions (Cox, 2000), comparative studies (De Champeaux et. al. 1992; Gu et.al. 2002; Kutar et al. 2002), comparing to ontology of systems (Opdahl et al. 2002) or evaluation based on a set of model quality criteria for business process modelling notation (Hommes et.al. 2003).

Several approaches to checking model quality has been proposed, e.g. checklists (Rational Unified Process, 2001), heuristics (Grotehen), object-oriented metrics with thresholds (Lorenz et al. 1994). Usually when applying them one finds out they are not complete and one misses a kind of framework for checking completeness. The problem is one does not know according to which quality criteria evaluations are made. Another problem in current approaches is that it is difficult to manage scope of evaluation when scope of models in the documentation or type of system under development changes.

The level of understanding of the quality criteria for models and usefulness of the proposed methods of evaluation is not satisfactory nowadays and the progress in this area is expected. But even assuming that universal lists of the quality criteria for models are possible to be defined, it is very likely that concrete evaluation will require only

limited scope of them. Therefore, instead of attempting to define yet another "final set of quality criteria", we want to present a kind of framework for dealing with these issues.

CONFIGURATION OF METHODS OF EVALUATION BASED ON QUALITY CRITERIA

The objective of our research was to provide a practical solution for increasing quality in the modeling technology. We assume that in order to achieve it one can manipulate on models or visual modeling languages. In this section we identify the requirements for the methods and their application area and then we describe a methodology for designing methods of evaluation.

With the current trend in the area of software processes to provide a framework with best practices, e.g. IBM Rational Unified Process, which could be customized and configured for a given type of projects depending on its characteristics, particular models, modeling and model checking activities are just a result of decisions made by process engineer. This observation leads to formulation of the first requirement for the methods of evaluation. They should be configurable for artifacts under evaluation.

The practice of software project shows that most projects are performed in the tough market conditions, they must meet limitation of resources and increasing quality requirements. On the other hand, it is known that quality assessment activities are essential, but there is an optimal point on the curve describing cost-to-effect. This perspective leads to the next requirements for the methods of evaluation. They should be as effective and efficient as possible. Since more advanced methods require more time to be performed, the methods of evaluation should be additionally manageable with respect to the scope and time of evaluation.

Furthermore, process engineer should be delivered with a solid knowledge about the consequences of using a given method of evaluation. Such knowledge would enable making rational decisions instead of using a coincidental set of checkpoints.

The above requirements can be fulfilled when delivering a methodology for designing methods of evaluation customizable for selected objects under evaluation which check out these objects against desired quality criteria. The methodology can be summarized operationally in the following steps:

1. Define objectives for your method of evaluation
2. Identify means you can manipulate – objects under evaluation
3. Define quality criteria
4. Make configuration of the method of evaluation.

This methodology applied to design of the method of evaluation for models during the software project can be used by software process engineers once during the configuration of the process for a given type of projects or when the changes to this process are introduced. Then, several evaluations of models can be made by members of the quality assurance group in several projects of this type. The methodology applied for designing methods of evaluation for visual modeling languages can be used by the members of the standard committees as well as language engineers working on visual modeling languages. The application in the area of support for improvement of the standard modeling languages is not a common activity but it has a great impact on usefulness of technology used by many users. With the increasing popularity of domain specific languages, the design of the modeling languages and methods of their evaluation becomes a more common activity.

Definition of the Objectives and Identification of Objects Under Evaluation

The first important thing when designing a method of evaluation is to define objectives. It requires making realistic decisions about expected results and elements to be manipulated. Hardly ever the process engineer has the freedom to make configuration of the process from scratch without any limitations. Without this specific point of reference, hardly any evaluation can be successful. The distinction between quality of language and quality of models increases precision in evaluation. It is useful to understand a language as an expression space and a model as a kind of expression. Thus, examples of objectives for models include:

- Find defects in the design diagrams,
- Analyze fit to the purpose of the documented system,
- Support domain expert in validation of analysis documents,
- Evaluate understandability of documentation for a project,
- Predict functional quality of a system on the basis of its documentation.

Depending on the expected results different methods would be useful.

As examples of objectives for visual modeling languages one can state:

- Evaluate application of a subset of UML for a given type of projects with respect to the fit to needs,
- Evaluate usability of UML diagrams,
- Compare expressiveness of several propositions for a domain specific language,
- Compare maturity of modeling technology using BPMN and business use case modeling including tool support and fit to software development process.

It is important to have realistic expectation what can be achieved by manipulating VML, models and tools. For example, in order to achieve "executable diagrams" one needs a VML which allows to make executable specifications, then models which are precise enough to deliver data for transformations, and finally the tools which make the transformations to the executable form. When attempting to assess correctness with respect to syntax it is useful to understand that VML defines correct models, then one can check models against the syntax, and tools support checking correctness against the syntax. They can disable incorrect constructions but additional check is needed in order to assess lack of incomplete work-in-progress ones. When evaluating expressiveness, VML defines what is possible to express and it can be evaluated against the fit of the expression space to the domain or purpose of modeling; models are kinds of expression within VML and they can be evaluated against how they use possibilities of VML to represent a system, and the role of tools is neutral – they just facilitate making models. When evaluating inspectability, VML can be checked against ease of defining criteria for inspection and relating them the model elements, the most important for models is understandability for inspectors and tools can be evaluated whether they support making inspections. Depending on the quality aspect the role of VML, models and tools changes.

Quality Criteria

Once decided about objectives and objects under evaluation the next step is to define quality criteria. It is difficult to define an orthogonal and complete set of quality criteria. The solution depends on several circumstances as well as internal aspects of VMLs. In order to understand better impact of quality criteria for models we use the following linguistic inspirations:

- Distinction into content and expression areas - which enables to predict consequences of several types of defects;
- Model of syntax, semantics and notation - and its application to evaluation of several aspects of VML; and
- Pragmatics – a promising approach which allows to define context of model usage and make more precise context-dependent evaluation.

For describing the quality model one can use, for example, McCall's framework or Goal Question Metric (GQM) approach.

Content and Expression Areas

Distinction between content and expression areas was inspired by the work of Hjelmslev (semiotician and linguist living in 1899-1965). In his perception of a language, a sign is a function between two forms, a content form and an expression form and every sign function is manifested by two substances: the content substance and the expression substance. The content substance is the psychological and conceptual manifestation of the sign, whereas the expression substance is the material substance wherein a sign is manifested. In simple words, it is a distinction between what one communicates and the means one uses to do it, e.g. sound, text, pictures, sign language, gestures, etc.

The implication for model quality evaluation is we can evaluate separtely content of models from their expression form. It allows to split apart these characteristics which have impact on solution from those which are only concerned with understanding. In the first group there are: completeness, correctness with respect to goals of the system etc. While the second group includes understandability, precision, adequate symbols and simplicity.

The content has direct impact on the system and these criteria can be used in order to predict quality of software. For example, the lack of completeness of use case diagram will result in the lack of functions in the system, the consequence of incorrect class diagram will be incorrect structure of the system, incorrect dynamic models will propagate to incorrect interactions between the user and the system. The expression criteria are indirectly concerned with the system quality, but they indicate for likely problems with understanding by their users and resulting defects.

Syntax, Semantics and Notation

The distinction between syntax, semantics, notation and pragmatics is inspired by the work of semioticians such as Morris and Peirce and chapters of contemporary books on linguistics which study separately syntax (grammar) when dealing with relations between signs, semantics concerned with relations between signs and reality, different forms of expressions and their rules (speech, writing, gestures) and pragmatics—dependence of communication on interpreters. The distinction between syntax, semantics and notation is successfully applied in formulation of UML description. An attempt to use distinction between syntax, semantics and pragmatics for understanding model quality has already been proposed (Lindland et al. 1994). However, this distinction has much greater potential for performing more precise methods of evaluation from the perspective of a given area as well as the perspective of relationships between given two areas.

Pragmatics

Pragmatics is the study of language which focuses attention on the users and the context of language use rather than on reference, truth, or grammar' (The Oxford Companion to Philosophy). It studies the use of language in context, and the context-dependence of various aspects of linguistic interpretation. Context is the situation in which language is used and it includes extralinguistic

factors: social, psychological and environmental ones. One of the topics of debate in linguistics is the semantics-pragmatics distinction (Bach). Semantics concerns context-independent meaning (the relation of signs to objects) and pragmatics deals with context-dependent meaning (the relation of signs to their interpreters). This distinction is best reflected in the following pairs of expressions: sentence vs. utterance; meaning vs. use; context-invariant vs. context-sensitive meaning; linguistic vs. speaker's meaning; literal vs. nonliteral use; or saying vs. implying.

Pragmatics in linguistics allows to deal with the context of use. It enables understanding aspects dependent on people who take part in conversations and their situations. It could play similar role in research on modeling in software engineering. VMLs also have several kinds of users with different social, psychological and environmental factors. The perception of models might differ depending on expectations related to the roles they play in software development activities. Application of pragmatics in practice would require definition and description of pragmatics profiles and evaluation of VML in the context of these pragmatics profiles.

Design of the Method of Evaluation

The input for the method of evaluation are objectives, quality criteria and objects under evaluation which can be changed depending on the results of evaluation. The results depend on the objectives. They include: lists of defects, metrics, suggestions of improvement, comparison results etc. The essence of the design of the method of evaluation is combination of the all relevant quality criteria with objects under evaluation. This can be as simple as intersection of criteria and objects under evaluation or as difficult as using several basic methods supporting the quality improvement and integrating them.

In our opinion, the method of evaluation is basically a support for human information processing. Although some tools automatically collect diagram metrics or automatically discover some kinds of low-level defects, still majority of model evaluation tasks and almost all VML evaluation tasks must be performed by professionals.

Thus, it is useful to have a look at a cognitive inspiration (without going into details of cognitive modeling.) One can notice that within an evaluation without any support two different types of information processing processes are performed:

- An organizational process – which is concerned with issues 'What shall I do next? What should be checked? How to do it? Is it enough?'
- A checking process – which performs several basic checks according to the organizational process.

These processes take place concurrently and can be informal, implicit and unordered. They might be more or less conscious and casual. Main problems and most of 'awaiting' are associated with the organizational process. The role of the method of evaluation is to deliver a pattern for the organizational process, and, thus, to make it more explicit, conscious, ordered and repeatable. As the most waste of time is concerned with this process, the method should result in improvement of the efficiency of evaluation.

Furthermore, modeling concepts and quality concepts are usually placed in different conceptual models in our minds. The role of the methods of evaluation which combine model elements with quality criteria is to drive evaluator's attention step by step to facilitate checking all important aspects. Any of these combinations is less prone for forgetting when there are lots of them or evaluator is working in hurry or has another motivation to finish the evaluation soon. Thus, the method supports effectiveness by forcing complete check.

Additionally, some strategies are useful when designing methods of evaluation, e.g. 'most important things first' which takes into consideration that people get tired during evaluation and their productivity can decrease, or the idea of 'building evaluators' knowledge' and thus checking related aspects together in time. A good practice is to design a space for 'other comments' just in case of finding by evaluators defects which are not covered by the method or to allow them to express their comments on the method.

One more important group of aspects to be taken into account when designing methods of evaluation are human factors: evaluators, their characteristics, their knowledge and their context of work. The differences might depend on culture or language. The evaluators might prefer e.g. command style or question style, long questionnaires with very simple questions or shorter questionnaires with more open and complex questions, discussions with authors or just formal reports from evaluation.

An interesting issue related to the design of the methods of evaluation is whether it is possible to automatically generate appropriate checklists. As tools can be designed to support any task, it is useful to pose additional questions about the quality of the generated checklists and effectiveness of generation, i.e. comparison of the effort required for the development of such tools and inserting necessary data with the effort required for re-designing the checklists when context of application or requirements change. Large benefits can be achieved with low-cost manually-made methods of evaluation. The tools can add the value of easy generation of multiple variants of checklists and allow for relating results of evaluation with the items of the method and processing them. However, one should be skeptical to automatically generated checklists and review them carefully for accuracy and style.

The main idea of the method to support organizational process during evaluator's work and to drive their attention seems to be universal, how-ever more research on strategies and evaluator's preferences would be useful.

CASE STUDIES

In order to demonstrate the practical application of the methodology of designing methods of evalua-tion, we present three case studies with design of diverse methods of evaluation. Two of them are related to models, but they have different objec-tives. The first method is a simple manageable checklist for the purpose of finding defects and the second uses every information on the models in order to deliver quality predictions (Bobkowska, 2001). The third case study summarizes a method for evaluating visual modeling languages from a cognitive perspective (Bobkowska, 2005).

Quality Criteria-Based Checklist

The objective of this method design was to pro-vide a simple checklist for verification of analysis models to be applied in teaching classes of systems modeling and analysis. It was required that the method fits well to the diagrams under evaluation and quality criteria for models should be explicitly stated. Additionally, the method should be efficient and easy to modify.

The object under evaluation was documen-tation of the analysis, which consisted of the vi-sion of the system (goals, scope, context) in the textual form, use case diagram for presentation of the system's functionality, class diagram and sequence diagrams for all use cases. Apart from the diagrams, non-functional requirements were specified in the textual form.

The quality criteria reflected the distinction between content and expression areas. The con-tent group included: completeness, correctness, consistency and fit to the vision of the system. The expression group included: understandability

of diagrams, their elegance, precision, simplicity and adequate level of abstraction.

While designing the method we have used additionally two 'strategies' which allowed for effective and efficient evaluation: 'direct users to check most important aspects first' and 'order questions around the diagrams not the quality criteria'. This resulted in a checklist to check content of the use case diagram, then content of the class diagram and sequence diagrams. Later consistency between all diagrams and fit to the vision were evaluated, and finally - expression criteria for all diagrams. The checklist ended with some space for summary. Each subsection related to checking a given diagram with a selected qual-ity criterion included direct instructions for users informing them what they should do.

For example, section '1. Content of use case diagram' consists of two subsections '1.1 Com-pleteness of use case diagram' with instruction to identify missing actors, missing use cases and missing relationships and subsection '1.2 Correctness of use case diagram' with instruc-tion to identify incorrect actors, use cases and relationships, i.e. spurious, these with wrong scope, wrong labels, wrong directions of arrows in relationships. Section '6. Expression of use case diagram' consists of the following subsections '6.1. Precision and understandability of labels and descriptions' with instruction to identify unclear, vague and difficult to understand labels and descriptions, '6.2. Elegance of icon place-ment on the diagram' with instruction to find defects related to placements and aesthetics of the diagram, '6.3. Simplicity' with instruction to identify unnecessarily complex descriptions and constructions on the diagram and finally subsection '6.4 Adequate level of abstraction' with instruction to identify mismatch of elements in respect to level of abstraction, e.g. some elements too general or others too detailed.

This checklist satisfies the requirements for-mulated when stating objectives. It is simple, it fits exactly for the diagrams under evaluation and it explicitly indicates for the criteria of evaluation. It is as efficient as possible and easy to modify when documentation or quality criteria change. We collected opinions of users of this checklist who have also used fragments of general purpose RUP checklist for these diagrams. The users said that clear instructions in context of these subsections facilitate finding defects and give a good understanding according to which criteria evaluation is made. The checklist was leading them through the review and without it they wouldn't find so many defects. They claimed it suited better to the diagrams under evaluation then the RUP checklist.

Software Quality Prediction

The objective of this method design was to use every information on the models indicating for quality of the final software to be developed and use it in order to make software quality predictions in early phases of software development. Such predictions should allow managers to control the development process with quantitative measures of software product (together with measures of software process taken from other sources).

The objects under evaluation were documents of software analysis and design. The scope of analysis was similar to one described in the previous section, and the documentation of design consisted of systems design which consisted of subsystem diagram and interactions between subsystems, decisions about environment, boundary conditions, style and trade-offs. Other documents contained user interface design, database design and subsystems design.

Since the objective was to predict quality factors of system under development, the meaningful attributes were functionality, maintainability and usability. They needed to be related to quality criteria of models such as completeness, correctness, precision, adequate structure, flexibility to probable changes, adequacy of designed algorithms etc. Additionally, the requirement of

quantitative measurement leaded to introduction of quality metrics for both quality factors and quality criteria in scale 0..1.

The schema of the relationships between items of the method for software quality prediction is shown in Fig. 1. The design integrates the quality model (made with the use of McCalls framework with its terms of quality factors, criteria and metrics) with UML model elements and related textual specifications, e.g. these which describe vision of the system or system design decisions.

The link between them consists of elementary quality data, which can be diagram metrics and their expected values, model evaluation in a scale and the lists of defects together with their metrics. Diagram metrics cover the idea of measurement of the UML diagrams and use of this information to reason about quality by comparing the results of measurements with expected values, which can be derived from historical data about similar projects. Diagram metrics are also the basis for local size calculation which can be used for defect metrics calculation. The diagram metrics are example of optimal features, and expected values indicate the right range. Evaluations with comments are concerned with the criteria that are difficult to measure objectively. Evaluations are numbers that represent subjective feelings about some aspects of the work, e.g. ease of understanding, aesthetics, precision, etc. They can be given in the scale and described as comments. They represent positive features. Defect collection according to the defect classification is an instantiation of the negative features in the model. These defects can be then counted and combined with the diagram size metrics.

Two steps are performed during the quality prediction:

- Elementary quality data collection which allows to gather elementary quality data on the basis of documentation;
- Reasoning about quality, which allows to transform elementary quality data into

Figure 1. Elementary quality data in context of the quality model and documentation with UML (©2007 Anna Bobkowska. Used with permission)

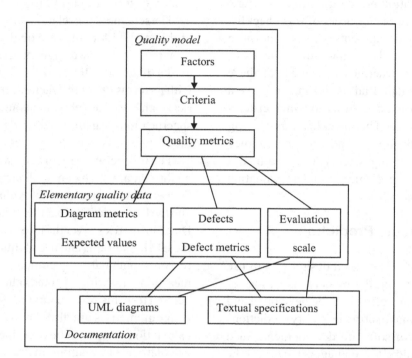

quality metrics, which can be made manually by quality expert or can be calculated according to formulas with parameters which represent the impact of given metrics or evaluations.

This method requires more work comparing to the previous case study. However, it satisfies its goal of delivering quantitative predictions of the software quality in early phases of software development. It allows to see consequences of defects in the documentation for the software quality and supports the control of the process of software development. The problem of software quality prediction is quite complicated and when designing a solution one meets the questions of missing data and thus uncertainty of predictions

as well as the problem of subjectivity of evaluations and reasoning. However, with questionnaires supporting elementary quality data collection and reasoning, even students of experimental group have performed predictions with satisfying results.

Evaluating VMLs from a Cognitive Perspective

The objective of this method design was to propose a tool for visual modeling language (VML) evaluation from a cognitive perspective and then evaluate with this method use case diagram. It is believed that cognitive fit of the technology to its users can increase efficiency, decrease cost, improve software quality and allow for easier learning, use and maintenance.

Since the methodology is configurable the object under evaluation can be any visual modeling language or any of its diagrams. In this case study we present customization for use case diagram, thus we operate are at meta-model level and objects under evaluation are UML model elements.

The quality criteria for this methodology were defined by a set of cognitive dimensions (Blackwell, Green, 2000):

- Viscosity - resistance to change,
- Visibility - ability to view components easily,
- Premature commitment - constraints on the order of doing things,
- Hidden dependencies - important links between entities are not visible,
- Role-expressiveness - the purpose of an entity is readily inferred,
- Error-proneness - the notation invites mistakes and the system gives little protection,
- Abstraction - types and availability of abstraction mechanisms,
- Secondary notation - extra information in means other than formal syntax,
- Closeness of mapping - closeness of representation to domain,
- Consistency - similar semantics are expressed in similar syntactic forms,
- Diffuseness - verbosity of language,
- Hard mental operations - high demand on cognitive resources,
- Provisionality - degree of commitment to actions or marks,
- Progressive evaluation - work-to-date can be checked at any time,

A schema of the approach to the design of the method is presented in Fig. 2. CD-VML template is a product of customization of the original cognitive dimensions (CD) questionnaire for visual modeling languages. It required some modification to increase precision of questions and their fit to visual modeling language terminology. Then, the next step in design is customization for the method of evaluation for a specific visual modeling language or one of its diagrams. We have designed a CD-VML-UC questionnaire - a product of the CD-VML methodology for the use case (UC) model in the default context of use of creating models, their usage and change.

In order to give an example, we present questions from the section of the questionnaire related to error-proneness. It starts with questions to find common mistakes whilst modeling and using diagrams: 'Whilst modeling, what kinds of mistakes are particularly common or easy to make? Which kinds of mistakes you must be careful not to make? Whilst using diagrams, which misunderstandings are very likely to happen?' They were followed by a table with listing of all model elements and notation elements and space for problem descriptions. The table was headed with the questions: 'Which model elements or constructions or notation element or visual mechanisms are these mistakes concerned with? What are the problems?' Below the table there was a space for explanations, examples, comments and suggestions for improvement of the VML or suggestions for special features of the CASE tool.

This method was verified in an experiment with students as participants. Students confirmed simplicity and usefulness of use cases, but they also discovered a large number of problems, gave reasonable explanations to them and quite often made suggestions for improvements. Their discoveries covered all the problems reported in the related work. The level of detail of the individual answers was satisfactory: problems usually were described with details and examples and even simple diagrams for illustration of the problem were added. In the section of comments they stated the following strengths of the methodology: the precision of questions, large area of covered issues and ease of use. Usefulness of the method was evaluated as high and results were considered as

Figure 2. Schema of the CD-VML methodology (©2007 Anna Bobkowska. Used with permission)

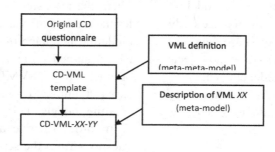

important for use case model improvement.

FUTURE TRENDS

In our opinion, the following areas need to be integrated into the research on quality of software models:

- Proper configuration of modeling tasks and artefacts in the context of software project;
- Integration of reuse technology with modeling technology;
- Need for methods which enable evaluation of the fit between the problem and modeling technology;
- Usability of the modeling technology;
- Visual modeling language engineering.

There is a need for knowledge which would enable proper configuration of the modeling artefacts and modeling tasks within the software project depending on the type of project. Modeling takes time and often does not result in increase of code (except from the situation where the full code is generated by tools). Thus, the suggestion is that the use of models is efficient and beneficial only to certain limits. Furthermore, unlike sug-

gestions in pure modeling solutions, in realistic projects still a lot of documentation is made in the textual form. It is worth to mention that quality of models and thus the quality of the system which is represented by these models depends on whether analysts and developers have enough time for making them. It depends also on the proper scope of modelling. Understanding of this impact requires more research and should result in guidelines on the scope of application of models in the software project depending on the project characteristics. Once the development process is customised, the proposed methodology of designing methods of model evaluation can be used to create proper methods of evaluation.

Integration of the reuse technology with the modeling technology is the next of the challenges. We have a lot of evidence about benefits of reuse for both efficiency and quality of software. However, there are some risks as well. The most important reuse solution related to modeling are patterns and components. The related questions include: How to use patterns effectively for the purpose of software development? How to study their impact for software quality? How the fit between a problem and the applied patterns matters? How components could be incorporated into models? How to analyse their impact for quality of software? The proposed method can facilitate approach to evaluation, but several new factors must be defined e.g. fit of the reuse method to the solution of the problem.

There is a need for methods which enable evaluation of the fit between a problem and given technical modeling solution. It is not a surprise that a problem which can be difficult in one technology can be easy to solve in another. Expert's knowledge is necessary to evaluate modeling solutions against the problem at hand. Examples of decisions include: whether to use UML or a domain specific language, object-oriented or aspect-oriented solutions; how to choose between several technical spaces? It is worth to remember that this perspective sets the space of achievable effects.

Much more work should be done on the usability side of modeling methods. Most decisions so far are technology-driven and result in difficult to use methods and tools. Focus on users of the modeling technology could surely result in better fit of the technology to support several roles of software development process and their activities. This area of research can use pragmatics by the means of identifying pragmatics profiles and their tasks and then evaluating how they are supported by modelling technology.

And finally, we would like to support the research in the discipline of visual modelling language engineering. The technology changes, modeling paradigms are passing by, but the activity of modeling is useful anyway. The role of visual modeling language engineering would be to capture the knowledge about modeling which is technology invariant. It could collect universal and consistent knowledge about models in the areas including:

- understanding the role of models;
- quality of models;
- guidelines for creating visual modeling languages;
- quality of visual modeling languages;
- guidelines for use of modeling technology in the software project.

The proposed method could be a part of visual modeling language engineering.

CONCLUSION

The objective of this chapter was to present an approach to dealing with model quality in a way which integrates quality criteria and methods of evaluation. The methodology for designing methods of evaluation customized for selected objectives and objects under evaluation which check out these objects against desired quality criteria fulfills the requirements which were stated before it. It is explicitly configurable to different objectives and objects under evaluation and thus it fits to configurable software development process in which particular models, modeling and model checking activities are results of decisions made by process engineer. With integrating quality criteria and methods of evaluation it is easy to manage scope of inspection and enable better fit to the objects under evaluation. Inspirations from linguistic theories provide a framework for understanding impact of given criteria for the quality of software under development and software development process. The proposed methodology is flexible and universal. The case studies have delivered an evidence of feasibility of the methodology and its coverage for a diversity of cases as well as usefulness of the results achieved with the use of designed methods of evaluation.

REFERENCES

Bach, K. The Semantics-Pragmatics Distinction: What It Is and Why It Matters, Retrieved in June 2005, from http://userwww.sfsu.edu/~kbach/sem-prag.html

Blackwell, A.F. & Green, T.R.G. (2000) A Cognitive Dimensions questionnaire optimised for users. In: *Proceedings of the Twelfth Annual Meeting of the Psychology of Programming Interest Group* (pp.137-152).

Bobkowska, A.E. (2005) A methodology of Visual Modeling Language Evaluation, In: *Proceedings of SOFSEM 2005*, LNCS 3381 (pp. 72-81).

Bobkowska, A.E. (2001) *Software Quality Prediction with UML*, Unpublished doctoral dissertation, Gdansk University of Technology.

Booch, G. (1994) *Object-Oriented Analysis and Design with Applications.* Benjamin/Cummings.

Cox, K. (2000) Cognitive Dimensions of use cases: feedback from a student questionnaire. In: *Proceedings of the Twelfth Annual Meeting of the Psychology of Programming Interest Group.*

De Champeaux, D.& Faure, P. (1992) A comparative study of object-oriented analysis methods. In: Journal of Object-Oriented Programming, 1(5) 21-33.

Firesmith, D., Henderson-Sellers, B., Graham, I.& Page-Jones, M. (1996) OPEN Modeling Language (OML). Reference Manual.

Gu A., Henderson-Sellers B.& Lowe D. (2002) Web Modeling Languages: The Gap Between Requirements And Current Exemplars. In *Proceedings Of The Eighth Australian World Wide Web Conference.*

Grotehen, T. & Dittrich, K.R. *The MeTHOOD Approach: Measures, Transformation Rules, and Heuristics for Object-Oriented Design*, Technical Report., retrieved in October 2003 from http://www.ifi.unizh.ch/groups/dbtg/MeTHOOD/index.html

Hommes, B.J.& van Reijswoud, V. (2000) Assessing the Quality of Business Process Modeling Techniques, In *Proceedings of the 33rd Hawaii International Conference on System Sciences.*

Hong, S. & Goor, G. (1993) A Formal Approach to the Comparison of Object-Oriented Analysis and Design Methodologies. In *Proceedings of the 26th International Hawaii International Conference on System Sciences.*

Kutar, M., Britton, C.& Barker, T. A. (2002) Comparison of Empirical Study and Cognitive Dimensions Analysis in the Evaluation of UML Diagrams. In *Proceedings of the Fourteenth Annual Meeting of the Psychology of Programming Interest Group.*

Lorenz, M. & Kidd, J. (1994) *Object-oriented Software Metrics. A Practical Guide.,* Prentice Hall.

Lindland, O.I., Sindre, G. & Sølvberg, A. (1994) Understanding Quality in Conceptual Modeling, *IEEE Software.*

Martin, J. (1993) *Principles of object-oriented analysis and design*, Prentice Hall

McGregor, J.D. (1998), The fifty-foot look at the analysis and design models, *Journal of Object-Oriented Programming* 11(4) 10-15.

Opdahl, A.L.& Henderson-Sellers, B. (2002) Ontological Evaluation of the UML Using the Bunge–Wand–Weber Model. *Journal of Software and System Modeling,* 1.

Rumbaugh, J. (1999) Notation Notes: Principles for choosing notation, In *Journal of Object-Oriented Programming,* 12, 4,.

Selic, B. (2003) The Pragmatics of Model-Driven Development, *IEEE Software* 9, 19-25.

Rational Unified Process (RUP) is a trademark of IBM

Unified Modeling Language (UML) and Business Process Modeling Notation (BPMN) are registered marks of OMG

ADDITIONAL READING

Basili, V., Green, S., Laitenberger O., Shull F., Sorumgaard S., & Zelkowitz M, (1996) The Empirical Investigation of Perspective-Based Reading, *Empirical Software Engineering: An International Journal*, vol. 1, 2 (pp.133-164) Another approach to reviews which is based on perspectives of people involved in the process.

Fenton N.E. & Pfleeger S.L. (1998), *Software Metrics: A Rigorous and Practical Approach, Revised,* Course Technology; 2 edition A book for quick and solid introduction to the role of metrics in software engineering.

Gilb T. & Graham D. (1993), *Software Inspection.* Workingham: Addison-Wesley. An introduction to inspections and reviews in software engineering.

Unhelkar B. (2005) *Verification and Validation for Quality of UML 2.0 Models*, John Wiley & Sons Inc.

A book describing checklists for syntactical correctness, semantics and aesthetics of models.

Section II
Evaluating the Model Quality

This section presents several chapters that are aimed at obtaining ob-jective data to support the evalu-ation of model quality. In general, the papers provide methods, criteria, and metrics that support the derivation of quality information from models and the practical use of the quality information obtained for steering development.

Chapter V
Evaluating Performance of Software Architecture Models with the Palladio Component Model

Heiko Koziolek
Universität Oldenburg, Germany

Steffen Becker
University of Karlsruhe, Germany

Ralf Reussner
University of Karlsruhe, Germany

Jens Happe
Universität Oldenburg, Germany

ABSTRACT

Techniques from model-driven software development are useful to analyse the performance of a software architecture during early development stages. Design models of software models can be transformed into analytical or simulation models, which enable analyzing the response times, throughput, and resource utilization of a system before starting the implementation. This chapter provides an overview of the Palladio Component Model (PCM), a special modeling language targeted at model-driven performance predictions. The PCM is accompanied by several model transformations, which derive stochastic process algebra, queuing network models, or Java source code from a software design model. Software architects can use the results of the analytical models to evaluate the feasibility of performance requirements, identify performance bottlenecks, and support architectural design decisions quantitatively. The chapter provides a case study with a component-based software architecture to illustrate the performance prediction process.

INTRODUCTION

To ensure the quality of a software model, developers need not only to check its functional properties, but also assure that extra-functional requirements of the system can be fulfilled in an implementation of the model. Extra-functional properties include performance, reliability, availability, security, safety, maintainability, portability, etc. Like functional correctness, these properties need to be addressed already during early development stages at the model level to avoid possible later costs for redesign and reimplementation.

Performance (i.e., response time, throughput, and resource utilization) is an extra-functional property critical for many business information systems. Web-based information systems rely on fast response times and must be capable of serving thousands of users in a short time span due to the competitive nature of internet businesses. Furthermore, the responsiveness of software used within companies is important to ensure efficient business processes.

Performance problems in large distributed systems can sometimes not be solved by adding more servers with improved hardware ("kill it with iron"). Large software architectures often do not scale linearly with the available resources, but instead include performance bottlenecks that limit the impact of additional hardware.

Therefore, it is necessary to design a software architecture carefully and analyse performance issues as early as possible. However, in the software industry, performance investigations of software systems are often deferred until an implementation of the system has been build and measurements can be conducted ("fix it later"). To avoid this approach, which might lead to expensive redesigns, software architects can use performance models for early, pre-implementation performance analysis of their architectures.

This chapter provides an overview of the Palladio Component Model (PCM), a domain specific modelling language for component-based software architectures, which is specifically tuned to enable early life-cycle performance predictions. Different developer roles can use the PCM to model the software design and its targeted resource environment. The models can be fed into performance analysis tools to derive the performance of different usage scenarios. Software architects can use this information to revise their architectures and quantitatively support their design decisions at the architectural level.

The chapter is structured as follows: Section 2 provides background and describes related work in the area of model-driven performance prediction. Section 3 introduces different developer roles and a process model for model-driven performance predictions. Section 4 gives an overview of the PCM with several artificial model examples, before Section 5 briefly surveys different model transformations to analysis models and source code. Section 6 describes the performance prediction for an example component-based software architecture and discusses the value of the results for a software architect. For researchers interested working in the area of model-driven performance prediction, Section 7 highlights some directions for future research. Section 8 concludes the chapter.

BACKGROUND AND RELATED WORK

Model-driven performance predictions aim at improving the quality of software architectures during early development stages (Smith et al., (2002)). Software architects use models of such prediction approaches to evaluate the response time, throughput, or resource utilization to be expected after implementing their envisioned design. The prediction model's evaluation results enable analysing different architectural designs and validate performance-related requirements (such as maximum response times or minimum throughput) of software systems. The advantage of using prediction models instead of testing implementations is the lowered risk to find performance problems in already implemented systems, which require cost-intensive redesigns.

Researchers have put much effort into creating accurate performance prediction models for the last 30 years. Queuing networks, stochastic process algebras, and stochastic Petri nets are the most prominent prediction models from the research community. However, practitioners seldom apply these models due to their complexity and high learning curve. Therefore, focus of the research community has shifted to create more developer-friendly models and use model transformations to bridge the semantic gap to the above mentioned analytical models.

From the more than 20 approaches in this direction during the last decade (Balsamo et al., (2004)), most use annotated UML models as a design model and ad-hoc transformations to create (layered) queuing networks as analytical models. Tools encapsulate the transformation to the analytical models and their solution algorithms to limit the necessary additional skills for designers. For these approaches, the Object Management Group (OMG) has published multiple UML profiles (SPT profile cf. OMG, (2005); QoS/FT profile; MARTE profile) to add performance-related annotations to UML models. However, these profiles remain under revision, are still immature, and are still not known to have been used in practise in a broader scope.

Component-based software engineering (CBSE) adds a new dimension to model-driven performance prediction approaches. CBSE originally targeted at improved reusability, more flexibility, cost-saving, and shorter time-to-market of software systems (Szyperski et al. (2002)). Besides these advantages, CBSE might also ease prediction of extra-functional properties. Software developers may test components for reuse more thoroughly and provide them with more detailed specifications. These specifications may contain performance-related information.

Hence, several research approaches have tackled the challenge of specifying the performance of a software component (cf. survey by Becker et al., (2006)). This is a difficult task, as the performance of a component depends on environmental factors, which can and should not be known by component developers in advance. These factors include:

- **Execution environment:** The platform a component is deployed on including component container, application server, virtual machine, operating system, software resources, hardware resources
- **Usage profile:** User inputs to component services and the overall number of user requests directed at the components
- **Required services:** Execution times of additionally required, external services, which add up to the execution of the component itself

Component developer can only fix the component's implementation, but have to provide a performance specification, which is parameterisable for the execution environment, the usage profile, and the performance of required services. The following paragraph summarises some of the approaches into this direction.

Sitaraman et. al (2001) model the performance of components with an extension to the O-calculus, but do not include calls to required services. Hissam et. al (2002) aim at providing methods to certify component for their performance properties. Bertolino et. al (2003) use the UML SPT profile to model component-based systems including dependencies to the execution environment, but neglecting influences by the usage profile. Hamlet et al. (2003) investigate the influence of the usage profile on component performance. Wu et al. (2004) model components with an XML-based language and transform this notation into layered queueing networks. The AP-PEAR method by Eskenazi et al. (2004) aims at predicting performance for changes on already built systems, and thus does neglect the influence of the execution environment. Bondarev et al. (2005) target components in embedded systems with the ROBOCOP component model. Grassi et al. (2005) develop an intermediate modelling language for component-based systems called KLAPER, which shall bridge the gap between different design and analytical models.

The Palladio Component Model (Becker et al., (2007)) described in this chapter is in line with these research approaches and tries to reflect all influences on component performance. Unlike some of the above listed approaches, the PCM does not use annotated UML as design model, but defines its own metamodel. This reduces the model to concepts necessary for performance prediction and does not introduce the high complexity of arbitrary UML models with a variety of concepts and views.

DEVELOPER ROLES AND PROCESS MODEL

The PCM metamodel is divided into several domain-specific modelling languages, which are aligned with developer roles in CBSE. This section introduces these roles and provides an overview of the process model for using the PCM.

An advantage of CBSE is the division of work between different developer roles, such as component developers and software architects. *Component developers* specify and implement components. They also have to provide a description of the component's extra-functional properties to enable software architects to predict their performance without deploying and testing them. *Software architects* compose components from different component developers to application architectures. They are supported by tools to predict the architecture's performance based on the performance specifications of the component developers. With the predicted performance met-

rics, they can support their design decisions for different architectural styles or components.

For performance predictions, the software architect needs additional information about the execution environment and the usage profile. The role of the *system deployer* provides performance-related information about the hardware/software environment of the architecture (such as processing rate of a CPU, throughput of a network link, scheduling policies of the operating system, configuration of the application server, etc.). Business *domain experts* provide knowledge about the anticipated user behavior (in terms of input parameters and call frequencies), and must assist software architects in specifying a usage model of the architecture.

Figure 1 depicts the overall development process of a component-based system including performance prediction (Koziolek et al. (2006)): Boxes model workflows, thick and grey arrows indicate a change of activity, and thin and black arrows illustrate the flow of artefacts. The workflows do not have to be traversed linearly; backward steps for revision are likely. After collecting and analysing requirements for the system to develop (Requirements), the software architect specifies components and the architecture based on input by component developers (Specification). With a fully specified architecture, performance predictions can be carried out by tools (QoS-analysis). The software architect can use the results to alter the specification or decide to implement the architecture. This is done either by obtaining existing components from third-party vendors or by implementing them according to their specification (Provisioning). Afterwards, the software architect can compose the component implementations (Assembly), test the full application in a restricted environment (Test), and then install and operate it in the customer's actual environment (Deployment).

During "Specification", the above introduced roles interact as follows (cf. Figure 2): The PCM provides a domain-specific modelling language

Figure 1. Component-based development process (©2007 Heiko Koziolek. Used with permission)

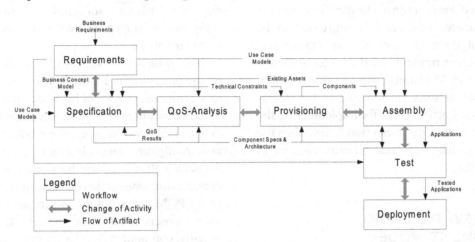

Figure 2. Specification and QoS analysis with the PCM (©2007 Heiko Koziolek. Used with permission)

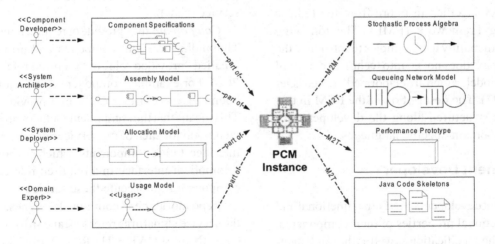

for each developer role, which is restricted to its known concepts. Component developers model performance-related component behaviour, software architects add an assembly model. System deployers model hardware/software resources and the components' allocation to these resources. Finally, domain experts provide a usage model. All specifications can be combined to derive a full PCM instance. Section 4 will elaborate on the PCM's specification languages.

During "QoS-Analysis", this model can be transformed into different analysis models, such as a stochastic process algebra or a queueing network. These models provide capabilities to derive performance metrics such as response times, throughputs, or resource utilisations for specific usage scenarios. Additionally, the PCM can be transformed into a performance prototype, which simulates the specified resource demands. This prototype enables pre-implementation performance measurements on the target platform. Finally, the PCM instance can be converted into Java code skeletons via model-2-text transformation, as a starting point for implementing the system's business logic. Section 5 describes the analysis models and code transformations in more detail.

OVERVIEW PALLADIO COMPONENT MODEL

This section provides an overview of the modeling capabilities of the PCM to describe component-based software architecture. The PCM is a metamodel specified in Ecore from the Eclipse Modelling Framework (EMF). The following section will mainly use examples to introduce the concepts, and does not go into technical details of the metamodel, which are elaborated in (Reussner et al., 2007). The description of the PCM in this section is structured along the developer roles and their domain-specific languages.

Component Developer

Component developers specify the functional and extra-functional properties of their components. They put the specification as well as the implementation in repositories, where software architects can retrieve them. This section will first introduce all entities, which can be stored in repositories and then focus on service effect specifications, which model the abstract behavior and performance properties of component services.

Component Repositories

Figure 3 shows an example PCM repository, which includes all types of entities that can be

specified. First class entities in PCM repositories are interfaces, data types, and components. They may exist on their own and do not depend on other entities.

The *interface* `MyInterface` is depicted on the upper left in Figure 3. It is not yet bound to a component, but can be associated as a provided or required interface to components. An example of interfaces existing without clients and an implementation in practice was the Java Security API, which had been specified by Sun before an implementation was available. Interfaces in the PCM contain a list of service signatures, whose syntax is based on CORBA IDL. Additionally, component developers may supplement an interface with protocols, which restrict the order of calling its services. For example, an I/O interface might force clients to first open a file (call service open()) before reading from it (call service read()).

Components may provide or require interfaces. The binding between a component and an interface is called "provided role" or "required role" in the PCM. For example, component A in Figure 3 is bound to `YourInterface` in a provided role. This means that the component includes an implementation for each of the services declared in the interface. Other components, which are bound to a compliant interface in a required role can use component A to execute these services.

Repositories need common data types, so that the service signatures refer to standardized types (e.g., INT, FLOAT, CHAR, BOOL, STRING, etc.). In the PCM, data types are either primitive types, collection types, or composite types (composed out of inner types). Figure 3 contains a primitive data type `INT` and a collection data type `INT-Array`, which contains `INT`s as inner elements.

The PCM supports modeling different types of components to a) reflect different development stages, and b) to differentiate between basic (atomic) components and composite components.

Figure 3. Example component repository (©2007 Heiko Koziolek. Used with permission)

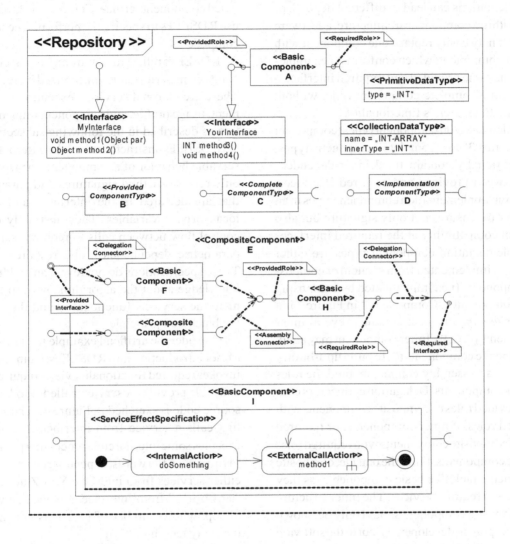

Different development stages are reflected by *provided, complete, and implementation component type*. Component developers can refine components during design from provided to implementation component types.

Provided component types (component B in Figure 3) only provide one or more interfaces, but include no mandatory required interfaces. Component developers can use these type of components

early during the development, when they know that a certain functionality has to be provided, but do not know whether other components are needed to provide this functionality.

Complete component types (component C in Figure 3) are provided component types, but additionally may contain mandatory required interfaces. However, the inner dependencies between provided and required interfaces are not fixed in complete component types, as different implementations can lead to different dependencies. Within a component architecture, a software architect may easily replace one component with another component, which conforms (i.e., implements the same provided and required interfaces) to the same complete component type, without affecting the system's functionality.

Implementation component types (component D in Figure 3) are complete component types, but additionally contain fixed inner dependencies between provided and required interfaces. Replacing implementation component types in an architecture ensures not only signature but also protocol compatibility at the required interface.

Implementation component types are either basic (i.e., implemented from scratch) or composite components (i.e., implemented by composing other components). Component E in Figure 3 is a *composite component*. It contains several inner components (F, G, H). Inner component may again be composite components (G) to build up arbitrary hierarchies. Assembly connectors bind the roles of inner components. Delegation connectors connect provided roles of composite components with provided roles of inner components, or required roles of composite components with required roles of inner components. From the outside, composite components look like basic components, as they provide and require services. The inner structure of a composite component should only be known to the component developer, but not to the software architect, who shall use the component as a unit and treat it the same as other components.

Finally, basic components are atomic and therefore cannot be further decomposed. They may contain a mapping for each provided service to required services, which is called resource demanding service effect specification.

Service Effect Specification

Resource demanding service effect specifications (RDSEFF) provide means to describe resource demands and calls to required services by a provided component service. Component developers use RDSEFFs to specify the performance of their components.

RDSEFFs reflect the environmental factors on component performance introduced in Section 2. These are external services, execution environment, usage profile, and component implementation as described in the following subsection.

RDSEFFs abstractly model the externally observable behavior of a component service. They only refer to method signatures and parameters that are declared in the interfaces and not to local, private variables. They abstractly model control flow between calls to required services, parametric dependencies, and resource usage. These specifications do not reveal any additional knowledge about the algorithms used to implement the service's functionality and thus retain the black-box principle.

Consider the artificial example in Figure 4 for a brief introduction into RDSEFFs. Component A invokes required functionality via its required X, Y, and Z. It provides a service called "do", whose source code is sketched in Figure 4. The service first calls a service from interface X, and then executes some internal code processing parameter "input1". Afterwards, depending on "input2", either services from interface Y or Z are called. "method2" from interface Y is located within a loop, whose number of iterations depends on the array length of "input3".

The corresponding RDSEFF for service "do" is located on the right hand side in Figure 4. As a graphical, concrete syntax, the illustration uses the UML activity diagram notation. However, in this case, the metamodel underlying the modeling constructs is not the UML metamodel, but the PCM, which is indicated by enclosing the PCM class names in brackets. In the following, the underlying concepts for control flow, resource demands, and parametric dependencies will be described.

Figure 4. Resource demanding service effect specification (©2007 Heiko Koziolek. Used with permission)

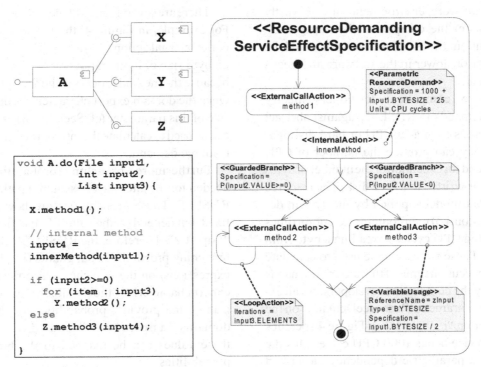

```
void A.do(File input1,
          int input2,
          List input3){

X.method1();

// internal method
input4 =
innerMethod(input1);

if (input2>=0)
   for (item : input3)
     Y.method2();
else
   Z.method3(input4);

}
```

Control Flow: Actions in RDSEFFs can either be internal actions (i.e., the component executes some internal code) or external call actions (i.e., the component calls a service declared in its required interface). RDSEFF offer as basic control flow constructs sequences, alternatives, loops, and parallel executions (forks). The order of these actions may influence performance properties of the service, because different services may concurrently use the same resources or synchronize each other, which induces delays for waiting.

Alternatives or branches split the control flow with an XOR semantic (with guards covering the whole input domain of parameters), while forks (not depicted in Figure 4) split the control flow with an AND semantic, i.e., all following actions

are executed concurrently. Loops have to specify the number of iterations, so that the execution times for actions within the loop can be added up a limited number of times.

Notice that the control flow in RDSEFFs is an abstraction from the actual inner control flow of the service. Internal actions potentially summarize a large number of inner computations and control flow constructs, which do not contain calls to required services.

Resource Demands: Besides external services, a component service accesses the resources of the execution environment it is deployed in. Ideally, component developers would provide measured execution times for these resource accesses in the RDSEFF. However, these measured times would be useless for software architects, who want to use the component, because their hardware/software environment can be vastly different from the component developer ones. The execution times of the service could be much faster or slower in the software architect's environment.

Therefore, component developers specify resource demands in RDSEFFs against abstract resource types such as a CPU or hard disk. For example they can provide the number of CPU cycles needed for execution or the number of bytes read from or written to a hard disk. The resource environment model supplied by the system deployer (Section 4.3) then contains execution times for executing CPU cycles or reading a byte from hard disk. These values can be used to calculate the actual execution times of the resource demands supplied by the component developers. As an example, the "ParametricResourceDemand" on the internal action "method1" in Figure 4 specifies that the service needs 1000 CPU cycles plus the amount of a parametric dependency (described in the next paragraph) to execute.

In addition to active resources, such as processors, storage devices, and network devices, component services may also acquire and release passive resources, such as threads, semaphores, database connections etc. Passive resources are not capable of processing requests and usually exist only a limited number of times. A service can only continue its execution, if the required amount of resources is available. Acquisition/Release of passive resources is not depicted in Figure 4.

Parametric Dependencies: To include the influence of the usage profile into the RDSEFF, component developers can specify parametric dependencies. When specifying an RDSEFF, component developers cannot know how the component will be used by third parties. Thus they cannot fix resource demands, branching probabilities or the number of loop iterations if those values depend on input parameters. Hence,

RDSEFFs allow specifying dependencies to input parameters.

There are several forms of these dependencies. For example, in Figure 4, the resource demand of the internal action "innerMethod" depends on byte size of input parameter "input1" (e.g., because the method processes the file byte-wise). Once the domain expert characterizes the actual size of this parameter (cf. Section 4.4), this value can be used to calculate the internal action's actual resource demand.

Furthermore, branching probabilities are needed for the alternative execution paths in this RDSEFF. These probabilities are however not fixed, but depend on the value of input parameter "input2". Therefore, the RDSEFF includes no branching probabilities but guards (i.e., Boolean expressions) on the branches. Once the domain expert characterizes the possible values of "input2" and provides probabilities for the input domains "input2>=0" and "input2<0", these values can be mapped to the branching probabilities.

The RDSEFF in Figure 4 also contains a parametric dependency on the number of loop iterations surrounding the external call to "method2" of component Y. Loop iterations can be fixed in the code, but sometimes they depend on input parameters. In this case the service iterates over the list "input3" and calls the external service for each of its elements. The RDSEFF specifies this dependency as the component developer cannot know in advance the lengths of the lists.

Finally, the service "do" executes the external call to "method3" in Figure 4 with an input parameter that in turn depends on an input parameter of the service itself. The service processes "input1", assigns it to a local variable "input4", and then forwards it to interface Z via "method3". While processing "input1", the service "do" reduces its byte size by 50% ("input1.BYTESIZE / 2"). The RDSEFF includes the specification of this dependency. Once the domain expert specifies the actual byte size

Figure 5. System example (©2007 Heiko Koziolek. Used with permission)

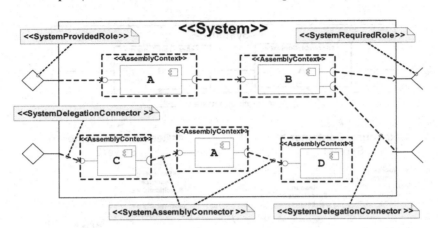

of "input1", the byte size of the input parameter of "method3" can be calculated.

Software Architect

Software architects retrieve components (including their RDSEFFs) from repositories and compose them to architectures. They can use several component instances of the same type in an architecture at different places. Hence, in the PCM, software architects put component instances in so called assembly contexts, which save the connections of a single component instance.

Software architects bind the roles of components in assembly contexts with system assembly connectors, as illustrated in the example in Figure 5. Notice that the component type A is used in two assembly contexts in this example (once connected with component B and once with C and D).

A set of connected assembly contexts is called *assembly.* An assembly is part of a *system,* which additionally exposes system provided roles and system required roles (cf. Figure 5). System delegation connectors bind these system roles with roles of the system's inner components. Domain experts later use system provided roles to model the usage of the system (Section 4.4). System

required roles model external services, which the software architect does not consider part of the architecture. For example, the software architect can decide to model a web service or a connected database as system external services.

There is a distinction between composite components and systems. For software architects and system deployers, composite components hide their inner structure and the fact that they are composed from other components. The inner structure is an implementation detail and its exposure would violate the information hiding principle of components. Opposed to this, the structure of assemblies is visible to software architects and system deployers. Therefore, system deployers can allocate each component in a system to a different resource. However, they cannot allocate inner components of composite components to different resources, because these stay hidden from them at the architectural level.

System Deployer

System deployers first specify the system's resource environment and then allocate assembly contexts (i.e., connected component instances) to resources.

Figure 6. Resource environment and allocation (©2007 Heiko Koziolek. Used with permission)

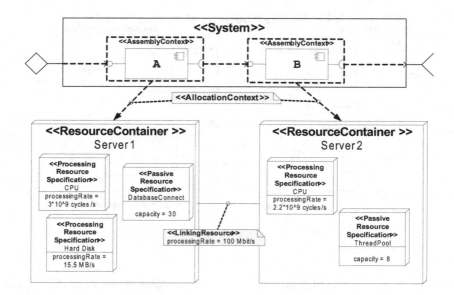

In *resource environments,* resource containers group resources. For example, in Figure 6, the resource container "Server1" contains a CPU, a hard disk, and a database connection pool. The PCM differentiates between processing resources, which can execute requests (e.g., CPU, hard disk, memory), and passive resources, which cannot execute requests, but only be acquired and released (e.g., threads, semaphores, database connections).

Processing resources specify a processing rate, which can be used to convert the resource demands in RDSEFFs into timing values. Passive resources specify a capacity. If a component acquires a passive resource, its amount of available units (i.e., its capacity) decreases. Once the capacity reaches zero, further components requesting the passive resource must wait until other services release it again. Linking resources connect resource containers and are themselves special processing resources.

System deployers use *allocation contexts* to specify that a resource container executes an assembly context. In Figure 6, the system deployer has allocated component A's assembly context to "Sever1" and component B's assembly context to "Server2".

System deployers can specify different resource environments and different allocation contexts to answer sizing questions. The PCM's resource model is still limited to abstract hardware resources. We will extend it in the future with middleware parameter, operating system settings, and scheduling policies.

Domain Expert

Domain experts create a usage model that characterizes user behavior and connects to system provided roles. In the example in Figure 7, users first log in to the system, then either browse or search, then buy an item, and finally log out. All

Figure 7. Usage model example (©2007 Heiko Koziolek. Used with permission)

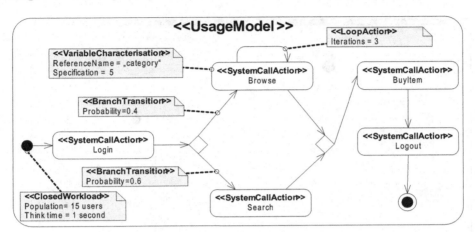

actions target system provided roles (i.e., services exposed by the system, cf. Section 4.2).

Domain experts can specify user behavior with control flow constructs such as sequence, alternative, and loop. They must specify branching probabilities for alternatives and the number of iterations for loops.

Additionally, domain experts specify the user workload. Workloads are either closed or open. Closed workloads specify a fixed number of users (population) circulating in the system. In Figure 7, the domain expert has specified a closed workload with 15 users, which perform the specified actions and then re-enter the system after a think time of 1 second. Open workloads specify a user arrival rate (e.g., 5 users/second), and do not limit the number of users in the system.

The PCM usage model also enables domain experts to characterize the parameter values of users. In Figure 7, variable "category" of action browse has been characterized with a constant (5) meaning that users always browse in the category with id number 5. Besides constants, the usage model offers specifying probability distribution functions over the input domain of a parameter, so that domain experts can provide a fine-grained

stochastic characterization of the user's input parameters. The reader may find details in Reussner et al. (2007).

Tool Support

We have implemented an Eclipse-based open-source tool called "PCM-Bench", which enables software developers to create instances of the PCM metamodel and run performance analyses (cf. Figure 8). The tool offers a different view perspective for each of the four developer roles and provides graphical model editors. Models of the different developer roles reference each other in the editor, which enables the creation of a full PCM instance. The PCM-Bench is an Eclipse RCP application and its editors have been partially generated from the PCM Ecore metamodel with support of the Graphical Modelling Framework (GMF).

The graphical editors provide an intuitive way of modeling component-based architectures analogous to UML modeling tools. They offer model validation by checking OCL-constraints (Object Constraint Language). The PCM-Bench visualizes violated constraints directly in the

Figure 8. Screenshot PCM-bench (©2007 Heiko Koziolek. Used with permission)

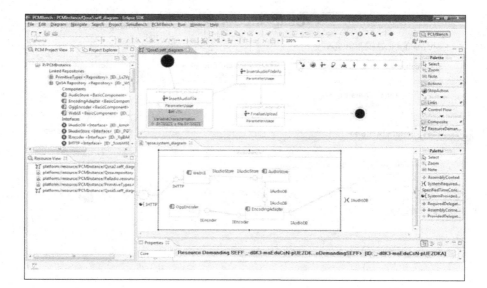

model diagrams. The editors support entering performance annotations with special input masks that offer syntax highlighting and code completion. Model instances can be serialized to XMI-files.

Besides graphical editors, the PCM-Bench is a front-end for the performance analysis techniques described in Section 5. Software architects can configure and run simulations. They can retrieve different performance metrics such as response times for use cases, throughputs, and resource utilizations. The PCM-Bench visualizes probability distribution functions of response times as histograms and provides standard statistical values such as mean, median, standard deviation etc. Furthermore, the PCM-Bench supports Model-to-Text transformations to generate Java code from PCM instances.

MODEL TRANSFORMATION AND PREDICTION METHODS

The PCM offers different performance evaluation techniques, which are still subject to research. For analyzing use cases without concurrency, a PCM instance can be transformed into a stochastic process algebra (SPA), which offers a fast way of predicting response times (Section 5.1). A PCM instance can alternatively be transformed into a queuing network based simulation model (Section 5.2). The simulation model is less restricted than the SPA, but its execution is usually more time consuming than solving the SPA. Finally, there are transformations to derive Java code skeletons from a PCM instance, to provide a starting point for implementing the modeled architecture (Section 5.3).

Stochastic Process Algebra

The PCM-Bench supports a model-2-model transformation of a PCM instance into an SPA called Capra (Happe et. al (2007), Koziolek et. al (2007c)). Capra includes concurrent processes, resources with current operating systems scheduling policies, and is able to efficiently incorporate timing values specified as arbitrary probability distributions into the analysis process. It employs a hybrid approach of analysis and simulation to conduct the performance prediction.

To transform a PCM instance into a Capra expression, a tool first solves the parametric dependencies within the RDSEFFs. They use the parameter characterizations provided by the domain expert in the usage model to transform parametric resource demands to resource demands, guards on branches to probabilities, and parameter dependent loop iteration specifications into iteration numbers. Afterwards, the transformation into Capra is straightforward (Koziolek et. al (2007a)). The remainder of this section gives a brief overview on Capra's syntax, semantics, and analytical capabilities.

The basic entities of a process are actions. In Capra, the set of actions *Act* is divided into a set of event actions *EAct* and demand actions *DAct*. Event actions represent atomic, indivisible behavior which is mainly used for process communication. Demand actions on the other hand represent the usage of resources, like processors and hard disks, for a certain time span. During the execution of a demand action other activities might happen in the system. A random variable $D_{a,r}$ specifies the demand issued by a demand action a to a resource r. It is characterized by a probability density function (pdf) $f_{a,r}(t)$. To create more complex behavioral structures, Capra offers a set of different operators for sequential and alternative composition as well as for the specification of recursive process behavior. The following describes the available operators.

Process $P \cdot Q$ denotes the *sequential composition* of two processes P and Q. It first executes P and then, after the successful termination of P, it executes Q.

The *alternative composition* models the execution of only one of the two processes P and Q. Capra distinguishes two types of alternative composition, depending on where the decision for the next activity is made. If the process itself decides on the next activity, the internal or probabilistic choice is used. Process $P \oplus_p Q$ selects process P with probability π and process Q with probability $1 - \pi$. On the other hand, the external or non-deterministic choice $P + Q$ models different possible behaviors. Here, the selection is determined by event actions issued by the process' environment, i.e. other processes running in parallel.

A process variable X can be used to define *recursive processes*. For example, $Do := a \cdot Do$ specifies a process that executes an infinite number of a actions. In real systems, the number of recursive calls is usually bounded. Furthermore, the limit is usually not fixed to a single value, but depends on the system's parameters. To approximate such behavior, Capra models the number of recursive calls as a discrete random variable specified by a probability mass function (pmf). Process $P^{*(Iter)}$ describes the *bounded loop* of a processes P. The random variable *Iter* characterized by a pmf $P(Iter = n)$ denotes the probability of executing the recursion n times (Koziolek et. al., 2007c).

Process $P \mid_A Q$ denotes the *parallel composition* of the processes P and Q. The processes communicate (and synchronize) over the event actions in the set A. Both processes compete for the available resources, which might delay their execution.

To reduce the complexity of the simulation, the total demand of some operations can be determined in advance. If two processes issue only demands to a single resource, their total demand can be computed for the operations sequential composition, probabilistic choice, and finite recursion. The following gives an impression on the possible analyses.

The total demand of a sequence of demand actions is the sum of the single demands. So, the random variable for the sequential demand is given by $D_{P;Q,r} = D_{P,r} + D_{Q,r}$. The sum of two random variables is the convolution of its pdfs. Thus, the pdf of $D_{P;Q,r}$ is $f_{P;Q,r}(t) = (f_{P,r} \otimes f_{Q,r})(t)$, where $\otimes$ denotes the convolution.

For the probabilistic choice $P \oplus_p Q$, the demand is either $D_{P,r}$ with probability π or $D_{Q,r}$ with probability $1 - \pi$. Thus, the pdf of $D_{P \oplus_p Q}$ is the weighted sum of the probability density functions:

$$f_{P \oplus_\pi Q,r}(t) = \pi \cdot f_{P,r}(t) + (1 - \pi) f_{Q,r}(t).$$

Finite recursion can be considered as large probabilistic choices over the n-time sequential composition of processes P and Q. The pmf $P(I = n)$ defines the probabilities for the probabilistic choice. Thus, function:

$$f_{\langle P[I]Q \rangle,r}(t) = \left(\sum p_I(i) \otimes_{j=1}^i (f_{P,r} \otimes f_{Q,r}) \right)(t)$$

computes the pdf for demand $D_{\langle P[I]Q \rangle}$.

With such combined resource demands, the number of required simulation steps is reduced significantly. The simulation itself is an event-discrete simulation based on the Desmo-J framework and yields as result the response time of a usage scenario as a probability distribution. Details on Capra and the simulation can be found in Happe et al. (2007).

Queuing Network Simulation

Many performance analysis methods use queuing networks as underlying prediction models because of their capability to analyze concurrent system interactions. Queuing models contain a network of service centers with waiting queues which process jobs moving through the network. When applying queuing networks in performance predictions with the PCM, some of the commonly used assumptions need to be dropped. As the PCM uses arbitrary distribution functions for the random variables, generalized distributed service center service times, arrival rates, etc. occur in the model. Additionally, the requests are routed through the queuing network according to the control flow specified in the RDSEFF. In contrast, common queuing networks assume probabilistic movement of the jobs in the network. As a result, only simulation approaches exist, which solve such models.

Hence, we use a model-to-text transformation to generate Java code realizing a custom queuing network simulation based on the simulation framework Desmo-J. The simulation generates service centers and their queues for each active resource. Passive resources are mapped on semaphores initialized with the resource's capacity. The transformation generates Java classes for the components and their assembly. Service implementations reflect their respective SEFF.

For the usage model workload drivers for open or closed workloads simulating the behavior of users exist in the generated code. For any call issued to the simulated system, the simulation determines the parameter characterizations of the input parameters and passes them in a so called virtual stackframe to the called service. Originally, the concept of a stackframe comes from compiler construction where they are used to pass parameters to method calls. In the PCM simulation, stackframes pass the parameter characterizations instead.

Utilizing the information in the simulated stackframes, the simulated SEFF issues resource demands to the simulated resources. If the resource is contented, the waiting time increases the processing time of the demand.

The simulation runs until simulation time reaches a predefined upper limit or until the width of the estimation for the confidence interval of the mean of any of the measured response times is smaller than a predefined width. After the end of a simulation run, the simulation result contains different performance indicators (response times, queue lengths, throughputs …) which the software architect can analyze to determine performance bottlenecks in the software architecture.

The computations described here reduce the complexity of Capra expressions allowing a more efficient and more accurate simulation. In the special case, that all demands are issued to the same resource and no concurrency is used, the whole expression can be solved analytically.

Java Code & Performance Prototype

The effort spent into creating a model of a software architecture should be preserved when implementing the system. For this, a model-2-text transformation based on the openArchitectureWare (oAW) framework generates code skeletons from PCM model instances. The implementation uses either Plain Old Java Objects (POJOs) or Enterprise Java Beans (EJBs) ready for deployment on a J2EE application server.

The transformation uses as much model information as possible for the generation of artifacts. Repository models result in components, assembly connectors in distributed method calls, the allocation is used to generate ant scripts to distribute the components to their host environment and finally, the usage model results in test drivers.

A particular challenge is the mapping of concepts available in the PCM to objects used in Java or EJB. Consider for example the mapping of composite components to Java. As there is no direct support of composed structures in Java, a common solution to encapsulate functionality is the application of the session façade design pattern.

Another issue with classes as implementing entities for components is the missing capabilities to explicitly specify required interfaces of classes in object oriented languages. A solution

for this is the application of the component context pattern by Völter et al. (2006). This pattern moves the references to required services into a context object. This object is injected into the component either by an explicit method call or by a dependency injection mechanism offered by the application server.

Finally, we can combine the EJB and the simulation transformation. This way, users can generate a prototype implementation which can be readily deployed and tested on the final execution environment. Internal actions of the prototype only simulate resource demands by executing dummy code which offers quality characteristics as specified in the model. By using the prototype, early simulation results can be validated on the real target environment to validate early performance estimates.

EXAMPLE

To illustrate the performance prediction approach with the PCM, this section provides a case study, in which we predicted the response time of a usage scenario in a component-based software architecture and compared the results with measured response times from executing an implementation.

The system under analysis is the "MediaStore" architecture, a web-based store for purchasing audio and video files, whose functionality is modeled after Apple's iTunes music store. It is a three-tier architecture assembled from a number of independently usable software components (Figure 9). Users interact with the store via web browsers, and may purchase and download different kinds of media files, which are stored in a database connected to the store's application server via Gigabit Ethernet.

We analysed a scenario, in which users purchase a music album (10-14 files, 2-12 MB per file) from the store. As a measure for copy protection, a component "DigitalWatermarking" shall

Figure 9. MediaStore architecture (©2007 Heiko Koziolek. Used with permission)

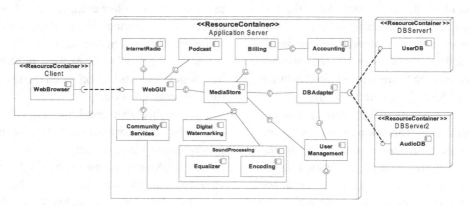

be incorporated into the store. This component unrecognisable attaches the user's ID to the audio files via digital watermarking. In case the audio files would appear illegally in public file sharing services, this enables tracking down the responsible user. However, this copy protection measure has an influence on performance, as it decreases the response time of the store when downloading files. With the model-driven performance prediction, we analysed whether the store is capable of answering 90% of all user download requests in less than 8 seconds.

Each component in the store provides RDSEFFs to enable performance analyses (three examples in Figure 10). The execution time in this use case mainly depends on the number and size of the files selected for download, which influences network traffic as well as CPU utilisation for the watermarking algorithm. The specifications of the the components' RDSEFFs have been calibrated with measurements on the individual components. In this case, we carried out the predictions using Capra.

Besides modelling the store, we also implemented the architecture assisted by the introduced model-to-text transformations

to Java code (EJB3). After generating code skeletons from the design, we manually added the implementation of the business logic of forwarding requests and watermarking audio files. The code generation also creates build scripts, test drivers, deployment descriptors, and configuration files. We weaved measurement probes into the code using AspectJ.

The results of prediction and measurement are compared in Figure 11. The diagram on the left hand side visualises the histograms of the response times. The dark columns indicate the prediction, while the bright columns on top of the dark columns indicate the measurement. The highest probability of receiving a response from the store with the mentioned parameters is at around 6 second. In this case, the prediction and the measurement widely overlap.

The diagram on the right hand side visualises the cumulative distribution functions of the response time prediction and measurements. This illustration allows to easily check our constraint of at least 90% of all responses in less than 8 seconds. It was predicted that 90% of all requests would be responded in 7.8 seconds even if watermarking was used in the architecture. The measurements

Figure 10. MediaStore service effect specifications (©2007 Heiko Koziolek. Used with permission)

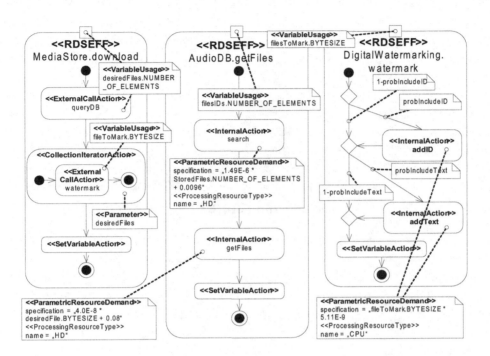

confirmed the predictions, because in our tests 90% of the request could be answered less than 7.8 seconds. There is a difference of 0.1 seconds or 1.3 percent.

In this case, the predictions were useful to quantitatively support the software architect's decision to introduce watermarking without violating a service level agreement. Note, that the predictions are not meant to be real-time predictions for safety-critical systems. They are useful at early development stages on the architectural level to support design decisions and lower the risk of performance problems in implementations. Safety-critical systems (e.g., airbag controls) instead need formal verifications of predictions to prevent harming human lives. That requires more fine grain specifications at lower abstraction levels, which developers can only create if most details of the system are known.

FUTURE RESEARCH DIRECTIONS

Model-driven performance prediction and quality assurance of software architecture models is still in its infancy and provides lots of opportunities for future research. Woodside et al. (2007) recently commented on the future of software performance engineering. We provide a list of future research directions from our viewpoint complementing their ideas:

- **Intermediate languages:** To bridge the gap between designer-friendly model notations and analytically-oriented formalisms, many approaches have developed ad-hoc model transformations. Several approaches aim at providing a standard interface, i.e., an intermediate modelling language, to ease the

Figure 11. Case study results (©2007 Heiko Koziolek. Used with permission)

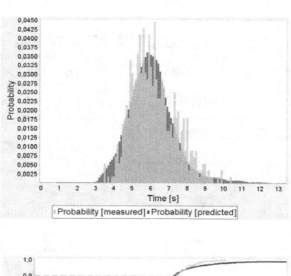

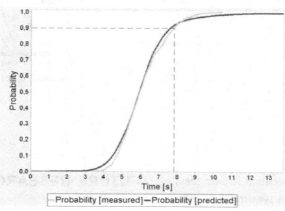

implementation of model transformations (Grassi et al. (2005), Petriu et. al. (2005))

- **Dynamic architectures:** The PCM is only targeted at static architectures, and does not allow the creation/deletion of components during runtime or changing links between components. With the advent of web services and systems with dynamic architectures changing during runtime, researchers pursuit methods to predict the dynamic performance properties of such systems (Caporuscio et al. (2007), Grassi et al. (2007)).

- **Layered resource models:** With OMG's MDA vision of platform independent models and platform specific models, it seems straight forward to follow this approach in performance modelling. For different system layers (e.g., component containers, middleware, virtual machine, operating system, hardware resources), individual models capturing performance-relevant properties could be built. These models could be composed with architectural models to predict the performance (Woodside et. al (2007)).

- **Combination of modeling and measurement:** Developers can only carry out performance measurements if the system or at least parts of it have been implemented. Measurement results could be used to improve models. In component-based performance modelling, measurements are useful to deduce the resource demands of components. A convergence of early-life cycle modelling and late-life cycle measurement can potentially increase the value of performance evaluations (Woodside et. al (2007)).

- **Performance engineering knowledge database:** Information collected by using prediction models or measuring prototypes tends to get lost during system development. However, the information is useful for future maintenance and evolution of systems. Systematic storage of performance-related information in a knowledge database could improve performance engineering (Woodside et. al (2007)).

- **Improved automated feedback:** While today's model-transformations in software performance engineering bridge the semantic gap from the developer-oriented models to the analytical models, the opposite direction of interpreting performance result back from the analytical models to the developer-oriented models has received sparse attention. Analytical performance results tend to be hard to interpret by developers, who lack knowledge about the underlying formalisms. Thus, an intuitive feedback from the analytical models to the developer-oriented models would be appreciated (OMG (2005), Woodside et. al (2007)).

CONCLUSION

This chapter provided an overview of the Palladio Component Model, a modelling language to describe component-based software architectures aiming at early life cycle performance predictions. The PCM is aligned with developer roles in CBSE, namely component developers, software architects, system deployers, and domain experts. Therefore, the PCM provides a domain specific modelling language for each of these developer roles. Combining the models from the roles leads to a full PCM instance specification, which can be transformed to different analysis models or Java code. An hybrid analysis model (SPA) provides a fast way to predict response times. Simulation of PCM instances is potentially more time-consuming, but offers more expressiveness than the hybrid approach. Finally, developers may use generated Java code skeletons from a PCM instance as a starting point for implementation. To illustrate the PCM's capabilities the chapter included a case study predicting the performance for a small component-based architecture.

The PCM is useful both for component developers and software architects. Component developers can specify the performance of their components in a context-independent way, thereby enabling third party performance predictions and improving reusability. Software architects can retrieve component performance specification from repositories and assemble them to architectures. With the specifications they can quickly analyse the expected performance of their designs without writing code. This lowers the risk of performance problems in implemented architectures, which are a result of a poor architectural design. The approach potentially saves large amounts of money because of avoided re-designs and re-implementations.

The chapter provided pointers for future directions of the discipline in Section 7. Future work for the PCM includes improving the resource model, supporting dynamic architectures and reverse engineering. The resource model needs to be improved to support different scheduling disciplines, concurrency patterns, middleware parameters, operating system features etc. Dynamic architectures complicate the model as they allow changing links between components and allow the creation and deletion of components during runtime. However, this is common in modern service-based systems, and thus should be incorporated into performance predictions. Finally, reverse engineering to semi-automatically deduce performance models from existing legacy code seems an interesting pointer for future research. Reducing the effort for modelling would convince more developers of applying performance predictions. The inclusion of legacy systems enables predicting the impact on performance of planned system changes.

REFERENCES

Balsamo, S. , DiMarco, A., Inverardi, P. & Simeoni, M. (2004). Model-Based Performance Prediction in Software Development: A Survey. *IEEE Transactions on Software Engineering, 30*(5), 295-310.

Becker, S.; Grunske, L.; Mirandola, R. & Overhage, S. (2005). Performance Prediction of Component-Based Systems: A Survey from an Engineering Perspective. In *Springer Lecture Notes in Computer Science Vol. 3938* (pp. 169-192).

Becker, S., Koziolek, H. & Reussner, R. (2007). Model-based Performance Prediction with the Palladio Component Model. In *Proceedings of the 6th Workshop on Software and Performance WOSP'07* (pp. 56-67). ACM Press

Bertolino, A. & Mirandola, R. (2004). CB-SPE Tool: Putting Component-Based Performance Engineering into Practice. In Crnkovic, I., Stafford, J. A., Schmidt, H. W. & Wallnau, K. C. (Ed.), *Proceedings of the 7ᵗʰ International Symposium on Component-Based Software Engineering, CBSE2004* (pp. 233-248). Springer Lecture Notes in Computer Science, Vol. 3054

Bondarev, E., de With, P., Chaudron, M. & Musken, J. (2005). Modelling of Input-Parameter Dependency for Performance Predictions of Component-Based Embedded Systems. In *Proceedings of the 31th EUROMICRO Conference (EUROMICRO'05)*

Caporuscio, M., DiMarco, A. & Inverardi, P. (2007), Model-based system reconfiguration for dynamic performance management. *Journal of Systems and Software, 80*(4), (pp. 455-473). Elsevier

Eskenazi, E., Fioukov, A. & Hammer, D. (2004). Performance Prediction for Component Compositions. In Crnkovic, I., Stafford, J. A., Schmidt, H. W. & Wallnau, K. C. (Ed.), *Proceedings of the 7ᵗʰ International Symposium on Component-Based Software Engineering, CBSE2004.* Springer Lecture Notes in Computer Science, Vol. 3054

Grassi, V., Mirandola, R. & Sabetta, A. (2005). From design to analysis models: a kernel language for performance and reliability analysis of component-based systems. In *Proceedings of the 5th international workshop on Software and performance, WOSP '05* (pp. 25-36). ACM Press

Grassi, V., Mirandola, R. & Sabetta, A. (2007). A Model-Driven Approach to Performability Analysis of Dynamically Reconfigurable Component-Based Systems. In *Proceedings of the 6th international workshop on Software and performance, WOSP '07* (pp. 142-153). ACM Press

Happe, J., Koziolek, H., & Reussner, R. H. (2007). Parametric Performance Contracts for Software Components with Concurrent Behaviour. In *Electronical Notes of Theoretical Computer Science, Vol. 182* (pp. 91-106), Elsevier.

Hamlet, D., Mason, D. & Woit, D. (2004). Properties of Software Systems Synthesized from Components. In Lau, K. (Ed.), *Component-Based Software Development: Case Studies* (pp. 129-159). World Scientific Publishing Company

Hissam, S. A., Moreno, G. A., Stafford, J. A. & Wallnau, K. C. (2002). Packaging Predictable Assembly. In *CD'02: Proceedings of the IFIP/ACM Working Conference on Component Deployment* (pp. 108-124). Springer-Verlag

Koziolek, H., Happe, J. & Becker, S. (2006). Parameter Dependent Performance Specifications of Software Components. In Hofmeister, C., Crnkovic, I., Reussner, R. & Becker, S. (Ed.) *Proceedings of the 2nd International Conference on the Quality of Software Architecture, QoSA2006* (pp. 163-179). Springer Lecture Notes in Computer Science, Vol. 4214

Koziolek, H., Happe, J. & Becker, S. (2007). Predicting the Performance of Component-based Software Architectures with different Usage Profiles. In Szyperski, C. & Overhage, S. (Ed.) *Proceedings of the 3rd International Conference on the Quality of Software Architecture, QoSA2007.* Springer Lecture Notes in Computer Science, To Appear

Koziolek, H. & Firus, V. (2007). Parametric Performance Contracts: Non-Markovian Loop Modelling and an Experimental Evaluation. In *Electronical Notes of Theoretical Computer Science,* Vol. 176 (pp. 69-87), Elsevier

OMG: Object Management Group (2005). UML Profile for Schedulability, Performance and Time. *http://www.omg.org/cgi-bin/doc?formal/2005-01-02*

Petriu, D. B. & Woodside, M. (2005). An intermediate metamodel with scenarios and resources for generating performance models from UML designs. *Springer Journal on Software and Systems Modeling*

Reussner. R. H., Becker, S., Happe, J., Koziolek, H., Krogmann, K. & Kuperberg. M. (2007). *The Palladio Component Model.* Internal Report Universität Karlsruhe (TH)

Sitaraman, M., Kuczycki, G., Krone, J., Ogden, W.F. & Reddy, A. (2001). Performance Specifications of Software Components. In *Proceedings of the Symposium on Software Reusability 2001* (pp. 3-10).

Szyperski, C., Gruntz, D. & Murer, S. (2002). *Component Software: Beyond Object-Oriented Programming.* Addison-Wesley

Wu, X. & Woodside, M. (2004). Performance modeling from software components. In *Proceedings of the 4th International Workshop on Software Performance, WOSP2004* (pp. 290-301). ACM SIGSOFT Software Engineering Notes

Völter, M. & Stahl, M. (2006). *Model-driven Software Development.* Wiley & Sons

Woodside, M., Franks, G. & Petriu D. C. (2007). The Future of Software Performance Engineering. In *Proceedings of 29th International. Conference on Software Engineering, ICSE'07.* Track: Future of Software Engineering.

ADDITIONAL READING

Bolch, G., Greiner, S., de Meer, H. & Trivedi, K. S. (2006). *Queueing Networks and Markov Chains: Modeling and Performance Evaluation with Computer Science Applications.* Wiley-Interscience, 2nd Edition

Cecchet, E., Marguerite, J. & Zwaenepoel, W.(2002) Performance and scalability of EJB applications. *ACM SIGPLAN Notes, 37*(11), 246-261

Chen, S., Liu, Y., Gorton, I. & Liu, A. (2005). Performance prediction of component-based applications. *Journal of Systems and Software, 74*(1), 35-43.

DiMarco, A. & Mirandola, R. (2006). Model transformations in Software Performance Engineering. *Springer Lecture Notes in Computer Science,* Vol. 4214, 95-110

Dumke, R., Rautenstrauch, C., Schmietendorf, A. & Scholz, A. (2001). *Performance Engineering: State of the Art and Current Trends.* Springer Lecture Notes in Computer Science, Vol. 2047

Grassi, V., Mirandola, R. & Sabetta, A. (2006). Filling the gap between design and performance/reliability models of component-based systems: A model-driven approach. *Journal of Systems and Software, 80*(4), 528-558.

Hermanns, H., Herzog, U. & Katoen, J. (2002) Process algebra for performance evaluation. *Theorectical Computer Science, 274*(1-2), Elsevier Science Publishers Ltd., 43-87

Jain, R. K. (1991). *The Art of Computer Systems Performance Analysis: Techniques for Experimental Design, Measurement, Simulation, and Modeling.* Wiley

Kounev, S. (2006). Performance Modeling and Evaluation of Distributed Component-Based Systems Using Queueing Petri Nets. *IEEE Transactions on Software Engineering, 32*(7), 486-502.

Lazowska, E.; Zahorjan, J.; Graham, G. & Sevcik, K. (1984). *Quantitative System Performance,* Prentice Hall

Liu, Y., Fekete, A. & Gorton, I. (2005). Design-Level Performance Prediction of Component-Based Applications. *IEEE Transactions on Software Engineering, 31*(11), 928-941.

Menasce, D. A. & Gomaa, H. (2000). A Method for Design and Performance Modeling of Client/Server Systems. *IEEE Transactions on Software Engineering, 26*(11), 1066-1085

Menasce, D. A. & Almeida, V. A.(2000) *Scaling for E-Business: Technologies, Models, Performance, and Capacity Planning,* Prentice Hall

Menasce, D. A. & Almeida, V. A.(2002) *Capacity Planning for Web Services,* Prentice Hall

Menasce, D. A., Dowdy, L. W. & Almeida, A.F. (2004). *Performance by Design: Computer Capacity Planning By Example,* Prentice Hall PTR

Reussner, R. H., Schmidt, H. W. & Poernomo, I. H. (2003). Reliability prediction for component-based software architectures. *Journal of Systems and Software, 66*(3), 241-252.

Rolia, J. A. & Sevcik, K. C. (1995). The Method of Layers. *IEEE Transactions on Software Engineering, 21*(8), 689-700

Smith, C. U. & Williams, L. G. (2001). *Performance Solutions: A Practical Guide to Creating Responsive, Scalable Software.* Addison-Wesley Professional

Verdickt, T., Dhoedt, B., Gielen, F. & Demeester, P (2005). Automatic Inclusion of Middleware Performance Attributes into Architectural UML Software Models. *IEEE Transactions on Software Engineering, 31*(8), 695-771.

Woodside, C. M., Neilson, J. E., Petriu, D. C. & Majumdar, S. (1995) The Stochastic Rendezvous Network Model for Performance of Synchronous Client-Server-like Distributed Software. *IEEE Transactions on Computers,* 44(1), 20-34.

Chapter VI
Integrating Measures and Redesigns in the Definition of Domain Specific Visual Languages

Esther Guerra
Universidad Carlos III de Madrid, Spain

Juan de Lara
Universidad Autónoma de Madrid, Spain

Paloma Díaz
Universidad Carlos III de Madrid, Spain

ABSTRACT

The goal of this work is to facilitate the task of integrating measurement and redesign tools in modelling environments for Domain Specific Visual Languages (DSVLs), reducing or eliminating the necessity of coding. With this purpose, we have created a DSVL called SLAMMER that includes generalizations of some of the more used types of product metrics and frequent model manipulations, which can be easily customised for any other DSVL in a graphical way. The metric customisation process relies on visual patterns for the specification of the elements that should be measured in each metric type, while redesigns (as well as other actions) can be specified either personalizing generic templates or by means of graph transformation systems. The provided DSVL also allows creating new metrics, composing metrics, and executing actions guided by measurement values. The approach has been empirically validated by its implementation in a meta-modelling tool, which has been used for several DSVLs. In this way, together with the DSVL specification, a SLAMMER model can be provided containing a suite of metrics and actions that will become available in the final modelling environment. In this chapter we show a case study for a notation in the web engineering domain. As ensuring model quality is a key success factor in many computer science areas, even crucial in model-driven development, we believe that the results of this work benefit all of them by providing automatic support for the specification, generation and integration of measurement and redesign tools with modelling environments.

INTRODUCTION

Diagrammatic notations are pervasive in software development, e.g. to specify, understand and reason about the system to be built. When the notations are constrained to a particular application domain, they are called Domain Specific Visual Languages (DSVLs) (Gray et al., 2004). These provide high-level, domain-specific, graphical primitives, having the potential to increase the user productivity for the specific modelling task. Being so restrictive they are less error-prone than general-purpose languages, and easier to learn.

DSVLs are frequently used in Model-Driven Software Development (MDSD) (Kent, 2002) as a means to capitalize the knowledge in a certain application domain. MDSD seeks increasing quality and productivity in software development by considering models as the primary asset, from which the application code is generated. Although its steep learning curve has been pointed out as one of its main disadvantages, its benefits outweigh the drawbacks, and the use of appropriate modelling tools can help developers to overcome this and other problems. Thus, many efforts are being currently spent in order to provide adequate tool support for the specification and generation of rich modelling environments for DSVLs (DSLTools, 2007; GMF, 2007; Lédczi et al., 2001; Pohjonen & Tolvanen, 2002) encompassing aspects of the MDSD process, such as facilities for code generation, reporting, formal verification, or quality assessment (Guerra et al., 2006), which is the topic of the present chapter.

Software quality is defined as *"the totality of features and characteristics of a software product that bear on its ability to satisfy stated or implied needs"* (ISO/IEC 9126, 1991). By stated needs we refer to explicit system requirements, mostly functional. Quality features of this type are product correctness, completeness and reliability, and the use of formal methods can help to achieve them. Implied needs are those ones that, although may be incomplete or not specified, if they are not present in the final product then this is considered to have less quality. Some features of this type are efficiency, usability, maintainability, extensibility or cohesion. Product metrics (Fenton, 1996) measure such features in order to control and improve the quality of software products. In this chapter, we are interested in generating tools to measure the quality of software system designs specified using any arbitrary (domain specific) visual notation. We will use the term *"model quality"* to refer to the quality properties of the software system that a model represents. Note that, as in MDSD code is generated from models, it is natural to lift up the mechanisms to check the quality and correctness of applications from code to models.

However, even if measurement is a key quality control activity in most engineering domains (Basili et al., 1994; Whitmire, 1997), this is sometimes neglected in Software Engineering. A factor that may attract a more widespread use is its support by tools, which is even more critical for automation-based processes such as MDSD. Its use helps detecting defects prior to implementation, saving time and budget. The problem is that adapting, implementing and integrating measurement mechanisms for the plethora of DSVLs and tools is costly and time-consuming, and usually does not take advantage of previous developments. Our goal is to reduce such cost, by making the customisation of measures for any kind of DSVL easy.

Additional techniques to enhance system quality from its very design are redesigns and design patterns. Redesigns are design modifications that do not change the functionality but improve model quality. This concept is similar to the concept of refactoring for code (Fowler, 1999). Design patterns (Gamma et al., 1995) are a catalog of best practices that can be applied in order to solve specific problems in software design. Again, the proliferation of notations and tools can hamper the automated application of redesigns and the use of patterns.

In this chapter we propose a novel DSVL called SLAMMER (Specification LAnguage for Modelling MEasures and Redesigns). The language allows the customisation of general predefined measures and actions to be applied to a specific DSVL. Measurement and redesign tools are automatically generated from SLAMMER models and integrated in the DSVL modelling environment. SLAMMER contains the main types of product metrics we have identified. The user can customise these metrics with visual patterns or create new ones. In addition, it is possible to specify threshold values for the metrics. Thresholds may have an associated action described either using a programming language, a graph transformation system (Ehrig et al., 2006) or customising a generic predefined template. This is useful if the action executes known redesigns that improve the model quality.

These ideas have been implemented in the AToM³ tool (de Lara & Vangheluwe, 2002), which allows the description of DSVLs by means of meta-modelling. We illustrate its use by defining a set of metrics and redesigns for Labyrinth (Díaz et al., 2001), a DSVL in the web domain.

Chapter organization. The chapter starts by studying related work. Then, it gives an introduction on meta-modelling for the generation of environments for DSVLs, and presents an ex-

ample of environment generation for Labyrinth. Next section introduces the main concepts of measurement and redesign. Then, SLAMMER is presented using examples with Labyrinth. After that, we show how SLAMMER was integrated in AToM³ and used to improve the environment for Labyrinth. Then, some methodological issues are discussed, regarding the use of these concepts in MDSD. Finally, the chapter ends with future trends and the conclusions.

STATE OF THE ART

As stated in the introduction, the purpose of the work presented in this chapter is to facilitate the generation of visual environments integrating mechanisms to quantify and improve model quality, regardless of the DSVL in which these models are specified. Therefore, the required mechanisms must be general enough to be reused or adapted to any notation. In this respect, some proposals for generic measurement and redesign are found in the literature, although they are usually oriented to a specific domain and focused on the implementation phase. For example (Mens & Lanza, 2002; Misic & Moser, 1997) present meta-model based approaches in order to specify generic metrics for object-oriented systems. They define meta-models that include domain abstract concepts, such as class or attribute. A generic metric is defined by using the meta-model concepts, and customised for a specific language by mapping the language concepts and the meta-model ones. However, these approaches are domain dependent as the calculation of the metrics depends on the concepts defined on the "generic" meta-model. They don't exploit metrics as software remodelling tools that allow guiding redesign execution either. The approach followed in SPQR/20 (SPQR/20, 1995) also provides an implementation of the measurement function (an extended version of function points) applicable to different languages. Finally, it is also worth mentioning the attempts to define ontologies for software measurement (García et al., 2006; Martín & Olsina, 2003).

With respect to the notion of generic refactoring, this is presented in (Lämmel, 2002). The framework consists of meta-programs written in Haskell that can be instantiated for different programming languages by means of parameters. However, the parameterisation is complex and implies knowing Haskell and the abstract syntax of the specific language. Search of candidate code to refactoring is exhaustive (consuming-time) and not guided by mechanisms that help to guide its application by detecting bad smells.

Recently, the necessity of new tools for modernization and evolution of software has been recognised by the OMG with its Architecture-Driven Modernization (ADM) Task Force. It has published a Request for Proposal (RFP) for Metrics and Refactoring Packages with the purpose of defining a meta-model that enables the interchange of metrics and refactorings, respectively, being flexible enough to adopt any new kind of metric. Its main goal is to facilitate the analysis, visualization, refactoring and transformation of existing software systems.

There are a variety of modelling tools that incorporate functionalities for obtaining measurements. Nonetheless, the provided metrics are usually hard-coded, oriented to a specific domain, and the extension possibilities are very limited. One exception is the SDMetric tool (SDMetric), which allows the definition of metrics for UML models using a relational-like language based on XML. In ATHENA (Tsalidis et al., 1992) the set of predefined metrics can be extended by using a textual language. The Moose Reengineering Environment (Lanza & Ducasse, 2002) implements an engine for language-independent object-oriented software metrics. It provides more than 30 predefined software object-oriented metrics with no possibility of extension, but that can be customised for any object-oriented language by its mapping to a language independent representation called FAMIX. As it can be seen, there is a need of more general approaches neither restricted to UML nor object orientation, being more easily adaptable and intuitive.

Regarding redesign capabilities, the ones provided by modelling tools are usually oriented to a specific language, with no possibility of extension, and the parts that need to be redesigned have to be detected by hand (e.g. the Refactoring Browser (Roberts et al., 1997) for Smalltalk code or Together Technologies for Java and UML models). There are only a few that allow an automatic detection of model refactoring opportunities, such as SOUL (Tourwé & Mens, 2003). This is a language built on the VisualWorks Smalltalk environment that detects existing bad smells by using logic meta-programming, and then proposes a set of appropriate refactorings that can solve them. Again, this tool is domain specific and the set of bad smells and refactorings cannot be enhanced.

In the area of meta-CASE tools, although there is a plethora of them (e.g. GME (Lédczi et al., 2001), MetaEdit+ (Pohjonen & Tolvanen, 2002) or the Eclipse Generic Modelling Framework (GMF)), to our knowledge none of them support the definition and customisation of metrics. Even though GMF provides a "metrics" package, it only allows defining metrics from scratch by coding them in OCL, making the process tedious, hard and time consuming. In order to define redesigns, some of them provide some transformation language, but in any case they do not provide support for the detection of the parts that should be reworked.

META-MODELLING FOR DOMAIN SPECIFIC VISUAL LANGUAGES

A meta-model is a model of a modelling language (Favre, 2004). That is, in order to describe a modelling language, one can make a model (e.g. using class or entity relationship diagrams) to describe the language *abstract syntax*. This contains the main concepts of the language and their relations. In addition, in order to restrict the number of valid models defined by meta-models, they may contain additional constraints expressed in textual languages such as OCL (Warmer & Kleppe, 2003).

As an example, Figure 1 shows an excerpt of the meta-model for Labyrinth, a DSVL oriented to the design of web applications (Díaz et al., 2001). In Labyrinth, a web application is modelled as a set of nodes where contents are located. Nodes and contents can be composed in order to create complex information structures. Navigation is expressed through anchors and links: a link defines a possible navigation path between nodes or contents, and the source and target of a link is defined through anchors. Besides, users can assume roles and belong to different teams from which they receive a set of permissions concerning the nodes and contents they are allowed to visit. These roles and teams can be nested in hierarchical

structures where permissions assigned to more general roles are inherited by more specific roles, and permissions assigned to teams are propagated to their members.

The meta-model of a DSVL has to be provided with information about the visualization of each one of its elements, which is known as its *concrete syntax* (de Lara & Vangheluwe, 2002). The simplest way is to assign an icon-like visualization to classes and arrow-like to associations.

Meta-modelling tools allow specifying the concrete and abstract syntax of a certain DSVL, and they automatically generate a modelling tool where end-users are allowed to edit models written in such notation. In this chapter, our purpose is to provide a mechanism to enrich such generated environment with capabilities for model quality measurement and improvement.

Figure 1. An excerpt of the labyrinth meta-model (©2007 Esther Guerra. Used with permission)

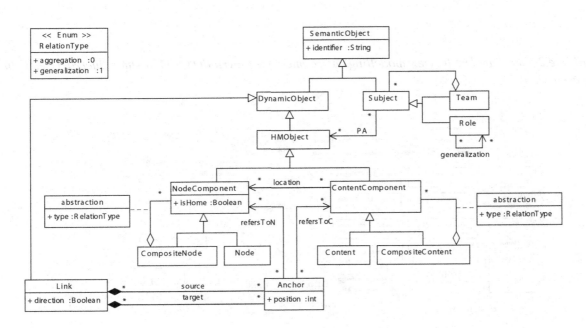

Multi-View Domain Specific Visual Languages

As systems become more complex, there is a trend to split their specification in smaller models, each one of them built by using the most appropriate notation. The family of notations that are used in combination for the description of the aspects of a system is called Multi-View DSVL (MV-DSVL). UML (UML, 2006) is one of its most prominent examples, although for a broader domain. It provides different diagram types for the specification of the static (e.g. class and object diagrams) and dynamics (e.g. statecharts and sequence diagrams) of a system. Similarly, the Ariadne Development Method (Díaz et al., 2005) defines a set of diagram types based on the Labyrinth meta-model to deal with various concerns of a web design, such as the information structure, navigation paths, presentation features and access control policies.

Modelling environments for MV-DSVLs must ensure not only intra-diagram consistency (i.e. conformance of a model to its meta-model), but also inter-diagram consistency for those cases when the same element belongs to different diagrams, therefore changes in one of them should

be propagated to the others. Our approach (implemented in AToM[3]) for the specification of such environments is to first define the meta-model of the complete language, and then define each diagram type as a subset of it (Guerra & de Lara, 2007). From this specification, a multi-view environment is generated where the end-user builds models conforming to some diagram type. Inter-diagram consistency is achieved by building a *repository* made of the gluing of the system models, from where changes are propagated to the rest of the views, as done in the Model-View-Controller pattern. This behaviour is performed by triple graph transformation (TGT) rules (Schürr, 1994) derived from the meta-model information (Guerra & de Lara, 2006). The generated multi-view environment can also check the inter-diagram semantic consistency by translating the repository into a semantic domain, executing an analysis method, and back-annotating the results into the original notation (Guerra et al., 2007).

For example, Figure 2 shows the generated multi-view modelling environment for Labyrinth by using AToM[3]. The background window allows defining system diagrams of different types. One diagram called `Role Hierarchy` of type Us-

Figure 2. Generated multi-view modelling environment for labyrinth (©2007 Esther Guerra. Used with permission)

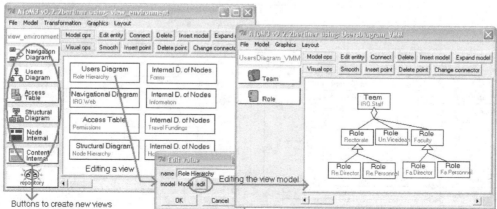

ers Diagram is being edited. The control dialog (named "Edit value") allows setting the property values for this "view" of the system, including the corresponding model (i.e. a role hierarchy), which is shown in the right-most window.

In multi-view environments, measurement becomes more complex because the information needed for its calculation is scattered in several models (of the same or different type). Similarly, certain redesigns or model refactorings may imply parallel modifications to several of the system models. Finally, after a redesign, changes should be appropriately propagated to the rest of the models so as to recover the inter-diagram consistency.

In following sections we present our proposal for the definition of measures and redesigns for single and multi-view DSVLs, and show how using it for enriching the previously presented environment for Labyrinth. Before, we give an introduction to measurement and redesign.

MEASUREMENT AND REDESIGN

Measurement is a basic tool for quality control in many engineering disciplines (Basili et al., 1994; Whitmire, 1997). Engineers make use of measures in order to provide feedback and assist in evaluation, creating a corporate memory and helping answering questions about the object being measured. In software engineering, the measurable objects are usually processes, resources, products (Fenton, 1996) and projects (Whitmire, 1997). Our work is focussed to measuring products, and in particular models, as they are the key concept in MDSD.

Products (and in general any measurable object) contain *internal* and *external* attributes. The former can be measured in terms of the product itself (e.g. its size). External attributes can only be measured with respect to how the product relates to its environment (e.g. its cognitive complexity, usability or maintainability), and are obtained by

testing, operating and observing the executable software. Our work is directed to measuring internal attributes, as they apply on the system models instead on the system itself.

Measurement can be *direct* or *indirect*. In the first case, the value is derived from an attribute that does not depend upon any other measure. Sometimes they are also called *base* measures. Indirect (or *derived*) measures are obtained by combining several direct or indirect measures. The term *indicator* is sometimes used to refer to indirect measures that have an associated analysis model made of a calculation procedure with decision criteria. The criteria can be a threshold, a target or a pattern used to determine the need for action or further investigation (García et al., 2006). As we will see in next section, SLAMMER supports direct and indirect measures, as well as indicators with thresholds. Thresholds indicate anomalies in the metric values (e.g. extreme values) and may trigger redesigns for improving the quality of the model.

Further classification of measures includes the *objectivity*, that is, whether they involve human (*subjective*) judgement, or they are quantifications based on numerical rules (i.e. *objective* methods). Finally, regarding the *automatization* degree, measurement methods can be *automatic, semi-automatic* or *manual*. Our approach is aimed at the automatization of the measurement in tools, thus we only consider objective metrics (as subjective measures cannot be made fully automatic).

Redesigns are changes in a design model for improving some quality attribute, such as understandability, performance, cohesion or coupling. When the redesign preserves the intended meaning (or behaviour) of the model, it is called model refactoring (Mens, 2006). Refactorings (Fowler, 1999) were originally defined as changes to software code in order to make it easier to understand and modify, without changing its observable behaviour. Model refactoring shifts code refactoring techniques to the model level. In MDSD, this is the right abstraction level, as the application code is generated from the models, which is then frequently treated as a "black box" (i.e. the generated code is not manually adapted).

The need for performing refactorings and redesigns is commonly detected through so-called "*bad smells*" (Fowler, 1999). They informally describe some design or code problem, and have a number of associated actions (one or more refactorings) to help in its solution. Some efforts have been recently placed in formally defining such *smells* through the use of metrics (Munro, 2005). In our proposal, we follow this trend by using thresholds associated to metrics in order to detect product anomalies, and possibly correct them through redesigns. Although automated, these redesigns usually require human supervision, either for additional input or simply for confirming that they are adequate in the given situation.

SLAMMER: SPECIFICATION LANGUAGE FOR MODELLING MEASURES AND REDESIGNS

SLAMMER is a novel DSVL that tries to facilitate the definition of measures and redesigns for a given DSVL, as well as to provide a framework for the automatic (model-driven) generation of measurement and redesign tools that can be integrated in the final modelling environment for the DSVL. SLAMMER can be used for any kind of DSVL (which may be used for describing

structure, behaviour, or any other system perspective). SLAMMER has been defined by means of a meta-model that takes into account related works on ontologies for software measurement (García et al., 2006), as well as on the international standard for software quality ISO 15939 (ISO/IEC 15939, 2002). In addition, it is based on the use of visual techniques (e.g. graphical patterns, graph transformation) to achieve its purposes.

In this section, we start by introducing the concept of graphical pattern and its instantiation in the context of SLAMMER, as patterns will be used to configure measures and redesigns. Then, we present the part of the SLAMMER meta-model for the definition of measures and actions. We illustrate the SLAMMER concepts with examples for Labyrinth.

Graphical Patterns in SLAMMER

In SLAMMER, the simplest form of pattern is a single positive graph. The application of a pattern to a model gives as result all occurrences of the positive graph in the model. The pattern can be initialised with a partial match, given as an argument of the pattern, and the output can be filtered in order to return a subgraph of the positive graph occurrences. Figure 3 shows to the left an example pattern. The positive graph is made of objects *Role* and *Node* related through a permission assignment (relationship *PA*). To the right, the pattern is instantiated in graph G. In step (i)

Figure 3. Example of graph pattern and instantiation (©2007 Esther Guerra. Used with permission)

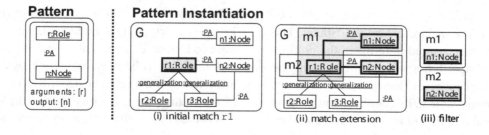

Figure 4. Example of graph pattern with positive and negative application conditions and instantiation (©2007 Esther Guerra. Used with permission)

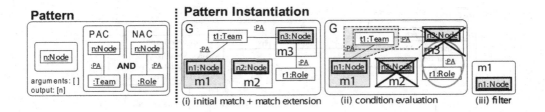

the match is initialised with the role r1, which is received as argument. In step (ii) the match is extended to the complete positive graph of the pattern. Two occurrences of the positive graph are found in G: one relating role r1 to node n1, and another one relating it with node n2. In step (iii) the matchings are filtered so that only the elements specified as output in the pattern are obtained as result. Thus, as the pattern specified node n as the output, only nodes n1 and n2 in the matchings are given as result.

The number of instantiations of a pattern can be restricted by means of one or more *application conditions* (Ehrig et al., 2006). These are made of a premise graph and a set of consequence graphs. If a pattern specifies some application condition, the pattern instantiation process is as follows. First, all occurrences of the positive graph are found in the model. Then, for each application condition, if an occurrence of the premise graph is found then some of the consequence graphs have also to be found for the occurrence of the positive graph to be considered valid. There are two special cases of application conditions. If only a premise is specified and no consequence, then it is called a *negative application condition* (NAC), and finding the premise in the model makes invalid the positive graph occurrence. On the other hand, if the premise is isomorphic to the positive graph and some consequence is specified, it is called a *positive application condition* (PAC). In this

case, some of the consequences have to be found on the model for the positive graph occurrence to be valid.

Figure 4 shows to the left an example of pattern with two application conditions. Its positive graph is made of an object *Node*, the PAC specifies that an object *Team* must have permission to access the node, and the NAC forbids an object *Role* to have access to the node. To the right, the pattern is instantiated in graph G. In step (i) all the matches of the positive graph are found. As the pattern has no arguments, there is no starting initial match, and thus all nodes in G are valid instantiations of the positive graph. In step (ii) the application conditions are evaluated for each match. An occurrence of the PAC and no occurrence of the NAC are found for match m1, therefore the match is valid. For match m2 no occurrence of the PAC is found, thus the match is discarded. Finally, for match m3 the PAC is satisfied, but an occurrence of the NAC is found, thus the match is also discarded. This is why in step (iii) only match m1 is obtained as result.

Figure 5 shows the package of the SLAMMER meta-model dealing with pattern definition. In SLAMMER we use patterns in order to customise generic measures and task templates for concrete DSVLs. Patterns allow visually specifying how model attributes (i.e. features that are going to be measured or modified) are expressed in a DSVL, as next subsection explains.

Figure 5. Domain specific visual language SLAMMER. Package "Pattern" (©2007 Esther Guerra. Used with permission)

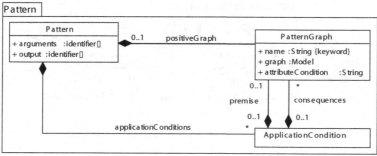

Specification of Measures in SLAMMER

A measure can be specified by providing the set of entities that are going to be characterized by the measurement (the *domain*), the relevant *attributes* for the measurement method, the *measurement method* itself (a function in the case of indirect metrics), the *scale* (the range of values it can take) and, in case of scales of type interval or ratio, a *measurement unit* (e.g. number of classes, lines of code). In addition, measures may include information about normal or unusual value ranges, pointing to *threshold* values in the measurement scale. It must be noted that the measurement method is domain independent and remains always the same. On the contrary, the domain, the properties to be measured and the threshold values are domain dependent, and have to be specified for each DSVL where we want to perform the measurement. SLAMMER uses this idea in order to specify a set of predefined generic metric templates that hide the measurement function and can be customised by providing only the domain-specific information in each case. The metric domain is specified as the list of types that

conform the domain space, the attributes to be measured are given as a set of patterns, the units are given as text, and the thresholds are boolean conditions evaluated on the metric value.

The package of the SLAMMER meta-model concerning the definition of measures is shown in Figure 6. Concrete classes inheriting from class *Measure* define metric templates that can be customised by giving the domain and properties for a specific DSVL. All measures contain a unique identifier *name* and a *goal*. Attribute *domain* is used to specify the metric domain as a list of types. Attribute *subtypeMatching* specifies if objects in the domain must have exactly the type specified in attribute *domain*, or also any of its subtypes is allowed. This makes measures more reusable, being defined once for a type, and used for all its subtypes. Attributes *scale* and *unit* are used to specify the range of values the measure can take and its magnitude, respectively. In addition, relation *dependency* allows a measure to use results calculated by other ones and thus metrics composition. In this way, measures can be reused and composed in order to build more complex composite ones. A meta-model constraint forbids cycles of recursive dependencies. A measure may have any number of *threshold* values, which are extreme values for it. A threshold has a *name*, a *description* and a *condition*. The latter is a logical expression over values of the measure.

Concrete measures in the SLAMMER meta-model are organized depending on its domain dimension and on the measurement function used to calculate the metric value. From the domain dimension point of view, they can be *model-oriented* if they take measures of global model properties (such as number of cycles and size); *element-oriented* if they refer to element features (e.g. permissions assigned to a role); and *group-oriented* if they measure features of groups of elements (e.g. their similarity or coupling). From the measurement function point of view, we sort out them either as *path-oriented* if they use a measurement function that traverses paths between elements of the same type (e.g. a navigation path joins nodes by means of anchors and links, and an inheritance path joins subjects or classes by means of inheritance relations) or

any of their subtypes, which is specified by attribute *type*; or as *user-defined* if the measurement function is provided by the user (and is different from the ones already provided by the SLAM-MER meta-model).

SLAMMER contains generalizations or abstractions of some of the more used types of metrics in software engineering, together with mechanisms for their combination. That is, we are not inventing new metrics, but reusing metrics that have been validated by other researchers and shown to work for specific purposes. In SLAM-MER metrics are visually customised for a given DSVL by means of graphical patterns (class *Pattern* in the meta-model) that identify how domain specific features are expressed in such language. The arguments of the pattern correspond to a value in the metric domain, and the output is the set of model attributes we want to obtain. In the remaining of this subsection, we explain the generic metrics included in SLAMMER.

Figure 6. Domain specific visual language SLAMMER. Package "Measures" (©2007 Esther Guerra. Used with permission)

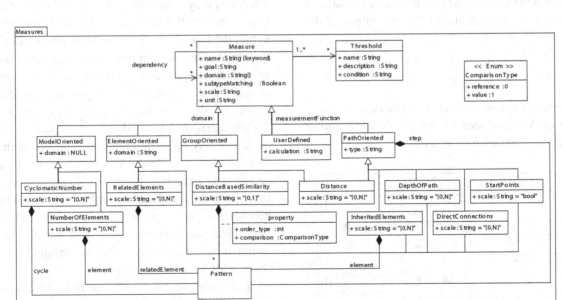

NumberOfElements allows counting the number of elements of certain type in a model. This is a model-oriented measure because it calculates a property of the model itself, and thus it is not necessary to specify the domain (i.e. it is the complete model). The type of the element to be counted is given as a pattern. As patterns are indeed models plus application conditions, we can count not only elements of a certain type, but also complex structures made of sets of different related elements.

As an example, the *Number of Navigational Contexts* (NNC) (Abrahao et al., 2003) is used in the web domain as indicator of the navigational model size. In Labyrinth, a navigational context is a node component that participates in a navigational link through the corresponding anchor. We can use SLAMMER in order to adapt the NNC to Labyrinth by customising a measure of type *NumberOfElements* with the pattern shown in Figure 7. This pattern has an application condition which allows counting the number of node components (simple and composite, see Labyrinth meta-model in Figure 1) that are source (consequence graph 1) or target (consequence graph 2) of a navigational link. Thus, one of the consequence graphs of the application condition has to be found, and we indicate it with an "OR". The output of the

pattern is the element to be counted, that is, the node component.

CyclomaticNumber counts the number of cycles in a model, thus being model-oriented. In this case a pattern showing the structure of a cycle in the given DSVL must be provided.

RelatedElements counts how many elements are related to a given element type, which is specified by attribute *domain*. This measure is element-oriented, and thus, it is calculated for each element of the specified type in a given model. The relation between the elements is given as a pattern, which allows expressing complex relations made of several elements as well.

For example, we can instantiate a measure of this type for Labyrinth, and customise it so as to count the number of nodes each role has permission to access. In this case attribute domain should contain type "Role", and the related element should be specified by the pattern shown in Figure 3. The metric is calculated for each role in the model and, in each case, the metric value is calculated as the number of times the pattern gets instantiated (two for role r1).

DistanceBasedSimilarity compares how similar a set of entities is by studying the set of attributes they share (Simon et al., 1999). It can take values in the interval [0, 1]: the higher the value, the bigger the distance between the entities, and the less similar they are. The types of the entities to compare are given as a list in attribute *domain*. For each one of the types, it must also be specified which are the properties used for the comparison. This is done with a pattern for each property (qualified relation *property* in the meta-model). The properties define an attribute *order_type* that relates them with the corresponding type in the list given by attribute *domain*. The comparison can be made either by reference (i.e. two objects are considered equal if they are the same) or by value (i.e. two objects are equal if all their fields have the same value).

This measure can be applied to Labyrinth in order to analyse how similar are each two roles

Figure 7. Customisation pattern for metric "Number of Navigational Contexts" (©2007 Esther Guerra. Used with permission)

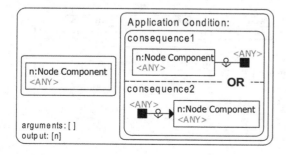

in the system, and thus detect redundancies in the defined security policy (Guerra et al., 2006). In this case, the domain contains type *Role* twice and the properties that make similar two roles are the permissions they define (expressed with a pattern).

Distance, as well as the following measures, allows measuring different properties of path-like structures where the nodes in the path have the same type and are connected through some specific relation. For example, the structure of a web navigation map is path-like, since we have information nodes that are connected through anchors and links. Another example is the users' hierarchy provided by Labyrinth, which contains subjects (i.e. roles and teams) connected by means of inheritance relations. In this measure, as well as in the remaining ones, it must be specified the element type to which the measure applies (attribute *domain*), as well as the fundamental step (e.g. the inheritance relationship in the users' hierarchy), which is specified as a pattern. Thus, the measure calculates the minimum number of necessary steps to reach each element from the other ones. From the point of view of the domain dimension, it is a group-oriented metric as it measures a property of a group of two model elements.

For example, Figure 8 shows a pattern specifying what a step is in the Labyrinth navigation map (i.e. two nodes related through a link and two anchors). The target node of a navigation step (output) is the source of the following step (argument). We may use such pattern to customise *Distance* so as

to define the Minimum Path Between Navigational Contexts (MPBNC) (Abrahao et al., 2003) for Labyrinth. This gives a measure of the usability of a navigational map by counting the number of links that must be traversed to reach certain information node from another one, and can be used to detect unreachable nodes. In the present example, assigning type "Node Component" as metric domain and selecting subtype matching would complete the customisation process.

StartPoints identifies all elements where a path begins, but to which no path arrives. These are the base classes in object-oriented notations.

DepthOfPath counts the minimum number of steps that are necessary in order to reach an element from a starting point. For example, it can be used to calculate the depth of the inheritance tree in object-oriented notations, or the Depth of a Node (D) (Botafogo et al., 1992) in web notations, which is the distance from the root node to a particular node in a navigation map. The bigger the distance, the harder becomes to reach the node. In order to adapt metric D for Labyrinth, it should be specified what a step is in the Labyrinth navigation map, which can be done with the same pattern that was shown in Figure 8.

InheritedElements applies to notations having some concept of inheritance. It calculates how many elements of certain type are inherited through the inheritance hierarchy. In this case, together with the type and the fundamental step, a pattern must be specified with the element to be inherited.

Figure 8. Customisation pattern for metric "Minimum Path Between Navigational Contexts" (©2007 Esther Guerra. Used with permission)

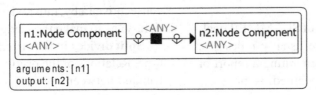

Figure 9. Customisation patterns for metric "Subject Inherited Permissions" (©2007 Esther Guerra. Used with permission)

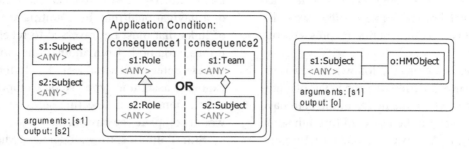

For example, Figure 9 shows the two necessary patterns for the definition of the metric Subject Inherited Permissions, which counts the number of inherited permissions through the hierarchy of roles and teams defined in Labyrinth. The pattern to the left specifies what a step in such hierarchy is, that is, two subjects joined by either a generalization (consequence graph 1) or an aggregation (consequence graph 2). The pattern to the right indicates which is the inherited element, that is, the permission to access a hypermedia object (i.e. a node or a content).

Finally, **DirectConnections** calculates the number of elements than can be directly reached in one step in a path-like structure. As before, only the type to which the measure applies as well as the fundamental step must be specified. This measure can be used by Labyrinth, for example, to calculate how many members belong to a team. Note that this information can be scattered in different user diagrams.

Specification of Actions in SLAMMER

Figure 10 shows the portion of SLAMMER dealing with actions. These are usually redesigns, although other tasks (e.g. generating a report or printing a model) can be specified. Actions are made of reusable tasks expressed either procedurally, by means of a graph grammar (Ehrig et al., 2006), or by customising task templates. They can be applied either when some measure reaches certain threshold value (relation *fires*) or directly by the end-user independently from metric values. In the first case, the action is executed for each value in the domain for which the measure makes the threshold condition true. Attribute *execution* in class *Action* selects whether this action is automatically executed, or it needs human supervision to confirm it.

SLAMMER defines four customisable tasks: merge, split, move and pull. **Merge** collapses two elements into a single one that brings together all the relationships of the formers. If the original entities defined the same relation, the merged entity contains it twice. Attribute *rel_duplication* allows selecting whether this is allowed or if duplicated relationships are deleted after the merging. Attribute *att_merging* specifies the attribute merging mechanism as the concatenation of the original values or taking one of them. For example, this task can be used to compact two consecutive Labyrinth nodes with little information, so as to make the navigation lighter.

Split divides in two an entity of the specified type. Relations of the original element are redistributed between the new ones either randomly

Figure 10. Domain specific visual language SLAMMER. Package "Actions" (©2007 Esther Guerra. Used with permission)

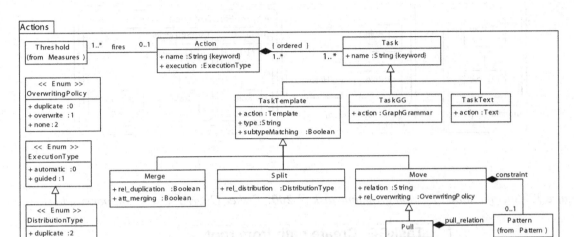

in equal parts or guided by the user (controlled by attribute *rel_distribution*). The task could be used, for example, in order to divide nodes with a large amount of information, so as to avoid a cognitive overload to the user.

Move moves relationships between entities of the same type. In addition to the entity type, it is necessary to specify the relation type to be moved (attribute *relation*), and the overwriting policy in case the relation already exists in the target entity (attribute *rel_overwriting*). Possible values for the overwriting policy are *duplicate* if we want to move the relation maintaining the existing one in the target; *overwrite* if the relationship is moved and overwrites the one in the target; and *none* if the relation is not moved. It is possible to restrict the number of relations to be moved by means of a pattern that receives as arguments the elements that take part in the action (i.e. the relation to move and the source and target elements). In this case the action is applied only if the pattern is satisfied.

Finally, **Pull** specializes task *Move* to those cases where the involved entities must be related. The relation is specified as a pattern with the entities as arguments and no output.

As an example, we can customise a task *Pull* for Labyrinth so as to pull up permissions to a parent role if all its direct children already define them. This is a model refactoring with the aim of promoting reuse of permissions by taking advantage of the inheritance concept. The task should be defined for type "Role" and relation "PA" (the one used for permission assignment in the Labyrinth meta-model). In order to pull up a permission, an inheritance relation must exist between the source and target roles, which is specified by the pattern to the left in Figure 11. This pattern corresponds to relation *pull_relation* in the SLAMMER meta-model. In addition, as we only want to pull up those permissions defined by all children roles, we constrain the applicability of the task by means of the pattern to the right in the same figure, which corresponds to relation

Figure 11. Specification of pull task (©2007 Esther Guerra. Used with permission)

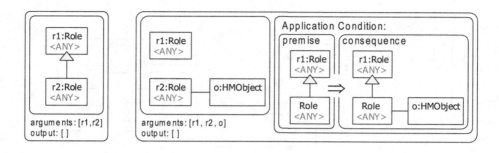

Figure 12. Specification of graph grammar task (©2007 Esther Guerra. Used with permission)

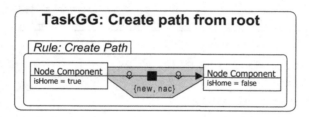

constraint in the SLAMMER meta-model. The pattern receives the permission to move and the source and target roles as input. The application condition checks the existence of such permission in each target role's child. Note that the model refactoring should be completed with an additional task that removes permissions in children roles if defined by their parents. The second task could be defined by means of a graph grammar, and be combined with the previous task to conform a single action.

In order to specify tasks by means of graph transformation we can use *TaskGG* objects. For example, Figure 12 shows a graph grammar task made of a rule that creates a navigational path from the root node of a web design (with attribute *isHome* to true) to a given node which is not root. The elements to be added by the rule application are shown in a coloured polygon and labelled as

"new". These elements form also a NAC, and thus the rule is not applied if such path already exists. We can use this task to create direct links from the home page of a web application to those nodes that are not reachable or where a high number of navigational steps are required to access them. In addition, it is possible to use a metric to detect to which nodes apply this redesign. For example, a customisation of *DepthOfPath* can be defined so as to count the number of steps to reach any node starting from the home page. Then, if we associate an appropriate threshold value to the metric (e.g. 0, which means that it is not possible to reach the node), we can detect the candidate nodes, and thus automatically fire the action on them.

IMPLEMENTATION IN ATOM³

Starting from the meta-models shown in previous sections, we have built a tool for SLAMMER that allows complementing a DSVL meta-model with a SLAMMER model, and generating a measurement and redesign tool for the given DSVL. For this purpose we took advantage of the code generation capabilities provided by AToM³. Thus, we defined the SLAMMER meta-model in AToM³, and automatically obtained a tool for building SLAMMER models. A code generator that synthesizes tools from the SLAMMER models was added to this tool. The synthesized tools generated this way make accessible the defined metrics and actions to the modelling environment generated for the DSVL. Finally, the new tool was integrated into AToM³ itself.

In order to be able to configure (to a certain degree) the features of the tools generated from the SLAMMER models, we have slightly modified the SLAMMER meta-model previously shown.

In particular, we have added an abstract class *UIButton* as the parent of classes *Measure*, *Action* and *Task*. This class has a single boolean attribute *button* that controls whether a button should be generated in the tool user interface in order to execute the corresponding measurement process, action or task. This is useful, for example, in case we want to prevent the direct calculation of a metric that is only used as auxiliary metric by others. In addition, class *Measure* has been provided with additional attributes to allow obtaining PDF reports with all the measurement results, or only the ones making some threshold condition true.

In addition, we have provided SLAMMER with the concrete syntax shown in Figure 13, where five metrics and two actions are being defined by using the generated tool for SLAMMER. In particular, measures are represented as rectangles with the measure type and name inside. Dependencies between measures are represented as arrows, where the arrowhead indicates the data

Figure 13. Generated tool for SLAMMER (©2007 Esther Guerra. Used with permission)

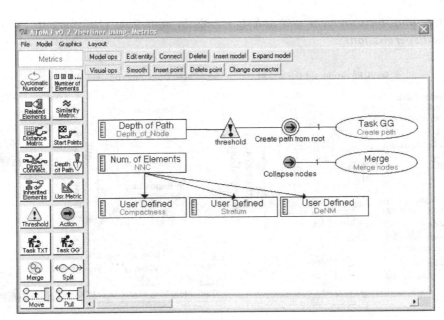

flow direction. For example, in the model of the figure, the result obtained by metric NNC is used to calculate metrics Compactness, Stratum and DeNM. Thresholds are shown as triangles with an exclamation mark inside, and related to the measures for which they are defined. Actions are depicted as circles with an arrow inside and the action name below. If their execution mode is automatic, they are shown as a double circle, as in the case of action Create path from root. Finally, tasks are visualized as ellipses with the task type and name inside. The tasks that are executed for a given action are related to it by means of lines, with the execution order above.

Figure 14 summarizes the process of defining, generating and using a modelling tool for a DSVL with AToM³. The left part of the figure shows the specification of the DSVL by the DSVL designer. In step 1 (of the left part), the DSVL definition is given by a meta-model. In the case of a MV-DSVL, the different diagram types (or viewpoints) have also to be specified. In addition, a quality expert can design a SLAMMER model

with the metrics and actions for the particular DSVL. The metrics are usually customisations of the suite offered by SLAMMER, thus only the domain (elements of the DSVL) and the specific attributes to measure (specified as patterns) have to be given. Actions are made of tasks that can be specified either procedurally (by using Python), by means of graph grammars, or by customising task templates with patterns. Although we have separated the roles of defining the DSVL meta-model and the specification of metrics and redesigns, in many occasions it is the same person who performs both activities.

Starting from this definition, AToM³ is able to automatically generate a modelling tool for the (MV-)DSVL. The use of such environment is schematised to the right of Figure 14. The end-user interacts with the generated tool user interface in order to build his models (step 1 of the right part). The tool automatically builds a repository with the gluing of the different models (or system views) and provides intra- and inter-diagram consistency. The repository properties can be evaluated (step

Figure 14. Integrating measurement and redesign tools in modelling environments (©2007 Esther Guerra. Used with permission)

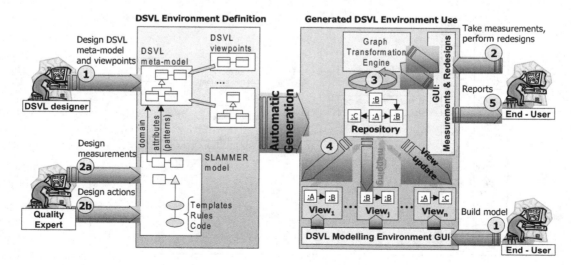

2) by using the metric specifications provided by the quality expert during the definition of the modelling environment, and the results are shown to the user as PDF reports (step 5). Note that measurement is performed in the repository, as it is the only model that contains all the system information. In addition, extreme values of metrics can trigger actions that modify the repository model with the purpose of improving the value of the metrics (step 3). Transforming the repository can leave the system design in an inconsistent state, as some elements can be added, edited or even deleted by the redesign. For this reason, once the redesign has been performed, the changes are propagated by the same consistency TGT rules that provide inter-diagram consistency in multi-view environments (step 4).

ENRICHING THE LABYRINTH ENVIRONMENT WITH METRICS AND REDESIGNS

Figure 15 shows a screenshot of the definition process of metrics and actions for Labyrinth. Window 1 in the background is the tool generated for SLAMMER and contains the metrics and actions defined for Labyrinth. In particular, the figure shows the customisation of the metric named Depth _ Of _ Node of type *DepthOfPath*, which is the upper one to the left in window 1. The metric counts the number of necessary steps to reach a node starting from the root node. The editing of its attributes is shown in dialog box 2. By clicking on button "step" a new window is opened where the user customises the basic step for the metric with a pattern. Window 3 contains the definition of the positive graph of such pattern, a navigation step in Labyrinth made of two nodes joined by a link and two anchors.

Figure 15. Customisation of "Measurement & Action" tool for the labyrinth environment (©2007 Esther Guerra. Used with permission)

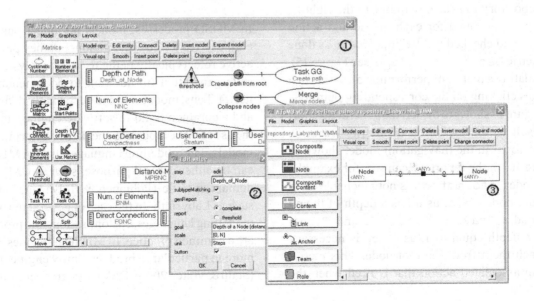

Figure 16. Generated environment, enriched with measurements and actions (©2007 Esther Guerra. Used with permission)

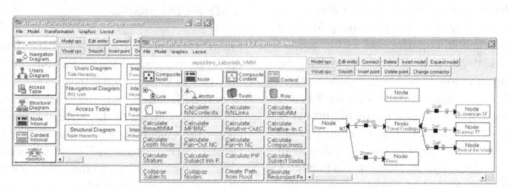

Note that metric `Depth _ of _ Node` defines a threshold value 0 for those nodes that are not root (yellow triangle). Action `Create path from root` (green circle) is executed for those nodes that make the threshold condition true. The action is made of the task shown in Figure 12, which creates a link from the web root node to a given node. In this way, if some node is not reachable from the root (i.e. it has a depth equal to 0), a link is created from the root to the node.

Figure 16 shows the environment automatically generated from the previous definition. In the repository interface (window to the right), a button is generated for each metric and action (if they had checked its attribute *button*, as done for metric `Depth _ of _ Node`, see Figure 15). Calculating a metric or performing an action just implies clicking on the corresponding button.

Figure 17 shows to the left the generated report as result of the execution of metric `Depth _ of _ Node` in the (navigation) model shown in Figure 16. In the report we can see, for example, that node `Information` is not reachable from the root node `Home`, as it has a depth of 0, and that nodes `Travel Fundings` and `Forms` have a depth equal to 1, as a step is necessary to reach them from the root node. This metric has an associated action that is fired when the

metric reaches a value of 0. Thus, it is executed for node `Information`. The resulting model is shown in the same figure to the right, where a link has been created from the root node `Home` to node `Information`. Note that the action is not executed for node `Home` because, although it has also depth 0, the threshold is fulfilled only for nodes that are not root.

USING SLAMMER IN A MDSD PROCESS

In MDSD processes, models no longer passive entities used for documentation, but they play an active role, typically being used for analysis and code generation (in addition to documentation itself). Thus, models have to be formally defined, and a common trend in software engineering is the use of meta-models to check the conformity of models. The modelling languages used in MDSD can be either general purpose, such as UML, or domain-specific (Pohjonen & Tolvanen, 2002), such as Labyrinth. In the case of general purpose modelling languages, customisations and profiles are a common practice. In MDSD processes, and more in particular in product family engineering (Stahl & Völter, 2006), DSVLs are frequently used

Figure 17. Generated report and model resulting from action execution (©2007 Esther Guerra. Used with permission)

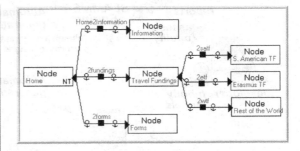

for the customisation of the variability of system families. In this case, developers are faced with the problem of generating modelling environments for the DSVLs. It is towards this scenario where a high automation is needed, together with customised tools, where our approach for the easy integration of measurement and redesign tools is directed.

One of the most successful scenarios for MDSD is product line engineering. Two processes are present in product line engineering (Greenfield et al., 2004): the product line development and the specific product development. The first process aims at analysing, designing and implementing reusable assets than can be used in the latter process so as to obtain the final product. In the specific product development, an application is generated by using a product configurator that is responsible of generating code and assembling the existing reusable components. In the most general case, the configurator is a DSVL plus a code generator. Note that this process is not very different from other MDSD processes (Stahl & Völter, 2006) in which a reference architecture has

to be defined (i.e. a fixed part of the applications to be generated), together with a code generator, and a DSVL or some other means to express the characteristics of the application to be generated (Czarnecki & Eisenecker, 2000).

Figure 18 shows a simplified scheme (e.g. we have not represented iterations) of a product line engineering process, showing how our approach can be integrated. This can be considered as an additional twist (with the addition of the generative techniques) of the classical process of developing for reuse/with reuse (Karlsson, 1995). To the right, the figure shows the product line development process where the framework and predefined components (i.e. the common part of the product family), the DSVL for configuration and the code generator are built. For simplicity, we don't explicitly show the usual process of first building one or more applications of the family, and then generalizing and exploiting that knowledge in the framework, components and generator. In addition, we propose building a SLAMMER model capturing additional domain knowledge. This includes known good modelling practices with the

Figure 18. Integrating quality assessment in a MDSD process (©2007 Esther Guerra. Used with permission)

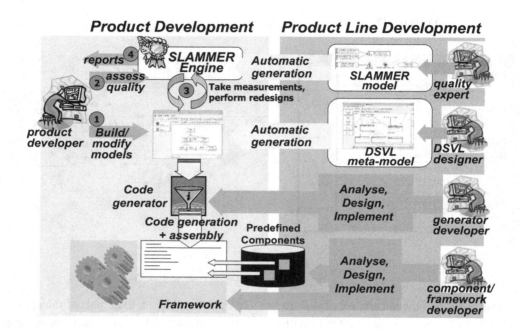

DSVL, which can be expressed as measures (with associated thresholds) and common redesigns and model refactorings. We have separated two roles in this process: one to design the DSVL and the other one as quality expert to design measures and redesigns. Note that the same person or group of people can assume both roles.

The left of the figure shows the process of using the artefacts generated by the development process to the right for developing specific products. In this way, the product developer can use the DSVL in order to obtain the final application. Note that sometimes, the generated code should be completed by manually written code, but we do not show this activity in the process for simplicity. Thus, our approach introduces quality assessment at the level of product configuration, as the product developer can use the measurement tool provided by the measurement expert in order to

check whether the model conforms to the quality standards or know good practices. In addition, he may have available redesigns implementing common or known structural changes to be applied on the models.

In summary, SLAMMER helps in quality assessment in two ways. First, SLAMMER models capture additional domain specific knowledge in terms of measures and redesigns. This knowledge is not only used for documentation, but in order to produce a real tool. Second, the generated tool allows developers to take advantage of the knowledge provided by experts in order to assess the quality of their models. The proposed framework is also model-driven, so code is automatically generated for the final user (vertically in the left-part of the figure) as well as for the developers working in the product development process (horizontally in the figure). That is, the DSVL and the measurement tools are generated from a meta-model and from a SLAMMER model. We believe this is the right approach, as one needs high levels of automation in order to be able to support short iterations, so common in this kind of developments.

FUTURE TRENDS

The presented framework can be extended by including additional metrics and action templates. It can also be interesting to study how to support other kinds of metrics, for example subjective and dynamic ones. The latter can be suitable in case of having executable models, with a precise operational semantics, for example defined through graph transformation rules. In addition, we are starting the study of mechanisms to support richer customisable template tasks. Providing further analysis tools (e.g. statistical) for studying the results, as well as more powerful visualization facilities for the results is also up to future work.

As stated in the introduction, the evolution of this field is moving towards an easy specification and generation of richer modelling tools for DS-VLs. There are many approaches for the generation of tools, which are merely visual editors. However, MDSD needs more functional tools, integrating for example quality control aspects. Some tools (e.g. OpenArchitectureWare, which however does not provide support for DSVLs) are moving towards this direction by integrating a number of additional tools helping in common MDSD tasks, such as code generation, model transformation and reporting. The fact that some of these tools are integrated in the Eclipse framework may make easier the interoperability with further tools. However, it is our view that all these related tools have to be customised (probably using the DSVL meta-model as the core of the customisation) and tightly integrated for the given domain.

CONCLUSION

In this chapter we have presented SLAMMER, a DSVL for the specification of measures and redesigns for other DSVLs, and its integration in a MDSD process. The work improves related approaches by decoupling the metrics meta-model and the language concepts, making the predefined metrics totally independent of the domain, and facilitating their integration with any DSVL. Our use of patterns allows a high level of abstraction and reusability, and makes easier the customisation of metrics in a graphical and declarative way. In addition, the SLAMMER meta-model includes entities modelling actions and its relation to metrics, making it more complete for software remodelling.

The framework has been implemented in the AToM³ meta-modelling tool. In this way, when a modelling environment is generated for a DSVL, AToM³ makes available the defined measures and redesigns to the final user. To the best of our knowledge, this feature is not available in any other meta-CASE tool. We have shown the usefulness of this approach by defining a set of metrics and redesigns for Labyrinth, a DSVL in the web domain. However, the approach is general enough to be used with other DSVLs or even general-purpose languages such as UML, by capturing in a SLAMMER model the appropriate measures and redesigns for the notation.

We believe this is a valuable approach especially in MDSD processes, as it simplifies the customisation of metrics and definition of redesigns for DSVLs. Moreover, the implementation supports a model-driven approach for the generation of measurement and redesign tools from the SLAMMER models, allowing fast iterations and easy changes in the SLAMMER models.

REFERENCES

Abrahao, S., Condori-Fernández, N., Olsina, L., & Pastor, O. (2003). *Defining and validating metrics for navigational models*. In Proceedings of 9th International Software Metrics Symposium, pp.: 200-210.

ADM: Architecture-Driven Modernization home page: http://adm.omg.org

Basili, V. R., Caldiera, G., & Rombach, H. D. (1994). *Goal Question Metric Paradigm*. Encyclopaedia of Software Engineering, pp.: 528-532. John Wiley&Sons.

Botafogo, R. A., Rivlin, E., & Shneiderman, B. (1992). *Structural analysis of hypertexts: identifying hierarchies and useful metrics*. ACM Transactions on Information Systems, Vol. 10(2). pp.: 142-180.

Czarnecki, K., & Eisenecker, E. (2000). Generative programming. Addison-Wesley Professional.

Díaz, P., Aedo, I., & Panetsos, F. (2001). *Modeling the dynamic behavior of hypermedia applications*. IEEE Transactions on Software Engineering, 27 (6), pp.: 550-572.

Díaz, P., Montero, S., & Aedo, I. (2005). *Modeling hypermedia and web applications: the Ariadne Development Method*. Information Systems, Vol. 30(8), pp.: 649-673.

DSLTools from Microsoft, 2007: http://msdn.microsoft.com/vstudio/DSLTools/

Ehrig, H., Ehrig, K., Prange, U., & Taentzer, G. (2006). *Fundamentals of algebraic graph transformation*. Monographs in Theoretical Computer Science. Springer.

Favre, J.-M. (2004). *Towards a basic theory to model driven engineering*. Workshop on Software Model Engineering, WISME 2004, joint event with UML'2004, Lisbon.

Fenton, N. E. (1996). *Software metrics: A rigorous and practical approach (2nd edition)*. International Thomson Computer Press.

Fowler, M. (1999). *Refactoring: Improving the design of existing code"*. Addison Wesley.

Gamma, E., Helm, R., Johnson, R., & Vlissides, J. (1995). *Design patterns, elements of reusable object-oriented software*. Professional Computing Series. Addison-Wesley.

García, F., Bertoa, M. F., Calero, C., Vallecillo, A., Ruiz, F., Piattini, M., & Genero, M. (2006). *Towards a consistent terminology for software measurement*. Information and Software Technology 48, pp.: 631-644. Elsevier.

GMF, 2007: The Eclipse Graphical Modeling Framework home page: http://www.eclipse.org/gmf

Gray, J., Rossi, M., & Tolvanen, J.-P. (2004). Special issue on Domain-Specific Modeling with Visual Languages of the Journal of Visual Languages & Computing, Vol. 15 (3-4). Elsevier.

Greenfield, J., Short, K., Cook, S., Kent, S., & Crupi, J. (2004). *Software factories: assembling applications with patterns, models, frameworks, and tools*. Wiley.

Guerra, E., Díaz, P., & de Lara, J. (2006). *Visual specification of metrics for domain specific visual languages*. In Proceedings of Graph-Transformation Visual Modelling Techniques.

Guerra, E., & de Lara, J. (2006). *Model View Management with Triple Graph Transformation Systems*. Proc. ICGT'2006. Lecture Notes in Computer Science, Vol. 4178, pp.: 351-366. Springer.

Guerra, E., & de Lara, J. (2007). *Meta-modelling and graph transformation for the definition of multi-view visual languages*. Chapter of the book "Visual Languages for Interactive Computing: Definitions and Formalization", Idea Group Publishers, edited by Fernando Ferri.

Guerra, E., Sanz, D., Díaz, P., & Aedo, I. (2007). *A transformation-driven approach to the verification of security policies web designs*. In Proceedings of the 7th International Conference on Web Engineering. L. Baresi, P. Fraternali, and G. J. Houben, Eds. Lecture Notes in Computer Science, Vol. 4607. Springer. pp.: 269-284.

ISO/IEC 9126 (1991). Software Engineering – Product Quality.

ISO/IEC 15939 (2002). Software Engineering – Software Measurement Process.

Karlsson, E-A. (1995). *Software Reuse: A Holistic Approach*. Wiley.

Kent, S. (2002). *Model Driven Engineering*. In Proceedings of the 3rd International Conference on Integrated Formal Methods. M. J. Butler, L. Petre, and K. Sere, Eds. Lecture Notes in Computer Science, Vol. 2335. Springer-Verlag. pp.: 286-298.

Lämmel, R. (2002). *Towards generic refactoring*. In Proceedings of the 2002 ACM SIGPLAN Workshop on Rule-Based Programming. ACM Press. pp.: 15-28.

Lanza, M., & Ducasse, S. (2002). *Beyond language independent object-oriented metrics: Model independent metrics*. In Proceedings of QAOOSE'02, pp.: 77-84.

de Lara, J., & Vangheluwe, H. (2002). *AToM³: A tool for multi-formalism modelling and meta-modelling*. In Proceedings of ETAPS/FASE'02. Lecture Notes in Computer Science, Vol. 2306, pp.: 174 - 188. Springer-Verlag. See the AToM³ home page: http://atom3.cs.mcgill.ca, and http://astreo.ii.uam.es/~jlara/doctorado.2006/ ATOM3_deploy.zip for the version described in this chapter.

Lédczi, A., Bakay, A., Marói, M., Vögyesi, P., Nordstrom, G., Sprinkle, J., & Karsai, G. (2001). *Composing domain-specific design environments*. IEEE Computer, pp.: 44-51.

Martín, M. A. & Olsina, L. (2003). *Towards an ontology for software metrics and indicators as the foundation for a cataloging Web system*. In Proceedings of LA-WEB. IEEE Computer Society.

Mens, T. & Lanza, M. (2002). *A Graph-Based Metamodel for Object-Oriented Software Metrics*. Electronic Notes in Theoretical Computer Science, Vol. 72(2)

Mens, T. (2006). *On the use of graph transformations for model refactoring*. In Proceedings of Generative and Transformational Techniques in Software Engineering, pp.: 219-257

Misic, V. B. & Moser, S. (1997). *From Formal Metamodels to Metrics: An Object-Oriented Approach*. In Proceedings of 24th International Conference on Technology of Object-Oriented Languages and Systems, pp.: 330-339.

Munro, M., J. (2005). *Product metrics for automatic identification of "bad smell" design problems in Java source-code*. In Proceedings of 11th International Software Metrics Symposium, IEEE Computer Society.

Pohjonen, R., & Tolvanen, J-P. (2002). *Automated production of family members: Lessons learned*. In Proceedings of International Workshop on Product Line Engineering The Early Steps: Planning, Modeling, and Managing, pp.: 49-57.

Roberts, D., Brant, J., & Johnson, R. (1997). *A refactoring tool for Smalltalk*. Theory and Practice of Object Systems, Vol. 3, pp.: 253-263.

Schürr, A. (1994). *Specification of graph translators with Triple Graph Grammars*. In Lecture Notes in Computer Science, Vol. 903, pp.: 151-163. Springer.

SDMetric home page: http://www.sdmetrics.com

Stahl, T., & Völter, M. (2006). *Model-driven software development.* Wiley.

Simon, F., Löffler, S., & Lewerentz, C. (1999). *Distance based cohesion measuring.* In Proceedings of 2ⁿᵈ European Software Measurement Conference, pp.: 69-83.

SPQR/20. (1995). *User Manual.* Software Productivity Research Inc.

Together Technologies home page: http://www.borland.com/us/products/together

Tourwé, T., & Mens, T. (2003). *Identifying refactoring opportunities using logic meta programming.* In Proceedings of 7ᵗʰ European Conference on Software Maintenance and Reengineering, pp.: 91-100.

Tsalidis, C., Christodoulakis, D., & Maritsas, D. (1992). ATHENA: a software measurement and metrics environment. *Journal of Software Maintenance* 4, 2. pp.: 61-81.

UML 2.0 specification at the OMG home page (2006). http://www.omg.org/UML

Warmer, J., & Kleppe, A. (2003). *The object constraint language: Getting your models ready for MDA*, 2ⁿᵈ Edition. Pearson Education. Boston, MA.

Whitmire, S. A. (1997). *Object oriented design measurement.* John Wiley & Sons, Inc.

ADDITIONAL READING

Graph Transformation, applications to Refactoring

Rozenberg, G. (ed). (1997). Handbook of Graph Grammars and Computing by Graph Transformations. Volume 1: Foundations. World Scientific.

This book presents the foundations of all the basic approaches to graph transformation.

Ehrig, H., Engels, G., Kreowski, H.-J., U., & Rozenberg, G. (ed). (1999). Handbook of Graph Grammars and Computing by Graph Transformations. Volume 2: Applications, Languages and Tools. World Scientific.

It includes applications of graph transformation to different domains, such as functional languages, visual and object-oriented languages, software engineering or mechanical engineering.

Ehrig, H., Kreowski, H.-J., Montanari, U., & Rozenberg, G. (ed). (1999). Handbook of Graph Grammars and Computing by Graph Transformations. Volume 3: Concurrency, Parallelism and Distribution. World Scientific.

The third book of the series presents the main results on concurrency, parallelism and distribution of graph grammars. An interesting field of application is the coordination of concurrent of systems.

Mens, T., Demeyer, S., & Janssens, D. (2002). *Formalizing behaviour preserving program transformations,* In Proceedings of International Conference on Graph Transformation, Lecture Notes in Computer Science, Vol. 2505, pp.: 286-301, Springer.

This paper introduces a graph representation of those aspects preserved by a code refactoring, and uses graph rewriting rules in order to formalize the refactoring transformations.

Mens, T., Taentzer, G., & Runge, O. (2007). *Analysing refactoring dependencies using graph transformation.* Software and Systems Modeling Journal, Springer.

In this paper, refactorings are formalized by means of graph transformation rules, so that implicit dependencies between refactorings can be studied by using critical pair analysis. The obtained results can help developers to choose which refactoring is more appropriate in a given context.

Additional Meta-Modelling and MDSD Tools

AndroMDA web page at: http://www.andromda.org/

GEMS (Generic Eclipse Modeling System) web page at: http://sourceforge.net/projects/gems

GME web page at: http://www.isis.vanderbilt.edu/projects/gme/

GMT web page at: http://www.eclipse.org/gmt/

MetaEdit+ web page at: http://www.metacase.com/

OpenArchitectureWare web page at: http://www.openarchitectureware.org/

OpenMDX web page at: http://www.openmdx.org/index.html

OptimalJ web page at: http://www.compuware.com/products/optimalj/default.htm

TIGER Project web page: http://tfs.cs.tu-berlin.de/~tigerprj/

UMT web page at: http://umt-qvt.sourceforge.net/

Model-Driven Software Development

Frankel, D. (2003). *Model driven architecture – Applying MDA to enterprise computing.* Wiley.

The Model Driven Architecture (MDA) is the OMG's proposal for Model Driven Development. This book explains this methodology and demonstrates how it can work with different technologies.

Kleppe, A., Warmer, J., & Bast, W. (2003). *MDA explained. The model driven architecture: Practice and promise.* Addison Wesley.

This is a useful second reference for researchers interested in MDA.

Proceedings of the Model Driven Engineering Languages and Systems (MoDELS) series of conferences: http://www.umlconference.org/, edited by Springer Lecture Notes.

Software Measurement and Refactoring

ISO/IEC 25000:2005 Software Engineering – Software product Quality Requirements and Evaluation (SQuaRE) – Guide to SQuaRE. Available at the web page of ISO: http://www.iso.org

Set of standards, including those for software measurement.

Kerievsky, J. (2004). *Refactoring to patterns.* Addison-Wesley.

The book is about improving system designs through the execution of sequences of low-level design transformations (refactorings) towards well-known design patterns. It provides useful examples.

Lindvall, M., Donzelli, P., Asgari, S. & Basili V. (2005). *Towards Reusable Measurement Pat-*

terns. Proceedings of the 11th IEEE International Software Metrics Symposium, pp.: 21-28.

The paper identifies a catalogue of measurement patterns that can be reused in different software measurement programs. The objective is to reduce the time and cost to develop new measurement tools, without starting their implementation from scratch.

Mens, T., & Tourwé, T. (2004). *A survey of software refactoring.* IEEE Transactions on Software Engineering, Volume 30, Number 2, pp.: 126-139.

This paper provides an overview of existing research in the field of software refactoring: supported activities and techniques, target artefacts, tool support, and integration on the software development process.

Pretschner, A., & Prenninger, W. (2007). *Computing refactorings of state machines.* Software and Systems Modeling Journal, Springer.

In this paper, refactorings are formalized as logical predicates and applied to the computation of semantically equivalent models.

Visual Languages

Luoma, J., Kelly, S., & Tolvanen, J.-P. (2004). *Defining domain-specific modeling languages: Collected experience.* Object-Oriented Programming Systems, Languages and Applications (OOPSLA) Workshop on Domain Specific Languages.

This paper explores several approaches to the identification and creation of modelling constructs when defining domain specific languages.

Marriot, K., & Meyer, B. (1998). *Visual language theory.* Springer-Verlag.

This book provides a broad survey concerning the definition, specification, structural analysis and theoretical foundations of visual languages. It is oriented to researchers interested in formal language theory, HCI, artificial intelligence and computational linguistics.

Chapter VII
Measuring Models

Martin Monperrus
ENSIETA & University of Rennes 1, France

Jean-Marc Jézéquel
University of Rennes 1 & INRIA, France

Joël Champeau
ENSIETA, France

Brigitte Hoeltzener
ENSIETA, France

ABSTRACT

Model-Driven Engineering (MDE) is an approach to software development that uses models as primary artifacts, from which code, documentation and tests are derived. One way of assessing quality assurance in a given domain is to define domain metrics. We show that some of these metrics are supported by models. As text documents, models can be considered from a syntactic point of view i.e., thought of as graphs. We can readily apply graph-based metrics to them, such as the number of nodes, the number of edges or the fan-in/fan-out distributions. However, these metrics cannot leverage the semantic structuring enforced by each specific metamodel to give domain specific information. Contrary to graph-based metrics, more specific metrics do exist for given domains (such as LOC for programs), but they lack genericity. Our contribution is to propose one metric, called σ, that is generic over metamodels and allows the easy specification of an open-ended wide range of model metrics.

INTRODUCTION

Model-Driven Engineering (MDE) is an approach to software development that uses models as primary artifacts, from which code, documentation and tests are derived. In this context, a model can be seen as the abstraction of an aspect of reality for handling a given concern in a specific domain.

In MDE, the meaning of a model is itself defined with another model, called a metamodel. Complex systems typically give rise to more than one model because many aspects are to be handled.

One way of assessing quality assurance in a given domain is to define domain metrics from expert know-how, best practices or statistical analysis. As text documents, models can be considered from a syntactic point of view i.e., thought of as graphs. We can readily apply graph-based metrics to them, such as the number of nodes, the number of edges or the fan-in/fan-out distributions (see for example [Edmonds, 1999, Van Belle, 2002]). However, these metrics cannot leverage the semantic structuring enforced by each specific metamodel to give domain specific information.

Contrary to graph-based metrics, more specific metrics do exist for given domains (such as LOC for programs), but they lack genericity. The lines of codes per method/function has been proven to be a software quality attribute [Kitchenham et al., 1990]. As LOC or other code-centric software metrics, each domain has its own quality metrics.

An applied research program named *Measurement of Complexity* [Chretienne et al., 2004] lists more than one hundred *metrics of complexity* of importance in engineering. As an application of this program, a human review of textual documents has been done on four real world systems to compute the *metrics of complexity*. Complexity is not an issue of our investigation. However this program concludes on the need to facilitate the definition and computation of metrics and motivates this work.

The scope of our research is the definition of metrics at a higher level of abstraction than code, independently of the domain, while remaining rich enough for the domain expert. Our contribution is to propose one metric, called σ, that is generic over metamodels and allows the easy specification of an open-ended wide range of model metrics

The remainder of this chapter is organized as follows. We first give an introduction on model measurement in section 2. In section 3, we then introduce a generic metric, grounded in set theory and first-order logic. This metric is questionned with established metric property frameworks. We then discuss implementation issues. To show the genericity of our approach, we present in section 4 three case studies from various domains,

and we show in section 5 that this also applies to the metamodel measurement. We finally discuss future research directions (section 6) and conclude.

STATE OF THE ART

Dedicated Model Measurement

Metamodel Measurement

Ma et al. [Ma et al., 2004] compare different versions of the UML metamodel using OO metrics defined in [Bansiya and Davis, 2002]. Ma et al. [Ma et al., 2005] define patterns linked to the lifecycle of metaclasses, and study them on different versions of the UML metamodel. This work is similar in spirit to those made at the OO level [Mattsson and Bosch, 1999, Bansiya, 2000, Gîrba et al., 2005].

MDE Processes Measurement

Berenbach et al. [Berenbach and Borotto, 2006] list a number of metrics for model driven requirements development and enounce some good practices. The Modelware project delivered three documents [Modelware Project, 2006a, Modelware Project, 2006b, Modelware Project, 2006c] in which several metrics about MDE processes are defined.

UML Models Measurement

Previous works about the measurement of UML models follows the same decomposition as the UML artifacts themselves. Some authors address the measurement of class diagrams (see [Genero et al., 2005] for a survey), others the measurement of dynamic models [Genero et al., 2002, Baroni, 2005], component models (e.g., [Mahmood and Lai, 2005]), and OCL expressions [Cabot and Teniente, 2006, Reynoso et al., 2003].

Synthesis

These works are dedicated to particular MDE artifacts, i.e., metamodels, processes, UML models. They do not note that all this artifacts are models too, w.r.t. a metametamodel, a process metamodel or the UML metamodel. These contributions do not leverage this idea for defining a generic metric usable at any moment of product life-cycle, from requirements to implementation.

Metamodel Based Measurement of OO Programs

Misic et al. [Misic and Moser, 1997] express a generic object-oriented metamodel using Z. With this metamodel, they express a function point metric using the number of instances of a given type. They also express a previously introduced metric called the *system meter*. Reissing et al. [Reissing, 2001] extends the UML metamodel to provide a basis for metrics expression and then use this model to specify known metric suites with set theory and first order logic.

Harmer et al. [Harmer and Wilkie, 2002] expose a concrete design to compute metrics on source code. The authors create a relational database for storing source code. This database is fed using a modified compiler. Metrics are expressed in SQL for simple ones, and with a mix of Java and SQL for the others. El Wakil et al [El Wakil et al., 2005] use XQuery to express metrics. Metrics are then computed on XMI files. Baroni et al. propose in [Baroni et al., 2002] to use OCL to specify metrics. They use their own metamodel exposed in a previous paper. Likewise, in [McQuillan and Power, 2006], the authors use Java bytecode to instantiate the Dagstuhl metamodel and specify known cohesion metrics in OCL.

These works are centered around the issue of OO metrics and are not metamodel independent. They show that it is useful to ground metrics into the semantic of source code, i.e., its metamodel. It seems possible to generalize the idea and define

precisely generic metrics on top of metamodels, set theory and logic. It is also to be noted that these approaches do not explore the modularity of metrics.

Generic Metrics for OO Measurement

Mens et al. [Mens and Lanza, 2002] define a generic object-oriented metamodel and generic metrics. They then show that known software metrics are an application of these generic metrics. Alikacem et al. [Alikacem and Sahraoui, 2006] propose a generic metamodel for object oriented code representation and a metric decription language.

These two contributions emphasize on a generic way to define metrics. However, they do not provide applications of the genericity outside the scope of OO metrics.

Generic Model Measurement

Saeki et al. [Saeki and Kaiya, 2006] specify the definition of metrics in OCL as part of the metamodel. Saeki et al. do not attach the definition of metrics to any particular domain and underlines in a future research agenda the need for defining various domain metamodels, domain metrics and supporting tools.

Guerra et al. [Guerra et al., 2006] propose to visually specify metrics for any Domain Specific Language and introduce a taxonomy of metrics. Tool support is provided in the Python and Atom3 environment. We share the motivation of this paper and provide further facts on the problem of model measurement and on the solution. Our case studies give a different perspective on the issue.

THE GENERIC Σ METRIC

In this section, we present a model metric, called σ. The σ metric is a generic metric. It means that an executable metric is a specialization of σ. The genericity allows high level specification of metrics and a simplified implementation. Considering the Goal Question Metrics approach [Basili et al., 1994], the σ metric is a generic answer to a set of questions related to model quality:

- **Goal** Improve the model quality from the modeler point of view.
- **Question #1** What model metrics can be related to functionality?
- **Question #2** What model metrics can be related to reliability ?
- **Question #3** What model metrics can be related to maintainability?
- **Metrics** The family of σ metrics.

In this section, we first define a model in the model-driven engineering (MDE) sense in order to clearly ground the generic metric. Then, we introduce the notion of filtering function which is the kernel of the proposed generic model metric. We close the presentation with theoretical arguments and implementation issues.

Definition of a MDE Model in Set Theory

A model, in the Model Driven Engineering (MDE) terminology, is at first glance a directed graph. A MDE model also contains information on nodes, sometimes refered as slots, which contain primary information. A model also embeds its structure i.e., the types of nodes, the types of edges, and the types of slots. The figure 1, inspired from [Kuehne, 2006], shows the different viewpoints on a model: a graph in the upper left part, a graph containing data in the upper right part, or a graph containing structured data in the lower left part where the structure is defined with a metamodel represented in the lower right part.

We define a model as:

Definition 1. *A model M is M=((V;E;S);(C;R ;A);T2$_v$;T$_e$;T$_s$ where: V is the set of nodes, E a set of directed edges between nodes, which are elements of (V×V), S is the set of slots, C is the set of classes, R is the set of relationships between classes i.e., elements of (C×C), A is the set of attributes of classes i.e., elements*

Figure 1. Models from different points of view

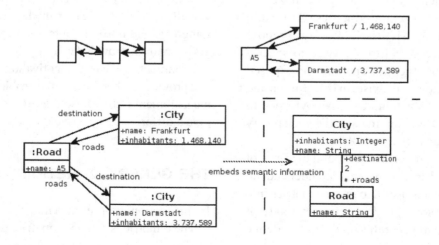

of (C×{*boolean,numeric,etc.*}), T_v contains bindings between nodes and classes i.e., a set of elements of (V×C), T_e contains bindings between edges and relationships i.e., a set of elements of (E×R), T_s contains bindings between slots and attributes i.e., a set of elements of (S×A).

Note that this definition includes support for languages such as Java or MOF, where one has classes and primitive types.

For convenience, we later use three functions:

- *source* which maps each edge to the source node of the edge;
- *target* which maps each edge to the target node of the edge;
- *type* which maps each node to a class $c \in C$.

The Filtering Functions

A filtering function is a function that tests a boolean condition on a given node. Applied to a set of nodes, it can be used as a filter.

Definition 2. *A filtering function φ is a morphism from the set of nodes to the truth values.*

$$\varphi : V \circledR \{true; false\}$$
$$x \mapsto \varphi(x)$$

φ is a boolean function, it thus can be a boolean formula of sub-filtering boolean functions. This function can be composed of an arbitrary unlimited number of conditions e.g., $\varphi = \varphi_1 \check{U} \varphi_2 \acute{U} \emptyset \varphi_3$. In figure 1, the filtering function φ(x)=(*type*(x)=*City*) is true for two out of three model elements: the *Frankfurt* node and the *Darmstadt* node.

We define the core filtering functions as: a test on the type, a test on a slot, a size test and a λ-test on a collection:

- **Test on the type** This tests the type of an object of the model with respect to the name of a class. It is equivalent to the *isInstance* method of the Java class *Class*.
- **Test on a slot value** This evaluates the value of a slot (a primitive type in Java, an EDataType in Eclipse Modeling Framework) with respect to a constant.
- **λ-Test on a collection** This evaluates a sub-filtering functions on each member of the multiplicity element. This test is either a test *at least one* or *for all* and introduces a λ parameter.
- **Test on the size of a collection** This evaluates the number of elements of a collection.

We chose these core filtering functions because they are sufficient for our case studies. Note that filtering functions are not closed in their definition and can include refinements so as to express more powerful statements. For example, it is conceivable to add regular expressions in slot tests on string values.

For instance, here are some examples of filtering functions refering to Figure 1:

- φ(x)=(*type*(x)=*City*)
- φ(x)=(x.*name*="A5")
- φ(x)=(*size*(x.*roads*)>3)
- $\varphi(x)=(\exists \lambda \in x.destination | \lambda.name=$"Darmstadt")
- $\varphi(x)=(\forall \lambda \in x.destination | \lambda.inhabitants>100000)$

Filtering functions involve information from the metamodel e.g., *City* or *inhabitants*. They involve elements of *C*,*R* and *A*. Hence, they are at the same level as metamodels and are grounded into the structure of the models. The evaluation of a filtering function relies on the binding between a model and its structure i.e., T_v, T_e, T_s.

Set of Nodes

As defined above, one of the components of a model is a set of nodes. It is possible to specify a subset of nodes X satisfying a filtering function. This is noted $SoN(\varphi)(V)$ (SoN is the acronym for *set of nodes*).

Definition 3. $SoN(\varphi)(V)=\{n \in V | \varphi(n)\}$.

Definition of the σ Metric

The generic σ metric is derived from *SoN* and is the cardinality of a set of nodes given a filtering function. σ refers to the classical Σ mathematical symbol which denotes an iteration over a set of elements.

Definition 4. $\sigma_\varphi V\hat{I}N=|SoN(\varphi)(V)|$.

The σ metric characterizes an open-ended wide range of model metrics that are illustrated in sections below.

Theoretical Validation

In this section, we confront the σ metric with theoretical matters: the type, the scale, the dimension and the reliability of the σ metric.

Type

Several frameworks exists for validating software metrics e.g., [Briand et al., 1996, Melton et al., 1990, Schneidewind, 1992]. We chose [Briand et al., 1996] to validate the metrics proposed in this paper because it is a formalized, yet convenient synthesis of previous works. Briand et al. enounced [Briand et al., 1996] formal properties for five types of software metrics: size, length, complexity, cohesion and coupling metrics. The σ metric satisfies the formal properties of size metrics *Size.1*, *Size.2* and *Size.3*:

Size.1 : Nonnegativity $\sigma(SoN(V)) \geq 0$ by definition of a set;

Size.2 : Null value if $SoN(V)=\varnothing \Rightarrow \sigma(SoN(V))=0$ by definition of a set;

Size.3 : Module Additivity $V=V1\grave{E}V2$ and $V1\c{C}V2=\textit{Æ} \Rightarrow \sigma(SoN(V))=\sigma SoNV1+\sigma SoNV2$ (idem for $E1,E2,E$)

The σ metric can then be considered as a generic size metric applicable to any domain.

Scale

The σ metric is a kind of count, hence is on an absolute scale. According to [Fenton, 1991], all arithmetic analysis of the resulting count is meaningful, and according to [Henderson-Sellers, 1996], this scale permits a full range of descriptive statistics to be applied. This is true for a given filtering function, as discussed in the next paragraph.

Dimensional Analysis

Dimensional analysis aims to determine a consistent assignment of units. A dimension is a generalization of a unit of measure [Henderson-Sellers, 1996]. Since the σ metric is generic, it has no dimension associated with. It's a number of objects according to a filtering function. To this extent, a filtering function defines a dimension per se. Hence, one cannot directly perform arithmetics on different σ i.e., $\sigma\varphi1V$ and $\sigma\varphi2V$. For instance, summing $\sigma\varphi1V$ and $\sigma\varphi2V$ raises the same issue as summing a time and a length in physics. Derived measurement from σ metrics should be made carefully.

Measurement Errors

The σ metric does not have any measurement errors. It is theoretically reliable. Note that implementations still need to be tested or statically verified with the adequate methods to ensure its practical reliability.

Conclusion

With respect to theoretical facts, the σ metric is a generic, reliable size metric on which descriptive statistics can be applied.

Implementation

We discuss below the reasons making the implementation of model metrics a difficult issue.

Non-Programmer Use

The most appropriate person for defining domain metrics is a domain expert. He rarely has skills in programming. Hence, he needs to specify what he wants and to delegate the implementation to others . This dramatically increases the cost of definition and collection of model metrics. This observation is a strong motivation to define a simple and intuitive DSL, a coherent interface to be used by the domain expert for defining metrics.

Libraries / Framework

Always for cost and productivity reasons, a good language for implementing metrics has the libraries to access models and their metamodels. It is very costly to develop an ad hoc and reliable parser, database connector, or binding to an existing modeling framework.

Ability to Access to the Metamodel

The language or library for implementing metrics should include an easy way to navigate through the model and to access to the metamodel. For instance, considering a model element, there should be a way to access to the referenced elements as well as the metaclass and its attributes.

Non-Intrusivity

We have experienced that it is often tempting to pollute models with metrics concerns. For example, to add an attribute *marked : boolean* to the root class of the domain model, to mark visited objects. However, this practice violates the separation of concerns principle. A good metrics design practice is totally non-intrusive with respect to the semantic of the model. In the previous example, the need to mark visited objects implies the use of *Map:Object®Boolean*.

Our Implementation

One can find in the literature several proposals for the implementation of model metrics (see section 2) e.g., Java, SQL, Python, Xquery, XML-based DSL, OCL, and a graphical language. Proposals mix some of these languages. These proposals do not adress all the issues cited above. We based our approach on the model-oriented programming language Kermeta [Muller et al., 2005].

Kermeta is a language based upon the EMF API. This facilitates the accesses to models and the navigation through models and metamodels. Furthermore, our industrial partners generally use Eclipse Modeling Framework (EMF) models. Kermeta features closures, which are of great help for the filtering functions. Indeed, a filtering function written in Kermeta is syntactically close to the underlying semantic hence very concise.

Polymorphism is useful to express modularized metrics. An example of code is shown on figure 2. An abstract class *SigmaMetric* encapsulates the generic code of the generic σ metric. A class *NumberOfCityMetric* is defined as a subclass of the SigmaMetric class. *NumberOfCityMetric* implements the filtering function φ and potentially delegates the definition of a subfiltering function φ1 to subclasses by polymorphism. *NumberOfCityConnectedToA5Metric* overrides φ1 to compute the number of cities connected to the road named *A5*.

Kermeta satisfies all the issues cited above, except the first one. Even if a filtering function written in Kermeta is syntactically close to its semantic, a domain expert can not feel comfortable with writing pieces of Kermeta code. It is outside of the scope of this contribution to specify visual or textual syntax usable by the domain expert.

The prototype[1] involves two main abstract classes *ReflectiveWalk* and *SigmaMetric*. To define a σ model metric, the user just need to create a new class inheriting from *SigmaMetric* and to write the associated filtering function.

APPLICATIONS OF THE Σ METRIC

In this section, we present three case studies so as to illustrate the genericity and the feasibility of the σ metric. We first show that the σ metric allows the computation of logical lines of code in usual languages such as Java, the value-added of this approach is the ease of use compared to equivalent existing approaches. Then, we go beyond software metrics and consider non code centric artifacts such as requirements and system engineering metrics. The application of the σ metric in these various domains shows the genericity of the σ metric. Finally, since metamodels can be considered as models too, we present results of the σ metric at computing metamodel metrics in a full section.

Figure 2. Implementation: Excerpt of Kermeta code

```
abstract class SigmaMetric {
  // generic implementation part of the sigma metric

  // specific part: an abstract method to be implemented
  operation phi(o : Object) : Boolean is abstract
} // end class


class NumberOfCityMetric inherits SigmaMetric {
  operation phi(o : Object) : Boolean is do
    result := (o.getMetaClass == City) and self.phi1(o)
  end

  operation phi1(o : Object) : Boolean is do
    return true
  end
} // end class


Class NumberOfCityConnectedToA5Metric inherits NumberOfCityMetric {
  operation phi1(o : Object) : Boolean is do
    return (o.asType(City).roads.exists{ x | x.name == "A5"})
  end
} // end class
```

Case Study: Lines of Code (LOC)

Kan states that "the lines of code (LOC) metric is anything but simple" [Kan, 1995] (p.88). Indeed, there are numerous definitions of LOC, depending on authors and language (see [Kan, 1995]). Early LOC definitions follow a physical i.e., a representational point of view. An example is the count of the non-blank lines in source files. More sophisticated LOC definitions focus on logical statements (see [Kan, 1995, Henderson-Sellers, 1996]). This raises the technical issue of parsing the source files to access the semantics. In this section, we do not propose yet another LOC definition. We demonstrate that considering traditional programs as model, one gets essential LOC building blocks by applying the generic σ metric.

LOC semantic building-blocks are an application of the σ metric. They are numerous, among them are the number of methods, number of conditionals, number of blocks. For sake of readability, we do not list all of them. A representative part of them is shown in the results of our case study.

In this case study, we consider the Java programming language because of its wide diffusion. Furthermore, numerous open-source Java software packages are available. Since our implementation is based on the Eclipse Modeling Framework (EMF), we needed a way to transform Java source code into EMF models (as XMI files).

We have used the SpoonEMF tool[2]. SpoonEMF is a binding between Spoon and EMF. Spoon [Pawlak et al., 2006] provides a complete and fine-grained Java metamodel where any program element (classes, methods, fields, statements, expressions, etc.) is accessible. This process finally transforms a whole Java software into a single XMI model file that can be natively processed with Kermeta.

The whole process is sketched on figure 3.

From this model, our prototype is able to compute the specific σ metrics values. For example, it produces the number of statements; number of assignments; number of conditionals; number of blocks.

To demonstrate the feasibility and the scalability of our approach, we have chosen five open-source Java software packages to be represented as models:

- **UmlGraph** UmlGraph allows the declarative specification and drawing of UML class and sequence diagrams.
- **log4j** log4j is a logging library. It provides an advanced service of logging, with emphasis on the performance of determining if a logging statement should be logged or not.
- **org.eclipse.osgi** org.eclipse.osgi is the heart of the Eclipse IDE. It's the Eclipse implementation of the Open Services Gateway Initiative (OSGI) standards.

Figure 3. The Java to EMF process

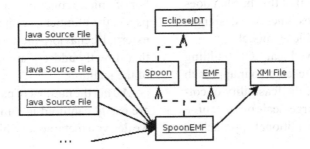

- **regexp** regexp provides a regular expression Java library.

BCEL BCEL is a Byte Code Engineering Library (BCEL) intended to give users a convenient possibility to analyze, create, and manipulate (binary) Java class files.

For the sake of replication, the models used in this case study are available on the web[3].

In Table 1, we show our results on the Java software packages listed above. Table 4.1 shows us that the σ metric is applicable to computer languages. Furthermore, it shows us that our approach scales with the model size (the org.eclipse.osgi model has 507798 model elements and 703360 references between them). Each line of the table compares the software packages under study with repect to a rigorously defined point of view. For instance, for a similar number of class, the BCEL software uses much less try/catch constructs than org.eclipse.osgi. Each column of the table is a vector that characterizes the software packages in a multi-dimensional space.

Measuring LOC with models as an application of the generic σ metric is easy. Spoon and SpoonEMF are components of our approach, yet have not been developed on purpose. One does not need to go inside a compiler or an interpreter, neither write a parser, which are both complex tasks.

One can object that much of the work has been moved on transformation from source code to models. But this task can be shared with other discplines such as aspect weaving or testing. Indeed, Spoon and SpoonEMF are not at all dedicated to metrics. Note that this burden does not exist for new languages when the designers make them directly available as models.

In this section, we showed that LOC building blocks are σ metrics. We presented our approach and our prototype to prove the feasibility of collecting LOC σ metrics on large-scale open-source software projects. Unlike traditional approaches,

measuring LOC with models is easy. Collecting semantic metrics on source code could be done before. The added value of our approach is the simplicity. Firstly, it is easier to define and compute metrics on code represented as a model than on raw source files. Secondly, the application of a generic metric inside a framework to compute logical LOC is no more than a few lines of code i.e., the filtering functions.

Case Study: Requirements Metrics

Since measurement is a tool to know if one is reaching the goal of building high quality requirements, several works have been done on defining requirements metrics (a survey can be found in [Medina Mora and Denger, 2003, Kandula and Sathrasala, 2005]). The need for requirements metrics is also illustrated by the metric features of commercial tools e.g., Telelogic Doors. In this section, we aim to show that some requirements metrics are a special case of the generic σ metric.

Our methodology consists of taking a previous contribution on requirements metrics, extracting a metamodel, and identifying σ metrics.

Davis et al. define [Davis et al., 1993] a set of attributes that contributes to evaluate the quality of a requirements specification. 18 of the 24 quality attributes presented in this article have a mathematical metric formulation. These formulae are derived from the following metrics building blocks: the total number of requirements; the number of correct requirements; the number of stimulus input; the number of state input; the number of functions currently specified; the number of unique functions specified; the number of pages; the number of requirements that describe external behavior; the number of requirements that directly address architecture or algorithms of the solution.

All but the number of pages are concepts which are easily captured in a metamodel. In figure 4, we derive a metamodel which permits to compute

Table 1. Results of the σ LOC metrics on large-scale Java software packages

NumberOf	log4j-1.2.14	umlgraph-4.1	eclipse.osgi-3.2	regexp-1.4	bcel-5.2
TypeParameterReference	125	0	306	3	54
Method	1353	63	3389	119	2569
FieldReference	3713	373	12061	1156	7947
Catch	156	3	498	24	133
TypeReference	44874	5781	145149	6290	85155
For	104	8	867	32	379
LocalVariableReference	3379	388	16107	991	6503
Field	768	58	2183	137	983
Assignment	941	117	2785	253	1612
VariableAccess	5436	638	23221	1362	11415
Case	111	9	287	181	556
If	898	109	4392	263	1502
Parameter	1340	75	3621	159	2831
Constructor	295	11	391	22	545
ExecutableReference	7624	785	22913	1345	15409
Class	247	11	334	16	345
ParameterReference	2057	250	7114	371	4912
BinaryOperator	1874	269	8165	705	4922
ArrayAccess	127	63	1890	151	905
Return	932	60	3368	181	1416
Literal	3584	493	11747	1071	6691
Invocation	4842	484	13959	847	9392
Block	2979	164	7754	557	5283
LocalVariable	1327	126	5136	239	2117
ArrayTypeReference	1104	314	14461	724	5801
FieldAccess	3713	373	12061	1156	7947
NewClass	725	51	1840	127	1105
PackageReference	43691	5415	139303	6047	83183
UnaryOperator	264	33	1750	226	752
Try	139	4	530	19	129

Figure 4. The requirements metamodel extracted from [Davis et al., 1993]

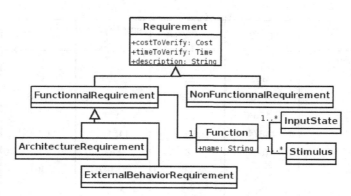

the metrics above. This is a backbone for a bigger requirements metamodel. Except for the number of unique functions specified, all these metrics are σ metrics.

Note that Davis et al. also use the following parameters: CR_i is the cost necessary to verify presence of requirement R_i; TR_i is the time necessary to verify presence of requirement R_i. The notations C and R (resp. *cost* and *requirement*) are from [Davis et al., 1993] and are totally different of the notations of section 3. The integration of this information in the metamodel is straightforward and represented in the figure 4.

It is possible, yet outside the scope of this chapter to apply this methodology to other requirements metrics contributions e.g., [Costello and Liu, 1995], so as to create a comprehensive requirements metamodel. We mainly aim to show the genericity of our contribution in the field of requirements engineering. A threat to our reasoning remains. One misses requirements models and case studies. Contrary to the previous section, where we have manipulated large scale models of source code , we are not able to produce metric values for this requirement metamodel due to the absence of models. However, the integration of model-driven requirements engineering in in-

dustrial processes shall solve this issue in a near future. Another solution to requirements metrics is to analyze natural language e.g., [Wilson et al., 1996, Fantechi et al., 2002]. It is to be noted that these methods are primarily at a syntactic level i.e., deals with natural language. Our approach is totally at the model level and deals with the concepts, not the syntax.

Case Study: System Engineering Metrics

As said in the introduction, an applied research program named *Measurement of Complexity* [Chretienne et al., 2004] driven by the DGA concludes on the need to automate the computation of system engineering metrics in a semantic manner for better reliability and affordable costs. This report grounds this case study.

This report lists 122 indicators that might measure a kind of complexity of the system. These indicators address a wide range of domains: requirements engineering; environment specification; software engineering; logical architecture; project management; mechanical and chemical architecture. This is a good artifact to illustrate the genericity of our contribution, genericity over the domain and over the product lifecycle.

For instance, from the metrics related to information systems, we have derived a metamodel i.e., we have listed the domain concepts of an information system e.g., Server, Protocol, Service, etc. The implementation in Kermeta is outlined in figure 5. This implementation of the metamodel associated with the σ metric enables the computation of most of the information system metrics identified in the report e.g., the number of protocols; the number of parallel databases; the number of file formats; the number of servers.

Exploring the whole list of indicators, it turns out than 45 out of 122 (37%) are metrics of the form *number of* i.e., an application of the σ metric. The table 2 shows that depending on the domain, the σ metric is more or less useful. The domain of software architecture is the best target, with 19 σ metrics out of 21 metrics. Thus, our approach really facilitates the definition and collection of metrics for model-based software architectures. The domain of mechanical and chemical architecture is the worst target of the σ metric. To our knowledge, the reason is that these engineering fields are better described with mathematical models. Hence, the associated interesting metrics also are at a mathematical level. The domain of requirements engineering seems to be partly covered by the σ metric. However, most of the sixteen non-sigma

metrics are totally subjective e.g., the distance of the required product from technological limits. In other words, computable requirements engineering metrics are well covered by the σ metric as discussed in the previous section.

This case study showed that a significant number of metrics identified outside the scope of model-driven engineering are applications of the σ metrics. Our contribution adresses totally 37% of metrics listed in the report. The other 63% metrics are mostly pure mathematical or physical ones, hence outside the scope of model-driven metric development. Our approach is promising since it solves the majority of logical metrics.

GENERICITY APPLIED TO METAMODEL METRICS

The generic metric addresses the issue of defining and collecting metrics for a given domain. If the considered domain is metamodeling, the generic metric gives information on metamodels themselves. Our last case study is the metamodel measurement. Indeed, metamodels are important artifacts in Model Driven Engineering and we believe that it is essential to know their size, quality and complexity. For these purposes, metrics

Figure 5. Excerpt of the metamodel implemented in Kermeta

```
class InformationSystem inherits System
{ reference servers : Server
 reference subSystems : InformationSystem[0..*] }
class Interface inherits Aspect::NamedElement,
        Aspect::VersionnedElement, Aspect::DescriptedElement {}
class NetworkService
{ reference protocols : Protocol[0..*] }
class PersistenceService inherits Service { }
class DataBase inherits PersistenceService
{ attribute replicated : DataType::boolean }
```

Table 2. Complexity indicators which are an application of σ

Requirements engineering	12/28
Ex: Number of requirements without an associated specified test	
Environment specification	2/6
Ex: Number of variables	
Software architecture	19/21
Ex: Number of external protocols for interoperability	
Logical architecture	9/34
Ex: Number of configurations	
Mechanical and chemical architecture	1/21
Ex: Number of materials	
Project management	2/12
Ex: Number of stakeholders	

are to be defined, validated and implemented. This permits to give a numerical and objective vision of metamodels. Considering metamodels as models, we show that some of these metrics are an application of the σ metric presented above.

Metamodels: Definition and Implementation

There is no clear consensus on the definition of a metamodel. In [Kuehne, 2006], Kühne makes a contribution to the clarification of the definition, that *"may drastically simplify disputes about fundamental issues, such as the metamodel definition"*. We refer to this paper for the essence of a metamodel and follow a practical approach to define a metamodel: based on the EMOF specification [OMG, 2004a], we outline the pratical differences between an EMOF metamodel and a class model, from typed object-oriented programming languages.

An EMOF model is composed of instances of classes from the EMOF package. The EMOF package is the result of the merge of five packages UML::Basic (from the UML infrastructure [OMG, 2004b]), MOF::Common, MOF::Identifiers, MOF::Reflection and MOF::Extension. The main differences with object-oriented models are:

1. collections are explicitly typed;
2. collections have explicit lower and upper bounds;
3. collections are explicitly unique and/or ordered;
4. associations are defined as the binding between two references;
5. references can have containment role.

Note also that: EMOF differentiates references to primitive types (integer, boolean, etc.) and references to classes; EMOF allows multiple inheritance.

Ecore is part of the Eclipse Modeling Framework [Budinsky et al., 2004] (EMF) developped by IBM. It is an implementation of EMOF. The core EMF framework includes Ecore for describing models and runtime support for the models including change notification, persistence support with default XMI serialization, and a very efficient reflective API for manipulating EMF objects generically. The EMF framework includes generic reusable classes for building editors for EMF models and code generation facility capable of generating everything needed to build a complete editor for an EMF model.

Since Ecore is reflective and bootstrapped, Ecore metamodels can be considered as models. In this section, we leverage this facility to apply the generic model metric proposed above to the measurement of Ecore metamodels.

Direct Application of the σ Metric for Metamodel Measurement

Genero notes in [Genero et al., 2005] that unlike class measurement, the object-oriented *system metrics*, also called *package-scope metrics* [Genero et al., 2000, Xenos et al., 2000] have been little investigated. Since the notion of metamodel seems to be much more central in MDE than the notion of package in object-oriented programming languages, we aim to define metamodel metrics, not restricted to a given class i.e., metrics considering the metamodel as a whole. Thus, in this section, we define 6 global and simple metamodel metrics, taken or inspired from object-oriented *system metrics*. In the remainder of this section, we study the direct application of the σ metric for metamodel measurement i.e., metrics at the metamodel level so as to give a numerical and objective vision of metamodels. We consider:

- **NoC** the number of classes.
- **NoD** the number of primitive datatypes. A datatype is a primary information type e.g., byte, short, int, etc.

- **TNoR** the total number of references. It is the sum of the number of references of each class. In the EMOF terminology, a reference points to another class i.e., its type is a class and not a primitive type. The T (like the first letter of *total*) denotes that one considers the metamodel level (without the T, one considers the number of references per class), thus $TNoR=\Sigma i\hat{I}CNoRi$.
- **TNoA** the total number of attributes. It is the sum of the number of attributes of each classes. Note that we use the EMOF terminology: an attribute is a relationship between a class and a dataype, it defines a slot for primary information. The T denotes that one considers the metamodel level (without the T, one considers the number of attributes per class), thus $TNoA=\Sigma i\hat{I}CNoAi$.
- **NoAC** the number of abstract classes;
- **NoE** the number of enumerations. An enumeration is a kind of datatype, hence $NoE \leq NoD$.

Since metamodels can be considered as models w.r.t. the metametamodel, let us consider Ecore metamodels as models in the Eclipse Modeling Framework (EMF). In this implementation, the metamodel metrics above are σ metrics. Here are the corresponding filtering functions (names refer to the ecore metamodel implemented in EMF):

- **NoC** $\varphi(x)=(type(x)=ecore::EClass)$;
- **NoD** $\varphi(x)=(type(x)=ecore::EDataType)$;
- **TNoR** $\varphi(x)=(type(x)=ecore::EReference)$;
- **TNoA** $\varphi(x)=(type(x)=ecore::EAttribute)$;
- **NoAC** $\varphi(x)=(type(x)=ecore::EClass$ and $x.abstract=true)$;
- **NoE** $\varphi(x)=(type(x)=ecore::EEnumeration)$.

In the next section, we show that the generic σ metric can be a building block for metrics which take into account the specificities of metamodels w.r.t. object-oriented models.

The σ Metric as a Building Block so as to Take Into Account Metamodel Specificities

Existing object-oriented metrics do no take into account some modeling facilities available in EMOF metamodels. In this section, we use the *Goal Question Metric* approach [Basili et al., 1994] to define three new metrics that leverage these facilities so as to prove the ability of the σ metric to ground other metrics.

Goal

Improve the knowledge about EMOF metamodels to identify bad and good practices, patterns and templates. This identification will finally improve the quality of produced or refactored metamodels.

Questions

- How to characterize the use of associations in EMOF metamodels from the metamodel designer and user point of view ?
- How to numerically characterize the use of containment in EMOF metamodels from the metamodel designer and user point of view?
- How to numerically characterize whether the EMOF metamodel is primitive data oriented or relationship oriented ?

The answers of these question can be the independent variables of an experiment where the dependent variable is a quality attribute (e.g., from [ISO/IEC, 2001]) of a MDE process. To this extent, our approach grounds the characterization of metamodel quality.

Metrics

The Navigability Metric

The navigability metric involves the number of associations of the metamodel and *TNoR* described above. The number of associations *TNoAss* of the metamodel is a σ metric. The navigability metric is further named *Nav*.

Definition 5. $TNoAss = \sigma\varphi/2$ *where* $\varphi(x) = (type(x) = ecore::EReference$ *and* $x.opposite \neq null);$

Definition 6. $Nav = (2*TNoAss)/TNoR$

Properties

$0 \leq Nav \leq 1$ since an association is made from two references i.e., $2*TNoAss \leq TNoR$.

Interpretation

If Nav = 0 the metamodel designer does not at all use EMOF associations and only uses simple references, if Nav = 1 the metamodel designer only uses EMOF associations i.e., all references are bound to the opposite one.

The Containment Metric

The containment metric evaluates the use of containments in the metamodel. It is further named *Cont*. The containment metric involves four quantities A,B,C and D. A is the number of associations with the containment role. B is the number of associations *TNoAss*. C is the number of references with the containment role not part of an association. D is the number of references non part of an association.

- $\varphi Ax = typex = ecore::EReference$ and $x.opposite \neq null$ and $x.containment=true);$
- $\varphi o5Bx = typex = ecore::EReference$ and $x.opposite \neq null);$
- $\varphi Cx = typex = ecore::EReference$ and $x.opposite=null$ and $x.containment=true);$

- $\varphi Dx=typex=ecore::EReference$ and $x.opposite=null$);

Definition 7. *Cont=(A/B+C/D)/2*

Properties

$0 \leq Cont \leq 1$. Proof: $0 \leq A,B,C,D$ since it is a σ metric. $A<B$ and $C<D$ since φA (resp. φC) is stronger than φB (resp. φD). Then $A/B,C/D \leq 1$. Finally, the division by 2 normalizes the metric to 1. If $B=0$ (resp. $D=0$), then $A=0$ (resp. $C=0$). Hence, if $B=0$ (resp. $D=0$), the whole term A/B (resp. C/D) is discarded.

Interpretation

If Cont = 0 the metamodel designer does not use at all EMOF containment, if Cont = 1 the metamodel designer always uses containment i.e., all relationships have a container role.

Data Quantity Metric

Metric. The data quantity metric is the ratio between the number of EMOF attributes (EAttribute) and the number of EMOF structural features (EStructuralFeature). It is further named Dat. It is based on global metamodel metrics defined above in section 5.2.

Definition 8. *Dat=TNoA/(TNoA+TNoR)*

Properties

$0<Dat<1$ by definition.

Interpretation

The data quantity metric is a kind of signature of the modeled domain and/or the modeling style.

Note that there is no a priori good or bad values for these 3 metrics. Future use and validation can clarify their meanings. In the next section,

we present empirical results of the nine metrics presented.

Empirical Results on Real Metamodels

Presentation of the Metamodels

We aim to demonstrate the applicability of the generic metric for metamodel measurement i.e., how the generic metric fits to metamodel metrics. More and more metamodels are publicly available, as part of open source projects or standardization effort e.g., [OMG, 2004b]. We have configured our generic prototype for the nine metamodel metrics previously exposed and computed them on the following metamodels:

- **AADL** Architecture Analysis & Design Language metamodel, AADL is a standard for real-time embedded systems driven by the Society of Automotive Engineers - the corresponding Ecore implementation is part of the standard;
- **UML2** the Unified Modeling Language metamodel - the corresponding Ecore implementation comes from the UML2 project of Eclipse.
- **Ecore** the EMF implementation of the EMOF metamodel;
- **XML Schema Definition** XML Schema Definition metamodel - the Ecore implementation comes from the EMF tool which provides support for converting between Ecore and XML Schema models;
- **KDM** Knowledge Discovery Metamodel of the OMG - the Ecore implementation comes from the Atlantic zoo[4];
- **Java** the Java 5 metamodel - the Ecore implementation has been extracted from the Spoon tool [Pawlak et al., 2006] in our team.

For the sake of replication, the Ecore implementation of these metamodels used in this case study is available on the web[5].

Results

In Table 3, we present the results obtained with our prototype.

It shows that the σ metric is adapted to the metamodel measurement; it also roots new metrics that leverage metamodel specificities; and it is implementable and scalable enough to be applied to real world metamodels.

The basic interpretation of this table is that NoC, TNoR, TNoA, NoDT enable an objective and numeric description of metamodels in a concise manner. That is to say, we can see without previous knowledge that all these metamodels are relatively different in their structure. NoAC and NoE are refinements of these metrics.

It also shows that the ratio between references and classes is discriminant: from more than two for XMLSchema to approximately one for KDM. We tend to think that there are two types of metamodels. The first type is element-dominant such as KDM, where the main goal is to explicit the concepts of a domain. The second type is reference dominant, such as XMLSchema, where the main goal is to describe relationships.

The metrics Nav, Cont and Dat are discriminant. We believe that these metrics give information on the modeled domain and the modeling styles and practices. However, the balance between the domain and the style cannot be determined. For instance, considering *Cont*, UML2 has a value of 0.50 while Java5 has a value of 0.01. To our opinion, this can be due to the fact that the Java5 modeler did not master the containment feature of Ecore, or to the fact that the Java5 programming language is not adapted to this modeling feature. The same reasoning concerns *Nav* and *Dat*. We showed in section 3.4 that, from a theoretical point of view, the σ metric is closely related to size. This is confirmed in this domain of application, where intuitive metamodel size metrics e.g., number of classes, are σ metrics. Note that metrics where σ is used as a building block, such as *Cont* are not size metrics.

To conclude, we showed that the generic metric application on metamodel measurement is possible i.e., permits to define existing metrics and new metrics which leverage the metamodel specificities.

FUTURE RESEARCH DIRECTIONS

Our contribution enables the easy definition of metrics and collection of metrics values. Thus,

Table 3. Results on EMOF metamodels

Name	NoC	NoAC	TNoR	TNoA	NoDT	NoE	Nav	Cont	Dat
KDM	259	51	263	31	7	1	0.56	0.35	0.10
UML2	228	48	437	91	19	13	0.36	0.50	0.17
AADL	189	39	387	34	13	8	0.12	0.28	0.08
Java5	73	1	92	39	13	0	0.12	0.01	0.30
XMLSchema	57	22	125	98	28	20	0	0.16	0.44
Ecore	18	5	34	3	32	0	0.50	0.49	0.48

the main research direction is to leverage the generic σ metric to identify and empirically validate quality attributes in a given domain.

The study of metamodel metrics through the generic σ metric led to the definition of the metrics *Nav*, *Cont* and *Dat*. While our goal was to demonstrate the applicability of the generic metric, we also aimed at defining new and valuable metrics. This would be a better point in favor of generic metrics. However, we did not empirically validate the relationships between these metrics and software quality attributes. Future research is needed for the validation.

Finally, an issue is that the application of the generic σ metric is unaccessible to a non-programmer. This practice excludes the domain expert from defining and testing metrics in an autonomous manner. To this extent, a metric specific language is needed. As a perspective, a metric specific language will be studied so as to provide an intuitive notation and a user-friendly interface accessible to non-programmers. Defining and computing metrics should be totally transparent so as to unleash the domain analysis and creativity.

CONCLUSION AND PERSPECTIVES

In this chapter, we defined a generic metric that support the measurement of domain-specific attributes. The generic metric σ is defined using set theory and first order logic. It is the cardinality of a subset of model elements satisfying a filtering function. The theoretical validity of the generic σ metric is questionned in regard to type, scale, dimensional analysis and measurement errors. This shows that it is closely related to size.

To illustrate the genericity of the σ metric, we presented four case studies. We showed that the σ metric is able to precise the concept of source lines of code. By rising up Java source code at the model level, we were able to produce σ metric values on open-source projects including Eclipse-OSGI and Apache-Log4j. Two others applications encompass a wider scope than code-centric metrics. System engineering is engineering in the large. Numerous relevant metrics identified by system engineering experts are applications of the generic σ metric. This is an argument to go from non-semantic document centric system engineering to model driven engineering. In a similar manner, the generic σ metric permits to express metrics on requirements. The σ metric can also ground metamodel metrics, which are a solution to have a concise and objective summary of their internal complexity, size and quality.

REFERENCES

[Alikacem and Sahraoui, 2006] Alikacem, E. and Sahraoui, H. (2006). Generic metric extraction framework. In *Proceedings of IWSM/MetriKon 2006*.

[Bansiya, 2000] Bansiya, J. (2000). Evaluating framework architecture structural stability. *ACM Comput. Surv.*, 32(1es):18.

[Bansiya and Davis, 2002] Bansiya, J. and Davis, C. (2002). A hierarchical model for object-oriented design quality assessment. *IEEE Transactions on Software Engineering*, 28(1):4–17.

[Baroni et al., 2002] Baroni, A., Braz, S., and Abreu, F. (2002). Using OCL to formalize object-oriented design metrics definitions. In *ECOOP'02 Workshop on Quantitative Approaches in OO Software Engineering*.

[Baroni, 2005] Baroni, A. L. (2005). Quantitative assessment of uml dynamic models. In *ESEC/FSE-13: Proceedings of the 10th European software engineering conference held jointly with 13th ACM SIGSOFT international symposium on Foundations of software engineering*, pages 366–369. ACM Press.

[Basili et al., 1994] Basili, V. R., Caldiera, G., and Rombach, H. D. (1994). The goal question metric approach. In *Encyclopedia of Software Engineering*. Wiley.

[Berenbach and Borotto, 2006] Berenbach, B. and Borotto, G. (2006). Metrics for model driven requirements development. In *ICSE '06: Proceeding of the 28th international conference on Software engineering*, pages 445–451, New York, NY, USA. ACM Press.

[Briand et al., 1996] Briand, L. C., Morasca, S., and Basili, V. R. (1996). Property-based software engineering measurement. *Software Engineering*, 22(1):68–86.

[Budinsky et al., 2004] Budinsky, F., Steinberg, D., Merks, E., Ellersick, R., and Grose, T. J. (2004). *Eclipse Modeling Framework*. Addison-Wesley.

[Cabot and Teniente, 2006] Cabot, J. and Teniente, E. (2006). A metric for measuring the complexity of ocl expressions. In *Model Size Metrics Workshop co-located with MODELS'06*.

[Chretienne et al., 2004] Chretienne, P., Jean-Marie, A., Le Lann, G., Stefani, J., Atos Origin, and Dassault Aviation (2004). Programme d'Étude Amont Mesure de la compléxité (marché n°00-34-007). Technical report, DGA.

[Costello and Liu, 1995] Costello, R. J. and Liu, D.-B. (1995). Metrics for requirements engineering. *J. Syst. Softw.*, 29(1):39–63.

[Davis et al., 1993] Davis, A., Overmyer, S., Jordan, K., Caruso, J., Dandashi, F., Dinh, A., Kincaid, G., Ledeboer, G., Reynolds, P., Sitaram, P., Ta, A., and Theofanos, M. (1993). Identifying and measuring quality in a software requirements specification. In *Proceedings of the First International Software Metrics Symposium*.

[Edmonds, 1999] Edmonds, B. (1999). *Syntactic Measures of Complexity*. PhD thesis, University of Manchester.

[El Wakil et al., 2005] El Wakil, M., El Bastawissi, A., Boshra, M., and Fahmy, A. (2005). A novel approach to formalize and collect object-oriented design-metrics. In *Proceedings of the 9th International Conference on Empirical Assessment in Software Engineering*.

[Fantechi et al., 2002] Fantechi, A., Gnesi, S., Lami, G., and Maccari, A. (2002). Application of linguistic techniques for use case analysis. In *RE '02: Proceedings of the 10th Anniversary IEEE Joint International Conference on Requirements Engineering*, pages 157–164, Washington, DC, USA. IEEE Computer Society.

[Fenton, 1991] Fenton, N. E. (1991). *Software Metrics: A Rigorous Approach*. Chapman & Hall.

[Genero et al., 2002] Genero, M., Miranda, D., and Piattini, M. (2002). Defining and validating metrics for uml statechart diagrams. In *Proceedings of QAOOSE'2002*.

[Genero et al., 2000] Genero, M., Piattini, M., and Calero, C. (2000). Early measures for UML class diagrams. *L'Objet*, 6(4):489–505.

[Genero et al., 2005] Genero, M., Piattini, M., and Caleron, C. (2005). A survey of metrics for UML class diagrams. *Journal of Object Technology*, 4:59–92.

[Guerra et al., 2006] Guerra, E., Diaz, P., and de Lara, J. (2006). Visual specification of metrics for domain specific visual languages. In *Graph Transformation and Visual Modeling Techniques (GT-VMT 2006)*.

[Gîrba et al., 2005] Gîrba, T., Lanza, M., and Ducasse, S. (2005). Characterizing the evolution of class hierarchies. In *Proceedings of 9th European Conference on Software Maintenance and Reengineering (CSMR'05)*, pages 2–11. IEEE Computer Society.

[Harmer and Wilkie, 2002] Harmer, T. J. and Wilkie, F. G. (2002). An extensible metrics extraction environment for object-oriented programming languages. In *Proceedings of the International Conference on Software Maintenance*.

[Henderson-Sellers, 1996] Henderson-Sellers, B. (1996). *Object-Oriented Metrics, measures of complexity*. Prentice Hall.

[ISO/IEC, 2001] ISO/IEC (2001). *ISO/IEC 9126. Software engineering – Product quality*. ISO/IEC.

[Kan, 1995] Kan, S. H. (1995). *Metrics and Models in Software Quality Engineering*. Addison Wesley, Reading, MA.

[Kandula and Sathrasala, 2005] Kandula, G. and Sathrasala, V. K. (2005). Product and Management Metrics for Requirements. Master thesis. Umea University.

[Kitchenham et al., 1990] Kitchenham, B. A., Pickard, L. M., and Linkman, S. J. (1990). An evaluation of some design metrics. *Softw. Eng. J.*, 5(1):50–58.

[Kuehne, 2006] Kuehne, T. (2006). Matters of (meta-) modeling. *Software and System Modeling*, 5(4):369–385.

[Ma et al., 2005] Ma, H., Ji, Z., Shao, W., and Zhang, L. (2005). Towards the uml evaluation using taxonomic patterns on meta-classes. In *Proceedings of the Fifth International Conference on Quality Software (QSIC'05)*, volume 0, pages 37–44.

[Ma et al., 2004] Ma, H., Shao, W., L.Zhang, Z.Ma, and Y.Jiang (2004). Applying OO metrics to assess UML meta-models. In *Proceedings of MODELS/UML'2004*. UML 2004.

[Mahmood and Lai, 2005] Mahmood, S. and Lai, R. (2005). Measuring the complexity of a uml component specification. In *QSIC '05: Proceedings of the Fifth International Conference on Quality Software*, pages 150–160, Washington, DC, USA. IEEE Computer Society.

[Mattsson and Bosch, 1999] Mattsson, M. and Bosch, J. (1999). Characterizing stability in evolving frameworks. In *TOOLS '99: Proceedings of the Technology of Object-Oriented Languages and Systems*, page 118, Washington, DC, USA. IEEE Computer Society.

[McQuillan and Power, 2006] McQuillan, J. A. and Power, J. F. (2006). Experiences of using the dagstuhl middle metamodel for defining software metrics. In *Proceedings of the 4th International Conference on Principles and Practices of Programming in Java*.

[Medina Mora and Denger, 2003] Medina Mora, M. and Denger, C. (2003). Requirements metrics. an initial literature survey on measurement approaches for requirements specifications. Technical report, Fraunhofer IESE.

[Melton et al., 1990] Melton, A. C., Baker, A. L., Bieman, J. M., and Gustafson, D. M. (1990). A mathematical perspective for software measures research. *Software Engineering Journal*, 5:246–254.

[Mens and Lanza, 2002] Mens, T. and Lanza, M. (2002). A graph-based metamodel for object-oriented software metrics. *Electronic Notes in Theoretical Computer Science*, 72:57–68.

[Misic and Moser, 1997] Misic, V. B. and Moser, S. (1997). From formal metamodels to metrics: An object-oriented approach. In *TOOLS '97: Proceedings of the Technology of Object-Oriented Languages and Systems-Tools - 24*, page 330, Washington, DC, USA. IEEE Computer Society.

[Modelware Project, 2006a] Modelware Project (2006a). D2.2 MDD Engineering Metrics Definition. Technical report, Framework Programme Information Society Technologies.

[Modelware Project, 2006b] Modelware Project (2006b). D2.5 MDD Engineering Metrics Baseline. Technical report, Framework Programme Information Society Technologies.

[Modelware Project, 2006c] Modelware Project (2006c). D2.7 MDD Business Metrics. Technical report, Framework Programme Information Society Technologies.

[Muller et al., 2005] Muller, P. A., Fleurey, F., and Jézéquel, J. M. (2005). Weaving executability into object-oriented meta-languages. In *Proceedings of MODELS/UML 2005*.

[OMG, 2004a] OMG (2004a). MOF 2.0 specification. Technical report, Object Management Group.

[OMG, 2004b] OMG (2004b). UML 2.0 superstructure. Technical report, Object Management Group.

[Pawlak et al., 2006] Pawlak, R., Noguera, C., and Petitprez, N. (2006). Spoon: Program analysis and transformation in java. Technical Report 5901, INRIA.

[Reissing, 2001] Reissing, R. (2001). Towards a model for object-oriented design measurement. In *ECOOP'01 Workshop QAOOSE*.

[Reynoso et al., 2003] Reynoso, L., Genero, M., and Piattini, M. (2003). Measuring ocl expressions:

a "tracing"-based approach. In *Proceedings of QAOOSE'2003*.

[Saeki and Kaiya, 2006] Saeki, M. and Kaiya, H. (2006). Model metrics and metrics of model transformation. In *Proc. of 1st Workshop on Quality in Modeling*, pages 31–45.

[Schneidewind, 1992] Schneidewind, N. F. (1992). Methodology for validating software metrics. *IEEE Trans. Software Eng.*, 18(5):410–422.

[Van Belle, 2002] Van Belle, J. (2002). Towards a syntactic signature for domain models: Proposed descriptive metrics for visualizing the entity fan-out frequency distribution. In *Proceedings of SAICSIT 2002*.

[Wilson et al., 1996] Wilson, W. M., Rosenberg, L. H., and Hyatt, L. E. (1996). Automated quality analysis of natural language requirement specifications. In *Proceeding of the PNSQC Conference*.

[Xenos et al., 2000] Xenos, M., Stavrinoudis, D., Zikouli, K., and Christodoulakis, D. (2000). Object-oriented metrics - a survey. In *Proceedings of the FESMA Conference (FESMA'2000)*.

Section III
Improving the Model Quality

This section presents several chapters on techniques and methods that help to improve the quality of models. The papers address approaches such as refactoring or model transformations from the viewpoint of quality criteria and describe how model-driven development might be-come quality-driven model-based development.

Chapter VIII
Model–Driven Software Refactoring

Tom Mens
University of Mons-Hainaut, Belgium

Gabriele Taentzer
Philipps-Universität Marburg, Germany

Dirk Müller
Chemnitz University of Technology, Germany

ABSTRACT

In this chapter, we explore the emerging research domain of model-driven software refactoring. Program refactoring is a proven technique that aims at improving the quality of source code. Applying refactoring in a model-driven software engineering context raises many new challenges such as how to define, detect and improve model quality, how to preserve model behavior, and so on. Based on a concrete case study with a state-of-the-art model-driven software development tool, AndroMDA, we explore some of these challenges in more detail. We propose to resolve some of the encountered problems by relying on well-understood techniques of meta-modeling, model transformation and graph transformation.

INTRODUCTION

In the current research and practice on software engineering, there are two very important lines of research for which tool support is becoming widely available. The first line of research is *program refactoring*, the second one is *model-driven software engineering*. To this date, however, the links and potential synergies between these two lines of research have not been sufficiently explored. This will be the main contribution of this chapter.

Model-Driven Software Engineering

In the realm of software engineering, we are witnessing an increasing momentum towards the use of models for developing software systems. This trend commonly referred to as model-driven software engineering, emphasizes on models as the primary artifacts in all phases of software development, from requirements analysis over system design to implementation, deployment, verification and validation. This uniform use of models promises to cope with the intrinsic complexity of software-intensive systems by raising the level of abstraction, and by hiding the *accidental complexity* of the underlying technology as much as possible (Brooks, 1995). The use of models thus opens up new possibilities for creating, analyzing, manipulating and formally reasoning about systems at a high level of abstraction.

To reap all the benefits of model-driven engineering, it is essential to install a sophisticated mechanism of *model transformation*, that enables a wide range of different automated activities such as translation of models (expressed in different modeling languages), generating code from models, model refinement, model synthesis or model extraction, model restructuring etc. To achieve this, languages, formalisms, techniques and tools that support model transformation are needed. More importantly, their impact on the quality and semantics of models needs to be better understood.

Program Refactoring

Refactoring is a well-known technique to improve the quality of software. Martin Fowler (1999) defines it as "A change made to the internal structure of software to make it easier to understand and cheaper to modify without changing its observable behavior".

The research topic of refactoring has been studied extensively at the level of programs (i.e., source code). As a result, all major integrated software development environments provide some kind of automated support for program refactoring.

As a simple example of a program refactoring, consider the refactoring *Extract Method*, one of the more than 60 refactorings proposed by Fowler. Essentially, it is applied to a method in which part of the method body needs to be extracted into a new method that will be called by the original one. The situation before this program refactoring on a piece of Java source code is shown in Figure 1, the situation after is shown in Figure 2. The code lines that differ between both versions are marked with an asterisk.

For program refactoring, a wide variety of formalisms has been proposed to gain a deeper understanding, and to allow formal analysis. One of these formalisms is graph transformation theory (Mens *et al.*, 2005). We mention it here explicitly, as we will show later in this chapter how this formalism can be applied to support model refactoring as well. It is, however, not our goal to provide a detailed overview of existing work on program refactoring here. For the interested reader, we refer to a detailed survey of the state-of-the-art in this domain (Mens & Tourwé, 2004).

Model-Driven Software Refactoring

A natural next step seems to explore how the idea of refactoring may be applied in a model-driven software development context. We will refer to this combination as *model-driven software refactoring* and we will explore the ramifications of this synergy in the current chapter.

One of the straightforward ways to address refactoring in a model-driven context is by raising refactorings to the level of models, thereby introducing the notion of *model refactoring*, which is a specific kind of model transformation that allows us to improve the structure of the model while preserving its quality characteristics. To the best of our knowledge, Sunyé *et al.* (2001) were the first to apply the idea of refactoring to models expressed in the Unified Modeling Language (UML).

A simple yet illustrative example of a UML model refactoring is shown in Figure 3. It depicts a class model in which two classes having attributes of the same type have been identified. The model refactoring consists of removing the redundancy

Figure 1. Java source code example before applying the Extract Method program refactoring (©2007 Tom Mens, UMH. Used with permission)

```
    protected LectureVO[] handleFindLecture
        (java.lang.String title, domain.Weekday day, domain.Time time)
        throws java.lang.Exception
*   { SearchCriteria c = new SearchCriteria();
*       c.setDay(day);
*       c.setTitle(title);
*       c.setTime(time);
        Collection coll =
         getLectureDao().findLecture(LectureDao.TRANSFORM _ LECTUREVO,c);
        LectureVO[] lectures = new LectureVO[coll.size()];
        return (LectureVO[])coll.toArray(lectures); }
```

Figure 2. Java example after applying the Extract Method refactoring (©2007 Tom Mens, UMH. Used with permission)

```
    protected LectureVO[] handleFindLecture
        (java.lang.String title, domain.Weekday day, domain.Time time)
        throws java.lang.Exception
*   { SearchCriteria c = this.initialise(title,day,time);
        Collection coll =
         getLectureDao().findLecture(LectureDao.TRANSFORM _ LECTUREVO,c);
        LectureVO[] lectures = new LectureVO[coll.size()];
        return (LectureVO[])coll.toArray(lectures); }
* protected SearchCriteria initialise
*       (java.lang.String title, domain.Weekday day, domain.Time time)
*       throws java.lang.Exception
* { SearchCriteria c = new SearchCriteria();
*       c.setDay(day);
*       c.setTitle(title);
*       c.setTime(time);
*       return c; }
```

by introducing an abstract super class of both classes, and moving up the attribute to this new super class.

The above example may look simple, but it should be seen in a more general context, which makes dealing with model refactorings considerable less trivial. Consider the scenario depicted in Figure 4. It clearly illustrates the potentially high impact a simple refactoring may have on the software system. We assume that a model is built up from many different views, typically using a variety of different diagrammatic notations (e.g., class diagrams, state diagrams, use case diagrams, interaction diagrams, activity diagrams, and many more). We also assume that the model is used to generate code, while certain fragments of the code still need to be implemented manually. Whenever we make a change (in this case, a refactoring) to a single view or diagram in the model (step 1 in Figure 4), it is likely that we need to synchronize all related views, in order to avoid them becoming inconsistent (step 2 in Figure 4) (Grundy *et al.*, 1998). Next, since the model has been changed, part of the code will

Figure 3. Example of a model refactoring on UML class diagrams (©2007 Tom Mens, UMH. Used with permission)

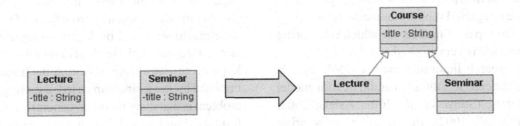

Figure 4. A scenario for model-driven software refactoring (©2007 Tom Mens, UMH. Used with permission)

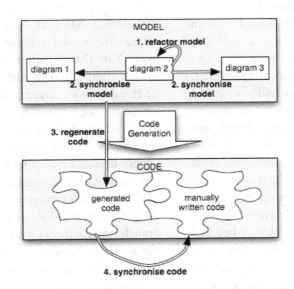

need to be regenerated (step 3 in Figure 4). Finally, the manually written code that depends on this generated code will need to be adapted as well (step 4 in Figure 4).

STATE-OF-THE-ART IN MODEL REFACTORING

At the level of models, research on refactoring is still in its infancy. Little research has been performed on model refactoring, and many open questions remain that are worthy of further investigation. For example, the relation between model refactoring and its effect on the model quality remains a largely unanswered question. From a practical point of view, only very few tools provide integrated support for model refactoring. Also, the types of models for which refactoring is supported is very limited.

In research literature, mainly UML models are considered as suitable candidates for model refactoring (Sunyé *et al.*, 2001; Astels, 2002; Boger *et al.*, 2002). In particular, refactoring of class models (e.g., UML class diagrams) has been investigated by various researchers. The advantage of such models is that they provide a representation that is relatively close to the way object-oriented programs are structured. As such, many of the refactorings known from object-oriented programming (Fowler, 1999) can be ported to UML class diagrams as well. For example, the refactoring shown in Figure 1 can also be considered as a class diagram refactoring, since a new method is created that will be visible in a class diagram. Of course, additional techniques are needed in order to ensure traceability and consistency between class diagrams and their corresponding source code when applying class diagram refactorings (Bouden, 2006).

When it comes to reasoning about the behavior preservation properties of class diagram refactorings, however, things become more difficult for various reasons. The main problem is that class diagrams provide an essentially structural description of the software architecture. Hence, behavioral information has to be expressed in a different way, either by resorting to OCL constraints, behavioral models (e.g., state diagrams or interaction diagrams), or by program code.

With respect to refactoring of behavioral models, not much work is available. We are only aware of a few approaches that address the problem of refactoring state diagrams, and try to prove their behavior preservation properties in a formal way. Van Kempen *et al.* (2005) use a

formalism based on CSP to describe statechart refactorings, and show how this formalism can be used to verify that a refactoring effectively preserves behavior. Pretschner and Prenninger (2006) provide a formal approach for refactoring state machines based on logical predicates and tables. Integrating these ideas into tool support is left for future work. Apart from some limitations imposed by the formalisms used, a more general problem is that there is still no generally accepted formal semantics for (UML) state diagrams. Many different interpretations exist and, obviously, this has an important effect on how the behavior is formally defined.

Though research on model refactoring is still in its infancy, a number of formalisms have already been proposed to understand and explore model refactoring. Most of these approaches suggest expressing model refactoring in a declarative way. Van Der Straeten *et al.* (2004) propose to use description logics; Van Der Straeten & D'Hondt (2006) suggest the use of a forward-chaining logic reasoning engine to support composite model refactorings. Gheyi *et al.* (2005) specify model refactorings using Alloy, a formal object-oriented modeling language. They use its formal verification system to specify and prove the soundness of the transformations. Biermann *et al.* (2006) and Mens *et al.* (2007) use graph transformation theory as an underlying foundation for specifying model refactoring, and rely on the formal properties to reason about and analyze these refactorings.

An important aspect of refactoring in a model-driven software development context that is typically neglected in research literature is how it interferes with code generation. Most contemporary tools for model-driven software development allow generating a substantial part of the source code automatically from the model, while other parts still need to be specified manually (see Figure 4). This introduces the need to synchronize between models and source code when either one of them changes. How such synchronization can be achieved in presence of automated refactoring support is a question that has not been addressed in detail in research literature. If a model is being refactored, how should the corresponding source code be modified accordingly? Vice versa, if source code is being refactored, how will the models be affected? These are the kind of questions that will be addressed in this chapter. To this extent, we will report on our experience with AndroMDA, a state-of-the-art tool for model-driven software development based on UML.

MOTIVATING EXAMPLE: MODEL-DRIVEN DEVELOPMENT WITH ANDROMDA

This section presents the model-driven development of a small web application for a simple university calendar. We will develop this calendar in two iteration steps using AndroMDA[1]. First the underlying data model is designed and a web application with a default web presentation is generated. Second, application-specific services and the web presentation are developed with AndroMDA. This means that use cases are defined and refined by activity diagrams that can use controllers and services. The development is not hundred percent model-driven, since service and controller bodies have to be coded by hand.

For both iteration steps, we first present the UML model using the AndroMDA profile and then discuss a refactoring step useful in that context.

Getting Started with Developing a University Calendar Using AndroMDA

One of the main tools for model-driven software development is AndroMDA. Its transformation engine is structured by cartridges. A number of pre-defined cartridges is already available realizing the generation of web applications from UML models. We illustrate model-driven software development based on AndroMDA by the example of a very simple university calendar.

In principle, the model-driven development process of AndroMDA is based on use cases. But in this initial example, we start with an even simpler way of using AndroMDA. We just design the underlying data model and AndroMDA generates a complete web application with a default web presentation from that.

A web application generated by AndroMDA has a three-tier architecture consisting of a service layer building up on a data base, controllers using the services defined, and a web presentation. The underlying data model, services and controllers are defined by an UML class diagram. Additionally, visual object classes are modeled, which are used for presenting data to the user, decoupled from the internal data model.

An example of an AndroMDA class diagram is shown in Figure 5. It depicts a simple data model for a university calendar. We can observe that the basic entities are Rooms that can be occupied for giving a Lecture or a Seminar. Based on this class diagram, AndroMDA can generate a default web interface for managing lectures, seminars and rooms. Users can add and delete instances, change attribute values and perform searches. The webpage for managing lectures is shown in Figure 6.

The UML profiles used in connection with AndroMDA can be considered as a domain-specific language, dedicated to the generation of web applications. This is achieved by giving a specific semantics to UML models by relying on that dedicated UML profiles. They extend the semantics of the UML by introducing specific stereotypes, to which additional constraints and tagged values are attached. For example, the stereotype «Entity» attached to a class is used to represent a data entity to be stored in a database. If, additionally, the «Manageable» stereotype is used, it causes AndroMDA to generate a default web

Figure 5. Data model for a simple university calendar (©2007 Tom Mens, UMH. Used with permission)

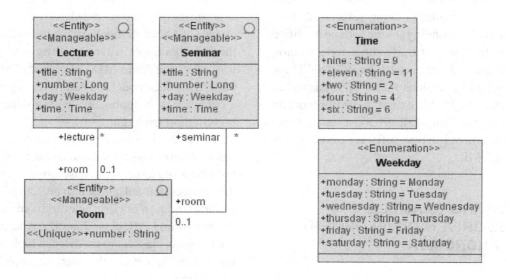

Figure 6. Webpage for managing lectures (©2007 Tom Mens, UMH. Used with permission)

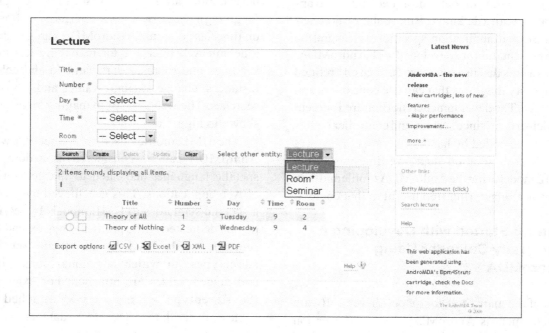

presentation for managing the corresponding entities. The use of such manageable entities has been illustrated in Figure 5.

First Refactoring of the University Calendar

Due to their compactness, large parts of An-droMDA UML models are used for generating user interfaces. Thus, model refactorings in this context are likely to cause changes in user interfaces as well. Following Fowler (1999) in a strict sense, refactorings should not change the user interface of software, since they are supposed to "preserve the observable behavior". This strict interpretation of refactoring, however, makes little sense if applied in a model-driven software development context, due to the side-effects that model refactorings may cause on the generated code, especially user interfaces. Thus, Fowler's definition of refactoring should be interpreted in a more liberal way, in the sense that it should not change the functionality offered by software. Modifications to the *usability* of the software or to other non-functional properties (such as interoperability, portability, reusability, adaptability and the like) should be allowed, if the goal of these modifications is to improve the software quality.

Figure 7. Data model for a simple university calendar after having applied the Pull Up Attribute refactoring (©2007 Tom Mens, UMH. Used with permission)

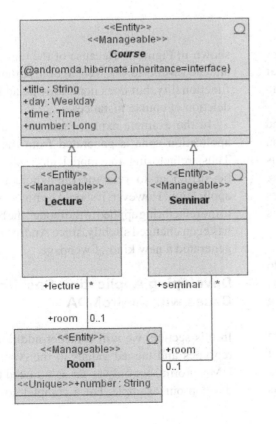
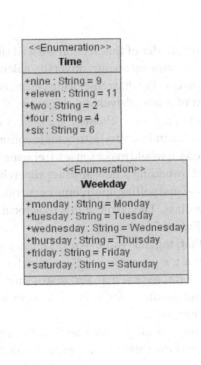

Figure 8. Webpage for managing courses (©2007 Tom Mens, UMH. Used with permission)

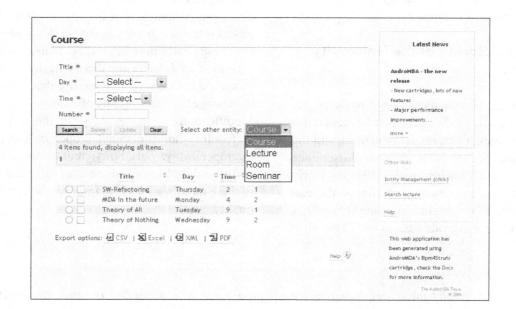

In the remainder of this section we will show a concrete refactoring on our university calendar case study to clarify what refactoring can mean in the context of model-driven development.

Since «Entity» classes Lecture and Seminar contain several attributes in common (see Figure 5), it would make sense to refactor this data model by adding a new abstract superclass, called Course, and pulling up all common attributes to this new class. The result of this refactoring is shown in Figure 7.

Note that tagged value @andromda. hibernate.inheritance has to be set to interface for restricting the management facilities for courses to searching functionalities only.

When regenerating a web application from the refactored data model in Figure 7, most of the user interface remains unaltered. But a new webpage will appear for managing courses, as shown in Figure 8. Because of the tagged value attached to Course, this webpage only offers search functionality, but does not allow the addition or deletion of course instances.

In the example explained in section 3.1, all application code is generated from the model. Thus, refactoring the model alone appears to be sufficient to refactor the whole software application. However, it should be noted that, due to the refactoring applied to the model, the behavior has been changed slightly, since AndroMDA has generated a new kind of webpage.

Developing Application-Specific Use Cases with AndroMDA

In this section, we will consider additional stereotypes and tagged values in the AndroMDA UML profile, but only as far as we need them to develop our example. For a complete overview of all available stereotypes and how to use them we refer to the AndroMDA website.

«Service»   is a class stereotype used to specify application-specific services. These services typically use one or more entities that store the data used by the services. For the model-driven development of a web presentation, we extend the model by use cases that are refined by activity diagrams. This model part describes the web presentation and its usage of controllers based on services. The development is not hundred percent model-driven, since service and controller bodies have to be coded by hand.

To illustrate the development of specific web applications we reconsider the university calendar and develop a specific use case diagram for lectures (see Figure 9). Use case Search lectures has two stereotypes being «FrontEndUseCase», which determines the use case to be visible to the user in form of a webpage, and «FrontEndApplication», which defines this use case to be the starting one.

Use case Search lectures is refined by an activity diagram that supports a search activity and the presentation of filtered lectures (see Figure 10). Activity Search lectures is an internal activity that calls the controller method showLectures(). Activity Present lectures has stereotype «FrontEndView» implying that this activity models a webpage. Both activities are connected by two transitions arranged in a cyclic way. After calling method showLectures() the result is transferred to the webpage by signal show , which has the resulting value object array as parameter. Signal search   and its parameters are used to model the web form for filtering the lectures.

The class model in Figure 5 is again used as data model. To show lectures, a special value object class for lectures is used, which is specified by stereotype «ValueObject» (see Figure 11). This makes sense in terms of encapsulation (think of security, extensibility, etc.) and corresponds to the layered model-view-controller approach. Necessary information of the business layer is packaged into so-called "value objects", which are used for the transfer to the presentation layer. Passing real entity objects to the client may pose a security risk. Do you want the client application to have access to the salary information inside the Lecturer entity?

An attribute room of type String was added to LectureVO in order to allow a connection to the unique number   of the Room class. Since value objects are used at the presentation layer, the types used are primitive ones; entity types are not used in that layer. A dependency relation between an entity and a value object is used to generate translation methods from the entity to its corresponding value object. Moreover, search criteria can be defined by a class of stereotype «Criteria»   .

Figure 9. Example of a use case model in AndroMDA (©2007 Tom Mens, UMH. Used with permission)

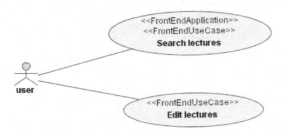

Figure 10. Example of an activity diagram specifying the Search lectures use case (©2007 Tom Mens, UMH. Used with permission)

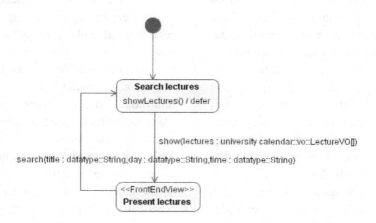

Figure 11. Value Object and Criteria classes (©2007 Tom Mens, UMH. Used with permission)

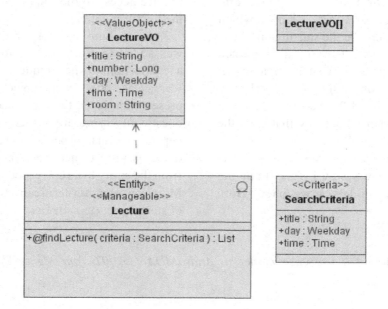

Figure 12. Service and controller classes (©2007 Tom Mens, UMH. Used with permission)

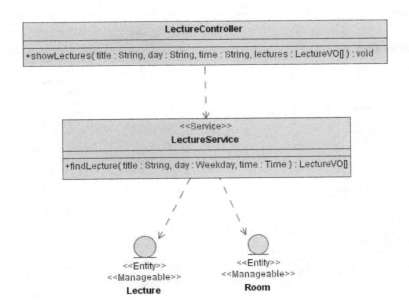

Method showLectures() that is called from activity Search lectures in Figure 10, is defined in LectureController, a class that relies on class LectureService. This class is stereotyped as «Service» and relies on entities Lecture and Room (see Figure 12). However, the bodies of service and controller methods cannot be modeled, but have to be coded directly by hand. For example, the implementation of service method findLecture() is shown in Figure 1. Because of special naming conventions of AndroMDA it has to be named handleFindLecture().

The web application generated by AndroMDA from the complete model given in the previous figures (together with manually written code parts) produces the webpage shown in Figure 13. Please note that the names used as page title, in the search form and for the buttons are generated from the model.

Further Refactoring of the University Calendar

As a second model refactoring[2], we will discuss the renaming of attribute time to starttime based on the model given in Section 3.3. We will argue that this refactoring affects the usability of the generated software. The refactoring is primarily performed on entity class Lecture, but since there is a value object class LectureVO for that entity, the corresponding value class attribute time has to be renamed into start-time, too (see Figure 14). The same is true in SearchCriteria. Thus, the standard refactoring method *Rename Attribute* becomes domain-specific and affects several classes in this domain-specific context.

Since the value object attribute is not used directly in other parts of the model, the model does not have to be updated any further. But the

Figure 13. Webpage for searching lectures (©2007 Tom Mens, UMH. Used with permission)

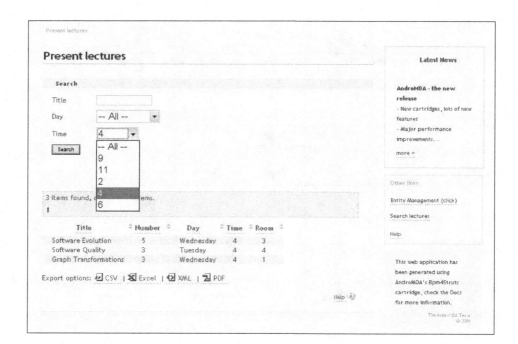

hand-written code (given in Figure 1) is affected, since accessor method `setTime()` is no longer available after regenerating the code. Thus, it has to be renamed as well, by calling method `setStarttime()` instead. After having performed this refactoring, the webpage for searching lectures has been changed slightly. As a result, the usability is affected, though not dramatically, since the column named "Time" of the presented table presented has changed into "Starttime" (see Figure 15).

Based on the analysis of both model refactorings carried out in this section, we can derive the following important preliminary conclusions:

- Generic model refactorings need to be adapted and refined in order to work properly in a domain-specific modeling language.

- Model refactorings may also affect, and require changes to the hand-written source code.

- Model refactorings may change external qualities as perceived by the user, such as usability aspects.

CHALLENGES IN MODEL-DRIVEN SOFTWARE REFACTORING

In this section, we will discuss some important challenges in model refactoring that have to do with the relation between model refactoring and model quality. It is not our ambition to solve all these challenges in the current chapter. In Sections 5 and 6 we will therefore only focus on those challenges that we consider being most urgent and most important and we will exemplify our

Figure 14. Value Object and Entity classes after renaming (©2007 Tom Mens, UMH. Used with permission)

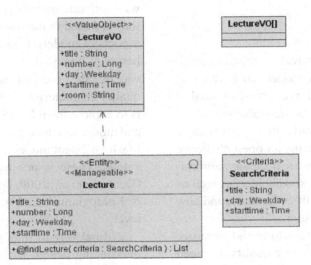

Figure 15. Webpage for searching lectures after renaming (©2007 Tom Mens, UMH. Used with permission)

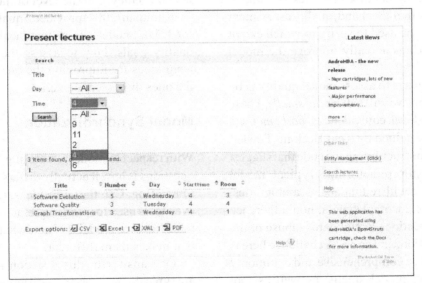

proposed solution using the case study introduced in the previous section.

Model Quality

A first challenge is to provide a precise definition of model quality. A model can have many different non-functional properties or quality characteristics that may be desirable (some examples are: usability, readability, performance and adaptability). It remains an open challenge to identify which qualities are necessary and sufficient for which type of stakeholder, as well as how to specify these qualities formally, and how to relate them to one another.

Since the main goal of refactoring is to improve certain aspects of the software quality, we need means to assess this quality at the model level in an objective way. On the one hand, this will allow software modelers to identify which parts of the model contain symptoms of poor quality, and are hence potential candidates for model refactoring. On the other hand, quality assessment techniques can be used to verify to which extent model refactorings actually improve the model quality.

One of the ways to assess model quality is by resorting to what we will call *model smells*. These are the model-level equivalent of *bad smells*, a term originally coined by Kent Beck in (Fowler, 1999) to refer to structures in the code that suggest opportunities for refactoring. Typical model smells have to do with redundancies, ambiguities, inconsistencies, incompleteness, non-adherence to design conventions or standards, abuse of the modeling notation, and so on. A challenge here is to come up with a comprehensive and commonly accepted list of model smells, as well as tool support to detect such smells in an automated way. What is also needed is a good understanding of the relation between model smells and model refactoring, in order to be able to suggest, for any given model smell, appropriate model refactorings that can remove this smell.

A second way to assess and control model quality is by resorting to *model metrics*. In analogy with software metrics (Fenton & Pfleeger, 1997) they are used to measure and quantify desirable aspects of models. It remains an open question, however, how to define model metrics in such a way that they correlate well with external model quality characteristics. Another important issue is to explore the relation between model metrics and model refactoring, and in particular to assess to which extent model refactorings affect metric values. These issues have been addressed by (Demeyer *et al.*, 2000; Du Bois, 2006; Tahvildari & Kontogiannis, 2004) though mainly at code level.

A final way to improve model quality is by introducing design patterns, which are proven solutions to recurring problems (Gamma *et al.*, 1994). At code level, Kerievsky (2004) explored the relation between refactorings and design patterns. It remains to be seen how similar results may be achieved at the level of models.

Kamthan (2004) provided a quality framework for UML models. It systematically studies the quality goals, how to assess them, as well as techniques for improving the quality, similar to the ones discussed above.

Model Synchronization

With respect to model refactoring, one of the key questions is how it actually differs from program refactoring. Can the same ideas, techniques and even tools used for program refactoring be ported to the level of models? If not, what is it precisely that makes them different?

One answer to this question is that models are typically built up from different views, using different types of diagrams, that all need to be kept consistent. This in contrast to programs, that are often (though not always) expressed within a single programming language.[3]

Perhaps a more important difference is that models are abstract artifacts whose main purpose is to facilitate software development by generating a large portion of the source code that would otherwise need to be written manually. However, full code generation is unfeasible in practice for most application domains. The additional challenge therefore consists in the need to synchronize and maintain consistency between models and their corresponding program code, especially when part of this program code has been specified or modified manually. In the context of model transformation, this implies that automated model refactorings (or other transformations) may need to be supplemented with code-level transformations in order to ensure overall consistency. Vice versa, program refactorings may need to be supplemented with model-level transformations to ensure their consistency.

Though no general solutions exist yet, the problem of model synchronization and model consistency maintenance is well known in literature. For example, (Van Gorp *et al.*, 2003) discuss the problem of keeping the UML models consistent with their corresponding program code. (Correa & Werner, 2004) explain how OCL constraints need to be kept in sync when the class diagrams are refactored and vice versa. Egyed (2006) proposes an incremental approach to model consistency checking that scales up to large industrial models. Liu *et al.* (2002) and Van Der Straeten & D'Hondt (2006) rely on a rule-based approach for detecting and resolving UML model inconsistencies, respectively. Van Der Straeten *et al.* (2003) bear on the formalism of description logics to achieve the same goal. Mens *et al.* (2006) propose to resolve inconsistencies in an incremental fashion by relying on the formalism of graph transformation. Grundy *et al.* (1998) report on how tool support can be provided for managing inconsistencies in a software system composed of multiple views. Goedicke *et al.* (1999) address the same problem by relying on the formalism of distributed graph transformation.

Behavior Preservation

Another important challenge of model refactoring has to do with *behavior preservation*. By definition, a model refactoring is supposed to preserve the observable behavior of the model it is transforming. In order to achieve this, we need a precise definition of "behavior" in general, and for models in particular. In addition, we need formalisms that allow us to specify behavioral invariants, i.e., properties that need to be preserved by the refactoring. The formalism should then verify which of these invariants are preserved by the model refactoring. Although formal research on behavior preservation is still in its infancy, in Section 2 we already pointed to a few approaches that carried out initial research in this direction. Another approach that is worthwhile mentioning is the work by Gheyi *et al.* (2005). They suggest specifying model refactorings in *Alloy*, an object-oriented modeling language used for formal specification. It can be used to prove semantics-preserving properties of model refactorings.

A more pragmatic way to ensure that the behavior remains preserved by a refactoring is by resorting to *testing* techniques. Many researchers have looked at how to combine the ideas of testing with model-driven engineering (Brottier *et al.*, 2006; Mottu *et al.*, 2006). Test-driven development is suggested by the agile methods community as good practice for writing high-quality software. In combination with refactoring, it implies that before and after each refactoring step, tests are executed to ensure that the behavior remains unaltered.

Domain-Specific Modeling

A final challenge is the need to define model refactorings in domain-specific extensions of the UML (such as AndroMDA), or even in dedicated domain-specific modeling languages. These refactorings should be expressible in a generic yet customizable way. Indeed, given the large number of very diverse domain-specific languages, it is not feasible, nor desirable, to develop dedicated tools for all of them from scratch.

Zhang *et al.* (2004) therefore proposed a generic model transformation engine and used it to specify refactorings for domain-specific models. Their tool is implemented in the Generic Modeling Environment (GME), a UML-based meta-modeling environment. A model refactoring browser has been implemented as a GME plug-in. Their tool enables the automation and user-defined customization of model refactorings using ECL (Embedded Constraint Language), an extension of the declarative OCL language with imperative constructs to support model transformation. As an example of the expressiveness of their approach, they illustrated how it can be applied to class diagrams, state diagrams and Petri nets. The solution that we will explore later in this chapter is related, in the sense that we will propose a generic approach for UML-based model refactoring based on graph transformation concepts.

In general, the main challenge remains to determine, for a given domain-specific modeling language, which transformations can be considered as meaningful refactorings. On the one hand, they will need to preserve some notion of "behavior" and, on the other hand, they need to improve some quality aspect. These notions of behavior and quality can differ widely depending on the domain under study. For domains that do not refer to software (e.g., business domains, technical domains, etc.) it is much harder to come to a meaningful definition of behavior, implying that the notion of refactoring would become much harder to define in that context.

Analyzing Model Refactorings

Even more advanced support for model refactorings can be envisaged if we have a precise means to analyze and understand the relationships between refactorings. This will enable us to build up complex refactorings from simpler ones; to detect

whether refactorings are mutually exclusive, in the sense that they are not jointly applicable and to analyze causal dependencies between refactorings. These techniques have been explored in detail by Mens *et al.* (2007), and promise to offer more guidance to the developer on what is the most appropriate refactoring to apply in which context. A short introduction to this line of research will be given in Section 6.

MOTIVATING EXAMPLE REVISITED

In Section 3 two concrete model refactorings have been applied to AndroMDA models: pulling up an attribute into a new superclass and renaming an entity. In this section, we explore some more refactorings for AndroMDA models.[4] We start by considering a set of "standard" model refactorings widely used to restructure class diagrams. As it will turn out, most of these refactorings have side-effects due to constraints imposed by AndroMDA's code generator. Therefore, these model refactorings need to be customized to take into account more domain-specific information. Next to these "standard" refactorings, we will also discuss entirely new "domain-specific" refactorings for AndroMDA models.

In the following, we will take a slightly broader view, and we discuss three categories of model transformations as follows:

(1) model refactorings that do not affect the user interface at all;

(2) model refactorings that do affect the user interface with respect to the usability, but that do not affect what the user can do with the application;

(3) model transformations that also affect the actual behavior/functionality of the application.

The latter category does not contain refactorings in the strict sense of the word, but it is nevertheless useful and necessary to deal with them. For example, it could be the case that what is perceived as a normal refactoring will actually *extend* the behavior as a side effect of the code generation process.

Pull Up Attribute

When pulling up an attribute to a super class, as explained in Section 3.2, the code generator will generate a new webpage corresponding to this super class, with search functionality for each manageable entity. Thus, this model transformation belongs to category (3).

Rename

The refactoring example in Section 3.4 is concerned with renaming an attribute of an entity class. This refactoring affects the user interface, if the entity is manageable. In this case, one of the columns in the table of the webpage has been renamed. Furthermore, in case that the entity class comes along with a value object class that is derived from the entity class, a renaming of an entity attribute has to be accompanied by a renaming of the corresponding attribute in its value object class. If, in addition, this value object attribute is used in some activity diagram, the name has to be adapted there as well. Furthermore, this value object attribute can occur in hand-written code, which implies that renaming has to be performed also in that part of the code.

A similar situation would arise if we renamed the entity class itself, as it would be reflected by a change in the title of the corresponding webpage for manageable entities. In case that the renamed entity class comes along with a value object class whose name is derived from the entity class name (e.g., in Figure 14, "LectureVO" is derived from "Lecture" by suffixing "VO"), renaming has to be accompanied by a renaming of its corresponding value object class. Furthermore, the renaming has to be propagated as discussed

for attributes. In all cases presented, although the user interface changes slightly, the functionality of the application is not affected. Hence, these refactorings belong to category (2).

Similar to entities, use cases can be renamed as well. This might have an effect on activity diagrams, since AndroMDA supports the connection of several activity diagrams via use case names. For example, an end activity of one activity diagram may be named as a use case, which means that the control flow would continue at the start activity of the corresponding activity diagram. In the generated web applications, use cases are listed on the right-hand side of each webpage. Again, a renamed use case would change the usability of the web application, but not its functionality, so the refactoring belongs to category (2).

In summary, we see that renaming in AndroMDA may have a high impact. Due to the fact that the code generator automatically produces new types of elements based on the names of existing elements, a seemingly simple change (in casu renaming) will propagate to many different places. A tool that would implement this model refactoring would therefore need to take these issues into account to ensure that the renaming does not lead to an inconsistent model or code. Furthermore, because the changes affect hand-written code, the refactoring may require a certain amount of user interaction.

Create Value Object

A domain-specific refactoring for AndroMDA models is the creation of value objects for entities. An example is visually represented in Figure 16. Given a class with stereotype «Entity» (for example, class Lecture), a new class with stereotype «Value Object» is created and the entity class becomes dependent on this new class. The value object class is named after its entity class followed by suffix "VO" (for example, value object class LectureVO).

Figure 16. Example of the domain-specific model refactoring CreateValueObject (©2007 Tom Mens, UMH. Used with permission)

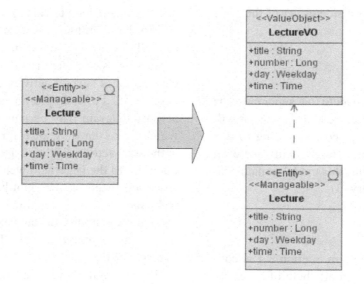

The entity attributes are copied to the value object class, keeping names and types, by default. If internal information should be hidden from the client, the corresponding attribute would not be copied. This refactoring belongs to category (1) and does not affect any other part of the model, since the value object class is only created without being used yet.

Merge Services

Another domain-specific model refactoring is *Merge Services*. It takes two «Service» classes and merges them as well as all their incoming and outgoing dependencies. Consider the following example where both a LecturServicevice and RoomService exist (see Figure 17). If we do not consider remote services and have only one controller class, it does not make sense to have two service classes. Therefore, both should

be merged into LectureService. After refactoring, the controller class will have only one outgoing dependency. As a result, the hand-written code for the controller method will be affected. Nevertheless, this restructuring will not modify the external behavior, so users of the generated web application will not notice any change. Hence, this refactoring falls into category (1).

Split Activity

The front-end of a web application is modeled by use cases and activity diagrams. A refactoring like the splitting of activities into two consecutive ones, linked by a transition, can directly affect the web presentation. If the original activity was a «FrontEndView», the corresponding webpage is split into two pages. If an internal activity was split, this refactoring has to be accompanied by a splitting of the corresponding

Figure 17. Service classes LectureService *and* RoomService *with dependencies (©2007 Tom Mens, UMH. Used with permission)*

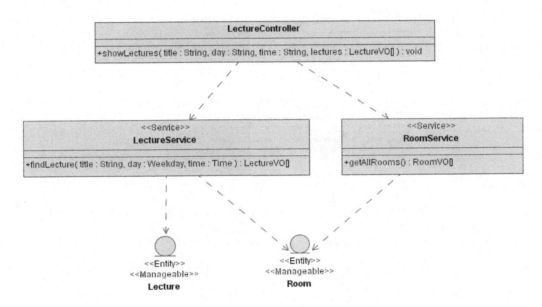

controller method called. In the first case, the refactoring belongs to category (2), in the second case it belongs to category (1).

Extract Method

Extract Method is a refactoring from the standard catalogue established by Fowler. In the context of model-driven development, and AndroMDA in particular, it can have new effects. Consider the scenario in Figure 19. First, we perform the extract method refactoring to the hand-written code, as illustrated in Figure 2 where a method, called initialise(), is extracted from a given service method handleFindLecture. To reflect this change at model level, we modify the class diagram by adding the extracted method to the class LectureService as well (see Figure 18). Consequently, the code generator will generate extra code for this method, which

requires the manually written code to be adapted to make it consistent again. In particular, method initialise() needs to be renamed into handleInitialise(), because this is the convention used by the code generator: all service methods need to be prefixed with "handle" at source code level. We can use this knowledge to constrain the Extract Method refactoring to make it domain-specific: When extracting a method, the name that the user needs to provide for the extracted method needs to follow the naming conventions imposed by the code generator. Not doing so will cause the precondition of the refactoring to fail.

The above scenario is generalized and visualized in Figure 19. It shows how a refactoring at source code level (step 1) may require synchronization of the corresponding model (step 2) which, after regenerating the code (step 3) involves another modification to the hand-written

Figure 18. Changes to the class diagram as a result of applying the Extract Method program refactoring (see Figure 2) (©2007 Tom Mens, UMH. Used with permission)

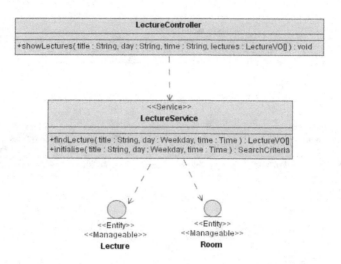

Figure 19. Another scenario of model-driven software refactoring, initiated by a refactoring of the hand-written source code (©2007 Tom Mens, UMH. Used with permission)

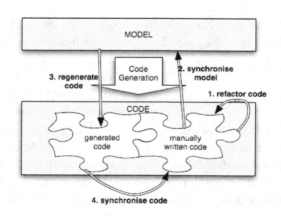

part of the code (step 4). The last step is not needed, if the user obeys the naming convention for the new method as discussed above.

SPECIFYING AND ANALYZING MODEL REFACTORINGS

In Section 5, the important challenge of domain-independent support for model refactoring was discussed. A possible formalism that can be used to specify and also analyze refactorings is the theory of *graph transformation* (Ehrig *et al.* 2006). Compared to other approaches it has a number of advantages: it allows one to specify program refactorings and model refactorings for various languages in a uniform and generic way, by representing the software artifact under consideration as a graph, and by specifying the refactorings as graph transformation rules. In addition, one can benefit from the formal properties of graph transformation theory to reason about refactoring in a formal way. For example, prop-

erties such as termination, composition, parallel dependencies, and sequential dependencies can be analyzed.

Since the Eclipse Modeling Framework (EMF) has become a key reference for model specification in the world of model-driven development, we rely our approach to model refactoring on EMF model transformation. This approach is presented in Section 6.1. To perform a formal analysis of EMF transformations we translate them to graph transformations, which is possible under certain circumstances. In Section 6.2, a conflict and dependency analysis of model refactorings is presented, assuming that the model refactorings are defined by graph transformation rules.

Technical Solution

From a technical point of view, we will discuss how to implement and execute model refactorings. In particular, we will consider how to realize model refactoring within the Eclipse Modeling Framework (EMF). As a prerequisite, a specifi-

Figure 20. Extract of AndroMDA meta-model as EMF model (©2007 Tom Mens, UMH. Used with permission)

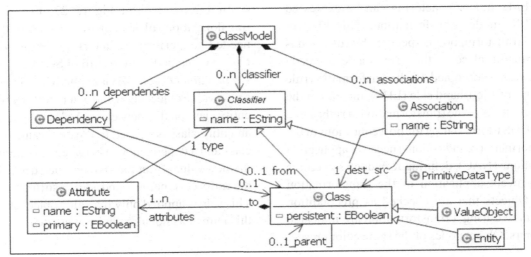

Figure 21. Entity class `Lecture` *with attributes in abstract syntax as EMF model instance (©2007 Tom Mens, UMH. Used with permission)*

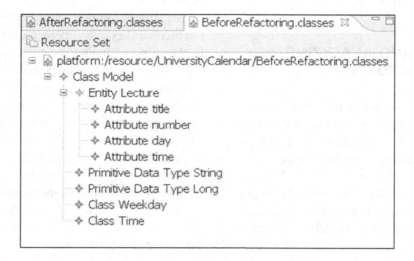

cation of the underlying modeling language is needed, which will be given by a meta-model. Figure 20 shows an EMF model that represents a simplified extract of the AndroMDA meta-model. Figure 21 shows an instance of this EMF model for the entity class `Lecture` of the simple university calendar.

Biermann *et al.* (2006) explain in detail how EMF model refactoring can be expressed by EMF model transformation. This kind of model transformation is specified by rules and is performed in-place, i.e., the current model is directly changed and not copied. Each transformation rule consists of a left-hand side (LHS), indicating the preconditions of the transformation, a right-hand side (RHS), formulating the post conditions of the transformations, and optional negative application conditions (NAC), defining forbidden structures that prevent application of the transformation rule. Objects that are checked as precondition preserved during a transformation are indicated by colors. Object nodes of the same color present

one and the same object in different parts of a rule. While attributes in the LHS may have constant values or rule variables only, they are allowed to carry Java expressions in the RHS, too. The same variable at different places in the rules means the same value at all places. In the following, we use this approach to EMF model transformation for specifying UML model refactorings.

In Figure 22 and Figure 23, two model transformation rules are shown, which both are needed to perform refactoring *Create Value Object* explained in Figure 16 of Section 5. Rule *CreateValueObjectClass* is applied once, creating a new value object class and a dependency of the entity class on this new class. A class model with an entity class is needed to create a value object class and a dependency in between. The name of this new value object class is constructed by taking the entity class name e and adding suffix "VO". This rule is applied only if a value object class of this name has not already been created.

Figure 22. EMF model transformation rule CreateValueObjectClass for refactoring method Create Value Object (©2007 Tom Mens, UMH. Used with permission)

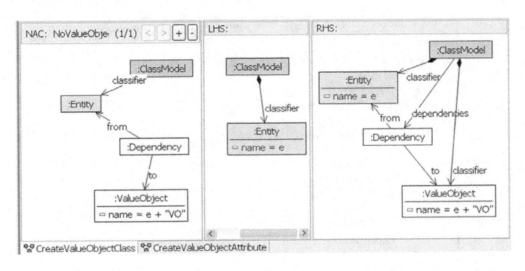

Figure 23. EMF model transformation rule CreateValueObjectAttribute for refactoring method Create Value Object (©2007 Tom Mens, UMH. Used with permission)

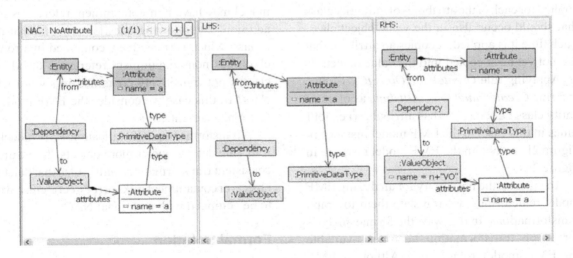

Figure 24. Entity class `Lecture` *with value object class* `LectureVO` *in abstract syntax as EMF model instance (©2007 Tom Mens, UMH. Used with permission)*

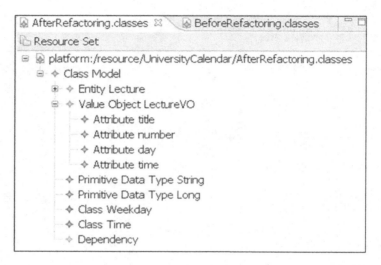

Thereafter, rule *CreateValueObjectAttribute* is applied for each of the attributes of the entity class that should occur also in the value object class. Each time it is applied, it copies an attribute that has not yet been copied into the value object.

Applying rule *CreateValueObjectClass* once and rule *CreateValueObjectAttribute* as often as entity class `Lecture` has attributes (i.e., four times in this case) to the EMF model instance in Figure 21, we obtain the EMF model instance in Figure 24.

To open up the possibility for analyzing EMF model refactorings, we translate them to graph transformations. In this way, the formal analysis for graph transformation becomes available for EMF model refactoring. Although EMF models show a graph-like structure and can be transformed similarly to graphs, there is an important difference between both. In contrast to graphs, EMF models have a distinguished tree structure that is defined by the containment relation between their classes. Each class can be contained in at most one other class. Since an EMF model may have non-containment references in addition, the following question arises: What if a class, which is transitively contained in a root class, has non-containment references to other classes not transitively contained in some root class? In this case we consider the EMF model to be inconsistent.

A transformation can invalidate an EMF model, if its rule deletes one or more objects. To ensure consistent transformations only, rules that delete objects or containment links or redirect them, have to be equipped with additional NACs.

Formal Solution

As an illustration of how refactoring dependency analysis may increase the understanding of refactoring, consider the following scenario. Assume that a software developer wants to know which refactoring rules need to be applied in order to restructure a software system. Typically, many

Figure 25. Sequential dependencies computed by AGG for a representative set of refactorings implemented as graph transformations (©2007 Tom Mens, UMH. Used with permission)

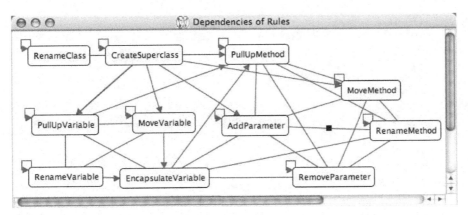

different refactoring rules may be applicable, and it is not easy to find out what would be the most optimal way to apply these rules. Joint application of some refactoring rules may not be possible due to parallel dependencies between them, and some refactoring rules may sequentially depend on other ones. Graph transformation theory allows us to compute such dependencies by relying on the idea of *critical pair analysis*. The general-purpose graph transformation tool AGG[5] provides an algorithm implementing this analysis.

Figure 25 gives an example of all sequential dependencies that have been computed between a representative, yet simplified, subset of refactorings expressed as graph transformation rules. For example, we see that there is a sequential dependency between the *CreateSuperclass* refactoring and the *PullUpVariable* refactoring. *CreateSuperclass* inserts a new intermediate superclass (identified by node number 2) in between a class (node 1) and its old superclass (node 3). *PullUpVariable* moves a variable contained in a class up to its superclass. The dependency between both transformation rules, as computed by AGG, is visualized in Figure 26. The effect of applying *CreateSuperclass* before

PullUpVariable will be that the variable will be pulled up to the newly introduced intermediate superclass instead of the old one. As such, there is a sequential dependency between both refactoring rules. It is even the case, in this example, that the application of both refactorings in a different order will produce a different result.

For a more detailed discussion of how critical pair analysis can be used to reason about refactoring dependencies, we refer to (Mens *et al.*, 2007) that provides a detailed account on these issues.

Related Work

Various authors have proposed to use some kind of rule-based approach to specify model refactorings, so it appears to be a natural choice:

Grunske *et al.* (2005) show an example in Fujaba[6] of how model refactoring may be achieved using graph transformation based on story-driven modeling. Bottoni *et al.* (2005) use distributed graph transformation concepts to specify coherent refactorings of several software artifacts, especially UML models and Java

Figure 26. Example of a sequential dependency between the CreateSuperclass and the PullUpVariable refactoring (©2007 Tom Mens, UMH. Used with permission)

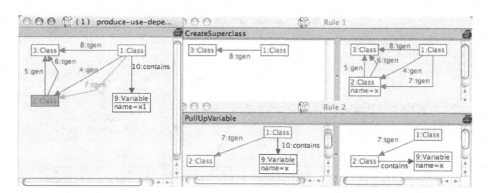

programs. Both kinds of artifacts are represented by their abstract syntax structures. Synchronized rules are defined to specify not only refactoring on models and programs separately, but to update also the correlation between different model parts and program. Synchronized rules are applied in parallel to keep coherence between model and program. Considering the special case where exactly two parts (one model diagram and the program or two model diagrams) are related, the triple graph grammar (TGG) approach could also be used (Schürr 1994; Königs & Schürr 2006). Originally formulated for graphs, TGGs are also defined and performed on the basis of MOF models by the modeling environment MOFLON[7].

(Porres, 2003) uses the transformation language SMW to specify model refactorings. This script language is also rule-based and resembles the Object Constraint Language (OCL). SMW is oriented at OCL for querying patterns, but also provides basic operations to realize transformations. A prototypical refactoring tool for UML models has been implemented based on SMW.

Van Der Straeten & D'Hondt (2006) suggest using a rule-based approach to apply model refactorings, based on an underlying inconsistency detection and resolution mechanism implemented in the description logics engine RACER[8].

We decided to specify model refactorings based on EMF model transformation, since EMF is developing to a standard format for models and to be compatible with upcoming UML CASE tools based on EMF. Moreover, our approach opens up the possibility for analyzing model refactorings, since EMF model transformations can be translated to algebraic graph transformations.

SUMMARY

Software complexity is constantly increasing, and can only be tamed by raising the level of abstraction from code to models. With the model-driven software engineering paradigm, automated code generation techniques can be used to hide the accidental complexity of the underlying technology (Brooks, 1995). This enables one to deal with complex software in a systematic way.

To guarantee high-quality software, it is also important to address concerns such as readability, extensibility, reusability and usability of software.

Software refactoring is a proven technique to reach these goals in a structured, semi-automated manner.

By integrating the process of refactoring into model-driven software development, we arrive at what we call *model-driven software refactoring*. Analogously to program refactoring, the first phase is to determine potential candidates for model refactorings, which can be obtained using "model smells" and "model metrics". The second phase consists of applying the selected refactorings. This would be a relatively straightforward issue, if hundred-percent code generation were achievable. In practice, for large and complex software systems, this is not the case. Full code generation is not even desirable in many situations since – at least for describing algorithms or data conversions – source code seems to be more adequate than behavioral models. An additional difficulty is the lack of a general accepted semantics of UML. This makes it very difficult to determine whether a given model transformation is behavior preserving, which is the main criterion to decide whether something can be called refactoring or not, according to Fowler (1999).

As a feasibility study, we have chosen AndroMDA to illustrate the model-driven development of web applications. We illustrated and discussed a number of standard and domain-specific restructurings. Since they often change the observable behavior of the software in some sense, we explored to what extent they can be considered as refactorings. All restructurings were categorized into three groups, ordered by the fulfillment degree of Fowler's criterion. The obtained results show that we should address the notion of model refactoring with care, and may serve as suggestions for better tool support:

- We may want to support refactorings that do not fully preserve behavior, as long as they improve other important software quality aspects. This also implies that we need

techniques to assess the effect of a model transformation on the software quality.
- We need to find a balance between, and provide user support for the ability to specify generic model refactorings, and the ability to adapt and refine these refactorings to work properly in a domain-specific modeling language;
- We need to provide an interactive round-trip engineering approach to refactoring. When performing model refactorings, it turns out that manual intervention is frequently required in order to keep the abstraction levels of *source code* and *model* consistent. Model refactorings may also affect and require changes to the hand-written source code.

From a theoretical point of view, we have suggested to use graph transformation to provide a formal specification of model refactorings. It has the advantage of defining refactorings in a generic way, while still being able to provide tool support in commonly accepted modeling environments such as EMF. In addition, the theory of graph transformation allows us to formally reason about dependencies between different types of refactorings. Such a static analysis of potential conflicts and dependencies between refactorings can be helpful for the user during the interactive process of trying to improve the software quality by means of disciplined model transformations.

FUTURE RESEARCH DIRECTIONS

In Section 4, we identified many important challenges in model-driven software refactoring. We only worked out some of these challenges in more detail: the need for a formal specification of model refactorings, the need to reason about behavior preservation, the need to synchronize models and source code whilst applying refactorings, the need to relate and integrate the aspects of model refactoring and model quality. There are still many other challenges that remain largely unaddressed:

When developing large software systems in a model-driven manner, several development teams might be involved. In this case, it would be advantageous if the model could be subdivided into several parts that could be developed in a distributed way. Considering refactoring in this setting, model elements from different submodels might be involved. Thus, several distributed refactoring steps have to be performed and potentially synchronized if they involve common model parts. Distributed refactoring steps could be considered as distributed model transformations (Goedicke *et al.*, 1999; Bottoni *et al.*, 2005).

The usual way to test refactorings is by testing the code before and after refactoring steps. Clearly, the code has to satisfy the same test cases before and after refactoring it. Considering refactoring within model-driven development, the same testing procedure should be possible, i.e., test cases for the generated code before and after refactoring should produce the same results. As we discussed within this chapter, model-driven software refactoring often does not fulfill Fowler's criterion in a stringent way. Future investigations should clarify the impact of this kind of restructuring on test suites (Van Deursen *et al.*, 2002).

An important pragmatic challenge that has not been addressed in this chapter has to do with performance and scalability. Is it possible to come up with solutions that scale up to industrial software? Egyed (2006) provided initial evidence that this is actually the case, by providing an instant model synchronization approach that scales up to large industrial software models.

Another interesting research direction is to apply refactorings at the meta-model level. This raises the additional difficulty of needing to convert all models that conform to this meta-model accordingly, preferably in an automated way.

REFERENCES

Astels, D. (2002). Refactoring with UML. In M. Marchesi, G. Succi (Eds.), *Proceedings of 3rd International Conference eXtreme Programming and Flexible Processes in Software Engineering* (pp. 67-70), Alghero, Italy.

Biermann, E., Ehrig, K., Köhler, C., Taentzer, G., & Weiss, E. (2006). Graphical Definition of In-Place Transformations in the Eclipse Modeling Framework. In O. Nierstrasz (Ed.), *Proceedings of International Conference on Model Driven Engineering Languages and Systems* (pp. 425-439), Lecture Notes in Computer Science 4199, Heidelberg: Springer.

Boger, M., Sturm, T., & Fragemann, P. (2002). Refactoring Browser for UML. In M. Marchesi, G. Succi (Eds.), *Proceedings 3rd International Conference on eXtreme Programming and Flexible Processes in Software Engineering* (pp. 77-81), Alghero, Italy.

Bottoni, P., Parisi-Presicce, F., Mason, G., & Taentzer, G. (2005). Specifying Coherent Refactoring of Software Artefacts with Distributed Graph Transformations. In P. van Bommel (Ed.), *Handbook on Transformation of Knowledge, Information, and Data: Theory and Applications* (pp. 95-125). Hershey, PA: Information Science Publishing.

Bouden, S. (2006). *Étude de la traçabilité entre refactorisations du modèle de classes et refactorisations du code*. Unpublished masters dissertation, Université de Montréal, Canada.

Brooks, F. P. (1995). No Silver Bullet: Essence and accidents of software engineering. In *The Mythical Man-Month: Essays on Software Engineering, 20th Anniversary Edition*. Reading, MA: Addison-Wesley.

Brottier, E., Fleurey, F., & Le Traon, Y. (2006). Metamodel-based Test Generation for Model Transformations: an Algorithm and a Tool. In

Proceedings 17th International Symposium on Reliability Engineering (pp. 85-94), IEEE Computer Society.

Correa, A., & Werner, C. (2004). Applying Refactoring Techniques to UML/OCL Models. In *Proceedings International Conference UML 2004* (pp. 173-187), Lecture Notes in Computer Science 3273, Heidelberg: Springer.

Demeyer, S., Ducasse, S., & Nierstrasz, O. (2000). Finding Refactorings Via Change Metrics. In *Proceedings International Conference OOPSLA 2000* (pp. 166-177). ACM SIGPLAN Notices 35(10), ACM Press.

Du Bois, B. (2006). *Quality-Oriented Refactoring*. Unpublished doctoral dissertation, Universiteit Antwepen, Belgium.

Egyed, A. (2006). Instant consistency checking for the UML. In *Proc. International Conference on Software Engineering* (pp. 31-390), ACM.

Ehrig, H, Ehrig, K. Prange, U. & Taentzer, G. (2006). *Fundamental Approach to Graph Transformation*. EATCS Monographs, Heidelberg: Springer.

Ehrig, H., Tsioalikis, A. (2000). Consistency analysis of UML class and sequence diagrams using attributed graph grammars. In *ETAPS 2000 workshop on graph transformation systems* (pp. 77-86).

Fenton, N., & Pfleeger, S. L. (1997). *Software Metrics: A Rigorous and Practical Approach* (2nd edition). London, UK: International Thomson Computer Press.

Fowler, M. (1999) *Refactoring: Improving the Design of Existing Code*. Addison-Wesley.

Gamma, E., Helm, R., Johnson, R., & Vlissides, J. (1994). *Design Patterns: Elements of Reusable Object-Oriented Languages and Systems*. Addison-Wesley.

Gheyi, R., Massoni, T., & Borba, P. (2005). A Rigorous Approach for Proving Model Refactorings. In *Proceedings 20th IEEE/ACM International Conference Automated Software Engineering* (pp. 372-375). IEEE Computer Society.

Gheyi, R., Massoni, T., & Borba, P. (2005). Type-safe Refactorings for Alloy. In *Proceedings 8th Brazilian Symposium on Formal Methods* (pp. 174-190). Porto Alegre, Brazil.

Goedicke, M., Meyer, T., & Taentzer, G. (1999). Viewpoint-oriented software development by distributed graph transformation: Towards a basis for living with inconsistencies. In *Proceedings International Conference Requirements Engineering* (pp. 92-99). IEEE Computer Society.

Grundy, J. C., Hosking, J.G., & Mugridge W. B. (1998). Inconsistency Management for Multiple-View Software Development Environments, IEEE *Transactions on Software Engineering*, 24(11), 960-981.

Grunske, L., Geiger, L., Zündorf, A., Van Eetvelde, N., Van Gorp, P., & Varro, D. (2005). Using Graph Transformation for Practical Model Driven Software Engineering. In S. Beydeda, M. Book, & V. Gruhn (Eds.), *Model-driven Software Development* (pp. 91-118). Heidelberg: Springer.

Kamthan, P. (2004). A Framework for Addressing the Quality of UML Artifacts. *Studies in Communication Sciences*, 4(2), 85-114.

Kerievsky, J. (2004). *Refactoring to Patterns*. Addison-Wesley.

Königs, A. & Schürr, A. (2006). Tool Integration with Triple Graph Grammars - A Survey . In R. Heckel (Ed.), *Proceedings of the SegraVis School on Foundations of Visual Modelling Techniques* (pp. 113-150). Electronic Notes in Theoretical Computer Science 148, Amsterdam: Elsevier.

Lehman, M. M., Ramil, J. F., Wernick, P. D., Perry D. E., & Turski, W. M. (1997). Metrics and laws of software evolution: The nineties view.

In *Proceedings of International Symposium on Software Metrics* (pp. 20-32). IEEE Computer Society Press.

Liu, W., Easterbrook, S., & Mylopoulos, J. (2002). Rule-based detection of inconsistency in UML models. In *Proceedings UML Workshop on Consistency Problems in UML-based Software Development* (pp. 106-123). Blekinge Insitute of Technology.

Markovic, S., & Baar, T. (2005). Refactoring OCL Annotated UML Class Diagrams. In L. Briand, C. Williams (Eds.), *Proceedings International Conference Model Driven Engineering Languages and Systems* (pp. 280-294). Lecture Notes in Computer Science 3713, Heidelberg: Springer

Mens, T. (2006). On the use of graph transformations for model refactoring. In *Generative and Transformational Techniques in Software Engineering* (pp. 219-257). Lecture Notes in Computer Science 4143, Heidelberg: Springer.

Mens, T., & Tourwé, T. (2004). A Survey of Software Refactoring. IEEE *Transactions on Software Engineering*, 30(2), 126-162.

Mens, T., Van Eetvelde, N., Demeyer, S., & Janssens, D. (2005). Formalizing refactorings with graph transformations. *Journal on Software Maintenance and Evolution*, 17(4), 247-276.

Mens, T., Van Der Straeten, R., & D'Hondt, M. (2006). Detecting and resolving model inconsistencies using transformation dependency analysis, In O. Nierstrasz (Ed.), *Proceedings International Conference on Model-Driven Engineering Languages and Systems* (pp. 200-214). Lecture Notes in Computer Science 4199, Heidelberg: Springer.

Mens, T., Taentzer, G., & Runge, O. (2007). Analyzing Refactoring Dependencies Using Graph Transformation. *Journal on Software and Systems Modeling*, 6(3), 269-285.

Mottu, J.-M., Baudry, B., & Le Traon, Y. (2006). Mutation Analysis Testing for Model Transformations. In *Proceedings 2ⁿᵈ European Conference on Model Driven Architecture – Foundations and Applications* (pp. 376-390). Lecture Notes in Computer Science 4066, Heidelberg: Springer.

Parnas, D.L. (1994). Software Aging. In *Proceedings of International Conference on Software Engineering* (pp. 279-287). IEEE Computer Society Press.

Porres, I. (2003). Model refactorings as rule-based update transformations. In: P. Stevens, J. Whittle, G. Booch (Eds.), In *Proceedings of 6ᵗʰ International Conference UML 2003 - The Unified Modeling Language. Model Languages and Applications* (pp. 159-174). Lecture Notes in Computer Science 2863, Heidelberg: Springer.

Pretschner, A., & Prenninger, A. (2007). Computing Refactorings of State Machines, *Journal on Software and Systems Modeling*. To appear.

Schürr, A. (1994). Specification of Graph Translators with Triple Graph Grammars. In: G. Tinhofer (Ed.), *WG94 20th International Workshop on Graph-Theoretic Concepts in Computer Science* (pp. 151-163). Lecture Notes in Computer Science 903, Heidelberg: Springer.

Spanoudakis, G., & Zisman, A. (2001). Inconsistency management in software engineering: Survey and open research issues. In *Handbook of Software Engineering and Knowledge Engineering* (pp. 329-80). World Scientific

Sunyé, G., Pollet, D., Le Traon, Y., & Jézéquel, J.-M. (2001). Refactoring UML models, In *Proceedings International Conference Unified Modeling Language* (pp. 134-138). Lecture Notes in Computer Science 2185, Heidelberg: Springer.

Tahvildari, L., & Kontogiannis, K. (2004). Improving Design Quality Using Meta-Pattern Transformations: A Metric-Based Approach, *Journal of Software Maintenance and Evolution*, 16(4-5), 331-361.

van Deursen, A., & Moonen, L. (2002). The Video Store Revisited: Thoughts on Refactoring and Testing, In M. Marchesi, G. Succi (Eds.), *Proceedings 3rd International Conference on Extreme Programming and Flexible Processes in Software Engineering* (pp. 71-76). Alghero, Italy.

van Deursen, A., Moonen, L., van den Bergh, A., & Kok, G. (2002). Refactoring Test Code, In G. Succi, M. Marchesi, D. Wells, & L. Williams (Eds.), *Extreme Programming Perspectives* (pp. 141-152). Addison-Wesley.

Van Der Straeten, R. (2005). *Inconsistency Management in Model-driven Engineering: An Approach using Description Logics.* Unpublished doctoral dissertation, Vrije Universiteit Brussel, Belgium.

Van Der Straeten, R., & D'Hondt, M. (2006). Model refactorings through rule-based inconsistency resolution. In *Proceedings Symposium on Applied computing* (pp. 1210-1217). New York: ACM Press

Van Der Straeten, R., Mens, T., Simmonds, J., & Jonckers, V. (2003). Using description logics to maintain consistency between UML models. In *Proceedings International Conference on The Unified Modeling Language* (pp. 326-340). Lecture Notes in Computer Science 2863, Heidelberg: Springer.

Van Der Straeten, R., Jonckers, V., & Mens, T. (2004). Supporting Model Refactorings through Behaviour Inheritance Consistencies. In T. Baar, A. Strohmeier, & A. Moreira (Eds.), *Proceedings of International Conference on The Unified Modeling Language* (pp. 305-319). Lecture Notes in Computer Science 3273, Heidelberg: Springer.

Van Gorp, P., Stenten, H., Mens, T., & Demeyer, S. (2003). Towards automating source-consistent UML refactorings. In P. Stevens & J. Whittle & G. Booch (Eds.), *Proceedings International Conference on The Unified Modeling Language* (pp. 144-158). Lecture Notes in Computer Science 2863, Heidelberg: Springer.

Van Kempen, M., Chaudron, M., Koudrie, D., & Boake, A. (2005). Towards Proving Preservation of Behaviour of Refactoring of UML Models. In *Proceedings SAICSIT 2005* (pp. 111-118).

Zhang, J., Lin, Y., & Gray, J. (2005). Generic and Domain-Specific Model Refactoring using a Model Transformation Engine. In *Model-driven Software Development - Research and Practice in Software Engineering.* Springer.

ADDITIONAL READING

General and up-to-date information about **graph transformation** *can be obtained via the website http://www.gratra.org/. For those readers wishing to get more in-depth information about what graph transformation is all about, we refer to the 3-volume "bible" of graph transformation research. Volume 1 focuses on its theoretical foundations; Volume 2 addresses applications, languages and tools; and Volume 3 deals with concurrency, parallelism and distribution.*

Rozenberg, G. (1997). *Handbook of Graph Grammars and Computing by Graph Transformation, Volume 1.* World Scientific.

Ehrig, H., Engels, G., Kreowski, H.-J., & Rozenberg G. (1999). *Handbook of Graph Grammars and Computing by Graph Transformation, Volume 2.* World Scientific.

Ehrig, H., Kreowski, H.-J., Montanari, U., & Rozenberg, G. (1999). *Handbook of Graph Grammars and Computing by Graph Transformation, Volume 3,* World Scientific.

Background information about **model-driven software engineering** *can be obtained via the website http://www.planetmde.org/. This includes*

tool support and events devoted to this very active research domain. Many books on this topic have been published. In particular, we found the following ones to be very useful and relevant:

Beydeda, S., Book, M., & Gruhn, V. (2005). *Model-Driven Software Development*, Springer.

Stahl, T., & Völter, M. (2006). *Model-Driven Software Development*, Wiley.

With respect to **software evolution** *research, we suggest to consult the website http://www.planet-evolution.org/. Many books on this topic have been published. In particular, we found the following ones to be very useful and relevant:*

Grubb, P., & Takang, A.A. (2003). *Software Maintenance: Concepts and Practice* (Second Edition). World Scientific.

Madhavji, N. H., Fernandez-Ramil, J., & Perry, D. (2006). *Software Evolution and Feedback: Theory and Practice*. Wiley.

Mens, T., & Demeyer, S. (2008). *Software Evolution*. Springer.

Seacord, R., Plakosh, D. & Lewis, G. (2003). *Modernizing Legacy Systems: Software Technologies, Engineering Processes, and Business Practices* (SEI Series in Software Engineering). Addison-Wesley.

Regarding **software refactoring** *in particular, we would like to point to some of the early work on refactoring, which has been published in the following PhD dissertations:*

Griswold, W.G. (1991). *Program Restructuring as an Aid to Software Maintenance*. Unpublished doctoral dissertation, University of Washington.

Opdyke, W.F. (1992). *Refactoring: A Program Restructuring Aid in Designing Object-Oriented Application Frameworks*. Unpublished doctoral dissertation, University of Illinois at Urbana-Champaign.

Roberts, D. (1999). *Practical Analysis for Refactoring*. Unpublished doctoral dissertation, University of Illinois at Urbana-Champaign.

O Cinnéide, M. (2000). *Automated Application of Design Patterns: A Refactoring Approach*. Unpublished doctoral dissertation, Trinity College, University of Dublin.

Tichelaar, S. (2001). *Modeling Object-Oriented Software for Reverse Engineering and Refactoring*. Unpublished doctoral dissertation, University of Bern.

There are many useful standards that have been published for software maintenance and software evolution. As is frequently the case, some of these standards may be somewhat outdated compared to the current state-of-the-art in research:

The ISO/IEC 14764 standard on ``Software Maintenance'' (1999)

The IEEE 1219 standard on ``Software Maintenance'' (1999)

The ISO/IEC 12207 standard (and its amendments) on ``Information Technology - Software Life Cycle Processes'' (1995)

The ANSI/IEEE 1042 standard on ``Software Configuration Management'' (1987)

ENDNOTES

[1] http://galaxy.andromda.org

[2] This model refactoring is actually domain-

specific, as will be discussed later in this chapter.

3   Of course, programs also need to be synchronized with related software artefacts such as databases, user interfaces, test suites and so on. Each of these kinds of artefacts may have been expressed using a different language.

4   It is not our goal to be complete here.

5   http://tfs.cs.tu-berlin.de/agg

6   http://www.fujaba.de

7   http://www.moflon.org

8   http://www.racer-systems.com

Chapter IX
A Pattern Approach to Increasing the Maturity Level of Class Models

Michael Wahler
IBM Zurich Research Laboratory, Switzerland

ABSTRACT

Class models are typically specified at a high level of abstraction and subsequently refined with textual constraints to obtain higher maturity levels. This task requires significant expertise and effort because constraints must be elicited and formalized. In this chapter, we identify typical refinement problems for class models that threaten model quality and show how a list of refinement tasks can be automatically compiled from a given model. We present constraint patterns that help to carry out these tasks semi-automatically and introduce a tool prototype for our approach.

INTRODUCTION

Models have been used in software engineering for illustration and documentation purposes for a long time. In the past few years, model-driven development approaches such as Model-Driven Engineering (MDE) have become popular, and with these approaches, models have enormously gained importance. Still used for illustration, models now also serve as semantic foundation for the development of whole systems in certain domains: they are abstract representations of vari-

ous aspects of a system and drive the development process. This new role requires a certain degree of formality for the syntax and the semantics of models: Whereas it was sufficient for the syntax and the semantics to be intuitively understandable in the age of "models-as-illustrations", they need to be formally specified in the MDE age because they are the basis of the generated code.

In MDE, the abstract syntax of a modeling language is defined by a meta-model, which is usually a class model that graphically specifies the elements of a modeling language, such as classes and their properties, and the dependencies between these elements. The dependencies between classes are especially important in this refinement: Since each model that complies with its meta-model must be a valid abstraction of the system, the dependencies between elements in the model must be precisely captured in the meta-model. Whereas these dependencies can only be coarsely constrained within the graphical model itself, textual constraint languages such as the Object Constraint Language (OCL) (Object Management Group (OMG), 2003) are used to express details about the dependencies.

Adding textual constraints to a class model rules out invalid instances, which increases the maturity level of the class model (Kleppe and Warmer, 2003). For visualizing this idea, we use a function I that maps a set of concepts to the set of all possible objects for these concepts. In particular, I(M) denotes the set of all objects in all possible instances of a model M and I(R) denotes the set of all possible objects in a real system. Figure 1 a) visualizes a model M with a low maturity level: A large part of I(M) is not inside I(R), i.e., I(M) contains many elements that are not representations of the real system. By adding constraints to M, a model M' can be developed with a higher maturity level. Figure 1 b) shows that there are less elements in the set I(M') − I(R), which means that significantly less invalid

instances can be derived from M' than from M. Thus, M' has a higher maturity level than M.

In this chapter, we focus on increasing the maturity level of models as one important quality aspect. Thus, the aim of this chapter is to identify a number of causes for low maturity levels of models in early stages of development, show how these causes can be found in a given model, and offer solutions to refine the model and increase its maturity level. We focus on reducing the size of I(M)−I(R) and provide general guidelines for creating class models of a high maturity level and thus, a high quality.

In order to refine a given class model, it must be thoroughly *analyzed* by the model developer. However, not all causes for low maturity may be detected manually, which can cause serious problems in the MDE process because the generated code may cause runtime exceptions. To simplify and partly automate *model analysis*, we have identified recurring problems in class models that require refinement by textual constraints. The first objective of this chapter is to present these problems, show examples of how they threaten the maturity of class models, and introduce tool support for their automatic detection.

Having identified these problems, constraints can be formulated that restrict the expressiveness and increase the maturity of the model. However, this is not an easy task: Besides theoretical and

Figure 1. Visualization of model maturity levels

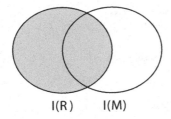

(a) Model *M*: Low maturity level.

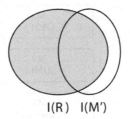

(b) Model *M'*: High maturity level.

practical arguments that point out various deficiencies of OCL (Chiorean et al., 2005, Süß, 2006, Cabot, 2006, Brucker et al., 2006), one important aspect needs to be taken into account: Class models can express complicated facts, including subtyping, reflexive relations, or potentially infinitely large instances, and constraining such facts requires addressing this complexity. To simplify the creation of constraints, the second objective of this chapter is using constraint patterns, which are predefined constraint expressions that can be parameterized. In particular, we present constraint patterns that can be instantiated to remedy the recurring problems that we have identified. Furthermore, we present how constraint patterns can be coupled with the analysis results to enable instant refinement.

This chapter is structured as follows. In Section 2, we provide background information on the Meta Object Facility (MOF), OCL, constraint patterns, and give an overview of related work. By analyzing MOF, we identify typical problems that require refinement in Section 3 and present examples to illustrate the potential dangers of low model maturity. In Section 4, we show how constraint patterns can be used to increase maturity and present tool support for our approach in Section 5. In Section 6, we draw conclusions, and we give an outlook on future research directions in Section 7.

BACKGROUND

In this section, we provide background information for the remainder of this chapter and give an overview of related work.

Meta Object Facility (MOF)

The MOF (OMG, 2006a) is a standard that defines the building blocks of modeling. Its core, the Essential MOF (EMOF), defines the facilities that are commonly found in object-oriented approaches such as types, classes, properties, and operations. Thus, it can be considered as the core of Unified Modeling Language (UML) class models, and the results of this chapter on MOF apply to UML class models as well.

MOF defines a hierarchy of model abstractions, which can comprise up to four layers (Atkinson and Kühne, 2003). In general, a model in layer n is called an instance of the model in layer $n+1$, which in turn is called its meta-model. In Figure 2, we illustrate these four modeling layers.

The most abstract layer, commonly perceived as M3, is the MOF meta-model, as shown in Figure 3. It defines the core modeling concepts and is defined recursively, i.e., a model on this layer is an instance of itself (Seidewitz, 2003). In contrast, the most concrete layer M0 represents the elements of the concrete system. For instance,

Figure 2. The four modeling layers of MOF

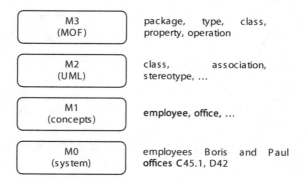

M3 (MOF)	package, type, class, property, operation
M2 (UML)	class, association, stereotype, ...
M1 (concepts)	employee, office, ...
M0 (system)	employees Boris and Paul offices C45.1, D42

Figure 3. Extract of the EMOF meta-model

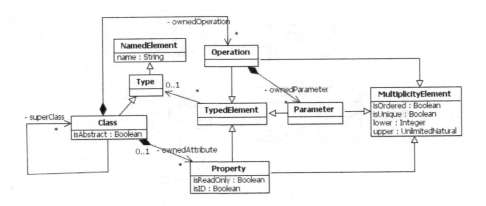

the model of a company could comprise elements such as an employee called "Boris" and an office labeled "C45.1". The models in layer M0 are instances of the models in layer M1, in which the concepts of a system are defined. In a company, examples of such concepts are classes such as Employee or Office. These concepts are defined using the MOF layer M3 as meta-model. Alternatively, another meta-modeling layer M2 can be used. A prominent example of an M2-layer model is the UML meta-model for class models, which defines modeling elements such as n-ary associations or stereotypes (OMG, 2006b).

In Figure 4, we illustrate an example M1-model company that is an instance of MOF. The elements in this model are instances of MOF elements, i.e., we use the MOF meta-model for both layers M2 and M3. In detail, the elements are defined as follows. Employee, Manager, Office, Single and Cubicle are instances of the MOF concept Class; name, salary, budget, headCount, isCEO, desks, employs, worksFor, inhabitant and worksIn are MOF Propertys, and they are used for defining associations between classes, which reflect relations between objects; String, Integer and Boolean are MOF types; hire is a MOF Operation of type Boolean; e is a MOF Parameter; 1..*, 0..1 and

* are MOF MultiplicityElements; and the generalization relations between Manager and Employee and Single/Cubicle and Office are instances of the MOF superClass relation.

In general, an instance of a model is defined by a set OID of object identifiers and a partial function A: OID×P9VAL that maps an object identifier o 2 OID and a property p 2 P of the object's class to a set of values. A binary relation R between objects o1 and o2 is represented by two properties p1, p2 with A(o1, p2) = o2 and A(o2, p1) = o1. A model instance can be considered as an object graph in which the nodes are the object identifiers and the edges are the relations between them.

Object Constraint Language (OCL)

MOF offers only limited support for defining the concepts of a model or a system. Whereas entities and basic relations can be described in terms of types, classes and their properties, relations and dependencies can be further specified by basic multiplicity (i.e., cardinality) constraints only. In order to express complex relations and restrictions in a model, OCL has been introduced (OMG, 2003), a textual constraint language for

Figure 4. Model "company": example instance of MOF

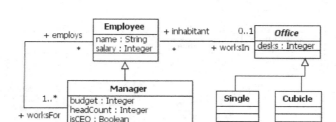

object-oriented modeling languages such as MOF or UML.

OCL is a first-order logic (FOL) with object-oriented extensions (Beckert et al., 2002). It serves two purposes: First, invariants can be specified for classes. An invariant is a predicate that holds for all instances of the constrained class. Second, contracts can be specified for operations, which consist of a precondition that restricts the applicability and a postcondition that describes the result of the operation. A detailed introduction to OCL and a reference manual can be found in (Kleppe and Warmer, 2003).

In the following, we illustrate some examples of invariants and operation contracts for the company model. The invariant for single offices restricts the inhabitants of these offices to objects of class Manager. The invariant for Manager states that the budget must not be negative. The precondition of hire requires that the employee who is supposed to be hired is not already employed, while the postcondition requires that after the operation has executed, the set of employees is the same as before the execution, except for the new employee who has joined this set. See Exhibit 1.

There are different ways of providing support for constraint checking in the generated code. This is not subject of this chapter and we therefore refer the reader to (Kleppe and Warmer, 2003)

in which a transformation from OCL to Java is discussed.

Constraint Patterns

In general, patterns describe generic solutions to recurring problems in a certain domain that can be reapplied to instances of the same problem. With the success of the object-oriented development paradigm, patterns have gained increasing momentum in software engineering. The most prominent publication, the "gang-of-four" (GOF) book on design patterns (Gamma et al., 1995), introduces a taxonomy of patterns for the construction of object-oriented software. Each pattern is presented with a name, classification, intent, structure, example, and other properties that describe its syntax, semantics, and pragmatics.

Patterns have also become popular in other areas of software engineering, such as software architecture (Buschmann et al., 1996), formal specification (Dwyer et al., 1998), or workflow design (van der Aalst et al., 2003). Recent publications have introduced constraint patterns that can be instantiated to constrain models (Ackermann and Turowski, 2006, Ahrendt et al., 2005, Costal et al., 2006, Miliauskaitė and Nemuraitė, 2005, Wah-ler et al., 2007).

Constraint patterns are parameterizable expressions in a logic such as OCL. An illustrative

Exhibit 1.

```
context Single
inv onlyManagers: self.inhabitant->forAll(x | x.oclIsTypeOf(Manager))

context Manager
inv budgetGreaterZero: self.budget >= 0


context Manager::hire(e: Employee): Boolean
pre: not self.employs->includes(e)
post: self.employs = self.employs@pre->including(e)
```

Exhibit 2.

```
pattern MultiplicityRestriction(navigation: Sequence(Property), operator: OclExpression,
                                value:OclExpression) =
   self.navigation->size() operator value
```

Exhibit 3.

```
context Office
inv sufficientDesks: self.inhabitant->size() <= self.desks
```

example is the *MultiplicityRestriction* pattern from (Wahler et al., 2007), which can be instantiated to constrain the number of elements in a relation. It is defined as shown in Exhibit 2.

Upon instantiation, the parameters of a pattern, which are printed *in italics* above, are replaced with actual values. An example constraint that can be expressed using this pattern is the following invariant for the company model: "An office must not be inhabited by more employees than there are desks in the office," which can be expressed in OCL as shown in Exhibit 3.

Instead of specifying the invariant in OCL, which is time-consuming and error-prone, we use the *MultiplicityRestriction* pattern. The following constraint expression replaces the parameter *navigation* with the property inhabitant and the parameter *value* with the property desks. See Exhibit 4.

In the literature, numerous constraint patterns have been defined. A comprehensive collection of patterns can be found in (Wahler et al., 2007) in which a taxonomy of constraint patterns is presented. The taxonomy comprises a set of atomic or elementary patterns as shown in Figure 5, to which we added the patterns that we introduce in this chapter. To simplify model refinement, users can choose and instantiate appropriate patterns from such taxonomies and use them in their constraint specifications. In the same paper, composite constraint patterns are introduced, i.e., higher-order patterns to logically combine pattern instances. Using composite patterns, complex constraints can be developed by composing elementary constraints. Elementary constraints are either instances of constraint patterns or literal OCL expressions. Thus, composite constraint patterns increase the expressiveness of the constraint

Exhibit 4.

```
context Office
inv sufficientDesks: MultiplicityRestriction(inhabitant, '<=', 'desks')
```

Figure 5. An example taxonomy of constraint patterns

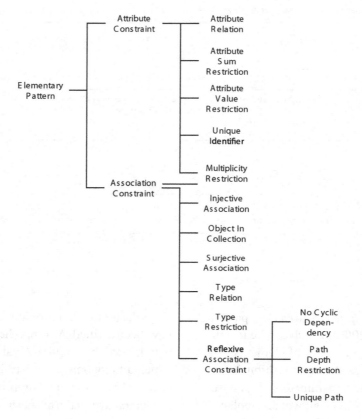

language. For example, the *IfThenElse* pattern allows one to model implication by selecting a set of elementary constraints as assumption (if) and one constraint each as conclusion (then) and alternative (else). See Exhibit 5.

We have prototypically implemented constraint patterns using the patterns framework of IBM Rational Software Architect (RSA) (IBM, 2007). Figure 6 shows a screenshot of how the constraint *sufficientDesks* is implemented in our

framework. Here, the pattern instance is represented by a rectangular box surrounded by a dashed line. The parameters and their actual values are listed in a table inside the pattern instance.

Related Work

In (Crosby, 1979), quality is defined as "conformance to requirements". We apply this definition

Exhibit 5.

```
pattern IfThenElse(assumption:Set(Constraint), conclusion:Constraint,
                   alternative:Constraint) =

if assumption
then conclusion
else alternative
endif
```

Figure 6. Constraint sufficientDesks as represented in RSA

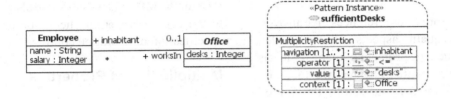

to class modeling by first defining the requirements for class models. On the one hand, class models must contain appropriate elements to express facts of the system modeled, i.e., coverage, and on the other hand, they must be specific enough such that models that represent valid facts of the system only can be modeled. Different kinds of models require different degrees of abstraction, e.g., analysis models are usually less detailed than design models. In general, models can have a high degree of abstraction and thus, a low maturity level at the beginning of an MDE process, but in the course of the process, they must be refined to achieve a higher level of maturity, and thus, quality.

Whereas quality assessment is well-established in software development (Chrissis et al., 2003, Schulmeyer and Mcmanus, 1999, Kan, 2002), it is a fairly new aspect in MDE, but has become an important topic, as addressed by the workshop "Quality in Modeling" (Kuzniarz et al., 2006). One of the papers presented in this workshop experimentally investigates the effect of using modeling conventions on the quality of a model (Bois et al., 2006) by evaluating a test group's perception of syntactic, semantic, and pragmatic aspects of test models. In (Lange and Chaudron, 2006), several threats to the quality of a model are identified and a survey is conducted on how easily such defects can be identified. In (Gamma et al., 1995), model quality is addressed indirectly by providing design patterns for class models in general. Patterns reflect best practices, and employing patterns in a model thus increases the overall quality of the model.

The quality of meta-models, which are typically specified in terms of class models, is discussed in (www.metamodel.com, 2007). The aspects scope, technical quality, extensibility, and quality of definitions of the documentation are defined and guidelines are given how class models can be created that are good in the respective aspect. In (Gitzel and Hildenbrand, 2005), different hierarchies of meta-modeling are illustrated. The quality of the hierarchies is evaluated according to their complexity, consistency, expressional strength, extensibility, and robustness to change. In (Davis and Bigelow, 2002), the quality criteria are goodness of fit, parsimony, identification of critical components, relative importance of model elements, and a good storyline. In this approach, a meta-model is derived from large models using statistical methods. An orthogonal aspect of meta-model quality is addressed in (Atkinson and Kühne, 2001) in which the problem of multi-level meta-model hierarchies are discussed and problems of frameworks such as MOF are pointed out.

Whereas the previous references give an overview of various quality aspects of a meta-model, they merely touch the problem of maturity levels of class models. In this chapter, we focus on identifying low maturity caused by the limited expressiveness of the MOF meta-model and show how models can be semi-automatically refined by using an automatic analysis and constraint patterns.

INCREASING CLASS-MODEL MATURITY LEVELS

As shown, only few restrictions on model instances can be applied by means of the graphical elements of a class model. In this section, we present limitations of the expressiveness of the MOF meta-model that typically require MOF-based class models to be refined with textual constraints. In the following, we present a list of the limitations we have identified, in which the term context denotes the objects and the values of their properties in a model instance:

1. The lower and upper multiplicity bounds of a MultiplicityElement cannot be related to its context,
2. the type of a TypedElement cannot be related to its context,
3. properties can cause reflexive relations, which can have side-effects that cannot be restricted,

4. the unique identifier for a class can only consist of a single Property, and
5. the value of a Property cannot be related to its context.

For each of these limitations, we show example object diagrams demonstrating that the expressiveness of the respective MOF elements is not sufficient for precise modeling and present OCL constraints necessary for restricting these examples. We focus on invariants, but our findings for the MOF class Property can also be applied to the class Parameter and hence be used in the specification of operation contracts.

Multiplicities of Properties

In MOF, relations between objects of two classes C1 and C2 are modeled using a property that is owned by C1 and is of type C2. Since Property is a MultiplicityElement (Figure 3), properties have a lower and an upper bound for the multiplicity, i.e., the cardinality of the domain of the relation. The lower bound reflects the minimum number and the upper bound reflects the maximum number of objects that need to be in the domain of the relation. As shown in Figure 3, the lower and upper boundary can be either a natural number or arbitrarily large, represented by the symbol *.

The upper multiplicity of an association is often unbound (*) because in most systems, the number of elements in a relation is not restricted to a fixed literal value. For instance, we used an unbound multiplicity for all associations in the company model (Figure 4), except for the property worksIn of Employee, because an employee can be related to at most one office in our system.

However, an unspecified number of elements in a relation can potentially cause a low maturity level of the model. In the company model, the employment relation is an example of low maturity: It allows managers to employ any natural number of employees and every employee may work for arbitrarily many managers (but at least

Figure 7. Two employees despite a maximum head count of 1

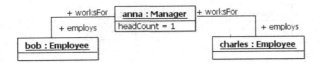

one). In the following, we present two cases in which this limited way of defining multiplicities in MOF causes low model maturity.

Multiplicities depending on an attribute value. In class Manager, we modeled an attribute headCount, which denotes the maximum number of employees that a manager can employ. MOF does not provide means to specify that the number of employees in the employment relation depends on the value of headCount. Therefore, the instance in Figure 7 is valid: Although anna has a maximum head count of one, she can employ two employees.

Since the instance shown in Figure 7 cannot be excluded in terms of the MOF meta-model, an OCL constraint is required that restricts the employment relation depending on the value of the headCount attribute. If the company model is annotated with the following invariant *headCountRestriction*, the instance shown above is invalid.

Context-unaware association semantics. Associations represent relations between classes. Often, associations are created with a certain semantics in mind, but the semantics is not specified. The relation between Employee and Manager in Figure 8 shows variables as lower and upper multiplicity bounds. The values for these variables determine the semantics of the relation. The relation can be a function ($x1=0$, $y1=*$, $x2=0$, $y2=1$), a total function (0..* / 1..1), an injective partial function (0..1 / 0..1), an injective total function (0..1 / 1..1), a surjective partial function (1..* / 0..1), a surjective total function (1..* / 1..1), or a bijective function (1..1 / 1..1).

The semantics of associations can be specified by assigning values for the multiplicities of each property involved in the association. However, if the semantics of an association depends on other elements in the model instance, e.g., the value of an attribute, this cannot be expressed in terms of MOF. The following example illustrates this problem: In the model in Figure 4, the association employs from Manager to Employee is surjective, i.e., every employee needs to work for at least one manager. This is a problem, since the CEO of the company should have no manager. Thus, surjectivity for the employment relation is only required for employees who are not the CEO. However, this cannot be expressed in MOF and thus requires a textual constraint, which we formalize in constraint *hasManager* as follows.

Note that the multiplicity of worksFor in the company model should be relaxed from 1..* to * to avoid contradictions with *hasManager*.

Exhibit 6.

```
context Manager
inv headCountRestriction: self.employs->size() <= self.headCount
```

Figure 8. A generic binary association between Employee *and* Manager

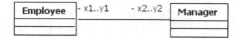

Exhibit 7.

```
context Manager inv hasManager:
if not self.isCEO
then self.employs.allInstances()->forAll ( y |
    self.allInstances()->exists( x | x.employs->includes(y)))
else true
endif
```

Property Types

According to the MOF meta-model in Figure 3, the type of a property can be a class. This allows one to create associations from one class to any other class, even to a class that has specialized subclasses. Thus, any subclass of the superclass can take the role of the superclass in the association. However, in some scenarios, this is unwanted but cannot be prevented by means of the MOF syntax.

Figure 9 shows an instance of our example model where anna, a Manager, works in a cubicle, while charles, an Employee, works in a single office. This instance is valid because it conforms to the meta-model.

However, a company policy may have the requirement that only managers may work in single offices. This constraint is violated by the instance in Figure 9. Therefore, a textual OCL constraint is necessary that restricts the usage of subclasses, which we specify as follows.

Reflexive Associations

Reflexive associations are an important means for modeling systems, since the concept of reflexivity is ubiquitous in many systems: The mother of a human being is a human being, the inverse of a color is a color, and the superior of a manager is a manager.

In general, reflexive associations need to be treated with care because they correspond to recursive definitions and allow objects to be related to themselves. In formal proof environments such as Isabelle/HOL (Nipkow et al., 2002), it must be explicitly proven that recursive definitions terminate. Often, additional constraints are necessary to rule out invalid relations, as in the following example. Although the successor of a natural number is a natural number, the Peano axioms, which can be considered a meta-model for natural numbers, ensure that the set of natural numbers is infinite and the successor relation is acyclic.

In class models, reflexive associations can cause a low maturity level for three reasons. First, they enable cycles in the object graph, second,

Figure 9. Manager and employee inhabiting "inappropriate" offices

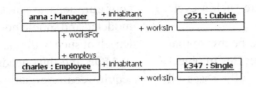

Exhibit 8.

```
context Single
inv onlyManagers: self.inhabitant->forAll(x | x.oclIsTypeOf(Manager))
```

Figure 10. A cyclic management relation

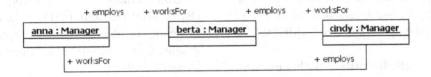

Exhibit 9.

```
context Manager

def: closureWorksFor(S:Set(Manager)) : Set(Manager) =
 worksFor->union((worksFor - S)->
 collect(m : Manager | m.closureWorksFor(S->including(self)))->asSet())

inv noCycles: self.closureWorksFor(Set{})->excludes(self)
```

they allow an arbitrary number of objects to be related in a chain, and third, they allow for so-called diamond configurations. In the following, we point out these problems in detail and show that textual constraints are needed to remedy the expressive deficiencies of graphical modeling languages such as MOF or UML.

Cycles. Reflexive associations can cause cycles in the object graph. Cycles may be desired in certain systems: For instance, in usual color spaces, the inverse of the inverse of a color is the color itself. However, cyclic relations are invalid abstractions for most systems: a person cannot be the mother of her mother, and a natural number is not the successor of itself. The reflexive association worksFor can cause cycles in instances of the company model. We illustrate such a cycle in Figure 10.

The model developer needs to be aware that reflexive associations can cause cycles in object graphs and it needs to be carefully assessed whether cycles are valid structures in the system that is modeled. If not, cycles can be excluded using OCL constraints.

For the definition of such constraints, an operation to compute the transitive closure of an operation is required. Since there is no such operation in OCL (Baar, 2003, OMG, 2003), the transitive closure of each association needs to be manually defined. In the following, we define a transitive closure operation for the worksFor association and state an invariant that the context object may not be a member of the transitive closure of its works-For association. We use a parameter S to ensure termination of the operation. See Exhibit 9.

Arbitrary path lengths. Another problem with reflexive associations is that navigation paths in the model instance can be arbitrarily long. For certain application domains, the maximum path length needs to be restricted. For instance, Figure 11 shows an instance of the company model with eight hierarchy layers, which could be restricted to 5 in order to keep the hierarchy in a company flat.

Reflexive associations also allow for infinitely long paths, involving infinitely many objects. Such configurations are not valid for most systems modeled and should not be allowed. However, the length of such paths cannot be restricted in terms of MOF and thus needs textual constraints that require recursive queries. The following constraint restricts the path length of the worksFor association to 5. It consists of two parts: a definition for the recursive query and the actual invariant, which uses the previously defined query. See Exhibit 10.

Diamond configurations. Reflexive associations can cause a third kind of undesired configuration, namely diamonds. Diamond configurations have been known for a long time (Newman, 1942) and have become known as "Nixon diamonds" in nonmonotonic reasoning (Reiter and Criscuolo, 1981) or "deadly diamonds of death" in object-oriented programming languages with multiple inheritance such as C++ (Martin, 1998).

In our company model, the reflexive association worksFor can cause diamond configurations between managers as shown in Figure 12: daniela has two managers berta and cindy, who work for the same manager anna. Such a configuration can cause the following problem: If anna tells berta to fire all employees and tells cindy to keep all employees, it is not specified what happens to daniela, who works

Figure 11. A company with eight management levels

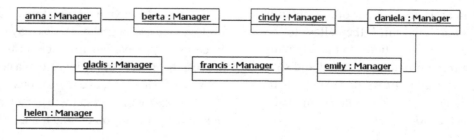

Exhibit 10.

```
context Manager

def: pathDepthWorksFor(max: Integer, counter: Integer): Boolean =
if (counter > max or counter < 0 or max < 0) then false
else if (self.worksFor->isEmpty()) then true
  else self.worksFor->forAll(m:Manager|m.pathDepthWorksFor(max, counter+1))
  endif
endif

inv smallHierarchy: self.pathDepthWorksFor(4,0)
```

Figure 12. Diamond configuration of managers

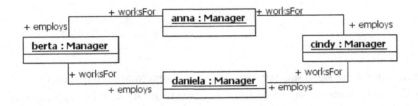

Exhibit 11.

```
context Manager inv noDiamond:
   self.worksFor->exists(m1,m2 |  m1->closureWorksFor(Set{})->intersect(
                                  m2->closureWorksFor(Set{}))->notEmpty()
                  implies m1=m2)
```

for both berta and cindy. Therefore, diamond configurations must be treated with special care and even may have to be excluded in many cases.

Such a configuration can be excluded with the following constraint *noDiamond* in which we re-use the previously defined operation closureWorksFor(). See Exhibit 11.

Unique Object Identifiers

Our example model of a company in Figure 4 is a data model. It is usually required for data models that objects can be uniquely identified, i.e., they must have a primary key. In MOF, a property of a class can be made a unique identifier by setting its isID attribute to true. However, only one property of a class may be a unique ID (OMG, 2006a), which excludes primary keys that are composed of several properties. In our example, the name of an Employee can be made a primary key in the company model in terms of MOF. However, if we want to compose the primary key from the properties name and worksIn, we need to add a textual constraint to the model because composed keys cannot be modeled in terms of MOF. Thus, Figure 13 shows a valid instance of the company model.

Figure 13. Two employees with the same name sharing an office

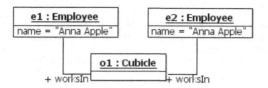

Exhibit 12.

```
context Employee
inv uniqueness: self.allInstances()->isUnique(e|Tuple(x=e.name,y=e.worksIn))
```

Using the OCL operation isUnique(), we can textually specify the tuple (name,worksIn) to be the primary key for class Employee. The constraint reads as in Exhibit 12.

Relations between Properties

Often, properties of the same class or of different classes are related because the value of one property depends on the value of other properties. The MOF meta-model does not provide any means to express such relations. In this subsection, we illustrate two examples for why this lack of expressiveness causes low maturity. We distinguish between simple and complex relations of properties.

Simple relations of attribute values. Two properties can be related by a binary operator such as less-than (<). However, such relations cannot be modeled in terms of the MOF meta-model. Figure 14 shows an instance of the company model that conforms to the meta-model although the employee charles has a higher salary than his manager anna, which may not conform to their company's policy.

To exclude such instances, the following OCL constraint *highestSalary* needs to be added to the company model. The constraint requires that the salary of a manager is higher than the salary of each employee. See Exhibit 13.

Complex relations of attribute values. In our example world, the budget of a manager is used to pay the salary of the manager's employees. Therefore, the budget must be at least the sum of the salaries of all employees whom a manager employs. However, this fact cannot be expressed in terms of MOF, and therefore, the instance in Figure 15 is a valid instance of the company model, although anna cannot pay the full salaries for bob and charles.

In order to exclude the instance from Figure 15, we annotate the company model with the following invariant, *budgetRestriction*. See Exhibit 14.

We have presented several cases in which the limited expressiveness of the MOF meta-model requires refinement of class models defined in terms of MOF, and we have shown how OCL constraints can be used to increase the maturity level of class models. However, writing a correct constraint specification for a class model is

Figure 14. An employee has a higher salary than his manager

Exhibit 13.

```
context Manager
inv highestSalary: self.employs->forAll( e | e.salary < self.salary )
```

Figure 15. Sum of employees' salaries is higher than the budget

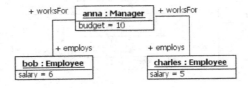

Exhibit 14.

```
context Manager
inv budgetRestriction: self.employs.salary->sum() <= self.budget
```

a time-consuming task that requires significant amount of expertise (Wahler et al., 2007). In the following section, we present how constraint patterns can be used to increase maturity levels with lower effort.

USING PATTERNS TO INCREASE MATURITY

In this section, we show how constraint patterns can be used to easily eliminate the sources of low maturity presented in the previous section. We represent each pattern as a function that maps parameters to an OCL expression. For each problem, we choose a constraint pattern and show how it can be parameterized to prevent the example instances shown in the previous section. This coupling of problem and solution paves the way for a semi-automatic refinement process.

Multiplicities of Properties

In Section 3.1, we showed that unbound multiplicities (*) for associations are on the one hand unavoidable in class models, and on the other hand, they are often a source of low maturity. In

Exhibit 15.

```
context Manager
inv headCountRestriction: self.employs->size() <= self.headCount
```

Exhibit 16.

```
pattern MultiplicityRestriction(navigation: Sequence(Property), operator: OclExpression,
                                value:OclExpression) =
   self.navigation->size() operator value
```

Figure 16. Constraint headCountRestriction as represented in RSA

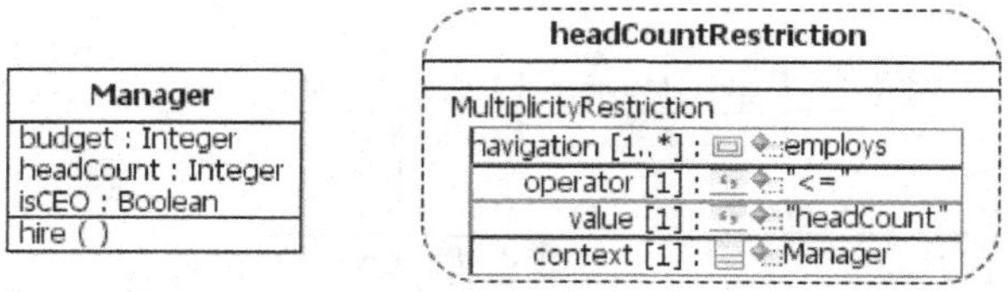

this subsection, we present patterns that allow one to restrict the cardinality of unbound associations depending on the context, i.e., attribute values of objects in the instance.

MultiplicityRestriction. In our company model from Figure 4, we modeled that managers can employ an arbitrary number of employees. In Figure 7, we showed that the number of employees of a manager m should depend on the value of the attribute headCount of m. Therefore, we defined the following OCL constraint (see Exhibit 15).

This constraint can be represented as an instance of the *MultiplicityRestriction* pattern, which is defined as in Exhibit 16.

This pattern has three parameters: *navigation*, which is a sequence of properties, thus allowing for the use of OCL navigation expressions such as self.employs.office, *operator*, and *value*, which can

be arbitrary OCL expressions. Typically, *value* is the name of an attribute. Using this pattern, the constraint *headCountRestriction* can be defined as shown in Figure 16 using our prototype for IBM Rational Software Architect (RSA).

InjectiveAssociation, SurjectiveAssociation, BijectiveAssociation. In Section 3.1, we showed that it is generally possible to define associations in MOF as injective, surjective, or bijective functions. However, if the semantics of an association depends on the context of the model instance, e.g., on attribute values, the semantics must be specified with an OCL constraint. The following constraint patterns can be instantiated to specify injectivity, surjectivity, and bijectivity. See Exhibit 17.

Using these patterns, we can express constraint *hasManager* from Section 3.1 in combination with

Exhibit 17.

```
pattern InjectiveAssociation(property:Sequence(Property)) =
    self.property->size() = 1 and
    self.allInstances()->forAll (x,y | x.property = y.property implies x=y)

pattern SurjectiveAssociation(property:Sequence(Property)) =
    self.property.allInstances()->forAll ( y |
        self.allInstances()->exists( x | x.property->includes(y)))

pattern BijectiveAssociation(property:Sequence(Property)) =
    InjectiveAssociation(property) and
    SurjectiveAssociation(property)
```

Exhibit 18.

```
context Manager inv hasManager:
    IfThenElse(Set{not self.isCEO}, SurjectiveAssociation(Sequence{employs}), true)
```

Figure 17. Constraint hasManager as represented in RSA

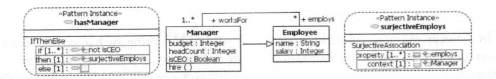

the *IfThenElse* pattern from Section 2.3 as follows. If a manager is not the CEO, the employs association must be surjective, i.e., the manager needs to work for another manager. See Exhibit 18.

Alternatively, the *MultiplicityRestriction* pattern can be used to express above constraint. In our tool, we represent *hasManager* as shown in Figure 17.

Property Types

In Section 3.2, we showed that properties that have a general type, e.g., the property worksIn of type Office, often require further specification, which is not possible in terms of MOF. Therefore, an OCL constraint needs to be defined that restricts the type of a property to a subset of the possible subtypes.

In our example, we want to constrain that employees may not work in single offices and thus defined the following OCL constraint. See Exhibit 19.

The constraint pattern *TypeRestriction* can be used to define this constraint in a simple and concise way. Using the parameter *allowedClasses*, a set of classes can be specified as allowed types for a navigation. This requires an additional existential quantifier, in contrast to the original constraint *onlyManagers*. See Exhibit 20.

Exhibit 19.

```
context Single
inv onlyManagers: self.inhabitant->forAll(x | x.oclIsTypeOf(Manager))
```

Exhibit 20.

```
pattern TypeRestriction(property:Property, allowedClasses:Set(Class)) =
    self.property->forAll(x | allowedClasses->exists(t | x.oclIsTypeOf(t)))
```

Figure 18. Instance of type restriction pattern

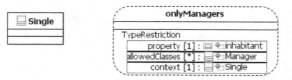

Figure 18 shows an example pattern instance of *TypeRestriction* that represents the *onlyManagers* constraint.

Reflexive Associations

In Section 3.3, we showed that unconstrained reflexive associations allow for instantiations that may be undesired. In particular, instances of reflexive associations can be cyclic, arbitrarily long, or multiple paths between two objects (i.e., diamonds) can exist. In this section, we present three patterns that can be instantiated to avoid such undesired instances.

NoCyclicDependency. Figure 10 shows a model instance with a cyclic path: anna works for berta, who herself works for cindy, who herself works for anna. In order to exclude such cycles, we defined the following constraint that ensures that a manager does not appear in the transitive closure of the worksFor association. See Exhibit 21.

To avoid writing such a verbose constraint, we use the pattern *NoCyclicDependency*, which is the inverse of the *CyclicDependency* pattern in (Wahler et al., 2007). This pattern instantiates the auxiliary pattern *closure*, which contains a definition for the transitive closure. See Exhibit 22.

In Figure 19, we illustrate the constraint *noCycles* as realized using the *NoCyclicDependency* pattern in RSA.

PathDepthRestriction. Unconstrained reflexive associations make it possible to create instances with arbitrarily long paths. Figure 11 shows a path of length seven between the managers anna and helen. We added the following OCL constraint to the model to exclude such instances. See Exhibit 23.

This constraint can be stated using the *PathDepthRestriction* pattern, which uses an auxiliary pattern *satisfiesPathDepth*. To instantiate the pattern, a parameter *property* specifying the as-

Exhibit 21.

```
context Manager

def: closureWorksFor(S:Set(Manager)) : Set(Manager) =
    worksFor->union((worksFor - S)->
    collect(m : Manager | m.closureWorksFor(S->including(self)))->asSet())

inv noCycles: self.closureWorksFor(Set{})->excludes(self)
```

Exhibit 22.

```
pattern NoCyclicDependency(property: Sequence(Property)) =
    self.closure(property)->excludes(self)

pattern closure(property: Sequence(Property)) =
    self.property->union(self.property.closure(property))
```

Figure 19. Constraint noCycles as represented in RSA

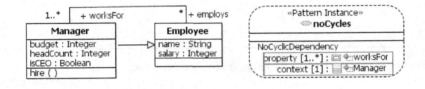

Exhibit 23.

```
context Manager

def: pathDepthWorksFor(max: Integer, counter: Integer): Boolean =
    if (counter > max or counter < 0 or max < 0) then false
    else if (self.worksFor->isEmpty()) then true
            else self.worksFor->forAll(m:Manager|m.pathDepthWorksFor(max, counter+1))
        endif
    endif

inv smallHierarchy: self.pathDepthWorksFor(4,0)
```

Exhibit 24.

```
pattern PathDepthRestriction(property: Sequence(Property), maxDepth:Integer) =
    self.satisfiesPathDepth(property,maxDepth-1,0)

pattern satisfiesPathDepth(property: Sequence(Property), max:Integer,
                                            counter:Integer) =
    if (counter > max or counter < 0 or max < 0) then false
    else if (self.property->isEmpty()) then true
            else self.property->forAll(m|m.satisfiesPathDepth(property, max, counter+1))
            endif
    endif
```

Figure 20. Instance of pattern PathDepthRestriction

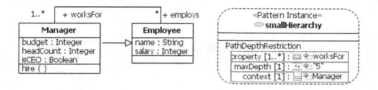

Exhibit 25.

```
context Manager inv noDiamond:
    self.worksFor->exists(m1,m2 | m1->closure(worksFor)->intersect(
                                            m2->closure(worksFor))->notEmpty()
                                        implies m1=m2)
```

sociation and a parameter *maxDepth* specifying the maximum path depth need to be specified. See Exhibit 24.

In Figure 20, we show an example of how the depth of the worksFor association can be restricted to five using this pattern. To this end, we choose worksFor as parameter value for *property* and 5 as value for *maxDepth*.

UniquePath. The third problem of recursive associations that we have identified is that they make it possible to create diamond configurations in the object graph. For instance, in Figure 12, anna has two employees berta and cindy, who are managers themselves. Both berta and cindy share one employee, daniela. We excluded such instances

with the constraint *noDiamond*. See Exhibit 25.

In (Wahler et al., 2007), the pattern *UniquePath* is defined. This pattern allows one to easily exclude diamond-shaped instances by parameterizing it with one parameter, *property*. The definition of the pattern reads as in Exhibit 26.

In Figure 21, we illustrate how constraint *no-Diamond* can be specified using the *UniquePath* constraint pattern.

Unique Object Identifiers

We showed in Section 3.4 that objects should be uniquely identifiable and that this can be easily accomplished if a single property of the object's class is the unique identifier. However, if the

Exhibit 26.

```
pattern UniquePath(property: Sequence(Property)) =
    self.property->exists(m1,m2 | m1->closure(property)->intersect(
                                        m2->closure(property))->notEmpty()
                                        implies m1=m2)
```

Figure 21. Constraint noDiamond as represented in RSA

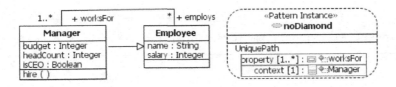

Exhibit 27.

```
context Employee
    inv uniqueness: self.allInstances()->isUnique(e|Tuple(x=e.name,y=e.worksIn))
```

Exhibit 28.

```
pattern UniqueIdentifier(property:Tuple(Property)) =
    self.allInstances()->isUnique(property)
```

unique key of an object is composed of several properties, we need to use an OCL constraint to express this fact. We used the following constraint to express that each employee can be uniquely identified by the name and by the office that the employee inhabits (see Exhibit 27 and 28).

Pattern *UniqueIdentifier*, which is a more general version of the *UniqueAttributeValue* pattern in (Wahler et al., 2007), can be used to easily express above *uniqueness* constraint.

Figure 22 shows an example instance of pattern *UniqueIdentifier*.

Relations between Properties

In Section 3.5, we showed that textual constraints are necessary to express relations between properties. In the following, we use two constraint patterns to express the previously introduced constraints.

AttributeRelation. Figure 14 showed an instance in which an employee has a higher salary than his manager. We added the constraint *highestSalary* to exclude such instances from the set of valid instances. See Exhibit 29.

This constraint can be expressed using the *AttributeRelation* pattern. Using this pattern,

Figure 22. Constraint uniqueness as represented in RSA

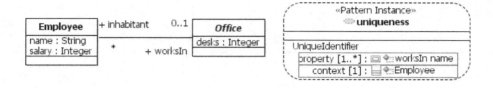

Exhibit 29.

```
context Manager
    inv highestSalary: self.employs->forAll( e | e.salary < self.salary )
```

Exhibit 30.

```
pattern AttributeRelation(navigation:Sequence(Property), remoteAttribute:Property,
                          operator: OclExpression, contextAttribute:Property)=
    self.navigation->forAll( x | x.remoteAttribute operator contextAttribute)
```

an attribute *contextAttribute* can be related to a *remoteAttribute* by an *operator*. The class containing the *contextAttribute* and the class containing the *remoteAttribute* are related by a navigation. See Exhibit 30.

Figure 23 shows a pattern representation of constraint *highestSalary*.

AttributeSumRestriction. In Figure 15, we showed a different source of

low maturity in which the cardinality of the association depends on the relation of several attributes. In this example, the number of employees a manager can employ depends on the budget of the manager and the salaries of the employees. The OCL constraint that expresses this dependency reads as in Exhibit 31.

To capture this constraint, we introduce a new pattern, *AttributeSumRestriction*. Besides the parameter *navigation*, which is analog to the *MultiplicityRestriction* pattern, this pattern has two parameters. Parameter *summation* refers to

the property in the context class that denotes the value that must not be exceeded, and *summand* refers to the property in the related class that is accumulated. See Exhibit 32.

In Figure 24, we show an example of how the constraint *budgetRestriction* is defined using the pattern *AttributeSumRestriction*.

With these patterns, we have introduced an easy-to-use remedy for each source of low maturity presented in Section 3. Furthermore, coupling specific constraint patterns with one of the expressive limitations of graphical modeling languages allows for pointing users to possible, predefined solutions to recurring specification problems. In the next section, we show how such coupling can be used to simplify model refinement in a Computer Aided Software Engineering (CASE) tool.

Figure 23. Constraint highestSalary as represented in RSA

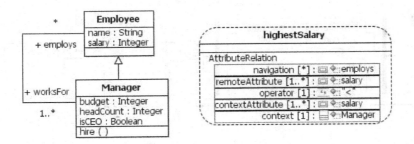

Exhibit 31.

```
context Manager
    inv budgetRestriction: self.employs.salary->sum() <= self.budget
```

Exhibit 32.

```
pattern AttributeSumRestriction(navigation: Sequence(Property),
                                summand: Property, summation: Property) =
    self.navigation.summand->sum() <= summation
```

Figure 24. Constraint budgetRestriction as represented in RSA

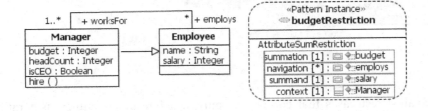

TOOL SUPPORT AND FIRST EXPERIENCES

In this section, we present prototypical tool support that analyzes a model for sources of low maturity and offers constraint patterns that can be instantiated to increase the model's maturity level. We also show how the tool helps to improve the MDE process and provide an experience report of applying the tools to a real-world case study.

Tool Support

Figure 25 illustrates a simplified traditional development process for MDE: After the model has been defined and a (potentially empty) constraint specification has been added, code is generated

Figure 25. Traditional workflow for constraint specification

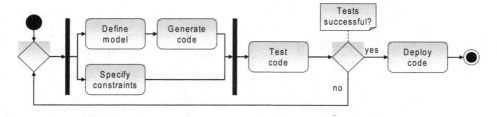

Figure 26. Workflow for constraint specification using patterns

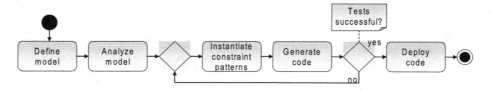

Figure 27. Invoking class model analysis

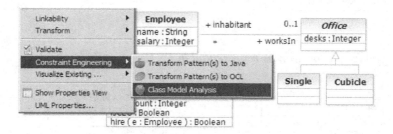

that is evaluated against test cases that correspond to the system requirements. If the code does not pass the tests, the model may need to be changed and/or constraints may need to be added to, removed from, or changed in the constraint specification. If the generated code passes the tests, it can be deployed. Such a process can be time-consuming because specifying constraints comprises identifying sources of low maturity and writing potentially complex OCL expressions. Often, problems are detected in the test phase only, which results in numerous iterations of the constraint specification task.

Tool support for our approach simplifies this traditional workflow by adding two new components, model analysis to automatically detect potential sources of low maturity and an implementation of constraint patterns. In the new workflow as depicted in Figure 26, the time-consuming iteration caused by such an "trial-and-error" approach is replaced by a structured approach comprising two new tasks, *analyze model* and *instantiate constraint patterns*. In the following, we highlight the features of our implementation.

The first new task, analyze model, can be invoked from the context menu of a model as shown in Figure 27. It analyzes the model for occurrences of insufficiently specified model elements as introduced in Section 3. As a result, the tool presents a class model analysis view as depicted in Figure 28, which contains a list of potential problems regarding low maturity. Each item in the list contains a description of the problem and the context element for which the problem occurs. For each item, the user has two choices: the problem can either be ignored by the user because model analysis searches for *potential* problems or the user can take counter-measures against the displayed problem.

In the second case when the user wants to increase the maturity level, the analysis view recommends constraint patterns for each item in the list. This is possible because of the coupling between problem and solution, as explained in Section 4. From the context menu of each item, an appropriate constraint pattern can be selected as instant fix and automatically be instantiated, as shown in Figure 28. The pattern instance is shown in the class diagram and certain parameters are automatically filled in, e.g., the name of properties that represent reflexive associations, while the remaining parameters are specified by the user.

After a pattern instance is fully parameterized, it can be automatically transformed into a textual constraint, e.g., in OCL.

Our prototype is a plug-in extension to the CASE tool IBM Rational Software Architect (RSA) and adds the following features to the functionality of RSA:

- A class model analysis that investigates a given model for occurrences of the limitations introduced in Section 3,
- An analysis view as shown in Figure 28, which presents the analysis results in a user-friendly way and allows users to instantiate appropriate constraint patterns with a single action;
- A transformation that transforms the instances of each constraint pattern into an OCL constraint.

Such tool support has the following advantages. First, the user is supported in detecting potential sources of low maturity. This task is usually time-consuming, requires a high level of expertise from the model developer, and some problems may be not identified, which may cause problems in the remainder of the development process. Second, the model developer can specify most constraints by simply instantiating and parameterizing constraint patterns instead

Figure 28. Results of class model analysis

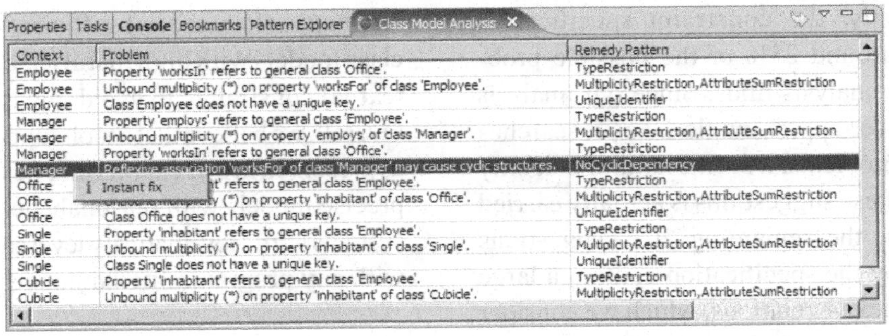

of manually writing OCL expressions, which is time-consuming and error-prone because some constraints are fairly complicated, e.g., constraints for reflexive associations (cf. Section 3.3). Third, our approach is independent of the constraint language, i.e., several transformations can be defined that transform pattern instances into different target languages, e.g., OCL, Java, or Alloy (Jackson, 2002).

Experience Report

In a larger case study (Chen et al., 2006), we refined a monitor model by formalizing 71 constraints that were provided in its specification in natural language. These constraints motivate our choice of the five limitations we introduced in Section 3, because the set of constraint patterns we used for formalizing the specification comprises

- multiplicity restrictions (around 25% of all constraints),
- type restrictions (around 15% of all constraints),
- no cyclic dependencies (4),
- unique identifiers (for around 15% of all classes), and
- attribute relations (around 20% of all constraints).

For the initial unconstrained model, our analysis provided 272 suggestions for refinement. After refining the model with the constraints from the specification, the analysis reported 203 remaining suggestions, which provides two interesting insights. Firstly, the constraint specification covers only around 25% of the possible problems that our analysis finds. Since our analysis provides an over-approximation, i.e., it searches for potential problems, it seems natural that only a fraction of these suggestions is actually carried out. However, the remaining 203 suggestions not handled by the specification contain a large number of reflexive relations, which we consider

one of the most important modeling concept that requires refinement, because reflexive relations can cause cycles in the object graph, which in turn can result in nonterminating computations. Thus, we suggest to extend the specification by some of the problems identified by our analysis. Secondly, the specification contains constraints not suggested by the analysis. This is caused by the fact that our analysis searches for problems that are independent of the application domain of the model, whereas the constraint specification for the monitor model contains domain-specific constraints.

CONCLUSION

In this chapter, we have identified several short-comings in the expressiveness of modeling languages such as MOF. We have shown how these shortcomings can cause low maturity, which is a threat to the quality of models because it allows invalid model instances to be created. We have presented how constraint patterns can be used as an easy and precise means to increase maturity levels, and we have presented an extension to the CASE tool IBM Rational Software Architect (RSA) that supports users in identifying and increasing maturity in class models by coupling the results of an automatic analysis with predefined constraint patterns.

Diagrammatic languages such as defined by MOF or UML have been successfully used in various development projects. However, model developers must be aware that diagrammatic languages alone are not sufficient for developing class models with high maturity, but they require textual constraints to avoid low maturity levels. Overall, we believe that a tool-supported approach as presented in this chapter enables users to create precise models with reasonable effort. After all, systems with a low maturity level can be developed with any programming language, and it may be harder to systematically analyze programs and detect low maturity than to analyze models.

FUTURE RESEARCH DIRECTIONS

From our experience, we have identified the five problems discussed in Section 3 as the most important ones for increasing the maturity level of class models. Future work can build on these problems and investigate further specification problems that frequently occur in the MDE process, both independent of the application domain and specific to certain domains. Future work can also comprise enhancing the tool support. In particular, we envision an improved view of the analysis results in which results are ordered or grouped according to certain priorities. Furthermore, pattern-mining techniques could be used to map existing OCL constraints to our patterns and thus incorporate existing constraints in the analysis.

Although increasing the maturity of models is a current problem, the inverse problem, over-specification, is another threat to the quality of a class model. In a nutshell, an overspecified model contains constraints that contradict each other, and as a consequence, no valid instance of the model can be created. Constraint specifications with contradictory constraints are inconsistent, and we are currently investigating the problem of consistent model refinement. We envision several directions for future research in this area. Since OCL is an undecidable logic (Cengarle and Knapp, 2004), consistency analysis is a challenge for tools and users. Whereas an interactive analysis approach that involves interactive theorem proving can be performed with approaches such as HOL-OCL (Brucker and Wolff, 2006), future research may focus on automatic, but necessarily incomplete, consistency analysis methods. Constraint patterns can play an important role in such automatic approaches, since their fixed structure can simplify consistency proofs.

Little work exists on the quality of class models, despite the fact that various quality aspects have been identified (www.metamodel.com, 2007, Gitzel and Hildenbrand, 2005, Davis and Bigelow, 2002, Gamma et al., 1995). These aspects need to be highlighted in more detail and from different perspectives in order to identify practices that are recommended and those that are discouraged, which will motivate further design patterns and anti-patterns. In particular, we consider the following quality aspects interesting: First, what are "correct" levels of abstraction for different kinds of class models, i.e., at what point of time in the MDE process is what maturity level desired? Second, what are the implications on the quality of a class model that is composed using different means of meta-model extension, e.g., profiles vs. extensions (Cook, 2000).

ACKNOWLEDGMENT

I thank Jana Koehler and Ksenia Ryndina for the constructive discussions on the subject of this chapter. Furthermore, I thank the anonymous reviewers for their helpful comments.

REFERENCES

Ackermann, J. and Turowski, K. (2006). A Library of OCL Specification Patterns to Simplify Behavioral Specification of Software Components. In *Proceedings of Conference on Advanced Information Systems Engineering*, volume 4001 of LNCS (Lecture Notes in Computer Science), pages 255–269.

Ahrendt, W., Baar, T., Beckert, B., Bubel, R., Giese, M., Hähnle, R., Menzel, W., Mostowski, W., Roth, A., Schlager, S., and Schmitt, P. H. (2005). The KeY Tool. *Software and System Modeling*, 4(1):32–54.

Atkinson, C. and Kühne, T. (2001). The Essence of Multilevel Metamodeling. In Gogolla and Kobryn, editors, *UML 2001 – The Unified Modeling Language. Modeling Languages, Concepts, and Tools: 4ᵗʰ International Conference*, Toronto, Canada, October 1-5, 2001, Proceedings, volume 2185 of LNCS. Springer, pages 19-33.

Atkinson, C. and Kühne, T. (2003). Model-driven Development: A Metamodeling Foundation. *IEEE Software*, 20(5):36–41.

Baar, T. (2003). The Definition of Transitive Closure with OCL – Limitations and Applications. In *Proceedings, Fifth Andrei Ershov International Conference, Perspectives of System Informatics*, Novosibirsk, Russia, volume 2890 of LNCS, Springer, pages 358–365.

Beckert, B., Keller, U., and Schmitt, P. H. (2002). Translating the Object Constraint Language into First-order Predicate Logic. In *Proceedings of VERIFY, Workshop at Federated Logic Conferences (FLoC)*.

Bois, B. D., Lange, C. F., Demeyer, S., and Chaudron, M. R. (2006). A Qualitative Investigation of UML Modeling Conventions. In (Kuzniarz et al., 2006), pages 79–94.

Brucker, A. D., Doser, J., and Wolff, B. (2006). Semantic Issues of OCL: Past, Present, and Future. In *Proceedings of the 6th OCL Workshop at the UML/MoDELS Conference 2006*, pages 213-228.

Brucker, A. D. and Wolff, B. (2006). *The HOL-OCL Book*. Technical Report 525, ETH Zurich, Switzerland.

Buschmann, F., Meunier, R., Rohnert, H., Sommerlad, P., and Stal, M. (1996). *Pattern-oriented Software Architecture: a System of Patterns*. John Wiley & Sons, Inc. New York, NY, USA.

Cabot, J. (2006). Ambiguity Issues in OCL Postconditions. In *Proceedings of the 6th OCL Workshop at the UML/MoDELS Conference 2006*, pages 194–204.

Cengarle, M. V. and Knapp, A. (2004). OCL 1.4/5 vs. 2.0 Expressions Formal Semantics and Expressiveness. *Software and Systems Modeling*, 3(1):9–30.

Chen, S.-K., Lei, H., Wahler, M., Chang, H., Bhaskaran, K., and Frank, J. (2006). A Model Driven XML Transformation Framework for Business Performance Management Model Creation. In *International Journal of Electronic Business*, volume 4, pages 281–301. Inderscience.

Chiorean, D., Bortes, M., and Corutiu, D. (2005). Proposals for a Widespread Use of OCL. In Baar, T., editor, *Proceedings of the MoDELS'05 Conference Workshop on Tool Support for OCL and Related Formalisms - Needs and Trends*, Montego Bay, Jamaica, October 4, 2005, Technical Report LGL-REPORT-2005-001, pages 68–82. EPFL, Lausanne, Switzerland.

Chrissis, M., Konrad, M., and Shrum, S. (2003). *CMMI: Guidelines for Process Integration and Product Improvement*. Addison-Wesley Professional.

Cook, S. (2000). The UML Family: Profiles, Prefaces and Packages. In Evans, A., Kent, S., and Selic, B., editors, *UML 2000 - The Unified Modeling Language, Advancing the Standard, Third International Conference*, York, UK, October 2-6, 2000, Proceedings, volume 1939 of LNCS, pages 255–264. Springer.

Costal, D., Gómez, C., Queralt, A., Raventós, R., and Teniente, E. (2006). Facilitating the Definition of General Constraints in UML. In Nierstrasz, O., Whittle, J., Harel, D., and Reggio, G., editors, *MoDELS 2006*, volume 4199 in LNCS, pages 260–274. Springer-Verlag.

Crosby, P. B. (1979). *Quality is Free. The Art of Making Quality Certain*. McGraw-Hill Book Company.

Davis, P. K. and Bigelow, J. H. (2002). Motivated Metamodels. In *Proceedings of the 2002 PerMIS Workshop*.

Dwyer, M. B., Avrunin, G. S., and Corbett, J. C. (1998). Property Specification Patterns for Finite-state Verification. In *FMSP '98: Proceedings of the second workshop on Formal methods in software practice*, pages 7–15, New York, NY, USA. ACM Press.

Gamma, E., Helm, R., Johnson, R., and Vlissides, J. (1995). *Design Patterns: Elements of Reusable Object-Oriented Software*. Addison-Wesley Longman Publishing Co., Inc., Boston, MA, USA.

Gitzel, R. and Hildenbrand, T. (2005). *A Taxonomy of Metamodel Hierarchies*. Working Paper 2/2005.

IBM (2007). Rational Software Architect. http://www-306.ibm.com/software/awdtools/architect/swarchitect/index.html.

Jackson, D. (2002). Alloy: A Lightweight Object Modelling Notation. ACM *Transactions on Software Engineering and Methodology*, 11(2):256–290.

Kan, S. H. (2002). *Metrics and Models in Software Quality Engineering*. Addison-Wesley.

Kleppe, A. and Warmer, J. (2003). *The Object Constraint Language. Second Edition*. Addison-Wesley.

Kuzniarz, L., Sourrouille, J. L., Straeten, R. V. D., Staron, M., Chaudron, M., Förster, A., and Reggio, G., editors (2006). *Proceedings of the 1st Workshop on Quality in Modeling. Co-located with the ACM/IEEE 9th International Conference on Model Driven Engineering Languages and Systems (MoDELS 2006)*, Genova, Italy.

Lange, C. F. J. and Chaudron, M. R. V. (2006). Effects of Defects in UML Models: an Experimental Investigation. In *ICSE '06: Proceeding of the 28th international conference on Software engineering*, pages 401–411, New York, NY, USA. ACM Press.

Martin, R. C. (1998). Java and C++: A Critical Comparison. In *Java Gems: Jewels from Java Report*, pages 51–68.

Miliauskaitė, E. and Nemuraitė, L. (2005). Representation of Integrity Constraints in Conceptual Models. *Information Technology and Control*, 34(4):355–365.

Newman, M. H. A. (1942). On Theories with a Combinatorial Definition of "Equivalence". *The Annals of Mathematics*, 43(2):223–243.

Nipkow, T., Paulson, L. C., and Wenzel, M. (2002). *Isabelle/HOL - A Proof Assistant for Higher-Order Logic*. Number 2283 in LNCS. Springer-Verlag Berlin Heidelberg New York.

Object Management Group (OMG) (2003). *UML 2.0 OCL Final Adopted Specification*. http://www.omg.org/cgi-bin/apps/doc?ptc/03-10-14.pdf.

OMG (2006a). *Meta Object Facility (MOF) Core Specification*. Version 2.0. http://www.omg.org/cgi-bin/doc?formal/2006-01-01.

OMG (2006b). *Unified Modeling Language: Superstructure. Version 2.1*. OMG document ptc/06-04-02. http://www.omg.org/cgibin/doc?ptc/2006-04-02.

Reiter, R. and Criscuolo, G. (1981). On Interacting Defaults. *Proceedings of the Seventh International Joint Conference on Artificial Intelligence (IJCAI'81)*, pages 94–100.

Schulmeyer, G. and Mcmanus, J. (1999). *The Handbook of Software Quality Assurance*. Prentice Hall.

Seidewitz, E. (2003). What Models Mean. *IEEE Software*, 20(5):26–32.

Süß, J. G. (2006). Sugar for OCL. *In Proceedings of the 6th OCL Workshop at the UML/MoDELS Conference 2006*, pages 240–251.

van der Aalst, W., ter Hofstede, A., Kiepuszewski, B., and Barros, A. (2003). Workflow patterns. *In Distributed and Parallel Databases*, Springer, 2003, 14, 5-51

Wahler, M., Koehler, J., and Brucker, A. D. (2007). Model-Driven Constraint Engineering. *Electronic Communications of the EASST*, 5.

www.metamodel.com (2007). *How do I tell a good metamodel from a bad one?* Online article. http://www.metamodel.com/staticpages/index. php?page=20021010225607569. Visited April 2007.

ADDITIONAL READING

Ackermann, J. (2005). Formal Description of OCL Specification Patterns for Behavioral Specification of Software Components. In Baar, T., editor, *Proceedings of the MoDELS'05 Conference Workshop on Tool Support for OCL and Related Formalisms - Needs and Trends*, Montego Bay, Jamaica, October 4, 2005, Technical Report LGL-REPORT-2005-001, EPFL, Switzerland, pages 15–29.

The author presents a few simple constraint patterns and shows how they simplify the specification process. Interesting reading for motivation on using constraint patterns.

Botiza, C., Carcu, A., Chioreau, D., Moldovan, S., and Pasca, M. (2003). Ensuring UML Models Consistency Using the OCL Environment. In *UML 2003 - Workshop: OCL 2.0 - Industry standard or scientific playground?*

The OCL Environment (OCLE) is a tool that supports users in the precise specification of class models with OCL. This is a valuable reference for readers who want to experiment with OCL.

Calì, A., Calvanese, D., De Giacomo, G., and Lenzerini, M. (2001). Reasoning on UML Class Diagrams in Description Logics. In *Proc. of IJCAR Workshop on Precise Modelling and Deduction for Object-oriented Software Development.*

The authors discuss consistency of class models. This paper is for readers who are interested in the semantic foundations of class models.

Ehrig, K., Küster, J. M., Taentzer, G., and Winkelmann, J. (2006). Generating instance models from meta models. In *Proceedings of the 8th IFIP International Conference on Formal Methods for Open Object-Based Distributed Systems*, Bologna, Italy, volume 4037 of LNCS, pages 156–170. Springer.

In this paper, an approach is introduced to automatically generate instances from class models. This approach may be interesting for readers who want to know whether constrained class models can be instantiated.

Foerster, A., Engels, G., and Schattkowsky, T. (2005). Activity Diagram Patterns for Modeling Quality Constraints in Business Processes. In *Proceedings of the MoDELS Conference*, volume 3713 of LNCS, pages 2–16. Springer.

The authors present a language for representing patterns for activity diagrams. This paper may be interesting for anybody who wants to learn more about using patterns in model-driven software development.

Gogolla, M. and Richters, M. (2002). Expressing UML Class Diagrams Properties with OCL. In *Object Modeling with the OCL, The Rationale* behind the *Object Constraint Language*, pages 85–114, London, UK. Springer-Verlag.

In this paper, it is investigated how the constraints that can be expressed in terms of class models, e.g., multiplicity constraints, can be represented OCL. Interesting reading as background on constraints and patterns.

Jackson, D., Schechter, I., and Shlyakhter, I. (2000). Alcoa: The Alloy Constraint Analyzer. *Proceedings of the International Conference on Software Engineering*, pages 730–733.

Alloy is an object-oriented specification language comparable to UML/OCL. This paper discusses the consistency analysis of Alloy specifications and may thus be interesting as background in constraint languages.

Koehler, J. and Vanhatalo, J. (2007). Process Anti-Patterns: How to Avoid the Common Traps of Business Process Modeling. *IBM WebSphere Developer Technical Journal*, 10.2/10.3.

The authors discuss anti-patterns for business process models and how to remedy them. An interesting witness for the importance of patterns in software engineering.

Chapter X
Transitioning from Code–Centric to Model–Driven Industrial Projects:
Empirical Studies in Industry and Academia

Miroslaw Staron
IT University of Göteborg, Sweden

ABSTRACT

Introducing Model Driven Software Development (MDSD) into industrial projects is rarely done as a "greenfield" development. The usual path is to make a transition from code-centric (CC) development in existing projects into MDSD in a step-wise manner. Similarly to all other software development activities, software quality assurance needs to be adjusted to meet the new challenges arising when using models instead of the code for the mainstream development. In this chapter we present a set of empirical data on the issues related to transitioning from CC to MDSD projects in industry. First, we present results from a set of experiments evaluating how a domain specific notation affects the effectiveness and efficiency of reading techniques used for inspecting models. Second, we present a comparison of productivity increase when changing to MDSD projects from one of the large Swedish companies. Finally we present a short survey on the prioritization of products, projects, and resource metrics in MDSD projects.

INTRODUCTION

Introduction of new development paradigms and technologies is never a simple task. It is even harder when we consider large software development organizations with a long history of using other methods and with a portfolio of long-lasting

software products. The long-term nature of these projects coupled with their continual development requires stable and reliable development methods. In contrast, the global economy with its competition drive companies to seek out and adopt new methods and tools to improve productivity and enhance their competitive position with innovative products of higher quality and rapid development cycles. Using modeling in software development promises improved quality and productivity through increased automation of the software development process.

Model Driven Software Development (MDSD) comes in many flavors – starting from using general-purpose modeling languages such as UML (Unified Modeling Language, (Object Management Group, 2004)), and ending with a set of integrated Domain Specific Modeling Languages (DSLs). The main characteristic of MDSD projects, regardless of the modeling notation used is that models play the central role in the process. Models are used for code generation, but also for early quality assessment activities (e.g. software inspections, testing executable models), or for estimations.

This chapter addresses the problem of providing empirical evidence on how much improvements could be expected in the first projects conducted according to the principles of MDSD. It also addresses the issue of which aspects should a project manager consider when undertaking the first projects in MDSD, and which metrics should be customized for MDSD already for the first project.

In order to address the problem we analyze a set of empirical studies performed both in industry (case studies at Ericsson) and in academia (experiment with software inspections). By providing empirical evidences and experiences from industry we support managers of future software projects in making informed decisions concerning adoption of MDSD.

The chapter presents experiences of improvements brought by model-driven development in industrial projects and the expected increase of effectiveness of software inspection of models elicited through experiments.

The chapter is structured as follows. Section 2 presents the background for the claims presented in the chapter, outlines the existing problems in detail and overviews the existing literature in the area.

Section 3 is the core of the chapter and presents the empirical studies, in the end discussing their validity. Section 4 presents a short meta-analysis of the series of studies presented in Section 3. Section 5 contains conclusions. The chapter concludes with a section on future research directions related to using reading techniques as a quality assurance technique for models, and research in productivity assessment in MDSD projects.

BACKGROUND

Based on the roadmap for research on MDSD (France & Rumpe, 2007) it shows that MDSD is not yet a fully established technology and it will still evolve. Therefore, an issue could be raised whether it is mature enough to be adopted or whether it delivers on its promises. The main challenge in the industrial adoption of MDSD is that MDSD needs investments to be effective: the larger the investments, the larger the benefits. In large software projects and in large companies the adoption of MDSD is burdened with all the problems of immature technology (how to justify real expenses based on promises?) and organizational resistance (how do we know that the technology actually improves our way of working?). Herein lies a challenge – how to gradually build up the confidence that using models in a project can help to increase productivity (or quality, or ideally – both). As we are able to show in the case study at Ericsson in Section 3.3, in addition to investing in technology, the investments should also contain costs of coaching (making sure that modeling knowledge is in place), model migration, or gradual migration process.

Transitioning of software practices from document and code centric into model driven can take several years, which is shown in a recent study from Motorola (Baker, Loh, & Well, 2005). The length of time depends on the size of the organization and the range of the products of the company. The long time span of the adoption activity needs to take into account the fact that technology changes during that time. This fact also means that the criteria for deciding whether to early adopt MDSD in industry are not the same as the decision criteria for the projects adopting MDSD a while later. The interpretation of the results from this study could indicate that there are several *flavors* of MDSD at large companies:

- using UML as the core modeling language of MDSD, and
- using Domain Specific Modeling Languages (DSLs) as the core languages of MDSD.

As it is currently observed, the first flavor is more popular. Therefore the "UML flavor" of MDSD forms the context of this chapter.

In this chapter we consider UML as the core modeling language in MDSD as all the presented studies use UML (both in the experiment and in industry). The studies presented here are based on the view of MDSD as a process of creating a sequence of models in a semi-automated way. The automation is achieved through the use of model transformations, which can be programs that transform one model into another or make updates to the same model. The process is semi-

automated since not all model transformations can be automated at the current state of technology. Such a view of MDSD can be presented in Figure 1 and it is adopted from one of the pioneer companies introducing MDSD into their processes (Staron, Kuzniarz, & Wallin, 2004a).

The process of using models (which should be inherent in the product development process) is realized by Model Driven Architecture (Mellor, Kendall, Uhl, & Weise, 2002; Miller & Mukerji, 2003). MDA realization of MDSD recognizes four kinds of models: Computation Independent Models (CIM), Platform Independent Models (PIM), Platform Specific Models (PSM), and Platform Models (PM). The models, expressed in UML, are used sequentially, as shown in Figure 1. The models differ in the abstraction levels and purposes. The horizontal and diagonal lines represent transformations; the transformations can be manual and automated[1]. The vertical lines in the right-hand side of the figure represent dependencies between code modules. This approach to MDSD can be referred to as the *generative approach* since new models are created from other, more abstract models, the models are used to generate the code and the code is then compiled. An alternative approach is the executable approach

Figure 1. Models in MDSD in the studied organizations (©2007 Miroslaw Staron. Used with permission)

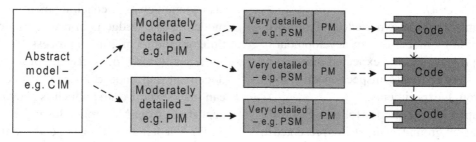

where the models are executed and verified – the code is embedded in the models (Mellor & Balcer, 2002; Starr, 2002). The transformations can themselves be expressed as models thus creating a set of interrelated models – called mega-models (Bézivin, 2005; Bézivin, Jouault, Rosenthal, & Valduriez, 2005).

Another flavor of MDSD can be seen as using DSLs as the core modeling notation. In the telecom domain, Jouault et al. (2006) show that this approach needs extra effort for integration of DSLs, which is required as the final product, is usually an embedded application. One of the major differences between DSLs and general-purpose languages (like UML) is the way of integrating models. In the UML case, the integration is easier, as the complete system can be expressed in one model, while in the previous case it is a set of models expressed in different DSLs. The practical problems with integrations of DSLs are that the extra effort is needed to create mechanisms for integration and the semantics of the integrations. Furthermore, Evans et al. (2003) show that creation of MDSD environments is usually a creation of a multitude of languages specific for dedicated purposes. Making these languages subsets of a single language like UML eases the integration and allows early verification and validation of the system (or its model).

The creation of modeling languages requires deep knowledge in the mechanism and techniques used for that purpose – the main one being metamodeling. As Atkinson and Kühne (2002) point out, metamodel creation is an essential part of MDSD and requires the competence of a language engineer. A way of simulating the creation of a brand-new modeling language is customization of an existing one. In the case of UML, stereotypes can be used for that purpose. The use of stereotypes has limitations, but it has also advantages – e.g. less strict requirements for knowledge from the creators of the customization (Staron & Wohlin, 2006).

France and Rumpe (2007) in their roadmap outline research needs in the area of MDSD and thus provide insight into the current challenges of MDSD. They identify 3 categories of challenges:

- Manipulating models – defining the challenges with automation of model transformations, e.g. the need for effective integration of models and increased research into mega-models (i.e. models of models and transformations between them).
- Supporting separation of design concerns – defining the challenges with creating separate views on the same phenomenon and integration of these views, e.g. Aspect Oriented Modeling.
- Modeling language – defining the challenges related to the use of high level modeling languages, e.g. managing language complexity and extensibility, domain specific modeling environments.

France and Rumpe also point out the need for executable models that can help to shrink the gap between problem domain and the solution space. They conclude that at the current stage, MDSD only contributes to the complexity of software and that the technologies of MDSD need more research into being effectively usable in industry.

A study at two Swedish companies willing to adopt MDSD (Staron, 2006) identifies additional challenges with large scale industrialization of model driven development. The outcome of that study indicated that the main challenges are:

- Maturity of modeling technology – indicating that the modeling environments are either restrictive (and simple, not well-suited for the problem at hand), or vast (and difficult, demanding large expertise in defining modeling languages and tool building).
- Maturity of modeling related methods – indicating that project need support in

quality management based on models and improving the ways the models are used in the process.

- Process compatibility – indicating that the processes cannot be "revolutionized" by the introduction of models, but rather gradually improve efficiency.
- Core language engineering expertise – indicating that at the current state of the technology the project team needs to understand details behind the construction of a modeling language – e.g., to understand the constraints of the modeling technology.
- Goal-driven adoption process – indicating that MDSD should be adopted gradually aligned with elevating the competence of the team.

In this chapter we focus on providing empirical evidences on how much improvements one could expect from effective and efficient use of models. First we present a survey of a focus group, which results in identifying that process automation, modeling knowledge, and model based quality assurance are the most important elements which the group would see solved.

ISSUES AND SOLUTIONS IN ADOPTING MDSD IN THE INITIAL PROJECTS

In this section we present a set of issues and controversies to address while transitioning to MDSD in large software organizations/projects. These issues are:

- How much can quality assurance benefit if domain-specific modeling notations are used?
- How much productivity improvement can we expect from the first project?
- Which are the most important investments in the first projects in MDSD?

These issues are addressed by proposing solutions which are in the form of results from several case studies and experiments both in academia and industry. Each study has a described background, motivation, outline of the design, and the results.

How Much Can QA Benefit if Domain-Specific Modeling Notations are Used?

From the perspective of quality assurance, MDSD promises increased quality of products, at the same time promising increased productivity. In order to verify these promises, we performed a series of experiments with domain specific notations and reading techniques. In the initial experiments we evaluated whether a domain specific notation, simulated by UML stereotypes, increases the level of understanding of models in comparison with the standard UML models (L. Kuzniarz, Staron, & Wohlin, 2004; Staron, Kuzniarz, & Wohlin, 2004, 2006). The outcome of the previous experiments was that the domain specific notation increased the understanding by up to 131% (the correctness of designs evaluated at Volvo IT). In the next experiment we evaluated whether a similar domain specific notation increased the effectiveness and/or efficiency of reading techniques, which are presented in this section. The experiment presented here is an extension of the experiment presented in (Staron, Kuzniarz, & Thurn, 2005).

The motivation behind this experiment was to evaluate whether a domain specific notation helps in increasing quality of models when structured reading techniques are used. We intended to check how much improvement in quality (correctness) one can expect when migrating from standard UML to domain specific notations. The characteristics of the study are as follows:

- Type: controlled experiment
- Treatments:

o   domain specific notation (simulated with UML stereotypes) and general purpose notation (UML)

- Sampling: Randomized Control Trial using blocking
- Analysis: Statistics: Shapiro-Wilk test for normality, paired t-test (or Wilcoxon depending on the results of Shapiro-Wilk)
- Results: Effectiveness is higher for a domain-specific notation than the general purpose notation; efficiency is the same

UML Stereotypes and Reading Techniques

As defined in the UML specification documents (Object Management Group, 2003), the main idea behind using stereotypes is to introduce new semantics to the existing model elements. The UML definition of stereotypes involves the definitions of other extension mechanisms – tagged values and constraints (c.f. (Gogolla & Henderson-Sellers, 2002; Ludwik Kuzniarz & Staron, 2002)). Stereotypes allow extending the language in a way, which is consistent with the definition of the language and they are useful in automatic model transformations, like for example code generation for a specific purpose (e.g. (Uhl & Lichter, 2002)).

In addition to the above, there is also another way of perceiving stereotypes – the original intention of introducing the notion of stereotypes. The stereotypes can provide a secondary classification of model elements. This concept was initially introduced in (Rebecca Wirfs-Brock, Wilkerson, & Wiener, 1994). Such stereotypes provide a means of expressing some classification of the stereotyped model elements, adding properties, which cannot be defined for all model elements of the same kind, but only for some. These stereotypes can be classified as *transitive stereotypes* (according to the classification presented in (C. Atkinson, Kühne, & Henderson-Sellers, 2002)),

Figure 2. Example of a UML stereotype presented using a graphical notation (©2007 Miroslaw Staron. Used with permission)

HIT-FM   Vaxjo-HIT-FM

because they are added to classifiers on the model level, but should also be recognized on the instance level. They are useful as a secondary classification mechanism (R. Wirfs-Brock, 1993) since they both brand the classifier and its instances with additional meaning. An example of a transitive stereotype is presented in Figure 2.

The figure presents two stereotyped elements – a class which is also a sender station and its instance – a particular sender in a city in Sweden.

Other important elements in the experiment design are the reading techniques. Different reading techniques are used to examine the artifacts during software inspections and to find errors. In the investigation presented in this paper, we use two specific reading techniques – checklist-based reading (CBR, (Fagan, 1976)) and perspective-based reading (PBR, (Basili et al., 1996)) and an unstructured reading (further referred to as the ad-hoc technique).

In the context of software inspections, the reading techniques are only a part of the whole process. Usually, the complete process consists of planning, overview, preparation, meeting, rework and follow-up. The details of all steps in the inspection process can be found in (Fagan).

Checklist based reading (CBR) is a reading technique in which the reader is given a checklist with specific kind of faults to look for. The items in the checklist can be expressed as questions or as statements. In particular, the checklist contains items that help in finding logical errors in the inspected documents – errors that cannot be verified in an automatic way by a modeling tool (in the case of UML models).

Perspective based reading (PBR) is a reading technique in which artifacts are examined from certain perspectives. Each perspective is intended to provide a different way of examining the document. Using different perspectives allow focusing on various aspects of the document (for example user's or designer's perspective). One of the assumptions of PBR is that the reader can better identify faults if he/she works in a structured manner. The PBR is a special kind of scenario-based reading techniques (Porter, Votta, & Basili, 1995).

The third kind of reading can be characterized as ad hoc reading. It denotes a technique which provides no guidelines and implies that the readers use their personal experience to find faults. Only a general description of the task is provided as part of the instructions for this reading technique.

Outline of Experiment Design

The goal of the experiment was to evaluate the effect of domain specific notation on the effectiveness and efficiency of reading techniques in software inspections. The reading techniques used in the experiment were the most widely adopted techniques – checklist-based reading (CBR), perspective-based reading (PBR), and unstructured reading.

The hypotheses in the experiment were:

$H_{0\text{-}effectiveness}$: *Introducing stereotypes does not influence the effectiveness of finding faults by subjects*

$H_{1\text{-}effectiveness}$: *Introducing stereotypes influences the effectiveness of finding faults by subjects*

$H_{0\text{-}efficiency}$: *Introducing stereotypes does not influence the efficiency of finding faults by subjects*

$H_{1\text{-}efficiency}$: *Introducing stereotypes influences the efficiency of finding faults by subjects*

The derived variables, effectiveness and efficiency, are calculated from the direct variables – time (T), number of faults found (FF), and total number of faults in the design (TF), in the following way:

$$effectiveness = \frac{F}{F} \text{ and } efficiency = \frac{F}{T}$$

The hypotheses are tested using the paired t-test and Wilcoxon (as efficiency was found non-normally distributed).

The experiment was done as a paired comparison design. The participants were divided into two groups (A and B). After the analysis between these two groups we observe the mean values for each reading technique, which are compared between the groups. However, due to the number of subjects (35) we did not use reading techniques as a factor level which would result in non-significant results caused not by the lack of effect, but by the insufficient number of subjects/data points.

Results

The basic descriptive statistics for the efficiency are presented in Table 1.

The descriptive statistics indicate that there is a small difference between the mean values of notations. The Shapiro-Wilk test for normality does not allow rejecting the assumption of the data being normally distributed with significance level of 0.322. Therefore the parametric paired t-test is used for testing of hypothesis $H_{0\text{-}efficiency}$. The paired t-test does not allow rejecting the null hypothesis as the significance level was 0.202. Thus the observed difference in efficiency is not statistically

Table 1. Descriptive statistics for efficiency

Factor level	Mean	Std. Deviation	Percentage
Domain specific (DS)	0.44	0.33	98%
General (G)	0.45	0.39	100%
Difference: DS-G	-0.01	0.45	2% = 0.01/0.45

Table 2. Descriptive statistics for effectiveness

Factor level	Mean	Std. Deviation	Percentage
Domain specific (DS)	0.63	0.20	129%
General (G)	0.49	0.20	100%
Difference: DS-G	0.14	0.20	29% = 0.14/0.49

significant. This in consequence means that the introduction of stereotypes does not influence the efficiency of the reading techniques.

The basic descriptive statistics for the effectiveness are presented in Table 2.

The descriptive statistics shows that using stereotypes in models resulted in an increase of effectiveness by 0.14 (relatively by 29%). The Shapiro-Wilk test for normality does not allow rejecting the assumption of the data being normally distributed with the significance level of 0.020; Wilcoxon is used for testing of $H_{0-effectiveness}$. After running this test the null hypothesis can be rejected with the significance level of 0.0003. This means that the use of domain specific notation improves the effectiveness of reading techniques.

In order to investigate which of the studied reading techniques was affected most by introducing stereotypes, we perform an analysis of the effect of introducing stereotypes for each method. The analysis is done only with descriptive statistics due to the small number of data points for

each reading technique. The mean values for the effectiveness by reading technique are presented in Figure 3.

The descriptive statistics indicate that the outcome of all reading techniques has been positively influenced, in terms of effectiveness, by the introduction of stereotypes. It seems that the most effective technique for using stereotypes is CBR which resulted in finding 79% of faults in design documents.

Since the checklists used in the experiment were general purpose checklists, we expect that using dedicated checklists would further improve these results – c.f. (Laitenberger, Atkinson, Schlich, & Emam, 2000). The fact that CBR was the most effective technique indicates that the checklists are a very useful help in the review process and provide the most structured reading when examining the documents.

The fact that the unstructured reading was better than PBR seems to be counter-intuitive. It could be caused by the fact that the perspectives

Figure 3. Summary of differences in effectiveness by reading techniques (©2007 Miroslaw Staron. Used with permission)

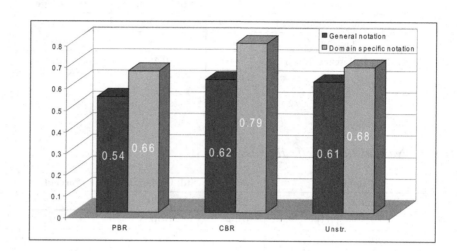

might have actually mislead the subjects and let them focus on aspects which were not important in the experiment, while the unstructured reading stimulated the respondents to more active thinking and more thorough examining.

The observed improvements in the effectiveness of reading techniques show results from an academic experiment. Although the experiment was not replicated in industry, we still believe the results in industry would be stronger. This belief is based on our previous experiments where the use of a domain specific notation caused much stronger effect in industry than in academia (c.f. Figure 4) when it comes to correctness of understanding the design as presented by Staron et al. (2006).

These results show that the transitioning from standard modeling notations to more advanced notations, which are closer to the problem domain than the solution space leads to increased effectiveness of fault finding techniques. This in turn leads to increased quality of the products, as faults

are found earlier in the development process. Although this is not an exhaustive study on quality, it shows what kind of improvements can be expected in an initial project adopting MDSD in terms of quality increase. The limitation of this study is its academic context, which was dictated by the need to obtain statistical power when it comes to results. The materials in the study were based on the materials from our industrial partners to ensure that the context of the experiments were as close to reality as possible, at the same time retaining controllability over factors. The complementary aspect to quality – productivity – would have a limited use if studied in the same manner. Therefore, we studied an industrial project at another industrial partner – Ericsson – in order to address the issue of expected productivity increase from the first project.

Figure 4. Differences between the improvements of industry professionals and university students in a series of experiments with a domain specific notation (©2007 Miroslaw Staron. Used with permission)

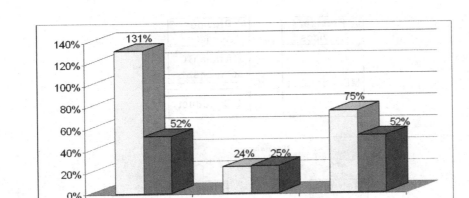

How Much Productivity Improvement Can We Expect From the First Project?

One of the crucial aspects in adopting a new technology is the issue of productivity and quality improvement after adoption. The project and product managers are eager to observe the improvement already in the first project. The increase, however, comes with a price. The first project needs to be given a high degree of freedom in adjusting the company processes to achieve measurable improvement in productivity and quality. The project described in this section is not a special case, but rather a representative situation with respect to controllability and conformance to standard company process description. This was our assumption which we checked in the study presented in Section 3.3. The same situation was observed in the first advanced MDSD project at Volvo IT (Staron, Kuzniarz, & Wallin, 2004b).

This study can be characterized as follows:

- Type: case study
- Sampling: convenience sampling (we used the most suitable project at the studied organization)
- Data collection: artifacts analysis, interviews
- Analysis: descriptive statistics
- Results: show that the MDSD project was 39.5% more efficient than a sister CC project

Outline of the Case Study Design

In order to assess the degree of initial productivity increase in the first MDSD project, we compared two similar projects run at Ericsson: the MDSD project and a sister code-centric (CC) project. The sister project used in the comparison was an old version of a similar technology[2]. The same platform was used, although a different approach was used to deploy the software in this platform. The positioning of the projects is shown in Figure 5.

Figure 5. MDSD project and the sister project – position in the architecture of the telecom systems (©2007 Miroslaw Staron. Used with permission)

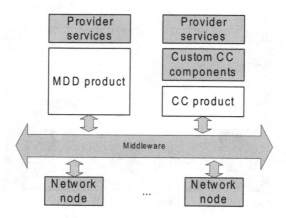

Both products operate above middleware that mediate communication with network nodes. Both products are providing a way of configuring the nodes according to the specifications of provider services. The CC project requires more configuration and development of custom components which mediate between the CC product-specific messaging and the provider-specific messaging. The MDSD product is intended to improve that and provide more flexible and adaptable environment where the creation and deployment of new services for providers is more efficient, faster, and by that much cheaper. Both projects were done in an iterative way and in the comparison we used the data for the completed projects. However, since the MDSD project was in progress (it was just after the 1st iteration) for that project we used the actual data from the 1st iteration and the updated estimations for the coming iterations.

Results

The effort distribution per phase (the sum for all iterations) is presented in Figure 6. It should be noted that the effort for analysis and design could not be distinguished in the model-driven project. The term analysis did not mean the same thing in the CC and MDSD projects, what was called analysis in the CC project was included in the design part of it. This could have been caused by the fact that MDSD was adopted in this project.

The figure shows that there is a difference between the effort distribution between the MDSD and CC projects. The MDSD project spends almost twice as much effort for designing as the CC project. It should be noted that in the case of the CC project the design was done using textual specifications and code fragments illustrating important design decisions. It should also be noted that the implementation effort in the MDSD project was much smaller than for the CC project. In the MDSD project the implementation was intended to fill in the code which cannot be generated automatically from models. This is due to the fact that the standard UML with some basic profile support is used in the project. Nevertheless, the long-term goal for subsequent

Figure 6. Effort distribution for code-centric and model-driven projects (©2007 Miroslaw Staron. Used with permission)

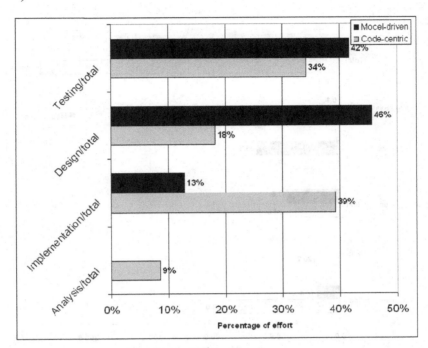

MDSD projects is to replace repetitive manual coding tasks by automated transformations. The resources released in this way could be used to develop new transformations and to focus on modeling of the core business functionality in the project.

Another important aspect was the effort per unit of size for both projects. For these two projects we chose the functionality of the product to be the determinant of size as the size cannot be measured uniformly in both projects (size of models vs. size of source code). We used an internal metric for the functionality (which cannot be given together with the data on productivity due to the confidentiality agreement with the industrial partner). The results for both projects are presented in Figure 7. The data has been transformed as the real data is sensitive to the company, although after the transformation the proportions are still the same.

The value of the total effort per unit of size shows that using models provides the means of decreasing the effort by 39.5%, which is a considerable value. Not surprisingly the most significant gains in efficiency are achieved in the implementation phase – 66.7% decrease in effort. Another interesting aspect is the reduction of effort for system testing and concurrent increase in the effort for function testing. This is caused by the fact that this first MDSD project expects to have problems with the software caused by the introduction of new paradigm and thus there is a need for compensating for that by increasing the effort for function testing (which is included in the planning). The initial productivity improvement seems promising and it does not require advanced

Figure 7. Effort per unit of size for code-centric and model-driven projects (©2007 Miroslaw Staron. Used with permission)

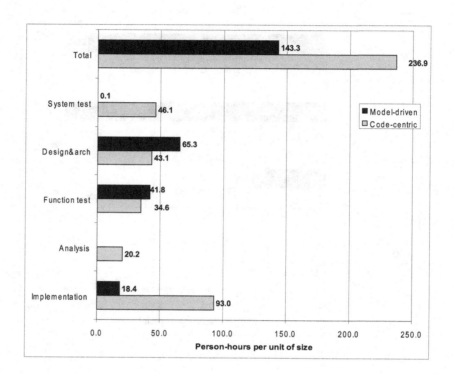

tool or language customizations, which require significant effort (Staron & Wohlin, 2006). Larger benefits, however, require significant additional effort in customization of the modeling environment, in particular to automate the process by the use of model transformations. The development of such model transformations needs to be carefully planned and introduced into the projects gradually.

Which are the Most Important Investments in the First Projects in MDSD?

One of the main issues in adopting MDSD is which elements of the project should be addressed in the first place when migrating to MDSD projects. In particular we were interested in the will to invest

in developing (or customizing existing) metrics for MDSD projects and artifacts; ISO/IEC 9126 (described in section 3.1.1) was used as the reference standard for this purpose. To obtain an empirical data on the investments, we provide data from a survey among 20 experts in the focus group of researchers (4) and practitioners (16) working with the adoption of MDSD (or with MDSD that is already adopted) at their companies: Ericsson, Motorola, and others. The prioritization technique ($100 technique) was used to prioritize particular issues. We asked the experts a series of questions about:

- prioritization of measurements defined in the ISO/IEC 9126 standards,
- prioritization of quality characteristics of the ISO/IEC 9126 standards,

- prioritization of potential improvements in the first MDSD projects, and
- the use of models in their work.

Finally we interviewed a project manager while he was deciding whether to adopt MDSD in his project. Our goal was to obtain qualitative data and his perception of the investments. The manager had several years of experience as the project manager and engineer, including model driven software development.

The motivation behind this study was to investigate which measurements are most important for MDSD projects and to investigate the context of making the decision about migration to MDSD. The context consists of the decision criteria, as well as the required initial investments.

This study can be briefly characterized as follows:

- Type: case study
- Sampling:

  o Survey: Randomized Control Trial; population: project managers, quality managers, design engineers, and architects working with MDSD projects
  o Migration project: Convenience sampling; population: project managers of mid-size sub-projects that are migrating from code-centric to MDSD

- Analysis: descriptive statistics
- Results: show that process and resource metrics are the most important metrics in MDSD projects; modeling knowledge and process automation are key aspects in MDSD projects; and the most important quality characteristics are functionality and maintainability

ISO/IEC 9126 Standard

One of the most widely adopted quality standards which includes the definition of software measurements meant to measure quality is the ISO/IEC 9126 standard (International Standard Organization & Commission, 2001). The standard defines the following quality perspectives (also called approaches to quality in the standard), with the associated types of metrics:

- Process quality: defines the quality of software processes followed during software development
- Internal quality: defines the details of software product quality that can be improved during code implementation, reviewing and testing,
- External quality: defines the quality when the software is executed, which is typically measured and evaluated while testing in a simulated environment,
- Quality in use: defines the quality of software product as perceived by the users

The perspectives are further divided into quality characteristics, which are further associated with specific metrics. Each quality characteristics has several metrics associated with it and the ISO/IEC 9126 has an example set of metrics. The metrics in the standard, however, are not dedicated for models, but for measuring code-based or document-based artifacts. Therefore, there is a need to develop (or customize the existing) metrics to reflect model driven software development.

The standard defines the following internal and external quality characteristics (the characteristics are defined for internal and external quality together – definitions are quoted after the standard):

- Functionality: the capability of the software product to provide functions which meet stated and implied needs when the software is used under specified conditions.

- Reliability: the capability of the software product to maintain a specified level of performance when used under specified conditions.
- Usability: the capability of the software product to be understood learned, used, and attractive to the used, when used under specified conditions.
- Efficiency: the capability of the software product to provide appropriate performance, relative to the amount of resources used, under stated conditions.
- Maintainability: the capability of the software product to be modified.
- Portability: the capability of the software product to be transferred from one environment to another.

These characteristics were used during the study presented in this section.

Outline of the Case Study Design

The first part of the study (survey on measurements) presented in this chapter was performed during a focus group meeting at the workshop on quality in modeling at the MODELS conference and at Ericsson in Sweden. The focus group consisted of architects, researchers, managers, and design engineers, who have experience in the field. The sampling technique was Randomized Control Trial as we have randomly chosen participants and not the whole group of experts.

The second part of the study (migration issues) was performed at Ericsson, by interviewing a project manager who was involved in making the decision whether the project should adopt MDSD and how the adoption should be done. The sampling was a convenience sampling as we only looked for the appropriate managers at Ericsson, our industrial partner, and no other company in the region.

Prioritization of Measurements in ISO/IEC 9126

The first question asked to the respondents was which of the measurements defined in the ISO/IEC 9126 they would see as most important – i.e. in which quality perspective (and the types of metrics associated with them) they were willing to invest and how much if they were to develop new measurements. Their rationale was that if the experts were to be part of the first MDSD project in their organization, which measurements they would need most to be able to ensure controllability of their work (which is different depending on the role – quality manager, project manager, architect, consultant, researcher, and designer). Figure 8 presents the average of the answers from the experts in the focus group.

The focus group prioritized the process metrics as the most important type of metrics although the product and resource metrics were not much less important. This indicates that in the first MDSD project, a strong focus should be put into having precise tools for collecting process metrics – e.g. efficiency of specific phase or effectiveness of the process of finding defects in models.

The resource metrics are prioritized quite high which shows that the results come from managers in a company who are very concerned by the costs of their project. This, in turn, is caused by the tight market in which the company has to operate, where the cost has a key role in success.

The project metrics are not highly prioritized as the way of working is potentially not altered to a large extent in the first project (since it is a transitioning from standard code-centric projects). Since MDSD changes the process of developing software, there is no doubt that the associated metrics must be changed as well. Productivity cannot be measured as size of the code produced per time unit, but rather as the size of model per time unit. The size of the model, however, needs to be specific for the phase (e.g. number of classes in high-level design, while the number of states

Figure 8. Prioritization of types of metrics from ISO/IEC 9126 (©2007 Miroslaw Staron. Used with permission)

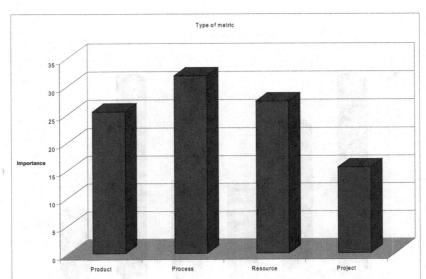

in the detailed design phase). The size metrics, nevertheless, are specific for the modeling notation used and the process followed.

The process metrics are important for ensuring that MDSD actually delivers in terms of productivity or increased efficiency and effectiveness of software processes. One should not, nevertheless, forget that the quality of the product that can be affected by adopting a new development technology.

Prioritization of Quality Characteristics

The experts in the focus group prioritized the quality characteristics of good software from ISO/IEC 9126. They were asked how much they would be willing to invest to improve each characteristic of the software. The results are presented in Figure 9.

The results show that the experts were still willing to prioritize the functionality and the maintainability of the product as top quality characteristics. The least important characteristic was portability. This is rather surprising since MDSD promises increased portability through exchangeable code generators and pluggable platform models.

Prioritization of Improvements in the First Project

The experts were also asked which improvements they expect to see in the first MDSD project, caused by introducing MDSD. The results are presented in Figure 10.

The results show that the top three expected improvements are:

- Process automation – which includes automating tedious tasks – e.g. writing very similar code several times in the same project.

Figure 9. Prioritization of ISO/IEC 9126 quality characteristics (©2007 Miroslaw Staron. Used with permission)

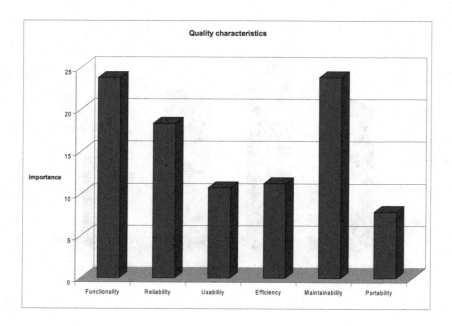

Figure 10. Prioritization of potential improvements in projects (©2007 Miroslaw Staron. Used with permission)

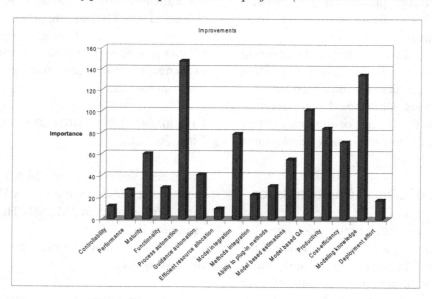

- Modeling knowledge – which includes the knowledge how to use abstractions effectively in software projects.
- Model based quality assurance – which includes using inspections of models rather than text documents to increase the effectiveness and efficiency of quality assurance of early stages of project artifacts.

The process automation should be considered in the context of productivity, namely how much productivity improvement we can expect in the first project by using automated code generation from design artifacts (as an example of process automation).

Presence of Models in Experts' Work

The final question in the survey with the focus group was aimed to examine the presence of models in various phases of software development. The experts were asked what percentage of artifacts in a particular phase are models. The

usage of models in the work of experts varies, and it is shown in Figure 11. The highest use of models is for architectural design – on average 42% of architectural design artifacts are models. The next highest usage is for detailed design with 35% of design artifacts being models.

The survey with the experts from the focus group provides an overview of the importance of metrics in the first projects. The survey, however, did not provide an insight on how the projects are chosen whether they can be migrated into MDSD projects.

Decision Factors in Adoption of MDSD

In order to establish such a set of decision criteria, we examined one small project at Ericsson. The project involved the developing of an algorithm used in a component in a mobile network. The size of the project is a few person months[3] and this project has been chosen to be the pilot project supporting the project management team in making a decision on how to proceed with the large

Figure 11. Use of models in the focus group work (©2007 Miroslaw Staron. Used with permission)

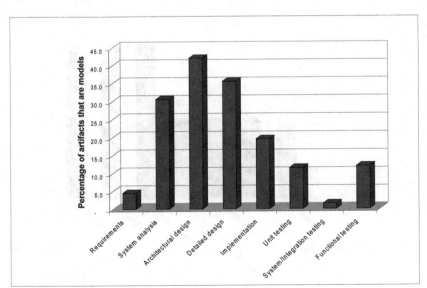

project. In our study we identified the following decision criteria:

- **Structure migration**: It is possible to migrate the core model structure (e.g. class diagrams) to the new model in a very cost-effective way (i.e. with rather low effort).
- **Independent co-existence:** It is possible to model the new part/model of the software independently from the legacy part/model (e.g. by developing new sequence diagrams in the new model).
- **Migration effort:** The effort for changing to the new model is low.
- **Controlled legacy changes:** It is possible to reference the legacy part, and there is no (or very limited/controlled) need for changing the legacy parts/models.
- **Model longevity:** The "new" *model* will be used for more than one project (e.g. to become product documentation).

- **Controlled initial change:** A limited group of people is going to be affected by the initial change.
- **Knowledge in place:** The modeling knowledge (in the new tool) is in place in the project and is not in the hands of one/two individuals.

Using the $100 technique the project manager prioritized these criteria, which resulted in identifying two levels of criteria as shown in Figure 12.

The results show that there are two classes of criteria defined by their importance. The higher prioritized criteria are related to project management. They address the question of what the project manager needs to minimize the risk of failing the migration process already during the first project. The project manager identified also additional issues that are pre-requisites for adopting MDSD from his perspective:

Figure 12. Prioritized criteria for migration to new models (©2007 Miroslaw Staron. Used with permission)

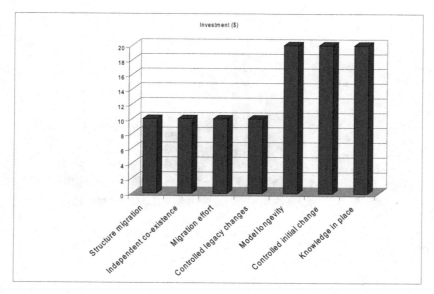

(i)   migration process should be longer than the span of a single project; in the studied organization, the migration process could not be automated due to the large legacy code base and the size of the products,

(ii)   the initial knowledge gap should be small (unless large investments were envisioned), and

(iii)   the old and the new documentation styles (code-centric and model-driven) can co-exist for some time since a lot of knowledge and documentation in large projects needs to be maintained and used in new projects (and there is no possibility of re-doing all documentation during the migration process).

Model migration was less important than model longevity, which could be seen as an unexpected situation. However, it is not the case in the studied organization. The effort of manual can be (and already) is spread over several projects and releases as no automated tools exist which would fulfil the migration purposes of the company.

The views of the project manager bring us to another issue – how to effectively adopt MDSD in industrial context. However, before diving into this issue, let us address another important aspect, directly related to quality assurance.

Validity Evaluation

This chapter presents a series of empirical studies performed both in academia (section 3.1) and in industry (section 3.2 and 3.3). There are some threats to the validity of the results from the studies. In this chapter we use the validity evaluation framework by Wohlin et al (2000).

The main *external validity* threats are related to the case studies. The choice of projects was dictated by their availability. Only the projects which were already using (or just before using) MDSD were chosen in the study (section 3.2 and 3.3 respectively). As we only examined two projects, this poses the threat that the results are not representative. We believe, however, that the results are representative, as they are in line with our other studies, not related to the studies presented in this chapter (Staron, Kuzniarz et al., 2004a; Staron & Wohlin, 2006).

The main *construct validity* threat is related to meta-analysis. The studies presented in this chapter were performed separately, and combined afterwards. Although we designed and performed the studies in order of appearance and using the experiences from the previous studies when designing new ones, we did not initially mean to perform meta-analysis. Therefore, there is a threat that some aspects might have been missed when performing the separate studies. In order to validate this, we performed a workshop (during the presentation of results) at Ericsson during which we presented and discussed our results. We did not miss any points according to the company representatives present during the workshop.

The main *internal validity* threats are different for each study in the chapter:

- Experiment (3.1): the order of presenting the treatments to the subjects could bias the results; to minimize this we performed repeated-measures experiment design with each group having ABBA and BAAB design (Wohlin et al., 2000).
- Productivity case study (3.2): we measured the effort data using the measurements provided by the company; since there are no uniform size metrics for MDSD and CC projects, we had to resolve to high-level metrics in order to be able to compare the productivity. This threat, however, seems to be minimal for the company as the metrics we used are also used at the company to assess project progress and size.
- Survey and migration case study (3.3): we presented the quality characteristics which are used at the company, whereas we could have performed a workshop beforehand and let the respondents decide which quality

model is best; we chose that as the company must adhere to adopted standards, which would render our results useless for the company if we did not adopt the ISO/IEC 9126 standard.

Finally, the main *conclusion validity* threat is related to the analysis of the results from case studies. Due to the small sample sizes, the results are very specific and might not reflect the trends in the general population. However, from the previously reported experiences, for example (De Miguel, Jourdan, & Salicki, 2002; Staron, 2006; Vokac & Glattetre, 2005), we find our results in line with the existing empirical evidence.

META-ANALYSIS

The studies presented in Section 3 show that introducing MDSD into software projects provides such benefits as increased quality (correctness) of artifacts and increased productivity. The increase in correctness was shown in the experiment, as this was the most adequate empirical method to provide evidence for this claim (due to sample size and controlled environment). The increase in productivity, however, cannot be assessed through an experiment since the productivity is best measured in a case study.

The above benefits can be considered in a context of costs of introducing MDSD in the first projects. Investments in adjusting methods, metrics, tools, and knowledge of engineers are unavoidable. The study presented in Section 3.3. shows that in the first projects, the most important metrics are process metrics and the most important investments should be put in elevating the knowledge of engineers as well as ensuring longevity of models.

The studies presented in this chapter provide evidence how much improvements MDSD can bring into an organization adopting it.

CONCLUSION

Transitioning from code-centric development into MDSD can be an effort and resource intensive process. In this chapter we outlined two main aspects that are important in the first projects that adopt MDSD in large organizations. The first was how much effectiveness and efficiency improvement we can expect when using a domain specific notation. The results showed that the effectiveness can be improved significantly with constant efficiency of the process. This leads to increased quality of the final product at a constant cost. The other main aspect is the productivity change in the first MDSD project. The industrial case presented in this chapter showed that the first project could improve the productivity by 39.5%. The other two supporting studies show that the group of experts prioritized quality assurance as one of the most important aspects in the first MDSD project.

Future Research Directions

The adoption of MDSD is moving from pilot projects and from small organizations into the phase where large organizations are adopting MDSD for their large, long-term projects. Aiming at the productivity increase, the large companies are pulling the technology forward, demanding advanced methods for working with models. Examples of needs that pull the development of MDSD project practices are configuration management techniques that are suited for models, supporting graphical identification of model differences and supporting model merging similar to code merging. Configuration management practices are necessary if the models are to increase the quality of software products. Ineffective configuration management will surely lead to delays in projects and inefficient verification and validation. This, in turn might lead to lower quality in the final product. Therefore, model-based CM is one of the future research trends within MDSD. The existing solutions, e.g. IBM/Rational Software Architect, support basic configuration management tasks, but fail to help developers in such situations as merging from several branched in a configuration tree. Although this problem also exists in code-based CM, it is easier to predict a result of merging more than two branches than it is when models are concerned.

Future trends in transitioning to MDSD lean towards adoption of DSLs as the core modeling languages. The use and integration of DSLs form the mainstream of the research in the field (France & Rumpe, 2007). Domain specific notations constitute a significant volume of research and several industry-quality tools have been released that support graphical DSLs – examples of these tools include Microsoft DSL toolkit for Visual Studio 2005, and MetaEdit. The interest of software development companies has risen significantly since the release of these tools as the DSL technology is no longer a research playground, but an industrial application. Defining the quality characteristics of domain specific modeling languages is still an open issue. The standard quality characteristics of the ISO and IEEE standards need to be adapted, as the definition of languages is done at the meta-level (compared to the definition of models of systems).

Another strong trend in MDSD and especially in integration of quality assurance is the introduction of executable models in large software projects. Runtime models (as they are sometimes called) facilitate early verification and validation techniques, but at the same time require skills that are not common at the current software engineering education – working with abstract models and very refined action code. This working at two levels seems to be the main challenge to address in order to increase the quality of executable models.

One future research direction is the creation of methods for defining domain specific checklists when developing domain specific languages. The use of these checklists should further improve the effectiveness of reading techniques. The checklists used in our experiments were general checklist for designs. However, it could be expected that the domain specific checklist, which takes into account design guidelines of the organization, should increase the effectiveness and efficiency of the verification process considerably.

The second research direction is creating model-based project management practices to facilitate making the most out of software projects done in the MDSD way. Together with the research on model-based project metrics (e.g. productivity measurements), the results of research in this direction would be of a great value for project managers.

The third direction is research into effective introduction of MDSD into industrial projects. Industrial adoption needs to progress gradually and companies need support in the process of adopting modeling notations. Some of the challenges that this research should address are: increasing the level of abstraction, ensuring stability of modeling techniques in the company, or continuous professional development of software engineers who finished their education before graphical modeling languages were taught at the universities.

Finally, the most important aspect to address in the transitioning to MDSD is to create a roadmap how the transition should be done at a particular company. Based on the experiences from the current state-of-the-art in MDSD and the existing roadmaps for related areas, e.g. education in engineering roadmap (Shaw, 2000), this roadmap would be of a great value for industry.

ACKNOWLEDGMENT

The author would like to thank the experts participating in the studies described in this paper. I would also like to thank Ericsson Lindholmen, Ericsson Region South, Blekinge Engineering Software Qualities (BESQ) project, Software

Architecture Quality Center (SAQC), and Ericsson SW Research for support in this study.

REFERENCES

Atkinson, C., & Kühne, T. (2002). *The Role of Metamodeling in MDA.* Paper presented at the Workshop in Software Model Engineering, Dresden, Germany.

Atkinson, C., Kühne, T., & Henderson-Sellers, B. (2002, 2002). *Stereotypical encounters of the third kind.* Paper presented at the 5th International Conference on the Unified Modeling Language «UML» 2002. Model Engineering, Concepts, and Tools., Dresden, Germany.

Baker, P., Loh, S., & Well, F. (2005). *Model-Driven Engineering in a Large Industrial Context - Motorola Case Study.* Paper presented at the Model Driven Engineering Languages and Systems - MoDELS, Montego Bay, Jamaica.

Basili, V. R., Green, S., Laitenberger, O., Shull, F., Sorumgard, S., & Zelkowitz, M. V. (1996). The empirical investigation of perspective-based reading. *Empirical Software Engineering, 1*(2), 133-164.

Bézivin, J. (2005). On the unification power of models. *Software and Systems Modeling, 4*(3), 171-188.

Bézivin, J., Jouault, F., Rosenthal, P., & Valduriez, P. (2005). *Modeling in the Large and Modeling in the Small.* Paper presented at the European MDA Workshops: Foundations and Applications, MDAFA 2003 and MDAFA 2004.

De Miguel, M., Jourdan, J., & Salicki, S. (2002). *Practical Experiences in the Application of MDA.* Paper presented at the The 6th International Conference on The Unified Modeling Language - «UML» 2002.

Evans, A., Maskeri, G., Sammut, P., & Willians, J. S. (2003). *Building Families of Languages for Model-Driven System Development.* Paper presented at the Workshop in Software Model Engineering, San Francisco, CA.

Fagan, M. E. (1976). Design and code inspections to reduce errors in program development. *IBM Systems Journal, 15*(3), 182-211.

France, R., & Rumpe, B. (2007). *Model-Driven Development of Complex Software: A Research Roadmap.* Paper presented at the 29th International Conference on Software Engineering, Minneapolis, MN, USA.

Gogolla, M., & Henderson-Sellers, B. (2002). *Analysis of UML Stereotypes in the UML Metamodel.* Paper presented at the UML 2002, Dresden.

International Standard Organization, & Commission, I. E. (2001). *Software engineering – Product quality Part: 1 Quality model.* Genevao. Document Number)

Jouault, F., Bézivin, J., Consel, C., Kurtev, I., & Latry, F. (2006). *Building DSLs with AMMA/ATL, a Case Study on SPL and CPL Telephony Languages.* Paper presented at the 1st ECOOP Workshop on Domain-Specific Program Development (DSPD).

Kuzniarz, L., & Staron, M. (2002). *On Practical Usage of Stereotypes in UML-Based Software Development.* Paper presented at the Forum on Design and Specification Languages, Marseille.

Kuzniarz, L., Staron, M., & Wohlin, C. (2004). *An Empirical Study on Using Stereotypes to Improve Understanding of UML Models.* Paper presented at the The 12th International Workshop on Program Comprehension, Bari, Italy.

Laitenberger, O., Atkinson, C., Schlich, M., & Emam, K. E. (2000). An experimental comparison of reading techniques for defect detection in

UML design documents. *The Journal of Systems and Software, 53*(2), 183-204.

Mellor, S. J., & Balcer, M. J. (2002). *Executable UML : a foundation for model-driven architecture.* Boston ; San Francisco ; New York: Addison-Wesley.

Mellor, S. J., Kendall, S., Uhl, A., & Weise, D. (2002). *Model-Driven Architecture.* Paper presented at the Object-Oriented Information Systems, Montpellier.

Miller, J., & Mukerji, J. (2003). MDA Guide. 1.0.1. Retrieved 2004-01-10, 2004, from http://www.omg.org/mda/

Object Management Group. (2003). Unified Modeling Language Specification v. 1.5. Retrieved 2003-10-01, 2003, from www.omg.org

Object Management Group. (2004, December 2003). Unified Modeling Language Specification: Infrastructure version 2.0. Retrieved 2004-02-20, 2004, from www.omg.org

Porter, A. A., Votta, L. G., Jr., & Basili, V. R. (1995). Comparing detection methods for software requirements inspections: a replicated experiment. *Software Engineering, IEEE Transactions on, 21*(6), 563-575.

Shaw, M. (2000). *Software engineering education: a roadmap.* Paper presented at the International Conference on Software Engineering, Limerick, Ireland.

Staron, M. (2006). *Adopting MDD in Industry - A Case Study at Two Companies.* Paper presented at the ACM/IEEE 9th International Conference on Model Driven Engineering Languages and Systems, Genova, Italy.

Staron, M., Kuzniarz, L., & Thurn, C. (2005). *An Empirical Assessment of Using Stereotypes to Improve Reading Techniques in Software Inspections.* Paper presented at the Third Workshop on Software Quality, St. Louis, MO.

Staron, M., Kuzniarz, L., & Wallin, L. (2004a). A Case Study on Industrial MDA Realization - Determinants of Effectiveness. *Nordic Journal of Computing, 11*(3), 254-278.

Staron, M., Kuzniarz, L., & Wallin, L. (2004b). *Factors Determining Effective Realization of MDA in Industry.* Paper presented at the 2nd Nordic Workshop on the Unified Modeling Language, Turku, Finland.

Staron, M., Kuzniarz, L., & Wohlin, C. (2004). *An Industrial Replication of an Empirical Study on Using Stereotypes To Improve Understanding of UML Models.* Paper presented at the Software Engineering Research and Practice in Sweden, Linköping, Sweden.

Staron, M., Kuzniarz, L., & Wohlin, C. (2006). Empirical assessment of using stereotypes to improve comprehension of UML models: A set of experiments. *Journal of Systems and Software, 79*(5), 727-742.

Staron, M., & Wohlin, C. (2006, June 12-14, 2006.). *An Industrial Case Study on the Choice between Language Customization Mechanisms.* Paper presented at the 7th International Conference, PROFES 2006, Amsterdam, The Netherlands.

Starr, L. (2002). *Executable UML: how to build class models.* Upper Saddle River, NJ: Prentice Hall.

Uhl, A., & Lichter, H. (2002). *A UML Variant for Modeling System Searchability.* Paper presented at the Object Oriented Information Systems, Monpellier.

Wirfs-Brock, R. (1993). Stereotyping: a technique for characterizing objects and their interactions. *Object Magazine, 3*(4), 50-53.

Wirfs-Brock, R., Wilkerson, B., & Wiener, L. (1994). Responsibility-driven design: Adding to your conceptual toolkit. *ROAD, 2*(1), 27-34.

Wohlin, C., Runeson, P., Höst, M., Ohlsson, M. C., Regnell, B., & Wesslèn, A. (2000). *Experimentation in Software Engineering: An Introduction.* Boston MA: Kluwer Academic Publisher.

Vokac, M., & Glattetre, J. M. (2005). *Using a Domain-Specific Language and Custom Tools to Model a Multi-tier Service Oriented Application - Experiences and Challenges.* Paper presented at the Model Driven Engineering Languages and Systems, Montego Bay, Jamaica.

ADDITIONAL READING

ATLAS research group website: http://www.sciences.univ-nantes.fr/lina/atl/

The practitioners interested in the issues of automating the generation of model transformations should read the material on the ATLAS research group. The material describes how the notions of transformations and definitions of models can be unified. The materials include several case studies on industrial applications of these techniques.

Atkinson, C., & Kühne, T. (2000). Strict Profiles: Why and How. Paper presented at the ACM/IEEE 3rd International Conference on UML.

Deeper understanding on the issues of defining profiles for theoreticians can be obtained by reading the material in the paper above. The paper explains the notion of instantiation which is important when defining model transformations. This material supports the reasoning in our experiment.

Atkinson, C., & Kühne, T. (2005). Concepts for Comparing Modeling Tool Architectures. Paper presented at the ACM/IEEE 7th International

Conference on Model Driven Engineering Languages and Systems.

A practitioner interested in details how UML model repositories are built should definitely read the above article. The article describes how meta-meta-models are related to models and meta-models in practice. It shows that modeling is usually done in multiple dimensions, which to a large extent can explain the limitations of the current UML tools.

Clark, T., Evans, A., Sammut, P., & Willans, J. (2004). Applied Metamodeling - A Foundation for Language Driven Development (1st ed.): Xactium.

The above material is dedicated for practitioners interested in understanding the practical aspects of creating modeling languages. This book is an essential reading for language engineers who want to increase the productivity of modeling beyond the limitations of standard, UML-based modeling.

Bell, A. E. (2004, March 2004). Death by UML Fever. *ACM Queue, 2,* 72-80.

Skeptics in the adoption of MDSD should definitely read this article and its references. The author explicitly names the most common types of adopters of MDSD and reveals wholes in their reasoning. The material is a very good counterpart and a set of negative (or realistic – as some researchers put it) view of MDSD.

Glass, R. L. (2004). On modeling and discomfort. *Software, IEEE, 21*(2), 104-103.

In the same tone as the previous article, Robert Glass presents a good debate on the use of domain specific modeling in industrial projects. The outcome of the debate is that the modeling community lacks empirical evidence that modeling indeed increases performance of software development.

Thomas, D. (2004). MDA: Revenge of the Modelers or UML Utopia? *IEEE Software, 21*(3), 15-18.

The article above contains a discussion and explanation of how MDA is an evolution of the known UML-based software development. The authors explore the notions of model transformations and domain specific modeling as the next step in the evolution of UML.

Uhl, A. (2003). Model Driven Architecture Is Ready for Prime Time. *IEEE Software, 20*(5), 70-72.

Practitioners interested in the discussion on whether MDA is mature enough to be used in industry should read the above article. In the article, the author explores the arguments for and against MDA being a viable alternative for industry in the time of its writing.

The readers interested in other industrial case studies can read:

Meservy, T. O., & Fenstermacher, K. D. (2005). Transforming software development: an MDA road map. *Computer, 38*(9), 52-58.

In this article, the practitioners can find an example of appropriate use of MDA in the context of a web application. The authors discuss the

levels of abstractions of CIM, PIM, and PSM and their relationships. They conclude that MDA still needs to mature, even though it has been around for a while.

ModelWare project, "MDD maturity levels", www.modelware-ist.org

When working with MDSD in practice the issue of maturity of the use of MDSD often arises. The ModelWare project developed an initial version of MDSD maturity model. The model contains five stages which define how mature a use of MDSD is in an organization.

Vokac, M., & Glattetre, J. M. (2005). Using a Domain-Specific Language and Custom Tools to Model a Multi-tier Service Oriented Application - Experiences and Challenges. Paper presented at the Model Driven Engineering Languages and Systems, Montego Bay, Jamaica.

In this article, the practitioners can find more evidence on effort required to develop an industry quality domain specific modeling language. The experiences of the authors show that the development of a good DSL require more than a few weeks of extra effort. This reading is a complementary to the evidence of the productivity increase presented in this chapter.

Knodel, J., Anastasopolous, M., Forster, T., & Muthig, D. (2005). An Efficient Migration to Model-driven Development (MDD). Electronic Notes in Theoretical Computer Science, 137(3), 17-27.

In practice, migration from code-centric to model-driven software development is a multi-stage process. The authors of this article show a simple process of migrating existing projects into

MDSD. This reading complements the material in this chapter when discussing the prioritization issues.

Zhang, Y. (2004). Test-driven modeling for model-driven development. Software, IEEE, 21(5), 80-86.

In this case study, the author summarizes the process of modeling and executing test cases using TTCN-3 at Motorola. This material is an interesting reading for practitioners who want to have more than just code generated from their models.

ENDNOTES

[1] Although manual transformations should constitute the minority of all transformations.

[2] Naturally, due to the sensitivity of the data presented in this paper we cannot give details about the products.

[3] Due to the confidentiality agreement we cannot provide the exact numbers.

Chapter XI
From Requirements to Java Code:
An Architecture–Centric Approach for Producing Quality Systems

Antonio Bucchiarone
IMT of Lucca, Italy

Davide Di Ruscio
University of L'Aquila, Italy

Henry Muccini
University of L'Aquila, Italy

Patrizio Pelliccione
University of L'Aquila, Italy

ABSTRACT

When engineering complex and distributed software and hardware systems (increasingly used in many sectors, such as manufacturing, aerospace, transportation, communication, energy, and health-care), quality has become a big issue, since failures can have economic consequences and can also endanger human life. Model-based specifications of component-based systems permit to explicitly model the structure and behaviour of components and their integration. In particular Software Architectures (SA) have been advocated as an effective means to produce quality systems. In this chapter by combining different technologies and tools for analysis and development, we propose an architecture-centric model-driven approach to validate required properties and to generate the system code. Functional requirements are elicited and used for identifying expected properties the architecture shall express. The architectural compliance to the properties is formally demonstrated, and the produced architectural model is used to automatically generate Java code. Suitable transformations assure that the code is conforming to both structural and behavioural SA constraints. This chapter describes the process and discusses how some existing tools and languages can be exploited to support the approach.

1. INTRODUCTION

Software Architectures (SAs) are typically used to specify high level design blueprints of the systems under development and later on for maintenance and reuse purposes (in order to capture and model architectural design alternatives). At the same time, SAs can be used in order to analyze and validate architectural choices, both behavioural and quantitative (by complementing traditional code-level analysis techniques). More recently, architectural artefacts have been used to implicitly or explicitly guide the design and coding process (ARCHJAVA Project, 2005; Fujaba Project, 2006). In summary, SA specifications are nowadays used for many purposes (Mustapic, 2004; Bril, 2005) like documenting, analysing, or guiding the design and coding process.

Even though SA documentation, analysis, and code generation have been intensively analyzed in isolation (e.g., Bernardo, 2003; Muccini, 2006; Fujaba Project, 2006) (code generation only very recently and partially), a tool supported process for selecting and documenting the right architecture and for successively propagating architectural design to the final system implementation is still missing. Analysis techniques and tools have been introduced to understand if the SA satisfies certain expected properties. By using model checking, testing, performance analysis (and others) at the architectural level, a software architect can assess the architectural quality and predict the final system characteristics. In the context of code generation, this verification phase assumes even a more central role, being the selected architectural model used for (automatically) deriving the system implementation. However, most of the analysis techniques rely on formal architectural specifications (e.g., (Bernardo, 2003)) of difficult application in industrial projects and of difficult integration in the software development process.

In this chapter we propose an architecture-centric development approach which enables the Java code generation of a software system from a high quality architectural model-based design. High quality architecture hereafter is referred to the SA ability to fulfil certain functional and temporal constraints as imposed by the requirements. Other qualities (i.e., performance, security, safety, reliability, etc..) are not explicitly taken into consideration. The formally verified SA is then the starting point of model transformations that produce a skeleton of the Java code implementing the specified system. The produced code reflects both structural and behavioural SA constraints and consequently assures the validity of defined, specified, and verified functional requirements.

Thus the goals of this work are twofold: to validate the model-based architectural specification with respect to defined requirements, and to use this validated model to guide the generation of a quality system implementation using model-driven techniques. Moreover, the approach promotes the following key benefits: *(i)* a model-based specification of the SA is provided, *(ii)* the conformance relation between functional requirements and architecture is validated, and *(iii)* Java code is automatically generated from architectural models. The generated code is obliged to respect both structural SA constraints (e.g., each component can only communicate using connectors and ownership domains (Aldrich 04) that are explicitly declared in the SA) and behavioural constraints (i.e., methods provided by components have to be invoked consistently with respect to the architectural specification). The approach is supported by automated tools, which allow formal analysis and permit code generation from the validated architecture. Overall, the approach encourages developers to make a more extensive and practical usage of SA specifications.

The remaining of the chapter is organized as follows: Section 2 outlines the state of the art on functional requirements specification, on SA modelling and analysis, and on code generation. Based on this background information, Section 3 describes our proposal for an architecture-centric model-driven and quality oriented development process from requirements to code. Section 4 introduces an ATM system running case study that is used for detailing the approach. Section 5 draws future research directions. Section 6 discusses related work, while Section 7 concludes the chapter.

2. BACKGROUND

This section provides background information on the state-of-the art on functional requirements specification (Section 2.1), on formal and model-based specification of SAs (Section 2.2), on architecture-level analysis (Section 2.3), and on existing code generation techniques from architectural specifications (Section 2.4).

2.1 Functional Requirements Specification

Some work have been proposed in the last years attempting to bridge the gap between an informal functional requirements description to a formal one. Works in this area, related to our proposed research, can be organized into three groups: *properties elicitation and formalization*, approaches for *bringing the gap between informal requirements' descriptions and formal ones*, and *requirements to software architecture transition*.

Properties elicitation and formalization: In the literature little attention has been put in the properties to be proven. In general, these are assumed to exist as part of the problem specification. Holzman in (Holzmann, 2002) states that one of the "most underestimated problem in applications of automated tools to software verification" is "the problem of accurately capturing the correctness requirements" (properties) "that have to be verified" and continues identifying the difficulty of such task. When the verification technique is model checking (Clarke, 2000), temporal logic is the standard method to express the correctness

requirements. In the same chapter, Holzman shows how Linear-time Temporal Logic (LTL) (Manna, 1992) formulae may be used to describe properties and how the level of sophistication required by them may allow one to specify properties in a wrong way. However, in an industrial context it is unfeasible to write by hand complex LTL formulae. To this extent, he proposes a tool to write temporal properties in a graphical notation.

In (Smith, 2002) the authors recognize the difficulty in writing properties correctly. They notice that this difficulty is not only related to the chosen notation: "no matter what notation is used, however, there are often subtle, but important, details that need to be considered". In order to mitigate this problem, they propose PROPEL introducing pattern templates previously identified, which are represented using both disciplined natural language and finite state automata.

Bringing the gap between informal requirements' descriptions and formal ones: Many languages and notations have been suggested and devised for use in requirements engineering. Less formal notations, such as scenarios and use cases, have proven to be more for elicitation and negotiation, while more formal notations have proven more effectiveness for requirements specification and analysis. Much work has been done over last years attempting to bridge the gap between informal requirement descriptions to formal ones. We here discuss only those works we believe closer to our approach.

Johannisson in his PhD thesis (Johannisson, 2005) investigates how to bridge the gap between formal and informal software specifications. This work makes use of interactive syntax-directed editor, parsers and linearizers, based on a grammatical framework that combines linguistic and logical methods. The approach proposed in this chapter is related to a number of other approaches that have been considered by researchers.

In (Zhu, 2003) the authors exploit a software tool that allows system engineers to write detailed use case descriptions using structured templates. The specification is guided by use case style guidelines, temporal semantics and an extensive dictionary of naval domain nouns. Once the use case description phase has been accomplished, system engineers derive use case specifications and, after parameterization, corresponding scenarios are automatically generated.

In the Specification Pattern Instantiation and Derivation EnviRonment (SPIDER) framework (Cheng, 2006), developers can create natural language specifications of properties that are automatically and transparently mapped to the property specification language of the targeted analysis tools, e.g., LTL.

Requirements to software architecture transition: The problem of deciding how requirements, architectures and implementation have to be mutually related is still open as advocated and investigated by many researchers (STRAW 2003; Nuseibeh, 2001; Grünbacher, 2003). In (STRAW 2003; Nuseibeh, 2001), ways to bridge the gap between requirements and SAs have been proposed. Grünbacher et al. propose ways to trace requirements to SA models (Grünbacher, 2003) and SA to the implementation (Medvidovic, 2003).

Considerations: One relevant problem that arises during the requirement engineering process is the result of failing to make a clear transition between different levels of requirements description. According to the terminology adopted in (Sommerville, 2004), the term "user requirements" is used to mean high-level abstract requirement descriptions and the term "system requirements" is used to mean detailed and possibly formal descriptions. Often in practice, stake-holders are able to describe user requirements in an informal way without detailed technical knowledge. They are rarely willing to use structured notations or formal ones. Transiting from user requirements to system requirements is an expensive task. In fact, we are speaking about decisions made during early phases of the software development process, when the system under development is vague also in the mind of the customer. A good answer to this need is W_PSC (Autili, 2006), a speculative tool that facilitates understanding and structuring requirements. By means of a set of sentences (based on expertise in requirements formalization and on a set of well-known patterns (Dwyer, 1999) for specifying temporal properties used in practice) and classified according to main keywords of temporal properties, W_PSC forces to make decisions that break the uncertainty and the ambiguity of user requirements.

The output of W_PSC is a temporal property expressed in Property Sequence Chart (PSC) (Autili, 2007). PSC is a simple and (sufficiently) powerful formalism for specifying temporal properties in a user-friendly fashion. It is a scenario-based visual language that is an extended graphical notation of a subset of UML 2.0 Sequence Diagrams. PSC can graphically express a useful set of both liveness and safety properties in terms of messages exchanged among the components forming the system. W_PSC supports also the user on taking many required decisions transiting from requirements to architecture. Indeed, automatically transforming informal requirements into formal temporal properties is not always possible (due to inconsistencies or under specifications) and may become time consuming. W_PSC, as all those related approaches previously summarized, makes an attempt to make the transition from informal requirements to formal properties easier and faster. Being W_PSC and PSC part of our proposal, further usage details will be provided in the following Section 3 and Section 4.

2.2 Software Architecture Specification

Two main classes of languages have been used so far to specify SAs: formal Architecture Description Languages (ADLs) and model-based specifications.

Table 1. The most known ADLs

ADL	Born Data	Tools	Still Supported	Notes
Rapide	1990	Rapide	NO	ADL and simulation
Darwin	1991	LTSA + SAA	YES	Focus on dynamic SA
Weaves	1991	Weaves	NO	Data-flow-architectures with high-volume of data
Adage	1992	—	NO	Avionics navigation and guidance Architecture Description
LILEANNA	1993	LILEANNA	NO	Modules connection language
MetaH & MetaS	1993	MetaH	YES	ADL for avionic domain
ArTek	1994	—	NO	Non conventional ADL
Resolve	1994	Resolve	NO	Focus on Component Specification
Wright	1994	Wright	NO	Focus on communications
Acme	1995	AcmeStudio Armani	YES	Interchange Language between ADLs
SADL	1995	Sadl tool	NO	Focus on Refinement
UniCon	1995	UniCon	NO	Focus on connectors and Styles
C2 SADEL & C2 AML	1996	Dradel, SAAGE ArchStudio	NO	ADL based on C2 style
GenVoca	1996	P3	NO	Non conventional ADL
Fujaba	1997	Fujaba	YES	Non conventional ADL
Jacal	1997	Jacal 2	YES	Focus on prototyping SA
Koala	1997	Koala tools	YES	ADL for product families
Little-JIL	1998	Little-JIL 1.0	NO	Non conventional ADL
Maude	1998	Maude 2.0	YES	Non conventional ADL
ADML	2000	ADML Enabled Tools	YES	XML-based ADL
xArch/xADL	2000	xADL 2.0	YES	XML-based ADL
AADL	2001	Osate	YES	Embedded real-time systems / Avionics systems
xArch/xAcme	2001	AcmeStudio	YES	Acme in XML
ABC/ADL	2002	ABC tool (prototype)	YES	ADL for component composition
Prisma	2002	PrismaCase	YES	Component-based systems
DAOP-ADL	2003	DAOP-ADTools	YES	Component and Aspect-based ADL

Many ADLs have been proposed in the last fifteen years, with different requirements and notations, and with the objective to support components' and connectors' specification and their overall interconnection, composition, abstraction, reusability, configuration, heterogeneity, and analysis mechanisms (Medvidovic, 2000). Table 1 shows the most known ADLs evidencing the ones still supported. The table contains also approaches which are usually classified as non-conventional ADLs since they possibly neglect fundamental aspects.

Even if much work has been done on this direction, the application of such techniques into industrial systems can still be very difficult due to some extra requirements and constraints imposed by realistic scenarios: the methodology must be tool supported, frequently based on semi-formal or informal notations, and typically based on partial models.

As a consequence, we cannot always assume that formal modelling of the software system exists. On the contrary, a semi-formal, easy to learn and possibly diagrammatic notation may reasonably offer enough pragmatic qualities.

With the introduction of UML as the de-facto standard to model software systems and with its widespread adoption in industrial contexts, many extensions and profiles have been proposed to adapt UML to model architectures. Many proposals have been presented so far to adapt UML 1.x to model SAs (e.g., (Robbins, 1998; Kruchten, 1995; Gomaa, 2001; Kande', 2002)). In such proposals, researchers have compared the architectural needs with UML concepts, extended or adapted UML, or created new profiles to specify architecture specific needs with UML.

Recently, several works propose UML 2.0 native specifications (i.e., without any profile or extension) for SA modelling. In (Eriksson, 2004) logical architectures, patterns and physical architectures are represented by using components, dependencies, and collaborations. In (Pender, 2003) components within a component diagram are used to model the logical and physical architecture. In order to bridge the gap between UML 2.0 and ADLs, some aspects still require adjustments, thus much work is still ongoing (Goulo, 2003; Roh, 2004; Ivers, 2004; Perez-Martinez, 2004).

The success of model-based specifications of SAs is proven by many profiles defined so far for UML-modelling of SAs (e.g., (AADL; SysML)).

2.3 Software Architecture Analysis

While how to model SAs has been for a long time the main issue in the SA community, how to select the right architecture has become one of the most relevant challenges in recent days. Model checking, deadlock detection, testing, performance analysis, and security are, among others, the most investigated analysis techniques at the architectural level. Among the techniques that allow designers to perform exhaustive verification of the systems (such as theorem provers, term rewriting systems and proof checkers), model checking (Clarke, 2000) has as main advantage that it is completely automatic. The user provides a model of the system and a specification of the property to be checked on the system and the model checker provides either true, if the property is verified, or a counter example is always generated if the property is not valid. The counter example is particularly important since it shows a trace that leads the system to the error.

While presenting a comprehensive analysis of the state of the art in architectural analysis is out of the scope of this chapter, this section will focus on architecture-level model checking techniques. For further reading on the topic, interested readers may refer to e.g., (Bernardo, 2003; Muccini, 2006; Dobrica, 2002).

Initial approaches for model checking at the architecture level have been provided by the Wright architectural language (Allen, 1997) and the Tracta approach (Magee, 1999). More recently, many other approaches have been proposed, as listed and classified in Figure 1. By focussing on the model-based approaches, Bose (Bose, 1999) presents a method which automatically translates UML models of SA for verification and simulation using SPIN (Holzmann, 2003). A component is specified in terms of port behaviours and performs the computation or provides services. A mediator component is specified in terms of roles and co-ordination policies, and safety properties are also checked. Lfp (Jerad, 2005) is a formal language dedicated to the description of distributed embedded systems' control structure. It has characteristics of both ADL and coordination language. Its model checker engine is Maude based on rewriting logic semantics. Fujaba (Fujaba Project, 2006) is an approach tool supported for real-time model checking of component-based systems: the system structure is modelled through UML component diagrams, the real-time behaviour is modelled by means of real-time statecharts (an extension to UML state diagrams), properties are specified in TCTL (Timed Computation Tree Logic) (Alur, 1990) and the UPPAAL (UPPsala and AALborg University) (Bengtsson, 1995) model checker is used as the real-time model checker engine. Arcade (Barber, 2001) (Architecture Analysis Dynamic Environment) applies model checking to a DRA (Domain Reference Architecture) to provide analysts and developers with early feedback from safety and liveness evaluations during requirements management. The properties are represented as LTL formulae and the model checker engine is SPIN. AutoFOCUS (AutoFOCUS Project) is a model-based tool for the development of reliable embedded systems. In AutoFOCUS, static and dynamic aspects of the system are modelled in four different views: structural view, interaction view, behavioural view, and data view. AutoFOCUS provides an integrated tool for modelling, simulation, and validation. AutoFOCUS2 (AutoFOCUS2 Project) advances and improves previous work on Auto-FOCUS by adding new modeling views.

CHARMY (Pelliccione, 2005; CHARMY, 2004; Inverardi, 2005) is our proposal to model-check SA compliance to desired functional temporal properties. It intends to fill this gap by providing an automated, easy to use tool for the model-based design and validation of SA. CHARMY main strengths are as follow:

1. **Informal vs formal:** Formal languages allows for automatic analysis, but they are generally time and cost consuming, while requiring certain specific skills. Informal languages, instead, are faster and easier to learn, by permitting lower automation. CHARMY tries to incorporate both advantages, and mitigate their respective weaknesses automatically completing informal and incomplete models: SA topology and behaviour are described via UML based specifications and automatically translated into a formal prototype. In particular, components and state diagrams, used to specify the SA topology and behaviour, are automatically interpreted to synthesize a formal Promela prototype, which is the SPIN model checker modelling language;

2. **SA simulation and checking:** CHARMY provides support for simulating the SA: it uses the SPIN simulation engine and offers simulation features which interpret SPIN results in terms of CHARMY state machines. Moreover, properties whose validity needs to be checked on the architectural model are modelled through scenarios, by expressing desired and undesired behaviours. Such scenarios are automatically translated into Büchi automata (Büchi, 1960), an operational representation for LTL formulae. SPIN is then used to check the conformance of the Promela prototype with respect to such behavioural properties;

3. **Automatic tool support:** The CHARMY approach for specifying and analyzing SAs is tool supported, and it hides most of the complexity of the modelling and analysis process. Model-based architectural specifications,

Figure 1. Model checking techniques based on formal or model-based architectural specifications (©2007 Computer Science Department – University of L'Aquila (Italy). Used with permission)

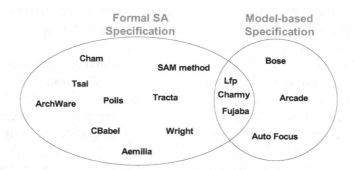

2.4 Code Generation from Software Architecture Specification

drawn using the CHARMY editors or standard UML tools, are automatically translated into a formal prototype. The prototype can then be automatically checked for correctness with respect to desired properties.

For further information on model-checking software architectures, a survey is available in (Zhang, 2007).

2.4 Code Generation from Software Architecture Specification

In this section we present an overview on the various techniques used to generate code from a SA specification. We focus the attention on languages that can be used to generate code starting from an architectural model of the system. They can be distinguished in Architecture Description Languages (ADLs), such as languages for describing SAs, and Architectural Programming Language (APL), such as languages that integrate SA concepts into programming languages. We conclude this section with a comparison among APLs. It is important to note that code generated from ADLs not necessarily contain architecture concepts. This can have impact on the readability of the code and can reduce its modifiability and maintainability. Furthermore, modifications on the generated code made by developers can invalidate architectural constraints. APLs have been introduced to solve this problem. All these aspects will be detailed in the following.

2.4.1 ADLs and Code Generation

Some ADLs support code generation from an architectural description of the system. In Table 2 we list some of them: it shows the ADL name, the tool support and the type of code that they produce as output. We have considered ADLs that are currently used in an industrial context and that are continuously updated showing the last release and the references.

While code generation is enabled starting from SA specifications, code generation approaches do no explicitly represent architectural notions at the code level. Thus, the notion of SA components, connectors and configurations is kept implicit and the implementation inevitably tends to loose its connection to the intended architectural structure during the maintenance steps. The result is "architectural erosion" (Perry, 1992).

Table 2. Code generation from ADLs

ADL	Born Data	Tools	Output Code	Last Update	Reference
Darwin	1991	LTSA-WS + SAA	C++	March 2007	(Magee, 1999)
Fujaba	1997	Fujaba	Java	July 2007	(Fujaba Project, 2006)
xArch/xADL	2000	ArchStudio + Apigen	XML	January 2005	(xADL 2.0, 2005)
AADL	2001	Osate	Ada, C, Java	April 2007	(AADL)
Prisma	2002	PrismaCase	C#	September 2007	(PRISMA)

2.4.2 Architectural Programming Languages (APLs)

APLs overcome the problem of architectural erosion in implementations by integrating SA concepts into programming languages.

By using APLs there is an inclusion of architectural notions, like components, ports with provided and required interfaces as well as protocols, connectors, and assemblies, into a programming language (typically Java). The basic idea of architectural programming is to preserve the SA structure and properties throughout the software development process so as to guarantee that each component in the implementation may only communicate directly with the components to which it is connected in the architecture. In fact our objective is to have a development process that guarantees the "Communication Integrity" between code and SA (xADL 2.0, 2005).

In this section we present ARCHJAVA and JAVA/A, which are the most famous and advanced APLs (Baumeister, 2006), in order to understand their main characteristics and to compare them with respect to aspects that we consider important for an APL. Then, based on the proposed comparison, we will choose one of the two technologies to be part of our SA-based quality process.

ArchJava

ARCHJAVA (ARCHJAVA Project, 2005) is an APL which extends the Java language with component classes (which describe objects that are part of the architecture), connections (which enable components communication), and ports (which are the endpoints of connections).

Components are hierarchically organized by using ownership domains (Aldrich, 2004), which can be shared along connections, permitting the connected components to communicate through shared data. Owernship domains are conceptual groups of objects with explicit domain names and explicit policies that govern references between them (Abi-Antoun, 2007).

A component in ARCHJAVA is a special kind of object whose communication patterns are explicitly declared using architectural declarations. Component code is defined in ARCHJAVA using *component classes*. Components communicate through explicitly declared ports. A *port* is a communication endpoint declared by a component. Each port declares a set of required and provided methods. A provided method is implemented by the component and is available to be called by other components connected to this port. Conversely, each required method is provided by some other component connected to this port. Each provided method must be implemented inside the component.

ARCHJAVA requires developers to declare the connection patterns that are permitted at run time. Once they have been declared, concrete connections can be made between components. All connected components must be part of an ownership domain declared by the component making the connection.

Communication integrity is the key property enforced by ARCHJAVA, ensuring that components can only communicate using connections and ownership domains that are explicitly declared in the architecture. ARCHJAVA guarantees communication integrity between an architecture and its implementation, even in the presence of advanced architectural features like run time component creation and connection. A prototype compiler for ARCHJAVA is publicly available for download at the ARCHJAVA web site (ARCHJAVA Project, 2005). Figure 2 shows a sample ARCHJAVA specification of the toy architecture[1] depicted on the upper side of the Figure by means of a UML composite component diagram.

The *OutService* component is made up of two subcomponents: the *AccidentAssistanceService* (AAS) and the *EmergencyService* (ES). The former has one *out* port and the latter an *in* port through which the two components are connected. A port is a communication endpoint declared by a component. For each port the language offers constructs to define *requires* and *provides* methods. ARCHJAVA requires developers to declare in the architecture the connection patterns that are permitted at run time.

Taking a look to the code for the specification in Figure 2 (top), the declaration "connect pattern" in our code permits the *OutService* component to make connections between the *out* port of its AAS subcomponents and the *in* port of its ES subcomponent. Once a connect pattern has been declared, concrete connections are admitted between components. For example the *constructor* for *OutService* connects the *out* port of the AAS component instance to the *in* port of the ES component instance. This connection binds the required methods (*AlertAccepted*, *AlertEmergencyService*, etc.) in the *out* port of AAS to a provided method with the same name and signature in the *in* port of ES component. Thus when AAS invokes *AlertAccepted* on its *out* port, the corresponding implementation in ES will be invoked.

Java/A

The basic idea of JAVA/A (Baumeister, 2006; Hacklinger, 2004) is to integrate architectural concepts, such as components, ports and connectors, as fundamental parts into Java (similarly to ARCHJAVA). The underlying component model is compatible with the UML component model (Hacklinger, 2004; OMG). This compatibility and the one-to-one mapping of these concepts allow software designers to easily implement UML2.0 component diagrams. They can express the notions present in these diagrams using built-in language concepts constructs of Java. Furthermore, the visibility of architectural elements in the JAVA/A source code prevents architectural erosion.

The basic concepts of the JAVA/A component model are *components, ports, connectors* and *configurations*. Any communication between JAVA/A components is performed by sending messages to ports. Each message must be an element of the required interface of the perspective port. The port will then forward the message to the attached connector, which itself will delegate the message

Figure 2. OutService composite component in ARCHJAVA (©2007 Computer Science Department – University of L'Aquila (Italy). Used with permission)

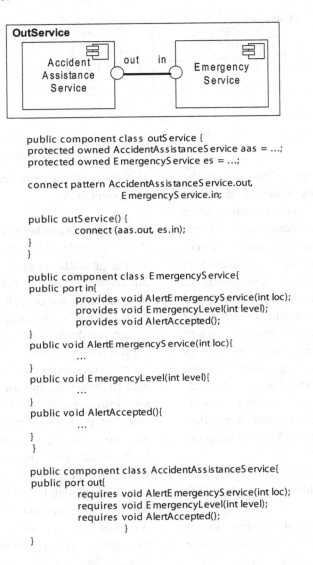

```
public component class outService {
protected owned AccidentAssistanceService aas = ...;
protected owned EmergencyService es = ...;

connect pattern AccidentAssistanceService.out,
                EmergencyService.in;

public outService() {
        connect (aas.out, es.in);
}
}

public component class EmergencyService{
public port in{
        provides void AlertEmergencyService(int loc);
        provides void EmergencyLevel(int level);
        provides void AlertAccepted();
}
public void AlertEmergencyService(int loc){
        ...
}
public void EmergencyLevel(int level){
        ...
}
public void AlertAccepted(){
        ...
}
}

public component class AccidentAssistanceService{
public port out{
        requires void AlertEmergencyService(int loc);
        requires void EmergencyLevel(int level);
        requires void AlertAccepted();
        }
}
```

to the port at its other end. Each port may contain a *protocol*. These protocols describe the order of messages that are allowed to be sent from and to the respective port. Any incoming and outgoing communication must conform to the protocol. Protocols are specified by UML state machines and ensure the soundness of a configuration at compile-time. A *Connector* in JAVA/A links two components by connecting ports they own.

The JAVA/A compiler is not yet complete and available but authors claim that it will transform JAVA/A components into pure Java code which can be compiled to byte code using the Java compiler. It will be possible to compile and

Figure 3. OutService composite component in JAVA/A (©2007 Computer Science Department – University of L'Aquila (Italy). Used with permission)

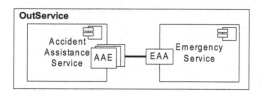

deploy each component on its own, since the component's dependencies on the environment are encapsulated in ports. The correctness of an assembly (i.e., deadlock-freedom) can be ensured using the UML state machine model checker HUGO (HUGO, 2005). Another important aspect that JAVA/A has is the *dynamic reconfiguration*. It summarises changes to a component-based systems at runtime, concerning creation and destruction of components and building up and removing connections between ports. JAVA/A supports each of these reconfiguration variants. JAVA/A has a semantic model that uses states as algebras approach (Baumeister, 2006) for representing the internals of components and assemblies, and the I/O-transition systems for describing the observable behaviour.

Figure 3 shows a composite component diagram of the same system already introduced for ARCHJAVA (in Figure 2).

The composite component contains an assembly of two components Accident Assistance Service (AAS) and Emergency Service (ES) whose ports are wired by a connector. The AAE port of the AAS component is depicted as stacked boxes since it is a dynamic port which can have an arbitrary number of port instances. In contrast, the static port EAA must have a single instance at any time. Port protocols are specified with UML state machines. A protocol describes the order and dependencies of messages which are sent and received by a port. The code corresponding

to this specification is described and illustrated in Appendix A.

Comparing ArchJava and Java/A

ARCHJAVA and JAVA/A employ similar approaches. Both augment Java with the concepts of component and connector. ARCHJAVA components have ports with required and provided interfaces. However, ports in ARCHJAVA do not have associated protocols. As a result the dynamic behaviour of ports is not captured in ARCHJAVA.

ARCHJAVA, as well as JAVA/A, allows hierarchical component composition. In JAVA/A there is no possibility of communicating with components other than sending messages to their ports, whereas in ARCHJAVA outer components can invoke methods of inner components directly, which breaks the encapsulation. While ARCHJAVA lacks a semantic model, JAVA/A provides a complete one based on algebras and I/O- transitions systems. As far as concern tool support, in (Schmerl, 2004) the authors have developed additional Eclipse plug-ins that integrates AcmeStudio (Acme) and ARCHJAVA. With this framework an architect can model an architecture using AcmeStudio, and have access to AcmeStudio's verification engines to check desired architectural properties. The architect can then generate ARCHJAVA code using the refinement plug-in. Once developers complete the implementation of the system, ARCHJAVA's checks help ensuring that the implementation conforms to the architect's design. Unfortunately

Table 3. APLs comparison

APL	Components	Ports	Configurations	Encapsulation
ArchJava	Yes	Yes	Implicit	Partial
Java/A	Yes	Yes	Explicit	Yes

APL	Behavioural Modeling	Distributed Applications	Asynchronous Communication	Tool Support
ArchJava	No	No	No	Total
Java/A	Yes	Yes	Explicit	Not yet

the existing ArchJava environment supports only the *verification* of architectural properties and it does not *force* the developers to respect the component behaviour described into the SA. For Java/A the tool support is not yet complete and it is one of future works. So far, a Java/A compiler should transform Java/A components into pure Java code which can be compiled to byte code using the Java compiler. However, this compiler is not yet publicly available.

Table 3 synthesizes the above discussion while providing an explicit way of understanding the key features and differences of ArchJava and Java/A.

Our SA-based approach makes use of the ArchJava language since the availability of the corresponding compiler has allowed us to develop each phase of the approach described in the next section leading to a prototypical implementation available for download at (Charmy, 2004).

3. MAIN THRUST OF THE CHAPTER: THE PROPOSED APPROACH

The model-based architecture-centric and automated analysis approach we are proposing aims at combining exhaustive analysis techniques (model checking) and SA-based code generation to produce highly-dependable systems in a model-based development process. Figure 4 shows the activities of the architecture-centric analysis and deployment approach. It is composed of four principal activities: *(i)* specification of functional requirements, *(ii)* model-based specification of SAs, *(iii)* validation of the SA specification with respect to requirements through model checking, and finally *(iv)* architecture-based code generation.

The architectural topology and behaviour is captured through a UML-based notation, part of the Charmy framework (Pelliccione, 2005; Inverardi, 2005). Properties are elicited from requirements by means of W_PSC (Autili, 2006) and modelled according to the Property Sequence Chart (PSC) language (Autili, 2007). Charmy is used to check the architectural model conformance with respect to identified functional properties. After this activity, the architecture is proven to be compliant with selected properties. In the SA-based code generation activity Charmy models are translated into ArchJava code by means of a developed code generator based on the Eclipse Java Emitter Template (JET) framework (part of the Eclipse Modeling Framework (Budinsky, 2003)). Finally, the ArchJava compiler is used to generate Java code and to ensure that the implementation conforms to the architectural specification.

Figure 4. The proposed approach (©2007 Computer Science Department – University of L'Aquila (Italy). Used with permission)

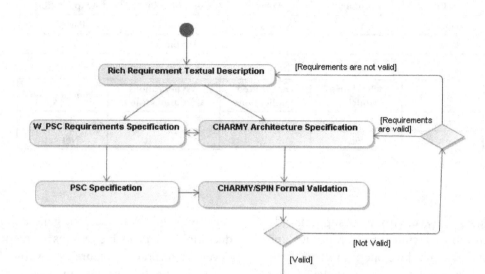

In the following, by referring to Figure 4, each activity of the proposed approach is individually described.

W_PSC Requirements Specification and Formalization in the PSC Language

Functional requirements are identified, modeled and analyzed. In order to automatically verify that the system SA satisfies the functional requirements, properties are elicited from requirements and expressed and formalized as formulae in temporal logics. Unfortunately, the level of inherent sophistication required by these formalisms too often represents an impediment to move these techniques from "research theory" to "industry practice". PSC facilitates the non trivial and error prone task of specifying, correctly and without expertise in temporal logic, temporal properties. PSC can graphically express a useful set of both *liveness* and *safety* properties in terms of messages exchanged among the components forming the system. Finally, an algorithm, called Psc2Ba (Autili, 2007), translates PSC into a temporal property representation understandable by model checkers.

Since the aim of this chapter is not to present PSC (presented elsewhere) we do not provide details about this language, but we refer to (Autili, 2007) for a fully description of both the textual and graphical language and its declarative and operational semantics. Moreover, in Section 4 we explain further aspects of the language as needed to fully understand the approach. While the translation process from PSC diagram to Büchi automata is fully automated, the selection of properties from requirements and their formalization in PSC is totally left to engineers' experience. Both tasks may become expensive and error prone, when applied to real projects. W_PSC aims at alleviating the engineers work in eliciting and formalizing properties bridging the gap between possibly informal requirement specifications (as found in practice) and formal ones (as needed in formal methods). It is a conversational tool that, by means of well structured and deep sentences, helps the software engineers in identify and formalize properties. It has been built selecting and classifying the PSC statements, and allows engineers to incrementally build PSC diagrams, starting from user requirements. W_PSC offers a user-friendly wizard helpful while translating a user requirements description into PSC scenarios. It is composed of several windows that present sentences helpful for requirements understanding and selection. The sentences are grouped according to a classification based on temporal properties keywords. Since PSC is built by taking into account the same keywords, W_PSC introduces an intuitive way to use all the subtle and precise instruments of PSC. In Section 4 we will provide

further details of W_PSC as needed for understanding the case study, while we refer to (Autili, 2006) for a complete description of it.

3.2 Software Architecture Model-Based Specification in CHARMY

The SA is designed in CHARMY (CHARMY, 2004; Inverardi, 2005) that allows software engineers to specify both the structure and the behaviour by using UML-based notations. We use CHARMY to design the SA since it provides automatisms for verifying the SA by means of model checking techniques. CHARMY allows the specification of the SA topology in terms of components and relationships among them, where components represent abstract computational subsystems. As shown in Figure 5, the internal behaviour of each component is specified in terms of CHARMY state diagrams. The CHARMY notation for state machines allows engineers to specify the intra-component and inter-component behaviours of architectural components and connectors (i.e., the internal behaviour of architectural elements and their integration, respectively). States of the state machines are connected by means of transi-

Figure 5. Chunks of the CHARMY metamodel (©2007 Computer Science Department – University of L'Aquila (Italy). Used with permission)

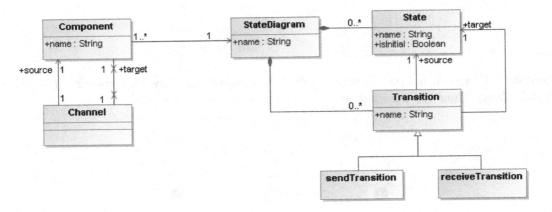

tions. Transitions are labelled with a name and could represent either a message sent or received, denoted by an exclamation mark "!" or a question mark "?", respectively.

In Figure 7 a sample CHARMY specification that will be considered throughout the section is depicted. In particular, it is a model that conforms to the metamodel in Figure 5 and it consists of the components *C1* and *C2* connected through the channels *C1_TO_C2* and *C2_TO_C1*. For each component, a corresponding state machine is provided in order to describe the admitted component behaviours.

3.3 Software Architecture Verification

CHARMY uses model checking techniques to validate the SA conformance to certain properties. Being the SA typically used as the driver for the entire development process, exhaustive analysis has been preferred instead of partial proofs or sampling.

Starting from the SA description CHARMY synthesizes, through a suitable translation into Promela (the specification language of the SPIN (Holzmann, 2003) model checker), a runnable SA prototype that can be executed and verified in SPIN. This model can be validated with respect to a set of properties expressed in the PSC language. By using CHARMY, thanks to a UML like notation used for the system design and the properties

specification, we have an easy to use, practical approach to model and check architectural specifications, *hiding the modelling complexity.*

Whenever the SA specification does not properly implement selected requirements ("Not valid" arrow in Figure 4), the SA itself needs to be revised. Thanks to the model-checker output in case of a not valid result (i.e., a counter example reproducing the error) we may either correct the SA specification (if we discover that there is an error in the SA specification) or correct the PSC property (if we discover that the property is not properly expressed).

3.4 JET/ARCHJAVA Code Generation

Whenever the SA is validated with respect to the desired requirements, Java code is automatically generated from the SA specification. According to Figure 6, this activity is performed through two main steps: starting from a validated CHARMY *Specification,* ARCHJAVA *code* is automatically obtained by means of a *JET-based Code Generator.* Then, by exploiting the existing ARCHJAVA *Compiler,* executable *Java code* is generated. Here we focus on the first step of the translation in Figure 6 which is based on the following directives:

(i)   Each CHARMY component becomes an ARCHJAVA component. For instance, the component *C1* in Figure 7.a induces the following ARCHJAVA specification:

Figure 6. JET/ ArchJava Code Generation (©2007 Computer Science Department – University of L'Aquila (Italy). Used with permission)

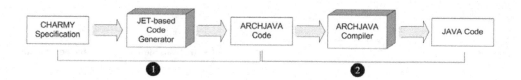

Figure 7. Sample Charmy specification (©2007 Computer Science Department – University of L'Aquila (Italy). Used with permission)

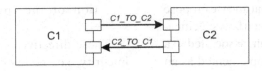

(a) Topology specification

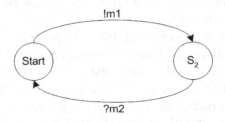

(b) C1 behaviour specification

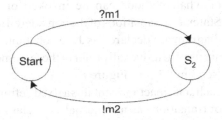

(c) C2 behaviour specification

```
public component class C1 {
...
}
```

(ii)   Each CHARMY component's sent and received message is used to synthesize the component ports. We recall that ARCHJAVA has both provided ports for provided services and required ports for required services. An ARCHJAVA port only connects a pair of components. This means that if a component needs to communicate with more than one component, it needs additional ports. Thus, the provided component services are partitioned into sets of services provided to different components. The same is done for required services. Accordingly, the suitable number of required and provided ports is declared into the ARCHJAVA specification of the component (containing the declaration of required and provided services, respectively). For instance, the sample SA in Figure 7.a gives place to the following ARCHJAVA code fragments concerning the *C1* component implementation:

```
public port C1_TO_C2 {
requires void m1();
}

public port C2_TO_C1 {
provides void m2();
}
```

(iii) For each CHARMY component an ARCHJAVA specification is generated to encode the associated state diagram. ARCHJAVA does not offer a direct support for that and we propose guidelines to extend the ARCHJAVA specifications so that a state diagram associated to a software component is implemented as an adjacency list. In particular:

- for each method invoked by a given component the corresponding state machine changes state accordingly so having trace of what methods can be invoked or not. States and transitions of the considered state diagram are declared as Java constants and are used to univocally refer to these elements (see lines 3-9 in Figure 8).
- each state machine contains a fixed definition of transitions as an internal Java class (see line 15-37 in Figure 8). The state diagram is defined as a *LinkedList*. The constructor of the state diagram class contains the definition of the state machine adding to the *LinkedList* of the state diagram an element for each state containing all existing transitions (for each existing transition a new object of the internal class transition is added) (see lines 40-50).
- each state machine class contains also a method that simulates the transition fire, i.e., this method gets as input the transition (according to the runtime behaviour of the system) and checks if it is possible, in the actual computation state, to perform the transition fire (see lines 52-63). If the behaviour is allowed then the actual state is updated to the transition target state, otherwise an exception is raised. In case a method cannot be invoked in a certain time, an exception is raised. The exception is defined as an additional ARCHJAVA specification, i.e., a java class extending the *java.lang.Exception* class.

(iv) A *main* ARCHJAVA specification is also generated to define the binding among component's ports and the instantiation of the involved state machines

These directives ensure the communication integrity, i.e., components can only communicate using connections and ownership domains that are explicitly declared in the SA. The rest of the section outlines the approach supporting the automatic generation of code that implements such directives. This automation is required since manual coding could diverge or not completely adhere to them.

As previously said, the code generator implementing the four directives above has been developed in JET (Budinsky, 2003). JSP-like templates define explicitly the target ARCHJAVA code structure and get the data they need from the CHARMY models. In particular, the code generator consists of four templates (see Figure 9): *main.jet* is a default template that gets data as input and applies the other templates. Being more precise, it applies the *componentMain.jet* template, which implements the directive *(iv)* previously described, producing the target *MAIN.archj* file (see line 2 in Figure 10). Then, for each component in the source CHARMY specification, the *component.jet* template is applied in order to generate the component implementation according to points *(i)* and *(ii)* above (see line 4-6 in Figure 10). Finally, for each source component the corresponding state machine encoding is generated by applying the *smComponent.jet* template that implements point *(iv)* (see line 8-10).

Due to space limitation, the templates are not reported here. However, interested readers can refer to (CHARMY, 2004) for downloading the full implementation of the proposed JET-based code generator.

In the next section we will apply the architecture-based approach we are proposing on a case study. We will focus principally on the code

Figure 8. Sample state machine encoding (©2007 Computer Science Department – University of L'Aquila (Italy). Used with permission)

```
1.   public class SM_C1 {
2.
3.       /** State encoding*/
4.       public final int S_startC1= 0;
5.       public final int S_S1= 1;
6.
7.       /** Transition encoding */
8.       public final int T_m1=0;
9.       public final int T_m2=1;
10.
11.  private int currentState=S_startC1;
12.
13.  private LinkedList states = new LinkedList();
14.
15.  private class transition{
16.          private int state;
17.          private int transition;
18.          private int send_receive;
19.
20.          public transition(int transition, int state, int send_receive){
21.                  this.transition=transition;
22.                  this.state=state;
23.                  this.send_receive=send_receive;
24.                  }
25.
26.          public int getTransition(){
27.                  return transition;
28.          }
29.
30.          public int getState(){
31.                  return state;
32.          }
33.
34.          public int getSendReceive(){
35.                  return send_receive;
36.          }
37.  }
38.
39.      /** State Machine constructor*/
40.  public SM_C1(){
41.          System.out.println("SM_C1.constr");
42.
43.          LinkedList startC1 = new LinkedList();
44.          startC1.add(new transition(T_m1, S_S1 ,1));
45.          states.add(startC1);
46.
47.          LinkedList S_S1 = new LinkedList();
48.          S_S1.add(new transition(T_m2, S_startC1,0));
49.          states.add(S_S1);
50.  }
51.
52.  public void transFire(int trans) throws SMException {
53.          LinkedList transitions = (LinkedList) states.get(currentState);
54.          for (int i = 0; i < transitions.size(); i++) {
55.            if (((transition) transitions.get(i).getTransition() == trans)
56.              currentState = ((transition) transitions.get(i).getState();
57.              System.out.println("User.trans allowed: ");
58.              return;
59.            }
60.          }
61.          System.out.println("trans not allowed: " + trans);
62.          throw new SMException();
63.  }}
```

Figure 9. JET-based Code Generator templates (©2007 Computer Science Department – University of L'Aquila (Italy). Used with permission)

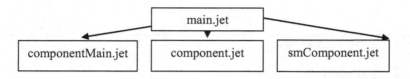

Figure 10. Fragment of the main.jet template (©2007 Computer Science Department – University of L'Aquila (Italy). Used with permission)

```
1.  ...
2.  <ws:file template="templates/componentMain.jet" path="{$org.eclipse.jet.resource.project.name}/src-
        generated/MAIN.archj"/>
3.
4.  <c:iterate select="$SAcomponent" var="component">
5.  <ws:file template="templates/component.jet" path="{$org.eclipse.jet.resource.project.name}/src-
        generated/{$component/@nome}.archj"/>
6.  </c:iterate>
7.
8.  <c:iterate select="$SAcomponent" var="component">
9.  <ws:file template="templates/smComponent.jet" path="{$org.eclipse.jet.resource.project.name}/src-
        generated/SM_{$component/@nome}.archj"/>
10. < /c:iterate>
```

generation activity, to be considered the main contribution of this chapter.

4. MAIN THRUST OF THE CHAPTER: A SAMPLE ATM SYSTEM

A bank has several automated teller machines (ATMs), which are geographically distributed and connected to a central server. Each ATM has a card reader, a cash dispenser, a keyboard/display, and a receipt printer. A user can withdraw cash or recharge a mobile phone credit. Assuming that the card is recognized, the system validates the ATM card to determine that the card has not expired and that the user-entered PIN (Personal Identification Number) is correct. If the user is authorized, it is prompted for withdraw or recharge transaction. Before these transactions can be approved, the bank determines that sufficient funds exist in the requested account. If the transaction is approved, the requested amount of cash is dispensed, the account is updated and the card is ejected. A user may cancel a transaction at any time with a logout operation.

4.1 Functional Requirements Specification

In this section we report only a subset of the requirements which are useful for explaining the approach. The requirements are presented in the following as use case tables. The first one, in Table

Table 4. User login use case

Use Case Name	User login
Description	The ATM System validates the USER PIN
Actors	USER, TM, AUTH
Pre-Conditions	ATM is idle, displaying a Welcome message
Process Steps	1. USER enters the PIN (*login*). 2. TM forwards the request (*login_auth*) to AUTH that checks whether the USER-entered PIN matches the card PIN maintained by the system. 3. If PIN numbers match, AUTH notifies it (*login_auth_ok*) to TM. 4. TM notifies to USER (*login_ok*) the login successful and prompts customer for transactions type (*withdraw* or *chargePhone*).
Post-Conditions	USER has been validated
Alternative Paths	If the USER-entered PIN does not match the PIN number of the card, AUTH notifies to TM an error (*login_auth_ko*) and TM asks USER to re-insert the PIN (*login_ko*).

4, is the User login use case that describes the user interactions to get access to the ATM.

The other use case, represented in Table 5, is the withdraw functionality of the ATM that allows the user to withdraw money from the bank. This use case includes the User login use case as precondition.

4.2 Software Architecture Specification in CHARMY

The architecture of the ATM system that we consider is composed of four components as shown in Figure 11: the user (USER component), the transaction manager (TM component), the bank account (BA component), and the authentication manager (AUTH component). The USER component communicates only with the TM component that forwards the service requests to the BA or AUTH component.

Moreover the behaviour of each component is described with the state machines depicted in Figures 12-14. The USER component (see Figure 12) handles three different requests, one for the authentication (*!login*) followed by two possible responses (*?login_ok* and *?login_ko*), one for withdrawing money from its account (*!withdraw*), and one for recharging the mobile phone credit (*!chargePhone*).

The TM component (refer to Figure 14) contains the logic of the ATM system. This component receives the login request from the User (*?login*) and forwards it to the AUTH component (*!login Auth*).

283

Table 5. Withdraw use case

Use Case Name	Withdraw
Description	USER withdraws a specific amount of money from a valid bank account
Dependency	Include Validate PIN Use Case
Actors	USER, TM, AUTH, BAWhich actor from the actor model initiates this course of the use case? All the different user roles and/or other systems that initiate the use case. Actors are external to the system.
Pre-Conditions	ATM is idle, displaying a Welcome message
Process Steps	1. Include User login use case. 2. USER selects *withdraw* and enters the amount of money to be withdrawn. 3. TM forwards the request to BA (*connect*). 4. If the request is accepted BA notifies the connection to TM (*connect_ok*). 5. TM checks whether USER has enough money by BA (*check_funding*). 6. If USER has enough money BA notifies it to TM (*funding_ok*). 7. TM dispenses the cash amount (*withdraw_ok*). 8. USER gets the amount of money and the card (*logout*).
Post-Conditions	USER money have been withdrawn
Alternative Paths	• If TM experiences problems that can compromise the operation, it sends an error to BA (*noconnection*) and the TM ejects the card (*logout*). • If BA determines that there are insufficient funds in the USER's account, it notifies it to TM (*funding_ko*) and TM ejects the card (*logout*).

Two are the possible responses that TM can receive from AUTH: login success (*?login_auth_ok*), and login failure (*?login_auth_ko*). The state diagram of the AUTH component is shown on the upper-hand side of Figure 13. In case of success, the user is habilitated to available services (i.e., withdraw money or recharge mobile phone). TM receives the response for both services and forwards them to the User component. The other component, BA (right-hand side of Figure 13),

manages the bank account services (i.e., withdraw, charge).

4.3 W_PSC Requirements Specification and formalization in the PSC Language

Starting from the two use cases selected in the previous subsection, a set of properties to be checked on the system are extracted. In the following we will focus on two properties and

Figure 11. Software Architecture of the ATM System (©2007 Computer Science Department – University of L'Aquila (Italy). Used with permission)

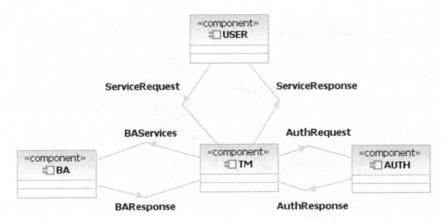

Figure 12. USER state diagram (©2007 Computer Science Department – University of L'Aquila (Italy). Used with permission)

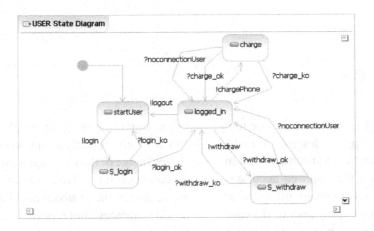

we will provide their descriptions as PSC. The formalization of the properties as PSC is made by using W_PSC.

Property 1: if the withdraw request has been performed (*withdraw*) and before no errors on the connection have been raised (*noconnection* is not sent), and the request of money is consis-

tent with the user funds (*funding_ok*), then TM must dispense the cash amount (*withdraw_ok*); the withdraw request is allowed only after a successful login request.

Having requirements well formulated as the ones considered in this chapter is an ideal situation not very common in real projects. W_PSC can be particularly useful in these situations since,

Figure 13. AUTH and BA state diagrams (©2007 Computer Science Department – University of L'Aquila (Italy). Used with permission)

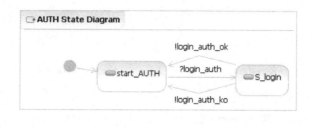

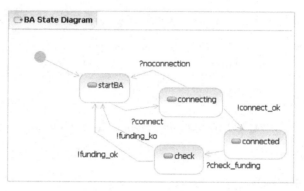

as already explained, it is not an automatic tool but it is a wizard that helps the designer to make decisions in formalizing the requirements and in restructuring them with the required accuracy. In the following we provide enough information on W_PSC and PSC for understanding the case study and we refer to (Autili, 2006; Autili, 2007) for further details.

An important aspect to be considered when formalizing the requirements is the distinction among *Mandatory, Forbidden,* and *Optional* operations. They are organized into W_PSC as different sentences contained into 3 different panels. Thus, reading Property 1 the first action that can be found is *login*. It is easy for the software engineer to understand if the considered part of the requirement is mandatory, forbidden, or optional. Making this decision the suitable tab

panel containing the pre-formulated sentences is chosen. *login* is clearly an optional operation since the exchange of the message *login* represents the precondition for *withdraw* and for the following messages. In the optional panel among the proposed sentences (and reported in the following), the software engineer selects the Sentence 1 since no other constraints on the login message are required.

Sentence 1 If the message < m > is exchanged then ...

Sentence 2 If the message < m > is exchanged and between this message and its predecessor (or the system startup) no other messages can be exchanged then ...

Figure 14. TM state diagram (©2007 Computer Science Department – University of L'Aquila (Italy). Used with permission)

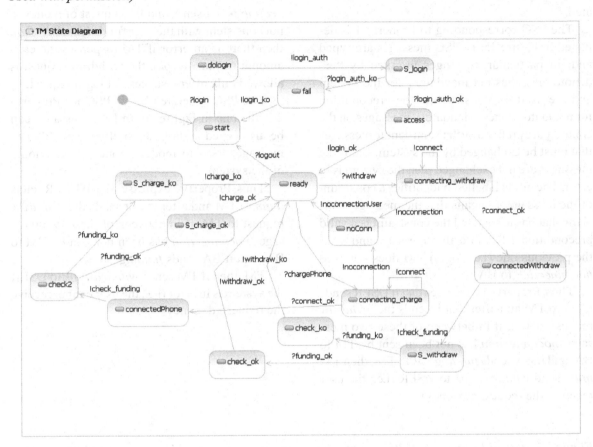

Sentence 3 If the message < m > is exchanged and between this message and its predecessor (or the system startup) < ... > then ...

Sentence 4 If the message < m > is exchanged and between this message and its successor (or after the last message) < ... > then ...

Sentence 5 If the message < m > is exchanged and between this message and its predecessor (or the system startup) < ... > and between this message and its successor (or after the last message) < ... > then ...

Following a similar reasoning, *withdraw* is identified as another optional message but in this case the selected sentence is Sentence 3 since *withdraw* is a valid precondition if and only if before this message no connection errors have been raised. *Funding* is another precondition, in this case without constraints, for the final message of the property that is *withdraw_ok*. *withdraw_ok* is a mandatory message (i.e., the correct sentence will be selected among the Mandatory sentences) since the system is in error if the this message is not exchanged.

When the formalization is finished in W_PSC the corresponding PSC is automatically generated.

The PSC corresponding to Property 1 is depicted in Figure 15. In PSC messages are typed and, in particular, messages prefixed by **"e:"** denote messages not mandatory for the system and are used for constructing the precondition for mandatory ones. Mandatory messages on the contrary are prefixed by **"r:"** and denote messages that must be exchanged by the system, i.e., if the messages are not exchanged then the system is in error. The circle labelled **b** identifies a constraint of the message. It means that the message *withdraw* that has associated the constraint is a valid precondition iff before this message and after the previous one (i.e., *login*) TM does not send *noconnection* to BA.

Thus, Property 1 expresses that if USER sends *login* to TM and after that it sends the *withdraw* request to TM, if in between of these two messages *noconnection* has not been by TM to BA, and if BA sends *funding_ok* to TM, then TM **must** send *withdraw_ok* to USER (i.e., the user receives the requested money).

Property 2: if the withdraw request has been performed (*withdraw*), there are no errors (*noconnection* is not sent), and the request of money is not consistent with the user funds (*funding_ko*), then there is an error if TM dispenses the cash amount (*withdraw_ok*); the withdraw request is allowed only after a successful login request.

The PSC generated by W_PSC for Property 2 is the one in Figure 16. In PSC messages can be also typed as fail, i.e., prefixed by **"f:"**, i.e., messages used to model erroneous behaviours of the system.

Thus, Property 2 expresses that if USER sends *login* to TM and after that it sends the *withdraw* request to TM, if in between of these two messages *noconnection* has been not sent by TM to BA, and if BA sends *funding_ko* to TM, then if TM sends *withdraw_ok* to USER the system is in error (i.e., the user cannot receive the requested money).

Figure 15. PSC of Property 1 (©2007 Computer Science Department – University of L'Aquila (Italy). Used with permission)

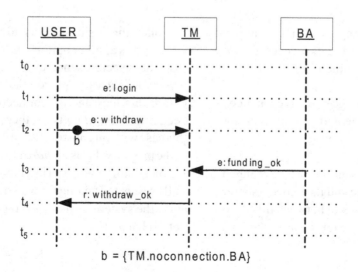

Figure 16. PSC of Property 2 (©2007 Computer Science Department – University of L'Aquila (Italy). Used with permission)

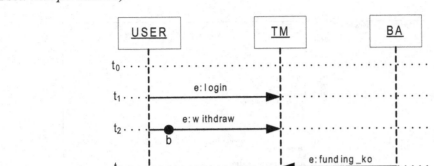

b = {TM.noconnection.BA}

4.4 Software Architecture Verification

The ATM software architecture presented in the previous section has been modelled in CHARMY, and the verification has been performed.

The first verification concerns the deadlocks detection. The verification is performed on a Pentium 1.73Ghz with 1,50 GB of RAM and took less than 1 minute using 2,582 MB of memory. The system specification is deadlock free and has 311 states and 663 transitions. Furthermore, there are no unreachable parts of the model.

The next step is the verification of the properties.

Property 1: this property is valid. The number of generated states is 1535, while the transitions are 33724. The memory used in this case is 2.622 MB of RAM.

Property 2: this property is also valid. The number of generated states is 951, with 2046 transitions. The memory used is 2.582 MB of RAM.

Now the software architecture is verified and then it can be used as the starting point for the implementation, as real blueprint for the development. The next section shows the code generation phase and shows how software architecture choices force the implementation.

4.5 JET/ARCHJAVA Code Generation

The application of the *JET-based Code Generator* (outlined in Section 3.2) on the CHARMY specification of the ATM case study produces a number of ARCHJAVA files listed on the left-hand side of the screenshot in Figure 17. In particular, for each component (e.g., *User*), the corresponding encoding is generated (e.g., *User.archj*). The state machine specifications are also synthesized (e.g., *SM_User.archj*) together with a *MAIN.archj* file (listed on the right-hand side of Figure 17) that

Figure 17. Generated code overview (©2007 Computer Science Department – University of L'Aquila (Italy). Used with permission)

enables the execution of the obtained system with respect to the modelled software architecture. Being more precise, in that main file all the components, the corresponding state machines and port connections are instantiated giving place to an encoding of the SA properties that constraint the execution of the hand-written code that will be filled in prearranged points (e.g., see the *try* statement in the code of Figure 17).

Focusing on the User component, a fragment of the corresponding generated code is listed in Figure 18. Essentially, it contains the declaration of the state machines that will be considered during the User component execution (hence the state machine of the User, TM, BA and AUTH components) (see lines 5-8 in Figure 18), the definition of the ports (TM_TO_User and User_TO_TM, lines 12-29) and the implementation of the provided

methods that have to be completed by the developer (lines 33-60). The generated method statements are devoted to fire the transitions of the involved state machines. For instance, the *withdraw_ko()* invoked by the TM component induces the state changes in the User and TM state machines. The former will reach the state *S_withdraw* from the *logged_in* one, whereas the latter change the state *check_ko* reaching the ready one, according to the state machines in Figure 12 and Figure 14.

In order to have a full application, the developer has to complete the generated code by implementing the logic of each provided method. The hand-written code can be filled in the predefined user regions like the one in lines 44-45. The code that will be written in such blocks will never be updated by subsequent generations. This facility is provided by the JET framework and it

Figure 18. Fragment of the generated User.archj (©2007 Computer Science Department – University of L'Aquila (Italy). Used with permission)

```
1.   public component class User {
2.   /**Declaration of the state machine variables
3.   *@ generated
4.   */
5.   private SM_User behaviour_User;
6.   private SM_TM behaviour_TM;
7.   private SM_BA behaviour_BA;
8.   private SM_AUTH behaviour_AUTH;
9.   /**TM_TO_User Port definition
10.  *@ generated
11.  */
12.  public port TM_TO_User {
13.  provides void login_ko() throws SMException;
14.  provides void login_ok() throws SMException;
15.  provides void charge_ko() throws SMException;
16.  provides void charge_ok() throws SMException;
17.  provides void withdraw_ko() throws SMException;
18.  provides void withdraw_ok() throws SMException;
19.  provides void noconnectionUser() throws SMException;
20.  }
21.  /**User_TO_TM Port definition
22.  *@ generated
23.  */
24.  public port User_TO_TM {
25.  requires void withdraw() throws SMException;
26.  requires void chargePhone() throws SMException;
27.  requires void login() throws SMException;
28.  requires void logout() throws SMException;
29.  }
30.  /**Implementation of the methods provided by the port TM_TO_User
31.  *@ generated
32.  */
33.  public void login_ok() throws SMException {
34.  System.out.println("User.login_ok");
35.  behaviour_User.transFire(behaviour_User.T_login_ok);
36.  behaviour_TM.transFire(behaviour_TM.T_login_ok);
37.  //WRITE YOUR CODE HERE
38.  //END YOUR CODE HERE
39.  }
40.  public void withdraw_ko() throws SMException {
41.  System.out.println("User.withdraw_ko");
42.  behaviour_User.transFire(behaviour_User.T_withdraw_ko);
43.  behaviour_TM.transFire(behaviour_TM.T_withdraw_ko);
44.  //WRITE YOUR CODE HERE
45.  //END YOUR CODE HERE
46.  }
47.  public void withdraw_ok() throws SMException {
48.  System.out.println("User.withdraw_ok");
49.  behaviour_User.transFire(behaviour_User.T_withdraw_ok);
50.  behaviour_TM.transFire(behaviour_TM.T_withdraw_ok);
51.  //WRITE YOUR CODE HERE
52.  //END YOUR CODE HERE
53.  }
54.  public void login_ko() throws SMException {
55.  System.out.println("User.login_ko");
56.  behaviour_User.transFire(behaviour_User.T_login_ko);
57.  behaviour_TM.transFire(behaviour_TM.T_login_ko);
58.  //WRITE YOUR CODE HERE
59.  //END YOUR CODE HERE
60.  }
61.  ...
62.  }
```

Figure 19. Fragment of the generated SM_User.archj (©2007 Computer Science Department – University of L'Aquila (Italy). Used with permission)

```
1.    ** User State Machine encoding
2.    *@ generated
3.    */
4.    public class SM_User {
5.    /** State encoding
6.    *@ generated
7.    */
8.    public final int S_startUser= 0;
9.    public final int S_S_login= 1;
10.   public final int S_logged_in= 2;
11.   public final int S_S_withdraw= 3;
12.   public final int S_charge= 4;
13.   /** Transition encoding
14.   *@ generated
15.   */
16.   public final int T_login_ok=0;
17.   public final int T_withdraw=1;
18.   public final int T_chargePhone=2;
19.   public final int T_charge_ko=3;
20.   public final int T_withdraw_ko=4;
21.   public final int T_withdraw_ok=5;
22.   public final int T_login=6;
23.   public final int T_login_ko=7;
24.   public final int T_logout=8;
25.   public final int T_charge_ok=9;
26.   public final int T_noconnectionUser=10;
27.   /** State Machine constructor
28.   *@ generated
29.   */
30.   public SM_User(){
31.   System.out.println("SM_User.constr");
32.   LinkedList startUser = new LinkedList();
33.   startUser.add(new transition(T_login, S_S_login ,0));
34.   states.add(startUser);
35.
36.   LinkedList S_login = new LinkedList();
37.   S_login.add(new transition(T_login_ok, S_logged_in ,1));
38.   S_login.add(new transition(T_login_ko, S_startUser ,1));
39.   states.add(S_login);
40.
41.   LinkedList logged_in = new LinkedList();
42.   logged_in.add(new transition(T_withdraw, S_S_withdraw ,0));
43.   logged_in.add(new transition(T_chargePhone, S_charge ,0));
44.   logged_in.add(new transition(T_logout, S_startUser ,0));
45.   states.add(logged_in);
46.
47.   LinkedList S_withdraw = new LinkedList();
48.   S_withdraw.add(new transition(T_withdraw_ko, S_logged_in ,1));
49.   S_withdraw.add(new transition(T_withdraw_ok, S_logged_in ,1));
50.   S_withdraw.add(new transition(T_noconnectionUser, S_logged_in ,1));
51.   states.add(S_withdraw);
52.
53.   LinkedList charge = new LinkedList();
54.   charge.add(new transition(T_charge_ko, S_logged_in ,1));
55.   charge.add(new transition(T_charge_ok, S_logged_in ,1));
56.   charge.add(new transition(T_noconnectionUser, S_logged_in ,1));
57.   states.add(charge);
58.   }
```

is a first step towards round-trip engineering and refactoring support even though a more advanced support is required and it is an issue that has to be deeply investigated in the future.

The generated specification of the *User* state machine that guarantees the code execution according to the admitted *User* component behaviour is listed in Figure 19. The states and the transitions are encoded as a linked list initialized in the lines 32-57 of the Figure. This specification forces the execution of the methods which are admitted in the current computation state with respect to both SA constraints and behavioural one: if a given *User* method can be invoked, then the current state is updated according to the information contained in the linked list. Otherwise an exception is raised. For instance, once the *User* component reach the *logged_in* state, only the *withdraw, chargePhone,* and *logout* transitions are admitted (see lines 41-45 in Figure 19), consistently with the *User* state diagram (see Figure 12). If a different transition is asked, an exception is raised stopping the system execution. The exception could be also handled defining different reaction policies to maintain the system running in a consistent state.

5. FUTURE TRENDS

In this chapter we presented an approach to automatically generate Java code starting from verified software architecture descriptions. The best of the state of the art, as presented in Section 2, is represented by ARCHJAVA that ensures the communication integrity, and by JAVA/A that constraints also the code to behave as defined in the port's protocols. These approaches (as they are today) can be used only in a context in which the system is completely implemented in-house, while neglecting the possibility of integrating external components. This because of acquired components which are not necessarily implemented following one of these approaches and thus it is not possible at runtime to enable the only admitted operations. Thus, an interesting future research direction consists on the ability of integrating in-house components code with automatically generated assembly code for acquired components, forcing the composed system to exhibit the properties specified at the architectural level. This integration would open the possibility of managing dynamic systems (i.e., systems in which some components have to change at runtime) where a re-generated "correct" assembly code assures that the composed system is forced to exhibit only the properties specified at the architectural level.

In the domain of system run-time validation, feedback generated by the run-time analysis of the generated code (through monitoring and testing techniques) could be automatically tracked back to the architectural model, so that whenever a change applies over the code, it is automatically reflected on the architectural model and vice-versa.

Another future research direction consists in investigating how to assure that the generated code respects non functional properties and quality aspects which have been proven to be valid at the architectural level.

6. RELATED WORK

The principal aspect related to our work is the use of "Software Architecture" in a development process of complex and distributed systems. Although the concept of "Software Architecture" was first described in the 60s, a significant interest among the research community is only 15 years old, and the industrial community's interest is very recent. Software Architecture's research results are widely ignored by the industrial community for which a good architect is mainly an experienced person. Currently the most used technique for distributed systems engineering is based on "best practices" documents that do not necessarily include precise models and descriptions.

There are few development methodologies covering architecture engineering. Some interesting initiatives covering architecture engineering are RUP (RUP , 2000), MDA (OMG), HP (HP, 1998) recommendations initially started in the Fusion 2.0 Project and the FIDJI project (FIDJI, 2001).

In RUP, UML models should be used to describe all the architecture artefacts. The famous "4+1" views (Kruchten, 1995) have been introduced to capture heterogeneous architectural properties that has to be understood by many people who have various jobs and therefore various background.

In the OMG Model Driven Architecture (MDA) the architecture is at the centre of software development. The key concepts are those of Platform Independent and Platform Specific models, and model transformation. A Platform Independent Models (PIM) is an abstract description of the system being developed. It exhibits a specified degree of platform independence so as to be suitable for use with a number of different technologies. A Platform Specific Model (PSM) is a view of a system from the platform specific viewpoint. A PSM combines the specifications in the PIM with architectural details and specifies how that system uses a particular platform. A model transformation is defined as "the process of converting one model to another model of the same system". The approach proposed in this chapter adheres to the MDA ideas through the realization of *model transformations* which take as input an architectural model and produces as output the source code skeleton.

Fusion 2.0 (HP, 1998) defines an architecture phase placed between analysis and design. It is split into "conceptual architecture" and "logical architecture"; the first one is more informal and abstract and the second one is very precise. This notion is very close to the PIM and PSM in MDA.

The intent of the FIDJI project is to define a methodology for distributed applications in Java. The approach is composed on four steps that are inspired from Fusion 2.0: *Requirements*, *Domain analysis*, *Architectural* and *Design*.

In the requirements step it is possible to define a set of use-cases inter use-cases relationships and contracts. Contracts are statements that have to be satisfied by the final system. The domain analysis step provides criteria to choose API and components that already exist. From domain analysis and requirements this approach is able to identify the architectural style that will act as guide for the remaining design. From the style and using a *framework specialization* tool (UML, ADL, etc...) the architecture is defined, developed and stabilized. The most difficult issue of this approach is to provide a concrete architecture that support the functional requirements and which validates its associated non-functional requirements.

Overall, the main distinction between our and existing approaches is that while they cover some of the steps in the software development process, we do cover the entire process from requirements to code. We specifically focus on the Software Architecture as the main artefact enabling the transition from requirements to code. Moreover, we especially focus on quality during the entire process.

7. CONCLUSION

Model-driven development is based on the idea that code can be generated from a model of the system. This chapter has provided a contribution in this direction, by showing how an architectural model defined in a model-based fashion can be used for code generation. An important aspect during this process consists of ensuring that the selected architecture provides the required qualities. We have shown how this is feasible in a specific context, where coordination properties are elicited from requirements, modelled, and verified against the architectural model. As soon as the architectural model is proven to be good enough, we demonstrated that it can be used for generating Java code, constraining the system execution according to the architectural decisions.

Indeed, this approach shall be considered as a mere feasibility study, which demonstrates one possible way of achieving the desired objectives, while motivating other researchers to pursue similar objectives.

ACKNOWLEDGMENT

The authors of this chapter wish to thank the anonymous reviewers for their careful and useful comments. This work has been partially supported by the Italian FIRB Project ART DECO (Adaptive InfRasTructures for DECentralized Organizations).

REFERENCES

(AADL) The SAE Architecture Analysis and Design Language (AADL). http://www.aadl.info/

(Abi-Antoun, 2007) Abi-Antoun, M., & Aldrich, J. (2007). Owernship domains in the real world. In IWACO workshop at ECOOP.

(Acme) The Acme Studio Homepage. http://www.cs.cmu.edu/~acme/ AcmeStudio/index.html.

(Aldrich, 2004) Aldrich, J., & Chambers, C. (2004). Ownership Domains: Separating Aliasing Policy from Mechanism. In Proc. of ECOOP'04 (pp. 1-25).

(Allen, 1997) Allen, R. , & Garlan, D. (1997). A Formal Basis for Architectural Connection. ACM Trans. on Software Engineering and Methodology, 6(3), (pp. 213-249).

(Alur, 1990) Alur, R., Courcoubetis, C., & Dill, D. L.(1990). "Model Checking for Real-Time Systems". In Proc. of IEEE Fifth Symp. Logic in Computer Science, (pp. 414-425).

(ArchJava Project, 2005) ArchJava Project. http://archjava.org/, 2005.

(Autili, 2006) Autili, M., & Pelliccione, P. (2006). Towards a Graphical Tool for Refining User to System Requirements. In: 5th GT-VMT'06 - ETAPS'06, to appear in ENTCS.

(Autili, 2007) Autili, M., Inverardi, P., & Pelliccione, P.(2007). Graphical Scenarios for Specifying Temporal Properties: an Automated Approach, published in the Automated Software Engineering (ASE) journal. DOI - 10.1007/s10515-007-0012-6.

(AutoFOCUS Project) AutoFOCUS Project. http://autofocus.in.tum.de/index-e.html.

(AutoFOCUS2 Project) AutoFOCUS2 Project. http://www4.in.tum.de/af2.

(Barber, 2001) Barber, K. S., Graser, T. , & Holt, J. (2001). Providing early feedback in the development cycle through automated application of model checking to software architectures. In Proc. of 16th IEEE International Conference on Automated Software Engineering, (pp. 341–345).

(Baumeister, 2006) Baumeister, H., Hacklinger, F., Hennicker, R., Knapp, A., & Wirsing, A. (2006). A Component Model for Architectural Programming. Electronic Notes in Theoretical Computer Science (160), (pp. 75–96).

(Bengtsson, 1995) Bengtsson, J., Larsen, K. G., Larsson, F., Pettersson, P., & Yi, W.(1995). Uppaal - a Tool Suite for Automatic Verification of Real-Time Systems. In Proceedings of the 4th DIMACS Workshop on Verification and Control of Hybrid Systems, New Brunswick, New Jersey, (pp. 22-24).

(Bernardo, 2003) Bernardo, M., & Inverardi, P. (2003). Formal Methods for Software Architectures, Tutorial book on Software Architectures and Formal Methods. SFM-03:SA Lectures, LNCS 2804.

(Bertolino, 2004) Bertolino, A., Marchetti, E., & Muccini, H. (2004) Introducing a Reasonably Complete and Coherent Approach for Model-based Testing. (In: Testing and Analysis of Component-Based Systems Workshop, Tacos).

(Bose, 1999) Bose, P.(1999). Automated translation of uml models of architectures for verification and simulation using spin. In Proc. of 14th IEEE International Conference on Automated Software Engineering, (pp. 102–109).

(Bril, 2005) Bril, R.J., Krikhaar, R.L., Postma, A. (2005). Architectural Support in Industry: a reflection using C-POSH. Journal of Software Maintenance and Evolution.

(Büchi, 1960) Büchi, J. (1960). On a decision method in restricted second order arithmetic. In: International Congress on Logic, Method and Philosophical Sciences.

(Budinsky, 2003) Budinsky, F. , Steinberg, D., Merks, E., Ellersick, R., & Grose, T.J. (2003). Eclipse Modeling Framework. Addison Wesley.

(CHARMY, 2004) CHARMY Project: CHARMY Web Site. http://www.di.univaq.it/charmy (2004).

(Cheng, 2006). Cheng, Betty H.C, & Konrad, S.(2006). Automated Analysis of Natural Language Properties for UML Models. Jean-Michel Bruel, editor, Satellite Events at the MoDELS 2005, n. 3844 in LNCS, (pp. 48-57). Springer Verlag.

(Clarke, 2000) Clarke, E. M., Grumberg, O., & Peled, D. A. (2000). Model Checking. The MIT Press, Cambridge, second edition.

(Dashofy, 2002) Dashofy, E. M., van der Hoek, A., & Taylor, R. N. (2002). An infrastructure for the rapid development of xml-based architecture description languages. In ICSE '02: Proceedings of the 24th Int. Conf. on Software Eng., (pp. 266–276), New York, NY, USA, ACM Press.

(Dobrica, 2002) Dobrica, L., & Niemela, E. A Survey on Software Architecture Analysis Methods. IEEE Transactions on Software Engineering, VOL. 28, NO. 7.

(Dwyer, 1999) Dwyer, M. B., Avrunin, G. S., & Corbett, J. C. (1999). Patterns in property specifications for finite-state verification. In ICSE, (pp. 411–420).

(Eriksson, 2004) Eriksson, H.-E. , Penker, M., Lyons, B., & Fado D. (2004). UML 2 Toolkit, chapter Ch. 7, Representing Architecture, (pp. 251–279). John Wiley and Sons..

(FIDJI, 2001) Guelfi, N., Hammouche, D., Sterges, P., & Biberstein, O. (2001). FIDJI Project Annual Activities Report, Applied Computer Science Department technical report n° TR-DIA-02-01, Luxembourg University of Applied Sciences, Luxembourg-Kirchberg, Luxembourg.

(Fujaba Project, 2006) Fujaba Project. http://ww-wcs.uni-paderborn.de/cs/fujaba/ publications/index.html. University of Paderborn.

(Gomaa, 2001) Gomaa, H., & Wijesekera, D. (2001). The Role of UML, OCL and ADLs in Software Architecture. In Proc. of the Workshop on Describing Software Architecture with UML, in ICSE 2001, Toronto, Canada.

(Goulo, 2003) Goulo, M., & Abreu, F.(2003). Bridging the gap between Acme and UML for CBD. In Specification and Verification of Component-Based Systems.

(Grünbacher, 2003) Grünbacher, P., Egyed, A., & Medvidovic, N. (2003). Reconciling Software Requirements and Architectures with Intermediate Models. Springer Journal of Software and System Modeling. Accepted for publication. Published online on SpringerLink.

(Hacklinger, 2004) Hacklinger, F. (2004). Java/A – Taking Components into Java. IASSE 2004, (pp. 163-168).

(Hofmeister, 2007) Hofmeister, C., Kruchten, P., Nord, R.L., Obbink, H.,Ran, A., & America, P. (2007). A general model of software architecture design derived from five industrial approaches. J. Syst. Softw., 80(1), (pp.106-126).

(Holzmann, 2002) Holzmann, G. J. (2002). The logic of bugs. In Proc. of Foundations of Software Engineering (SIGSOFT 2002/FSE-10).

(Holzmann, 2003) Holzmann, G.J. (2003).The SPIN Model Checker: Primer and Reference Manual. Addison-Wesley.

(HP, 1998) Hewlett-Packard, Engineering Process Summary (fusion 2.0), Draft version January 1998.

(HUGO, 2005) HUGO. http://www.pst.ifi.lmu.de/projekte/hugo. 2005.

(Inverardi, 2005) Inverardi, P., Muccini, H., Pelliccione, P. (2005). CHARMY: an extensible tool for architectural analysis. In: ESEC/FSE-13: Proceedings of the 10th European software engineering conference, New York, NY, USA, ACM Press (pp.111–114).

(Ivers, 2004) Ivers, J. , Clements, P., Garlan, D., Nord, R., Schmerl, D., & Silva, J. R. O. (2004). Documenting Component and Connector Views with UML 2.0. Technical Report CMU/SEI-2004-TR-008, Carnegie Mellon University, Software Engineering Institute.

(Jerad, 2005) Jerad, C., & Barkaoui, K. (2005). On the use of rewriting logic for verification of distributed software architecture description based lfp. In Proc. Of 16th IEEE International Workshop on Rapid System Prototyping (pp. 202-208).

(Johannisson, 2005) Johannisson, K. (2005). Formal and Informal Software Specifications. PhD thesis, C. Technology and Göteborg Univ., SE-412 96 Göteborg, Sweden.

(Kande', 2002) Kande', M. M. , Crettaz, V. , Strohmeier, A. & Sendall, S. (2002). Bridging the gap between IEEE 1471, Architecture Description Languages and UML. Software and System Modeling, 2 (pp. 98–112)

(Kruchten, 1995) Kruchten, P. (1995). Architectural Blueprints - The "4+1" View Model of Software Architecture. IEEE Software, 12(6) (pp. 42–50).

(Magee, 1999) Magee, J., Kramer, J., & Giannakopoulou, D. (1999). Behaviour Analysis of Software Architectures. In I Working IFIP Conf. Sw Architecture, WICSA.

(Manna, 1992) Manna, Z., & Pnueli, A. (1992). The temporal logic of reactive and concurrent systems. Springer-Verlag New York, Inc.

(Medvidovic, 2000) Medvidovic, N. & Taylor, R. N. (2000). A Classification and Comparison Framework for Software Architecture Description Languages. IEEE Transactions on Software Engineering, 26(1).

(Medvidovic, 2002) Medvidovic, N. , Rosenblum, D. S. , Redmiles, D. F., & Robbins, J. E. (2002). Modeling Software Architectures in the Unified Modeling Language. *ACM Transactions on Software Engineering and Methodology (TOSEM)*, 11(1).

(Medvidovic, 2003) Medvidovic, N. , Grünbacher, P. , Egyed, A., & Boehm, B. (2003). Bridging Models across the Software Life-Cycle. Journal for Software Systems (JSS), 68(3) (pp. 199–215).

(Muccini, 2006) Muccini, H. & Hierons, R. Editors (2006). ROSATEA 2006: The Role Of Software Architecture in Testing and Analysis. ACM Digital Library.

(Mustapic, 2004) Mustapic, G., Wall, A., Norstrom, C., Crnkovic, I., Sandstrom, K., & Andersson, J. (2004). Real world influences on software architecture - interviews with industrial system experts. In: Fourth Working IEEE/IFIP

Conference on Software Architecture, WICSA (pp. 101–111).

(Nuseibeh, 2001) B. Nuseibeh. Weaving Together Requirements and Architectures. IEEE Computer, 34(3):115–117, March 2001.

(OMG) The Object Management Group (OMG). http://www.omg.org.

(Pelliccione, 2005) Pelliccione, P. (2005). CHARMY: A framework for Software Architecture Specification and Analysis. PhD thesis, Computer Science Dept., U. L'Aquila.

(Pender, 2003) Pender, T. (2003). UML Bible, chapter Part V: Modeling the Application Architecture, page 940. Wiley Pub.

(Perez-Martinez, 2004) Perez-Martinez, J. E., & Sierra-Alonso, A. (2004). UML 1.4 versus UML 2.0 as languages to describe Software Architectures. In Proc. EWSA 2004. LNCS n. 3047.

(Perry, 1992) Perry, D. E., & Wolf, A. L. (1992). Foundations for the Study of Software Architecture. ACM SIGSOFT Softw. Eng. Notes, 17(4), (pp. 40–52).

(PRISMA) PRISMA: Official Web Site: http://prisma.dsic.upv.es/.

(Robbins, 1998) Robbins, J. E. , Medvidovic, N. , Redmiles, D. F., & Rosenblum, D. (1998). Integrating architecture description languages with a standard design method. In Proc. 20th Int. Conf. on Software Engineering.

(Roh, 2004) Roh, S., Kim, K., & Jeon, T. (2004). Architecture Modeling Language based on UML2.0. In Proocedings of the 11th Asia-Pacific Software Engineering Conference (APSEC).

(RUP, 2000) Kruchten, P. (2000). The rational Unified Process An Introduction, second edition, Addison-Wesley.

(Schmerl, 2004) B. Schmerl, D. Garlan. AcmeStudio: Supporting Style-Centered Architecture Development. Proc. International Conference on Software Engineering, ICSE'04, pages 704-705, Edinburgh, Scotland, May 2004.

(SysML) The Systems Modeling Language (SysML) open source specification project. http://www.sysml.org/

(Smith, 2002) Smith, R. L. , Avrunin, G. S., Clarke, L. A., & Osterweil, L. J. (2002). PROPEL: An Approach Supporting Property Elucidation. In Proc. of 24th International Conference on Software Engineering (ICSE), (pp 11–21).

(Sommerville, 2004) Sommerville, I.: Software engineering (7th ed.). Addison-Wesley Longman Publishing Co., Inc., Boston, MA, USA (2004).

(STRAW, 2003) STRAW '03: Second Int. Workshop From Software Requirements to Architectures, May 09, 2003, Portland, Oregon, USA.

(xADL 2.0, 2005) xADL 2.0 Architecture Description Language. http://www.isr.uci.edu/projects/xarchuci/, 2005.

(Zhang, 2007) Zhang, P. C., Muccini, H. , & Li, B. X. (2007). A comparative study of model checking methods on software architecture. Technical Report, Chair of Software Testing and Verification, Southeast University. http://cse.seu.edu.cn/people/bx.li/en/cstv.htm

(Zhu, 2003) Zhu, X., Maiden, N., & Pavan, P. (2003). Scenarios: Bringing requirements and architectures together. In 2nd International Workshop on Scenarios and State Machines: Models, Algorithms, and Tools.

ENDNOTE

[1] Borrowed from Sensonia, Research supported by the EU within the FET-GC2 IST-2005-16004 Integrated Project Sensoria (Software Engineering for Service-Oriented Overlay Computers)

APPENDIX A: Java/A CODE GENERATION

The following code shows parts of the Java/A declaration of the component *OutService* described in Figure 3:

```
1.    simple component AccidentAssistanceService {
2.      dynamic port AAE {
3.      provided {
void AlertAccepted();
void AlertNotAccepted();
void EmergencyAccepted();
void EmergenctNotAccepted();
}
4.      required {
signal AlertEmergencyService(Location Loc);
signal EmergencyLevel(int Level);
void AlertAccepted();
}
5.
6.      try{
7.              Component aas = componentLookUp (this,
                    "AccidentAssistenceService");
8.              Port aae = aas.getPort ("AAE");
9.              ConnectionRequest cr = (this, this, EAA, aas, aae, new
                    Connector());
                    reconfigurationRequest(cr);
10.     }
11.     Catch (ReconfigurationException e) {...}
12.     }
13.     simple component EmergencyService{
14.     port EAA {
15.     provided{
signal AlertEmergencyService(Location Loc);
signal EmergencyLevel(int Level);
void AlertAccepted();
    }
16.     required{
        void AlertAccepted();
void AlertNotAccepted();
void EmergencyAccepted();
void EmergenctNotAccepted();
17.     }
18.     <! // protocol of EAA
```

```
    states {
initial Initial;
simple Q1,Q2,Q3,Q4;
    }
    transitions {
Initial -> Q1;
Q1 -> Q2 {trigger AlertEmergencyService();}
Q2 -> Q1 {effect AlertNotAccepted();}
Q2 -> Q3 {effect AlertAccepted();}
Q3 -> Q4 {trigger EmergencyLevel();}
Q4 -> Q3 {effect EmergencyNotAccepted();}
Q4 -> Q1 {effect EmergencyAccepted();}
}
!>


19.  }


20.   composite component OutService
21.   {
22.   assembly {
component types {AccidentAssistenceService,
EmergencyService
                        }
23.   connector types {
AccidentAssistenceService.AAE;
EmergencyService.EAA;
}
24.   initial configuration {
    AccidentAssistenceService AS = new AccidentAssistenceService();
    EmergencyService ambulance = new EmergencyService();
    EmergencyService police = new EmergencyService();
     Connector cn0 = new Connector();
        cn0.connect(ambulance.EAA, AS.AAE);
        connector cn1 = new Connector();
       cn1.connect = (police.EAA, AS.AAE);
                        }
            }
              }
25.  }
```

In lines 1-12 and 13-19 the two simple components (Accident Assistence Service (AAS) and Emergency Service (ES)) are declared while in lines 20-25 a composite component *"OutService"* is declared as an assembly of the two previous ones. In lines 2 and 14, the ports AAE and EAA are defined. Each port declaration contains a set of provided operations (i.e., lines 3 and 15) and a set of required operations (i.e., lines 4 and 16). Port protocols are specified by UML state machines which are textually represented using the UTE notation (HUGO, 2005). For instance, lines 18-19 show the UTE representation of the UML state machine for the port EAA. In line 24 a possible configuration of the *OutService* composite component is declared. It presents two instances of the ES component (ambulance and police) that are attached at the AAS by the EAA and AAE ports. JAVA/A also allows to cope with *"dynamic reconfiguration"* in order to describe changes to a component-based system at run-time (e.g., creation and destruction of components, building up and removing of connections between ports). This is made with a code like the one in lines 6-11 where a possible reconfiguration in the *OutService* composite component (i.e., the connection and disconnection of ES) is presented. An idle ES disconnects from the AAS and reconnects whenever there is an accident and the AAS alerts the ES. When AAS alerts the ES executes the code in the 6-11 lines which realised the (re)connection of an ES to the AAS.

Chapter XII
Quality–Driven Model Transformations:
From Requirements to UML Class Diagrams

Silvia Abrahão
Valencia University of Technology, Spain

Marcela Genero
University of Castilla – La Mancha, Spain

Emilio Insfran
Valencia University of Technology, Spain

José Ángel Carsí
Valencia University of Technology, Spain

Isidro Ramos
Valencia University of Technology, Spain

Mario Piattini
University of Castilla – La Mancha, Spain

ABSTRACT

Model-Driven Architecture (MDA) is a software engineering approach that promotes the use of models and model transformations as primary development artifacts. Usually, there are several ways to transform a source model into a target model. Alternative target models may have the same functionality but may differ in their quality attributes (e.g., understandability, modifiability). This chapter presents an approach to deal with quality-driven model transformations. Specifically, it focuses on a specific set of transformations to obtain UML class diagrams from a Requirements Model. A set of alternative transformations are identified, and the selection of the best alternative is done through a controlled experiment.

The goal of the experiment is to empirically validate which alternative transformation produces the UML class diagram that is the easiest to understand. This evidence can be further used to define high-quality transformation processes, as it will be based on empirical knowledge rather than on common wisdom and the intuition of the researchers and developers.

INTRODUCTION

Nowadays, the software development community is moving towards model-driven development processes whose goal is the development of software at a higher level of abstraction based on models and model transformations. Within this context, the Model-Driven Architecture (MDA) initiative (OMG, 2003) has attracted interest from both the research community and software practitioners. This approach comprises the use of models in all the steps of a software development project, until the delivery of the software on a given platform.

A MDA development process basically transforms a platform-independent model (PIM) into one or more platform-specific models (PSM), which are transformed into code (code model – CM). The CM is just the actual code generated from PSMs through transformation. Here, the goal is to decouple the way, in which software systems are currently defined, which is dependant on the technology they use (OMG, 2003).

A model transformation is a process of converting one model to another model. A model may be transformed to several alternative models that may have the same functionality but different quality attributes. For example, one model may be more reusable while another model may be more comprehensive to its stakeholders. Therefore, it is necessary to identify those transformations that produce models with the desired quality attributes.

To cope with the problem of selecting alternative transformations, this chapter presents an approach for quality-driven model transformations. The mechanisms to choose the appropriate

alternatives can greatly differ depending on the nature and the domain of the transformations as well as the quality perspective that is chosen. We focus on a set of transformations defined to obtain UML class diagrams from a Requirements Model (Insfran, 2003). Assuring quality in representing the system's conceptual model from requirements is particularly important, as the traceability between these models is not properly dealt with. Moreover, a conceptual model of good quality can help to minimize communication problems and misunderstandings of requirements among the stakeholders.

The quality perspective that we are interested in is the *pragmatic quality*[1] (Lindland, Sindre & Sølvberg, 1994). This quality category addresses the comprehension aspect of the model from the stakeholders' perspective. Pragmatic quality captures how the model has selected an alternative "from among the many ways to express a single meaning", and it essentially deals with making the model *easy to understand*.

The comprehension goal specifies that all audience members (or interpreters) completely understand the statements in the model that are relevant to them. This is an import quality attribute since it is recognized as one of the main factors that influences maintainability (Selic, 2003) (Otero & Dolado, 2004) (Reinhartz-Berger & Dori, 2005) (Genero et al., 2005; 2007). A UML class diagram must first be understood before any desired changes to it can be identified, designed, or implemented. In terms of the Lindland et al. framework, improving pragmatic quality means increasing the degree of correspondence between the set of statements in the model and the set of statements that the user thinks the model presents (i.e., their understanding of the model).

Therefore, our main goal is to empirically evaluate which of the alternative transformations produces the UML class diagram that is easiest to understand. This evidence can be further used to define high-quality transformation processes, as it will be based on empirical knowledge rather than on common wisdom and the intuition of the researchers and developers.

The structure of the chapter is as follows. Section 2 presents the state-of-the-art for quality in model-driven development. Section 3 describes how UML class diagrams can be obtained from a Requirements Model using different transformation alternatives. This section also shows the definition of these transformations using QVT and their execution in a platform for model management called MOMENT. Section 4 describes the design and the results of the experiment carried out to empirically validate the selection of the alternative transformations according to the 'understandability' quality attribute. Section 5 describes our conclusions. Finally, section 6 presents a discussion on future research directions.

Table 1. Comparison of approaches for quality in model-driven development

Proposal	Purpose	Type of	Input Artifact	Quality attributes	Automation
Zou and Kontogiannis, 2003	Reverse engineering (migration)	Vertical (CM-to-PIM)	Program code	Coupling and cohesion	No
Rottger and Zschaler, 2004	Refinement	Horizontal	Context Models	Response Time	Partial
Merilinna, 2005	Refactoring	Horizontal (PIM-to-PIM)	Architectural models	Performance, availability, reliability,	Yes
Kurtev, 2005	Synthesis	Vertical (PIM-to-PIM)	UML class models	Adaptability	Yes (Mistral)
Markovic and Baar, 2005	Refactoring	Horizontal (PIM-to-PIM)	UML class models	Syntactical correctness	No
Sottet et al., 2006	–	–	Interface models	Compatibility, error protection, homogeneity-consistency	No
Ivkovic and Kontogiannis, 2006	Refactoring	Horizontal (PIM-to-PIM)	Architectural models expressed in UML	Maintenance, performance and security	No
Kerhervé et al., 2006	Synthesis, refinement	Horizontal and Vertical	Information models	Response time, network delay, network bandwidth	No
				(–) means that the proposal does not provide this information	

STATE-OF-THE-ART OF QUALITY FOR MODEL-DRIVEN SOFTWARE DEVELOPMENT

In the last few years, some proposals that deal with the quality of model transformations from the perspective of a quality attribute have been proposed. An organized chronological summary of these studies is presented in Table 1.

Zou and Kontogiannis (2003) proposed a quality-driven reengineering framework for object-oriented migration. Analysis tools, transformation rules, and non-functional requirements for the target migration systems characterize this framework. During the migration process, the source-code transformation rules are associated with quality features of the target system (i.e., coupling and cohesion). This approach was applied to transform a set of gnu AVL libraries into an UML class diagram.

Röttger and Zschaler (2004) proposed an approach for refining non-functional requirements based on the definition of context models and their transformations. This approach has been defined in a software development process that separates the roles of the measurement designer and the application designer. It is the measurement designer's responsibility to specify measurements, context models and transformations among these models. Then, the application designer can apply the transformations when developing a system. Röttger and Zschaler defined a XML-based language for the specification of transformations between abstract and concrete context models. The transformations used the response time quality attribute.

Merilinna (2005) proposed a tool for quality-driven model transformations for software architectures. Two types of quality attributes are considered: attributes related to software execution (e.g., performance, availability, reliability) and attributes related to software evolution (e.g., maintenance, modifiability, reusability). The transformations are described according to MDA

and a proprietary transformation rule language. The approach only considers horizontal transformations (PIM-to-PIM transformations).

Kurtev (2005) proposed a formal technique for the definition of transformation spaces that support the analysis of alternative transformations for a given source model. This technique provides operations for the selection and reduction of transformation spaces based on certain desirable quality properties of the resulting target model. Specifically, this approach deals with the adaptability of model transformations. To generate the transformation space, the process takes a source model and its metamodel, the target metamodel, and the quality properties as input. The proposal has been applied to a set of transformations to obtain XML schemas from UML class diagrams.

Markovic and Baar (2005) defined a set of transformation rules for the refactoring of UML class diagrams. The rules have been defined using the Query/View/Transformation (QVT) standard of OMG (OMG, 2005). The refactoring is applied to UML class diagrams containing annotated OCL constraints that are preserved when the transformations are applied. Therefore, the syntactical correctness of the target model is preserved.

Similar to this proposal, Ivkovic and Kontogiannis (2006) presented an approach for the refactoring of software architectures using model transformations and semantic annotations. In this approach, the architectural view of a software system is represented as a UML profile with its corresponding stereotypes. Then, the instantiated architectural models are annotated using elements of the refactoring context, including soft goals, metrics, and constraints. Finally, the actions that are most advisable for a refactoring context are applied after being selected from a set of possible refactorings. The proposal has been applied to a case study to demonstrate that the refactoring transformations improve the maintenance, performance and the security of a software system.

Sottet et al. (2006) proposed an approach for model-driven mappings for embedding the description and control of usability. A mapping describes a model transformation that preserves properties. The mapping properties provide the designer with a means for both selecting the most appropriate transformation and previewing the resulting design. A case study that illustrates an application of the mapping metamodel using usability criteria (compatibility, error protection, and homogeneity-consistency) was presented.

Kerhervé et al. (2006) proposed a general framework for quality-driven delivery of distributed multimedia systems. The framework focuses on Quality of Services (QoS) information modeling and transformations. The transformations between models express the relationships among the concepts of the different quality information models. These relationships are defined in quality dimensions and are used to transform instances of a source model to a target model. Different types of transformations are applied to different layers and services: vertical transformations are applied to transform information between the different layers (user, service, system, and resource), and horizontal transformation are applied to interchange information between services of the same layer.

In summary, some proposals focus on defining horizontal transformations for model refactoring (Merilinna 2005) (Markovic & Baar 2005) (Ivkovic & Kontogiannis 2006). Other proposals are aimed at providing vertical transformations for model refinement (Rottger & Zschaler, 2004), synthesis (Kerhervé et al., 2006) (Kurtev, 2005), or reverse engineering (Zou & Kontogiannis, 2003). Of these studies, only the one by Kurtev (2005) presents a more systematic approach for selecting alternative transformations according to a given quality attribute.

All these approaches propose quality criteria that can be used to drive the transformations, but very few of these approaches (Kurtev, 2005) (Markovic & Baar, 2005) illustrate them by means of practical examples. With the exception of Markovic and Baar (2005) and Kurtev (2005), the transformations are poorly defined. Therefore, more systematic approaches to ensure quality in MDA processes are needed. Another weakness of these proposals is that they are not empirically validated. The practical applicability of model transformations is reported based on the intuition of the researcher. As pointed out by Czarnecki and Helsen (2006), there is a lack of controlled experiments to fully validate the observations made by the researchers.

A QUALITY-DRIVEN MODEL TRANSFORMATION APPROACH

This section presents a systematic approach to ensure quality in model-driven development processes. It takes a different approach to drive the selection of transformations, which is to empirically validate the selection of alternative transformations through controlled experiments. The rationale of this approach is to be able to automatically select the alternative transformation that an experienced software developer would select if the transformation process were manually applied.

In order to operationalize this approach, we propose the use of *quality attributes* to drive the selection of the most appropriate alternative transformation that contributes to the improvement of the target model according to a given quality attribute. A quality attribute is a measurable physical or abstract property of an entity (i.e., a conceptual model) (ISO, 2001).

Currently, our controlled experiments are oriented to empirically validating the selection of the alternative transformation that maximizes the 'understandability' quality attribute. Fig. 1 presents an overview of our quality-driven model transformation approach.

According to Fig. 1, a *transformation* is executed taking a *transformation definition* as input. A

Figure 1. Quality-driven model transformation approach

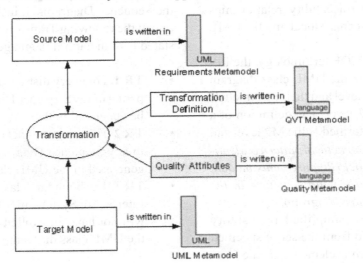

transformation definition contains transformation rules that relate constructs in the source model to constructs in the target model. These rules can be represented using the Query-View-Transformations (QVT) language proposed by the Object Management Group (OMG, 2005).

Another input for the transformation process is the definition of the *quality attributes* together with the corresponding empirical evidence gathered from the controlled experiments. This information will feed the transformation process with the criteria to choose the alternative transformation that maximize the selected quality attribute. Our final objective is to execute these transformations in a platform for Model Management called MOMENT (Boronat, Carsí & Ramos, 2005; 2006).

The following sections show a specific domain for applying our quality-driven model transformation approach using a Requirements Model as source model, a UML class diagram as target model, and "understandability" as the quality attribute to drive the transformations.

TRANSFORMING REQUIREMENTS MODELS INTO UML CLASS DIAGRAMS

The Requirements Model (Insfran, 2003) (Insfran, Pastor & Wieringa, 2002) defines the structures and the process followed to capture the software requirements. It is composed of a *Functions Refinement Tree (FRT)* to specify the hierarchical decomposition of the system, a *Use Case Model* to specify the system communication and functionality, and *Sequence Diagrams* to specify the required object-interactions that are necessary to realize each Use Case. Consequently, as only functional software requirements are gathered (business requirements are excluded), the Requirements Model can be placed at the PIM level. The Requirements Model is supported by a Requirements Engineering Tool[2] (RETO).

Following a MDA strategy of model transformation, once the Requirements Model has been specified, a conceptual model including a UML class diagram can be obtained by applying a set of transformation rules from a Transformation

Rules Catalog[3] (Insfran, 2003). These transformations establish traceability relationships between the Requirements Model and the UML class diagrams.

According to the MOF terminology, the Requirements Model and the UML class diagram are located in the M1 level and their metamodels are located in the M2 level. The definition of a transformation is performed at the M2 level and implies that *"a certain structural pattern is identified in the source model (Requirements model), which corresponds to a valid structure in the target model (UML class diagram)"*.

Fig. 2 describes a simplified traceability relationship map to go from the set of specified requirements to specific elements in the conceptual schema. These traceability relationships may be simple (*one-to-one* relationships). For example, the generation of classes for the UML class diagram is a process that is based on the

analysis of participating actors and classes in all the Sequence Diagrams. It includes the application of the following Transformation Rules (TR), stated here in natural language:

- **TR 1.** For every distinct actor class participating in any Sequence Diagram, a class will be generated in the UML class diagram.
- **TR 2.** For every distinct class participating in any Sequence Diagram, a class will be generated in the UML class diagram.
- **TR 3.** The boundary classes (usually called Interface or System) in Sequence Diagrams will not have an explicit representation in the UML class diagram.

However, the traceability relationships can also be *many-to-many* relationships. This is due to the variability of the transformations, which allows multiple possible representations in the UML

Figure 2. Traceability from requirements to conceptual models

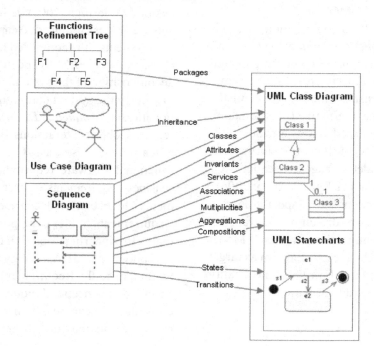

class diagram that satisfy a given requirement pattern identified in the Requirements Model. If this occurs, a single alternative mapping must be properly selected according to some predefined quality attribute.

Subsection 4.1 and 4.2 briefly introduce the requirements and the UML class diagram metamodels. The remainder of the section focus on transformations that have multiple valid representations in the UML class diagram that satisfy a given requirement pattern.

The Requirements Metamodel

Metamodeling is a key concept of the MDA paradigm and is used in Software Engineering (SE) to describe the basic abstractions that define the models and their relationships. A metamodel can be viewed as a class model whose classes and associations encode the concepts of the model and the relationships among them. The Meta Object Facility (MOF) (OMG, 2004) provides a framework for defining a metamodel and querying and manipulating the resulting models.

Fig. 3 shows an excerpt of the relevant parts of the Requirements Metamodel used as source in the transformation process. The *Use Case* class represents the functions of the system. Each Use Case is specified in detail by means of one or more Sequence Diagrams. Sequence Diagrams are composed mainly of *Entities* and *Messages*. We distinguish three types of Entities when describing a Sequence Diagram: Actor, Interface and Class. *Actor* represents the users of the Use Case (and may or may not be a class); *Interface* represents the boundary among the actors and the internal classes of the system; *Class* represents the different entity classes that participate in the realization of the Use Case.

Finally, in order to characterize the different nature of interaction between objects, we identify four types of messages: *Signal, Service, Query*, and *Connect*. Signal messages represent the interaction between actors and the interface. Service messages represent object interactions with the purpose of modifying the system (creation, deletion or update). Query messages represent object interactions to query the state of an object or a

Figure 3. Requirements metamodel

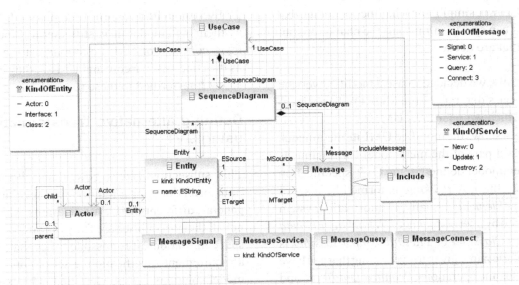

set of objects. Connect messages represent object interactions to establish a relationship between them.

The UML Class Diagram Metamodel

Once the source metamodel is defined, the UML target metamodel (OMG, 2006) must also be defined. At least three alternatives are possible:

- To use the UML2 metamodel directly. This has the advantage that the result can be used by all the tools that use this metamodel. However, the problem is the size of the metamodel and its complexity. The use of the UML2 metamodel makes transformation rules difficult to specify and understand.
- To use the Ecore metamodel. This has the advantage that many tools directly use this metamodel, and it is also very well integrated in the Eclipse environment (www.eclipse.org). However, we could not represent two of the three types of relationships (*association class* and *aggregation*) that we needed to generate in this metamodel.
- To use the class diagram metamodel defined in the MOF QVT Final Adopted Specification (OMG, 2005). This metamodel is well known, simple, and it has the advantage that it can specify almost all the characteristics that are needed.

Finally, we decided to use a modified version of the class diagram of the MOF QVT specification, which we refer to as UMLite.

Fig. 4 shows the modified UMLite metamodel. The main part of the metamodel is the same as the metamodel defined in the QVT specification (OMG, 2005). A *Package* is formed by a set of *PackageElements*. Usually, an information system is formed by a set of *Packages*. A *PackageElement* can be a *Classifier* or a *Relationship*. *Classifier* is the generic name given to everything that can have attributes and operations. *PrimitiveDataTypes* and *Classes* are both *Classifiers*. The class *PrimitiveDataType* defines the Abstract Data Types used in the definition of a system. Typical *PrimitiveDataTypes* are integers, doubles, strings, and so on. Instances of the *Class* class will belong to a specific *Package*. A *Class* is formed by a set of *Attributes*. Each one of the *Attributes* has a name inherited from *UMLModelElement* (in fact, everything has a name because every class inherits from the *UMLModelElement* class) and its type must be a *Classifier* that was previously defined. The IS-A relationship between classes is maintained with the reflexive association relationship defined in the *Class* class. The *Relationship* class defines the relationships that can exist between two classes (the source and the destination classes).

In order to be able to define the characteristics of relationships between classes, two modifications have been added to the metamodel:

- An attribute named *kind* in the *Relationship* class to express the kind of relationship between two classes (association, aggregation, or composition).
- A new relationship between the *Relationship* and *Class* classes to express that a relationship has an association class.

Even though there are no tools that use UMLite as their metamodel, it is still useful. Since the main concepts of UMLite are almost the same as the concepts in Ecore and UML2, they can be easily transformed to these metamodels.

Defining Alternative Transformations using QVT

This subsection shows how some alternative transformations for a requirement specification generate different UML class diagrams. Although not all the possibilities are fully explained due to space limitations, it is possible to see that, given a requirement specification, a set of conceptual model solutions can be identified. The example

Figure 4. The UMLite metamodel

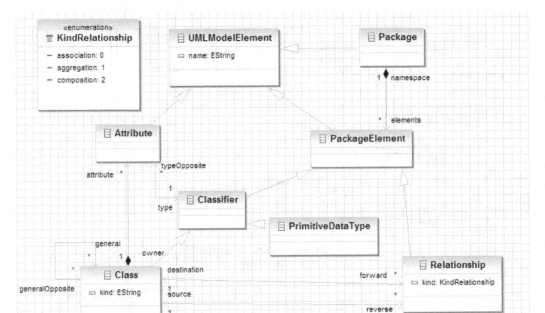

used to illustrate these alternative transformations is taken from the specification of a Car Rental system.

A Sequence Diagram is used to specify the necessary object interactions to realize the Use Case *Create Insurance* that is initiated by the *Administrator* actor. This Use Case represents the creation of a car *Insurance* policy that must be bought from an *Insurance Company* and assigned to the *Car* before using the car for rentals. Fig. 5 shows the Sequence Diagram for the Use Case *Create Insurance*. After introducing the necessary data and checking the existence of the corresponding car, a new *Insurance* object is created (messages 1 to 5). In addition, an *Insurance Company* object and a *Car* object must be connected to the new created Insurance policy (messages 6 and 7).

In our approach, this information is used to transform the requirements specification into a UML class diagram[4] following an MDA approach. It is important to remark that, for an automated transformation process to be considered useful, it must make decisions about which transformations are more suitable to produce the expected result by the analyst or a result that maximizes a quality attribute (in our case the *understandability* attribute).

The analysis of the requirement specified as object interactions shown in Fig. 5 indicates that the messages 6 and 7 satisfy the transformation rule TR 15:

- **TR15:** For every message between two classes labeled with the stereotype «connect», THEN an *association relationship* will be generated.

Figure 5. Sequence Diagram showing the required interactions for the Use Case Create Insurance

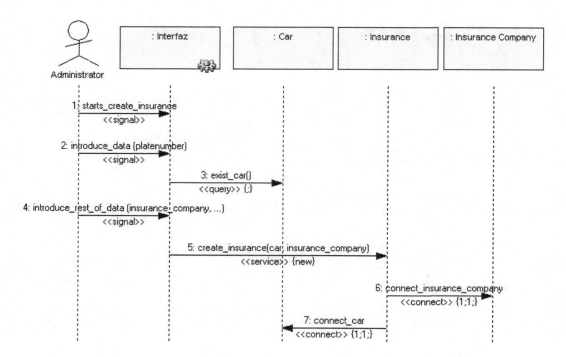

As a result, this transformation rule is applied twice. This means that two association relationships are established in the target model: one from *Insurance* to *Car* and another from *Insurance* to *InsuranceCompany* (Fig. 6a, **association**). An association relationship indicates a connection (link) between two classes.

Alternatively, there are other interpretations to the object interactions shown in Fig. 5. As a second alternative, the new created object *Insurance* can be represented as a component of both the *Insurance Company* compound class and the *Car* compound class (Fig. 6b, **aggregation**). This is because an aggregation is a special form of an association, specifying a whole-part relationship between two objects. This means that there is a connection between classes but also implies an additional semantics which indicates that an object 'is made up of other objects'. We are aware

that not always an association relationship can be represented as an aggregation relationship, as this decision depends on the problem domain. However, in our example, both relationships can be applied as an Insurance "could be *related to* an insurance company and a car" or "be *part of* an insurance company and a car".

A third alternative is to consider the *Insurance* as an association class related to the association relationship between *Insurance Company* and *Car* (Fig. 6c, **association class**). This means that when an instance of an *InsuranceCompany* class is associated with an instance of a *Car* class, there will also be an instance of an *Insurance* class.

These three types of relationships can be alternative representations for the object interactions shown in Figure 5. In general, an association class can always be replaced by two association or aggregation relationships. Consequently, we

Figure 6. Partial UML class diagram for the analyzed Sequence Diagram

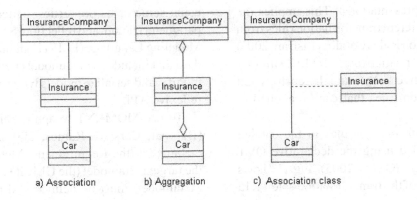

| a) Association | b) Aggregation | c) Association class |

Table 2. Three alternative structural relationships and their corresponding transformation rules

Alternatives	Transformation Rules
A1 (association)	**TR 14.** For every message between two classes labeled with the stereotype «service/new» where both classes are distinct from the "interface" class THEN an association relationship between these classes will be generated.
	TR 15. For every message between two classes labeled with the stereotype «connect», THEN an association relationship between these classes will be generated.
	TR 16. For every message with the stereotype «service/new» or «connect» where classes using role names appears THEN an association relationship between these classes will be generated using these role names on the ends of the relationship.
A2 (aggregation)	**TR 28.** For every message with the stereotype «service/new» between two classes A and B, which are distinct from the "interface" class, THEN an aggregation relationship between these classes will be generated.
A3 (association class)	**TR 39.** For every message with the stereotype «service/new» from the class A to the class B, if there exist two messages with the stereotype «connect» starting from the class B to the classes C and D respectively, THEN a new association class will be generated (called B) AND also an association relationship between C and D related to the new association class B will be generated.
	TR 40. For every message with the stereotype «connect» from the class A to the class B, if there exist a message with the stereotype «service/new» starting from the class A or B to the class C THEN a new association class will be generated (called C) AND also, an association relationship between A and B related to the new association class C will be generated..

have identified three types of structural relationships to represent object interactions (there may also be other representations). This implies the application of different transformation rules from the Transformation Rules Catalog (Insfran, 2003) to produce these relationships. Table 2 summarizes the alternative structural relationships and the transformation rules that can be applied to produce them.

All the transformation rules in the catalog are being specified using the declarative QVT relations language (OMG, 2005). Fig. 7 shows the specification of the transformation rule TR15 in QVT.

Executing the Alternative Transformations in MOMENT

MOMENT (Boronat, Carsí & Ramos, 2005) is a framework for model management that is fully integrated in the Eclipse environment. MOMENT combines the best features of Maude and Eclipse. First, it uses Maude (Clavel et al., 2005) as a backend. Maude is a reflective language and system supporting equational and rewriting logic

specification. Maude has been used as a rapid prototyping environment to develop MOMENT using some of its properties: pattern matching, parameterization, and reflection. Second, Eclipse Modeling Language (EMF) is an industrial standard that includes a metamodel (Ecore) to define, modify, and serialize models with a very efficient reflexive API.

To use MOMENT to apply transformations (Boronat, Carsí & Ramos, 2006), the source metamodel (the Requirements Metamodel) and the target metamodel (the UMLite class diagram Metamodel) must be defined and registered as Ecore models. MOMENT is used to define the QVT-Relations transformation *ReqModelToUMLite*. This transformation is composed of a set of rules that defines how to transform information belonging to a model that conforms to the Requirements Metamodel into a model that conforms to the UMLite class diagram Metamodel.

Finally, a configuration for the MODELGEN operator is defined. This configuration is composed of the *ReqModelToUMLite* transformation, a source model that is defined with the RETO tool, and the name of the target UML model.

Figure 7. TR15 specified using QVT-Relations

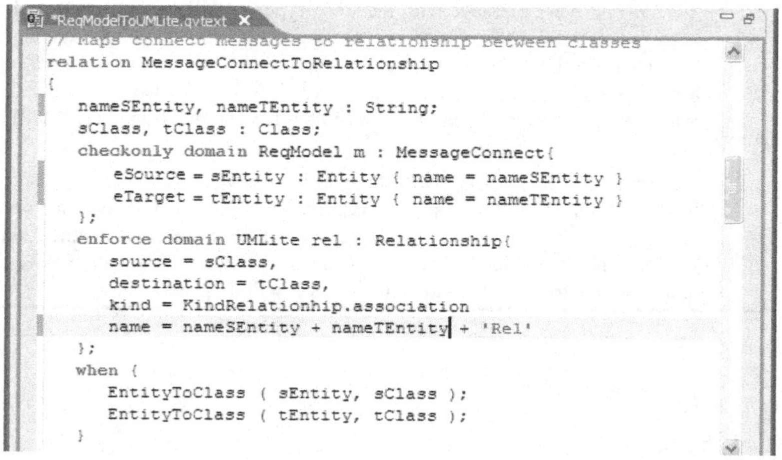

```
// Maps connect messages to relationship between classes
relation MessageConnectToRelationship
{
    nameSEntity, nameTEntity : String;
    sClass, tClass : Class;
    checkonly domain ReqModel m : MessageConnect{
        eSource = sEntity : Entity { name = nameSEntity }
        eTarget = tEntity : Entity { name = nameTEntity }
    };
    enforce domain UMLite rel : Relationship{
        source = sClass,
        destination = tClass,
        kind = KindRelationhip.association
        name = nameSEntity + nameTEntity + 'Rel'
    };
    when {
        EntityToClass ( sEntity, sClass );
        EntityToClass ( tEntity, tClass );
    }
```

Additionally, a traceability model is generated to relate the elements of the source model with the elements of the target model.

Fig. 8 shows MOMENT integrated in the Eclipse environment. On the left side, the Package Explorer shows all the files related to the transformation: *ModelGen.mop* is the model that defines the generic operator MODELGEN; *reqModel. ecore* is the model that defines the Requirements Metamodel used as the source in the transformation; *UMLite.ecore* is the metamodel used as the target in the transformation; *rentacar.reqmodel* is a model that defines the rentacar system (instance of the metamodel reqModel); *rentacar.umlite* is the model (instance of UMLite metamodel) resulting from the application of the transformation to rentacar.reqmodel; *rentacar.traceabilitymodel* is the traceability model that maps elements of the source and target models; *ReqModelToUMLite. qvtext* is the transformation expressed in QVT-Relations. The top of the figure shows part of the

UMLite metamodel. The bottom of the figure shows a part of the ReqModelToUMLite transformation inside the QVT text editor.

An additional transformation called *UMLite2UML2* was defined to transform UMLite class diagram models into UML2 class diagram models (see section 3.2).

Once a transformation has been executed, a traceability model is generated. The traceability model relates the elements of both models. There is a special view designed for this information. This view allows the analyst to see the transformation rules that have been executed and what the results are.

Fig. 9 shows the traceability model generated after executing the *reqModel2UMLite* transformation. The first column shows the domain model, which is the *rentacar* requirements model. The third column shows the range model, which is the generated *rentacar* UMLite model. Finally, the second column shows the traceability links

Figure 8. MOMENT environment

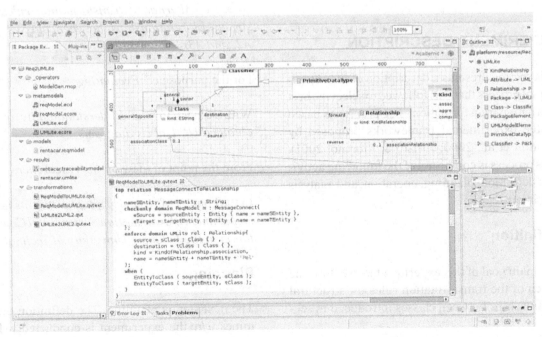

Figure 9. Traceability model generated by applying the ReqModelToUMLite transformation.

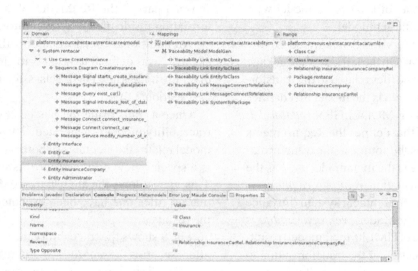

(mappings) that relates the elements of the domain and range models. A traceability link, which is the result of applying the transformation rule *EntityToClass* is highlighted. This traceability link relates the *Insurance* entity with the *Insurance* class.

EXPERIMENT DESCRIPTION

This section presents a description of the experimental process that was followed to select the best alternative transformation. The process is based on the experimental frameworks proposed by (Wohlin et al., 2000; Juristo & Moreno, 2001). This process is composed of the following activities: definition, planning, operation, and analysis and interpretation.

Definition

The main goal of this experiment is to determine which of the transformation rules for structural relationships between classes introduced in sec-

tion 4.3 (A1, A2, A3, and A4) obtained the easiest to understand UML class diagram. Therefore, using the GQM (Basili & Rombach, 1988) template for goal definition, the goal of our experiment is defined as follows:

Analyze: *Alternative transformation rules for structural relationships between classes (A1, A2, and A3)*

For the purpose of: *Evaluating*

With respect to: *the Understandability of the obtained UML class diagrams*

From the point of view of: *the researchers*

In the context of: *Undergraduate students at the Department of Information Systems and Computation at the Valencia University of Technology*

Planning

The next step is planning. The definition determines *why* the experiment is conducted, while the planning prepares *how* the experiment is to be conducted. The main characteristics of the planning phase are the following:

Subjects. The participants were 39 fourth-year students in Computer Science at the Valencia University of Technology, who were taking part in the second Software Engineering course. We took a "convenience sample" (i.e. all the students in the class). The subjects had six months of experience in modeling with UML and three years of experience in the OO paradigm. The subjects were encouraged to participate by offering them an extra point in the final grade for performing the required tasks correctly.

Variable selection. The independent variables were the transformation rules for structural relationships between classes (i.e., A1, A2, and A3). The dependent variable was understandability.

Experimental material and tasks. The experimental material and tasks consisted of:

- 9 Sequence Diagrams from three different case studies, with 3 UML class diagrams each. These were obtained by applying the alternative transformation rules. An example of the experimental material is shown in Appendix A. The rest of experimental material is available at: www.dsic.upv.es/~einsfran/experiment.
- Each Sequence Diagram has a questionnaire attached consisting of 6 Yes/No questions to test the subjects' understanding of the Sequence Diagrams. The effectiveness of the subjects in answering the questionnaires (number of correct answers/number answers) was used as a criterion to exclude those observations that did not fulfill a minimum level of quality. Observations with a value less than or equal to 0.5 were excluded. If the subjects did not understand

the Sequence Diagrams, their questionnaires were excluded.

- Each of the three UML class diagrams had a questionnaire attached (with 6 questions) for assessing which alternative UML class diagram was better understood by the subjects. In addition, the subjects had to write down the starting and ending times for completing the questionnaires. We obtained three measures for understandability from this understanding task:

Understandability Time, which reflects the time, in seconds, that the subjects spent answering each questionnaire (calculated by the difference between the ending time and the starting time). Each subject completed 3 questionnaires detailing 3 alternatives (A1, A2, and A3). Three understandability time measures (A1Time, A2Time, and A3Time) were obtained.

Effectiveness, which reflects the correctness of the answers (calculated by dividing the number of correct answers by the number of answers). Three understandability effectiveness measures (A2Effec, A2Effec, and A3Effec) were obtained.

Efficiency, which reflects the correctness of the answers by time (calculated by dividing the number of correct answers by the understandability time). Three measures for understandability efficiency (A2Effic, A2Effic, and A3Effic) were obtained.

- The final task of each test consisted of asking the subjects which of the three alternative UML class diagrams best reflected the problem modeled in the Sequence Diagram. In this way, we obtained a subjective measure (*Alternative Selected*) based on the subjects' perception.

Hypothesis formulation. The following hypotheses were formulated:

- **$H1_0$**: The use of different alternative transformations (A1, A2, and A3) does not affect the Understandability Time (A1Time, A2Time, and A3Time). $H1_1 = \neg H1_0$
- **$H2_0$**: The use of different alternative transformations (A1, A2, and A3) does not affect the Understandability Effectiveness (A1Effec, A2Effec, and A3Effec). $H2_1 = \neg H2_0$
- **$H3_0$**: The use of different alternative transformations (A1, A2, and A3) does not affect the Understandability Efficiency (A1Effic, A2Effic, and A3Effic). $H3_1 = \neg H3_0$
- **$H4_0$**: There is no correlation between the Alternative Selected and the means of objective Understandability variables (Understandability Time Effectiveness, and Efficiency). $H4_1 = \neg H4_0$

Operation

The experiment started with an introductory session in which the main concepts of the Requirements Model (e.g., the notation of Sequence Diagrams) were reviewed. The goal of the experiment was not disclosed to the subjects. Then, the subjects were shown an example of the experimental material, which was similar to what they would be using during the execution of the experiment.

Each subject was given all the experimental material, including nine tests (balanced within-subject design). The diagrams were assigned in different order to limit learning effects. The alternatives were also organized in a different order across subjects in order not to favor one alternative over another. In total, eighteen types of tests were prepared. The subjects were instructed how to develop the experimental tasks and they had a maximum of two hours to complete all the tasks.

Data Analysis and Interpretation

After the experiment took place, we collected the experiment data. It consisted of a table of 351 rows (9 diagrams x 39 subjects) and 9 columns (A1Time, A2Time, A3Time, A1Effec, A2Effec, A3Effec, A1Effic, A2Effec, A3Effec). We then performed a "data cleaning", excluding the observations that were not complete because the subjects had not written down the time or because the subjects did not selected the best alternative. Since all the questions in each questionnaire were complete, the completeness of the performed tasks was guaranteed. We also excluded the observations that had a value of effectiveness of 50% or less for each Sequence Diagram. The final data for testing the hypotheses were 325 observations.

The following statistical analyses were performed to analyze the data:

- A descriptive study was done to characterize the dependent variables.
- Hypotheses H1, H2, and H3 were tested using an ANOVA test with repeated measures.
- Hypothesis H4 was tested using the Spearman correlation coefficient.

We used SPSS (SPSS, 2002) to carry out the data analyses presented in this study.

Descriptive Statistics

The descriptive study was performed by first analyzing the variable *Alternative Selected* and then analyzing the measures of *Understandability Time*, *Effectiveness*, and *Efficiency*.

From Table 3 (which shows the frequency of each type of alternative (A1, A2, and A3) for each diagram) and Fig. 10 (which shows the percentages of selection for each type of alternative) we can infer the following:

- A1 is the alternative transformation that was most selected by the subjects, i.e., the subjects believed that the use of associations allowed to obtain the best UML class diagram (the easiest to understand).

- A3 is the alternative transformation that was least selected by the subjects, i.e., the subjects believed that it was the least appropriate alternative transformation.

The descriptive statistics for the *Understandability Time*, *Effectiveness*, and *Efficiency* are shown in Table 4. They are ranked in ascendant order by the value of the mean.

Table 4 reveals that, on average, the subjects spent less time performing the tasks related to alternative A2. However, the difference with the other tasks was not very significant (approximately 8 seconds for A1 and A3). The subjects were more effective and efficient performing the

tasks related to alternative A1; but the difference in effectiveness with the other alternatives was not very significant.

In summary, the descriptive statistics show a slight tendency in favor of A1, which is the transformation based on associations.

Testing Hypotheses

To test the hypotheses H_1, H_2, and H_3, we carried out an ANOVA for repeated measures. The results show hypotheses $H1_0$, $H2_0$, and $H3_0$ can be rejected (with a significance level = 0.05). This means that each alternative transformation really does affect the *Understandability Time*, *Effectiveness*, and *Efficiency*.

Moreover, we compared the means for each measure by pairs of alternatives. There was a significant difference between the following pairs:

Table 3. Frequency of transformation alternatives per diagram

Diagrams/ Alternatives	D1	D2	D3	D4	D5	D6	D7	D8	D9	Total
A1	6	12	13	25	18	14	16	18	7	129
A2	8	4	7	8	9	12	6	5	13	72
A3	19	20	10	5	11	12	15	14	18	124
Total	33	36	30	38	38	38	37	37	38	325

Figure 10. Percentages for alternative selected

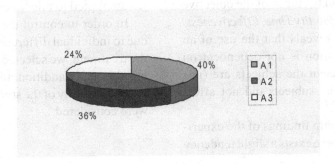

Table 4. Descriptive statistics for understandability time, effectiveness and efficiency

	Min.	Max.	Mean	St. Dev.
A2TIME	23	449	93.4338	57.9701
A1TIME	12	611	101.9046	79.1776
A3TIME	15	734	106.5077	72.2032
A2EFFEC	0.167	1	0.8701	0.1528
A3EFFEC	0.167	1	0.8844	0.1821
A1EFFEC	0.167	1	0.9111	0.1548
A3EFFIC	0.006	0.4	0.0677	0.0419
A2EFFIC	0.011	0.24	0.0757	0.0436
A1EFFIC	0.005	0.5	0.0803	0.0531

- The pairs A1-A2, A1-A3 in the values of the *Understandability Time*.
- The pairs A1-A2, A1-A3 and A2-A3, in the *Understandability Effectiveness*.
- The pairs A1-A3, A1-A3 and A2-A3, in terms of the *Understandability Efficiency*.

This comparison shows that there is a significant difference between A1 (related to associations) and the other alternatives (A2 and A3).

To test hypothesis H_4, we carried out a correlation analysis using the Spearman Correlation, separately per each diagram. We did not find any correlation between the subjective measure (*Alternative Selected*) and the mean of the objective measures (*Understandability Time, Effectiveness,* and *Efficiency*). This reveals that the use of an alternative transformation is not dependent on how effective or efficient the subjects are (i.e., the performance of the subjects did not affect their perception).

In summary, the main findings of the experimentation show that there exists a slight tendency in favor of using associations. In other words, the subjects are a slightly more effective and efficient when performing tasks related to association relationships (instead of aggregations or association classes). Assuming that the three alternatives are alternatives, this indicates that transformations related to association relationships are the most appropriate when the understandability quality attribute is selected.

Threats to Validity

This section discusses several issues that can affect the validity of the empirical study and how we attempted to alleviate them.

In order to control the risk that the variation due to individual differences is larger than due to the treatment, we selected a homogeneous group of subjects. In addition, to attempt to control the internal validity of the study, the following issues were considered:

- *Differences among subjects.* Using a within-subjects design, error variance due to differences among subjects was reduced. In addition, we randomly assigned the tests to the subjects in different order. This procedure cancels out a possible learning effect (due to similarities in the treatments) and a confounding effect (due to the order in which the alternatives were presented).
- *Knowledge of the universe of discourse.* We used the same requirement specification document for all subjects. It specifies the requirements of a Car Rental System for a company. This is a well-known universe of discourse.
- *Fatigue effects.* On average, each subject took two hours to solve the experimental tests, so fatigue was not very relevant.
- *Persistence effects.* In order to avoid persistence effects, the experiment was carried out by subjects who had never done a similar experiment.
- *Subject motivation.* We motivated students to participate in the experiment by offering them an extra point in the final grade of the course.

One limitation to the external validity of this study is the fact that the three alternative transformation rules cannot be applied simultaneously to all modeling situations. For instance, to establish an association class relationship (A4), at least one «service/new» message and two «connect» messages are needed in the source model. The goal of this experimentation was to gather empirical evidence for the specific case when the three alternative transformations can be applied to obtain a relationship between classes. We are aware that, more alternatives may be possible to represent structural relationships between classes. More experimentation is needed to validate these other combinations.

Another limitation is the use of only students as participants. In general, our students have no working experience in conceptual modeling. The use of student participants may present a threat to the study's external validity. However, the students who participated in the experiment were fourth-year students in Computer Science. Therefore, they can be considered as representative of novice users of conceptual modeling approaches. To increase external validity, the current study needs to be replicated using experienced practitioners from the industrial sector who are experienced in UML and/or students with higher levels of training in order to confirm our results.

CONCLUSION

This chapter has presented an approach for quality-driven model transformations. Specifically, it described a controlled experiment to investigate the selection of alternative QVT transformations to obtain UML class diagrams from a Requirements Model. The goal of the experiment was to gather empirical evidence about which alternative transformation produces the UML class diagram that is easiest to understand.

The results show that there is a slight tendency to favor the use of association relationships when the three alternatives can be applied. This indicates that transformations related to association relationships are the most appropriate when the understandability quality attribute is selected. A possible reason for this could be that this relationship has less semantic strength than the other kinds of relationships. When an aggregation relationship is chosen instead of an association relationship, analysts know that they are defining a *part-of* relationship. However, when an association class is chosen, the same relationship can be represented using two association or aggregation relationships.

These results provided first evidence about the understandability of a model obtained through a model transformation process. The study was conducted in the context of the UML class diagram that is the most-used specification for model-driven software development in industry. Although this evidence is specific to this domain, and in particular, to the relationships among classes, it should be generalized to other elements in a UML class diagram, other UML diagrams, and also to other domains. Therefore, more experimentation is needed to verify the generalizability of our approach.

The results that we have obtained through experimentation are promising. However, they must be considered as preliminary results. We plan to replicate this experiment with students from the University of Castilla-La Mancha in Spain and also with more experienced practitioners from the industrial sector in order to confirm these results. We believe that the level of experience in UML modeling can considerably influence the performance of the subjects.

FUTURE RESEARCH DIRECTIONS

Our literature review has shown that there are very few studies that deal with quality in model-driven development. As far as we know, there is no study encompassing the empirical validation of model transformations. The study of quality for model-driven development is of great relevance to software development organizations faced to the adoption of this technology in industry.

The empirical study presented in this chapter shows how model transformations can be empirically validated with regard to a given quality attribute. This work is part of a project on quality-driven model transformations whose goal is the definition of a quality metamodel to drive the selection of model transformations according to multiple quality attributes. Therefore, our current research efforts are focused on the validation of the remaining transformations of the Transformation Rules Catalog (Insfran 2003). We also plan to study other quality attributes (i.e., efficiency, understandability, usability, modifi-

ability) and possible conflicts that could arise when more than one quality attribute is chosen. Our ultimate goal is to build an empirically validated quality metamodel to drive the selection of model transformations in different domains (e.g., Bioinformatics and Data Warehouse). This quality metamodel will be fully integrated in the MOMENT environment.

There is an urgent need for more research studies of this type to complement and extend the current empirical study. Empirical evaluation of model transformations will help software developers assess the usefulness of different sets of transformations according to the quality of the resulting target model and/or transformation needs.

While several studies (including this one) have studied model transformations and its properties, it would be interesting to survey or interview domain-specific engineers and ascertain the importance of certain model transformations to define heuristics to drive the transformations. In our study, a heuristic could be the type of traceability (i.e., strong and weak) assigned to each transformation rule. This could be an additional criterion to be used during the transformation process.

Another area of future research needs to examine other quality perspectives (i.e., syntactic quality, semantic quality). Syntactic quality in the context of model-driven development is trivial due to all the models are compliant to their respective metamodel. However, assessing semantic quality will allow to verify which alternative transformation will produce a target model that is more correct and relevant to the problem domain.

Finally, the applicability or dependence of model transformations to the type of domain of the application being developed would be an interesting study.

REFERENCES

Basili, V. & Rombach, H. (1988). The TAME project: towards improvement-oriented software environments. *IEEE Transactions on Software Engineering*, 14(6), 728-738.

Boronat, A., Carsí J.A., & Ramos I. (2006). *Algebraic Specification of a Model Transformation Engine*. Proceedings of the Fundamental Approaches to Software Engineering (FASE'06). ETAPS'06. Vienna, Austria, 262–277.

Boronat, A., Carsí, J.Á., Ramos, I. (2005). *MOMENT: a formal MOdel manageMENT tool*. School on Generative and Transformational Techniques in SE. Braga, Portugal.

Clavel, M., Durán, F., Eker, S., Lincoln, P., Martí-Oliet, N., Meseguer, J., & Talcott, C. (2005). Maude 2.2 manual and examples, from http://maude.cs.uiuc.edu/maude2-manual

Czarnecki, K., & Helsen, S. (2006). Feature-based survey of model transformation approaches. *IBM Systems Journal*, 45(3), 621–645.

Genero, M., Manso, M., Visaggio, A., Canfora, G. & Piattini, M. (2007) Building measure-based prediction models for UML class diagram maintainability. *Empirical Software Engineering* (to appear).

Genero, M., Moody, D., & Piattini, M. (2005). Assessing the capability of internal metrics as early indicators of maintenance effort through experimentation. *Journal of Software Maintenance and Evolution: Research and Practice*, 17, 225-246.

Insfran, E. (2003). *A Requirements Engineering Approach for Object-Oriented Conceptual Modeling*, PhD Thesis, DSIC, Valencia University of Technology, Spain.

Insfran, E., Pastor, O. & Wieringa, R. (2002). Requirements Engineering-Based Conceptual Modelling. *Journal of Requirements Engineering*, 7 (2), 61–72, Springer-Verlag.

ISO, ISO/IEC 9126-1, (2001). Software Engineering – Product quality – Part 1: Quality model.

Ivkovic, I., & Kontogiannis, K. A. (2006). *Framework for Software Architecture Refactoring using Model Transformations and Semantic Annotations*, Proc. of the Conference on Software Maintenance and Reengineering (CSMR'06), 135–144.

Jurista, N. & Moreno, A. M. (2001). *Basics of Software Engineering Experimentation*. Kluwer Academic Publishers.

Kerhervé, B., Nguyen, K. K., Gerbé, O., & Jaumard, B. A. (2006). Framework for Quality-Driven Delivery in Distributed Multimedia Systems, Proc. of the Advanced International Conference on Telecommunications and International Conference on Internet and Web Applications and Services (AICT/ICIW 2006), 195–205.

Kurtev, I. (2005). *Adaptability of Model Transformations*. PhD Thesis, University of Twente, The Nederlands.

Lindland, O. I., Sindre G., & Sølvberg A. (1994). Understanding quality in conceptual modeling. *IEEE Software*, 11(2), 42–49.

Markovic, S., & Baar, T. (2005). *Refactoring OCL annotated UML class diagrams*. In Proc. of the 8th Int. Conference on Model Driven Engineering Languages and Systems, 280–294.

Merilinna, J. (2005). *A Tool for Quality-Driven Architecture Model Transformation*. Espoo, VTT Electronics, VTT Publications.

OMG, (2006). OMG, UML 2.1 Unified Modeling Language™

OMG, (2005). OMG, MOF 2.0 Query/Views/Transformations Final Adopted Specification, Object Management Group, from http://www.omg.org/cgibin/apps/doc?ad/05-11-01.pdf

OMG, (2004). Meta Object Facility (MOF) 2.0 Core Specification, ptc/04-10-15.

OMG, (2003). MDA Guide, from http://www.omg.org/docs/omg/03-06-01.pdf. Version 1.0.1.

Otero, M. C., & Dolado, J. J. (2004). Evaluation of the Comprehension of the Dynamic Modeling in UML. *Information and Software Technology*, 46(1), 35-53.

Reinhartz-Berger, H. & Dori, D. (2005). OPM vs. UML—Experimenting with Comprehension and Construction of Web Application Models. *Empirical Software Engineering*, 10, 57–79.

Rottger S., & Zschaler, S. (2004). Model-Driven Development for Non-functional Properties: Refinement through Model Transformation, In LNCS Volume 3273, The Unified Modelling Language (UML) Conference, pp. 275–289.

Selic, B. (2003). The Pragmatics of Model-Driven Development. *IEEE Software*, 20 (5), 19-25.

SPSS, SPSS 11.5, Syntax Reference Guide. 2002, SPSS Inc.: Chicago, USA.

Sottet, J. S., Calvary, G., & Favre, J. M. (2006). Mapping Model: A First Step to Ensure Usability for sustaining User Interface Plasticity, In: Proc. of the MODELS 2006 Workshop on Model Driven Development of Advanced User Interfaces.

Wohlin C., Runeson P., Höst M., Ohlson M., Regnell B. and Wesslén A. (2000). *Experimentation in Software Engineering: An Introduction.* Kluwer Academic Publishers.

Zou, Y., Kontogiannis, K. (2003). Quality Driven Transformation Framework for OO Migration. In. *Proc. 2nd ASERC Workshop on Software Architecture*, Banff, Canada, pp. 18–24.

ADDITIONAL READING

Endres, A. & Rombach, D. (2003). *A Handbook of Software and Systems Engineering: Empirical Observations*, Laws and Theories. Addison Wesley.

Frankel, D. S. (2003) *Model driven Architecture: Applying MDA to Enterprise Computing*, Wiley.

Juristo, N. & Moreno, A. M. (2001). *Basics of Software Engineering Experimentation.* Kluwer Academic Publishers.

Maxwell, K. (2002). *Applied Statistics for Software Managers.* Software Quality Institute Series. Prentice Hall.

Stahl, T., Voelter, M., & Czarnecki, K. (2006) *Model-Driven Software Development: Technology, Engineering, Management, Wiley.*

Unhelkar, B. (2005) *Verification and Validation for Quality of UML 2.0 Models*, Wiley-Interscience.

Wohlin C., Runeson P., Höst M., Ohlson M., Regnell B. and Wesslén A. (2000). *Experimentation in Software Engineering: An Introduction.* Kluwer Academic Publishers.

APPENDIX A. AN EXAMPLE OF THE EXPERIMENTAL MATERIAL

TEST R1

The following Sequence Diagram represents the creation of a *Car* for a car rental company. All the cars of the company have an assigned *Rate*. In addition, they must have an *Insurance* policy from an *Insurance Company*.

Figure 11. Sequence diagram "creation of a car"

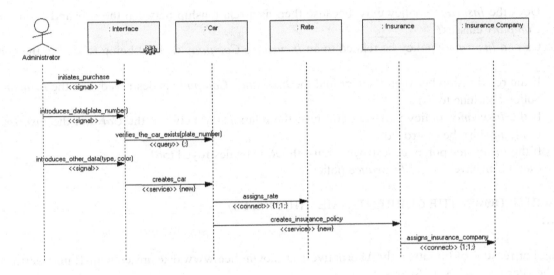

SECTION A: Understandability

WRITE DOWN THE CURRENT TIME (HH: MM: SS) _____

Answer the following Yes/No questions:

1. Is it possible in this scenario to create several *Cars*? _____
2. Can a *Car* have several *Insurance* policies in addition to the obligatory one for accidents?; for example, a policy for theft _____
3. Are there four classes in this Sequence Diagram? _____
4. If an appropriate *Rate* for a *Car* does not exist, can a new type of *Rate* be created and then assigned to the *Car*? _____
5. Can a *Car* be created without an obligatory *Insurance* policy? _____
6. Is it possible to associate an *Insurance* policy of another *Car* to the *Car* being created? _____

WRITE DOWN THE CURRENT TIME (HH: MM: SS) _____
Section B: Alternatives of Representation
Note: As an example of the three alternatives obtained from the Sequence Diagram shown in Fig. 11, we include the one based on the association class relationship.

Alternative 1:

WRITE DOWN THE CURRENT TIME (HH: MM: SS) _____
Answer the following Yes/No questions:

1. Does the *Insurance* policy exist because there is a relationship between the *Car* and *Insurance Company* classes? _____
2. Can an *Insurance* policy be related to an *Insurance Company* without being related to the *Car*? _____
3. If the relationship between the *Car* and the *Insurance Company* is destroyed, can the *Insurance* policy continue to exist? _____
4. If the *Insurance* policy is destroyed, must the relationship between the *Car* and the *Insurance Company* also be destroyed? _____
5. If the *Insurance* policy is destroyed, must the *Rate* be destroyed too? _____
6. Can a *Car* have several *Insurance* policies? _____

WRITE DOWN THE CURRENT TIME (HH: MM: SS) _____
...

Note: For reasons of brevity, only Alternative 1 is shown. See www.dsic.upv.es/~einsfran/experiment for the alternatives 2-3 (in Spanish).

SECTION C: Rating tasks
In your opinion, which one of the UML class diagrams presented in Section B best represents the scenario illustrated in the Sequence Diagram of Fig. 11? (Mark your choice with an "X")

Alternative 1 ( )   Alternative 2 ( )   Alternative 3 ( )

Chapter XIII
A Framework for Understanding and Addressing the Semiotic Quality of Use Case Models

Pankaj Kamthan
Concordia University, Canada

ABSTRACT

As software systems become ever more interactive, there is a need to model the services they provide to users, and use cases are one abstract way of doing that. As use cases models become pervasive, the question of their communicability to stakeholders arises. In this chapter, we propose a semiotic framework for understanding and systematically addressing the quality of use case models. The quality concerns at each semiotic level are discussed and process- and product-oriented means to address them in a feasible manner are presented. The scope and limitations of the framework, including that of the means, are given. The need for more emphasis on prevention over cure in improving the quality of use case models is emphasized. The ideas explored are illustrated by examples.

INTRODUCTION

A characteristic common to the majority of present software systems is interaction. There is a broad variety of interactive software systems in use today, including those that run on automatic banking machines (ABMs), on mobile devices, and on the Web, to name a few.

The users can play a central role in the engineering of an interactive software system. Therefore, it is critical to precisely understand, identify, and document the services that an interactive software system will provide from the viewpoint of its potential users. A large and important class of models that these services encapsulate is *use cases* (Jacobson et al., 1992).

Indeed, in the last few years, the use case approach (Jacobson & Ng, 2005) has become indispensable as means for behavioral modeling of interactive software systems. They play a crucial role in various activities, including estimating software development cost (Anda, 2003), eliciting software (external) behavioral requirements (Bittner & Spence, 2003; Leffingwell & Widrig,

2003), contributing to software architecture views (Kruchten, 1995), defining test cases (Alexander & Maiden, 2004), and authoring a user manual.

As the integration and deployment of use cases in software process environments becomes pervasive, the question of their quality arises. If left unaddressed, these models, for example, may become incommunicable or unmanageable to their stakeholders. This could seriously compromise the utility of use cases as early artifacts and potentially threaten their broad acceptance. At the same time, an approach to the improvement of the quality of use case models may not be effective if it is ad hoc and infeasible. A systematic quality-centered approach for use case model engineering is necessary.

The rest of the chapter is organized as follows. We first outline the background and related work necessary for the discussion that follows and state our position. This is followed by the presentation of a framework for understanding and systematically addressing the semiotic quality of use case models by process- and product-oriented means in a feasible manner. To place the discussion into perspective, the scope and limitations of the framework, including that of the means, are given. Next, a detailed example is presented, and then concluding remarks are given. Finally, challenges and directions for future research are outlined.

BACKGROUND

In this section, we present the terminology necessary for the discussion that follows and briefly review the significance of quality in use case models.

There are several interpretations (Seidewitz, 2003) of the term model. For the sake of this chapter, we define a *model* as a simplified description of some entity from a particular viewpoint of interest.

As indicated by the model-driven approach to software development (Beydeda, Book, & Gruhn, 2005; Völter et al., 2006), models are becoming first-class members of organizations and software process environments that embrace them. The need to model software can arise due to various reasons. These include assessing the viability of or planning software systems to be built, optimizing use of resources in response to inevitable changes in business, social, or technological environments, or simply understanding existing software systems. Modeling, particularly during early phases of software development, is playing an increasingly important role in software engineering profession and education (Cowling, 2005). The use case models are one important class of models, which we discuss next.

An Overview of Use Case Models

Since there are variations in the literature, we will closely follow one set of terminology of the use case domain in the following that provides a basis for further discussion.

A *use case* models the behavior of a software system, which yields an observable result of value to an actor of the system (Jacobson et al., 1992). In doing so, a use case intends to capture typical interactions between the actors and the software system being built. The use cases can be classified into *problem use cases* (those addressing the problem domain during analysis and sometimes labeled as business use cases or essential use cases) and *solution use cases* (those addressing the solution domain during synthesis and sometimes labeled as system use cases). The *system boundary* is a means to illustrate the separation of actors and use cases.

A use case has a unique *goal*. A use case is successfully executed if its goal is satisfied. There can be multiple use cases of a system, each with a different goal.

An *actor* is an external entity that interacts with each instance of a use case. An actor could be a (human) user or another program. Each actor plays a unique *role* with respect to a use case from the viewpoint of the system. There can be multiple actors of a system each with a different role. The actors can be classified into *primary actors* (those initiating a use case) and *secondary actors* (those supporting the goal of a primary actor).

Both the start and the end of a use case have conditions associated with them. There are certain necessary conditions that must be true at the start of a use case, and these are known as *pre-conditions*. There are certain guarantees that must be given at the end of a use case, and these are known as *post-conditions*: irrespective of whether the use case goal is achieved, there are certain guarantees and these are known as *minimal post-conditions*; if the use case goal is achieved, there are certain guarantees and these are known as *maximal post-conditions*.

A *flow* is a course through a use case. There can be single or sometimes multiple flows in a use case. A flow can be classified as being either *normal* (also known as *basic* or *main*) or *non-normal*. A normal flow will be carried out if everything goes according to the plan in the use case; otherwise a non-normal flow will be carried out. There can be different types of non-normal flows such as an *alternate* (also known as *variant*) flow or an *exceptional* flow. A flow follows a *path*. There can be one or more paths in a flow of a use case. Thus, in general, there are multiple paths through a use case.

A use case is an abstraction of the real-world use of a system. A *scenario* is a concrete realization or an *instance* of a use case: it takes actual values as input from a specific primary actor, it performs actions that cause changes to the system's internal state, and it makes actual decisions during the execution of the actions. For example, a scenario for a `Withdraw Money` use case for an ABM is the actual description of what occurs when John attempts to withdraw $100 from his savings account at a specific ABM on a certain day/time. This obviously leads to the classification of scenarios as normal or non-normal. A scenario will carry out one of the paths through a use case

in a concrete manner. An *abstract* use case does not have any instances.

In a use case model, multiple use cases can be related. There are three possible types of (binary and non-reflexive) relationships among use cases: "include," "extend," and "generalization." In a use case model, multiple actors of a system can also be related. There is one possible type of (binary and non-reflexive) relationship among actors: "generalization." For example, let UC_1 and UC_2 be two use cases and A_1 and A_2 are two actors for UC_1. Then, there is an include relationship from UC_1 to UC_2 if an instance of UC_1 includes the behavior of UC_2. There is an extend relationship from UC_1 to UC_2 if an instance of UC_2 is extended by the behavior of UC_1. The extend relationship is optional. There is a generalization relationship from UC_1 to UC_2 if an instance of UC_1 inherits the behavior of UC_2 where the inherited behavior is perhaps refined. In the object-oriented sense, UC_2 is a parent and UC_1 is a child. A generalization relationship from A_1 to A_2 can be understood in a similar manner.

The set of all actors and all use cases describing the complete usage of a software system is known as the system's *use case model*.

Representation of Use Case Models

A use case model needs to be represented in some form for the purpose of communication to both humans and to machines. In terms of formality, a use case model can be represented on the following discrete spectrum: informal (natural language), semi-formal, and formal (mathematical). In general, the formalization of use case models has been discouraged (Jacobson, 2003). In terms of modality, there are currently two common (and complementary) means of representing a use case model: as structured text and as a graphic.

Each means of representation has its own advantages and limitations, and a detailed discussion of this issue is beyond the scope of this chapter. While a representation in a natural language can include more details and preferred by technical stakeholders, a graphic tends to be more compact and preferred by novice or non-technical stakeholders. A *combination* of textual and graphical representation is recommended (Cockburn, 2001; Fowler, 2003) when the use of only one is deemed insufficient.

A UML View of Use Case Models

The Unified Modeling Language (UML) (Booch, Jacobson, & Rumbaugh, 2005) is a standard language for visually modeling the structure and behavior of object-oriented software systems.

The diagram types in UML can be used to provide different views of the use case domain knowledge: the Use Case Diagram to represent use case models, the Activity Diagram to represent the sequential order in which a use case is executed, and the Sequence Diagram to represent scenarios. These UML diagram types could be associated with a UML Note construct to provide annotations informally in natural language text or formally in a script in the Object Constraint Language (OCL) (Warmer & Kleppe, 2003). For example, the pre- and post-conditions in a use case model may be formally expressed in OCL.

The aforementioned relationships among actors or among use cases are represented in a Use Case Diagram using special arrows and arrowheads. Furthermore, the "include" and "extend" relationships are labeled using *stereotypes* in UML where their names are delimited using guillemets («»), resulting in «include» and «extend», respectively.

There is much support in the literature for expressing use case models in UML (Bittner & Spence, 2003). In this chapter, we will limit ourselves to use case models in UML unless specified otherwise. At the same time, we also acknowledge that even though UML has evolved over the years, the graphical notation alone is not sufficiently expressive in representing certain complex cases (Glinz, 2000).

Use Case Modeling and Software Process

The modeling of use cases needs to take place within the context of a software process. Indeed, the use case technique has been adopted by some recent software process environments.

Extreme Programming (XP) (Beck & Andres, 2005) is a broadly-used and well-tested agile methodology (Highsmith, 2002) aimed towards small-to-medium size software projects. XP does not have explicit support for use case modeling. However, it deploys *user stories* as means to elicit requirements, which could be viewed as an informal text-based representation of use cases for non-technical stakeholders.

Crystal Clear (Cockburn, 2005) is an agile methodology that aims to be human- and communication-centric. It consists of a framework of related methods, each addressing characteristics specific to a software project, and has explicit support for use case modeling.

The Unified Process (UP) (Jacobson, Booch, & Rumbaugh, 1999) is an archetype of a use case-driven process *framework* aimed towards large-scale software projects. An customization of UP for software systems in an enterprise setting is the Rational Unified Process (RUP) (Kruchten, 2004) and its customization in an educational setting is the Unified Process for EDUcation (UPEDU) (Robillard, D'Astous, & Kruchten, 2003).

The ICONIX Process is a use case-driven software development methodology (Rosenberg & Scott, 1999; Rosenburg, Stephens, & Collins-Cope, 2005). It is less agile than XP and lighter than UP.

Finally, we note that like other software artifacts, the use case approach to modeling has its own scope of applicability, advantages, and limitations (Jacobson, 2003), and a discussion of these is beyond the scope of this chapter.

Related Work on the Quality of Use Case Models

There are different views of quality (Wong, 2006). We need to understand and address the quality of software models for a variety of reasons. These include software development becoming increasingly (implicitly and/or explicitly) dependent on models, problems in early models may lead to their propagation in later artifacts (Moody, 2005), and difficulties in communicating the models can lead to more time being spent by others in understanding them correctly or managing their number as it grows across different collections.

There are various reasons (Rosenberg & Scott, 1999; El-Attar & Miller, 2006) due to which the quality of a use case model can be compromised, including lack of understanding of the underlying domain, lack of knowledge or skills in the modeling language, or limitations imposed by modeling tools.

There are currently limited efforts towards addressing the quality of use case models comprehensively, which we now consider chronologically.

The Cognitive Dimensions of Notations (CDs) (Green, 1989) is a generic framework for describing the utility of information artifacts by taking the system environment and the user characteristics into consideration. A questionnaire-based analysis of the CDs of the UML Use Case Diagram in an academic setting has been carried out (Cox, 2000). It is shown that the students find use case relationships in a Use Case Diagram hard to understand, although in general the graphical notation scores well.

An empirical experiment for detecting differences in understanding of a use case model and possible reasons for the differences has been carried out (Anda, Sjøberg, & Jørgensen, 2001). However, the attributes that impact understandability of a use case model are not adequately treated, and means for improving the understanding are minimal (namely, only guidelines).

The question of the quality of use case models has been asked (Adolph et al., 2003), but is neither systematically approached, nor adequately answered.

The expressiveness, consistency, and completeness of textual use case models has been analyzed using linguistic techniques (Fantechi et al., 2003), and as part of this initiative, a quality model and metrics are presented. However, the results do not exclusively carry over to graphical use case models.

Semiotics (Nöth, 1990) involves the study of communicative properties of signs and their representations. The question of the semiotic quality of UML models in general has been addressed (Kamthan, 2004; Kamthan, 2005; Genova, Valiente, & Nubiola, 2005; Bolloju & Leung, 2006) but use case model-related specifics are not discussed.

There have been initiatives to understand the notion of quality of use case models by decomposing it into attributes. A set of quality attributes, namely ambiguity, completeness, volatility, and traceability, for graphical use case models have been given (McCoy, 2003). However, the list is not systematically derived, is strongly related to software requirements, and the means for improvement are not discussed. Inspired by the IEEE Standard 830-1998, the quality attributes of correctness, consistency, unambiguousness, completeness, readability, and level of detail have been proposed and, by means of guidelines, used to evaluate the textual use case models at the Volvo Car Corporation (Törner et al., 2006). However, the list of attributes is neither systematic, nor complete, and the approach suffers from limitations inherent to the use of guidelines. A defect classification for UML models in general and UML Use Case Diagram in particular has been given (Lange & Chaudron, 2006). However, the classification does not appear to be exhaustive. A model-driven requirements process that integrates certain metrics for the improvement of quality of use case models has been proposed (Berenbach

& Borotto, 2006). However, the rationale for the selection of quality attributes is unclear. A discussion on the attributes for quality, namely correctness, consistency, and understandability of graphical use case models have been reported (El-Attar & Miller, 2006). However, these attributes represent only a partial list and have been intrinsically associated with software requirements. Furthermore, it has been simplistically concluded that an improvement in correctness and consistency will lead to an improvement in understandability.

Using theories of text comprehension, a collection of attributes for communicability of textual use case models and guidelines (heuristics) for realizing these attributes have been introduced (Phalp, Vincent, & Cox, 2007). These guidelines are then used to inspect use case models. The work provides some credence to the previous effort on use case guidelines (Cockburn, 2001). However, terms like "abstraction," "coherent," and "consistent," that tend to have multiple interpretations, are used in the guidelines but are not defined; the trade-offs among the attributes or the trade-offs among the guidelines are not considered; and (apart from the annotations) the results do not entirely carry over to graphical use case models.

A SYSTEMATIC APPROACH FOR UNDERSTANDING AND ADDRESSING THE SEMIOTIC QUALITY OF USE CASE MODELS

Using ISO/IEC 9126-1:2001 Standard, we could formally but broadly define the quality of a use case model as *the totality of characteristics of a use case model that bear on its ability to satisfy stated and implied needs*.

In this section, we propose a framework for understanding and systematically addressing the semiotic quality of use case models. Our approach rests on the following hypothesis:

Hypothesis 1. Modeling of software in general and that of use cases in particular has a significant place in the software development process adopted and followed by the organization.

Hypothesis 2. The quality of use cases is given a *first-class* consideration in the use case development process. The organization has for example shown that *explicitly* by dedicating resources for a quality-centered use case development process.

A use case model development process would usually be a *sub-process* of the overall software development process such as Crystal Methods or the RUP. Since non-trivial use case models are likely to evolve, this sub-process is also likely to be both iterative and incremental.

Among several proposed approaches for quality of conceptual models in general (Eppler, 2001; Moody, 2005), we adopt and extend the treatment in one case (Lindland, Sindre, & Sølvberg, 1994). The steps of the construction are as follows:

1. **Identification and Decomposition of Relevant Quality Concerns.** From a semiotics viewpoint, we view a use case on three interrelated levels: syntactic, semantic, and pragmatic. The pragmatic level depends on the semantic level, which in turn depends on the syntactic level. These levels can be further decomposed if necessary.

2. **Identification and Assignment of Relevant Means for Addressing the Quality Concerns.** We consider means for improving the quality concerns at each level. These means can be placed in process-oriented and product-oriented "tiers" where the former can make use of the latter. These means could also be broadly classified into those that are preventative (provide assurance) and those that are curative (focus on evaluation). The mapping between a semiotic level and the means is many-to-many.

Table 1. A framework for the semiotic quality of use case models

Semiotic Level	Means for Quality Assurance and Evaluation		Decision Support
• Pragmatic • Semantic • Syntactic	• Process-Oriented: Pair Modeling, Inspections, Refactoring • Product-Oriented: "Expert" Body of Knowledge (Principles, Guidelines, Patterns and Anti-Patterns), Metrics	Tools	Feasibility

3. **Practical Consideration for Realization.** Any quality expectations and considerations must be realistic. We therefore consider the feasibility of the previous two steps.

Table 1 summarizes this construction.

We now describe each of the components of the proposed framework in detail.

Feasibility

Our approach for addressing the semiotic quality of use case models is realistic, not perfective. This echoes the notion of *agile modeling* (Ambler, 2002). The identification of relevant quality attributes and the selection of appropriate means to address them does not have to be a matter of "all-or-nothing."

There are inevitable constraints associated with respect to allocation of resources (say, time, effort, budget, or personnel) in any initiative towards quality improvement, and the same applies to use case models. For example, hiring software engineers with the "best" knowledge of the use case domain or acquiring the "best" use case modeling tool may not be feasible, not to mention it may be economically challenging. Also, the use of any means of quality improvement mentioned above could require personnel training, which may

not be free-of-cost. The expectations of improving the quality of a use case model must therefore be feasible in order to be practical.

The quality concerns at a semiotic level could be viewed as *hard or soft* goals to be achieved. A hard goal is either *satisfied* or *not satisfied*. A soft goal cannot be completely satisfied; it can only be satisfied to a certain degree, that is, *satisficed* (Simon, 1996). If a soft goal is not satisficed, then it is *denied*.

The quality concern at the syntactical level is a hard goal, while those at the semantic and pragmatic levels are in general soft goals. Therefore, as compared to the syntactical level, the quality concerns at the semantic and pragmatic levels of a use case model are more susceptible to the need for feasibility analysis. For example, assuming that the project team has *complete* understanding of a new application domain or attempting to construct a use case model that will be acceptable in every aspect to *all* stakeholders at *all* times are not realistic.

The issue of feasibility analysis is evidently related to decision making (Clemen, 1996) and should be a consideration within the overall project management in general and use case model development process in particular. Further discussion of this aspect is beyond the scope of this chapter.

Semiotic Quality Concerns

In this section, we discuss the details of the use case quality concerns at each semiotic level.

Syntactic Quality

For the sake of this chapter, we view syntactic quality as a *contract* between a use case model and the (use case) modeling language.

There is only one concern at the syntactic level, namely that of *correctness*. This is a hard goal. A use case model in UML is syntactically correct if and only if every construct in it conforms to UML.

For example, consider a use case model M represented in UML version n. Then, the presence of any non-UML construct in M or the presence of a construct from UML version m ≠ n in M would make the model syntactically incorrect.

Semantic Quality

For the sake of this chapter, we view semantic quality as a *contract* between a use case model and the knowledge of the domains, namely of the use case domain and of the application domain, under study.

The two complementary concerns at the semantic level are *completeness* (relevant behavioral knowledge of the use case domain and the application domain is captured in the use case model) and *validity* (all constructs in the use case model conform to the use case domain and/or the application domain). For non-trivial cases, both of these are soft goals. The weaknesses in the behavioral semantics of UML meta-model have been reported to be the source of defects related to completeness (Lange, 2006). The attributes such as incorrectness, inconsistency, or redundancy suggested in previous work are subsumed by semantic validity.

For example, if a `Withdraw Money` use case for an ABM does not consider the possibility of re-

turning the user's bank card, then it is semantically not complete. A use case model for the problem that, for example, contains user interface-specific information, refers to internal design details, has the presence of a relationship between two use cases (such as the UML association relationship) that shows that they "communicate" with each other, or has a use case with include relationship to an alternate use case is semantically not valid. We also note that it is straightforward to construct a use case model, say in UML, which is syntactically correct but neither semantically valid, nor semantically complete.

In general, non-trivial violations related to semantic quality can be the hardest to detect, irrespective of any modeling language or tools used. It is also the author's contention that attaining "absolute" semantic quality, particularly via automation, for an *arbitrary* application domain is infeasible as that would require "perfect" knowledge and formal representation of the knowledge of the domains involved. This leads to two issues. First, although there are partial efforts, a formalization of the use case domain that is complete and is broadly acceptable in the software engineering community is yet to be seen. Second, not all application domains and not all information in a given application domain is amenable to formalization.

A *partial* solution to the aforementioned issue is to represent the declarative knowledge of the use case domain and for the application domain as formal ontologies (Gruber, 1993). Such knowledge artifacts can not only support use case modeling, but can have the added benefit of being useful throughout the software project. Since one may not have a complete knowledge of the use case domain or the application domain at the time of construction, these ontologies should be allowed to evolve. In other words, for the purpose of extension, these ontologies need to be based upon an "Open World Assumption." We can then limit the checking of semantic quality of the use case model with respect to the union of these domain models (ontologies).

Pragmatic Quality

For the sake of this chapter, we view pragmatic quality as a *contract* between a use case model and a stakeholder.

We can identify two broad classes of *stakeholders* with respect to a use case model: a *producer* is the one who develops or maintains the use case model, and a *consumer* is the one who uses the use case model for some purpose. Modeling specialists and even requirement engineers are examples of producers while business analysts, testers, and user manual writers, are some examples of consumers of a use case model.

It is the author's contention that pragmatic quality is a multi-dimensional concept, and therefore we decompose it broadly into *maintainability* (of which modifiability, portability, and reusability are special cases) and *usability* (of which comprehensibility and readability are special cases). The significance of these attributes is shown in a later example. We note that while maintainability is a producer's concern, usability is exclusively a consumer's concern. For non-trivial cases, these are soft goals.

For the definitions of these quality attributes, we resort to the IEEE Standard 1061-1998, the ISO Standard 9241-11:1998, and the ISO/IEC Standard 9126-1: 2001. It is also the author's contention that these quality attributes are necessary but make no claim of their sufficiency.

Relationships among Semiotic Levels

The conformance of a use case model to one quality attribute or semiotic level does not automatically mean conformance to another.

For instance, consider a use case UC that is represented in UML and is syntactically correct with respect to UML. Let the entire functionality of UC be essentially distributed in other included use cases UC_1, UC_2,..., UC_n. That is,

$$UC = \bigcup_{i=1}^{n} UC_i .$$

Then this construction encourages readability and perhaps even comprehensibility as each UC_i, for some i, is small and cohesive. However, if UC is not doing anything on its own (and therefore is not of any value to an actor), then it violates semantic validity. The construction is also unfavorable to reusability if none of the UC_i's are being used in any other use case.

Means for Addressing Semiotic Quality Concerns

In this section, we discuss the process- and product-oriented means that are outlined in Table 1 for addressing the semiotic quality of use case models. To keep the argument in perspective, we point out both the benefits and the limitations of each of these means.

Process-Oriented Means

We begin with the discussion of the process-oriented means, namely Pair Modeling, inspections, and refactoring.

Pair Modeling

Pair Modeling (Kamthan, 2005) is a practice that involves two people such that one person (the primary person or the pilot) works on the model using some input device, while the other (the secondary person or the co-pilot) provides support in decision making and provides input and critical feedback on all aspects of the model as it evolves. Thus, Pair Modeling falls on the "boundary" of assurance and evaluation.

We note that the focus in Pair Modeling is more on the *process* of creating the use case model rather than on the outcome of the process (the model itself). The underlying assumption here is that the improvements in the former will bring about improvements in the latter (Nelson & Monarchi, 2007). To that regard, we note that Pair Modeling is one way to help steer the use case development process.

Pair Modeling could be deployed to improve the semiotic quality of use case models in a few ways. For example, the partners can share the responsibility in playing the role of actors and of the use cases in formulating candidate choices, the partners can debate the appropriateness of guidelines, patterns or anti-patterns, the co-pilot can provide feedback to the pilot during the construction of the use case model, and so on.-

There are a few shortcomings of Pair Modeling. First, the project team must be able to dedicate two people for the task of use case modeling, which may be a constraint on very small teams. Second, there are inevitable issues of differentials in domain knowledge and modeling skills, compatibility in personalities, and mutually agreeable schedules between the partners. Finally, the commitment of double the number of people for the same activity can imply double the salary but does not automatically imply double the productivity.

Inspections

Inspections (Wiegers, 2002) are a rigorous form of auditing based upon peer review that, when practiced well, can help in prevention of semiotic quality-related issues in use case models. Since there are differences between how people read text narratives and graphical constructs, special-purpose reading techniques for UML models in general have been suggested (Conradi et al., 2003) and could be used with graphical use case models as well. The use of checklists (that are usually inspired by guidelines) has been made to identify defects in use case models (Anda, 2003).

However, the effectiveness of inspections lies strongly on the reading technique deployed. The efficacy of traditional checklist-based reading techniques that focus on the *quantity* (number)

rather than quality (significance) of defects has been brought into question (Thelin, Runeson, & Wohlin, 2003). Furthermore, inspections entail an initial cost overhead of training each participant in the structured review process followed by the logistics of checklists, forms, and reports involved.

Refactoring

In this chapter, we view use case modeling as an iterative process. Indeed, once developed, use case models may need to evolve for reasons such as discovery of "impurities" or "smells" (Kerievsky, 2005), or obsolescence. These could manifest themselves as worsening or the absence of one or more semiotic quality attributes.

The idea of refactoring suggests a revisitation of an artifact for the purpose of eliminating undesirable properties. Refactoring methods are structural transformations that provide a systematic way of eradicating the undesirables from a software artifact while preserving its behavioral semantics. The notion of refactoring originated in micro-architecture design and source code context (Fowler et al., 1999) and can be broadened to apply to models in general and to use case models (Rui & Butler, 2003) in particular.

There is parity between refactoring and patterns and anti-patterns. Indeed, we can interpret the presence of "impurities" as anti-patterns and therefore the *rationale* for refactoring. We can use patterns as "targets" of refactoring (Kerievsky, 2005). For example, during refinement, we may need to *RedistributeTheWealth* if a use case is getting too large or may have to *MergeDroplets* if there are use cases that are too small to exist on their own, or simply *CleanHouse* if there are use cases that do not add value to any actor any more.

There are a few limitations in current use case model refactoring efforts. The refactoring methods specific to use case models are in their infancy. The identification of "impurities" and a precise mapping between "impurities" and the refactoring methods is missing. There also seems to be a lack in software community of a common ground on what constitutes behavioral semantics of use case models, and therefore its preservation during refactoring. This raises the potential of refactoring methods becoming non-transferable across problem domains. Finally, a large-scale refactoring will inevitably require automated tool support in order to be practical.

Product-Oriented Means

We now move on to the discussion of product-oriented means, namely "expert" body of knowledge and metrics. For "expert" body of knowledge, we restrict ourselves to principles, guidelines, patterns and anti-patterns, but also note that there are other such, albeit less-known, entities (Garzas & Piattini, 2005).

Principles
The presence of time-invariant principles is a hallmark of maturity of a discipline, and software engineering is no different. In this chapter, we will focus on the principles that specifically address product quality (Ghezzi, Jazayeri, & Mandrioli, 2003). In general, the mapping between principles and semiotic levels (or quality attributes) is many-to-many. The principle of *Rigor and Formality* enables one to address syntactic quality of a use case model. The principles of *Separation of Concerns* and *Abstraction* enable one to address semantic quality of a use case model. For example, the names of actors in a use case model could be abstracted to reflect the roles they play (as opposed to their human names or titles they hold). The principles of *Abstraction, Anticipation of Change, Incrementality, Generality*, and *Modularity* enable one to address pragmatic quality (specifically, maintainability) of a use case model. For example, `Withdraw Money` use case and `Deposit Money` use case in a use case model for an ABM could be generalized to a new (and abstract) `Perform Transaction` use case in

anticipation that other forms of transactions could be added to the model in future.

In spite of their usefulness, in general, the descriptions of principles do not include directions of how to apply them successfully. Also, principles are stated at such a high-level that they tend to be more useful for an expert rather than a novice.

Guidelines
There are style guidelines for documenting use case models textually and graphically. The textual guidelines (Cox & Phalp, 2000; Cockburn, 2001; Leffingwell & Widrig, 2003) could be used for improvement of the semantic and to a certain extent the pragmatic quality of use case models. For example, there are guidelines that suggest that actor names should be singular nouns and use case names should be strong verbs, that user interface details should not be a part of use case description, and so on.

The graphical guidelines (Ambler, 2003) could be used for improvement of the syntactic, pragmatic, and to a limited extent semantic quality of use case models. For example, there are guidelines that suggest that the use case model should drawn on a "grid architecture," the actor-to-use case relationships should not be depicted by arrowheads, the lines depicting the relationships among use cases should not cross, and so on. The usefulness of guidelines for documenting use cases has been shown by some empirical studies (Anda, 2003).

In lieu of supporting pragmatic quality of use case models, the theoretical foundation of some of the graphical guidelines (Ambler, 2003) could be strengthened via notions from cognitive psychology. The secondary notation (Petre, 1995) is one of the CDs and is defined as the use of layout and perceptual cues to clarify information or to give hints to the stakeholder. The secondary elements of UML that affect the readability and comprehensibility of a use case model in UML are (Kamthan, 2006): color, directionality, labeling, level of abstraction and refinement, morphology, positioning, typography, and white space. As an example, the level of abstraction of a UML Sequence Diagram should be oriented to the stakeholder: it, for instance, need not show the operations (such as private methods) for actor stimuli and system response to a non-technical stakeholder (and thereby improve the likelihood that the model is understood). As another example, the presence of crooked nodes and zigzag vertices are cognitively ineffective (Di Battista et al., 1999), while the introduction of white space at appropriate places can improve readability. The labels in use case models could be based on natural naming (Keller, 1990), a technique initially used in source code contexts, that encourages the use of names that consist of one or more full words of the natural language in preference to acronyms or abbreviations. For example, actor names such as ABM are easier to be misinterpreted to have a variety of different meanings compared to their natural name counterpart such as `Automatic Banking Machine`.

In spite of their usefulness, guidelines assume a certain level of knowledge and therefore are more suitable for an expert than for a novice. The comparisons of guidelines for documenting use case models (Cox, Phalp, & Shepperd, 2001) suggest that some guidelines are rather complex to apply. The guidelines for use case modeling rarely discuss the trade-offs of their use or the relationships among them. As an example, a guideline like "inclusion of alternative paths in the main flow reduces readability" (Phalp, Vincent, & Cox, 2007) is not absolute. Furthermore, a guideline such as "make the use case easy to read" (Cockburn, 2001) can seem rather general and a guideline like "apply «extend» associations sparingly" (Ambler, 2003) can seem vague to a user particularly when there is widespread use of «extend» available in the literature and it is hard to quantify the term "sparingly." Finally, a guideline that is metaphorically-inclined such as

"who has the ball?" (Cockburn, 2001) may not be transferable across cultures.

Patterns and Anti-Patterns

The reliance on past experience and expertise is critical to any development, and patterns and anti-patterns are exemplars of that. A pattern is a proven solution to a recurring problem in a given context (Appleton, 1997). A unique aspect of a pattern (as opposed to other entities of knowledge such as a guideline) is that it not just describes how but *why* a certain solution works, the scope within which it works, and is preventative rather than curative (Dromey, 2003) in its approach towards quality improvement. There are patterns available for both developing and documenting use case models (Biddle, Noble, & Tempero, 2001; Angay, 2002; Adolph et al., 2003; Björnvig, 2003; Övergaard & Palmkvist, 2005).

In general, the mapping between patterns and semiotic levels (or quality attributes) is many-to-many. For example, let us consider patterns from one such collection (Adolph et al., 2003), names of which for the rest of the chapter are highlighted in italics and presented in camel case for the sake of identification. The *ExhaustiveAlternatives* pattern suggests the inclusion of all non-normal flows in a use case model, and thereby contributes to semantic completeness. The *TechnologyNeutral* pattern suggests *not* including non-application domain specifics (such as implementation details), and thus contributes to semantic validity. The *Adornments* pattern allows inclusion of metadata information in a use case model and thereby aims to improve the readability of the use case. The *PreciseAndReadable* pattern aims to improve the comprehensibility and readability of a use case, and in doing so targets both the user and the engineer. The *RedistributeTheWealth*, *MergeDroplets*, and *CleanHouse* patterns aim to improve the maintainability of a use case.

The benefits of "non-examples" in use case modeling education have been emphasized (Beus-Dukic & Myers, 2005). An anti-pattern is a frequently faced "negative" solution to a recurring problem (Appleton, 1997). If a pattern reflects a "best practice," then an anti-pattern reflects a "lesson learned." There are some anti-patterns available for use cases (El-Attar & Miller, 2006). An anti-pattern will not explicitly improve any quality attribute of a use case model; instead avoiding the anti-pattern will simply allow some quality attribute not to get worse. For example, the anti-pattern of having *a single use case that does everything for a software system* is an impediment to comprehensibility. To ameliorate this, one can for example use the *LargeUseCase:MultiplePaths* pattern (Övergaard & Palmkvist, 2005) where each of the longer flows can be modeled as a separate use case.

In spite of their usefulness, there are certain caveats in the adoption of patterns or anti-patterns towards quality improvement. A pattern may not have gone through adequate review or broad use by the community and therefore may not be mature enough for use. The reuse of any knowledge, including the use of patterns or anti-patterns in the development of use case models, is neither automatic, nor free; there is a cost of learning and adaptation involved in any reuse (Boehm et al., 2001). It is also possible that patterns are not adequately described such as when each pattern is presented as an isolated entity (independent of other patterns) or when the consequence(s) of applying a pattern are not always given (Övergaard & Palmkvist, 2005). Finally, for a given problem there simply may not be any suitable pattern or anti-pattern available. For example, interviewing the client is part of the use case elicitation process. However, none of the aforementioned collections provide any patterns for conducting such interviews.

Metrics

The significance of measurement in conceptual models has been emphasized recently (Moody, 2005). Metrics can provide a quantitative measure for semiotic quality improvement of use case models.

There are elementary metrics available for use case models that are expressed in UML (Kim & Boldyreff, 2002). They aim to measure the "size" and "structural complexity" (both of which can impact the comprehensibility and the modifiability) of a use case model in different ways, including counting the number of actors, the number of use cases, the number of relationships among use cases, and the number of associations between actors and use cases in it. There is also a rudimentary provision to associate "weights" with each of these to denote relative importance.

For example, a large number of include relationships from a use case would imply heavy reuse, which may reduce work (favorable to maintainability) but at the price of cognitive overload as to understand one use case would require an understanding of several others (which is unfavorable to comprehensibility). Similarly, the absence of extend relationships from the use case model for a system with diverse set of users could be an indication of semantic non-completeness.

There are currently certain obstacles in the use of metrics. Most of the metrics are introduced and used on empirical grounds, and are not formally validated against the representational theory of measurement (Fenton & Pfleeger, 1997). Also, since use cases model *usage* of a software system, metrics oriented towards absolute or relative counting are limited in scope (McQuillan & Power, 2006). Calculations using metrics and subsequent data analysis can become tedious and error prone if carried out manually, however, support for metrics in modeling tools is at present sketchy. Also, it seems that there are currently no metrics available for textual use case models.

Tools

The tools sensitive to the use case domain can aid towards automated development of use case models. They can indeed assist semiotic quality improvement by directly or indirectly supporting other means. For example, some modeling tools such as the IBM Rational Rose XDE, place restrictions on the use of UML syntactical constructs and provide some support for software design patterns, while others such as Borland Together provide some support for software design metrics.

However, both commercial and non-commercial use case modeling tools vary broadly with respect to their adoption (Davies et al., 2006); features; learning curve; ergonomics (Unhelkar, 2005); conformance to the official definition of UML and its different versions; implementation of layout algorithms; degree of support for refactoring, guidelines, patterns/anti-patterns, and metrics; and available import/export formats. Indeed, some UML modeling tools are known (El-Attar & Miller, 2006) to create use case models that violate one or more aforementioned quality attributes.

Relationships among Means

The aforementioned means are not mutually exclusive and can implicitly or explicitly aid each other. Indeed, the process-oriented means can utilize the product-oriented means towards their goal of quality improvement.

It is known that patterns often rely on principles to suggest solutions: the solutions suggested by patterns aim for the principle of *Abstraction* so as to be as general as possible in their applicability in different situations. Also, any patterns that target maintainability are, implicitly or explicitly, following the principle of *Anticipation of Change*. We have already seen the use of patterns in refactoring use case models. There are other possible relationships among means. For example, consider the use case (process) pattern *SmallWritingTeam*, which suggests restricting the number of people refining a use case model. This pattern, when restricted to two people, could be realized in practice during Pair Modeling. Furthermore, an inspections' session could follow the use case *TwoTierReview* (process) pattern to have two sets of inspections, one carried out by

inspectors internal to the team and the other by inspectors external to the team; use checklists derived from guidelines as means against with which to inspect the use case models; make use of metrics to compare two use case models; or look for the presence of certain patterns or anti-patterns in a use case model.

The Framework for Semiotic Quality of Use Case Models in Perspective

In this section, we briefly discuss the scope and limitations of the framework for semiotic quality of use case models presented above.

First, it appears that a complete formalization of the framework particularly that of certain quality attributes may not even be possible. Although the framework is rigorous, it does not provide formal definitions of syntax, semantics, or pragmatics, or of the quality attributes therein. On one hand, this makes the discussion accessible to non-technical stakeholders. On the other hand, it can make the application of certain means, and quantification and automatic verification of quality improvement, difficult.

Second, the framework does not discuss the quality of annotations associated with a use case model such as any text or OCL script within a UML Note construct.

Third, the resources pertaining to any software projects are limited: there is no *a priori* guarantee that an organization may be able to allocate resources (such as the time or budget for training personnel) to any of the means of use case model quality improvement that have been discussed. In general, the level of organizational process maturity (Paulk et al., 1995) may inhibit the extent (if at all) of such an adoption. This may become all the more challenging if it is anticipated that more than one means is necessary.

Fourth, there is no discussion in the framework on how the resource allocation for addressing the quality of use case models should be balanced with respect to *other* modeling activities.

Figure 1. The UML Use Case Diagram for the use case model M₁ with various semiotic quality issues.

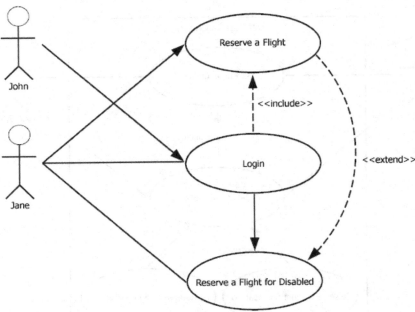

Finally, the framework is based on established work, and represents a first step towards systematically understanding and addressing the quality of use case models. However, like the use case domain itself, it is not a "standard."

Example

In this section, we present a simple example that exemplifies the use case model quality framework.

Figures 1 and 2 illustrate iterative *and* incremental development of use case models M_1 and M_2 for a Flight Reservation System, respectively. Figure 1 shows two actors named John and Jane and three use cases named Reserve a Flight, Login, and Reserve a Flight for Disabled. After M_1 was developed, the issue of quality arose and further information became available. M_2 is an iteration and an incre-

ment of M_1 for the purpose of semiotic quality improvement.

Figure 2 shows two actors named Customer and Airline System and four use cases named Get Authentication, Reserve a Flight, and Reserve a Flight for Disabled, and Reserve a Flight for VIP.

We now briefly explain the evolution from M_1 to M_2 from a semiotic quality perspective. By splitting the system functionality into different use cases, M_1 supports maintainability. M_1 follows some of the guidelines for labeling, typography, and white space to improve readability. However, M_1 as compared to M_2 will take longer to develop, and has multiple syntactic, semantic, and pragmatic quality-related violations. Specifically, M_1 issues include the following:

1. **Syntactic:** the actor-to-use case and use case-to-use case relationships and directionality are represented incorrectly;

Figure 2. The UML Use Case Diagram for the use case model M₂ that is a result of inspecting, iterating (refactoring), and incrementing M₁ to improve its semiotic quality.

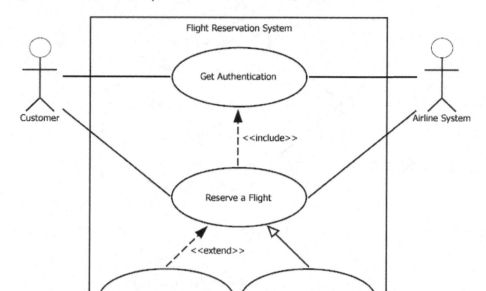

2. **Semantic;** actor names are not abstract;
3. **Pragmatic:** use case dependencies are not obvious; and it is hard to comprehend due to crossing relationships and non-readily-intuitive vertical placement of use cases.

The evolution from M_1 to M_2 takes place using multiple means available. M_2 deploys patterns such as *VisibleBoundary* pattern (Adolph et al., 2003) to set the system boundary, and *Multiple Actors: Common Roles* (Övergaard & Palmkvist, 2005) and *ClearCastOfCharacters* (Adolph et al., 2003) to reduce the number of actors to a minimal. Furthermore, it makes use of the guidelines for directionality and positioning to alleviate some of the aforementioned issues.

Finally, we note that M_2 is the second iteration of the model and do not claim that it is complete.

Further iterations are not discussed due to considerations of space. If necessary, a UML Note construct could be attached to constructs in M_2 to associate any metadata information (like the project title, author name, or date/time) or to, say, associate constraints on the number of flights available for each category of users. Also, there could be a consideration for reserving a flight for a VIP who is disabled. Furthermore, a Flight Reservation System may have other functionalities besides those shown in Figure 2, and likely needs to be administered and maintained. Therefore, M_2 should also evolve to include other actors such as an administrator and a maintainer, and other use cases such as those for presenting flight schedules, for access rights (authentication), and for payment. For example, a Get Authentication use case (that subsumes the Login use case of M_1) could be added to M_2 with an «include» relationship directed from the `Reserve a Flight` use case to the `Get Authentication` use case.

CONCLUSION

If there is any constant in the evolution of today's information-based software systems, it is the movement towards interaction. Use cases are abstractions that provide a service-oriented view of an interactive software system. The conceptual models of these services must strive for high-quality throughout the software development process (Bourque et al., 2002) and beyond so as to be amenable to their stakeholders. It is our hope that the work presented in this chapter provides one step towards making quality a *first-class* concern in use case modeling.

For a true realization of "exorcism" in software (Blunden, 2003), we must address the quality concerns as early as possible. One way to do that is to start with the quality of early models. Indeed, any initiative of an organization towards improving the quality of artifacts such as use case models begins with the acknowledgment of current process maturity and the emphasis in the process on addressing quality *early*. This is followed by an in-depth feasibility analysis of relevant quality attributes and the selection of one or more means to address them.

An investment in a quality-centric approach to use case modeling is neither automatic, nor free, but can benefit both the engineers and the users and, in the long-term, can outweigh the costs. It is important that the software engineers of the future must not only be trained in the syntax and semantics (namely, the primary notation) of a modeling language for use case models but cotemporally also in the pragmatics or style of its use (namely, the secondary notation). The focus on preventative means (provide assurance) should be at least as much as those that are curative (provide

evaluation). We hope that this chapter motivates the need for doing so.

In conclusion, like documents were two decades ago (Weinberg, 1998), it is the author's contention that models are the "castor oil" of the future software engineering. If that turns out to be the case, then like documentation (Kaner, 1995), striving for quality in software models may not only become an ethical and moral obligation but also a legal imperative.

FUTURE RESEARCH DIRECTIONS

The work presented in this chapter can be extended in a few different directions, which we now briefly discuss.

Formalization of Use Case Domain Terminology

The use case technique, and therefore the terminology (Winters, 2005) that ensues from adopting it, is *not* a "standard" per se. This has led to an apparent "terminological explosion" and proliferation of synonyms and homonyms in the literature. There is an urgent need for some form of consensus on what precisely constitutes the use case domain, namely a standard metamodel. This metamodel for the use case domain also needs to be adequately represented. As mentioned previously, the establishment of a publicly open formal ontology for the use case domain could be helpful in that regard. Among the given possibilities, the OWL Web Ontology Language (Dean & Schreiber, 2004), appears to be a promising candidate for such an ontology as it provides a balance between expressivity, decidability (of reasoning), and support of tools for authoring, processing, and reasoning.

Table 1 provides a structured but informal way of expressing the relationships among quality attributes, and between quality attributes and means for addressing them. We hope that further investigations into formalization of the concept of quality would lead to an upper-level ontology that will allow precise definition and organization of such relationships, and enable reasoning with them. The initial work on the ontology for software quality as defined in the Guide to the Software Engineering Body of Knowledge (SWEBOK) (Mendes & Abran, 2004) could provide input in this direction.

Some Potential Extensions of the Framework

A natural evolution of the aforementioned framework would be to increase the number of semiotic levels and to increase the *granularity* of the quality attributes at each semiotic level. For example, a *social level* (Shanks, 1999) could be introduced on the top of the other three. The social level could be defined as contract (or a social agreement) among the stakeholders with respect to the use case model. For example, social quality concerns would include credibility (Fogg & Tseng, 1999) and legality of the model. To address these concerns would also require an extension of the currently available means and is likely to involve associating appropriate metadata information with the model. However, we also note that as we move from technical to social levels, addressing the quality concerns (and their soft goals) becomes increasingly challenging.

The details of the aforementioned framework have largely been limited to the problem domain rather than for the solution domain. The previous discussion could be extended from problem use cases to solution use cases, and in that case an investigation into the quality of use case scenarios would be of interest.

While use cases provide abstractions of services that a system should perform, *misuse cases* (Alexander & Maiden, 2004) describe actions (such as security breaches) that should not be possible in a system. The UML notation of misuse cases is similar with the exception that

the colors of both the actors and use cases are reversed from transparent (or white) to black. With minimal effort at syntactic and semantic quality levels, our quality framework could be extended and applied to use case models that include misuse cases.

An investigation towards resolving the issues pointed out in the selection, adoption, and application of the means for improving the semiotic quality of use case models could be yet another extension of the work presented here. Specifically, the need for stable and robust tool support for guidelines, patterns, and metrics for textual use case models is particularly critical.

There are certain properties of a software system, labeled as "crosscutting concerns," that can not be (readily) separated from each other, and therefore can not be isolated and modularized. The crosscutting concerns are encapsulated in separate modules known as *aspects*. In recent years, aspect-oriented software development (Filman et al., 2005) has been put forward as an approach that aims at addressing crosscutting concerns by providing means for their systematic identification, separation, specification, representation, and composition. The term "early aspects" (Brito, 2004) refers to dealing with crosscutting concerns at the early stages of requirements engineering, specifically during the development of use cases (Jacobson & Ng, 2005). It will remain crucial that these extensions of the use case models preserve and adhere to quality, and if necessary, the proposed framework could be extended to provide an avenue to support that.

Quality in Use Case Education

Use case models have been given a place in efforts for "streamlining" undergraduate software engineering education (IEEE-CS/ACM, 2004). However, there have been very few efforts in introducing the significance of quality in use case modeling in education (Cox, 2000; Beus-Dukic & Myers, 2005). Therefore, the educational implications of quality in use case modeling (within say the UPEDU) would be worth examining. In particular, incorporating pedagogical patterns (currently available within the auspices of the Pedagogical Patterns Project or otherwise) into teaching, both inside and outside the classroom, would be of special interest. For example, the *FixerUpper* pattern (Bergin, 2000) suggests that it is useful to introduce artifacts that have errors in them that the students are asked to correct. This could help students "discover" the significance of quality attributes at different semiotic levels on their own and help appreciate the means to address them when introduced on a "need to know" basis.

Quality in Other Software Modeling Artifacts

Often, different application domains can lead to the choice of different modeling abstractions using special means. To that regard, addressing the quality of artifacts in other special-purpose visual languages such as Feature Modeling (Czarnecki & Eisenecker, 2000) for domain analysis, Object Role Modeling (ORM) (Halpin & Bloesch, 1998) for conceptual data modeling, and Use Case Maps (UCM) (Buhr, 1998) for reactive systems would also be of interest.

ACKNOWLEDGMENT

The author would like to thank Hsueh-Ieng Pai, Mitra Nami, and Maryam Shiri (Concordia University, Montreal, Canada) for early comments, and the reviewers for feedback and suggestions for improvement.

REFERENCES

Adolph, S., Bramble, P., Cockburn, A., & Pols, A. (2003). Patterns for Effective Use Cases. Addison-Wesley.

Alexander, I., & Maiden, N. (2004). Scenarios, Stories, Use Cases through the Systems Development Life-Cycle. John Wiley and Sons.

Ambler, S. W. (2002). Agile Modeling: Effective Practices for Extreme Programming and the Unified Process. John Wiley and Sons. 2002.

Ambler, S. W. (2003). The Elements of UML Style. Cambridge University Press.

Anda, B. C. D. (2003). Empirical Studies of Construction and Application of Use Case Models. Ph.D. Thesis, University of Oslo, Oslo, Norway.

Anda, B. C. D., Sjøberg, D. I. K., & Jørgensen, M. (2001). Quality and Understandability in Use Case Models. The Fifteenth European Conference on Object-Oriented Programming (ECOOP 2001), Budapest, Hungary, June 18-22, 2001.

Angay, H. (2002). Template Use Case Pattern. Appropriate Process Group White Paper. 2002.

Appleton, B. A. (1997). Patterns and Software: Essential Concepts and Terminology. Object Magazine Online, 3(5), 20-25.

Beck, K., & Andres, C. (2005). Extreme Programming Explained: Embrace Change (Second Edition). Addison-Wesley.

Berenbach, B., & Borotto, G. (2006). Metrics for Model Driven Requirements Development. The Twenty Eighth International Conference on Software Engineering (ICSE 2006), Shanghai, China, May 20-28, 2006.

Bergin, J. (2000). Fourteen Pedagogical Patterns. The Fifth European Conference on Pattern Languages of Programs (EuroPLoP 2000), Irsee, Germany, July 5-9, 2000.

Beus-Dukic, L., & Myers, C. (2005). Use and Abuse Cases. The First International Workshop on Requirements Engineering Education and Training (REET 2005), Paris, France, August 29-September 2, 2005.

Beydeda, S., Book, M., & Gruhn, V. (2005). Model-Driven Software Development. Springer.

Biddle, R., Noble, J., & Tempero, E. (2001). Patterns for Essential Use Cases. Technical Report CS-TR-01/02. School of Mathematics, Statistics and Computer Science, Victoria University of Wellington, Wellington, New Zealand. May 20, 2001.

Bittner, K., & Spence, I. (2003). Use Case Modeling. Addison-Wesley.

Björnvig, G. (2003). Patterns for the Role of Use Cases. The Eighth European Conference on Pattern Languages of Programs (EuroPLoP 2003), Irsee, Germany, June 25-29, 2003.

Blunden, B. (2003). Software Exorcism: A Handbook for Debugging and Optimizing Legacy Code. Apress.

Boehm, B. W., Abts, C., Brown, A. W., Chulani, S., Clark, B. K., Horowitz, E., Madachy, R., Reifer, D., & Steece, B. (2001). Software Cost Estimation with COCOMO II. Prentice Hall.

Bolloju, N., & Leung, F. S. K. (2006). Assisting Novice Analysts in Developing Quality Conceptual Models with UML. Communications of the ACM, 49(7), 108-112.

Booch, G., Jacobson, I., & Rumbaugh, J. (2005). The Unified Modeling Language Reference Manual (Second Edition). Addison-Wesley.

Bourque, P., Dupuis, R., Abran, A., Moore, J. W., Tripp, L., & Wolff, S. (2002). Fundamental Principles of Software Engineering - A Journey. Journal of Systems and Software, 62(1), 59-70.

Brito, I. (2004). Aspect-Oriented Requirements Engineering. The Seventh International Conference on the Unified Modeling Language (<<UML 2004>>), Lisbon, Portugal, October 11-15, 2004.

Buhr, R. J. A. (1998). Use Case Maps as Architectural Entities for Complex Systems. IEEE Transactions on Software Engineering, 24(12), 1131-1155.

Clemen, R. T. (1996). Making Hard Decisions: An Introduction to Decision Analysis (Second Edition). Duxbury Press.

Cockburn, A. (2001). Writing Effective Use Cases. Addison-Wesley.

Cockburn, A. (2005). Crystal Clear: A Human-Powered Methodology for Small Teams. Addison-Wesley.

Conradi, R., Mohagheghi, P., Arif, T., Hegde, L. C., Bunde, G. A., & Pedersen, A. (2003). Inspection of UML Diagrams using OORT - An Industrial Experiment. European Conference for Object-Oriented Programming (ECOOP 2003), Darmstadt, Germany, July 21-25, 2003.

Cowling, A. J. (2005). The Role of Modelling in the Software Engineering Curriculum. Journal of Systems and Software, 75(1-2), 41-53.

Cox, K. (2000). Cognitive Dimensions of Use Cases: Feedback from a Student Questionnaire. The Twelfth Annual Meeting of the Psychology of Programming Interest Group, Corigliano Calabro, Italy, April 10-13, 2000.

Cox, K., & Phalp, K. (2000). Replicating the CREWS Use Case Authoring Guidelines Experiment. Empirical Software Engineering Journal, 5(3), 245-267.

Cox, K., Phalp, K., & Shepperd, M. (2001). Comparing Use Case Writing Guidelines. The Seventh International Workshop on Requirements Engineering: Foundation for Software Quality, Interlaken, Switzerland, June 4-5, 2001.

Czarnecki, K., & Eisenecker, U. W. (2000). Generative Programming: Methods, Tools, and Applications. Addison-Wesley.

Davies, I., Green, P., Rosemann, M., Indulska, M., & Gallo, S. (2006). How do Practitioners

Use Conceptual Modeling in Practice? Data and Knowledge Engineering, 58(3), 358-380.

Dean, M., & Schreiber, G. (2004). OWL Web Ontology Language Reference. W3C Recommendation. World Wide Web Consortium (W3C). February 10, 2004.

Di Battista, G., Eades, P., Tamassia, R., & Tollis, I. G. (1999). Graph Drawing: Algorithms for the Visualization of Graphs. Prentice-Hall.

Dromey, R. G. (2003). Software Quality - Prevention Versus Cure? Software Quality Journal, 11(3), 197-210.

El-Attar, M., & Miller, J. (2006). Matching Antipatterns to Improve the Quality of Use Case Models. The Fourteenth International Requirements Engineering Conference (RE 2006), Minneapolis-St. Paul, USA. September 11-15, 2006.

Eppler, M. J. (2001). The Concept of Information Quality: An Interdisciplinary Evaluation of Recent Information Quality Frameworks. Studies in Communication Sciences, 1(2), 167-182.

Fantechi, A., Gnesi, S., Lami, G., & Maccari, A. (2003). Applications of Linguistic Techniques for Use Case Analysis. Requirements Engineering, 8(3), 161-170.

Fenton, N. E., & Pfleeger, S. L. (1997). Software Metrics: A Rigorous & Practical Approach. International Thomson Computer Press.

Filman, R, Elrad, T., Clarke, S., & Mehmet, A. (2005). Aspect-Oriented Software Development. Addison-Wesley.

Fogg, B. J., & Tseng, S. (1999). The Elements of Computer Credibility. The ACM CHI 99 Conference on Human Factors in Computing Systems, Pittsburgh, USA, May 15-20, 1999.

Fowler, M. (2003). UML Distilled: A Brief Guide to the Standard Object Modeling Language (Third Edition). Addison-Wesley.

Fowler, M., Beck, K., Brant, J., Opdyke, W., & Roberts, D. (1999). Refactoring: Improving the Design of Existing Code. Addison-Wesley.

Genova, G., Valiente, M. C., & Nubiola, J. (2005). A Semiotic Approach to UML Models. The First Workshop on Philosophical Foundations of Information Systems Engineering (PHISE 2005), Porto, Portugal, June 13, 2005.

Ghezzi, C., Jazayeri, M., & Mandrioli, D. (2003). Fundamentals of Software Engineering (Second Edition). Prentice-Hall.

Glinz, M. (2000). Problems and Deficiencies of UML as a Requirements Specification Language. The Tenth International Workshop on Software Specification and Design (IWSSD-10), San Diego, USA, November 5-7, 2000.

Green, T. R. G. (1989). Cognitive Dimensions of Notations. In: Sutcliffe, V. A., & Macaulay, L. (Eds.). People and Computers. Cambridge University Press, 443-460.

Gruber, T. R. (1993). Toward Principles for the Design of Ontologies Used for Knowledge Sharing. In: Formal Ontology in Conceptual Analysis and Knowledge Representation. Kluwer Academic Publishers.

Halpin, T. A., & Bloesch, A. (1998). A Comparison of UML and ORM for Data Modeling. Third International Workshop on Evaluation of Modeling Methods in Systems Analysis and Design (EMMSAD 1998), Pisa, Italy, June 8-9, 1998.

Highsmith, J. (2002). Agile Software Development Ecosystems. Addison-Wesley.

IEEE-CS/ACM. (2004). Software Engineering 2004: Curriculum Guidelines for Undergraduate Degree Programs in Software Engineering (SE 2004). Institute of Electrical and Electronics Engineers Computer Society (IEEE-CS)/Association for Computing Machinery (ACM) Steering Committee. August 23, 2004.

Jacobson, I. (2003). Use Cases: Yesterday, Today, and Tomorrow. IBM developerWorks, November 20, 2003.

Jacobson, I., Booch, G., & Rumbaugh, J. (1999). The Unified Software Development Process. Addison-Wesley.

Jacobson, I., Christerson, M., Jonsson, P., & Övergaard, G. (1992). Object-Oriented Software Engineering: A Use Case Driven Approach. Addison-Wesley.

Jacobson, I., & Ng, P.-W. (2005). Aspect-Oriented Software Development with Use Cases. Addison-Wesley.

Kamthan, P. (2004). A Framework for Addressing the Quality of UML Artifacts. Studies in Communication Sciences, 4(2), 85-114.

Kamthan, P. (2005). Pair Modeling. The 2005 Canadian University Software Engineering Conference (CUSEC 2005), Ottawa, Canada, January 14-16, 2005.

Kamthan, P. (2006). How Useful are Your UML Models? The 2006 Canadian University Software Engineering Conference (CUSEC 2006), Montreal, Canada, January 19-21, 2006.

Kaner, C. (1995). Liability for Defective Documentation. Software QA Quarterly, 2(3).

Keller, D. (1990). A Guide to Natural Naming. ACM SIGPLAN Notices, 25(5), 95-102.

Kerievsky, J. (2005) Refactoring to Patterns. Addison-Wesley.

Kim, H., & Boldyreff, C. (2002). Developing Software Metrics Applicable to UML Models. Sixth ECOOP Workshop on Quantitative Approaches in Object-Oriented Software Engineering (QAOOSE 2002), Malaga, Spain, June 11, 2002.

Kruchten, P. B. (1995). The 4+1 View Model of Architecture. IEEE Software, 12(6), 42-50.

Kruchten, P. (2004). The Rational Unified Process: An Introduction (Third Edition). Addison-Wesley.

Lange, C. F. J. (2006). Improving the Quality of UML Models in Practice. The Twenty Eighth International Conference on Software Engineering (ICSE 2006), Shanghai, China, May 20-28, 2006.

Lange, C. F. J., & Chaudron, M. R. V. (2006). Effects of Defects in UML Models: An Experimental Investigation. The Twenty Eighth International Conference on Software Engineering (ICSE 2006), Shanghai, China, May 20-28, 2006.

Leffingwell, D., & Widrig, D. (2003). Managing Software Requirements: A Use Case Approach (Second Edition). Addison-Wesley.

Lindland, O. I., Sindre, G., & Sølvberg, A. (1994). Understanding Quality in Conceptual Modeling. IEEE Software, 11(2), 42-49.

McCoy, J. (2003). Use Case Quality Attributes. The Third Annual NASA Office of Safety and Mission Assurance Software Assurance Symposium (OSMA SAS 2003), Morgantown, USA, July 30-August 1, 2003.

McQuillan, J. A., & Power, J. F. (2006). Some Observations on the Application of Software Metrics to UML Models. The First Workshop on Model Size Metrics, Genoa, Italy, October 3, 2006.

Mendes, O., & Abran, A. (2004). Software Engineering Ontology: A Development Methodology. Metrics News, 9(1), 64-71.

Moody, D. L. (2005). Theoretical and Practical Issues in Evaluating the Quality of Conceptual Models: Current State and Future Directions. Data and Knowledge Engineering, 55(3), 243-276.

Nelson, H. J., & Monarchi, D. E. (2007). Ensuring the Quality of Conceptual Representations. Software Quality Journal, 15(2), 213-233.

Nöth, W. (1990). Handbook of Semiotics. Indiana University Press.

Övergaard, G., & Palmkvist, K. (2005). Use Cases: Patterns and Blueprints. Addison-Wesley.

Paulk, M. C., Weber, C. V., Curtis, B., & Chrissis, M. B. (1995). The Capability Maturity Model: Guidelines for Improving the Software Process. Addison-Wesley.

Petre, M. (1995). Why Looking Isn't Always Seeing: Readership Skills and Graphical Programming. Communications of the ACM, 38(6), 33-44.

Phalp, K. T., Vincent, J., & Cox, K. (2007). Assessing the Quality in Use Case Descriptions. Software Quality Journal, 15(1), 69-97.

Robillard, P. N., D'Astous, P., & Kruchten, P. (2003). Software Engineering Process with the UPEDU. Addison-Wesley.

Rosenberg, D., & Scott, K. (1999). Use Case Driven Object Modeling with UML: A Practical Approach. Addison-Wesley.

Rosenberg, D., Stephens, M. & Collins-Cope, M. (2005). Agile Development with ICONIX Process. Apress.

Rui, K., & Butler, G. (2003). Refactoring Use Case Models: A Metamodel. The Twenty Sixth Australasian Computer Science Conference (ACSC 2003), February 4-7, 2003, Adelaide, Australia.

Saeki, M. (1999). Reusing Use Case Descriptions for Requirements Specification: Towards Use Case Patterns. Sixth Asia-Pacific Software Engineering Conference (APSEC 1999), Takamatsu, Japan, December 7-10, 1999.

Seidewitz, E. (2003). What Models Mean. IEEE Software, 20(5), 26-32.

Shanks, G. (1999). Semiotic Approach to Understanding Representation in Information Systems. Information Systems Foundations Workshop, Sydney, Australia, September 29, 1999.

Simon, H. (1996). The Sciences of the Artificial (Third Edition). The MIT Press.

Thelin, T., Runeson, P., & Wohlin, C. (2003). An Experimental Comparison of Usage-Based and Checklist-Based Reading. IEEE Transactions on Software Engineering, 29(8), 687-704.

Törner, F., Ivarsson, M, Pettersson, F., & Öhman. P. (2006). An Empirical Quality Assessment of Automotive Use Cases. The Fourteenth International Requirements Engineering Conference (RE 2006), Minneapolis-St. Paul, USA. September 11-15, 2006.

Unhelkar, B. (2005). Verification and Validation for Quality of UML 2.0 Models. John Wiley and Sons.

Völter, M., Stahl, T., Bettin, J., Haase, A., & Helsen, S. (2006). Model-Driven Software Development: Technology, Engineering, Management. John Wiley and Sons.

Warmer, J., & Kleppe, A. (2003). The Object Constraint Language: Precise Modeling with UML (Second Edition). Addison-Wesley.

Weinberg, G. M. (1998). The Psychology of Computer Programming (Silver Anniversary Edition). Dorset House.

Wiegers, K. (2002). Peer Reviews in Software: A Practical Guide. Addison-Wesley.

Winters, G. (2005). Use Case Terminology. IEEE Software, 22(2), 67.

Wong, B. (2006). Different Views of Software Quality. In: Measuring Information Systems Delivery Quality. E. Duggan & J. Reichgelt (Eds.). Idea Group, 55-88.

ADDITIONAL READING

The following publications introduce the notion of a pattern in the domain of urban architecture and planning, and paved the way to the introduction of patterns in software engineering in general and use cases in particular:

Alexander, C. (1979). The Timeless Way of Building. Oxford University Press.

Alexander, C., Ishikawa, S., & Silverstein, M. (1977). A Pattern Language: Towns, Buildings, Construction. Oxford University Press.

The following publications motivate the need for formality in use case models using different formalisms and specification languages:

Anderson, B. (2005). Formalism, Technique and Rigour in Use Case Modelling. Journal of Object Technology, 4(6), 15-28.

Butler, G., Grogono, P., & Khendek, F. (1997). A Z Specification of Use Cases: A Preliminary Report. The Fourth Asia-Pacific Software Engineering and International Computer Science Conference (APSEC 1997/ICSC 1997), Clear Water Bay, Hong Kong, December 2-5, 1997.

Riebisch, M., & Hübner, M. (2004). Refinement and Formalization of Semi-Formal Use Case Descriptions. The Second Workshop and Session on Model-Based Development of Computer Based Systems: Appropriateness, Consistency and Integration of Models, Brno, Czech Republic, May 27, 2004.

The following publication presents an empirical study of the effectiveness of use case guidelines aggregated from different sources:

Cox, K., Aurum, A., & Jeffery, R. (2004). An Experiment in Inspecting the Quality of Use Case Descriptions. Journal of Research and Practice in Information Technology, 36(4), 211-229.

The following publications motivate a systematic, "engineering-like" approach towards modeling, of which quality management is a part:

France, R., & Rumpe, B. (2003). Model Engineering. Journal on Software and System Modeling, 2(2), 73-75.

Williams, C., Kaplan, M., Klinger, T., & Paradkar, A. (2005). Toward Engineered, Useful Use Cases. Journal of Object Technology, 4(6), 45-57.

The following publications are standards for quality in general and software in particular:

IEEE. (1998). IEEE Standard 1061-1998. IEEE Standard for a Software Quality Metrics Methodology, IEEE Computer Society.

ISO. (1998). ISO 9241-11:1998. Ergonomic Requirements for Office Work with Visual Display Terminals Part 11: Guidance on Usability. International Organization for Standardization (ISO).

ISO. (2001). ISO/IEC 9126-1:2001. Software Engineering -- Product Quality -- Part 1: Quality Model. International Organization for Standardization (ISO).

The following publication presents the genesis of the concept of a use case in both a rigorous and a practical setting:

Jacobson, I. (1985). Concepts for Modeling Large Real Time Systems. Ph.D. Thesis, The Royal Institute of Technology, Stockholm, Sweden.

The following publications take a UML-based use case driven approach towards modeling a software system and carrying it throughout the development process:

Section IV
QA for MDSD
in Specific Domains

This final section presents several chapters on using quality assurance techniques for model-driven development in specific domains. Most pa-pers are devoted to the domain of embedded systems (i.e., systems that are composed of hardware and software) and report about experience collected in specific industrial environments.

Chapter XIV
Assuring Maintainability in Model–Driven Development of Embedded Systems

Stefan Wagner
Technische Universität München, Germany

Florian Deissenboeck
Technische Universität München, Germany

Stefan Teuchert
Durchstreichen, MAN Nutzfahrzeuge AG, Germany

Jean-François Girard
Durchstreichen, MAN Nutzfahrzeuge AG, Germany

ABSTRACT

In model-driven software development as much as in classical code-driven development maintenance costs make up the bulk of the total life cycle costs of a software system. However, as development methods in MDSD differ from classical methods, assuring the maintainability of systems built with MDSD requires companies to adjust their quality assurance to work with the new paradigm and the novel type of development artefacts. As the automotive industry has already applied model-driven approaches for some time (usually in the form of Matlab/Simulink) it proves to be a fertile ground to advance assurance methods for the maintainability of model-based systems. In this chapter we describe a two-dimensional quality metamodel and present an instance that defines maintainability for MDSD with Matlab/Simulink and TargetLink. We exemplify how such a model serves as the basis of all quality assurance activities and report on experiences made in an industrial case study with one of the leading international providers of commercial vehicles and transport solutions.

INTRODUCTION

Maintenance costs constitute the major part of the total life cycle costs of a software system (Lientz, Bennet, Swanson, & Burton, 1980; Boehm, 1981; Erlikh, 2000). Besides organisational issues such as knowledge management and labour turnover, the long-term maintenance costs are largely pre-determined by various quality attributes of the software system itself, such as its comprehensibility and modifiability.

In model-driven software development (MDSD) as much as in classical code-driven development organisations need methods and processes to continuously monitor these quality attributes to ensure the maintainability of software systems. However, as development methods in MDSD differ from classical methods, assuring the maintainability of systems built with MDSD requires companies to adjust their quality assurance to work with the new paradigm and the novel type of development artefacts.

In the development of embedded systems in general and automotive systems in particular, model-driven approaches become more and more common. Up to 80% of the production code deployed on embedded control units today is generated from models specified using domain-specific formalisms (Beine, Otterbach, & Jungmann, 2004). Several major companies develop software with model-based tools like Matlab/Simulink and TargetLink. As these technologies enabled companies to apply model-based software development already some time ago, this field proves to be a fertile ground to advance assurance methods for the maintainability of model-based systems.

Although model-driven architecture (MDA) is often proposed to ease the maintenance of systems, maintainability is also an issue in MDSD (Seifert, Beneken, & Baehr, 2004). The MDA approach is mainly concerned with technology - especially platform – change. The problems connected with changing the underlying technologies are simplified by layering models that abstract from such technological details. However, as also stated in (Seifert et al., 2004) portability and hence changing the technology is only one of many challenges in maintenance. Therefore, the other issues need also to be dealt with in MDSD.

In this chapter we give a short introduction on model-based approaches, especially in the field of embedded systems development, and describe how the maintainability of such models can be assured. We introduce a unique quality metamodel that enables us to rigorously define maintainability and present a model instance that has been developed in an industrial case study with MAN Nutzfahrzeuge, a supplier of commercial vehicles and transport systems. We illustrate how such a model can be used as versatile basis for maintainability-related quality assurance techniques. These techniques include manual activities like model reviews as well as automated quality assessments like static model analyses. We conclude by highlighting the differences between quality assurance for MDSD and classical development.

EMBEDDED SYSTEMS DEVELOPMENT WITH MATLAB/ SIMULINK/TARGETLINK

We investigate a slightly different flavour of MDSD than the MDA approach proposed by the OMG. In embedded systems development model-based tools such as Rhapsody, ASCET or Matlab/Simulink are commonly used. However, there is no explicit need to have different types of models on different levels and the modelling language is often not UML. Nevertheless, many characteristics are similar and quality-related results can easily be transferred to an MDA setting.

Matlab/Simulink is a tool commonly used in the automotive industry. It constitutes a representative example for a model-based tool-chain in embedded systems development. The original

Figure 1. Simulink and Stateflow examples

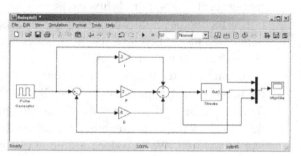
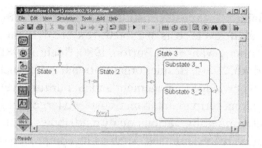

Simulink has its focus on continuous control engineering. Its counterpart Stateflow is a dialect of statecharts that is used to model the event-driven parts of a system. Fig. 1 shows example screenshots of the Simulink and Stateflow modelling environment.

The Simulink environment already allows simulating the model in order to validate it. In conjunction with a code generator such as the Embedded Coder from MathWorks, it enables the complete and automatic transformation of models to runnable code. TargetLink from dSpace offers a similar environment to Simulink, but additionally provides different attributes to better control its code generator. Both of these environments are commonly used in the embedded systems domain to transform models into runnable code. In our case study, we present an example using TargetLink.

MAINTENANCE AND MAINTAINABILITY

Maintenance

Since the early 1980ies it has been known that the bulk of the life cycle costs (50%-90%) for software systems is not consumed by the development of new software but by the maintenance of existing software (Lientz et al., 1980; Boehm, 1981; Erlikh, 2000). However, it is important to note that less than 20% of the efforts are devoted to fixing bugs. 18% are used for adapting systems to new operating environments and about 65% for the implementation of new requirements (Lientz et al., 1980; Nosek & Palvia, 1990). These figures show that software maintenance is not mainly concerned with maintaining the status quo of a software system but creates new business value by adding new functionality. Consequently, software maintenance should be rather seen as a chance and not as a problem (Glass, 1989).

Due to the economical importance of software maintenance, virtually any software dependent organisation has a vital interest in optimising its software maintenance productivity. In addition to financial savings, for many organisations, the time needed to complete a software maintenance task largely determines their ability to adapt their business processes to changing market situations or to implement innovative products and services. There is some hope that model-driven software development approaches may help to improve maintenance productivity. However, studies of the factors that influence maintenance productivity show that the technical issues (e. g. the applied development paradigm) have a limited impact on the overall productivity in comparison to organisational issues like personnel turnover

(Lientz et al., 1980). Therefore, we do not regard model-driven software development itself as a key to high maintenance productivity. We rather assume that the key factors for maintenance productivity for classical code-driven development apply for model-driven development in the same or a similar form. Likewise, we assume that problems like code decay (Parnas, 1994; Eick, Graves, Karr, Marron, & Mockus, 2001; Gurp & Bosch, 2002) or cloning (Lague, Proulx, Mayrand, Merlo, & Hudepohl, 1997), that are known to hamper maintenance productivity, do affect the model-based development approach, too. In fact, due to the lack of advanced tools for reengineering activities like refactoring (Dobrzanski & Kuzniarz, 2006), maintenance of software models may, at the moment, prove to be more demanding than the maintenance of classic code.

Maintainability

Next to non-technical issues like personnel turnover or the quality of maintenance processes, properties of software product itself are known to influence the maintenance productivity. These properties are usually subsumed as quality or, more specifically, maintainability. Researchers and practitioners alike have spent tremendous efforts to define, improve and assess the maintainability of software systems.

However, these efforts have not led to a comprehensive and commonly accepted definition of maintainability yet (Deissenboeck, Wagner, Pizka, Teuchert, & Girard, 2007). In fact, every software organisation of significant size seems to have its own definition of maintainability. For model-based development the situation appears to be even worse as many approaches to assess and improve maintainability were designed with a strong focus on code-based development. Although their core ideas are applicable for models, too, their concrete instances need to be adapted accordingly. Moreover, different organisations use different approaches for the definition and

evaluation of maintainability. Typical candidates are guidelines-based approaches, metrics-based approaches and quality models.

GUIDELINES

A commonly applied practice are guidelines that state what developers should do and what they should avoid in order to improve the quality of software artefacts. The MAAB guideline (MAAB, 2001) is an example of a quality guideline for model-based development with Matlab/Simulink. MISRA[1] and dSpace (dSpace, 2006) provide additional examples of guidelines for Simulink, Stateflow and TargetLink.

Unfortunately, such guidelines typically do not achieve the desired effect as developers often read them once, tuck them away at the bottom of a drawer and follow them in a sporadic manner only. According to our experience (Broy et al., 2006), this is often due to the fact that guidelines fail to motivate the required practices or provide very generic explanations, e. g. "Respecting the guideline ensures readable models" in (MAAB, 2001). In addition to this, guidelines are often not followed simply because it is not checked if they are followed or not. This is all the more unfortunate as for some guidelines rules compliance could be assessed automatically.

METRICS-BASED APPROACHES

Several groups proposed metrics-based methods to measure attributes of software systems which are believed to affect maintenance, e. g. (Berns, 1984; Coleman, Ash, Lowther, & Oman, 1994). Typically, these methods use a set of well-known metrics like lines of code, Halstead volume (Halstead, 1977), or McCabe's Cyclomatic Complexity (McCabe, 1976) and combine them into a single value, called *maintainability index* by means of statistically determined weights. With the exception of (Genero, Piattini, Manso, & Cantone, 2003) and (Kiewkanya, Jindasawat, & Muenchaisri, 2004) there is currently little work on maintainability metrics for models.

Although such indices may indeed often expose a correlation with subjective impressions and economic facts of a software system, they still suffer from serious shortcomings. First, they do not explain how the measured system properties influence the system's maintainability. This makes it hard to convey their findings to the developers. Second, they focus on properties which can be measured automatically by analysing source code and thereby limit themselves to syntactic aspects. Unfortunately, many essential quality issues, such as the usage of appropriate data structures and meaningful documentation, are semantic in nature and can inherently not be analysed automatically.

QUALITY MODELLING

A promising approach developed for software quality in general are *quality models* which aim at describing complex quality criteria by breaking them down into more manageable sub-criteria. Such models are designed in a tree-like fashion with abstract quality attributes like *maintainability* or *reliability* at the top and more concrete ones like *analysability* or *changeability* on lower levels. The leaf factors are ideally detailed enough to be assessed with software metrics. This method is frequently called the decompositional or *Factor-Criteria-Metric* (FCM) approach and was first used by McCall (McCall & Walters, 1977) and Boehm (Boehm et al., 1978). More recent approaches for code-driven development are (P. Oman & Hagemeister, 1992; Dromey, 1995; Marinescu & Ratiu, 2004; ISO, 2003). A quality model for UML-based software development was presented in (Lange & Chaudron, 2005). A model for the assessment of the maintainability of communication protocols based on their

formal specifications is discussed in (Huang & Lai, 2003).

Unfortunately, these approaches have failed to establish a broadly acceptable basis for quality assessments so far. We believe this is due to the lack of a clearly defined decomposition criterion that leads to a "somewhat arbitrary selection of characteristics and sub-characteristics" (Kitchenham, Linkman, Pasquini, & Nanni, 1997; Kitchenham & Pfleeger, 1996). Moreover, we see their fixed number of model levels as a problem. For example, FCM's 3 level structure is inadequate. High level goals like *maintainability* cannot be broken down into assessable properties in only two steps.

DISCUSSION

There is an abundance of further highly valuable work on software quality in general and maintainability in particular that we do not explicitly mention here, as it is either out-of-scope or does not fundamentally differ from the work already mentioned. Overall, this is and has been a very active field of research. However, as we show in (Deissenboeck, Wagner, Pizka, Teuchert, & Girard, 2007), most existing approaches to assess and improve software maintainability suffer from a number of shortcomings. Most importantly, none of the previous approaches explicitly explains the influence of system properties (e. g. modularity) on maintenance activities (e. g. impact analysis). As the maintenance activities are one of the main cost factors in software maintenance, previous approaches are not directly capable of explaining how system properties influence the maintenance effort.

Besides this, most quality models contain a number of criteria that are too coarse-grained to be assessed directly and fail to give a detailed account of the impact that specific criteria (or metrics) have on software maintenance. Moreover, existing models often lack a consistent criterion of decomposition and thereby exhibit inhomogeneous sets of quality criteria. Most times, quality models are expressed in prose and graphics only. They accompany the development process in the form of documents but are not operationalised as an integral artefact that is tightly coupled with the quality assurance activities.

To address these shortcomings we developed the two-dimensional quality metamodel QMM that explicitly models maintenance activities. In this chapter the quality model is used as a framework for structuring the diverse quality criteria presented in the next section.

QUALITY CRITERIA

As we discussed above, managing the maintainability of a software system is a difficult task. Although model-driven software development eases the problem because the used models are typically more abstract - and hence easier to comprehend - than current source code, the general issue is just lifted on a higher level. The models still need to be understood and changed independently of the level of abstraction used. Hence, it is necessary to have a set of quality criteria for the maintainability of models. This set needs to be used to assure the quality of the models. Unfortunately, this has not been investigated in the detail it deserves. Mainly guideline documents for various modelling languages have been created. We developed a comprehensive set of quality criteria for the maintainability of Stateflow and Simulink/TargetLink models based on various sources. These criteria are encoded in detail in a quality model but we give an overview of our quality criteria first. We categorise the criteria in three parts:

- Refinement of general criteria, e. g. program redundancy (Baxter, Yahin, Moura, Sant'Anna, & Bier, 1998), to match the MDSD approach.

- Criteria that deal with MDSD-only topics like presentational issues, e. g. model layout and model colouring.
- Criteria that define the legal subsets of Simulink/TargetLink/Stateflow that are reliably supported by C-code generators.

General Criteria

There is a plethora of maintainability criteria for code that is directly applicable to model-driven development. For example, dead code is considered a problem for maintaining a system. It extends the time needed to read the code and hampers the understanding of the system. This can obviously be directly transferred to models. It is possible in Simulink/TargetLink and Stateflow to create blocks, states or variables that are never executed or used. These *dead model elements* result in similar problems as dead code.

Another example is the classical observation: "Goto statement considered harmful" (Dijkstra, 1968). It is also valid in the case of Simulink/TargetLink where *From* and *Goto* blocks allow to change the control flow. Similarly, when using these blocks, the control flow is more complex and hence the model is more difficult to understand.

Moreover, in code-driven development, there usually are constraints on the size and scope of procedures, classes or methods. For example, it is often required that a class should not have more than a certain amount of methods in order to be comprehensible. Although we believe too rigid constraints to this end are critical, a guideline for the developers is still useful. This is also the case for model-driven development. Despite the fact that models are more abstract than code - and hence are easier to comprehend - their size and scope needs to be limited. It has often been experienced in practice that models grow to a size that is not manageable any more. UML class diagrams with hundreds of classes or state machines with dozens of control states are not comprehensible. Hence, we have quality criteria w.r.t. various size aspects of the Simulink/TargetLink and Stateflow models. For example, the maximum number of states in a Stateflow model or the maximum number of blocks in a Simulink/TargetLink model are defined. This should be based on the experiences of the developers.

Another general criterion is the complete and consistent documentation of the design and implementation. This equally holds for models as well. Therefore, it is desired that for Simulink/TargetLink and Stateflow models, the interfaces are well documented. Especially the parameters need to be explained in detail. This allows a quick understanding of the model and the interplay of different models.

MDSD

One aspect that is special for model-driven development are consistent display settings. Also in code-driven development the correct displaying of the code is important. However, in model-driven development, this is much more complex, especially when graphical models are used. Then the zoom factor makes a large difference w.r.t. the readability of the model. Also other settings are important such as whether specific tool bars or status bars are activated. They can hide parts of the model that are overlooked when making changes.

In graphical models, the colouring is a further very important issue. Having colours can improve the comprehension of models by "typing" different blocks with different colours. However, this needs to be done consistently. Otherwise, the colours will confuse more than they help. Similarly, the alignment and arrangement of the elements on the screen has huge effects. We know from (textual) code that indentation is very important for a quick comprehension (P. W. Oman & Cook, 1990). Graphical models increase the complexity by introducing a second dimension that the model elements can be arranged in. Moreover, there is a third dimension because often elements can be in front of other elements and hence hide them. This

way, important annotations can be overlooked. Also the crossing of lines - no matter whether they are Simulink/TargetLink signals, Stateflow transitions or associations in UML class diagrams - hampers the readability of the models.

The close relationship between Stateflow and the UML statecharts allows reusing empirical results. A study on hierarchical states in UML statecharts (Cruz-Lemus, Genero, Manso, & Piattini, 2005), for example, showed that the use of hierarchies improves the efficiency of understanding the model in case the reader has a certain amount of experience. Hence, it is desired to structure states in Stateflow models with appropriate substates. Such a simple state-space decomposition is not possible in code-driven development.

Code Generation

Finally, conformity to certain standards can be an issue. This is especially the case when the models will be used for code generation. For Simulink and Stateflow models, there are several tools available that generate production-ready C code for embedded systems. Hence, it is also a quality criterion to adhere to the standards given by the code generator. Under the hood of Simulink and Stateflow, there is the huge functionality provided by Matlab which is a general mathematical tool. It is possible to use this functionality inside Simulink in various ways. For example, one can use Matlab functions inside blocks or complex algebraic expressions in state transitions of Stateflow. It is obvious that this introduces a large complexity for the code generators. Hence, this is usually forbidden. Other issues are specific blocks in Simulink that are not supported or that specific reserved names, e. g. *exp*, are not allowed to be used.

THE QUALITY METAMODEL

These quality criteria are too large and complex to simply document them in prose. Hence they demand a systematic framework that does not only allow describing the single criteria in detail but also enables one to reason about their inter-dependencies. For this purpose we use our own activity-based quality metamodel that addresses the problems encountered with existing models.

The initial version of the model was developed in the context of a commercial project in the field of telecommunication (Broy et al., 2006). The extended version of the model discussed here was presented in (Deissenboeck et al., 2007) where more details about the metamodel can be found. The following sections explain the basic concepts of our model and discuss the differences to classical hierarchical models.

Hierarchical Models

The idea of explicitly modelling maintenance activities was based on our experiences with building large hierarchical quality models. With growing model size it became harder and harder to maintain a consistent model that adequately describes the interdependencies between the various quality criteria. A thorough analysis of this phenomenon revealed that our model and indeed most previous models mixed up nodes of two very different kinds: maintenance *activities* and *characteristics* of the system to maintain. An example for this problem is given in Fig. 2 which shows the maintainability branch of Boehm's

Software Quality Characteristics Tree (Boehm et al., 1978).

Though (substantiated) adjectives are used as descriptions, the nodes in the gray boxes refer to activities whereas the uncoloured nodes describe system characteristics (albeit very general ones). So the model should rather read as: When we *maintain* a system we need to *modify* it and this activity of *modification* is (in some way) influenced by the *structuredness* of the system. While this difference may not look important at first sight, we claim that this mixture of activities and characteristics is at the root of most problems encountered with classical models. The semantics of the edges of the tree is unclear or at least ambiguous because of this mixture. And since the edges do not have a clear meaning they neither indicate a sound explanation for the relation of two nodes nor can they be used to aggregate values!

As the actual maintenance efforts strongly depend on both, the type of system and the kind of maintenance activity, it should be obvious that the need to distinguish between activities and characteristics becomes not only clear but imperative. This can be illustrated by the example of two development organisations where company *A* is responsible for adding functionality to a system while company *B*'s task is merely fixing bugs of the same system just before its phase-out. One can imagine that the success of company *A* depends

Figure 2. Software quality tree

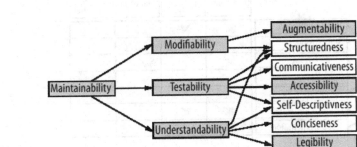

on different quality criteria (e. g. architectural characteristics) than company *B*'s (e. g. a well-kept bug-tracking system). While both organisations will pay attention to some common attributes such as documentation, *A* and *B* would and should rate the maintainability of *S* in quite different ways because they are involved in fundamentally different *activities*.

An Activity-Based Model for Maintainability

The consequent separation of activities and facts leads to a new 2-dimensional quality model that regards *activities* and *facts* as first-class citizens for modelling maintainability. The set of relevant activities depends on the particular development and maintenance process of the organisation that uses the quality model, e. g. the IEEE 1219 standard maintenance process (IEEE, 1998).

The 2nd dimension of the model, the facts about the product under maintenance, are modelled similar to an FCM model but without activity-based nodes like *augmentability*. We follow the FCM approach in the product tree by breaking down high level facts into detailed, tangible ones which we call atomic facts. An *atomic* fact is a

fact that can or must be assessed without further decomposition either because its assessment is obvious or there is no known decomposition.

To achieve or measure maintainability in a given project setting we now need to establish the interrelation between facts and activities. Because of the tree-like structures of activities and facts it is sufficient to link atomic facts with atomic activities. This relationship is best expressed by a matrix as depicted in the simplified Fig. 3.

The matrix points out what activities are affected by which facts and allows to aggregate results from the atomic level onto higher levels in both trees because of the unambiguous semantics of the edges. So, one can determine that *History Junctions* in Stateflow diagrams have an impact on *Debugging* and the *Impact Analysis* as they make statecharts harder to comprehend. Please note that this also applies for UML state machines. The names chosen for Simulink/TargetLink blocks (or UML model elements) have an impact on the modelling activity as they make the model more or less readable. But they also influence the code generation in case reserved names where chosen that make the generated code non-compilable.

To comprehensively describe the *maintenance efforts* of a system, one needs to evaluate not only

Figure 3. Example maintainability matrix

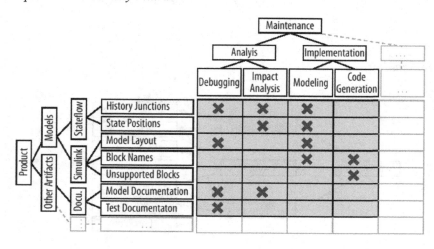

the system itself. It is well known, that factors like the capability of the team, established software processes or the existence of tools have a major impact on maintenance costs. Our model is designed to include such factors by extending the scope of the product tree by making it describe not only the system itself but the whole development situation (Broy et al., 2006; Deissenboeck et al., 2007). For brevity's sake, however, in the following we focus on the system's characteristics.

The example depicted here uses a simple Boolean relation between facts and activities and therefore merely expresses that there is a relation between a fact and an activity. To express different directions and strengths of the relations, more elaborate scales can be used here.

Attributes and Impacts

To be able to express more elaborate impact relations, one needs to create a more fine-granular decomposition of the product tree. It is, for example, not enough to express that the model documentation influences the impact analysis. We rather want to be able to pinpoint the properties of the documentation, e. g. its completeness, conciseness or redundancy, that do have a positive or negative influence on the activity.

We found that this decomposition inevitably leads to a high number of repetitions as the same properties apply to different kind of artefacts. For example, *consistency* is obviously required for the names used in models as well as for the layout of the models themselves.

Therefore, our model further decomposes facts into entities and attributes where entities "are the objects we observe in the real world" and attributes are "the properties that an entity possesses" (Kitchenham, Pfleeger, & Fenton, 1995). Hence, entities describe a plain decomposition of the product. Examples are *documentation*, *models*, *variables* or *states*. Entities are associated with one or more attributes like *consistency*, *redundancy*, *completeness* or *superfluousness*.

So, the facts defined in the product tree are actually tuples of entities and attributes: [Entity e | ATTRIBUTE A]. They describe properties of the product that are desired or undesired in the context of maintainability. Examples are [Identifiers | CONSISTENCY], [Documentation | COMPLETENESS] or [Unsupported Blocks | EXISTENCE] that simply describes the presence or absence of Simulink blocks that are not supported by the code generator.

Note that the separation of entities and attributes does not only reduce redundancy but allows for a clean decomposition of the product. This can be illustrated by an example of the quality taxonomy defined in (P. Oman & Hagemeister, 1992): *System Complexity*. As *System Complexity* appears too coarse-grained to be assessed directly, it is desirable to further decompose this element. However, the decomposition is difficult as the decomposition criterion is not clearly defined, i. e. it is not clear what a subelement of *System Complexity* is. A separation of the entity and the attribute as in [System | COMPLEXITY] allows for a cleaner decomposition as entities themselves are not valued and can be broken up in a straightforward manner, e. g. in [Subsystem | COMPLEXITY] or [Class | COMPLEXITY].

IMPACTS

Using the notation introduced for facts we can elegantly express the impact a fact has on an activity with a three-valued scale where "+" expresses a positive and "-" a negative impact (the non-impact is usually not made explicit):

$$[\text{Entity } e \mid \text{ATTRIBUTE A}] \xrightarrow{+/-} [\text{Activity } a]$$

Examples are [Unsupported Blocks | EXISTENCE] $\xrightarrow{-}$ [Code Generation], that describes that the existence of an unsupported Simulink block has a negative influence on the activity code generation. [Model Layout | CONSISTENCY]

$\xrightarrow{\ +\ }$ [Impact Analysis] describes that a consistent model layout has a positive impact on the impact analysis activity. [State | SUPERFLUOUSNESS] $\longrightarrow$ [Model Reading] describes that an unreachable state in a Stateflow chart hampers the reading of the model. Like most of the impacts discussed here, this can easily be transferred to the MDA-world where we would expect a state machine to have no unnecessary states, too. To provide justifications that explain the rationale behind these guidelines, in our model each impact is additionally equipped with a detailed description.

ASSESSMENT

Obviously, the facts are the elements of the model that need to be assessed in order to determine the maintainability (or maintenance effort) of a product. Since many important facts are semantic in nature and inherently not assessable in an automatic manner, we carefully distinguish three fact categories:

1. Facts that can be assessed or measured with a tool. An example is an automated check for unused output ports of a Simulink block ([Simulink | COMPLETENESS]). A typical example in the MDA-context is the check for multiple inheritance in UML class diagrams if the implementation language does not support multiple inheritance.

2. Facts that require manual activities; e. g. reviews. An example is a review activity that checks if Stateflow is actually used for state oriented parts of the system and not as a workaround ([Stateflow Chart | APPROPRIATENESS]). An example for MDA is the check for conformance to well-known object-oriented design patterns (Gamma, Helm, Johnson, & Vlissides, 1995) in UML class diagrams.

3. Facts that can be manually assessed from automated proposition. An example is the layout of Simulink/TargetLink models that should follow some basic rules, e. g. data flow is from left to right. Here a tool can help to find suspicious parts of the model but the final decision is left to the user ([Layout | CONSISTENCY]). Similar properties can be analysed for UML class diagrams.

THE METAMODEL

Fig. 4 shows a UML class diagram representing a simplified form of the quality metamodel with the elements discussed above: entities, attributes, facts, activities and impacts. Please note, that the figure shows only the core elements and omits details like the explanation texts that are associated with each element. Moreover, it does not show that the model features a generalisation mechanism that allows attribute inheritance. It is, for example, possible to specify an attribute SUPERFLUOUSNESS for the entity Component and inherit it to the entity Class.

Tool Support

Comprehensive maintainability models typically contain several hundred model elements. For example, the model that was developed for a commercial project in field of telecommunication (Broy et al., 2006) has a total of 413 model elements consisting of 160 facts (142 entities and 16 attributes), 27 activities and 226 impacts. Hence, quality models demand a rich tool set for their efficient creation, management and application just like other large models, e. g. UML class diagrams. Due to the fact that our quality models are based on an explicit metamodel we are able to provide a model editor that does not only allow the initial development of quality models but also supports other common tasks like browsing, persistence, versioning and refactoring[2].

Figure 4. The quality metamodel QMM

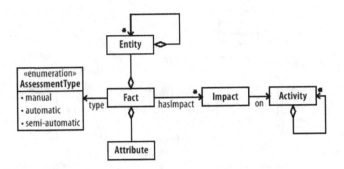

One of the most powerful features of the model editor is the automatic generation of guideline documents from the quality model. This enables us to transfer the abstract definition of quality stored in the model to a format developers are familiar with. However, unlike classic, hand-written guidelines the automatically generated ones are guaranteed to be synchronised with the quality model that explicitly captures the understanding of quality within a project or a company. Guideline documents can be tailored to specific needs by defining selected views on the model. For example, a guideline document could be specifically generated to be used during documentation review sessions.

QUALITY ASSURANCE BASED ON A QUALITY MODEL

In contrast to other quality models that are expressed in terms of prose and graphics only, our maintainability model is truly integrated in the software development as basis of all quality assurance activities. As Fig. 5 shows, the model can be seen as project- or company-wide quality knowledge base that centrally stores the definition of quality in a given context. Of course, an experienced quality engineer is still needed for designing the quality models and enforcing them with manual review activities. However, he can rely on a single definition of quality and is supported by the automatic generation of guidelines. Moreover, quality assessment tools like static analysers that automatically assess artefacts can be directly linked to the quality model and do not operate isolated from the centrally stored definition of quality. Consequently, the quality profiles generated by them are tailored to match the quality requirements defined in the model. We refer to this approach as model-based quality controlling.

The quality model acts as a central knowledge base of the quality-related relationships in the product and process. We document in a structured way how properties of the system, team, and organisation influence different activities. Therefore, it is the perfect basis for quality assurance (QA). It can be used in several ways for constructive as well as analytical QA.

Constructive QA

The knowledge documented in the quality model helps all developers to get a common understanding of the domain, techniques, and tools and thereby avoids misunderstandings. Improvements of the quality model are part of a continuous learn-

Figure 5. Model-based quality controlling

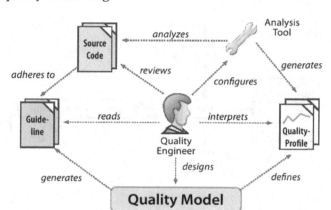

ing process for all developers. For example, by describing the properties of the system artefacts, a glossary or terminology is built and can be easily generated into a document. This glossary is a living artefact of the development process because it is not only paperwork but inside and part of a structured model. Hence, learning and improving the way developers work helps to avoid defects being introduced.

Analytical QA

The identified relationships in the quality model can also be used for analytical quality assurance. Because we aim with our quality model to break down the properties and attributes to a level where we can measure them, we are easily able to give concrete instructions in analytical QA. In particular, we are able to generate guidelines and checklists for reviews from the model. The properties and attributes are there and subsets can easily be selected and exported in different formats so that the developers and reviewers always have the appropriate guidelines at hand.

Moreover, we annotate the attributed properties in the model whether they are automatically, semi-automatically or only manually assessable.

Hence, we can identify straight-forwardly quality aspects that can be analysed automatically. Thus, we are able to use all potential benefits from automation. Finally, more general analyses and predictions are possible based on the quality model. One reason to organise the properties and activities in a tree structure is to be able to aggregate analyses to higher levels. This is important to get concise information about the quality of the system. However, we do not aggregate these measures into a single "maintainability metric" but analyse various aspects that reflect the multiple facets of maintainability.

CASE STUDY

Environment

The MAN Nutzfahrzeuge Group is a German-based international supplier of commercial vehicles and transport systems, mainly trucks and busses. It has over 34,000 employees world-wide of which 150 work on electronics and software development. Hence, the focus is on embedded systems in the automotive domain. The organisation brought its development process to a high level of maturity by investing enough effort to redesign it according to best practices and safety critical system standards. The driving force behind this redesign was constantly focusing on how each activity contributes to the global reliability and effectivity. Most parts of the process are supported by an integrated data backbone developed on top of the eASEE framework from Vector Consulting GmbH.

This backbone provides version control and configuration management support. With it, MAN follows a *single source* strategy: the development team enters information only once and refers to it in all the appropriate entities. To better assist the developer in their work, the backbone employs a metaphor close to the application domain. It represents the main domain entities (e. g., ECU, software, function, parameter, port, bus) as atomic elements explicitly. Their relations and descriptions are captured in configurations that the user can build by drag and drop during the development. A user requirement, for example, is first put under the ECU, it is then refined into one or more technical requirements that are first put under the software and later under the functions that will implement it. From this point on, the backbone offers full *traceability*: when modifying one of these requirements, the backbone can report where each requirement has been implemented and its complete context. This feature can be used for *impact analysis*: a project manager, for example, can analyse the impact of different changes in requirements and take the appropriate actions.

The backbone systematically exploits the single source strategy to generate consistent documents. Each domain entity like buses, ports and even signals are described only once and the more complex entities (functions, software or hardware) simply refer to them. When a function specification is generated, for example, the generator fetches the relevant information from the signals and ports to which it refers. Thus saving effort and reducing the error potential.

On top of this backbone, a complete model-based development approach has been established using the tool chain of Matlab/Simulink and Stateflow as modelling and simulation environment and TargetLink of dSpace as C-code generator. The *tool integration* does not stop there: report generators, a hazard assessment tool, as well as different test tools are also seamlessly integrated in the environment.

We describe the application and adoption of our model to this concrete situation and the generated benefits. The study led to the adoption of the model and the generated guidelines into the MAN standard development process

Experiences

In the case study, we adapted the maintainability model for the situation at MAN with a focus on the TargetLink and Stateflow parts. The model contains all the quality criteria relevant for that kind of MDSD described above. They are based on three types of sources: (1) existing guidelines for Simulink/TargetLink/Stateflow, (2) scientific studies about model-based development and (3) expert know-how of MAN's engineers.

Specifically, our main source was a consolidation of the four guidelines available for using TargetLink and Stateflow in the development of embedded systems: the MathWorks documentation (MathWorks, 2006), the MAN-internal guideline, the guideline provided by dSpace (dSpace, 2006) and the guidelines published by the MathWorks Automotive Advisory Board (MAAB) (MAAB, 2001).

Because of space and confidentiality reasons, we are not able to fully describe the MAN-specific model here. However, we present examples that demonstrate how our approach works in the context of MDSD. We start with a simple translation of the existing MAN guidelines for Stateflow models into the maintainability model. For example, the MAN guideline requires the current state of a Stateflow chart to be available as a measurable output. This simplifies testing of the model and improves the debugging process. In terms of the model this is expressed as [Stateflow Chart | ACCESSIBILITY] $\xrightarrow{+}$ [Debugging] and [Stateflow Chart | ACCESSIBILITY] $\xrightarrow{+}$ [Test].

We describe the ability to determine the current state with the attribute ACCESSIBILITY of the entity Stateflow Chart. The Stateflow chart contains all information about the actual statechart model. Note that we carefully distinguish between the chart and the diagram that describes the graphical representation. In the model the facts and impacts have additional fields that describe the relationship in more detail. These descriptions are included in generated guideline documents.

CONSOLIDATION OF THE TERMINOLOGY

In the case study we found that building a comprehensive quality model has the beneficial side-effect of creating a consistent terminology. By consolidating the various sources of guidelines, we discovered a very inconsistent terminology that hampers a quick understanding of the guidelines. Moreover, we found that even at MAN the terminology has not been completely fixed (e. g., synonyms were used). Fortunately, building a quality model automatically forces the modeller to give all entities explicit and consistent names. The entities of the facts tree of our maintainability model automatically define a consistent terminology and thereby provide a glossary.

One of many examples is the term subsystem that is used in the Simulink documentation to describe Simulink's central means of decomposition. The dSpace guideline, however, uses the same term to refer to a TargetLink subsystem that is similar to a Simulink sub-system but has a number of additional constraints and properties defined by the C-code generator. MAN engineers on the other hand, usually refer to a TargetLink subsystem as TargetLink function or simply func-

tion. While building the maintainability model, this discrepancy was made explicit and could be resolved.

RESOLUTION OF INCONSISTENCIES

Furthermore, we are not only able to identify inconsistencies in the terminology but also in contents. For the entity Implicit Event we found completely contradictory statements in the MathWorks documentation and the dSpace guidelines.

- MathWorks (MathWorks, 2006) "Implicit event broadcasts [...] and implicit conditions [...] make the diagram easy to read and the generated code more efficient."
- dSpace (dSpace, 2006) "The usage of implicit events is therefore intransparent concerning potential side effects of variable assignments or the entering/exiting of states."

Hence, MathWorks sees implicit events as improving the readability while dSpace calls them intransparent. This is a clear inconsistency. After discussing with the MAN engineers, we adopted the dSpace view.

REVELATION OF OMISSIONS

An important feature of the quality metamodel is that it supports inheritance. Its importance became obvious in the case study after modelling the MAN guidelines for TargetLink variables and Stateflow variables. We model them with the common parent entity Variable that has the attribute LOCALITY that expresses that variables must have the smallest possible scope. As this attribute is inherited by both types of variables, we found that this important property is not expressed in the original guideline. Moreover, we see by modelling that there was an imbalance between the TargetLink and Stateflow variables. Most of the guidelines related only to TargetLink variables. Hence, we transferred them to Stateflow as well.

Usage of the Model

The quality modelling process resulted in a quality model with 87 new facts specific for Simulink and Stateflow. In the further case study, we concentrated on checklist generation and some preliminary automatic analyses. Those were chosen because they promised the highest immediate pay-off.

CHECKLIST GENERATION

We see quality models as central knowledge bases w.r.t. quality issues in a project, company, or domain. This knowledge can and must be used to guide development activities as well as reviews. However, the model in its totality is too complex to be comprehended entirely. Hence, it cannot be used as a quick reference. Therefore, we use the tool support for the quality model to select subsets of the model and generate concise guidelines and checklists for specific purposes. These generated guidelines are able to completely replace the existing hand-written ones.

Automatic generation of guideline documents was perceived to be highly valuable as the documents could be structured to be read conveniently by novices as well as experts. Therefore, the documents feature a very compact checklist-style section with essential information only. This representation is favoured by experts who want to ensure that they comply with the guideline but do not need any further explanation. For novices the remainder of the document contains a hyper linked section providing additional detail. Automatic generation enables us to conveniently change the structure of all generated documents. More importantly, it ensures consistency within

the document which would be error-prone in hand-written documents.

AUTOMATIC ANALYSES

As the model is aimed at breaking down facts to a level where they can be assessed and they are annotated with the degree of possible automation, it is straight-forward to implement automatic analyses. So far, we have not fully exploited the possibilities but we are able to show that several facts can be checked in Simulink/TargetLink and Stateflow models. For this, we wrote a parser for the proprietary text format used by Matlab to store the models. Using this parser we are able to determine basic size and complexity metrics of model elements like states, blocks, and so on. Moreover, we can use the parser to automatically identify model elements that are not supported by the C-code generator. By integrating these analyses in our quality controlling toolkit ConQAT[3] (Deissenboeck, Pizka, & Seifert, 2005) we are able to create aggregated quality profiles and powerful visualisations of quality data. Alternatively, those checks could have been implemented directly in the Simulink Model Advisor. However, this would have prevented the easy integration into a toolkit like ConQAT.

Discussion

Our metamodel and the corresponding method for modelling maintainability proved to be applicable to model-driven software development in an industrial environment. Especially the model's explicit illustration of impacts on activities was seen as beneficial as it provides a sound justification for the quality rules expressed by the model. Moreover, the general method of modelling - that inherently includes structuring - improved the guidelines: although the initial MAN guideline included many important aspects, we still were able to reveal several omissions and inconsistencies. Building the model, similar to other model building activities in software engineering (Pretschner et al., 2005), revealed these problems and allowed to solve them.

Another important result is that the maintainability model contains a consolidated terminology. By combining several available guidelines, we could incorporate the quality knowledge contained in them and form a single terminology. We found terms used consistently as well as inconsistent terminology. This terminology and combined knowledge base was conceived useful by the MAN engineers.

Although the theoretical idea of using an explicit quality metamodel for centrally defining quality requirements is interesting for MAN, the main interest is in the practical use of the model. For this, the generation of purpose-specific guidelines was convincing. We not only build a model to structure the quality knowledge but we are able to communicate that knowledge in a concise way to developers, reviewers and testers. Finally, the improved efficiency gained by automating specific assessments was seen as important. The basis and justification for these checks is given by the model.

FUTURE TRENDS

Automatic Quality Controlling

An obvious direction for future work is the improvement of automatic quality analysis and assessment tools for the artefacts of the model-based development approach. Using a relatively simple parser and our quality controlling toolkit CONQAT we were able to quickly develop automatic checks for the most simple quality rules. However, we see major benefits in the extensions of this approach to more complex automatic or semi-automatic assessments. One interesting candidate is the detection of clones (redundancy) in Simulink/TargetLink/Stateflow models that

completely lacks tool support at the moment. Including this and similar analyses in a continuous quality controlling process would not only help to ensure maintainability but is expected to significantly reduce the efforts for manual quality assurance activities.

Integrated Quality Modelling

This chapter provides an in-depth discussion of the *maintainability* of software models. However, quality is known as "[...] a complex and multifaceted concept." (Garvin, 1984) that includes aspects as different as maintainability, safety, reliability, performance or even usability. Currently all these different aspects are dealt with by a plethora of different models and techniques. Examples are quality models for maintainability, failure mode and effects analysis (FMEA) for safety (Leveson, 1986), reliability growth models for reliability (Tian, 2004), execution environment measurements for performance (Yilmaz et al., 2005) and specialised models for usability (Seffah, Donyaee, Kline, & Padda, 2006).

All these techniques haven been proven to be highly valuable. But unfortunately, today these techniques are not integrated and usually applied in isolation. As we showed in (Wagner & Deissenboeck, 2007) the lack of a systematic concept to integrate the existing quality approaches renders a comprehensive analysis of software difficult and causes overlaps as well as inconsistencies in definitions of quality. Moreover, the current situation hampers the systematic discussion of quality trade-offs as they can be sometimes observed for maintainability and performance.

We are convinced that ultimately our goal must be a truly economically justified practice of quality engineering that enables us to reason about the different quality aspects and their interdependencies in a quantitative manner. Hence, we believe that an integrated discussion of different quality attributes will be a topic of major interest.

Reuse

In the context of classical software development reuse has often been called the "the holy grail of software engineering" as it promises tremendous productivity gains (Jacobson, Griss, & Jonsson, 1997). Of course, this is every bit as true for model-driven development. Unfortunately, in MDSD efficient reuse is even less common than in classical development. This is mainly due the week reuse mechanisms provided by currently used tools. Simulink, for example, has a library mechanism that proves to be too inflexible for the purpose of code generation in a real-world environment.

We claim, that the solutions found for reuse challenges in code driven development need to be transferred to MDSD, too. Furthermore, future work on unsolved reuse problems, e. g. efficient product line engineering, should be discussed in the context of MDSD from the beginning on.

DISCUSSION AND CONCLUSION

Comparison with Classical QA

In general, the quality assurance for maintainability in MDSD is not completely different from code-driven development. The main issues such as readability and changeability of the artefacts are still there but on a higher level of abstraction. To ensure that the models are easy to comprehend, we have to develop an understandable control and data flow similar to those used for source code. Simulink even has a *Goto* block and *implicit events* that can cause jumps in the control flow. Hence, we face the same challenges here. Also a clear modularisation and size constraints apply to models as well as to code. Obviously, other issues related to modularisation such as clear and simple interfaces and typing are very important in both cases.

On the other hand, there are clear differences. Quality assurance in MDSD needs far more emphasis on the two-dimensional arrangement of the elements. Even the third dimension plays a role because different model elements can hide each other. Also colouring and typing by graphical icons are unique issues. Finally, conformance to other tools - mainly code generators – introduce further constraints that need specific consideration in a quality model and in modelling guidelines for MDSD. However, as models typically are more abstract than code, they hide some of the platform details. Hence, in MDA as well as Simulink, changes in the underlying technology are easier to deal with.

Benefits and Drawbacks

We propose to use an explicit quality model to manage the maintainability of models in MDSD. This quality model acts (1) as a general knowledge base of the maintainability-related issues and (2) as basis for quality assurance. Obviously, the development and maintenance of the quality model itself constitutes a significant effort. In our experience, those models tend to become large and detailed. However, this is necessary for a structured management of maintainability. Moreover, there are several benefits that outweigh the costs: Firstly, the explicit modelling of the quality-related relationships enhances the completeness and consistency of the rules used in the company. This way, possibilities for process improvements become visible. Secondly, the quality model is a well-suited basis for quality assurance. We showed in the case study with MAN that specific guideline documents can be generated automatically from the model. This ensures that maintainability-related issues are not neglected, for example in reviews. Moreover, we were able to automate the checking of a variety of rules for Simulink/TargetLink and Stateflow models based on the quality model. Hence, we save review costs and give the developers a quick feedback on the quality of their models. In summary, we found that maintainability is as equally important in MDSD as in code-driven development and that an explicit quality model can serve as a structured basis for the quality assurance in MDSD.

REFERENCES

Baxter, I. D., Yahin, A., Moura, L., Sant'Anna, M., & Bier, L. (1998). Clone detection using abstract syntax trees. In *Proc. international conference on software maintenance (ICSM '98)* (p. 368). Washington, DC: IEEE Computer Society.

Beine, M., Otterbach, R., & Jungmann, M. (2004). Development of safety-critical software using automatic code generation. In *Proc. SAE world congress*. Society of Automotive Engineers.

Berns, G. M. (1984). Assessing software maintainability. *Communications of the ACM*, 27 (1), 14-23.

Boehm, B. W. (1981). *Software engineering economics*. Englewood Cliffs, NJ: Prentice-Hall.

Boehm, B. W., Brown, J. R., Kaspar, H., Lipow, M., Macleod, G. J., & Merrit, M. J. (1978). *Characteristics of software quality*. New York, NY: North-Holland.

Broy, M., Deissenboeck, F., & Pizka, M. (2006). Demystifying maintainability. In *Proc. the 4th workshop on software quality*. New York, NY: ACM Press.

Coleman, D., Ash, D., Lowther, B., & Oman, P. W. (1994). Using metrics to evaluate software system maintainability. *Computer*, 27 (8), 44-49.

Cruz-Lemus, J. A., Genero, M., Manso, M. E., & Piattini, M. (2005). Evaluating the effect of composite states on the understandability of UML statechart diagrams. In *Proc. 8th int. conf. on model driven engineering languages and systems*. Berlin, Heidelberg: Springer-Verlag.

Deissenboeck, F., Pizka, M., & Seifert, T. (2005). Tool support for continuous quality assessment. In *Proc. 13th IEEE international workshop on software technology and engineering practice (STEP '05)* (p. 127-136). Los Alamitos, CA: IEEE Computer Society.

Deissenboeck, F., Wagner, S., Pizka, M., Teuchert, S., & Girard, J.-F. (2007). An activity-based quality model for maintainability. In *Proc. 23rd international conference on software maintenance (ICSM '07)*. Washington, DC: IEEE Computer Society.

Dijkstra, E. W. (1968). Goto statement considered harmful. *Communications of the ACM*, 11 (3), 147-148.

Dobrzanski, L., & Kuzniarz, L. (2006). An approach to refactoring of executable UML models. In Proc. *2006 ACM symposium on applied computing (SAC '06)* (pp. 1273-1279). New York, NY: ACM Press.

Dromey, R. G. (1995). A model for software product quality. *IEEE Transactions on Software Engineering*, 21 (2), 146-162.

dSpace. (2006). *Modeling guidelines for MATLAB/ Simulink/ Stateflow and TargetLink*.

Eick, S. G., Graves, T. L., Karr, A. F., Marron, J. S., & Mockus, A. (2001). Does code decay? assessing the evidence from change management data. *IEEE Transactions on Software Engineering*, 27 (1), 1-12.

ISO 9126-1 Software engineering - Product quality - Part 1: Quality model (International Standard). (2003). ISO.

Erlikh, L. (2000). Leveraging legacy system dollars for e-business. *IT Professional*, 2 (3), 17-23.

Gamma, E., Helm, R., Johnson, R., & Vlissides, J. (1995). *Design patterns, elements of reusable object-oriented software*. Reading, MA: Addison-Wesley.

Garvin, D. A. (1984). What does product quality really mean? *MIT Sloan Management Review*, 26 (1), 25-43.

Genero, M., Piattini, M., Manso, E., & Cantone, G. (2003). Building UML class diagram maintainability prediction models based on early metrics. In *Proc. 9th international symposium on software metrics (Metrics '03)* (pp. 263-275). Washington, DC, USA: IEEE Computer Society.

Glass, R. L. (1989). Software maintenance is a solution, not a problem. *System Development*, 9 (1), 8-9.

Gurp, J. van, & Bosch, J. (2002). Design erosion: problems and causes. *The Journal of Systems and Software*, 61 (2), 105-119.

Halstead, M. (1977). *Elements of software science*. New York, NY: Elsevier Science Inc.

Huang, S.-J., & Lai, R. (2003). Measuring the maintainability of a communication protocol based on its formal specification. *IEEE Transactions on Software Engineering*, 29 (4), 327-344.

IEEE. (1998). 1219 Software maintenance (Standard).

Jacobson, I., Griss, M., & Jonsson, P. (1997). *Software reuse: architecture, process and organization for business success*. New York, NY: ACM Press and Addison-Wesley.

Kiewkanya, M., Jindasawat, N., & Muenchaisri, P. (2004). A methodology for constructing maintainability model of object-oriented design. In *Proc. fourth international conference on quality software (QSIC '04)* (pp. 206-213). Washington, DC, USA: IEEE Computer Society Press.

Kitchenham, B., Linkman, S., Pasquini, A., & Nanni, V. (1997, September). The SQUID approach to defining a quality model. *Software Quality Journal*, 6 (3), 211-233.

Kitchenham, B., & Pfleeger, S. L. (1996). Software quality: The elusive target. *IEEE Software*, 13 (1), 12-21.

Kitchenham, B., Pfleeger, S. L., & Fenton, N. (1995). Towards a framework for software measurement validation. *IEEE Transactions on Software Engineering*, 21 (12), 929-944.

Lague, B., Proulx, D., Mayrand, J., Merlo, E. M., & Hudepohl, J. (1997). Assessing the benefits of incorporating function clone detection in a development process. In *Proc. International conference on software maintenance (ICSM '97)*. Washington, DC: IEEE Computer Society.

Lange, C. F. J., & Chaudron, R. V., Michel. (2005). Managing model quality in UML-based software development. In *Proc. 13th IEEE international workshop on software technology and engineering practice* (pp. 7-16). Washington, DC: IEEE Computer Society.

Leveson, N. G. (1986). Software safety: why, what, and how. *ACM Computing Surveys*, 18 (2), 125-163.

Lientz, B. P., Bennet, P., Swanson, E. B., & Burton, E. (1980). *Software maintenance management: A study of the maintenance of computer application software in 487 data processing organizations*. Reading: Addison Wesley.

MAAB. (2001). Controller style guidelines for production intent using Matlab, Simulink and Stateflow.

Marinescu, R., & Ratiu, D. (2004). Quantifying the quality of object-oriented design: The factor-strategy model. In *Proc. 11th working conference on reverse engineering (WCRE '04)*. Washington, DC: IEEE Computer Society.

MathWorks. (2006). Simulink reference.

McCabe, T. (1976). A complexity measure. *IEEE Transactions on Software Engineering*, SE-2 (4), 308-320.

McCall, J., & Walters, G. (1977). *Factors in software quality*. Springfield, VA: The National Technical Information Service (NTIS).

Nosek, J. T., & Palvia, P. (1990). Software maintenance management: changes in the last decade. *Journal of Software Maintenance*, 2 (3), 157-174.

Oman, P., & Hagemeister, J. (1992). Metrics for assessing a software system's maintainability. In *Proc. international conference on software maintenance (ICSM '92)*. Washington, DC: IEEE Computer Society.

Oman, P. W., & Cook, C. R. (1990). Typographic style is more than cosmetic. *ACM Communications*, 33 (5), 506-520.

Parnas, D. L. (1994). Software aging. In *Proc. 16th international conference on software engineering (ICSE '94)* (pp. 279-287). Washington, DC: IEEE Computer Society.

Pretschner, A., Prenninger, W., Wagner, S., Kühnel, C., Baumgartner, M., Sostawa, B., et al. (2005). One evaluation of model-based testing and its automation. In *Proc. 27th international conference on software engineering (ICSE '05)*. New York, NY: ACM Press.

Seffah, A., Donyaee, M., Kline, R. B., & Padda, H. K. (2006). Usability measurement and metrics: A consolidated model. *Software Quality Control*, 14 (2), 159-178.

Seifert, T., Beneken, G., & Baehr, N. (2004). Engineering long-lived applications using MDA. In *Proc. IASTED international conference on software engineering and applications* (pp. 241-246). Calgary: IASTED/ACTA Press.

Tian, J. (2004). Quality-evaluation models and measurements. *IEEE Software*, 21 (3), 84-91.

Wagner, S., & Deissenboeck, F. (2007). An integrated approach to quality modelling. In *Proc. 5th workshop on software quality (5-WoSQ)*. Washington, DC: IEEE Computer Society.

Yilmaz, C., Krishna, A. S., Memon, A., Porter, A., Schmidt, D. C., Gokhale, A., et al. (2005). Main effects screening: a distributed continuous quality assurance process for monitoring performance degradation in evolving software systems. In *Proc. 27th international conference on software engineering (ICSE '05)* (pp. 293-302). New York, NY: ACM Press.

ADDITIONAL READING

Colgren, R. (2006). *Basic Matlab, Simulink and Stateflow*. AIAA (American Institute of Aeronautics & Ast).

Introductory book on Matlab, Simulink and Stateflow that is also recommended by The MathWorks, Inc.

Deissenboeck, F., & Pizka, M. (2006). Concise and consistent naming. *Software Quality Journal*, 14 (3), 261-282.

This paper describes the impact of program (or model) identifiers on program comprehension and introduces rules for good naming. Due to the paramount importance of naming this is worth reading for developers as wells as quality managers.

Fenton, N. (1994). Software measurement: A necessary scientific basis. *IEEE Transactions on Software Engineering*, 20 (3), 199-206. This is the fundamental basis for measuring software. It introduces a measurement theory and shows what analyses are possible.

Glass, R. L. (1998). Maintenance: Less is not more. *IEEE Software*, 15 (4), 67-68. Glass convincingly describes the true relevance of software maintenance and argues against the common prejudices about maintenance work.

Kaner, C., & Bond, W. P. (2004). Software engineering metrics: What do they measure and how do we know? In *Proc. 10th international software metrics symposium*. Washington, DC: IEEE Computer Society.

This paper discusses the sense and senselessness of software metrics and explains common problems with the interpretation of metric values. Worth reading for quality managers to improve metric programs and developers to argue against senseless metric thresholds imposed on them.

Krueger, C. W. (1992). Software reuse. *ACM Computing Surveys: A seminal paper on software reuse*, 24 (2), 131-183.

Lindvall, M., Komi-Sirvi, S., Costa, P., & Seaman, C. (2003). *Embedded software maintenance* (A DACS State-of-the-Art Report). Fraunhofer Center for Experimental Software Engineering. This report discusses the peculiarities of software maintenance for embedded systems. Worth reading for anyone who maintains embedded software systems.

Parnas, D. L. (1994). Software aging. In *Proc. 16th international conference on software engineering (ICSE '94)* (pp. 279-287). Washington, DC: IEEE Computer Society. This paper explains the inevitable aging of software through a comparison with the ageing of the human body. This is a seminal paper on software aging, evolution and maintenance and should be read by every software engineer.

Schach, S. R. (1994). The economic impact of software reuse on maintenance. Journal of Software *Maintenance: Research and Practice*, 6(4), 185-196. This paper illustrates that economic impact of software reuse on maintenance is even more pronounced than the impact on the initial development. Worth reading for team managers and engineers responsible for reuse strategies.

Weinberg, G. M. (1971). *The psychology of computer programming*. Van Nostrand Reinhold Co. This book discusses the influence on human psychology on the productivity of software development. In particular, in introduces the concept of egoless programming. This worth reading especially for development team leaders

Wilson, J. Q., & Kelling, G. L. (1982). Broken windows. *The Atlantic Monthly*, 249 (3), 29-38. This paper describes Zimbardo's experiments about the Broken Window Effect. Today, this effect is known to be one of the main reasons for rapid quality decay in software systems. This is worth reading for quality managers as well as software developers.

TRADEMARKS

MATLAB, Simulink, Stateflow are registered trademarks of The MathWorks, Inc. TargetLink is a registered trademark of dSPACE GmbH.

ENDNOTES

[1] The Motor Industry Software Reliability Association, http://www.misra.org.uk/

[2] A beta version of the editor can be downloaded from http://www4.cs.tum.edu/~ccsm/qmm/

[3] ConQAT can be downloaded from http://conqat.cs.tum.edu

Chapter XV
Quality Improvement in Automotive Software Engineering Using a Model–Based Approach

Tibor Farkas
Fraunhofer Institute FOKUS, Germany

ABSTRACT

Premium quality and innovation are the cornerstones of the leading positions of car manufacturers and suppliers in the world market. The permanently increasing complexity of in-car electronics and the rapidly growing amount of automotive software running on embedded electronic control units, places higher demands on quality assurance for the future. Quality cannot be implemented into software on embedded control units after their development. Methods for defects detection have to be constituted to automatically stop development to fix a problem before the defect continues downstream. In addition preventive actions have to be taken in respect of front-loading quality and reliability. An automatic and tool independent check of custom development rules, quality standards and enterprise wide guidelines can support the quality assurance process in the development of automotive control software. In the domain of automotive software engineering there is a lack of automated checking for standard conformance. Especially, a formal and tool independent notation of rules to follow is missing. In this chapter, the model-based design of automotive vehicle functions is taken as an example to show how textual rules describing development standards to be met can be transformed into a formal notation using the open standards Meta Object Facility and Object Constraint Language. Thereafter these rules can be checked automatically. The feasibility of this approach is shown by a software demonstrator.

1. INTRODUCTION

Premium quality and innovation are the cornerstones of the leading positions of car manufacturers and suppliers in the world market. Quality assurance starts in early development phases and is a joint responsibility of both, the car manufacturers and their suppliers. The use of electronic control units (ECU) has grown rapidly in modern vehicles. This has gone along with an increase in variety and complexity of these electronic systems and their networking over different busses. New functions are preferably implemented in embedded software that is distributed on a rising number of networked control devices (VDI, 2005). Having nowadays approximately 10 to 20 different ECUs on a single vehicle network, the integration of software from many different suppliers is a difficult task (Mercer, 2001).

X-by-wire systems are an upcoming technology in the automotive industry that replaces the traditional mechanical and hydraulic control systems with electronic control systems using electromechanical actuators and human-machine interfaces. They constitute the basis for vehicle control systems and assistance systems that support and relieve the driver during his driv-ing assignment. Purely mechanical or hydraulic systems will be replaced by mechatronic systems. They are integrated into the vehicle environment intelligently. As a result, software will become a technology that is critical for the business competition especially in the automotive manufacturing domain (Jackman, 2005). High demands for quality of these systems and the great complexity as well as the rapidly growing interaction between single subsystems lead to strong requirements on development methods and development tools. As an example, Figure 1 shows the increasing number of software inside telephone-hands-free equipment (an automotive telematics application) over a period of 10 years (Form, 2006).

While simple functions like displaying the digits were realized on an embedded display device, nowadays rich functions such as voice dialing and phone book synchronization are controlled by embedded software.

Coping with future system complexity under stringent quality requirements on the one hand and the expected lead in innovation on the other hand are important factors of business success for automotive manufacturers and their suppliers (Liggesmeyer, 2005). Nevertheless, the quality losses of the electronic devices in the vehicle are still engraving. According to the current

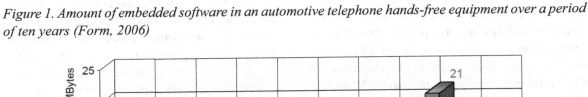

Figure 1. Amount of embedded software in an automotive telephone hands-free equipment over a period of ten years (Form, 2006)

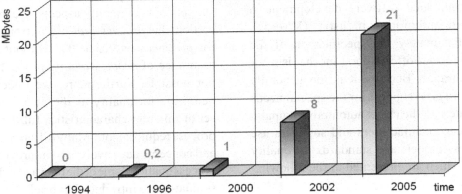

Figure 2. Largest proportion of the failures is situated in the area of electrical units, connections and software (ADAC, 2007)

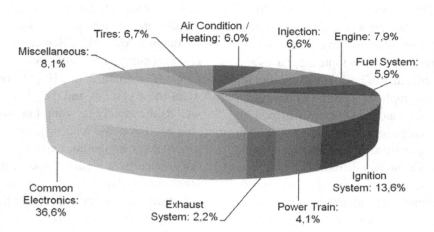

breakdown statistic (ADAC, 2007) of the year 2006 published by the ADAC (General German Automobile Association) up to 70% of breakdowns have been caused by failures occurred in the area of the electrical units, connections and software (see Figure 2). Also the other portions are influenced by electrical units (e.g. Injection System).

Quality cannot be implemented or tested into embedded control software after their development. Therefore it is essential to support aspects of quality and reliability by constructive measures in the early phases of the V-Model. The V-Model is a general process model (also further staged versions like V-Model XT) mostly used for embedded software development in the German automotive industry (VModel, 1997). Unfortunately the specification of the V-Model does not offer a good mechanism for quality assurance. Because it is too generally defined, there is no support for the special needs and the context of the target automotive domain. Therefore car manufacturers and suppliers use other process models and standards for quality assurance, which are presented in the following section.

2. BACKGROUND, STATE OF THE ART, CHALLENGES

In the system development the use of common standards are a prerequisite for each type of a quality assurance. However, most quality standards and other approaches for quality assurance focus on one specific quality aspect. With the development of embedded systems mainly two different aspects on the quality are to be differentiated, namely *product quality* and *process quality*. In this section common standards for *product quality* and *process quality* are introduced briefly, because the presented approach in section 3 targets on the support of both quality aspects. We make an assertion, that *process quality* is a strong perquisite for *product quality*, so that without having an assurance of *process quality* product quality is not possible. Furthermore, we understand the definition for quality as the degree to which a set of inherent characteristics fulfils product or process requirements. Many different techniques and concepts have evolved to improve product or process quality. Some of the relevant and important standards are introduced in brief.

Figure 3. Quality model for external and internal quality (ISO9126, 2001)

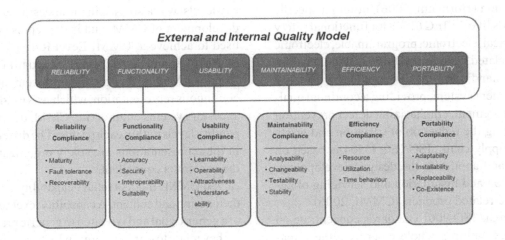

The international quality standard ISO/IEC 9126 defines the *product quality* of software in a quality model for external and internal quality (ISO9126, 2001). External quality is the totality of characteristics of the software product from an external view. It is the quality when the software is executed, which is typically measured and evaluated while testing in a simulated environment with simulated data using external metrics. Internal quality is the totality of characteristics of the software product from an internal view. Internal quality is measured and evaluated against the internal quality requirements. Details of software product quality can be improved during code implementation, reviewing and testing, but the fundamental nature of the software product quality represented by internal quality remains unchanged unless redesigned. The ISO/IEC 9126 quality standard categorizes software quality attributes into six characteristics:

(a) reliability,
(b) functionality,
(c) usability,
(d) maintainability,
(e) efficiency and
(f) portability.

The characteristics are further subdivided into sub characteristics (Figure 3, ISO9126, 2001). The sub characteristics can then be measured by internal or external metrics.

In such a quality model guidelines for software development exist, like the software development standard MISRA (MISRA, 1998). MISRA-C defines a set of rules for a common and fault-clearing use of the C language in manual coding of embedded software. Its aims are to facilitate code portability and reliability in the context of automotive engineering. While not all rules are applicable to deterministic automatic code generation, an auto-code generation nonetheless should comply with most of the MISRA-C rules.

For the quality assurance on the process level, there are a lot of different kinds of standards for process improvement like the ISO 9001:2004 (ISO9001, 2004) family or derived standards for the automotive domain like the ISO/TS 15504

(ISO15504, 1998) also known as SPICE — Software Process Improvement and Capability Determination (Hörmann, 2006), or target specific standards like the IEC 61508 for functional safety of electrical, electronic, programmable, electronic safety-related systems (ISO61508, 1998). The aim of these standards is the development of a quality management system, providing a continual quality improvement, emphasizing defect prevention and having the reduction of variation and waste in the supply chain. ISO/IEC 15504 is based on CMMI and applies to the design, development, production and installation and servicing of automotive-related products (CMMI, 2006).

Whereas ISO 9001 standards concentrate on processes within a whole enterprise the Capability Maturity Model Integration (CMMI) is a process improvement approach that provides organizations with the essential elements of effective processes (Kneuper, 2006). It consists of best practices that address development and maintenance activities that cover the product lifecycle from conception through delivery and maintenance. The CMMI defines two different representations: staged and continuous. The staged model, which groups process areas into five maturity levels, was also used in the ancestor software development of CMM, and is the representation used to achieve a 'CMMI Level Rating' from a SCAMPI appraisal (SCAMPI: Standard CMMI Appraisal Method for Process Improvement). The continuous representation, which was used in the ancestor systems engineering CMM, defines capability levels within each profile. The differences in the representations are solely organizational, the content is equivalent.

All CMMI models reflect capability levels in their design and content. A capability level consists of a generic goal and is related to generic practices as they relate to a process area, which can improve the organization's processes associated with that process area. The capability levels in a staged representation are shown in Figure 4 (Kneuper, 2006). The six capability levels, designated by the numbers 1 through 5, are as follows:

(1) Initial — sometimes divided into two levels Incomplete and Performed,

Figure 4. CMMI capability levels in staged representation (Kneuper, 2006)

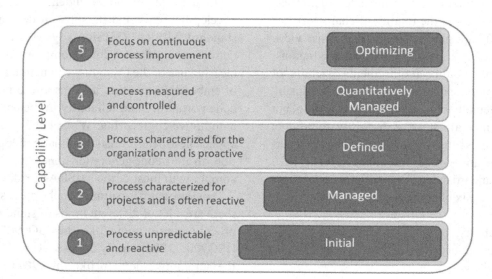

(2)   Managed,

(3)   Defined,

(4)   Quantitatively Managed and

(5)   Optimizing.

CMMI is a widely used approach especially in the area of systems engineering and development of embedded software for ECUs – not only in the automotive domain.

Quality systems like the ISO 9001:2004 family, derived standards like ISO/TS 16949 (ISO16949, 2002) for the automotive industry or process improvement approaches like the Capability Maturity Model Integrated (CMMI) describe criteria to reach goals and to achieve good processes, but they do not describe a particular instantiation for such a process. This instantiation is up to the organization implementing the quality model to a quality assurance system. Quality standards describe generically 'what' has to be done, but

not 'how' the quality requirements have to be realized. It is a general perception that such an instantiation should be supported by a concrete methodology and by software tools. Moreover the mentioned quality systems were developed for large organizations, therefore an optimal methodology and useful tooling should be customizable and scalable even for small organizations and medium enterprises as well. These are requirements on our approach for quality assurance that is presented in the third section.

Certification to an above mentioned standard does not guarantee compliance and therefore does not guarantee good quality of end products and services. However, it certifies that consistent business processes are being applied.

The use of different kind of complex artifacts in the development of automotive embedded control systems gains in importance, although new methods of resolution for the challenges for quality

Figure 5. Observance of consistency and standard conformance is difficult to enforce because of different artifacts, file formats and notations

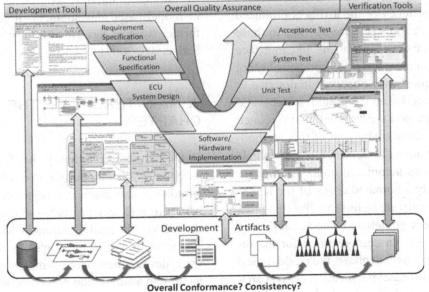

assurance have to be found. Carefully selected methods and tools for the development are of largest importance, since only efficient methods, tools and error preventing processes could master this competition (Farkas+03, 2007).

Different kind of tools for the requirements engineering, the model based design of vehicle functions, development environments for embedded C code, target compiler and finally tool suites for testing are used in one (or even more) specific phase. However, the tools are not specially customized for the special needs of embedded software development for the automotive-domain. Hence they do not cover the overall quality assurance of a given textual standard, like development guidelines.

To evaluate a very simple quality constraint for instance, like the examination of a general name convention, the consistency is not automatically provable. Even if only one artifact is considered, like the model based design of vehicle functions, the developer has to observe thousands more model elements to check compliance with the naming convention. This is of course very time consuming and inefficient. Problematic concerning the consistency of different artifacts it proves that the used tool chains cannot guarantee spreading consistency of the artifacts produced in the respective tools (Figure 5). Due to these circumstances, frequent problems, like interface inconsistency, or incorrect or comprehensibly not transferred requests, are observed in practice.

In the next section an integrated, scalable and model-based method is presented, that is related to (Farkas+06, 2006). The goal of this methodology is to enhance the development of vehicle functions with an automated quality assurance through an early automated check of the resulting embedded software against quality standards and development guidelines. The feasibility of this method has been demonstrated for the requirements management phase, the model-based design and the test case specification in a research project (Farkas+10, 2006). For lack of space, we focus only on the phase of model-based design of vehicle functions.

In the beginning of the next section the often used tools MATLAB, Simulink and Stateflow (MLSLSF, 2007) for the model-based development of automotive functions as well as a sample model are introduced briefly. Then a guideline catalogue "*Control Algorithm Modeling Guidelines Using MATLAB, Simulink, and Stateflow*" (CAMG, 2007) developed by The MathWorks Automotive Advisory Board (MAAB, 2007) for Simulink and Stateflow is referred to. Automotive manufacturers use enterprise specific guidelines as referenced in (Farkas+03, 2007) that are similar to the MAAB guidelines. Each guideline may consist of several textual rules. Some aspects of model checking are shown on the basis of example rules from this catalogue. A short outline of the chosen technology Meta Object Facility (MOF) for meta-modeling (MOF, 2003) follows. Building upon the MOF the OCL-Object Constraint Language (OCL, 2003) is used to formally describe rules and to show how textual guidelines like (CAMG, 2007) can be transformed into a formal specification. The section finishes with the presentation of a software prototype as a solution to automatic standard conformance checking in model-based development. It is based upon former work as described in (Farkas+01, 2007; Farkas+03, 2007).

3. MAIN THRUST OF THE CHAPTER

In the automotive industry the development of embedded system software needs modeling, simulation and analysis of dynamic system behavior in early design phases of the V-Model by the OEM (Original Equipment Manufacturer). The modeling of a function's algorithm in software development environments goes hand in hand with a simulation of its behavior on the PC (virtual prototyping). Rapid prototyping tools and technologies are used to develop and optimize new control concepts. The use of a model as an executable specification, the primary means for knowledge capture and transfer, represents the key benefit of model based software development. Software development tools provide a basis for the continuous, automated and efficient application of a model-driven development process for electronic control units. The automatic generation of target code from the implementation model is used to create the production C code of new functions for the ECU based on the results obtained in the preceding steps. To this end, the maximum benefit of model based software development is attained in terms of efficiency and reusability. Models have to be accepted in all phases of development by system engineers and they have to be integrated seamlessly into existing processes of the enterprise.

The next tool supported development phase after the requirement analysis is the development of automotive functions (functional specification). In this phase the concept from earlier development phases and the specifications from the recorded requirements are substantiated by a model-based design. The resulting control and feedback control systems allow the development of real, physical models that cannot only be modeled but that can also be simulated in a development environment. The tools for functional design have to realistically replicate simulation models of vehicle functions, e.g. models describing the driving dynamics or the power train. So called system behavior models that describe the general input and output behavior as well as the different states of the system and their interactions are created.

However, behavior models do not yet completely realize the concrete functions. Ideally, transformation engines are built into the tools that would provide the automated generation of platform specific code from parts of the simulation model for the ECU. This would allow early examination of the software functionality of a control feedback system. System behavior

models complement textual requirements in the tools for functional design under different aspects. The tools Simulink and Stateflow form an integrated software suite based upon MATLAB with a graphical user interface to model, simulate and analyze dynamic and state based systems (MLSLSF, 2007). They support editing and simulating linear and non-linear systems whether the systems use discrete or continuous time. This software suite is widely used in the automotive industry for the development of vehicle functions and should serve as an example to prove our methodology. Alternative tools with similar functionality are SCADE or ASCET that are not discussed within this chapter (SCADE, 2007; ASCET, 2007).

Especially within the development of embedded software systems Simulink and Stateflow are used in early development to model functional and behavioral models. A behavioral model acting as specification needs to be of much higher quality than one produced only for rapid prototyping.

The "engine timing model" from the examples provided by Simulink (MLSL, 2007) is shown in Figure 6. We use this model to demonstrate rule checking in this section. The simple model is based on (Crossley, 1991) and acts as a comprehensible sample for readers that are not familiar with Simulink. It describes the functional behavior of a four cylinder spark ignition internal combustion engine. Different subsystems model the throttle and manifold compression, combustion, the vehicle dynamics and the valve timing. A signal is generated by the valve timing subsystem. It triggers the compression subsystem twice per revolution of the crank.

After a simulation the engine speed and the throttle angle compared to the load torque can be shown graphically. Skipping the details of the subsystem components and their mode of operation the model shows the possible degrees of freedom in system modeling with Simulink. The freedom in modeling is provided by different graphic representations, semantics and structure

Figure 6. A sample artifact – a simple engine timing model (MLSL, 2007)

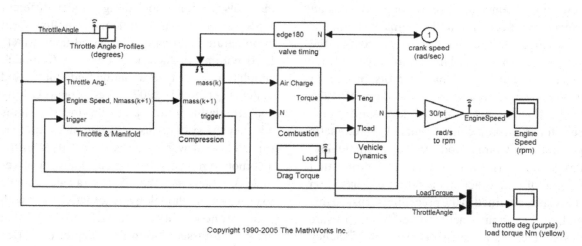

as well as different parameter settings. However, the tools Simulink and Stateflow are not specialized on the development of automotive embedded systems. Therefore the modeled systems are very sensitive to problems during further processing, e.g. the creation of control software in embedded devices – may it be code automatically generated from the model or may the model be the specification for manually created code. So, the question arises, how such models and the resulting software intensive vehicle functions can be validated against safety and reliability concerns expressed via existing standards and guidelines.

While modeling reliable applications a number of different guidelines, standards and norms regarding quality, introduced before, as well as legal regulations are employed in the automotive industry. These are not discussed here in detail, but it is obviously desirable to check a model for compliance against these rules already in the modeling phase of the development. Ideally, the check is automated to safeguard the development process and the resulting artifacts in a sustainable way.

A practical example of a modeling catalogue for Simulink models in the context of automotive systems is *"Control Algorithm Modeling Guidelines Using MATLAB, Simulink, and Stateflow"* (CAMG, 2007). The initial MAAB is an association of leading automotive manufacturers such as Ford, Daimler or Toyota and their suppliers in order to harmonize models. The published catalogue contains more than one hundred guidelines: different modeling rules for Simulink and for Stateflow categorized by context, importance and automatic verifiability. Figure 7 shows an excerpt of such a guideline on the usage of specific model elements. Divided into lemma, priority, scope, preconditions, description and a reasoning this guideline describes special functional units that could be used in Simulink models in general, but should not be used in automotive vehicle function models.

The guideline schematically and simplified represents the topical existing and current guidelines for behavior and implementation models in the industry. They are partly vendor independent. Only the enforcement of guidelines can assure that certain standards, like mentioned

Figure 7. Prohibited Simulink standard blocks inside controllers. Excerpt from the Control Algorithm Modeling Guidelines Using MATLAB, Simulink, and Stateflow. (CAMG, 2007)

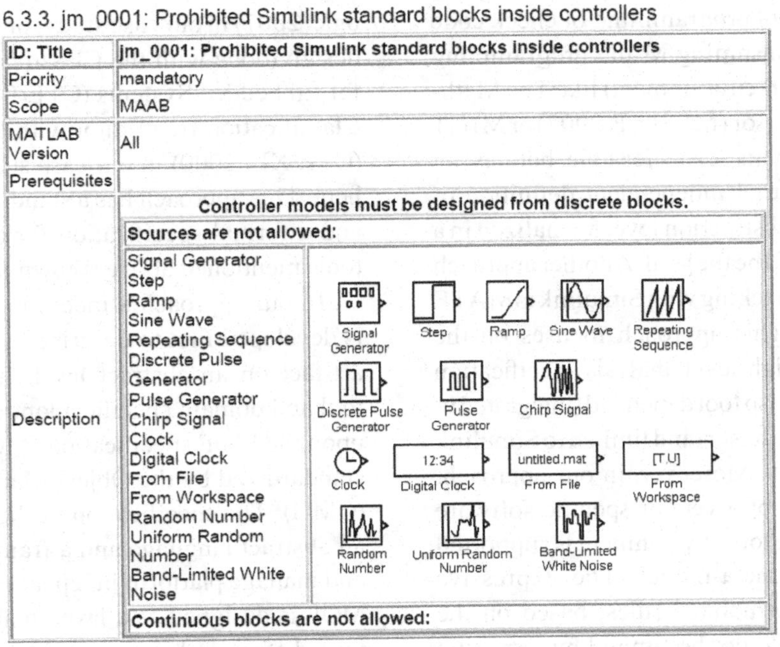
6.3.3. jm_0001: Prohibited Simulink standard blocks inside controllers

ID: Title	**jm_0001: Prohibited Simulink standard blocks inside controllers**
Priority	mandatory
Scope	MAAB
MATLAB Version	All
Prerequisites	
Description	**Controller models must be designed from discrete blocks.** **Sources are not allowed:** Signal Generator Step Ramp Sine Wave Repeating Sequence Discrete Pulse Generator Pulse Generator Chirp Signal Clock Digital Clock From File From Workspace Random Number Uniform Random Number Band-Limited White Noise **Continuous blocks are not allowed:**

standards in the second section, are met and sufficient consistency between a manufacturer and its suppliers is reached. This is very relevant for models of safety critical systems. Safety must be considered from the beginning as required by a safety standard like IEC 61508. Standards such as IEC 61508 define basic safety regulations for safety related systems used in vehicles (ISO61508, 1998). A prerequisite for road certification is that operational safety of the systems can be attested. In the area of software development, this can either be achieved by manual code reviews or greatly supported by the use of certified tools for code generation. To meet this requirement, a code generator has to be certified by organizations like the TÜV (Technical Control Board) for Safety Integrity Level (SIL).

Guidelines for quality regulations are written mostly in a textual representation with different kind of graphical illustrations included. Paper documented guidelines on model checking and standard conformance have considerable disadvantages. First, there is insufficient automatic verifiability during the use of such guidelines in a model-based development. Complex functional models with more than thousands of model elements, a model size that is easily reached today, cannot be feasibly checked by human visual examination.

Additionally, quality assurance is lacking an adequate means for analysis and protocol in order to monitor reoccurring guideline violations for further projects and process improvement. Further, the selection of a subset of the existing guidelines for a project, a business division or an enterprise is difficult and time consuming in a paper based guideline set. Not all guidelines are applicable for all models everywhere and every time. We will illustrate automation in the next section at several examples.

A first approach to automate rule checking would be an in-tool programming of check code (here the time-consuming M-file programming with the MATLAB environment) like The Math-Works Model Advisor (MLSLSF, 2007) or MINT (Ricardo, 2007). This seems feasible, but it is not sustainable. The tool independent definition of rules on a higher abstraction level formalized in a meta-model should be the goal. Another approach of conformance checking with Simulink is MATE (MATE, 2007). This approach focuses on the application of a high-level analysis specification language, but it is also tool depended (integrated in Simulink Model Advisor) and limited to Simulink and Stateflow only. Moreover, in our approach, the independence of a vendor specific software implementation or tool environment is supported with an overall meta-model. The expressive strength of the formalized rules, based on the meta-model, should not be limited by a specific software application.

Instead of a proprietary solution an open and scalable approach also suited for requirements engineering (done with Telelogic DOORS (Telelogic, 2007) in our case study) or test specification design (done with the Classification-tree Editor for Embedded Systems (CTE/ES, 2007) and the Classification-tree Editor with Extended Logics (CTE/XL, 2000) in our case study) is presented here. This approach has a standardized structure and a formal specification for the development tools mentioned above (shown in Figure 8).

In our approach a meta-model for each tool is developed first to describe the structure of an artifact on an abstract level. It contains some tool and domain specific adoptions and is based upon the MOF specification (MOF, 2003) that is standardized by the Object Management Group (OMG). The specification of the MOF proposes an abstract language and a framework to create and manage platform independent meta-models. MOF is designed as a layered architecture with four different abstraction layers. The architec-

Figure 8. First meta-models were built for different artifacts

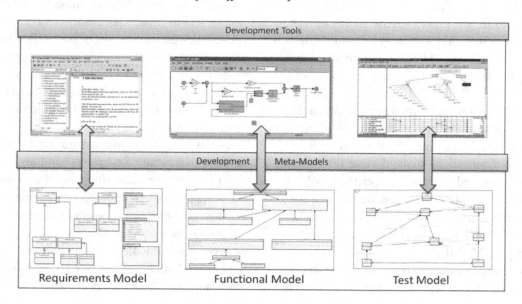

ture of MOF is based on a four-layer approach to meta-modeling:

- **Layer L3—The meta-meta-model:** The definition of the elements and the structure for the description of a meta-model.
- **Layer L2—The meta-model:** The definition of the elements and the structure of a concept space (i.e. the modeling language). An L2-layer model consists of instances of the L3-layer.
- **Layer L1—The model:** Definition of the structure and behavior of a system using a well defined set of general concepts. An L1-model consists of L2-layer instances. A Simulink model would be at this layer.
- **Layer L0—The instances:** Information or data that describe a concrete system at a fixed point in time. This layer consists of instances of elements of the L1-layer.

The MOF specification defines these concepts as well as supporting concepts in detail. Because there is no explicit notation for MOF, the UML notation has been deliberately used to visualize selected concepts.

In a standard modeling process the designer of a model has to consider implicit and explicit development guidelines. Such an explicit guideline could indicate naming conventions like all class names have to start with a capital letter. An implicit rule could be that the designer designates names meaningfully. With a set of such development guidelines it is possible to make the model more readable and clear. Design guidelines influence the system in an indirect way. The developed system has no preference whether a class name starts with a capital letter or not. Therefore design guidelines must not be strict. Hence if a model breaks a guideline this must not result in an error, in fact it could result in a kind of a warning.

Before we can bring our textual guidelines to a formalized representation and evaluate them,

we have to build a meta-model for the specific artifact. Figure 9 shows an excerpt of a MOF meta-model for Simulink and Stateflow that is used for the OCL examples below.

In this meta-model a generic, abstract element *ASDElement* is modeled to provide common attributes of all system elements. It is used by the Simulink specific block element *SLBlock* to derive basic attributes. Further down the hierarchy there are specific blocks like in and out ports (*SLInportBlock* and *SLOutportBlock*) for signal inputs and signal outputs, sinus generators for signal generation (*SLSineBlock*), signal terminators (*SLTerminatorBlock*) consuming signals or signal amplifiers (*SLGainBlock*) that transform signals. As the MOF defines only primitive data types, but Simulink allows using many complex data types, the modeling of these complex types becomes very important. An example is given by the type *ASDCoordinate* that contains tool dependent position coordinates. The developer gains not only a formal and structured representation by the developed meta-model, but also the possibility to define constraints via the OCL.

The OCL is a declarative constraint language that provides concepts of functional languages to evaluate expressions on a finite set of objects. It is predestinated to describe invariants in class diagrams as well as to state conditions in state or sequence diagrams. To take advantage of it textual guideline descriptions (as shown in Figure 7) have to be transferred into the formal OCL notation.

The usage of OCL constraints in MOF can be defined through OCL's specification as well as MOF's specification of constraints. OCL allows stating pre- and post-conditions of operations and, more importantly here, invariants. In combination with the evaluation policies as defined in MOF the following constraint categories are found:

- **Immediate invariants:** Constraints on instance objects which must hold all the time.

Figure 9. Simulink meta-model excerpt

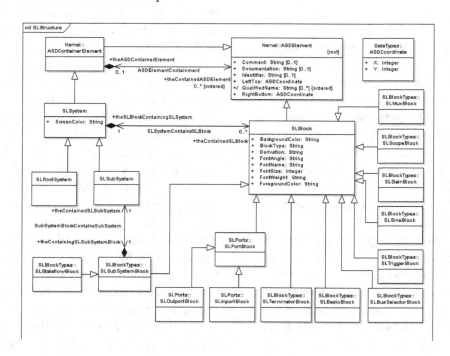

- **Deferred invariants:** Constraints on instance objects which must hold at a user specified point in time.
- **Pre- and post-conditions:** Constraints on operations which must hold before respectively after operation execution. Differentiation between immediate and deferred verification does not apply here.

OCL lists also several other places where formal expressions might be useful, for example, to define the value of derived attributes or the semantics of an operation, but such usage specifies an implementation and not a constraint and, therefore, doesn't need any monitoring inside a repository. Thus, it is out of the scope of this work, although some of the results found here might prove useful when implementing support for OCL in other MOF contexts.

For a better understanding of how OCL constraints can be used within a MOF model, an example is depicted in Figure 10. The example OCL constraint is taken from the MOF specification itself. It formally states that all members of a namespace must have different names. It is not well specified in any of OMG's documents how to manage the constraint definitions. One possibility is to store those in a separate text file (e.g. in XML format) where the context of each constraint is specified through the keyword "context" followed by the name of the classifier. It is proposed to keep the constraint definitions together with the meta-model, as it makes it easier for meta-modelers to define constraints while designing the meta-model; it also emphasizes the constraints because they are visible along with the meta-model. To allow use of existing UML modeling tools which do not have a special visualization for constraints, the following notation

Figure 10. Example OCL constraint

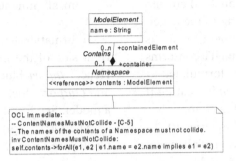

is suggested: OCL constraints are written inside "Notes" which are attached to the Classifier which defines their Context. To distinguish between normal notes and OCL constraint definitions, each OCL constraint definition could start with a keyword *OCL* followed by the constraint's evaluation policy. Adding OCL constraints to a MOF meta-model is a semantic enrichment of the meta-model. Constraints can serve as a source of documentation of the meta-models among software designers and programmers. But it is also desirable to enforce these constraints inside the modeling infrastructure (inside the repositories), and to react reasonably on constraint violation. Thus, whenever a client tries to store a meta-object in the repository, the meta-model's constraints are evaluated and, if any constraint is violated, the client is informed, and the violation can be resolved via a rollback. Please note that the behavior of MOF repositories for constraints is currently not specified in any standard.

To enable constraint monitoring and evaluation inside MOF repositories, the OCL constraints have to be transferred from the meta-model definition into the generated repositories. Computer code has to be generated to evaluate the constraints and to monitor the elements which are constrained. To enforce consistency of a repository, it is also necessary to decide what action should be undertaken upon violation of immediate constraints, whether

the client is responsible to put the repository back into a consistent state, or if the repository itself performs a rollback.

Monitoring and evaluating the constraints inside the repository can be computationally expensive. Therefore, it is necessary to develop a monitoring mechanism which calculates the minimum set of constraints to be checked on each change of the repository's state, and to generate efficient evaluation code. Also, the costs for evaluation can be reduced by following some rules for the definition of OCL constraints; semantically equivalent OCL expressions can have different evaluation costs. Besides the monitoring of constraints to assure structural consistency and validity in source and target models, OCL can further be used to query and transform models. The following subsection will explain how OCL can be used as core of a quality validation language. As mentioned before, an optimal methodology and useful tooling should be customizable and scalable. The scalability of this approach is ensured. An OCL constraint cannot change the model. Therefore multiple constraints can be checked in parallel on a single model. Additionally, the finite set of objects that an OCL constraint is checked on can be divided into several subsets. They can be checked independently from each other in parallel.

Subsequently, some modeling guidelines are taken from (CAMG, 2007). We transfer them into the notation of the OCL according to the developed meta-model. For this example a model is considered to be standard compliant if it conforms to these rules. OCL rules can be formulated as an invariant that returns a *Boolean* indicating if a certain guideline is met. In this example we formalize the guidelines as OCL queries (`OclVoid`). Each rule returns a collection of all model elements that violate a certain guideline, i.e. a model is standard conform if all rules return an empty collection. A non-empty collection can then be used to highlight the problematic blocks in the modeling tool (Simulink or Stateflow in our example). Complex guidelines consisting of several aspects connected by a logical 'and' are formalized as multiple OCL constraints. In this way it is easier to identify the cause if a block is considered to be problematic (see also Figure 11).

(1) **Quality Characteristic:** Guideline for common appearance

The arbitrary use of color can be misleading. Therefore, the background color of all model elements of the type block has to be set to white. See Exhibit A.

(2) **Quality Characteristic:** Guideline for misalignment of ports

Information has to flow from the left to the right side of the model to increase readability. Hence, *Inport* blocks must be on the left side and *Outport* blocks must be on the right side of a model. See Exhibit B.

The OCL expression to check that *Outport* blocks are located on the right is similarly formulated.

(3) **Quality Characteristic:** Guideline for block layout

The common reading direction in English is from top to bottom. Thus, trigger blocks that determine whether other model elements are considered at all must be located above all other blocks. See Exhibit C.

(4) **Quality Characteristic:** Guideline for text layout

Formatting model elements arbitrarily encumbers the readability. Thus, the font size of all block captions must be set to the value *10*. Text weight and text alignment can be checked alike. See Exhibit D.

Exhibit A.

```
context OclVoid inv: SLStructure ::
SLBlock.allInstances() -> reject
( x | x.BackgroundColor = 'white')
```

Exhibit B.

```
context SLStructure::SLSystem inv: let center _ x =
(self.LeftTop.X - self.RightBottom.X) / 2 in
self.theContainedSLBlock -> select
( x | x.oclIsTypeOf (SLPorts :: SLInportBlock )) ->
reject ( x | x.LeftTop.X < center _ x)
```

Exhibit C.

```
context SLStructure :: SLSystem inv:
let limit_y = self.theContainedSLBlock -> select ( x |
x.oclIsTypeOf ( SLBlockTypes :: SLTriggerBlock ) ) ->
 iterate ( x : SLStructure :: SLBlock;
acc : Integer = SLStructure :: SLRootSystem.
allInstances().asSequence().at(1).RightBottom.Y |
acc.min( x.RightBottom.Y ) in let other_blocks =
self.theContainedSLBlock -> select ( x | not (
x.oclIsTypeOf ( SLBlockTypes :: SLTriggerBlock ) ) )
in other_blocks -> reject ( x | x.LeftTop.Y > y_limit)
```

Exhibit D.

```
context OclVoid inv: SLStructure :: SLBlock.allInstances()
-> reject( x | x.FontSize = 10 )
```

Exhibit E.

```
context OclVoid inv: Kernel :: ASDElement.allInstances()
-> reject( x | x.Identifier.size() <= 31)
```

Exhibit F.

```
context Kernel :: ASDElement inv: let valid_characters =
Set{'a','b','c','d','e','f','g','h','i','j','k','l','m','n','
o','p','q','r','s','t','u','v','w','x','y','z'} in
allInstances() -> reject ( x | valid_characters ->
includesAll ( Set { 1 .. x.Identifier.size () } -> iterate
( i: Integer; sum: Sequence ( String )
= Sequence {} | sum ->
append (x.Identifier.substring(i, i)))))
```

Exhibit G.

```
context SLStructure :: SLSystem inv:
self.theContainedSLBlock -> exists ( x | x.oclIsTypeOf
( SLStructure :: SLSubSystemBlock )) implies
self.theContainedSLBlock -> forAll ( x | x.oclIsTypeOf
( SLStructure :: SLSubSystemBlock ) or x.oclIsTypeOf
( SLPorts :: SLInportBlock ) or x.OclIsTypeOf
( SLBlockTypes :: SLMuxBlock ))
```

(5) **Quality Characteristic:** Guideline for name convention

Some tools used for further processing of a model, like a target C code compiler and linker, cannot deal with very long names (e.g. function names). To demonstrate the check of the name length, in this scenario the identifier of all model elements must not exceed 31 characters. See Exhibit E.

(6) **Quality Characteristic:** Guideline for syntax

Similar to the constraint shown in rule five, certain characters cannot be processed by compilers. Therefore we have to ensure just a specific allowed character set. In this example only lower case letters can be used to name model elements. See Exhibit F.

(7) **Quality Characteristic:** Guideline for separation of concerns

The reuse of model elements can be simplified by constructing orthogonal subsystems. Then the quality of the orthogonal subsystems can be assured independently from each other as a preparation for the quality assurance of a collection of subsystems. In this example a subsystem is considered to be orthogonal if it is either a basic block that cannot contain other blocks or it is a *SLSubSystemBlock* that contains only certain other blocks. See Exhibit G.

(8) **Quality Characteristic:** Guideline for semantics

Some concepts like an analog sine wave generator can be simulated on a computer easily, but might be hard to implement on real embedded hardware. A part of MAAB guideline 6.3.3 from Figure 7 is realized by the following expression:

The usage of the block element *SLSineBlock* (Sine Wave) in all systems is forbidden. (analog for Block Scpo) See Exhibit H.

For other block types this expression can be applied, if only the type is changed.

(9) **Quality Characteristic:** Guideline for amount of state control logic

If discrete state control logic modeled with Stateflow is spread too widely in a model, it is difficult to capture the actual state of a system if it is executed for simulation. Consequently, only one state chart from Stateflow is allowed within each model level. See Exhibit I.

Similar transformations have been applied for the state machines modeled with the tool Stateflow. Guidelines and conventions that have to be met can be identified in this context, too.

Whereas the concise rules of presentation and formatting options improve the readability and understandability of models, the quality rules for semantics and syntax address special concerns in safety critical standards. The use of invalid or untested system components that might have been bought from an external supplier, the use of not grounded busses or signal pathways (signal not terminated, signal not connected etc.), nonconformance to a special name syntax or a certain allowed set of characters for the automatic code generation (how should a space character or a carriage return be interpreted) emphasize that early avoidance of known deficiencies improves the reliability and safety of information technological systems in a sustainable way. The effort necessary to test such systems (Zander-Nowicka, 2006) is reduced as a benefit of this approach.

Case Study: Automated Evaluation of Quality Standards

Our sample model (see Figure 11) in a slightly modified form (coloring) serves as an example for the automatic check of guidelines. The fol-

Exhibit H.

```
context SLStructure :: SLSystem inv:
theContainedSLBlock -> select
( b | b.BlockType = 'SineWave' or b.BlockType = 'Signal
Generator')
```

Exhibit I.

```
context SLStructure :: SLSystem inv:

let control_structures = self.theContainedSLBlock -> select
( x | x.oclIsTypeOf ( SLBlockTypes :: SLStateflowBlock ))
in

if control_structures.size() > 1 then
  control_structures
  else {}
endif
```

Figure 11. Vehicle model with different guideline violations

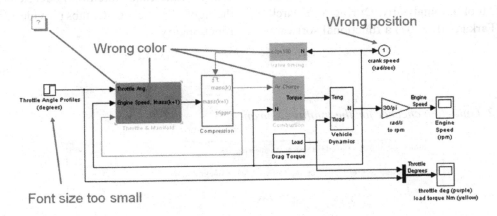

lowing modeling errors are found in the modified model:

a. **Violation of rule 1:** The background color of a block element is topical blue and differs from the required value white.

b. **Violation of rule 4:** The font size of a block element does not fulfil the demanded value 10.

c. **Violation of rule 8:** The model element of the type Scope occurs multiple times, although it is forbidden completely.

d. **Violation of rules 5 and 6:** An illegal carriage return character is used. The name length exceeds the maximum of 31 characters.

As a result, this sample model (Figure 11) does not conform to the before introduced modeling guidelines (1)-(9) that must be met in accordance to our quality standard. A wrong specification like this implemented in an early phase of the V-Model would affect ongoing development phases. So, code generation or the implementation by suppliers can be erroneous. Summarized the quality of the system would not to be guaranteed any more.

The violation of guidelines is clearly identifiable by the developer within this simple model. In complex models this would be impossible or at least very time consuming. For the automated check of our sample model we have to introduce a software prototype that automated these guidelines. This software integrates in Simulink and is presented now.

Modeling rules and design guidelines as OCL constraints could be evaluated with a corresponding OCL tool automatically. During a research project (Farkas+01, 2007) a functional software prototype for guideline examination in MATLAB, Simulink and Stateflow has been developed by the Fraunhofer Institute for Open Communication Systems (FOKUS). It is based upon a MOF compliant Simulink and Stateflow meta-model (see Figure 9) and supports the evaluation of OCL constraints on a MOF-compliant repository. The engine for the evaluation of OCL expressions bases on (OSLO, 2007). OSLO is an acronym and stands for Open Source Library for OCL. It is based on the Kent OCL library. Likewise the Kent OCL library, OSLO supports the evaluation of OCL constraints against meta-models. This feature is essential for verification of modeling rules and design guidelines. In Figure 12 the basic graphical user interface of this checking tool is shown.

The developer finds the so-called '*Model Explorer*' on the left side, a hierarchical tree structure of all Simulink and Stateflow model elements. On the right side, the register tabs provide additional functionality:

Figure 12. Guideline checker for the quality assurance

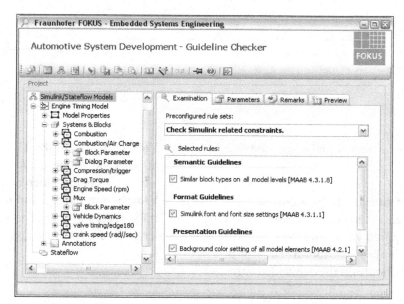

a. A customized selection of guidelines or characteristic guideline sets can be preconfigured and easily applied for the whole model by selecting specific rules from a list, before an evaluation is executed.

b. The quality standard in textual representation or a guideline catalog that can be displayed in an HTML representation (website). This is because an updated version is loaded every time from a web server; it could be possible that the catalog was recently updated by a quality manager.

c. For the quality assurance process further information has to be specified before an evaluation is started. This meta-information about the observation is defined here. This could be additional model information such as author or versioning information.

d. For the development of OCL constraints, an integrated rule editor is included to create new or edit existing rules. The OCL expressions could then be saved as XML files and loaded by the checker-tool before the evaluation.

e. A screenshot feature to archive the Simulink model together with its visual representation is implemented. This simplifies the navigation in a huge set of models without opening them in Simulink or Stateflow. The screenshot could be saved for later analysis by the responsible department.

If the developer likes to check his artifact, the complete Simulink/Stateflow model is read directly from the internal MATLAB memory into an integrated repository for the model evaluation. Thereafter the repository contains the model as an instance model of the meta-model. The OCL constraints are evaluated directly on the instance model in the repository and the results are shown in the analysis tool, the analysis feature of the software prototype, shown in Figure 13.

A detailed analysis is performed after checking each OCL constraint. It allows the developer to identify which guidelines are violated by which model element. A textual description can be shown which is taken directly from the textual quality standard catalogue. Different severity

Figure 13. Generated report for analysis of a guideline examination

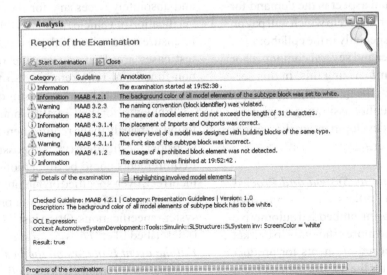

levels identify the magnitude of the violation. If a warning or an error occurs, the developer can jump directly onto the specific artifact (here a model element) in the development tool to correct the problem. The feature of an automated correction of an implementation error is not included in the software prototype yet; however, it was conceptually worked out already.

4. SUMMARY, FUTURE RESEARCH DIRECTIONS

Mastering challenges like the high system complexity and the still increasing diversity of the ECUs going along with a high demand for safety and reliability are the future challenges for the efficient quality assurance in the context of automotive engineering. This is important for all involved parties, the car manufacturers and their suppliers. As a result, a good quality assurance and quality management system includes the scenario of a world-wide distributed development.

Concerning the development of ECUs in the automotive context there are several boundary conditions one has to take into consideration. In comparison to other industrial domains, automotive electronic systems have very high production volumes. An additional aspect is the demand for integrity of the electronic system which will pay an ever increasing role especially in the collaboration between manufacturer and several component or system suppliers. Summarizing this, in this section we have to discuss the question, what are the cornerstones of the quality assurance, especially for the model-driven development, in the context of automotive engineering?

Quality Managements System and Process Assessment — are the pillars for ensuring high quality. The effort to bring embedded automotive electronics quicker and more efficiently to market not only sets by strict requirements for product development but also for the quality management

system (QMS) and the process assessment. In case of model-driven development the integration of methods and concepts from (MDA, 2003) the Model-Driven Architecture into a QMS is just at the beginning. At this time the applicability and support for the model-driven development is not adequate considered by international quality standards, which were introduced in the second part of this chapter. Standards (e.g. like ISO/IEC 9126) define the product quality of software in a quality model without having a relation to modeling languages like MOF and UML. Standards for programming compliance (like MISRA-C) do not include the fact that thousands of lines of code could be generated automatically from implementation models. Such standards should be updated to cope with model-based techniques. New or updated quality models will be necessary for model-driven development processes backing up on MDA-concepts. In the future, this will have especially an impact on the quality management systems and the way people do assessments.

Prospective Development — represents the basis of quality assurance. Quality assurance – in the model based development – is unfortunately often reduced to only one aspect of quality assurance: *testing*. Testing, of course, is a very important and absolutely necessary for the validation and verification of vehicle functions. More difficult is to ensure the quality of the test cases. However, test cases are derived from the functional and non-functional requirements. So the quality of the requirements has to be assured as well.

Problems for bad quality output are to be found primarily in the requirements engineering. Consider the different types of possible causation: Requirements could be ambiguous, incomplete, incorrect, over-specified or outdated. Incompleteness is one of the most common problems in the system specifications. Often just the functionality is described like:*"The system should do function **F** if the event **E** occurs on the bus"*. In this little example requirement, it is not defined, what happens if *E* does not occur or *E* is received too late. Then it's up to the way of implementation, how this issue is solved. However, at the implementation phase the component developer does not know much about the surrounding system. So it is difficult to implement robust functionality without knowing the periphery or other surrounding aspects.

Conciseness and Clarity — most specification is written in narrative text. Unfortunately, mostly narrative textual documents often leave readers in disagreement on the meaning of the specifications.

Requirements must be unambiguous. This is a strong requirement for the model-based design too. Also models can be interpreted differently. For this purpose, every stakeholder of the system development, like requirement engineers, system engineers, software developers, testers and other domain experts should all be capable of a common reading of specifications and models to derive the same understanding of the systems functionality.

Correctness — Informal, textual descriptions of development guidelines mostly cannot be executed or automatically analyzed.

Ensuring the correctness of a requirement is a difficult task. Moving more and more towards a model-based development — beginning at requirements specification, over functional design and simulation down to the code development — the quality assurance especially for the model-based development has to be further worked out. Integrated automatisms for ensuring the correctness of a model by guideline checking and especially formal and tool independent notations of the rules for quality assurance currently are not implemented satisfactorily for the use in a model-driven way of development.

Consistency — is a prerequisite for a quality management system. The trace of artifacts (e.g.

model-elements) could be a recorded link between source and target elements. Primary use of traces is for analysis purpose and to make transformation processes more comprehensible (e.g. for debugging). A quality management system must have the ability to mark artifacts for which traces are recorded. Further, the storage of traces and management of stored traces for un-do facilities is another aspect that should be addressed by a transformation engine. Traceability could not be fully directed to a transformation meta-model but always implies more technical aspects for a concrete implementation. Therefore, management of traces targets rather at the tool that implements transformations than the transformation language itself which must only provide a kind of "annotation" concept for traces. Beside traceability, consistency management and synchronization of models within the source and target repositories are further requirements for transformation executions.

Typically, a transformation does not operate on an empty target repository and must therefore be able to weave-in changes into existing models. These models may exist as result of former transformation processes or created by a user.

Completeness — is a main driver to reach total quality. As introduced before, quality consists of more than one characteristic, like functionality, reliability, usability, efficiency, maintainability and portability. If system designers just concentrate on only one aspect, e.g. the assurance of system functionality, and miss criteria for maintainability, then an uncertain system is received as a result. In addition, the high-class quality management systems must also be feasible. Just producing tons of paper with metrics and measurements does not support the quality of the end-product.

Predictions — an intelligent way of quality engineering. To front-load quality in the development process, predictions of quality statements have to be made. Whenever a change request is intended, it should be possible to do a quality analysis before the implementation of the request has begun. This is possible if actual measures are collected for estimation in the development process. Also associated information is needed to construct the estimates. This could be project planning parameters that constitute typical indicators of project progress and performance and include different attributes of work products like tasks, cost, effort or schedule. Metrics could be defined then on attributes of the artifacts that include such items as complexity, code size, form, depth or function. In case of model-driven development these attributes are also to be defined in the MOF meta-model of an artifact and can then be measured (evaluated) by query languages, like OCL evaluation in our approach. Then a tool supported monitoring is possible (like our rule-checker) that typically involves measuring of the actual values of project parameters, comparing actual values to the estimates in the plan and identifying significant deviations. A persistent recording is necessary to gather actual values of the development project and included recordings of associated contextual information to help understand the measures. This could be stored inside a repository according to the meta-model. An analysis of the impact that significant deviations have on determining what corrective actions to take is then initiated by the OCL expression evaluation engine upon the instance models inside the repository.

The mentioned characteristics like the Quality Managements System and Process Assessment, Prospective Development, Conciseness and Clarity, Correctness, Consistency, Completeness and Predictions are just the basics of an overall quality management system. The range of assessed processes and products covers more than we have space here to discuss. Within a model-driven quality framework further aspects are relevant, like the capability of problem resolution, the right project management, lifecycle and configuration management of models or supplier monitoring

if models implemented by third parties, just to name a few. As the development of automotive electronics move toward a model-based development, a lot of challenges in the quality assurance are to master. Concepts and techniques from MDA could help the current established processes in the systems engineering. Nevertheless, the quality engineering in the model-driven development has to be improved much more in the future.

5. CONCLUSION

This chapter presented a model-based method using the open standards Meta-Object Facility (MOF) and the Object Constraint Language (OCL) from concepts of the Model-Driven Architecture (MDA) to support quality assurance by enriching the embedded systems engineering in the context of the automotive domain. The model-based development of vehicle functions was equipped with an automated evaluation of development guidelines for the quality assurance of different artifacts. A selected tool suite for model-based design (Simulink and Stateflow) with a graphical user interface for functional modeling, simulation and analysis of dynamic and state based systems, which are increasingly used in the automotive industry, was used to demonstrate this concept. It was shown how the approach could be constituted on other artifacts, like requirements or test cases; if an artifact specific meta-model is developed. For the vehicle function modeling and reliable applications a multitude of different development guidelines, international standards and norms concerning quality, safety and reliability assurances as well as legal regulations were introduced that are used within areas of the automotive industry. Textual documented guidelines have obvious disadvantages and especially a missing formal notation that could be used for automatic checking. To avoid this lack an approach of formalizing narrative rule descriptions to computable expressions was introduced. For this purpose a tool dependent artifact was modeled to a MOF-conform meta-model. It was shown how textual guidelines can be transferred into a formal notation by means of OCL. The practical use of automatic guideline checking and guideline violation analysis was demonstrated on the basis of a software prototype. With the presented approach modeling errors and defects during the development process can be avoided in the future. Further it is possible to formalize even rules that concern more than one tool and check them automatically. Additionally it was stated, that OCL could also be used for the evaluation of quality metrics and measurements to achieve estimations. In the end comparisons were carried out between quality standards and the model-driven development of software intensive systems on relevant characteristics like quality management system, process assessment, prospective development, Conciseness, Clarity, Correctness, Consistency, Completeness and Predictions.

REFERENCES

(ADAC, 2007) General German Automobile Association (ADAC) (2007): *The ADAC-Breakdown statistic 2006*. ADAC Paper Manual Nr. 5, May 2007. Retrieved from URL: http://www.adac.de

(ASCET, 2007) ETAS GmbH (2007): ASCET Product Family, ASCET-MD (Modeling & Design). URL: http://en.etasgroup.com /products/ascet

(CAMG, 2007) MAAB The MathWorks Automotive Advisory Board (2007): *Control Algorithm Modeling Guidelines Using MATLAB, Simulink, and Stateflow, Version 2.0*. Retrieved from http://www.mathworks.com/industries/ auto/maab.html (MAAB_Style_Guide_pdf_v2_00.zip)

(CMMI ,2006) SEI Software Engineering Institute (2006): *CMMI - Capability Maturity Model Integration. CMMI for Development*. Standard Version 1.2, August 2006. URL: http://www.sei.cmu.edu/cmmi

(Crossley, 1991) P. R. Crossley & J. A. Cook (1991): *Control 91*. Conference Publication 332, IEEE International Conference, March 1991, Edinburgh, U.K.

(CTE/ES, 2007) Razorcat Development GmbH: *CTE for Embedded Systems*, URL: http://www.razorcat.com

(CTE/XL, 2000) Lehmann, E. & Wegener, J. (2000): *Test Case Design by Means of the CTE XL*. Proc. 8. Europ. Int. Conf. on Software Testing, Analysis & Review (EuroSTAR 2000), Copenhagen, Denmark.

(Farkas+01, 2007) Farkas, T. & Röbig H. (2007): *Automatisierte, werkzeugübergreifende Richtlinienprüfung zur Unterstützung des Automotive-Entwicklungsprozesses*. M. Conrad, H. Giese, B. Rumpe, B. Schätz (Ed.): Proceedings of the Dagstuhl-Workshop MBEES: Modellbasierte Entwicklung eingebetteter Systeme III., Informatics-Report 2007-01, Technical University Braunschweig, January 2007, Dagstuhl, Germany.

(Farkas+03, 2007) Farkas, T. & Grund, D. (2007): *Rule Checking in Model Based Development of Safety Critical Software and Information Technical Systems*. 8th International Symposium on Autonomous Decentralized Systems (ISADS 2007), pp. 287-294, IEEE International Conference, March 2007, Sedona, USA.

(Farkas+06, 2006) Farkas, T., Hein, C. & Ritter, T. (2006): *Automatic Evaluation of Modeling Rules and Design Guidelines*. European Conference on Model Driven Architecture - Foundations and Applications (ECMDA2006), Lecture Notes in Computer Science, ISBN-10: 3540359095, Springer-Verlag, July 2006, Bilbao, Spain.

(Farkas+10, 2006) Farkas, T., Leicher, A. & Röbig H., et al. (2006): *Werkzeugübergreifende Konsistenzsicherung von Artefakten bei der*

Entwicklung softwarebasierter Systeme im Automobil. 4th Workshop on Automotive Software Engineering, Informatik 2006, Jahrestagung der Gesellschaft für Informatik, October 2006, Dresden, Germany.

(Form, 2006) Form, T. (2006): *Systems Engineering im Spannungsfeld von Architekturen und Prozesse*. 10. EUROFORUM-Jahrestagung Elektronik-Systeme im Automobil, Technical University Braunschweig, Munich, Germany.

(Hörmann, 2006) Hörmann, K., Dittmann, L., Hindel, B. & Müller, M. (2006): *SPiCE in der Praxis - Interpretationshilfe für Anwender und Assessoren*, dPunkt Verlag, ISBN-13 978-3898643412, Heidelberg, Germany.

(ISO15504, 1998) ISO International Organization for Standardization & IEC International Electrotechnical Commission (1998): *ISO/IEC TR 15504 - Information technology: Process assessment and the Assessment Requirements for CMMI.*

(ISO16949, 2002) ISO International Organization for Standardization & IEC International Electrotechnical Commission (2002): *ISO/TS 16949:2002 Automotive Quality Standard.*

(ISO61508, 1998) ISO International Organization for Standardization & IEC International Electrotechnical Commission (1998): *IEC-61508 Functional safety of electrical/electronic/programmable electronic safety-related system.*

(ISO9001, 2004) ISO International Organisation for Standardisation (2004): *ISO 9000 family of Quality management system. ISO 9001:2004.*

(ISO9126, 2001) International Organisation for Standardisation (2007): *ISO/IEC 9126, Software engineering — Product quality. Part 1-4,* URL: http://www.iso.org

(Jackman, 2005) Jackman, B. & Sanyanga, S. (2005): *A Software Component Architecture for Improving Vehicle Software Quality and Integra-*tion. Society of Automotive Engineers (SAE) Centenary World Congress, Detroit, USA.

(Kneuper, 2006) Kneuper, R. (2006): *CMMI: Verbesserung von Softwareprozessen mit Capability Maturity Model Integration.* dPunkt Verlag, ISBN-10: 3898643735, Heidelberg, Germany.

(Liggesmeyer, 2005) Liggesmeyer, R. & Rombach, D. (2005): *Software Engineering eingebetteter Systeme.* Spektrum Akademischer Verlag, 1st Edition, ISBN-10: 3827415330, Munich, Germany.

(MAAB, 2007) The MathWorks Inc. (2007): *The MathWorks Automotive Advisory Board (MAAB),* URL: http://www.mathworks.com/industries/auto/maab.html

(MATE, 2007) Stürmer, I., Kreuz, I., Schäfer, W. & Schürr, A. (2007): *The MATE Approach: Enhanced Simulink and Statfelow Model Transformation.* Proc. of MathWorks Automotive Conference, Jun. 19-20, Dearborn (MI), USA.

(MDA, 2003) OMG Object Management Group (2003): *Model Driven Architecture. MDA Guide Version 1.0.1,* Retrieved from http://www.omg.org/docs/omg/03-06-01.pdf

(Mercer, 2001) Kalmbach, R. & Dannenberg, J. (2001): *Automobiltechnologie 2010. Technologische Veränderungen im Automobil und ihre Konsequenzen für Hersteller, Zulieferer und Ausrüster.* Study of the HypoVereinsbank and Mercer Management Consulting, Munich, Germany.

(MISRA, 1998) MISRA Consortium, The Motor Industry Software Reliability Association (1998): *MISRA-C - Guidelines for the Use of the C Language in Vehicle Based Systems,* ISBN-10: 0952415690. URL: http://www.misra.org.uk

(MLSL, 2007) The MathWorks Inc. (2007): *Automotive Applications - Examples in Documentation, Simulink Demos,* MATLAB/Simulink/Stateflow, Part of the MATLAB Product, Release 2007a.

(MLSLSF, 2007) The MathWorks Inc. (2007): *MATLAB/Simulink/Stateflow*, Products in the Release 2007a. URL: http://www.mathworks.com

(MOF, 2003) OMG Object Management Group (2003): *Meta Object Facility 2.0 Specification*, Retrieved from URL: http://www.omg.org/cgi-bin/doc?ptc/03-10-04.pdf

(OCL, 2003) OMG Object Management Group (2003): *UML 2.0 OCL Specification*, Retrieved from URL: http://www.omg.org/docs/ptc/03-10-14.pdf

(OSLO, 2007) Fraunhofer Institute FOKUS (2007): *OSLO – Open Source Library for the Object Constraint Language (OCL)*. Retrieved from URL: http://oslo-project.berlios.de

(Ricardo, 2007) Ricardo UK (2007): *Mint—Style checker for Simulink and Stateflow*. Retrieved from URL: http://www.ricardo.com

(SCADE, 2007) Esterel Technologies, Inc. (2007): *SCADE Product Suite*. URL: http://www.esterel-technologies.com/products/scade-suite

(Telelogic, 2007) Telelogic, *DOORS Release 8.0*, URL: http://www.telelogic.com /products/doors

(VDI, 2005) VDI — Society for Automotive and Traffic Systems Technology (2005): *Electronic Systems for Vehicles*. 12th International Conference, Baden-Baden, Germany.

(VModel, 1997) EStdIT - Entwicklungsstandard für IT-Systeme des Bundes (1997): *V-Modell - Vorgehensmodell Kurzbeschreibung*. Retrieved from URL: http://www.v-modell.iabg.de

(Zander-Nowicka, 2006) Zander-Nowicka, J., Schieferdecker, I. & Farkas, T. (2006): *Derivation of Executable Test Models From Embedded System Models using Model Driven Architecture Artifacts - Automotive Domain*. Proceedings of the Dagstuhl-Workshop MBEES: Modellbasierte Entwicklung eingebetteter Systeme III., Informatics-Report 2006-01, Technical University Braunschweig, January 2006, Dagstuhl, Germany.

ADDITIONAL READING

Two additional resources providing information about product quality and process quality in the domain of embedded systems and vehicle manufacturing:

The German book *Embedded Systems – quality-oriented development* (Bender, 2005) aims to provide an authoritative overview of the state-of-the-art in the domain of embedded systems engineering with a strong emphasis on quality aspects: (Bender, 2005) Bender, K. et. Al (2005): *Embedded Systems – qualitätsorientierte Entwicklung*. ISBN-10: 3540229957, 2005, Springer-Verlag, Berlin Heidelberg New York.

The Toyota Way (Liker, 2004) gives a good overview for a general audience that explains manufacturing, management principles and business philosophy of the car manufacturer Toyota and its worldwide reputation for quality and reliability: (Liker, 2004) Liker, J.K. (2004): *The Toyota Way: 14 Management Principles from the World's Greatest Manufacturer*. ISBN-10: 0071392319, Mcgraw-Hill Professional, New York, USA.

Chapter XVI
Quality–Aware Model–Driven Service Engineering

Claus Pahl
Dublin City University, Ireland

Marko Bošković
University of Oldenburg, Germany

Ronan Barrett
Dublin City University, Ireland

Wilhelm Hasselbring
University of Kiel, Germany

ABSTRACT

Service engineering and service-oriented architecture as an integration and platform technology is a recent approach to software systems integration. Quality aspects ranging from interoperability to maintainability to performance are of central importance for the integration of heterogeneous, distributed service-based systems. Architecture models can substantially influence quality attributes of the implemented software systems. Besides the benefits of explicit architectures on maintainability and reuse, architectural constraints such as styles, reference architectures and architectural patterns can influence observable software properties such as performance. Empirical performance evaluation is a process of measuring and evaluating the performance of implemented software. We present an approach for addressing the quality of services and service-based systems at the model-level in the context of model-driven service engineering. The focus on architecture-level models is a consequence of the black-box character of services.

INTRODUCTION

With software services becoming a strategic capability for the software sector, a service engineering discipline needs to address service development problems based on suitably flexible modelling and composition support. An increasing need for flexibility in this area is caused by changing user requirements, evolving services, and varying deployment contexts. Software services are application that are provided 'as-is' at certain locations in order to be integrated into existing applications or composed to larger systems. Essential in this process are abstract descriptions or models of the service functionality and other service characteristics. This makes model-driven software development both a highly suitable, but actually also necessary framework to adequately develop service-based software systems. Composition and integration-oriented modelling has already been successfully utilised for model-driven services development. The high complexity of modern software makes its development costly and error-prone. Model-driven development (MDD) is an approach that deals with software complexity by making software models primary artefacts of the software development process. MDD utilises two aspects of models. Firstly, in various engineering disciplines, predictions about a software system can be made based on a model. Secondly, even complete implementations for different platforms and languages can be generated from models.

The aim of this chapter is to address quality aspects of model-driven service engineering. We address two specific facets of quality assurance for model-driven software development: the model-driven design and development of high-quality software and the identification of quality aspects in model-driven development. Some specific aspects that we discuss in the context of quality aspects in model-driven service development are:

- modelling and architecture are concept that are closely linked in the context of model-driven development and service-oriented architecture,
- patterns for the model-driven development of service architectures to structure models and to enhance the integration task,
- model-based design and analysis of specific quality aspects for service-based systems.

We aim to demonstrate that model-driven architecture and design of this specific type of service-based software systems can yield high-quality software. Based on an analysis of the state of the art of service engineering and its platform and application requirements supported by a case study analysis, we identify the central quality aspect pertinent to services. This analysis is necessary in order to justify techniques for the quality-aware model-driven service engineering. Factors that impact the quality are:

- network and platform characteristic impacting on for instance performance,
- service-orientation to enhance interoperability and reusability,
- evolution and change as inevitable factors impacting on maintainability.

Service engineering and service-oriented architecture as an integration and platform technology is a recent approach to service-based software systems integration. Quality aspects, however, have not been addressed in sufficient depth in this context. Our technical contribution is an architecture- and pattern-based model-driven service engineering framework that aims at high-quality models as well as quality implementations. While functionally oriented design patterns have been widely used to support the development of large-scale software systems, we combine a service-specific range of these patterns with distribution patterns, which directly impact service-specific quality aspects such as performance. We complement this architectural perspective with an empirical, model-driven performance evaluation technique. To provide trustworthy software, quality attributes have to be satisfied. Performance is a quality attribute that shows the degree to which a software system or its components meet the objectives for timeliness. Quality attributes such as performance are of central importance for the integration of heterogeneous, distributed service-based systems.

We start this investigation with an introduction to model-driven development and service engineering in Section 2. Quality aspects are outlined in Section 3. Architecture modelling notations are introduced in Section 4 and applied in the service architecture context in Section 5. Distribution patterns as an MDD solution are discussed in Section 6 and model-driven performance evaluation is investigated in Section 7.

MODEL-DRIVEN SERVICE ENGINEERING

Service-oriented architecture as the architectural methodology and the Web Services as the deployment platform have implications on a corresponding service engineering framework. This section motivates model-driven service engineering as our framework:

- We introduce service engineering as a software engineering discipline and service-oriented architecture as an architectural framework.
- Web services as a specific platform for service-oriented architecture within a service engineering context are introduced.
- An overview of model-driven service development aspects concludes this section.

This section aims to clarify the principles of service-based software systems and their development support through model-driven approaches.

Service Engineering

A service in the context of service-oriented architecture (SOA) is a software component provided at a given location. Services are usually used 'as-is', based on an abstract description published by the service provider in directories and used by potential clients to locate suitable services. Several aspects characterise the targeted service platform (Alonso et al., 2004):

- **Distribution:** This deployment aspect characterises the services platform as a distributed infrastructure.
- **Independent deployment:** This development aspect refers to the independent, black-box deployment of services where different organisations are involved as clients and providers. This requires suitable description techniques to communicate service requirements and properties.
- **Process-orientation:** The development of services is tightly linked to the notions of architecture and process-centric configuration. The composition at various levels ranging from business workflows to service processes is central (Allen & Garlan, 1997; Plasil & Visnovsky, 2002). Orchestration and choreography are two perspectives on service process composition (Alonso et al., 2004).
- **Software value chain:** The notion of a software value chain emphasises the step-wise process of software development based on layered modelling techniques covering all stages from client-orientation to implementation by adding to models until a deployable service product is realised (Weber, 2005).

The composition of services to orchestrated processes is a major concern in current Web service research (Allen & Garlan, 1997; Plasil & Visnovsky, 2002; Bass et al., 2003). These developments have strengthened the importance of architectural questions such as service composition and configuration.

Model-driven development (MDD) emphases automation and encourages model reuse. Service-oriented architecture focuses on reuse-as-is in service form. We propose here central cornerstones of a model-driven development framework for service-based software. Composition-centric modelling shall address services, processes, and layered reuse in order to improve quality for instance in terms of maintainability. We have identified a number of aspects by reviewing case studies, which are facets that characterise the framework and that reflect factors that have impacted the design of our proposed development approach.

- Rigorous and formal foundations – the foundations of the modelling notation and techniques in terms of formal models.
- Service development and deployment process – the software process lifecycle with its stages and activities based on MDD.
- Development methods and techniques – composition-centric modelling and service architecture to support the activities.
- Standards and interoperability – the technology environment with its opportunities and constraints focusing on model and service interoperability.

Model-Driven Development

The general idea of model-driven development (MDD) is to introduce a model as a first-class entity. With models, the development focus is moved to the problem domain. Models often enable the exploitation of formal mathematical methods. With abstraction, the understanding of the problem and its realisation in a software system can be improved. Often, a complete implementation can be generated without discontinuities (Selic, 2003). Model Driven Architecture (MDA) is one approach for MDD initiated by the OMG

(OMG, 2003), a consortium of software vendors and users. The MDA initiative consists of three complementary ideas (Selic, 2003):

- direct representation to shift the focus of software development away from technology toward the ideas and concepts of the problem domain,
- automation to mechanize the relation of semantic concepts from a problem domain and from an implementation domain,
- open standards to enable interoperability, often in an application-specific context to close the semantic gap between domain problems and implementation technologies.

Our aim is to enable the evaluation of service performance when the primary artefact is a service (or service process) model.

Model-Driven Service Engineering

Modelling can support architectural questions that arise in service-oriented architecture. Behaviour and interaction processes are central modelling concerns for service-based software architectures. Fig. 1 illustrates how a UML activity diagram can be used to express a service orchestration. Four services that provide e-learning activities – system login, lecture participation, lab participation, and system logout – are orchestrated into a process starting with a login, then allowing a user to iteratively choose between lecture and lab activities, before logging out.

Explicit descriptions and exchangeable models enable developers and clients of services to create reliable service architectures using tool support. A model-driven development approach can even be utilised to support automated code generation and performance analysis. Assuming that concrete, provided services are already attached to each service element, then an executable WS-BPEL process for the Web service platform

Figure 1. Service process modelled using a UML activity diagram (©2007 Claus Pahl. Used with permission)

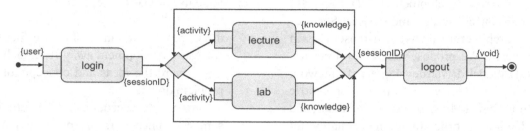

can be automatically generated. As we are going to demonstrate later on, the service composition model can be instrumented for empirical performance analysis and executable processes including performance monitoring functionality can be generated.

Model-Driven Service Engineering Case Study

The techniques of our framework shall be illustrated in the context of a re-engineering of the IDLE case study system as a service-based software system. IDLE is the Interactive Database Learning Environment – a Web-based learning and training system for database modelling and programming (Pahl et al., 2004). IDLE is a challenging application in terms of its need to provide multimedia and interactivity across a distribute server and user base. It allows us to focus on three essential quality aspects of service-based software systems: performance, reusability, and maintainability. We illustrate quality-aware model-driven service engineering using a recent re-engineering of IDLE as a fully service-oriented infrastructure.

QUALITY IN SERVICE-BASED SOFTWARE SYSTEMS

An analysis of the IDLE case study software system and other systems based on a literature review shall clarify quality considerations in the context of model-driven service engineering. This section

- aims to identify system-critical quality aspects and their determining factors from an empirical analysis of IDLE,
- evaluates the IDLE case study findings in the context of existing literature and discusses the requirements for quality-aware model-driven service engineering,
- introduces quality aspects in software systems, focusing on maintenance and performance as two specific quality attributes.

As individual quality attributes vary in the way they can be described, measured and analysed, we are not able to discuss all attribute-specific techniques in detail. We have selected attributes relevant to SOA as an integration technique – such as maintainability, reusability, interoperability and performance – and illustrate the common and generic features of our framework using these attributes. Before looking at IDLE, we introduce the quality and performance principles.

ISO 9126 Software Engineering – Software Product Quality

The ISO/IEC 9126 standard on software product quality (ISO, 2001) defines a two-part model for software product quality consisting of quality attributes (internal quality and external quality) and quality in use aspects.

- The first part of the model specifies six characteristics for internal and external quality, which are further subdivided into subcharacteristics. The six categories are functionality, reliability, usability, efficiency, maintainability, and portability. The subcharacteristics are manifested externally when the software is used as a part of a computer system, and are a result of internal software attributes.
- The second part of the model specifies four quality in use characteristics. The quality in use characteristics are effectiveness, productivity, safety and satisfaction. Quality in use is the combined effect for the user of the six software product quality characteristics.

In principle, the internal quality determines the external quality and external quality determines quality in use.

- Internal metrics measure the software itself. Internal metrics are those which do not rely on software execution (static measures).
- External metrics measure the behaviour of the computer-based system that includes the software. External metrics are applicable to running software.
- Quality in use metrics measure the effects of using the software in a specific context of use. Quality in use metrics are only available when the final product is used in real conditions.

IDLE Software Quality

We use the IDLE system to illustrate our approach (Pahl et al., 2004). IDLE is based on a Web software architecture that provides a range of educational services:

- It is a multimedia system that uses different mechanisms to provide access to learning content, e.g. Web server and a (synchronised) audio server.
- It is a composite, interactive system that integrates components of a database development environment (a design editor, a programming interface, and an analysis tool) into a teaching and learning context.
- It is a constructive environment in which learners can develop their database applications, supported by shared storage and workspace facilities and knowledge-level interactions between learner and system.

A comprehensive discussion of all quality aspects is beyond the scope of this chapter. However, some specific aspects shall be singled out.

- Portability. In particular interoperability shall be addressed. We identify two dimensions – generic, often middleware-induced and domain-specific – that are relevant for IDLE. On the architectural levels these are captured through architectural styles and reference architectures. Architectures suitable to be supported by the Web services platform need to be considered. Additionally, in order to allow specific components to be reused or exchanged, compliance with domain-specific reference architectures such as the Learning Technology System Architecture standards (LTSA) might be required. A current problem is the integration of components and content of the system into a national learning resource repository that allows these resources to be shared among third-level institutions. Interoperability is an absolute necessity, but other qualities such as reliability and performance are important as well.

- Maintainability. IDLE is a system that has been developed over a period of more than 10 years in several phases. Maintainability has been a critical problem due to high fluctuation of developers and an often experimental style of development driven by research aspects. Model-driven development can here be a contributor to improved maintainability. A number of different Internet-based technologies have been used in IDLE's implementation, ranging from audio processing with specific formats and servers to Java servlet-based middleware applications and storage solutions. An integrated infrastructure based on Web services is a current re-engineering problem in order to achieve maintainability and scalability. Knowledge-level interactions of users with the system using subject-specific editors and processing tools have equally made maintenance difficult. Only semantically enhanced information architectures and models can provide solutions here.
- Efficiency. IDLE as a bandwidth-demanding, distributed service-based Web software system is due to its needs arising from distributed multimedia delivery of content a system where performance is a critical factor. Performance evaluation – an aspect of the efficiency category – is important in order to provide users with a satisfactory usage experience.

In other distributed and Web-based applications, other qualities might be equally important – security and availability are two typical examples – but we have decided to focus in the ones relevant to IDLE, since a comprehensive account is beyond the scope of this chapter.

Discussion of Quality Aspects

Quality in the context of service-based software development is different from traditional software development and implementation. Services are black-box entities, i.e. they are used as-is. Determining or observing qualities through the inspection of service internals is in general not possible and would violate the principle of service computing. Consequently, quality needs to be considered at the architectural level. In particular, service compositions and service activations across a network, possibly distributed infrastructure are important and determine the categories we have singled out, i.e. portability, maintainability, and efficiency.

We can identify a number of central quality aspects pertinent to services. Factors that impact the quality are:

- internal, i.e., development and lifecycle-oriented static attributes:
- portability and reusability as a consequence of service-orientation and architectural style compliancy,
- maintainability as a consequence of model-driven controlled evolution and change,
- external, i.e. deployment- and execution-oriented observable attributes:
- performance as a consequence of for instance network characteristics,

Specific techniques of model-driven service engineering in the context of those specific quality categories are:

- modelling of architecture constraints in the form of styles and reference architectures addressing portability,
- patterns for structured model-driven development addressing maintainability,
- analysis and evaluation of quality-aware models addressing performance.

A sufficiently rich and tailored modelling language is necessary to adequately address and achieve quality for service-based systems at the architecture model level, which is outlined in the next section.

ARCHITECTURAL MODELLING

Before addressing the specific aspects architecture constraints, architecture patterns and performance evaluation, we introduce some basic elements of a notation that we use for architecture modelling.

The objective of software architecture (Bass et al., 2003) is the separation of computation and communication. Architectures are about components (i.e. loci of computation) and connectors (i.e. loci of communication). This allows a developer to focus on structures and the dynamics between components separately from component implementation. Various architecture description languages (ADLs) and modelling and development techniques have been proposed (Medvidovic & Taylor, 1997; Garlan & Schmerl, 2006; Cuesta et al., 2005; Oquendo et al., 2005). An architectural model captures common concepts found in a variety of architectural description languages: components provide computation, interfaces provide access to black-box components, and connectors provide connections between components.

Although UML is the most widely used modelling language, we use a mix of notations here. Textual notations are common for architectural description languages; we use them for instance for specific aspects such as architectural types and interaction behaviour. UML is the predominant notation for model-driven development; we use UML often as a visualisation of textual model specifications to emphasise the link to model-driven development. We use the textual notations as they demonstrate the link to formal specification notations and their underlying mathematical theories, such as process calculi or description logics, which is important if reasoning capabilities are to be exploited.

An Architecture Ontology

At the core of the notation is an architecture ontology that defines the central concept of the modelling notation. The central concepts are five core types of architectural elements

Configuration, Component, Connector, Role, Port

These are all derived from a general concept called *Element* that captures all architectural notions.

Components und connectors are the core elements of architecture descriptions. Components encapsulate computation and connectors represent communication between the components. Components can communicate through ports. Connectors connect to these ports, whereby the connection can play a specific role. Configurations are compositions of components and connectors with their ports and roles.

The vocabulary of the five elements shall be defined formally in terms of a simple logical formulation. This is loosely based on description logics, which often act as formal models of ontology languages such as the Web Ontology Language OWL.

$$Component \lor Connector \lor Role \lor Port \lor Configuration \subseteq Element$$

and

$$Configuration = \exists hasPart . (Component \lor Connector \lor Role \lor Port)$$

$$Component = Element \land \exists hasInterface . Port$$

$$Connector = Element \land \exists hasInterface . Role$$

The subset relation expresses subsumption, i.e. the subclass-superclass relationship. The predicates hasPart and hasInterface are predefined relationships between architecture elements. For instance, a configuration has parts such as component, connector, role or port. The existential qualifier describes that these components might exist. In terms of architecture models, these elements are types, i.e. are meta-level constraints for a concrete architecture.

Service Architectures, Processes and Dynamic Dependencies

Process and interaction behaviour is an essential part of modelling software architectures (Plasil and Visnovsky, 2002), in particular for service-based software systems. Interaction processes are central for the understanding of the behaviour of a software system. For instance, (Kazman et al., 2000) use scenarios – descriptions of interactions of a user with a system – to operationalise requirements and map these to a system architecture. We have extended the notion of interaction and also considered system-internal interactions. We also allowed interaction processes to be composite. Interaction process descriptions are forms of dependencies between components based on the connectors that need to be captured and addressed explicitly.

A service is defined as a coherent set of operations. An abstract service interface description is usually available. More recently, research has focussed on the composition of service to processes (Alonso et al., 2004). Existing components can be reused and assembled to form business or workflow processes. The principle of architectural composition that we look at here is process assembly.

Architecture Modelling Notation

We introduce a notation for the architectural modelling of service compositions and interaction that extends the previous structural focus of the architecture ontology. Our objective is to identify features of an architectural engineering language for services. This could be mapped or embedded into a full-scale architecture description language (ADL). Interaction behaviour for architecture configurations is an important feature for service architectures. Process calculi are often used in ADLs to express this type of information. Two elements define our notation.

- Firstly, a description notation is needed to capture architectural properties of a service-based software system.
- Secondly, the notation is complemented by modelling and analysis techniques.

The notation is defined in terms of the π-calculus (Sangiorgi & Walker, 2001) for two reasons. Firstly, a simulation notion allows us to formalise the transformation into executable code – for instance for empirical performance evaluation and instrumentation. Secondly, mobility is similar to changes in context – which gives us a formal framework in which to define change and address maintainability. We have introduced a new notation in order to tailor the π-calculus: firstly, to hide some of the more mathematical constructs and, secondly, to provide a focused set of operators for service composition.

The basic element describing process activity is an action. Actions are combined to process expressions. Given a service x and data item a, actions can be divided into invocations *inv x (a)* of other services and activations receive *rcv x (a)* and reply *rep x (b)* through other services. The process combinators are:

- Sequences are represented by the ';'-notation $a;P$, meaning that action a is executed and the system transfers to the remainder in the form of process P where the next action of P is executed.
- Choice means that one a_i from *choice* $a_i;P_i$ $(i=1,..,n)$ is chosen.

- Multichoice **mchoice** $a_i;P_i$ ($i=1,..,n$) allows any number of the processes $a_i;P_i$ to be chosen and executed in concurrently.
- Iteration **repeat** P executes process P an arbitrary number of times.
- Parallel composition **par** (P_1,P_2) executes processes P_1 and P_2 concurrently.

Additionally, process abstractions shall be introduced. The following example introduces *Coach* as an abstraction, which is defined as a repeated choice of three individual actions (one of which is a sequence). Results of invocations can be assigned to variables.

$Coach :=$ **repeat** (**choice** (**rcv** *getPref*();
  rep *getPref*(*prefInfo*),
    rcv *setPref*(*prefInfo*), *uri* =
      inv *locator* (*resource*)))

We cover the different aspects of architectural interaction modelling with this notation. Workflow operators are directly integrated as operators. An architectural design pattern can be formulated as an expression of a number of concurrently executing processes. Reference architectures and styles can be modelled on the level of abstractions in terms of the architecture ontology.

The architecture modelling notation is complemented by modelling and analysis techniques that suit the architectural engineering needs. A notion of satisfaction is needed to capture equivalence and refinement – an essential element of the modelling aspect. A simulation definition, adopted from the π-calculus, satisfies this requirement for the processes. A simulation needs to match all actions of the original process in the same ordering.

Modelling Approach: Overview

We have used textual notations for both the architecture ontology and also the behavioural specification constructs. Both could have been represented in terms of UML diagrams such as class and activity diagrams, with some OCL extensions. In order to clarify the formal background of these aspects, we have opted to represent them in terms of logics and process calculi notations.

The outline modelling notation support the three aspects identified earlier on. These three will be addressed in depth in the next three sections.

- A Styles and Reference Architectures Section aims at the internal attributes portability, interoperability and also reusability questions at the design level. Domain-specific and middleware-induced architectural constraints will be investigated.
- A Patterns Section looks at patterns in the form of architectural, workflow and distribution patterns with two aims: firstly, to deal with maintainability at design level; secondly, to address performance and in principle also reliability, availability and other external attributes at the code level.
- An Instrumentation Section looks at performance as a specific external attribute at the code level. Explicit instrumentation is an addition to the architecture modelling in terms of constraints and patterns.

Deployment and execution of instrumented code will also be addressed briefly, although our focus is on the modelling aspects.

SERVICE ARCHITECTURE: STYLES AND REFERENCE ARCHITECTURES

A central contributor to quality at architectural level is reuse. The reuse of architecture and components leads to better architectures in two aspects:

- maintainable through well understood structural and behavioural aspects,

- interoperable through standards-compliancy in terms of architectural aspects.

Architectural styles and reference architectures are related concepts that both constrain architectures, although with different objectives.

- Architectural Styles. We look at generic styles, like pipe-and-filter, which introduce a vocabulary of architectural element types with specific structural properties in terms of connectivity. The aim is to support interoperability and reuse from an internal, middleware- and platform-oriented perspective.
- Reference Architectures. We look at domain-specific reference architectures such as the IEEE Learning Technology System Architecture LTSA for learning technology systems. Their aim is often to support interoperability and reuse from an external, cross-organisational perspective.

The Architecture Ontology from Section 4.1 provides here the central notation.

Software architectures often act as a bridge between the client-oriented requirements and the software implementation-oriented design stages. The architectural style language for service architectures is directly based on the architecture ontology presented earlier. The style language is structural and connectivity-oriented. Styles are abstract models that aim to either

- reflect quality high-level design of software systems, i.e. aim typically at internal quality attributes, or
- constrain towards specific middleware and platform technologies, i.e. aim at interoperability.

They are therefore an integral part of a quality-aware model-driven service architecture framework.

Architectural Styles Principles

Architectural styles are reusable, recurring patterns in software architectures that are proven to have specific quality attributes (Abowd et al., 1995; Spitznagel et al., 1998; Baresi et al; 2004; Cortellessa et al., 2006; Giesecke, 2006). Typical examples are client-server, n-tiered, or pipe-and-filter architectures. These architectures share a common vocabulary, defining the elements of the architecture, and common constraints, defining the structural and behavioural restrictions that might apply.

Most ADLs focus on the component and connector view, i.e. model a system in terms of the components that will be implemented and executed and their connectivity. An architectural style language for this context needs to provide a type language – such as our architecture ontology – that allows basic element types – such as component, connector, or port – to be instantiated. The possibility to augment these types by structural and behavioural constraints is another necessary part of a style language.

Architectural Style Modelling

Defining architecture styles is actually done by extending the basic vocabulary of core types from the architecture ontology. The subsumption relationship serves to introduce the specific types that form an architectural style. This shall be illustrated using the pipe-and-filter style. We start with an extension of the hierarchy of architecture types in order to introduce style-specific components and ports:

$$PipeFilterComponent \subseteq Component$$
$$PipeFilterPort \subseteq Port$$

These new elements shall be further detailed and restricted to express their semantics. We distinguish three types of pipe-filter components, *DataSource*, *DataSink* and Filter. Their respective connectivity through input and output ports is defined as follows:

$$DataSource = \leq 1\ hasPort \wedge \exists\ hasPort . Output$$
$$DataSink = \leq 1\ hasPort \wedge \exists\ hasPort . Input$$
$$Filter = =2\ hasPort \wedge \exists\ hasPort . Input \wedge \exists\ hasPort . Output$$

DataSource, *DataSink*, and *Filter* are defined as components of a pipe-and-filter architectural style. Each of these components is characterised through the number and types of component ports using so-called predicate restrictions on a numerical domain and the usual concept descriptions. The expression $\leq n$ is used to express *hasPort.*($n \mid n \leq 1$) for instance. In addition to these more structural conditions that define the connections between the component types, a number of semantic constraints can be formulated that further refine the initial enumeration of pipe-filter components.

- Disjointness requires the individual components to be truly different:

$$DataSouce \wedge DataSink \wedge Filter = \perp$$

- Completeness requires pipe-and-filter components to be made up of only the three specified types:

$$PipeFilterComponent = DataSource \vee DataSink \vee Filter$$

Reference Architectures

Reference architectures are high-level specifications representing common structures of architectures specific to a particular domain or platform. If they exist, they can play an essential role in the architectural definition of a software system. Theys often emerge in an abstracted and standardised form from successful architectures. Reference architectures define accepted structures and processes that help to build maintainable and interoperable systems. In our context, these architecture abstractions can be represented similar to architectural styles, i.e. at a meta-level in terms of architectural element types and their properties. What we add to our illustration of reference architectures is the behavioural perspective. We allow them to be described in terms of service interactions.

In the context of educational software systems, the Learning Technology Standard Architecture LTSA provides a service-oriented reference architecture (IEEE, 2001). It captures common structural and behavioural features of learning technology systems. We can describe IDLE's architectural characteristics using the LTSA.

- An abstract structural representation of the LTSA in a notation resembling UML class diagrams can be found in Fig. 2. In terms of the architecture ontology, we would describe as follows for the component definition.

$$LearnerEntity \vee Delivery \vee Evaluation \vee$$
$$Learning\ Resources \vee Coach \vee LearnerRecords$$
$$\subseteq Component$$

- The interaction behaviour (of the delivery parts) of the LTSA in terms of the interaction calculus can be described as follows.

LearnerEntity : =
prefInfo = **inv** *getPref* (); **inv** *setPref* (*alter*(*prefInfo*));
learnRes = **inv** *multimedia* ()
Coach :=
repeat (**choice** (**rcv** *getPref*(); **rep** *getPref*(*prefInfo*),
   rcv *setPref*(*prefInfo*), *uri* = **inv** *locator* (*resource*)))
Delivery :=
rcv *locator*(*uri*); *learnRes* = **inv** *retrvRes* (*uri*); **rep** *multimedia* (*learnRes*)
LearningResources : =
rcv *retrvRes*(*uri*); **rep** *retrvRes*(*retrieve*(*uri*))

An important goal of using a (service-oriented) reference architecture in our context is the identification of services in the original IDLE system:

Figure 2. A structural overview of the LTSA Reference Architecture (©2007 Claus Pahl. Used with permission)

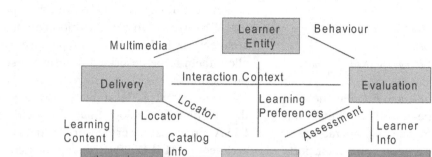

- Some of the components are already services – an SQL execution element that is part of the lab resources and delivery subsystem is an example.
- Some components (implemented as Java objects) are not services – a feedback system is not encapsulated as a service; another example is the workspace function. We have decided to realise the workspace function, which could have been integrated into either learning resources or learner records, as a separate service in the re-engineered system.

Quality-Driven Architecture

Architectures and the architectural styles and reference architectures they are based on have a critical impact on the quality of a software system. The use of styles in architecture design implies certain properties of software systems, as these styles are abstractions of successfully implemented systems that are usually easy to understand, to manage, to maintain etc. While of course functional properties of services are vital, non-functional quality aspects ranging from availability, performance, and maintainability

guarantees to costing aspects are equally important and need to be captured to clearly state the quality requirements. The reliability of a service-based system, the availability of services, and the individual service and overall system performance are often crucial. Links exist between functionally-oriented architecture models and quality properties of these systems (Garlan & Schmerl, 2006; Spitznagel & Garlan, 1998). A mere statement of required quality properties is therefore often not sufficient to actually guarantee these properties. We look at architectural styles and reference architectures to illustrate this point.

- A catalogue of architectural styles (Barrett et al., 2006) may be used by software architects to determine general patterns that would lead to architectures that exhibit some desired quality properties. Each of the styles in the catalog is associated with certain quality characteristics, which would be exhibited during the deployment and execution of system compositions. We return to this aspect later on in the context of patterns.
- Reference architectures are different in that large catalogues of these are usually not available. Reference architectures are often

prescribed. The quality benefit is in terms of interoperability and reuse. Associated qualities, as for styles, are not the primary aim.

Quality-driven development requires quality attributes to be evaluated and confirmed. As architectural styles are often extensible and composable, the qualities of newly derived styles cannot always be taken for granted. Only through empirical evaluations can these expected qualities be confirmed. For instance, the Goal-Question-Metric (GQM) approach to quality goal evaluation (Basili et al., 1994), a method which allows metrics to be derived from abstract quality criteria, can support this quality evaluation endeavour. Implemented systems can be evaluated using the metrics derived from the quality goals via GQM, but this approach can also be used to address internal quality attributes. We will return to this aspect later on in the specific context of performance evaluation where a specific combination of goals and metrics is used.

PATTERN-BASED MODELLING, ARCHITECTURE, AND DEVELOPMENT

The use of patterns in architecture design implies certain properties of services and systems, as these patterns are – similar to the higher-level styles and reference architectures – abstractions of existing system aspects that exhibit certain qualities. The implementation model of services in general and Web services in particular are based on the idea of service provider and service client being business partners. This constellation requires contracts to be set up, based on service-level agreements (SLAs). While of course functional properties of services are vital elements in these SLAs, non-functional aspects – ranging from availability, performance, and maintainability guarantees to costing aspects – are equally important and

need to be captured in SLAs to clearly state the quality obligations and expectations of provider and client. Explicit models can support SLAs for service-based systems deployment.

Based on the requirements for quality-aware model-driven service engineering, this section covers specific techniques for model-driven development with pattern-based modelling using a UML-compliant technique based on functional and distribution patterns for service architectures at its core. The impact of the techniques on quality – of both the models and the final system – is highlighted. Layered pattern modelling with a strong emphasis on distribution patterns emerges as the crucial element.

We distinguish workflow patterns (van der Aalst et al., 2003) and architectural design patterns (Garlan & Schmerl, 2006). Workflow patterns relate to connector types that are used in the composition of services or components – they are actually provided as built-in operators of the calculus. Architectural design patterns are structural and behavioural constraints formulated on a number of components with particular roles. We join here design patterns (Gamma et al., 1995) and architectural patterns (Garlan & Schmerl, 2006) into one architectural design pattern concept.

Service Composition Meta-Model

Our core notation for service configurations as interaction processes and remote activations was based on a process calculus. A service process based on the orchestration, or composition, of individual services can be also formulated in terms of the UML activity diagram in order to use a common visual notation. Its (simplified) definition as a process language based on activity nodes and edges is presented in Fig. 3.

The process-centric architecture modelling notation and these UML activity diagrams are related. Here, the structural connectivity in terms of service composition operators such as sequence, choice or parallel composition can be

Figure 3. Meta-model for UML activity diagrams (©2007 Claus Pahl. Used with permission)

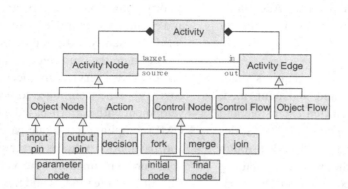

represented in terms of UML using control flow nodes and edges such as decision, fork, merge and join. Thus, we combine textual architecture descriptions (typical for ADLs such as ACME) and visualisations in terms of UML (which is also used extensively for architecture modelling).

Layered Service Systems Modelling

A layered conceptual service architecture model that is tailored towards the needs of service and process-oriented platforms shall address the different levels of abstraction in service-based architectures:

- Architectural design patterns are medium-scale patterns – usually referred to as design patterns or architectural frameworks.
- Workflow patterns are process-oriented patterns that represent common business or workflow processes in an application domain.

Some of these patterns qualify as distribution patterns, which are platform-oriented patterns with certain quality characteristics attached. These patterns are extensions of architectural styles. While the styles were more structurally

oriented, these patterns put an emphasis on interaction and processes. Similar to styles, their aim is reuse.

Design patterns are recognised as important building blocks in the development of software systems (Gamma et al., 1995). Their purpose is the identification of common structural and behavioural patterns in these systems. A rich set of design pattern has been described, which can be used to structure a software design at an intermediate level of abstraction. Design patterns in Web services architectures are discussed in (Topaloglu & Capilla, 2004). Usually, architectural patterns (such as client-server or model-view-controller) are distinguished from design patterns (such as factory, composite, or iterator). We see both forms of patterns as constraints on a system architecture, i.e. on services and on their patterns of interaction.

An example of an architectural design pattern for service architectures is the client-dispatcher-server pattern (Topaloglu & Capilla, 2004), represented in Fig. 4. In IDLE, a learner requests content from a resources server. This involves the learner (client), a coach (dispatcher), and the resources and delivery subsystem (server). The pattern is not identical to the structure found in the IDLE

Figure 4. Client-dispatcher-server design pattern (©2007 Claus Pahl. Used with permission)

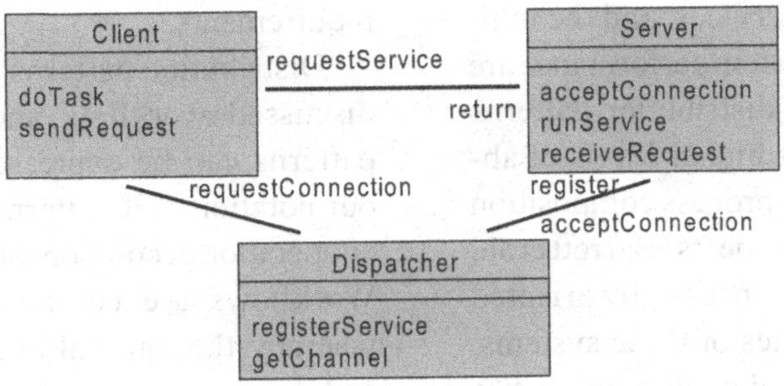

system. However, the client-dispatcher-server pattern is simulated by the composite process

par (*LearnerEntity,Coach,Delivery*)

of an IDLE reformulation in LTSA terminology, i.e. the pattern is a good abstraction of IDLE functionality. Abstracted pattern definitions such as client-dispatcher-server can act as building blocks in higher-level architectural specifications. Patterns are defined as process expressions and made available as process abstractions.

Workflow patterns are small-scale process patterns. These are small compositions of basic activities. The multichoice pattern is an example:

mchoice (*Lecture, Tutorial, Lab*)

expresses that a selection of IDLE services *Lecture*, *Tutorial*, and *Lab* can be used concurrently. Workflow patterns and the problems they cause when implemented in Web services infrastructures are described in (van der Aalst et al., 2003). To identify these patterns is important since often not all of them are supported by the implementation languages. In this case, predefined architectural transformations can be reused in an MDD environment that generates executable processes automatically.

The IDLE storage/workspace feature can be integrated as a service:

WorkSpace :=
choice (*repeat* (*rcv* retrieve (*resId*); *inv* provide (*res*));
repeat (*rcv* store (*resId, res*)))

This explicit storage and workspace service would require for instance the services *LearnerEntity* and *Delivery* to be modified in their interaction patterns.

The central aim of patterns is reuse, which leads to improved quality as a result. The reuse of architectural design is one issue. For instance, the client-dispatcher-server pattern is a common pattern that divides functionality and achieves loose coupling, which is a way to improve maintainability and replaceability. Reuse in this case also means reuse of predefined transformations, as the mchoice-based workflow pattern shows.

Service Distribution and Topology Modelling

While patterns in general can influence some of a system's quality characteristics, such as understandability or maintainability, for service-centric software systems specific properties arising from the distributed and cross-organisational context are of central importance. The reliability of a system, the availability of services, and the individual service and overall system performance are often crucial. We introduce distribution patterns to provide a framework for higher levels of abstraction beyond the service process composition that addresses these quality aspects (Barrett et al., 2006). Links exist between functionally oriented models and quality properties of these systems. A mere statement of required quality properties is often not sufficient to actually guarantee these properties. We look at distribution properties of service-centric software systems to illustrate this point.

Distribution, i.e. the consideration of locations of services in a complex system, affects qualities of the software systems such as reliability, availability, and performance. We use the term service topology to refer to the modelling of service compositions as collaborating entities under explicit consideration of the distribution characteristics.

Based on experience in designing and implementing service-centric software systems, a number of standard architectural topologies have emerged for distributed, service-based systems (Thone et al., 2002; Skogan et al., 2004; Vasko & Duskar, 2004). They include centralised configurations such as the hub-and-hpoke or decentralised ones such as peer-to-peer architectures. These standard topologies, or configurations, can be abstracted into distribution patterns for the SOA platform. Distribution pattern modelling expresses how a composed system is to be deployed in a distributed environment (Skogan et al., 2004).

The goal is to enable the generation of architecturally flexible Web service compositions that have the desired quality characteristics and whose quality characteristics can be evaluated and altered at design level – we will address the latter aspect in the Section 7. Having the ability to model, and thus alter the distribution pattern,

allows an enterprise to configure its systems as they evolve, and to meet varying non-functional requirements.

Distribution patterns and also the previously discussed workflow and architectural design patterns can be expressed in the same way in our notation. All patterns refer to the high-level cooperation of components, termed collaboration. Workflows are compositional orchestrations, whereby the internal and external messages to and from services are modelled. Distribution patterns are, similar to design patterns, abstract compositional choreographies, where the focus is on external message flow between services. A choreography expresses how a system would be deployed in a distributed environment. We denote these compositions as distributed compositions by annotating the composition operators, e.g. for the hub-and-spoke, which is often called Centralised, the specification

*Centralised = **d-par** (Hub, Spoke$_1$, . . . , Spoke$_n$)*

denotes a parallel distribution.

This annotation of a composition is of importance if, for instance, an executable service process is generated. In an MDD solution to service engineering, the predominant execution language for service compositions is the process execution language WS-BPEL. In WS-BPEL, process partners would be configured as distributed services. Semantically, we follow the architecture description language ACME (Garlan & Schmerl, 2006) here and introduce a type language for architectural elements, i.e. processes are typed. The identifiers *Hub* and *Spoke* are actually service types that can be instantiated, for instance by *Coach* and *Learner* services, respectively. The distribution annotation denotes a distribution constraint that will have to be satisfied by a concrete implementation. Although code generation is an integral element of MDD, in the context of the Web service platform, WS-BPEL is the predominant executable service composition language. The transformation from the activity diagrams (or the interaction calculus) is uncritical; we therefore keep our focus on modelling activities. It is worth noting that architectural modelling constraints such as styles and reference architectures are meta-level constraints on architecture, i.e. need to be considered during architecture modelling and need to be satisfied by concrete architectures, but do not have to be considered for code generation.

Our framework comprises a catalogue of distribution patterns (Barrett et al., 2006). Each of the patterns in the catalogue is associated with certain internal and external quality characteristics. The patterns in the catalogue are split into three categories: core patterns, auxiliary patterns and complex patterns. Core patterns represent the simplest distribution patterns most commonly observed in Web service compositions. Auxiliary patterns are patterns which can be combined with core patterns to improve a given quality characteristic of a core pattern, the resultant pattern is a complex pattern. This catalogue assists software architects in choosing a distribution pattern for a given application context. The catalog categories are briefly outlined below:

- Core patterns are *Centralised* and *Decentralised*.
- An auxiliary pattern is the *Ring*.
- Complex patterns are *Hierarchical, Centralised Ring, Decentralised Ring*, and *Centralised and Decentralised Hybrid*.

We describe one pattern that can be applied in IDLE in detail to illustrate distribution patterns and their quality relevance. We consider here the hub-and-spoke pattern. This pattern abstracts a system that manages a composition from a single location, the hub, which is normally the participant initiating the composition. The composition controller (the hub) is usually remotely accessed by the participants (the spokes). This is the most popular and usually default distribution configuration for Web service compositions (van der Aalst et al., 2003). We specify *Hub* and *Spoke* as components, i.e. $Hub \subseteq Component$ and $Spoke \subseteq Component$. Suitable completeness and disjointness constraints would need to be added.

$$Hub = \exists\, hasPort\,.\,Input \text{ and } Spoke = \exists\, hasPort\,.\,Output$$

explain that hubs receive incoming requests from spokes. Further constraints could limit the number of hubs to one, whereas spokes can be instantiated in any number. The dynamics can be specified as follows:

$$Centralised = \boldsymbol{d\text{-}par}\,(Hub, Spoke_1, \ldots, Spoke_n)$$

with

$$Hub = \boldsymbol{repeat}\,(\,\boldsymbol{rcv}\,invocation(\ldots);\, \boldsymbol{rep}\,reply(\ldots)\,)$$
$$Spoke_i = \boldsymbol{inv}\,result = invocation(\ldots)$$

Centralised is at activity level; *Hub* and *Spokes* are at interaction level. This could be specified in terms of UML Activity and Interaction Diagrams.

A sample application of the *Centralised* pattern in the IDLE context consists of the often widely distributed *Learner* client applications as the spokes and the centralised *Delivery* educational service provider as the hub.

The advantages of the *Centralised* or hub-and-spoke pattern in terms of quality aspects are:

- Composition is easily maintainable, as composition logic is all contained at a single participant, the central hub.
- Low deployment overhead as only the hub manages the composition.
- Composition can consume participant services that are externally controlled. Web service technology enables the reuse of existing services.
- The spokes require no modifications to take part in the composition. Web service technology enables interoperability.

The main disadvantages are:

- A single point of failure at the hub provides for poor reliability/availability.
- A communication bottleneck at the hub results in restricted scalability. SOAP messages have considerable overhead for message de-serialisation and serialisation.
- The high number of messages between hub and spokes is sub-optimal. SOAP messages are often verbose resulting in poor performance for Web services.
- Poor autonomy in that the input and output values of each participant can be read by the central hub.

All patterns have their advantages and disadvantages. The selection is determined by the context requirements. The hub-and-spoke pattern is typical for learning technology systems, for which maintainability and interoperability are central. Failure is not a highly critical problem and the number of users is predictable – which allows us to neglect two of the major disadvantages.

PERFORMANCE-DRIVEN MODELLING AND EVALUATION

We have looked at quality aspects of service-based software systems. Services as black-box entities limit this almost to the architectural level. In this section, however, we investigate a model-driven approach to the empirical quality evaluation of external quality properties. We focus on performance as one specific aspect.

We introduce an evaluation cycle, using a GQM approach for goal-to-measurement mapping. We extend service architecture modelling through an explicit and empirical way of dealing with quality. An empirical performance-oriented MDSE with instrumentation and measurement as example of one quality approach shall be presented.

Although model-based evaluation methods for performance exist, for example simulation and analytic methods, we choose an empirical approach here. Its benefits are accuracy and empirical validation. Our aim is to explore the potential of this technique under the given constraints given by the architecture-centricity of SOA and the black-box character of services to demonstrate the possibility of validated qualities.

Software Performance, Evaluation and Motivation

Performance is considered as the degree to which a software system or component meets its objectives for timeliness (Snodgrass, 1987). It can be evaluated with simulation techniques, with analytical modelling or using empirical methods (Lilja, 2000):

- Simulation is an imitation of a program execution. In simulations, only selected important parts of an execution are imitated. It is less expensive then building a full-scale software system for empirical evaluation. It is also flexible as changes can be dealt with easily if the simulation is derived automatically. However, simulation can suffer from a lack of accuracy.
- Analytical modelling is a technique where a system is mathematically described. Results of an analytical model can be less accurate than real-system measurements. However, analytical models are often easy to construct.
- Empirical evaluation is performed by measurements and metrics calculation. They provide the most accurate results as no abstractions are made.

We consider here model-based empirical performance evaluations in order to demonstrate the potential and limits of service-based quality evaluation through code-based measurement.

Empirical evaluation can be seamlessly integrated into a model-driven development methodology, as we will demonstrate.

While code-level instrumentations and evaluation techniques for services exist, we feel that in model-driven software development, observations of behaviour and their evaluation should be done in the terms of modelling constructs. Instrumentation for observing software should be done in terms of modelling constructs in order to prevent the software architecture from having to deal with transformation details. A necessary part of empirical performance evaluation is the execution data collection, which is achieved through instrumentation. The next subsection gives an overview of the instrumentation problem.

Instrumentation, Measurement and Evaluation

In software engineering, instrumentation is the process of adding software probes to a program for observing system behaviour and evaluating system properties (Snodgrass, 1987). Software probes are pieces of code for collecting data about the software execution. Generally, there are two techniques for collecting data about a program execution, sampling and event tracing:

- Sampling is a technique where parts of a program are sampled during its execution in some time interval – an example is sampling the program stack to follow program execution. It is a statistical technique in which a representative sample of the data about the program during execution is taken. An advantage of this approach is that the impact on the performance of the program does not depend on the execution of the program. However, collected samples are different from run to run. The possibility that infrequent events are missed is another drawback.

- Event tracing is a process of generating traces of events in the software execution. A program trace is a dynamic list of events generated by the program as it executes (Lilja, 2000). A trace contains the time-ordered events and can be used to characterize the overall program behaviour. Problems that can be encountered with event tracing are system perturbations due the measurement and the amount of resources that tracing requires. Each newly added probe causes execution overhead (performance) and event traces require resources (memory).

Due to its greater reliability, we utilised event tracing. We represent traces in a relational format using temporal database concepts. Temporal databases are databases that support a notion of time (Snodgrass, 1987). In contrast to conventional, non-temporal databases, in which only facts are stored, each fact stored in a temporal database is associated with some time information. These facts can be related to a valid time dimension and to a transaction time dimension (Snodgrass, 1988). The valid time dimension is related to the time when the fact was true in reality. The transaction time dimension is related to the presence of the fact in the database. Temporal databases which store only facts about the past are called historical databases (Sarda, 1990). Historical databases define two kinds of relations, event and interval relations. Interval relations are used for storing facts which were true for some time interval. Event relations are used for storing facts which were true at some particular point of time.

Model-Driven Service Development and Instrumentation

At present, most research in model-driven development is dedicated to simulation and performance prediction with mathematical analysis methods (Balsamo et al., 2004; Park & Kang, 2004). Nevertheless, predictions have to be validated when the software system is implemented and deployed. Validation should be based on modelling constructs as predictions are made according to them. Currently, timing behaviour is analysed based on source code constructs such as method execution time. In MDD, the level of abstraction is raised. Consequently, observations need to be based on modelling constructs such as states, activities, or methods.

We introduce an approach for the model-driven empirical performance evaluation of service-based software systems. We need to define a model-based language for service instrumentation. Instrumentation languages can enforce data collection in a relational format. We focus on compositions (orchestrations) of services to processes and address their performance behaviour. Our approach comprises:

- An instrumentation notation for service models that allows specific service model elements such as services or composition and flow operators to be annotated and marked as providing performance-relevant time information at execution time. We use UML activity diagrams to express service compositions and base our instrumentation language on this UML diagram format.
- Model-driven transformation techniques that generate executable code including the monitoring instructions necessary to record time information.
- A trace analysis query language that provides the ability to calculate performance metrics. The evaluation is based on the temporal databases theory (Zaniolo et al., 1997). The temporal databases theory relates facts stored in a relational format with time information. A relational program trace is a dynamic list of events and timing information generated by the program as it executes (Lilja, 2000).

The hypothesis of our approach is that the execution of a program, which is defined by modelling elements of a modelling language, can be characterised as either an event or an interval. The most important concepts in this basic package are thus interval trace and event trace. For instance, if an element of a modelling language models a part of the program execution which lasts for some time interval, it will be instrumented by a specialisation of the interval trace.

Model-Based Instrumentation Language

The instrumentation technique is developed around an instrumentation language. This is going to be integrated with the service modelling language, i.e. is an extension of the UML activity diagrams that we have used to model service orchestrations. Both the orchestration language and the instrumentation language can be defined in terms of the Meta Object Facility (MOF) (OMG, 2006). Our instrumentation notation comprises of two parts.

- Firstly, a basic trace package that captures the notion of traces and its two variants, event and interval traces, and operations to capture these traces (Fig. 5).
- Secondly, the instrumentation of activity diagrams using the MOF profiles extension mechanism (Fig. 6).

The basic trace package reflects the required time dimensions and the recording concepts. The activity diagram instrumentation utilises these concepts. This separation allows the basic instrumentation principles to be reused across a range of problem-specific or even model-specific applications. In the given instrumentation, actions such as the central elements of activity diagrams and all six control nodes are annotated. The execution of actions, which represent services at the model level, takes some time, i.e. an interval trace

Figure 5. Basic trace package (©2007 Marko Bošković. Used with permission)

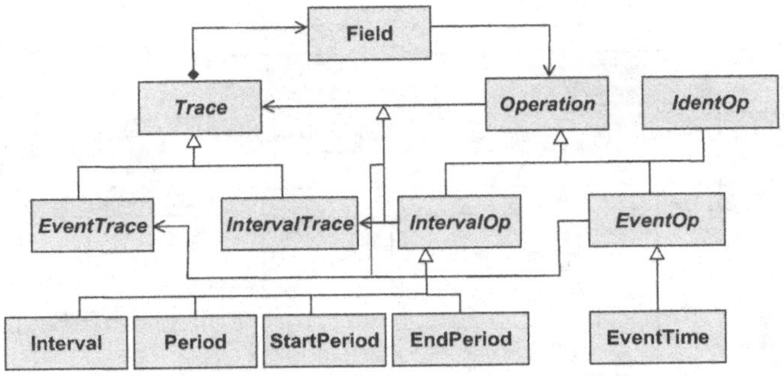

Figure 6. UML activity diagram instrumentation (©2007 Claus Pahl. Used with permission)

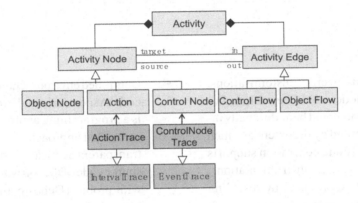

should be recorded at performance evaluation or execution time. We assume control flow decisions such as the start and end of the overall process, choices or mergers as instantaneous events.

Instrumentation Application

The application of the instrumented activity diagram is illustrated in Fig. 7. Two types of model elements – actions such as login or transfer and control nodes such as the start or the first decision point – are instrumented. An interval consisting of begin and end time of the service executions that implement the actions are recorded as a

consequence of this instrumentation. Events, i.e. individual time stamps, are recorded for the control nodes.

For the modeller and service architect, it is import to find an adequate instrumentation that provides answers to the relevant performance questions. For instance, in a particular situation only the (average or maximum) response times of particular services, such as the lecture and lab activity services, are of interest. Then, the instrumentation needs to reflect these requirements.

While we consider this instrumentation of actions and control nodes to be the standard case, the approach is actually flexible enough to

Figure 7. Application of the instrumentation to the IDLE activity selection process (©2007 Claus Pahl. Used with permission)

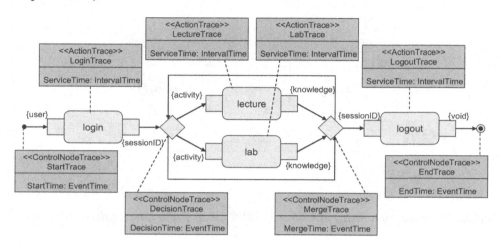

accommodate context-specific customisations. Some of the control nodes could be excluded or other modelling elements could be additionally included. This is only limited by the extent to which the transformation and code generation supports the different model element instrumentations. Some guidance could be provided by disabling the instrumentation of elements that are difficult to implement or whose analysis would not provide useful performance information.

Performance Monitoring

The actual implementation of the instrumentation is critical insofar it should be, firstly, easy to realise and, secondly, implemented without significant overhead. Aspects and interception techniques can be used to implement the instrumentation and data collection.

In the services context, often the problem arises that the addition of probes into the service implementation is not possible due to the nature of services as black-box software components. We therefore distinguish two scenarios:

- Controlled environments that allow access to code. Aspect Oriented Programming (AOP) is a programming approach, suitable for the controlled approach, which can be used for transparent software instrumentation. The source code of the software is here not mixed with probes (Debusmann & Geihs, 2003). Marenholz et al. (2002) use AspectC++ for the instrumentation of operating systems for debugging, profiling/measurement, and runtime surveillance/monitoring. AOP is a technique that enables the separation of instrumentation from the development of the core software functionality. With AspectJ and AspectC++, instrumentation can also be done by adding a transparent software layer to the application for collecting execution data.

- Open environments in which services are black-box components. For a transparent instrumentation of service systems, interceptors can be used. Interceptors are similar to AOP and can intercept method invocations to transparently instrument a program (Klar et al., 1991; Debusmann et al., 2002, Yeung et al., 2004). For instance, software probes are predefined and placed in stubs and skeletons during an interface description compilation (Debusmann et al., 2002). The measurement probes can be turned on and off at runtime. Diaconescu et al. (2004) introduce an approach where a transparent proxy layer for data collection is automatically generated at deployment time.

The JBoss Application Server, for instance, enables the transparent aspect-oriented addition of functionality. Its AOP features allow the interception of events and addition of trigger functionality based on those events. AOP, interceptors, and bytecode and platform instrumentation are approaches that enable the collection of data without influencing the functionality code. We can employ these ideas to collect data about the software execution at the model level as a separate concern.

The first step, however, is the generation of executable and instrumented code. Activity diagrams that model service orchestrations can be converted into executable WS-BPEL Web services processes if invocation information such as service location is added to the abstract service process description:

- AOP concepts are used to generate the instrumented executable service code.
- Interception mechanisms are used to add the instrumentation and data collection.

We suggest using the ATL transformation language and tool from the ATLAS project to transform activity diagrams into executable code. The instrumentation includes monitoring and data collection functionality. Data is stored in a temporal or historical database – or by using the time extensions of traditional relational databases. Fig. 8 shows a sample recording based on the instrumentation defined in Fig. 7.

Performance Evaluation

Performance-relevant information needs to be extracted from the basic times stored in the database in order to allow a software architect to assess the overall performance of individual services and also orchestrated service processes. Temporal and historical databases are usually extensions of traditional relational databases. SQL is therefore available as a query language to retrieve and aggregate information based on the recorded event and interval times. We argue that SQL is actually

Figure 8. Collected Data for Learning Activity Process Instrumentation (©2007 Claus Pahl. Used with permission)

LectureTrace: ServiceTime: IntervalTime	
2:22	2:45
3:03	3:12
3:15	3:29

DecisionTrace: DecisionTime: EventTime
2:19
2:50
3:01
3:10
3:35

sufficient as a query language to formulate the relevant performance assessment queries. More advanced solutions like data warehouses with their extended evaluation support are not required for typical performance assessments. Two central performance assessments issues are:

- Response time assessment: response times of activities are usually recorded as intervals. The SQL aggregate functions, such as average (AVG) or maximum (MAX), provide the relevant answers.
- Frequency and distribution of invocations: the distribution of invocations (workload) between the individual services can be determined based on the calculation of ratios between total numbers of invocations.

The database representation directly reflects the modelling layer, as the representation is generated from the model instrumentation. The queries are consequently formulated in terms of relevant model elements – which is one of the central objectives of our model-driven performance evaluation approach.

The average response time for service *Lecture* can be determined as follows:

SELECT AVG (ServiceTime)
FROM LectureTrace

The determination of the maximum time would be formulated in a similar way. In the context of SOA, where individual services are often provided by external organisations, this information is often part of contracts and service-level agreements.

The proportion of *Lecture* invocations in relation to all user selections (decisions) can also be formulated:

SELECT COUNT (ServiceTime) / COUNT (Decision-Time)
FROM LectureTrace, DecisionTrace

This allows a software architect to judge the frequency of individual service activations in typical application scenarios.

CONCLUSION

Since the service platform is based on a business model involving service-level agreements between providers and users, more than the service's functionality needs to be agreed upon. Internal qualities such as maintainability, but also external and observable quality attributes such as performance or security are of central importance for clients and providers.

Quality assurance is, however, a challenge as a consequence of the black-box character of services, at least from the client perspective. Service-oriented architecture (SOA) is an integration approach and consequently architecture-centric. Modelling in general and quality-aware modelling techniques in particular need to provide tailored service- and architecture-centric solutions.

In the context of this arising need to address quality for services in a model-driven service engineering discipline, we have investigated the crucial quality aspects and techniques that can be employed to actually address these through modelling activities at the service architecture level.

- Abstract architectural constraints in the form of styles and reference architectures guide architectural modelling towards interoperability and maintainability.
- Pattern-based modelling of service architectures is a further step towards reuse and maintainability.
- Empirical evaluation techniques, for instance for performance, complement the previous focus in internal quality attributes by external quality considerations.

The focus on one specific aspect, performance, in the evaluation context shows that although architectural approaches allow referring to and addressing a variety of qualities as far as modelling is concerned, more specific techniques are needed to evaluate these qualities. Performance, security, or maintainability require different approaches to be integrated in a quality-aware service engineering discipline.

As such a service engineering discipline is only emerging, we have discussed our findings as part of a roadmap to a comprehensive quality-aware service engineering approach. Although quality assurance is difficult to achieve due to the character of services, with the architectural modelling focus and the empirical evaluation we have suggested two ways of dealing with internal and external quality attributes of service-based software systems, respectively.

FUTURE RESEARCH DIRECTIONS

Model-driven development for service-oriented architecture (SOA) might initially seem easy to tackle since SOA is an integration approach at the software and system architecture level. Abstraction is already given and code generation seems easy due to the service platform principles and predominate execution languages. Difficulties, however, arise as this simplification becomes a problem if quality assurance is an issue.

SOA also creates other still unsolved problems for model-driven development (MDD).

- Modelling of service-based systems itself is intrinsically different from traditional software modelling. Service-based systems are process-centric compositions. Adequate modelling and architecture notations need to be provided for an MDD approach.
- Due to the heterogeneity of SOA targets, information integration is another integration dimension in addition to service-level integration. The SOA community already investigates semantically enhanced models and descriptions in the form of ontologies – for both information and service aspects. Besides consistency across applications, a higher degree of automation would be enabled through semantic enhancements. A similar trend can be observed in the context of MDD, where currently an ontology definition metamodel to support semantic modelling is being standardised by the OMG.

Quality-aware model-driven service architecture needs to be linked to the service platform in order to deliver validated quality guarantees. We have only introduced platform instrumentation and interception mechanisms briefly here, but an in-depth investigation would allow the trade-off, for instance between accuracy and overhead, to be discussed in detail.

More within the concrete framework of our approach than the semantic enhancements, a number of issues have remained unaddressed. We have only looked at performance as one of the highly important external, observable qualities of a service-based system. Due to the distribution of service systems and the openness of the service platform in terms of communications infrastructure, security is another important quality. Corresponding modelling concepts for security mechanisms ranging from encryption to access control to trust control need to be integrated. This is at least an equally complex endeavour to our solution of model instrumentation, monitoring and evaluation for performance considerations.

The idea of semantically enhanced models can lead to a solution in the security and trust context. Certified semantic descriptions of functional and quality properties of service and system, formalised in terms of ontologies, can support service-level agreements, even automated composition of services from different providers.

This, however, is a vision that is far from being investigated sufficiently.

REFERENCES

van der Aalst, W.M.P., Kiepuszewski, B., ter Hofstede, A.H.M. and Barros, A.P. (2003). Workflow Patterns. *Distributed and Parallel Databases*, *14*, 5–51.

Abowd, G., Allen, R. and Garlan, D. (1995). Formalizing style to understand descriptions of software architecture. *ACM Transactions on Software Engineering and Methodology*, *4*(4), 319–364.

Allen, R. and Garlan, D. (1997). A Formal Basis for Architectural Connection. *ACM Transactions on Software Engineering and Methodology*, *6*(3), 213–249.

Alonso, G., Casati, F., Kuno, H. and Machiraju, V. (2004). *Web Services – Concepts, Architectures and Applications*. London, UK: Springer-Verlag.

Baresi, L., Heckel, R., Thöne, S. and Varro, D. (2004). Style-based refinement of dynamic software architectures. *Proc. 4th Working IEEE/IFIP Conference on Software Architecture WICSA* (pp. 155–164).

Barrett, R., Patcas, L.M., Murphy, J. and Pahl, C. (2006). Model Driven Distribution Pattern Design for Dynamic Web Service Compositions. *International Conference on Web Engineering ICWE'06* (pp. 129-136).

Basili, V., Caldiera, G., and Rombach, D. (1994). The Goal/Question/Metric approach. *Encyclopedia of Software Engineering*, Volume I, 528–532. Los Alamitos, CA: Wiley.

Bass, L., Clements, P. and Kazman, R. (2003). *Software Architecture in Practice*. SEI Series in Software Engineering. Boston, MA: Addison-Wesley.

Cortellessa, V., Di Marco, A. and Inverardi, P. (2006). Software performance model-driven architecture. *Proc. ACM Symposium on Applied Computing SAC'06* (pp. 1218–1223).

Cuesta, C. E., del Pilar Romay, M., de la Fuente, P. and Barrio-Solorzano, M. (2005). Architectural Aspects of Architectural Aspects. *Proc. 2nd European Workshop on Software Architecture EWSA 2005*. Springer LNCS 3047.

Debusmann, M. and Geihs, K. (2003). Efficient and Transparent Instrumentation of Application Components using an Aspect-oriented Approach. *Proc. IFIP/IEEE Workshop on Distributed Systems: Operations and Management DSOM 2003* (pp. 209–220). Springer LNCS 2867.

Debusmann, M., Schmid, M. and Kroeger, R. (2002). Measuring End-to-End Performance of CORBA Applications using a Generic Instrumentation Approach. *Proc. 7th Int. Symp. on Computers and Communications ISCC '02* (pp. 181–186).

Diaconescu, A., Mos, A. and Murphy, J. (2004). Automatic Performance Management in Component Based Systems. *Proc. 1st Int. Conf. on Autonomous Computing ICAC'04* (pp. 214–221).

Gamma, E., Helm, R., Johnson, R. and Vlissides, J. (1995). *Design Patterns: Elements of Reusable Design*. Boston, MA: Addison Wesley.

Garlan, D. and Schmerl, B. (2006). Architecture-driven modelling and analysis. *Proc. 11th Australian Workshop on Safety Related Programmable Systems SCS'06*, volume 69 of Conferences in Research and Practice in Information Technology.

Giesecke, S. (2006). A Method for Integrating Enterprise Information Systems based on Middleware Styles. *Proc. International Conference on Enterprise Information Systems ICEIS'06*, Doctoral Symposium (pp. 24–37).

IEEE Learning Technology Standards Committee LTSC (2001). *IEEE P1484.1/D8. Draft Standard for Learning Technology - Learning Technology Systems Architecture LTSA.* IEEE Computer Society.

ISO/IEC. *ISO 9126 Software Engineering – Product Quality – Part 1: Quality Model.* Published Standard.

Kazman, R., Carriere, S.J. and Woods, S.G. (2000). Toward a Discipline of Scenario-based Architectural Evolution. *Annals of Software Engineering, 9*(1-4), 5–33.

Klar, V., Quick, A. and Soetz, F. (1991). Tools for a Model–driven Instrumentation for Monitoring. *Proc. 5th Int. Conf. on Modelling Techniques and Tools for Computer Performance Evaluation* (pp. 165–180).

Lilja, D. J. (2000). *Measuring Computer Performance: A Practitioner's Guide.* Cambridge, UK: Cambridge University Press.

Mahrenholz, D., Spinczyk, O. and Schroeder-Preikschat, W. (2002). Program Instrumentation for Debugging and Monitoring with AspectC++. *Proc. 5th Int. Symp. on Object-Oriented Real-Time Distributed Computing ISORC'02* (pp. 249–256).

Medvidovic, N. and Taylor, R.N. (2000). A Classification and Comparison Framework for Software Architecture Description Languages. *IEEE Transactions on Software Engineering, 26*(1), 70-93.

Object Management Group (2003). *MDA Model-Driven Architecture Guide V1.0.1.* OMG.

Object Management Group (2004). *MOF 2.0, OMG document ptc/04-10-15.* web: http://www.omg.org/cgibin/apps/doc?ptc/04-10-14.pdf.

Oquendo, F., Warboys, B.C., Morrison, R., Dindeleux, R., Gallo, F., Garavel, H. and Occhipinti, C. (2005). ArchWARE: Architecting Evolvable Software. *Proc. 2nd European Workshop on Software Architecture EWSA 2005.* Springer LNCS 3047.

Pahl, C., Barrett, R. and Kenny, C. (2004). Supporting Active Database Learning and Training through Interactive Multimedia. *Proc. Intl. Conf. on Innovation and Technology in Computer Science Education ITiCSE'04.*

Park, D. and Kang, S. (2004). Design phase analysis of software performance using aspect-oriented programming. *Proc. 5th Aspect-Oriented Modeling Workshop*, UML'2004.

Plasil, F. and Visnovsky, S. (2002). Behavior Protocols for Software Components. *ACM Transactions on Software Engineering, 28*(11), 1056-1075.

Sangiorgi, D. and Walker, D. (2001). *The π-calculus – A Theory of Mobile Processes.* Cambridge, UK: Cambridge University Press.

Sarda, N. (1990). Extensions to SQL for Historical Databases. *IEEE Transactions on Knowledge and Data Engineering, 2*(2), 220–230.

Selic, B. (2003). The Pragmatics of Model-Driven Development. *IEEE Software, 20*(5), 19–25.

Skogan, D., Grønmo, R. and Solheim I. (2004). Web Service Composition in UML. *Proc. 8th International IEEE Enterprise Distributed Object Computing Conference EDOC'2004* (pp. 47-57).

Snodgrass, R. (1987). The temporal query language tquel. *ACM Trans. Database Syst., 12*(2), 247–298.

Snodgrass, R. (1988). A Relational Approach to Monitoring Complex Systems. *ACM Transactions on Computer Systems, 6*(2), 157–196.

Spitznagel, B. and Garlan, D. (1998). Architecture-based performance analysis. *Proc. Conference on Software Engineering and Knowledge Engineering SEKE'98.*

Thöne, S., Depke, R. and Engels, G. (2002). Process-Oriented, Flexible Composition of Web Services with UML. *Proc. Joint Workshop on Conceptual Modeling Approaches for e-Business eCOMO 2002.*

Topaloglu, N.Y. and Capilla, R. (2004). Modeling the Variability of Web Services from a Pattern Point of View. *Proc. European Conf. on Web Services ECOWS'04* (pp. 128–138). Springer LNCS 3250.

Vasko, M. and Duskar, S. (2004). An Analysis of Web Services Flow Patterns in Collaxa. *Proc. European Conf. on Web Services ECOWS'04* (pp. 1–14). Springer LNCS 3250.

Weber, H. (2005). From Programme Engineering to Software Engineering. *Proc. Theory and Practice of Software Development TAPSOFT'2005.* (invited talk).

Yeung, K., Kelly, P.H.J. and Bennett, S. (2004). Dynamic Instrumentation for Java Using a Virtual JVM. *Performance Analysis and Grid Computing*, 175–187.

Zaniolo, C., Ceri, S., Faloutsos, C., Snodgrass, Subrahmanian, V. S. and Zicari, R. (1997). *Advanced Database Systems.* San Fransisco, CA: Morgan Kaufmann Publishers.

ADDITIONAL READING

Architecture and Service Ontologies
General Background

Baader, F., McGuiness, D., Nardi, D. and Schneider, P.P. (Eds) (2003). The Description Logic Handbook. Cambridge University Press.

A handbook on description logics that provides a comprehensive coverage of basics, extensions and applications of description logics, targeted at readers with some familiarity in formals aspects of computing.

Meyer, B. (1992). Applying Design by Contract. Computer, Oct. 1992, 40–51.

A seminal paper that outlines foundations and benefits of design-by-contract as a software design approach for the general computing audience.

Service-Specific Background

Lara, R., Stollberg, M., Polleres, A., Feier, C., Bussler, C. and Fensel, D. (2005). Web Service Modeling Ontology. Applied Ontology, 1(1), 77–106.

A research article introducing the Web service modelling ontology WSMO

DAML-S Coalition (2002). DAML-S: Web Services Description for the Semantic Web. Proc. First International Semantic Web Conference ISWC 2002, 279–291. Springer LNCS 2342.

A research article introducing the Web service modelling ontology OWL-S (formerly named DAML-S).

Semantic Web Services Language (SWSL) Committee (2006). Semantic Web Services Framework (SWSF). http://www.daml.org/services/swsf/1.0/.

A Web site that provides access to material (foundations and theory, specification, applications and case studies, tool support) on the Semantic Web Services Framework, which carries work started on OWL-S further.

Standards

Object Management Group (2006). Ontology Definition Metamodel, Submission (OMG Document: ad/2006-05-01). OMG.

An OMG Standard that defines the relationship between different knowledge representation frameworks or conceptual modelling languages such as ontology languages (OWL), topic maps, UML, and Entity-Relationship diagrams.

Pattern-Based Modelling
General Background

Kent, S. (2002). Model Driven Engineering. Proc. 3rd Int. Conf. on Integrated Formal Methods IFM '02, 286–298, Springer-Verlag.

A research article that introduces the principles of model-driven development.

Service-Specific Background

Schlingloff, B.-H., Martens, A. and Schmidt, K. (2005). Modeling and Model Checking Web Services. Electronic Notes in Theoretical Computer Science: Issue on Logic and Communication in Multi-Agent Systems, 126, 3–26.

A research article that investigates the principles of using formal methods (here model checking) to verify service system properties.

Selected Approaches

Dijkman, R. and Dumas, M. (2004). Service-oriented Design: A Multi-viewpoint Approach. Intl. Journal of Cooperative Information Systems, 13(4), 337–368.

This paper provides an example of a methodology to develop service-based software system.

Magee, J., Dulay, N., Eisenbach, S. and Kramer, J. (1995). Specifying Distributed Software Architectures. Proc. 5th European Software Engineering Conf. ESEC'95, Springer LNCS 989, 137–153.

A seminal paper on aspects on distributed systems and their formal specification.

Allen, R. and Garlan, D. (1997). A Formal Basis for Architectural Connection. ACM Transactions on Software Engineering and Methodology, 6(3), 213–249.

A seminal paper that provides a formal basis for architectural description languages.

Performance Evaluation
General Background

Hasselbring, W. and Reussner, R. (2006). Toward trustworthy software systems. Computer, 39(4), 91–92.

A short research paper introducing the context of software quality and trustworthiness of software.

Smith, C.U. and Williams, L.G. (2001). Performance Solutions: A Practical Guide to Creating Responsive, Scalable Software. Addison-Wesley, Massachusetts, Boston, USA.

A textbook that focuses on performance as a critical aspect in the development of software.

Selected Approaches

Balsamo, S., Marco, A. D., Inverardi, P. and Simeoni, M. (2004). Model-Based Performance

Prediction in Software Development: A Survey. IEEE Transactions on Software Engineering, 30(5), 295–310.

A survey paper that outlines a range of approaches to model-based performance predication.

Hollingsworth, J.K., Niam, O., Miller, B.P., Xu, Z., Goncalves, M.J.R. and Zheng, L. (1997). MDL: A Language And a Compiler For Dynamic Program Instrumentation. Proc. Int. Conf. on Parallel Architecture and Compiler Techniques PACT'97, 201–213. IEEE Comp. Society.

The paper describes a technique (based on a language and compiler) that can be used to instrument program with probes.

Liao, Y. and Cohen, D. (1992). A Specificational Approach to High Level Program Monitoring and Measuring. IEEE Transactions on Software Engineering, 18(11), 969–978.

A research paper that introduces a high-level, model-oriented approach to instrument (monitor and measure) program properties.

Petriu, D.B. and Woodside, M. (2004). A metamodel for generating performance models from UML designs. Proc. 7th Int. Conference on the Unified Modelling Language: Modelling Languages and Applications, 41–53. Springer LCNS 3273.

The paper describes a metamodel that allows the definition of performance models for existing UML-based software models.

Standards

Object Management Group (2005). UML Profile for Schedulability, Performance, and Time Specification, OMG document formal/05-01-02.

OMG Standard that defines notions in the context of performance and related software qualities. It uses the UML profile mechanism to define a performance extension to an existing model.

The Open Group (1998). Application Response Measurement (ARM). Technical Standard, Version 2, Issue 4.0.

The ARM defines the collection of performance data. It provides interfaces to library components for performance measurement.

Chapter XVII
Model–Driven Integration in Complex Information Systems:
Experiences from Two Scenarios

Sven Abels
Abelssoft GmbH, Germany

Wilhelm Hasselbring
University of Kiel, Germany

Niels Streekmann
OFFIS – Institute for Information Systems, Germany

Mathias Uslar
OFFIS – Institute for Information Systems, Germany

ABSTRACT

This chapter introduces model-driven integration in complex information systems by giving two practical examples. It relies on the experiences the authors have made in two different research projects at the public utilities domain. The chapter starts with a short introduction of the general problem domain and it gives detailed background information about the current state of the art in model-driven integration. Afterwards, the two research projects are introduced. The purpose of the first project (MINT) was to provide an integration approach allowing interoperability among several different legacy systems. Hence, the project itself was only acting as a "bridge" between the systems. The second project (DER) was built from scratch and got the challenge of integrating several existing third party systems into the newly designed system. In this project, the main system is a core element and only needed to integrate existing legacy systems for specific tasks.

1. INTRODUCTION

Business processes today usually involve several different information systems. A study by Marx Gómez and Brehm in 2007 with 658 participating SME companies in Germany turned out that 90.3% of all companies are using more than one product for their financial business needs (i.e. ERP related tasks). More then 53% are using 4 or more products and almost 15% of all companies are using 10 or more different products, most of them being produced by different software vendors (Details can be found in Marx Gómez & Brehm, (2007). Considering those figures reveals the strong need for integrating different software systems into a coherent solution. This is usually achieved by creating interoperability between software systems. As defined by the IEEE, interoperability is „the ability of two or more systems or components to exchange information and to use the information that has been exchanged" IEEE, (1990). At the I-ESA 2007 conference, Jeusfeld argues that this topic is often neglected in the design of modern information systems (Jeusfeld, (2007)). For example, he describes that the well known Software Engineering Body of Knowledge (Swebok, (2004)) mentions interoperability only twice, once as an example for a system requirement and the second time as a title of a standard library of data models. Interoperability and the possibility to integrate different heterogeneous systems in a coherent architecture is, however, a key of the MDA strategy as defined by the OMG (Object Management Group) (OMG, (2003)). The following sections focus on this complex area and they put it in context of the model-driven software development (MDSD). This chapter demonstrates how to cope with integration and interoperability issues by explaining the intermediate results of two research projects, namely MINT and DER.

The examples, used in this chapter are settled in the public utilities domain. Within utilities, several systems have a very long lifetime compared to systems from other domains. Once a company has chosen a SCADA (supervisory control and data acquisition system), it is unlikely to ever change it again in the next years or decades. Therefore, one has to deal with a lot of legacy systems which have to be integrated in both technical and business-related systems. The critical aspect in this context is that modern software systems are expected to quickly adapt to changing business processes by considering quality and reliability issues at the same time. This requires a flexible yet robust architecture and an approach to easily connect and enhance information systems.

2. BACKGROUND ON THE TECHNIQUES USED

Integration of software systems may take place on different levels. The OMG defines CIM (Computation Independent Model), PIM (Platform Independent Model), PSM (Platform Specific Model) and code levels. Those are defined and described in detail earlier in this book. We will therefore focus on putting those levels into the domain of our specific problem of integrating information systems. Considering this, the following figure visualizes the current state of the art using CIM, PIM and PSM as different stages of abstraction.

The figure shows two different information systems with their levels of abstraction. Within one system, the OMG defines the following levels that can be distinguished when modelling, creating and refactoring systems in the Model-Driven Software Development (MDSD) approach:

* CIM which is an abstract description of the system, mostly created by domain experts.
* PIM that defines the "What and How" of an information system independently from the actual technology.
* PSM that describes the "What and How" in a technologic dependent model and

Figure 1. Integration on CIM, PIM, PSM and Code-Level (©2007 Sven Abels, Wilhelm Hasselbring, Niels Streekmann, and Mathias Uslar. Used with permission)

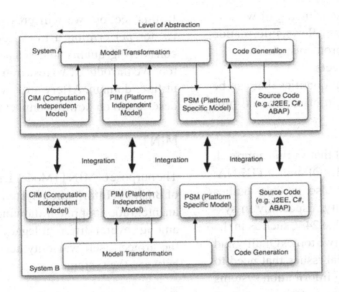

- Code Level that contains the actual source code (e.g. C#, Oracle SQL, etc.) being the most technology dependent level of this approach.

The main idea of the overall approach is to use model transformation between CIM, PIM and PSM and automatic code generation between PSM and Code Level. This allows software engineers to perform software development on a high level of abstraction and to handle very complex information systems.

When dealing with more than one information system it is, however, necessary to connect those information systems in order to either

i. exchange information between two equal systems, integrating them into an overall system that consists of different components or to

ii. exchange information between one main system and several sub systems that are integrated into the main system seamlessly.

This integration may happen on basically all levels of abstraction. There can be an early integration on CIM level, PIM or PSM level as well as a message-based integration on Code-Level. The two major European projects in Interoperability issues, namely INTEROP[1] and ATHENA[2] explicitly distinguish between the different integration of those levels for example in (Elvesæter et al., (2005)).

Beside those different levels of integration Elvesæter et al. also suggest to distinguish between the integration of different aspects which they call "Conceptual Integration" (Elvesæter et al., (2005)). They distinguish between the integration of

1. **Information aspects**
   Information aspects are related to the messages or structures exchanged, processed and stored by software systems or software components

2. **Service aspects**
   Services are an abstraction and an encap-

sulation of the functionality provided by an autonomous entity

3. **Process (and Rules) aspects**

Processes describe sequencing of work in terms of actions, control flows, information flows, interactions, protocols, etc.

4. **Non-functional aspects**

Additional functional qualities that can be applied to services, information and processes

It should be mentioned that in this approach of the two projects, INTEROP and ATHENA, "Non-functional aspects" also includes issues such as quality and security. Especially in systems that need to be available 24/7, such as in the public utilities domain, the two topics Quality and Security are usually crucial issues that need to be solved when integrating information systems in order to guarantee a coherent and consistent solution.

From a technical point of view, the area of integration can be distinguished. This defines where the integration takes place (see e.g. Reussner, (2005)). Considering this, we can define the following technological areas of integration:

i.   Integration at persistence level
ii. Integration at functionality level
iii. Integration at service or process level
iv. Integration at presentation level

In the past, practical approaches incorporated integration on the persistence level, e.g. different systems using the same database, or the function logic level, where applications directly called functions of other applications. Current approaches towards the integration of legacy systems focus on integration on the level of business processes using service-oriented architectures. These allow for the decoupling of functional aspects and their implementation.

3. CASE STUDIES FOR MODEL-DRIVEN INTEGRATION

In this section, we will present two case studies for performing a model-driven integration considering quality and scalability constraints, too. We introduce two research projects from the utilities domain. Afterwards, we will give a brief description on how to connect them.

MINT

The purpose of MINT (Model-Driven INTegration of Business Information Systems) was to provide an integration approach allowing interoperability among several different legacy systems. Hence, the project itself was only acting as a "bridge" between the systems.

Service Identification and Extraction

As stated in the last section, the integration in MINT will be performed at the service and business process level. The problem of this kind of integration is that the functionality provided by legacy systems was not designed and not implemented under the consideration of service-orientation. Actually, the legacy systems that needed to be integrated have been up to 10 years old and consisted of a monolithic architecture.

We use a practical approach to solve this problem by implementing adapters for legacy systems in the form of WebServices. To build these adapters and describe the orchestration of the WebServices we applied a model-driven approach. This approach based on the BALES methodology (van den Heuvel, (2000)). The BALES methodology combines forward and reverse engineering techniques in order to create models for the generation of adapters.

Integrating legacy systems and modern systems by employing service-oriented architectures and especially WebServices can be seen as a proven solution. The success of this method was shown in several case studies as in Hasselbring, (2004) and Zimmermann, (2005). The extension of the service-based integration by the generation of service adapters from architectural models is the subject of current research that has been carried out in our project. Besides the MINT project, there are some other approaches that use a similar approach as described in Winter, (2006) and Ziemann, (2006).

A challenge of the integration of legacy systems is to identify adequate services, because legacy systems were not designed to provide services for other applications. The identification and design of these services is a non-trivial problem since usually manifold requirements have to be considered. Service design should therefore follow certain rules. Hess, (2006) introduced such rules. The first rule is that the components that implement the services should be built by functional criteria. This principle is followed in MINT. Service adapters for legacy systems are derived from business process descriptions in the CIM. The challenge is to find the right granularity of a service and match the services derived from the CIM to the interfaces of legacy systems.

Business Requirements

Our approach follows the MDA standard and especially concentrates on the interdependence between CIM and PIM, because it defines the connection between business requirements and the interfaces of the legacy systems. The consideration of business requirements at CIM level allows us to add new functionality by considering new requirements. Of course this means that new requirements defined on CIM level must be transferred to the PIM level and afterwards the information needs to be used to create a service-interface that is able to provide WebServices for the legacy systems being involved in MINT. Thus, the proper transformation from CIM to PIM is one of the major aspects for the quality assurance of legacy integration. MINT thereby

focuses on process descriptions on a computation independent level from which architectural models are derived. These models are combined with interface models of the legacy systems to generate service adapters and orchestrations. We propose the use of model-driven and generative techniques to achieve this. The first allows the quick and consistent change of the requirements of the system by domain experts. Generative techniques as described in Czarnecki, (2000) allow the fast implementation of a software system in a standardized engineering manner. In a model-driven environment this can be achieved by reusable transformations. These transformations encapsulate design decisions and recurring implementation details. Thus changing requirements can be implemented fast and traceable.

Considering Domain Experts

The integration of legacy systems on the process level has two important issues from the software architecture point of view. The first is the generation of adapters to fit a legacy system into a modern software architecture or modern system landscapes. The second is the orchestration of these services according to the business process.

An important quality aspect for process-based integration is the correct conversion of domain-specific concepts into the generated adapters. This requires the participation of domain experts and system experts in the integration process. The system experts need to model the interfaces of legacy systems in an interface-based model of these systems. The domain experts on the other hand model the processes that integrate legacy systems in modern applications and are needed to match the concepts of the different systems to gain a correct integrated system. The involvement of domain experts is the base of MINT to guarantee quality issues.

A related approach to include models in the development process and thereby ensure the quality of the resulting software is domain-driven design as described by Evans, (2004). The approach also puts domain models into the centre of the software development process, but does not consider the generation of code from domain models.

To support the work of domain experts and system experts and to bring their work together in a consistent way new tools are required. Model-driven development is a promising method to achieve this. Models are able to capture all necessary information for the integration of software systems. Views on the models adjusted to the corresponding stakeholders and transformations between models on different levels of abstraction make it possible to offer an adequate working environment to each expert.

Model Transformation

To realize adequate views on the same model special modelling languages for each expert have to be employed. The MDA standard (OMG, (2003)) recommends the usage of UML to describe software systems. In our point of view the UML is an appropriate language for many tasks of software architects and developers. But since the UML offers a very technical view on software systems, it is not appropriate for all tasks that need to be fulfilled by domain experts describing their view and requirements on the integrated system. For this reason, we propose the usage of domain-specific languages (DSL) for the computation independent viewpoint of the MDA standard.

Furthermore the transformation from computation independent models to architectural models is in our view an important part of the software development process. To assist this by the utilization of DSL and automated model transformations is a step towards an engineering approach to software development that incorporates all necessary steps from the definition of requirements to the generation of code.

The main influences on the software architecture are decisions of the software architect based on the requirements of domain experts. Architectural decisions therefore strongly influence the transformation from CIM to PIM. Since the CIM only includes domain knowledge and requirements, it is clear that the decision for certain architectural aspects cannot be made out of the CIM alone, but also requires the knowledge of experiences with the influences of architectural decisions. These can be encapsulated in CIM-to-PIM transformations and made configurable, which is proposed by Zimmermann, (2006). To weigh up the requirements and make a decision for a specific architecture is the task of the software architect, but the transformation can encapsulate former design decisions that proved of value in certain situations. E.g. architectural decisions can have a fixed influence on the usage and configuration of design patterns, which e.g. is proposed by Becker, (2006) to introduce an engineering approach to component adaptation.

In MINT, we have focussed on the quality of former and future architectural decisions based on both incorporating more existing knowledge from the legacy systems and the software engineers into future decisions. While this work mainly deals with quality as a non-functional requirement and takes code transformations into account to ease the development, the use case described in the next section will have a different focus.

DER

The project DER (Distributed Energy Resources) is a scientific project dealing with a lot of problems coming from the domain of renewable energies. Therefore, we are going to provide an introduction to the IEC 61970 Common Information Model CIM.

Due to the fact that the MDA also uses the word CIM as an abbreviation, we are going to change the abbreviation to IEC-CIM for this contribution. While MINT had a different focus which was driven by the software architecture rather than the domain, DER strongly takes the domain semantics into account. In the following, we are going to provide some insights to the new drivers which lead to new objects and therefore semantics to be exchanged between systems in the utility domain.

Legal Unbundling

Running an energy grid is a commerce often combined with generating energy. In the European Community, those monopolistic functions provided in certain domains like transport (railways), communications (cellular, phone) and energy are subject to a dissembly which should lead to new competitors entering the (formerly) monopolistic markets Bundesministerium für Wirtschaft (2004), European Parliament (2003). In the utility domain, there must be a dissembly of energy generation and energy distribution through grids. This applies to both electricity and gas.

Summarizing the impact of the legal unbundling, it becomes clear that the changed processes have new entry points for third-party participants which have to be satisfied using IT-technology. Unfortunately, all the hundreds of different formats used by those companies cannot be easily integrated and processed.

New processes are being developed and the whole communication structure must be changed. Databases formerly used by the now unbundled distribution and generation structures must be split and kept in sync while their data schemes must be dissembled. This imposes both a threat and a chance to the systems. The chance is that new data schemes and techniques can be incorporated which better fit the needs of the market and provide less efforts needed when developing new adaptors and interfaces for exchanging data with new systems or third-party companies Robinson, Greg (2002)a, Robinson, Greg (2002)b.

Different standards and frameworks have been developed all over the world to cover this needed communication and data exchange structure. The two most prominent ones are the NRECA

MultiSpeak 2.0 (see MultiSpeak, 2003) standard and the IEC Common Information Model (IEC-CIM) standard (see IEC (2003), Podmore, Robin et al. (1999)). The IEC-CIM has proven to be the better choice (e.g. Neumann (2003)) and is being further described within this contribution.

Not only the new legal requirements impose changes, also environmental changes and increasing needs for new and different energy producers lead to changes in processes, data models and field level communication. The concept of decentralized energy producers like bio mass plants, wind power plants and fuel cells must be coordinated and their fed into the electricity power grid must be properly controlled and predicted Brand, Klaus-Peter & Buchholz, Bernd (2003). This leads to completely new function blocks and data models which have to be integrated in EMS and SCADA systems and must also interact with the commercial system like SAP.

To summarize the imposed requirements, we get to know that there is a strong need for coupling both new and old systems which have to deal with the proper semantics for the payloads. In order to use common semantics, we strongly make use of an existing domain ontology which is described in the next section.

IEC-CIM

The previous paragraph showed the two main drivers nowadays changing the IT-landscape in a utility company. Both data exchange processes and models heavily change with regard to complexity and sheer number of used standards. New standards must take this into account. As mentioned before, the IEC-CIM is the most prolific approach to deal with these problems. Due to the length of this chapter, more about the IEC-CIM and its object semantics has to be found in Uslar et al. (2005). Anyway, there are still many problems unsolved when adopting the IEC-CIM norm.

We have chosen the IEC TC 57 framework which incorporates the model as one sub-norm as the data model and communication standards framework. This lowers the amount of efforts which have to be spend on developing a domain model for the utility domain and market/substation communication. The IEC-CIM can serve as a global ontology for the utility domain and covers when converted into OWL (Web Ontology Language) about 2.500 RDF triples IEC (2004). Using the IEC-CIM ensures a high quality of the data format within the DER project since it is build on a solid base and since it has been evaluated and applied in various practical scenarios.

Currently, the IEC-CIM is mostly used for a message-based coupling and the exchange of power grid data. We are going to focus on the integration of heterogeneous system within this contribution. In order to achieve this, we created a RDF representation of the CIM format which will be transported as payload information using WebServices and SOAP, allowing all systems in the DER project to communicate and exchange information in a semantically standardized way.

Representing IEC-CIM Using RDF and XML

Although the IEC-CIM itself is modelled as an UML diagram and provides useful insight to the important objects within the power industry, it is difficult to exchange data due to the fact that object related databases are available but not widely used. Instantiated objects must be represented via serialization formats which can be exchanged in binary or ASCII format.

The IEC proposed RDF as a proper way to exchange topology (power grid) data in a common format IEC (2004)b. The RDF schema is documented as the IEC standard 61970-501. Like any other XML based format, it has several advantages over binary formats. Due to XML based mechanisms, it is possible to extend the model with versioning mechanisms and, more important, namespaces as a mechanism which is easily extensible and supports site-specific needs.

RDF is both machine and human readable and self-describing, although it is primarily intended

Figure 2. Defining payloads for EAI and EMB in the context of CIM (©2007 Sven Abelss, Wilhelm Hasselbring, Niels Streekmann, and Mathias Uslar. Used with permission)

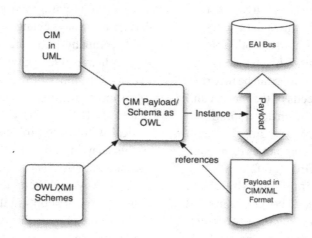

for programmatic access by tools which support the Document Object Model (DOM) API. Current web standards can be met when using a RDF based representation of the data.

IEC standard 61970-501 defines standards mechanisms to convert the UML model into an RDF model. The conversion of the Rational based UML file can be done manually or tool-supported by the Xpetal converter. It reads the Rational Rose .mdl file and creates RDF or XML schemes from the corresponding model. Still, one valid RDF representation can differ from other valid representations. Furthermore, RDF models often tend to become quiet complex having nested tags and a large overhead of administrative meta-data compared to the actual data used. Often, large files describing topologies have to be exchanged while e.g. only some of the breakers have changed. The IEC standard 61970-503 IEC (2004)b therefore defines a simplified RDF syntax being an actual subset of RDF but still valid RDF and an differential model providing the chance to exchange tiny subsets of changes instead of complete model status snapshots. The amount of data exchanged between energy management systems or even companies can become very large. Processing this data is most often time-critical.

Even though XML related data has proven to be useful due to its self-description capabilities (see Dag, Hasan & Urkan, Ulmut (2004), Zhou, E.Z. (2000)), nested tags instead of a simple serialized structure lead to slower process times as described in deVos, Arnold (2000). At implementation level, the IEC proposed a slightly changed syntax to a common RDF/XML representation, the so called simplified CIM/XML exchange format IEC (2004)b; deVos & Widergren & Zhu (2001). RDF provides many ways to represent the same set of data, e.g. an association between two resources can be written either with a resource attribute or by nesting one element within the other. This makes processing via XSLT tools sometimes a bit more difficult. The reduced syntax is still compatible with available RDF-de-serialization tools but provides a generally faster access to the data due to its pure simplicity. One improvement of the data structure is useful for the exchange of partial or full model data exchange. Another improvement in processing speed can be achieved by optimizing the amount of data exchanged

Figure 3. A simplified extract of a CIM/XML file modeling idle power (q) and effective power (p) (in RDF) (©2007 Sven Abels, Wilhelm Hasselbring, Niels Streekmann, and Mathias Uslar. Used with permission)

```xml
<?xml version="1.0" ?>
- <rdf:RDF xmlns:rdf="http://www.w3.org/1999/02/22-rdf-syntax-ns#"
    xmlns:cim="http://iec.ch/TC57/2000/CIM-schema-cimu09b#">
  - <cim:Substation rdf:ID="_28159176D77E2467">
      <cim:Naming.name>LEGAZZI</cim:Naming.name>
      <cim:Substation.MemberOf_SubControlArea
        rdf:resource="#_55D3DE366B2AD032" />
    </cim:Substation>
  - <cim:EnergyConsumer rdf:ID="_2963867E4A4B1669">
      <cim:EnergyConsumer.pfixed>19.78</cim:EnergyConsumer.pfixed>
      <cim:EnergyConsumer.qfixed>06.10</cim:EnergyConsumer.qfixed>
      <cim:EnergyConsumer.LoadArea
        rdf:resource="#_9C1602456B178B75" />
      <cim:Equipment.MemberOf_EquipmentContainer
        rdf:resource="#_A9D1427B3784CD78" />
      <cim:Naming.name>4711</cim:Naming.name>
    </cim:EnergyConsumer>
  </rdf:RDF>
```

between companies. After the initial data is exchanged, only updates need to be exchanged deVos & Rowbotham (2001) afterwards.

This mechanism is mostly used within the scope of topology exchange, the mechanisms dealing with EAI messages differ a bit in terms of serialization and tooling.

When looking at enterprise level data exchange, we have to deal with more simple structures, in our case XML documents and schemes. The overall process is illustrated in figure 2.

Starting with an XMI (XML metadata interchange) model, a different tool from XPetal is used, the so called open source CIMTool (http://www. cimtool.org). The CIMTool loads the IEC-CIM model as XMI file, this provides the proper base model for the code transformations. Afterwards, a wizard based interface is used to create an OWL representation of the needed payload. After completing those steps, we have a fully thorough semantic definition of our needed EAI payload. Having different base models, we can still use our generic editor to create the payload's semantic description. Afterwards, we have to do different steps to complete the xml scheme needed. We once more start the CIMTool, but instead of creating an OWL description, we create a flat or a nested xml schema based on code transforma-

tions of the OWL model. This leads to a proper fully semantically and syntactically compliant IEC-CIM based XML scheme. It is possible to include one's own namespaces and routing headers for the used EAI platform and the schema is ready to deploy.

This overall process really simplifies the creation of meaningful payloads for EAI and increases the overall semantic quality of the needed messages. The approach has several advantages over the existing ones:

- Meaningful semantics are supplied by the IEC-CIM that is used as a domain ontology. A common language can be established on the whole enterprise message bus.
- Model-driven development facilitates the ease of creating the payloads.
- Tools provide both a generic and deterministic way of creating the XML schemes which makes both for ease validation and introduction into the development department.
- Most of the tools available are provided as open source tools. This lowers the costs of getting acquainted with the new technology.

Figure 4. Choices of the CIMTool wizard (©2007 Sven Abels, Wilhelm Hasselbring, Niels Streekmann, and Mathias Uslar. Used with permission)

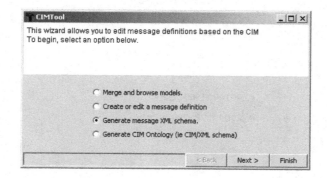

- Within the creation process, domain experts are mainly needed when defining the messages. Afterwards, the deployment engineers can transform the OWL descriptions into proper and more technology oriented payloads.

Anyway, there are still some disadvantages.

- A proper versioning of the underlying models is needed in order to structure the code generation process. The semantics of the different artefacts incorporated in the process must be kept consistent.
- The maturity of the used tools differs between the different code levels. While the XML tools already have reached a good maturity, the OWL tools have far less overall capabilities and functions. This sometimes restricts the engineer in modelling the proper payloads (e.g. when constraining objects).
- The overall amount of data exchanged is increased due to the use of XML in comparison to pure CSV (Comma Separated Value) or binary data.

The overall approach is successfully used in the project and has proven to be a good decision. Rapid prototyping of the needed payloads with agreed semantics has been extremely easy compared to the previous approaches. The use of IEC-CIM, MDD, UML and UMM (UN/CEFACT Modeling Methodology) has increased the overall quality and decreased time-to-deployment for the needed payloads for coupling heterogeneous systems.

4. SCOPES OF THE TWO USE CASES

As described in the last sections, MINT and DER are two completely independent projects. We described how to create a flexible architecture and semantically standardized payloads. For both projects, it results in a comprehensive set of services which are provided as SOAP-based WebServices. This allows for performing interactions between both projects by connecting their concepts on a service level.

Figure 5 shows which roles DER and MINT play in the integration of two systems and indicates where their intersection is. The systems

Figure 5. The projects: roles in system integration (©2007 Sven Abels, Wilhelm Hasselbring, Niels Streekmann, and Mathias Uslar. Used with permission)

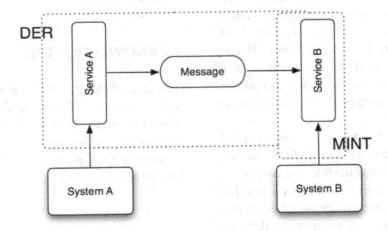

are integrated using services which interact by exchanging messages. DER concentrates on the generation of standardized messages. One of the focuses of MINT on the other side is the generation of service adapters for legacy systems and the orchestration of these services. Hence the intersection point of the projects would be the orchestration and generation of adapters that use generated standard messages.

Lessons Learned

In the course of the two projects, the authors learned some lessons that can help readers when taking the decision of using MDI and MDSD based approaches. Compared to a traditional development approach, our approach clearly needs more preparation time. There are two reasons for that. On the one hand, the approach is new and therefore somewhat unknown for all participants, which results in a learning curve at the beginning of the project.

On the other hand the success of our projects highly depends on the modelling and the 'ground work'. This means that it is even more important to ensure a high-quality yet flexible conceptualisation. In order to assure this, we involved domain experts at an early stage in MINT and used standards in DER. This has helped us to ensure a high quality and a standard-compliant solution.

We also realized that our approach is easier for new participants to join an ongoing project. The reason for that is the clear structure that is the result of our model based approach. Having this in mind, we result in a more transparent solution that should also be easier to maintain in the future (this statement of course has to be validated by the time).

Another fact is the necessity for interoperability techniques such as a clear interface specification and the usage of a flexible and easy to use intermediate exchange format. This is required because of the high number of different (and more or less independent) components that need to communicate within the solution. Approaches such as Services-Oriented Architectures can help achieving this.

5. CONCLUSION AND FURTHER ACTIONS

Within this chapter, the model-driven integration approach in complex information systems was introduced by giving two practical examples. The chapter used the experiences the authors have made in two different research projects in the public utilities domain. The result of this chapter is a brief introduction of this topic and it demonstrated the different possibilities to solve the problem. While MINT relies on WebServices to integrate systems on a message level, the DER project focuses on creating a common information model on a semantic basis (RDF) and uses WebServices only for transportation and technical integration between the heterogeneous IT landscape.

In order to ensure quality, MINT uses domain experts that should ensure the validity and the applicability and DER addresses quality issues by using a well defined standard (IEC-CIM) as a basis for creating the RDF messages. The two approaches can be combined to improve the quality of software development using MDI and MDSD techniques.

ACKNOWLEDGMENT

The research project MINT is supported by the German *Federal Ministry of Education and Research* in the scope of the *Forschungsoffensive Software Engineering 2006*. The DER project is supported and partly funded by the *EWE AG*, Oldenburg, Germany.

ADDITIONAL READING

Integration and migration of legacy systems in the focus of model-driven software development is also an issue that is faced by standardization organizations like the OMG, who introduced the Architecture-Driven Modernization Initiative (ADM).

In the practice of software engineering there are different approaches to increase the quality of software by using domain models to reduce the linguistic gap between domain experts and software engineers. These approaches differ from the ones described above since they do not focus on the integration of existing systems. Examples are the Eclipse Modeling Framework (Eclipse, 2007), Microsoft's Software Factories (Greenfield, 2004) and language workbenches (Fowler, 2005).

In addition to the model driven integration approach, an interesting and up to a certain extent even completing approach is the usage of ontologies for different formats that are connected using Ontology Mapping or Alignment approaches. An overview about different concepts of this is given in (Doan & Madhavan & Domingos, & Halevy, 2002), (Ehrig & Sure, 2004), (Abels & Haak & Hahn, 2005) and Rahm & Bernstein (2001).

More on the CIM and its scopes for message-based integration can be found in Uslar et al., (2005). Other scopes of use are a bit outside the model-driven development process, more general info on the CIM can be found in Shahidehpour & Yang, (2003). This source provides a useful overview on how to use the IEC TC 57 standard and the CIM in context with both SCADA technology and message-based coupling of systems.

FUTURE (NEEDED) RESEARCH

The future of software development tends toward model-driven development. Some of the main questions are addressed in the chapter: the role of standards, integration of existing systems and communication with domain experts. These will also be the topics in future research. The emerging standards in the MDA/ADM surroundings and domain specific standards like the IEC-CIM will be the basis for future high quality software. One of the main drivers will be on how fast the maturity of the overall process models and the tooling grows.

Domain models and domain-specific languages will play a more central role in software development. But still a lot of research has to be done on usability and the granularity of the languages and the decision on when to use standard models and transformations and when to use specific models and specialized languages and transformations.

REFERENCES

Abels & Haak & Hahn (2005). Identification of Common Methods Used for Ontology Integration Tasks. In: Proceedings of the first international ACM workshop on Interoperability of Heterogeneous Information Systems (IHIS05), CIKM conference proceedings. ACM, Sheridan publishing.

ADM Task Force. Why do we need standards for the modernization of legacy systems. White Paper. Retrieved June, 1, 2007, from http://adm.omg.org/legacy/ADM_whitepaper.pdf

Becker, Steffen & Brogi, Antonio & Gorton, Ian & Overhage, Sven & Romanowsky, Alexander & Tivoli, Massimo (2006). Towards an Engineering Approach to Component Adaptation. In Architecting Systems with Trustworthy Components, *Proceedings of Dagstuhl Seminar 04511.*

Brand, Klaus-Peter & Buchholz, Bernd (2003). *Systemanforderungen an interoperable Geräte und Systeme der Stationsautomatisierung.* In

(Schwarz, Karlheinz (Edt.): Offene Kommunikation nach IEC 61850 für die Schutz- und Stationsleittechnik.

Bundesministerium für Wirtschaft (2004). *Gesetz für den Vorrang Erneuerbarer Energien* (EEG) in der Fassung vom 21.7.2004, BGBL, I:1918

Czarnecki, Krzysztof & Eisenecker, Ulrich (2000). *Generative Programming - Methods, Tools, and Applications*. Addison-Wesley.

Dag, Hasan & Urkan, Ulmut (2004). *An XML Based Data Exchange Model for Power System Studies*. ARI - The Bulletin of the Istanbul Technical University, 2.

deVos, Arnold (2000). *Simplified RDF Syntax for Power System Model Exchange*. Longdale Consultants, 2000, available at http://www.langdale.com.au/CIMXML/.

deVos & Rowbotham (2001). *Knowledge Representation for Power System Modeling*, In (IEEE Publishing Edt.): Proceedings of the PICA 2001 (The 22nd International Conference on Power Industry Computer Applications), IEEE Power Engineering Society.

deVos & Widergren & Zhu (2001). *XML for CIM Model Exchange*. In (IEEE Publishing Edt.): Proceedings of the PICA 2001 (The 22nd International Conference on Power Industry Computer Applications), IEEE Power Engineering Society.

Doan & Madhavan & Domingos, & Halevy (2002). Learning to map between ontologies on the semantic web. In: Proceedings of the Eleventh International WWW Conference, Hawaii, US.

Ehrig & Sure (2004). Ontology Mapping - An Integrated Approach. Proceedings of the First European Semantic Web Symposium. Lecture Notes in Computer Science, Vol. 3053, Springer Verlag, Heraklion, Greece, May 2004, S. 76-91.

Elvesæter, Brian & Hahn, Axel & Berre, Arne-Jørgen & Neple, Tor (2005). Towards an Interoperability Framework for Model-Driven Development of Software Systems, Proceedings of the 2005 International Conference on Interoperability for Enterprise Software and Applications (I-ESA 2005).

European Parlament (2003). Richtlinie 2003/54/EG des Europäischen Parlaments und des Rates vom 26.Juli 2003 über die gemeinsamen Vorschriften für den Elektrizitätsbinnenmarkt und zur Aufhebung der Richtlinie 96/92/EG.

Evans, Eric (2004). *Domain-Driven Design – Tackling Complexity in the Heart Of Software*. Addison-Wesley.

Fowler, Martin (2005). Language Workbenches: The Killer-App For Domain-Specific Languages? Retrieved 2007/05/30, from http://www.martinfowler.com/articles/languageWorkbench.html

Greenfield, Jack & Short, Keith & Cook, Steve & Kent, Stuart (2004). *Software Factories: Assembling Applications with Patterns, Models, Frameworks, and Tools*. Wiley.

Hasselbring, Wilhelm & Reussner, Ralf & Jaekel, Holger & Schlegelmilch, Jürgen & Teschke, Thorsten & Krieghoff, Stefan (2004). The Dublo Architecture Pattern for Smooth Migration of Business Information Systems: An Experience Report. *Proceedings of the 26th International Conference on Software Engineering* (pp. 117-126). IEEE Computer Society Press.

Hess, Andreas & Humm, Bernhard & Voss, Markus (2006). Regeln für serviceorientierte Architekturen hoher Qualität. *Informatik-Spektrum, 29*(6), 395-411.

Van den Heuvel, Willem-Jan & Hasselbring, Wilhelm & Papazoglou, Mike (2000). Top-Down Enterprise Application Integration with Reference Models. *Australian Journal of Information Systems, 8*(1), 126-136.

IEC (2003). IEC - International Electrotechnical Commission: IEC 61970-301: *Energy manage-*

ment system application program interface *(EMS-API) – Part 301: Common Information Model (CIM) Base*. International Electrotechnical Commission.

IEC (2004). IEC - International Electrotechnical Commission: IEC 61970-501: *Energy management system application program interface (EMS-API) – Part 501: CIM RDF Schema – Revision 4*. International Electrotechnical Commission.

IEC (2004)b. IEC - International Electrotechnical Commission: Draft IEC 61970: *Energy Management System Application Program Interface (EMS-API) – Part 503: CIM XML Model Exchange Format - Draft 3b*. International Electrotechnical Commission.

IEEE (1990). Institute of Electrical and Electronics Engineers: IEEE Standard Computer Dictionary: A Compilation of IEEE Standard Computer Glossaries.

Jeusfeld, Manfred A. & Backlund, Per & Ralyté, Jolita (2007). Classifying Interoperability Problems for a Method Chunk Repository, Proceedings of the 3rd International Conference on Interoperability for Enterprise Software and Applications (I-ESA 2007).

Object Management Group, OMG (2003). MDA Guide Version 1.0.1.

Marx Gómez & Brehm (2007). *KMU-Software-Umfrage 2006 zur Nutzung betrieblicher Standardsoftware kleiner und mittelständischer Unternehmen in Deutschland,* Dep. of Business Information Systems, University of Oldenburg, Study.

MultiSpeak (2003). *MultiSpeak Version 2.2* Specification (10/07/03), NRECA, Virginia, available online at http://www.multispeak.org.

Neumann (2003). *Comparison of IEC CIM and NRECA* MultiSpeak, UISOL.

Podmore, Robin et al. (1999). *Common Information Model - a Developer's Perspective.* In

(Sprague, R. Edt.): Proceedings of the 32nd Hawaii International Conference on System Sciences, IEEE Publishing.

Rahm & Bernstein (2001). A survey of approaches to automatic schema matching, The VLDB Journal, 10, 2001.

Reussner, Ralf (2005). *MINT – Modellgetriebene Integration von Informationssystemen,* Description of Work, Forschungsoffensive „Software Engineering 2006".

Robinson, Greg (2002)a. *Key Standards for Utility Enterprise Application Integration* (EAI), Proceedings of the Distributech 2002, Miami, Pennwell, 2002.

Robinson, Greg (2002)b. *Model Driven Integration (MDI) for Electric Utilities,* Proceedings of the Distributech 2002 Miami, Pennwell, 2002.

Shahidehpour, Mohammad & Wang, Yaoyu (2003). *Communication and Control in Electric Power Systems: Applications of Parallel and Distributed Processing,* IEEE Press Series on Power Engineering, 2003.

Uslar, Mathias et al (2005): *Interaction of EMS related Systems by Using the CIM Standard,* In: Walter Leal Filho, Jorge Marx Gómez, Claus Rautenstrauch (Hrsg.): ITEE 2005: Second International ICSC Symposium on Information Technologies in Environmental Engineering: Proceedings, Otto-von-Guericke Universität Magdeburg, Shaker Verlag, 2005.

Winter, Andreas & Ziemann, Jörg (2006). *Model-based Migration to Service-Oriented Architectures.* In U. Kaiser, P. Kroha, A. Winter (Eds.), *3. Workshop Reengineering Prozesse (RePro 2006) Software Migration* (pp. 16-17). Mainz: Johannes Gutenberg University Mainz.

Zhou, E.Z. (2000). *XML and data exchange for power system analysis.* In (IEEE Edt.): IEEE Power Engineering Review, 20, 66-68.

Ziemann, Jörg & Leyking, Katrina & Kahl, Timo & Werth, Dirk (2006). Enterprise Model driven Migration from Legacy to SOA. In R. Gimnich, A. Winter (Eds.), *Workshop Software-Reengineering und Services* (pp. 18-27). Koblenz: University of Koblenz-Landau.

Zimmermann, Olaf & Doubrovski, Vadim & Grundler, Jonas & Hogg, Kerard (2005). *Service-oriented architecture and business process choreography in an order management scenario: rationale, concepts, lessons learned.* In OOPSLA Companion (301-312).

Zimmermann, Olaf & Köhler, Jana & Leymann, Frank (2006). *The Role of Architectural Decisions in Model-Driven Service-Oriented Architecture Construction.* In L.A. Skar, A.A. Bjerkestrand, *Best Practices and Methodologies in Service-Oriented Architectures, OOPSLA 2006 Workshop.*

ENDNOTES

1 http://www.interop-noe.org
2 http://www.athena-ip.org

Chapter XVIII

High–Quality Software Models of the Mid–Infrared Instrument for the James Webb Space Telescope

Jane M. C. Oh
Jet Propulsion Laboratory, California Institute of Technology, USA

Martin S. Feather
Jet Propulsion Laboratory, California Institute of Technology, USA

Mori A. Khorrami
Jet Propulsion Laboratory, California Institute of Technology, USA

ABSTRACT

This chapter examines the experience of using model-based design in the context of development of critical software. The software is being developed to control a science instrument that it to fly as part of NASA's James Web Space Telescope. The chapter discusses the context and nature of this software development effort, and why they motivated the choice of a model-based development approach. Illustrations are provided of the elements of model-based design that are proving to be beneficial. The chapter also considers how software assurance practices are being adapted to work with this approach.

1. INTRODUCTION

The work described in this chapter covers a software development effort being conducted at the Jet Propulsion Laboratory, software for control of an instrument that is to be a part of a deep-space observatory. While at first glance this may appear to be far removed (in not only physical distance) from concerns that permeate conventional software development, in fact many of the key factors will be familiar concerns to many developers of terrestrial software. As we will discuss, it was consideration of these factors that led to the choice of model based development as the software development approach to follow. We will describe how our experiences to date suggest this was a good choice. We will also describe some of the ramifications of this choice – changes to existing software development practices that are occurring to accommodate the changed nature of software development stemming from adoption of model based development.

The software development effort discussed in this chapter is the ongoing development of "Flight Software" (i.e., software that will be executed by computers on board the spacecraft) for a science instrument, the Mid Infra-Red Instrument (MIRI). As its name suggests, it will measure light in the mid-infrared spectrum, for astronomy purposes. MIRI is one of four science instruments that together form the Integrated Science Instrument Module (ISIM) element. ISIM is in turn one of three elements that comprise the Observatory Segment, and that in turn is one of the three segments that comprise the James Webb Space Telescope (JWST). This is a large space telescope, scheduled for launch in 2013. It is being developed jointly by the United States' National Aeronautics and Space Administration (NASA) and the European Space Agency; for details, see http://www.jwst.nasa.gov/.

This chapter will focus on the main challenges that pervade the development of this mission-critical software.

2. BACKGROUND AND CHALLENGES

NASA's spacecraft operate across the solar system performing a wide range of missions, including planetary surface exploration using rovers,

planetary observation using orbiters, and solar and astronomical observations using observing platforms at a variety of locations. As this fleet continues to expand in both number and complexity, there is a pressing need for increasing the role that on-board spacecraft software plays in controlling those spacecraft. This will relieve the growing burden levied on Earth-based ground control, and alleviate the bottleneck of communication back to earth. Furthermore, increased autonomy on the spacecraft themselves will enhance their capabilities – responding autonomously to investigate interesting but short-lived phenomena, increasing the capabilities of surface rovers to traverse terrain and to perform more intricate science experiments, etc. This all requires more sophisticated software in the spacecraft/rover itself. Without some change in the software development process, such more complex software systems will take longer to develop and verify, potentially increasing overall mission cost, introducing delays, and potentially introducing additional risk. Model based design is being investigated as a means to improve the development process for spacecraft software so as to help overcome some of these problems. The work reported here describes ongoing use of model-based design in a spacecraft setting, and the particular areas of benefit it conveys. Because of the risk-averse nature required of the development of NASA's spacecraft (in most cases well beyond reach of rescue or repair), ensuring the quality of the software remains of paramount importance. Also reported here is how software assurance techniques are being adapted to work with model-based design. One of the important synergies between model based design and software assurance is the opportunity to detect an increased fraction of software related defects earlier in the development process than would otherwise be the case, thus leading to net savings of cost and schedule, while ensuring quality.

3. EXPERIENCE WITH MODEL-BASED DESIGN FOR A COMPLEX SPACECRAFT SYSTEM'S SOFTWARE

Issues, Controversies, Problems

MIRI's flight software will control the operation of MIRI, including its interface with the rest of the spacecraft (both hardware subsystems, and other software, e.g., for data transfer). The Jet Propulsion Laboratory (JPL) has overall responsibility for MIRI (including design, development and testing) of the MIRI Instrument (both software and hardware). Hardware development is proceeding concurrently with software development, and in some instances at geographically separated locations. In particular, MIRI will incorporate optics that are being designed and delivered by the European Space Agency (ESA), as their development continues. For these reasons it was anticipated that the requirements for the MIRI software would undergo significant changes from the form they took at inception, due to concurrent development of the novel spacecraft instrument hardware.

MIRI's software, together with flight software for the other instruments, will become part of the overall ISIM flight software. In order to achieve compatibility, the elements of ISIM, MIRI included, must comply with an agreed upon development paradigm:

- Modeled using IBM's Rational Rose Real-Time
- Implemented using the C++ programming language
- Hosted on the VxWorks Real-Time Operating System (RTOS)
- Execute on a Power PC 750 Flight Processor

Lastly, MIRI's software must interface to elements that are being developed outside of this paradigm, specifically:

- Focal Plane Electronics and Instrument Control Electronics that have been implemented using Field Programmable Gate Arrays. These FPGA's firmware interfaces with the MIRI software.
- The MIRI Cooler system, which has its own micro-controller and software; it too interfaces with the MIRI software.

From the above description it is possible to discern key factors of MIRI's software development effort: fundamentally, MIRI software is part of an embedded, real-time system; its development must comply with a pre-established paradigm; it must interface with elements developed outside of this paradigm; it must utilize preordained computing platform capabilities; its requirements may be expected to change (because of concurrent development of the hardware it is to control); prior to receipt of actual hardware, its development and testing has had to proceed using software simulations that approximate the behaviour anticipated of that hardware; it is part of a geographically dispersed development effort; lastly, it has to produce highly reliable software (since mistakes in its control and operation of MIRI could compromise the science data it is designed to return, waste precious resources such as coolant, or threaten the health of the instrument itself and potentially even the health of the spacecraft). These are factors that recur in many software development efforts, most notably those for high-reliability embedded systems. Furthermore, these are often viewed as risks factors for a software development effort (e.g., volatile requirements).

It was in response to these that the MIRI development team selected model based development as their development paradigm, described next.

Solutions and Recommendations (1). Use of UML-RT Concepts and Technology

The MIRI development team chose to use model based development, specifically UML-RT (Unified Modeling Language – Real Time), to express MIRI's interface and behaviour. The primary benefits that stem from this decision are the ability to use UML-RT's agreed-upon notations to serve as an agreed-upon and technically rigorous vehicle of communication among the project personnel, and to allow the use of automatic code generation from the models expressed using these notations.

In particular, MIRI's interface and behaviour are being specified, and code generated, using this approach. UML-RT is being used to model these aspects using Capsule Structure Diagrams to express interfaces, and UML State Diagrams to express behaviour. We show examples of using a UML-RT Capsule Structure Diagram to express MIRI's interface, followed by use of a UML State Diagram to express key aspects of MIRI's behaviour.

The main functionality of the MIRI flight software includes (1) receiving commands from the surrounding ISIM element's software, (2) in response to those commands, controlling three hardware components (Focal Plane Electronics, Instrument Control Electronics and Cooler Control Electronics), (3) monitoring the status and heath of those hardware components, and (4) reporting their status and heath to the ISIM element. The structure of MIRI's interface that allows it access to the information and control is described using the Capsule Structure Diagram in Figure 1. A UML-RT "Capsule" represents an active object that can communicate, and indicates the protocols (sets of allowable communications) associated with the various ports on the object's interface.

The diagram employs the following UML-RT concepts:

- a *capsule* (denoted by the outermost large square red border)
- *ports* (denoted by the smaller red-coloured squares; those on the boundary are *public* ports, those in the interior *protected* ports)
- *protocols* (denoted by the small yellow-coloured rectangles).
- Were the diagram to be broadened to also include the ISWIM capsule, *connections* between the MIRI and ISWIM capsules would also be portrayed.

The meaning of these is as follows:

- *Public* ports (e.g., the one on the right hand border labelled cmdfePort) provide communication access to MIRI for software both inside and outside of the MIRI capsule. The six public ports seen in the diagram are used to (1) receive commands, hardware telemetry packets, timer and time services, (2) send control commands, event messages and housekeeping telemetry, and (3) perform tables operations and maintenance.
- *Protected* ports (e.g., the port labelled mrCmdClientPort) provide communication access to MIRI for only software within the MIRI capsule. In particular, protected ports provide access to the capsule's *state machine,* which we will describe shortly.

Naming conventions are followed to be indicative of the roles these ports play. For example, telemetryPort has the role of handling telemetry duties, cmdfePort has the role of a command front end (from which the abbreviation cmdfe is derived) to receipt of commands from the ISIM element, etc. Since our focus is on the MIRI interface and its overall behaviour, we will skip the details of what specific processing occurs in fulfilling these duties (details that are specific to the spacecraft instrument itself).

Figure 1 depicts the MIRI FSW Capsule Structure Diagram and Table 1 lists different ports and their types as used in the MIRI FSW capsule.

Figure 1. MIRI FSW Capsule Structure Diagram

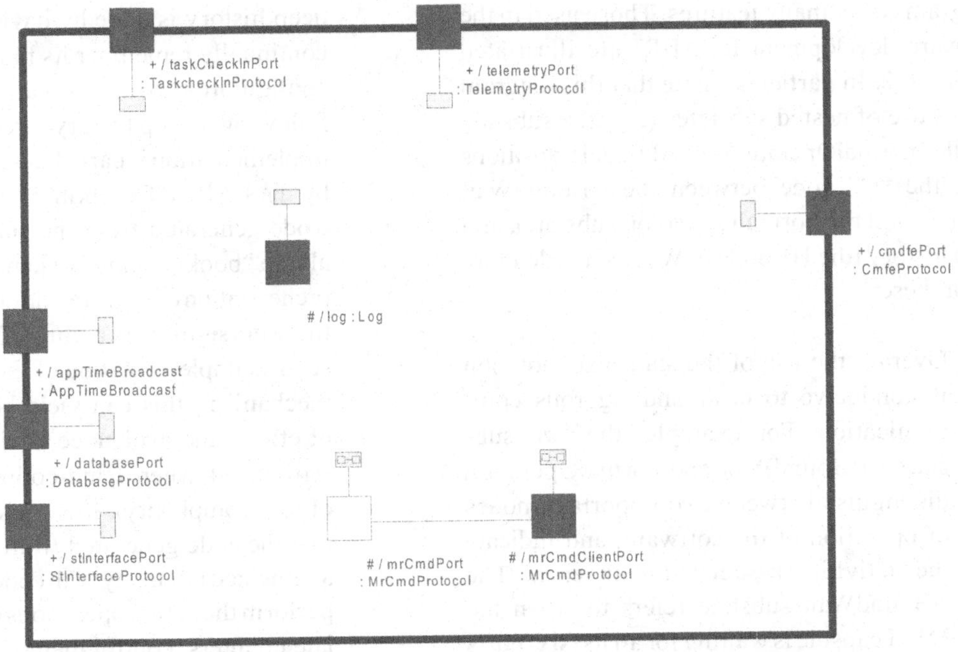

Table 1. Ports and their types used in the MIRI FSW Capsule

Port Name	Termination	Connection	Visibility	Protocol Name
taskCheckInPort	end	non-wired	public	TaskcheckInProtocol
telemetryPort	end	non-wired	public	TelemetryProtocol
appTimeBroadcast	end	non-wired	public	AppTimeBroadcast
databasePort	end	non-wired	public	DatabaseProtocol
stInterfacePort	end	non-wired	public	StInterfaceProtocol
cmdfePort	end	non-wired	public	CmfeProtocol
mrCmdPort	end	wired	protected	MrCmdProtocol
mrCmdClientPort	end	wired	protected	MrCmdProtocol
log	end	non-wired	protected	Log

MIRI's overall behaviour is described using a UML State Diagram. In general, UML State Diagrams offer many features. Those used in the software development for MIRI are illustrated in Figure 2. In particular, note that this diagram makes use of nested substates (e.g., the substate labelled normalOperation), conditional transitions (e.g., the "C" node between the rtBoundWait substate and the normalOperation substate), and deep history (the H* nodes). We say a little more about these:

- Overall, the use of the statechart notation is conducive to clear and rigorous communication. For example, the two substates, rtBoundWait and normalOperation distinguish between two important modes of operation of the software, and indicate the activities associated with each. The rtBoundWait substate refers to when the MIRI capsule is waiting for all its (six) ports to be connected successfully; the normalOperation substate refers to when the MIRI capsule is connected and performing normal operations with no erroneous conditions.

- State transitions defined in MIRI FSW may deal with events that require a *choice* between transition path segments. The Choice Point mechanism denoted as the circles C icon in Figure 2 addresses this situation. This mechanism allows a single transition (e.g., rtBounds) to be split into two outgoing transition segments (moreToBound and allPortsBound), each of which may terminate on a different state.

- Events that require immediate action may occur while MIRI software is engaged with ongoing activities. These events require that MIRI's activity be interrupted, those events dealt with, and upon completion of their handling MIRI is to continue its interrupted activity. The UML State Diagram's deep history mechanism is used to denote this. As can be seen in the figure, the transition to history mechanism is a widely used pattern in MIRI FSW. Implementation of deep history is done by having the system continually remember its most recent state configuration so that it can return to that following a deep history interruption. This implementation is part of the code generated by the UML-RT toolkit.

- Code generated from the statecharts does all the "bookkeeping" to handle the overall orchestration of state transitions, thus saving the users significant coding effort. For cases such as implementation of the deep history mechanism, this can yield both a savings of effort, and avoidance of risk (of defects introduced when hand-coding something of this complexity). It is important to note that the code generated from UML is then augmented manually with code fragments to perform the actual operations (e.g., manipulate counters, control memory, etc). Below is a code example where the hand-coded portion is highlighted (for the purposes of this presentation) in bold, the remainder being autogenerated:

```
static const char * const rtg_state_names[] =
{
        "TOP", "rtBoundWait", "normalOperation"
};
INLINE_METHODS void MIRIappMain_Actor::rtBoundWait_
rtBounds( const void * rtdata, RTProtocol * rtport )
{
        mrRtBoundCnt--;          //decrement the port connection
counter
}
```

Solutions and Recommendations (2). Software Assurance Techniques Applied

NASA's missions' flight software developments commonly have stringent reliability needs. MIRI's flight software is no exception to this. What is different from usual, however, is MIRI's adoption of the model-based development paradigm. Despite the allure of this paradigm, it could be disadvan-

Figure 2. MIRI FSW Capsule State Diagram

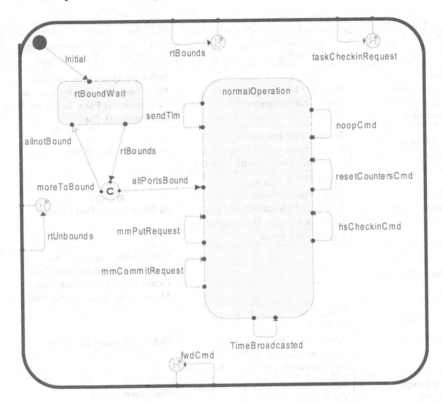

tageous if software models were generated by developers who did not understand appropriate use of UML-RT concepts. In order to minimize this risk, all the project team members have been sufficiently trained on UML-RT concepts and on how to use the toolset. Furthermore, software models have been generated by following the UML-RT design rules and guidelines, they have been iteratively and incrementally grown in size and complexity, and they have been periodically reviewed by peers and experts. This last item is an instance of the need to adapt software quality assurance to model-based development, considered in more detail in this section.

Until the advent of model-based design, software quality assurance practiced within JPL has been applied predominantly to the design artefacts and development processes of software developed by "traditional" means. In the model based development paradigm, novelty stems from the fact that many of the artefacts are in machine manipulable representations, not simply paragraphs of textual descriptions or drawings intended purely for human viewing. Furthermore, using tools that support the model-based paradigm allows code automated generation to be employed, yielding significant portions of machine-generated source code as significant parts of the development ef-

Table 2. Software assurance activities and their work products

Software Assurance Activities	Software Assurance Artefacts relatively unchanged during Model based development	Software Assurance Artefacts *with high potential for change* during Model based development
Software Development Process and Monitoring	Software Development Plan, Project Management Plan	**Software Quality Assurance Plan, Software Configuration Management Plan, Software Risk Management Plan**
Subcontractor Controls	Requests for Proposals, Procurement Requisitions, Pre-award Vendor Software Surveys	**Statements-Of-Work**
Software Requirements Analysis	Level 1, 2, 3, 4, and 5 Requirements Documentation, Functional Specification, Interface Control Documentation, Operational Specs	**Bi-Directional Traceability**
Software Reviews		**Code Walkthrough, Unit Test Walkthrough, Test Case Generation, Code Run-time Monitoring, Code Static Analysis**
Formal Reviews	Conceptual Design Reviews, Preliminary Design Reviews, Architecture Reviews, Test Readiness Reviews, Assembly and Operation Readiness Reviews	**Detailed Design Reviews**
Management Reviews	Fever Chart, Project Insight and Oversight	**Risk Assessment**
Peer Reviews	Inheritance Documentation, Test Plans and Procedures	**Software Reuses, Test Results Verification**
Software Delivery Reviews	Release Description Document, Acceptance Test Plan/Procedures/ Report	**Software Review Certification Records, End Item Data Packages**
Software Safety Hazard Analysis	Safety/Hazard Analysis Report	**Safety-critical Components Assessment**
Software FMECA and Fault Tree Analysis	Software Failure Modes Effect and Criticality Analysis	**Software Fault Tree Analysis**
Software Configuration Management	Engineering Change Requests, Change Control Report	**Configuration Management Report, Build List**
Software Problem/ Failure Reporting	Problem/Failure Report, Root Cause Analysis Report	**Action Items Report, Test Traceability Matrix**
Verification and Validation	**Subsystem Validation, System Validation, Hardware Review Certification Records**	**Unit Test, Integration Test, System Test, User Acceptance Test**

forts. We discuss the consequences of this next.

The objective of software assurance process is to improve the quality of mission-critical software and the productivity of software development process by detecting and removing errors and defects early in the life cycle. Table 2 lists in the leftmost column software assurance activities, and in the middle and right columns the artefacts dealt with in those activities; the middle column's artefacts are those relatively unchanged by the shift to a Model based development paradigm, while the right column's artefacts are those with a high potential for change, generally change for the better (faster and/or more thorough).

We give a more detailed example of the kind of adjustments to software assurance that result from the switch to model based design, focusing on the use of checklists in support of formal inspections done during reviews. Inspections are widely recognized as a highly cost-effective assurance technique (see (Shull et al, 2002) for a recent discussion), and they have long been in use at JPL; (Kelly et al, 1992) describes measurements calculated of the efficacy of JPL's tailoring of Fagan's original inspections process (Fagan, 1976). Checklists themselves are a commonly used means to "provide reviewers with hints and recommendations for finding defects during the examination of a workproduct" (quoting from (Brykczynski, 1999), which surveys 117 software inspection checklists from 24 sources).

Manual Inspection Checklist for Models

The following is a partial list of checklist questions used during manual inspection to guide a reviewer inspecting a model. This covers questions that relate to areas of conformance with traceability, consistency and completeness measures in general, and correctness measures for each specific type of model:

Completeness

- Does the model meet its requirements?
- Is there wrong, missing, or incomplete logic?
- Does the model correctly accommodate all required inputs, outputs, and database elements according to the required format, content, data rate, etc.?

Consistency

- Are variables named and used consistently throughout each component and its interfaces?
- Are models of all interfaces consistent with each other and with the interface requirements?
- Does the model fully describe the system?
- Are the models for similar or related components consistent?

Traceability

- Is each component of the design traced back to requirements?
- Have detailed requirements for each component been specified?
- Have component requirements been traced to the architectural design?

Correctness

- Class diagram
  - Is the aggregation relationship correct?
  - Is aggregation mixed up with composition?
  - Is generalization relationship correct?
  - Is the navigability direction consistent with ownership?
  - Is the multiplicity number correct?
- Capsule structure diagram
  - Does the diagram identify all the possible capsules and ports?
  - Are all the connectors between ports identified?

- Statechart diagram
  - ° Does the diagram identify all the possible states?
  - ° Are all the possible transitions between states identified?
  - ° Are all the events triggering each state's transition identified?
  - ° Are the necessary guard conditions labelled?
  - ° Are the necessary actions of event identified?
  - ° Does the state chart have an initial (and, if necessary end) state?

Observations

MIRI's adoption of model-based development, specifically in the form of UML-RT, was motivated by the characteristics (e.g., expectation of changing requirements) discussed earlier. The expectation was that this adoption would enable the development team to follow an iterative development style, and in particular help focus on rigorous yet understandable specification of interfaces and behaviour, with consequent benefits to the effort as a whole. In this section we summarize the effects we have been able to discern to date on aspects of quality, flexibility, communication and productivity.

Quality

From the efforts to date, we have seen indications of quality-improving activities successfully occurring in the context of model-based design. For example, we have seen that MIRI software engineers are actually finding requirements flaws (e.g., incompleteness and incorrectness) *early in the software development lifecycle*, by answering questions such as:

- Does the model meet its requirements?
- Is there wrong, missing, or incomplete logic?

- Does the model correctly accommodate all required inputs, outputs, and database elements according to the required format, content, data rate, etc.?.

These indications suggest that the artefacts of model-based design can be dealt with by the gamut of quality assurance practices that are needed for critical software.

Flexibility

The modelling approach provided a platform for the MIRI flight software to be developed so as to be more flexible and less impacted by hardware changes. Notably, the software design encapsulated hardware control elements to allow changes to be made to the hardware with little or no impact on the other parts of applications. This need for, and success of, this flexibility has been evident in the effort to date, during several years of which the requirements for the control of the instrument's cooling mechanism and interface to that were in a state of flux, while design trade-off studies were being conducted. The modelling approach allowed for the software development to progress even while these uncertainties remained, and to be readily able to adapt to the requirements and interfaces that ultimately emerged.

Communication

The designs artefacts (capsule diagrams, statecharts, etc) that the MIRI software development team has constructed by following the model-based approach are being exchanged between the development team (based in the United States) and the test team and partners (based in Europe). They have proven to be a useful form of conveying this information between these distinct groups. It is also encouraging to note that within the software development team, software engineers are actually exchanging information in terms of models and/or critiques of models, and are not reverting to informal descriptions (charts and textual documents).

Productivity

The hope was that using common tools and a common process would save time and effort, especially critical in a budget constraint environment. Over the course of multiple incremental deliveries of hardware and software for testing, the experience of the test team, software team and the hardware team indicates that we have done it more efficiently than the traditional way.

Internal to MIRI's software development, the practice has been to express the design as the model, and thereafter utilize the modelling tool suite to generate sequence diagrams and code itself. Experience to date indicates that this has been a tremendous help in implementation, testing, documenting and preparing for the design reviews.

4. FUTURE TRENDS

To understand where others are with respect to model-based design, a working group within JPL conducted a benchmarking study to compare JPL's engineering capability to seven different industries: Automobiles (Ford), Aerospace (Raytheon), Industrial Automation (Honeywell), Nuclear Energy (Sandia National Laboratories), Networks (AT&T), Airlines (United), and Weapons Systems (Los Alamos National Laboratory). Ford, Raytheon, and LANL showed strengths in model-based design as follows:

- Ford has invested in model-based engineering for competitive advantage and adopted model-based requirements and design analysis, with emphasis on design practices.
- Raytheon has used model-based design and simulation to address mission assurance requirements and made the domain expert and software engineer jointly responsible for model validation.
- Los Alamos National Laboratory has a mature capability and mindset for using virtual testbeds because of inherent domain limitations on physical testing.

The results of this study indicated how those industries took advantage of model-based design. However, JPL develops and builds one-off, novel spacecraft and systems (instruments, rovers), a situation that is somewhat different from those industry cases. Thus the advantages seen in industry will not necessarily apply to JPL. For example, JPL does not have the luxury of building multiple test units, nor can those test units recreate the deep space environments that spacecraft will experience, so our focus on early-lifecycle assurance is more critical than for those other industries. There is a continuing need for research to adapt/invent the processes that can utilize to good effect model-based design practices for JPL's mission- and safety-critical systems.

5. CONCLUSION

The objective of the use of high-quality software models is to improve quality, productivity and flexibility during development of critical software. We have described an instance of this in ongoing application in development of control software for a spacecraft component. We have illustrated how this development effort makes use of key notations of model based design as a vehicle for effective communication about key aspects of the software's design (notably its interface and overall behaviour). This development effort is also taking advantage of the automated code generation capabilities offered by the modelling tool to generate code directly from models.

The success of model-driven software development approach hinges on:

1. creation of a good quality (e.g., correct, complete, consistent, testable, etc.) model for a physical, mathematical, or logical representation of a system, entity, phenomenon, or process and

2. correct implementation of the model in software.

We have described some of the infusion and adaptation we are doing to apply leading software assurance techniques within the model based development approach, and so help ensure the quality of these models. It is also important to include all the necessary detail in the model so that automatic code generator can be used to automatically generate complete implementations. Following this approach has proven quite successful in this project, since doing so leads to detection of defects early in design stage (rather than later in the test stage), compared to the traditional development approach. In addition, the approach helps us more readily accommodate software changes forced by changes to hardware components and technologies used. Finally, it has proven helpful that the complex embedded real-time software system is designed with a sound architecture. For (2), ensuring correctness of the automated code generation step is also a concern, but has not been addressed by this chapter.

Future Research Directions

A model-driven software development approach offers a plethora of techniques for software modelling, and UML in particular has undergone several iterations (e.g., UML 0.9 in 1996, UML 1.1 in 1997, UML 1.4 in 1999, UML-RT in 2000, UML 2.0 in 2005). However, this form of modelling often requires that a level of detail below that covered by the models be provided. In the case of MIRI flight software, such detail takes the form of hand-coded software that fits in at the appropriate locations within the autocode generated from the models. The extent to which model based development can better accommodate and support this level of detail is an open research area.

We discusses how we believe that inspections have the potential to be equally effective for model-based design, and have begun to evolve them so as to achieve this potential. We believe this need for evolution will hold true of a broad range of quality assurance techniques. An important part of future research will be to identify which of these techniques have the potential to be highly effective on model based designs, and evolve them accordingly.

In addition, future research will invent new techniques specifically for V&V. The need for this is indicated by, among others, a JPL-conducted study (NASA 1998), which reported: "Organizations exercising existing techniques with a high degree of discipline are experiencing 'quality ceilings.' In these projects, traditional verification techniques have been improved and fine-tuned to the point that major quality improvements can no longer be achieved, even though some defects still remain in the developed product." The formal methods community is well placed to fill this role, and, it seems, particularly well suited to align with the semantically meaningful artefacts that predominate in the course of model-based development. Rather than requiring the separate (and hence costly, slow and disconnected) development of formal models for purposes of input to V&V tools, there is considerable interest in using model-based design's artefacts as inputs to V&V. For example, see the range of techniques for checking of UML statechart specifications in (Pap et al, 2001). Model-based design also holds promise as a means to improve other analysis methods, including testing. For example, (Blackburn, 1992) showed how model-based testing could have found the flaw in the logic of the Mars Polar Lander mission's landing control software (a flaw which is thought to have been responsible for the mission failure).

REFERENCES

Blackburn, M., Busser, R. Nauman, A. Knickerbocker, & Kasunder, R. (2002). Mars Polar Lander fault identification using model-based testing. In *26th NASA Goddard Software Engineering Workshop*, Greenbelt, MD (pp. 128-135) IEEE/NASA.

Brykczynski, B. (1999, January) A survey of Software Inspection checklists. *ACM SIGSOFT Software Engineering Notes* 24(1), 82-89.

Fagan, M.E. (1976) Design and Code Inspections to Reduce Errors in Program Development. *IBM Systems Journal*, 15(3), 182-211.

Kelly, J.C., Sherif, J.S., & Hops, J. (1992, February). An Analysis of Defect Densities Found During Software Inspections. *Journal of Systems and Software*. 17(2), 150-166.

NASA. (1998). *Formal Methods Specification and Verification Guidebook for Software and Computer Systems, Volume I: Planning and Technology Insertion*. NASA/TP-98-208193 http://eis.jpl.nasa.gov/quality/Formal_Methods/document/NASAgb1.doc

Pap, Z. Majzik, I., Pataricza A., & Szegi, A. (2001 April). Completeness and Consistency Analysis of UML Statechart Specifications, *Proceedings of the DDECS 2001 Workshop*, Győr, Hungary (pp. 83-90).

Shull, F.; Basili, V.; Boehm, B.; Brown, A.W.; Costa, P.; Lindvall, M.; Port, D.; Rus, I.; Tesoriero, R.; Zelkowitz, M. (2002 June). What we have learned about fighting defects"; *Proceedings. Eighth IEEE Symposium on Software Metrics* (pp. 249 – 258).

Selic, B., & J. Rumbaugh, J. (1998). *Using UML for Modeling Complex Real-Time Systems*.

ADDITIONAL READING

Ambler, S.W. (2003). The Elements of UML™ Style. Cambridge University Press.

Ambler, S.W. (2005). The Elements of UML™ 2.0 Style. Cambridge University Press.

Alexandre, D., Möller, M. O., & Yi, W. (2002). Formal Verification of UML Statecharts with Real-Time Extensions, Fundamental Approaches to Software Engineering, 5th International Conference, FASE 2002 (pp 208-241).

Bass, L., Clements, P., & Kazman, R. (1998). Software Architecture in Practice. Addision-Wesley, 1998.

Booch, G. (1994). *Object-Oriented Analysis and Design with Application*, 2nd edition. Redwood City, CA: Benjamin-Cummings Publishing Company.

Booch, G., Jacobson, I., & Rumbaugh, J. (2005). The Unified Modeling Language Reference Manual, Second Edition. Addison-Wesley.

Damm, W., Josko, B., Pnueli, A., & Votintseva, A. (2002). Understanding UML: A formal semantics of concurrency and communication in real-time UML. *Proceedings of the 1st Symposium on Formal Methods for Components and Objects* (pp. 70-98).

Douglass, B.P. (2000). Real-Time Design Patterns. Addison-Wesley.

Douglass, B.P. (1997). Real-Time UML: Efficient Objects for Embedded Systems. Addison-Wesley.

Gamma, E., Helm, R., Johnson, R., & Vlissides, J. (1995). *Design Patterns: Elements of Reusable Object-Oriented Software*. New York, NY: Addison-Wesley Publishing Company.

Gomaa, H., & D. Wijesekera, D. (2003, October). Consistency in Multiple-View UML Models: A

Case Study. Workshop on Consistency Problems in UML-based Software Development, San Francisco.

Jackson. M. (1993). System Development. Prentice Hall.

Jacobson I., Booch, G., & Rumbaugh, J. (1999). The Unified Software Development Process. Addision-Wesley.

Lange, C. F. J., Bois, B. D., Chaudron, M. R. V., & Serge Demeyer, S. (2006). An Experimental Investigation of UML Modeling Conventions. MoDELS 2006 (pp 27-41).

Lange, C. F. J., & Chaudron, M. R. V. (2006). Effects of defects in UML models: an experimental investigation. 28th International Conference on Software Engineering (pp 401-411).

Lange, C. F. J., & Chaudron, M. R. V. & Muskens, J. (2006, March). In Practice: UML Software Architecture and Design Description. IEEE Software 23(2), 40-46.

Lange, C.F.J. (2006, May). Improving the Quality of UML Models in Practice. 28th International Conference on Software Engineering (pp 993-996).

Lindland, O.I., Sindre, G., and Solvberg, A. (1994, March). Understanding Quality in Conceptual Modeling. IEEE Software 11(2), 42-49.

Martin, G., L. Lavagno, L. & Louis-Guerin, J. (1998). Embedded UML: A merger of real-time UML and co-design. Proceedings of Hot Interconnects 6.

Mitchell, R., Graff, P., & Bacvanski, V. (2004, January). High-quality modeling in UML. Infer-Data Corporation, USA.

Robbins, J., Redmiles, D. (1999, May). Cognitive Support, UML Adherence, and XMI Interchange in Argo/UML. Proceedings of the Conference on Construction of Software Engineering Tools, Los Angeles, CA (pp. 61-70).

Selic, B., & and J. Rumbaugh, J. (1998, March). Using UML for Modeling Complex Real-Time Systems. IBM Rational Technical Library, 1998

Selic, B., Gullekson, G. & Ward, P. (1994). Real-Time Object-Oriented Modeling. New York: John Wiley & Sons.

Selic, B. (2001). Using UML for Modeling Complex Real Time System Architectures. Object-Oriented Modeling of Embedded Real-Time Systems (pp. 16-21).

Selic, B., Gullekson, G., and Ward, P., Real-Time Object-Oriented Modeling, John Wiley & Sons, New York, NY, 1994.

Selic, B. (1999, October). Turning Clockwise: Using UML in the Real-Time Domain. Communications of the ACM, 42(10), 46-54.

Unhelkar, B. (2005). Verification and Validation for Quality of UML 2.0 Models. John Wiley & Sons, Inc.

Unhelkar, B. (2003). Process Quality Assurance for UML-Based Projects. Boston: Addison-Wesley.

Compilation of References

(Acme) The Acme Studio Homepage. http://www.cs.cmu. edu/~acme/ AcmeStudio/index.html.

(ARCHJAVA Project, 2005) ARCHJAVA Project. http://archjava.org/, 2005.

(AutoFOCUS Project) AutoFOCUS Project. http://autofocus.in.tum.de/index-e.html.

(AutoFOCUS2 Project) AutoFOCUS2 Project. http://www4.in.tum.de/af2.

(CAMG, 2007) MAAB The MathWorks Automotive Advisory Board (2007): *Control Algorithm Modeling Guidelines Using MATLAB, Simulink, and Stateflow, Version 2.0.* Retrieved from http://www.mathworks. com/industries/ auto/maab.html (MAAB_Style_Guide_ pdf_v2_00.zip)

(CHARMY, 2004) CHARMY Project: CHARMY Web Site. http://www.di.univaq.it/charmy (2004).

(CTE/ES, 2007) Razorcat Development GmbH: *CTE for Embedded Systems*, URL: http://www.razorcat.com

Abels & Haak & Hahn (2005). Identification of Common Methods Used for Ontology Integration Tasks. In: Proceedings of the first international ACM workshop on Interoperability of Heterogeneous Information Systems (IHIS05), CIKM conference proceedings. ACM, Sheridan publishing.

Abi-Antoun, M., & Aldrich, J. (2007). Owernship domains in the real world. In IWACO workshop at ECOOP.

Abowd, G., Allen, R. and Garlan, D. (1995). Formalizing style to understand descriptions of software architecture. *ACM Transactions on Software Engineering and Methodology, 4*(4), 319–364.

Abrahao, S., Condori-Fernández, N., Olsina, L., & Pastor, O. (2003). *Defining and validating metrics for navigational models.* In Proceedings of 9th International Software Metrics Symposium, pp.: 200-210.

Abreu, B. F., & Melo, W. (1996). Evaluating the impact of object-oriented design on software quality. *Third International Software Metrics Symposium (METRICS '96)*, 90-99.

Ackermann, J. and Turowski, K. (2006). A Library of OCL Specification Patterns to Simplify Behavioral Specification of Software Components. In *Proceedings of Conference on Advanced Information Systems Engineering*, volume 4001 of LNCS (Lecture Notes in Computer Science), pages 255–269.

ADM Task Force. Why do we need standards for the modernization of legacy systems. White Paper. Retrieved June, 1, 2007, from http://adm.omg.org/legacy/ ADM_whitepaper.pdf

ADM: Architecture-Driven Modernization home page: http://adm.omg.org

Adolph, S., Bramble, P., Cockburn, A., & Pols, A. (2003). Patterns for Effective Use Cases. Addison-Wesley.

Ahrendt, W., Baar, T., Beckert, B., Bubel, R., Giese, M., Hähnle, R., Menzel, W., Mostowski, W., Roth, A., Schlager, S., and Schmitt, P. H. (2005). The KeY Tool. *Software and System Modeling, 4*(1):32–54.

Aizenbud-Reshef, N., Nolan, B.T., Rubin, J., & Shaham-Gafni, Y. (2006). Model traceability. *IBM Systems Journal, 45(3)*, 515-526.

Aldrich, J., & Chambers, C. (2004). Ownership Domains: Separating Aliasing Policy from Mechanism. In Proc. of ECOOP'04 (pp. 1-25).

Aleman, J.L.F., & Alvarez, A.T. (2000). Can intuition become rigorous? Foundations for UML model verification tools. *Proceedings of the 11th International Symposium on Software Reliability Engineering*, 344-345.

Alexander, I., & Maiden, N. (2004). Scenarios, Stories, Use Cases through the Systems Development Life-Cycle. John Wiley and Sons.

Alikacem, E. and Sahraoui, H. (2006). Generic metric extraction framework. In *Proceedings of IWSM/MetriKon 2006*.

Allen, R. , & Garlan, D. (1997). A Formal Basis for Architectural Connection. ACM Trans. on Software Engineering and Methodology, 6(3), (pp. 213-249).

Alonso, G., Casati, F., Kuno, H. and Machiraju, V. (2004). *Web Services – Concepts, Architectures and Applications*. London, UK: Springer-Verlag.

Alur, R., Courcoubetis, C., & Dill, D. L.(1990). "Model Checking for Real-Time Systems". In Proc. of IEEE Fifth Symp. Logic in Computer Science, (pp. 414-425).

Ambler, S. W. (2002). Agile Modeling: Effective Practices for Extreme Programming and the Unified Process. John Wiley and Sons. 2002.

Ambler, S. W. (2003). The Elements of UML Style. Cambridge University Press.

Ambler, S.W. (2005). *The elements of UML 2.0 style*. New York: Cambridge University Press.

Anda, B. C. D. (2003). Empirical Studies of Construction and Application of Use Case Models. Ph.D. Thesis, University of Oslo, Oslo, Norway.

Anda, B. C. D., Sjøberg, D. I. K., & Jørgensen, M. (2001). Quality and Understandability in Use Case Models. The Fifteenth European Conference on Object-Oriented Programming (ECOOP 2001), Budapest, Hungary, June 18-22, 2001.

Angay, H. (2002). Template Use Case Pattern. Appropriate Process Group White Paper. 2002.

Antoniol, G., Caprile, B., Potrich, A., & Tonella, P. (2000). Design-code traceability for object-oriented system. *Annals for Software Engineering, 9*, 35-58

Appleton, B. A. (1997). Patterns and Software: Essential Concepts and Terminology. Object Magazine Online, 3(5), 20-25.

Astels, D. (2002). Refactoring with UML. In M. Marchesi, G. Succi (Eds.), *Proceedings of 3rd International Conference eXtreme Programming and Flexible Processes in Software Engineering* (pp. 67-70), Alghero, Italy.

Atkinson, C. and Kühne, T. (2001). The Essence of Multilevel Metamodeling. In Gogolla and Kobryn, editors, *UML 2001 – The Unified Modeling Language. Modeling Languages, Concepts, and Tools: 4th International Conference*, Toronto, Canada, October 1-5, 2001, Proceedings, volume 2185 of LNCS. Springer, pages 19-33.

Atkinson, C. and Kühne, T. (2003). Model-driven Development: A Metamodeling Foundation. *IEEE Software*, 20(5):36–41.

Atkinson, C., & Kühne, T. (2002). *The Role of Metamodeling in MDA*. Paper presented at the Workshop in Software Model Engineering, Dresden, Germany.

Atkinson, C., Kühne, T., & Henderson-Sellers, B. (2002, 2002). *Stereotypical encounters of the third kind*. Paper presented at the 5th International Conference on the Unified Modeling Language «UML» 2002. Model Engineering, Concepts, and Tools., Dresden, Germany.

Aurum, A., Petersson, H., & Wohlin, C. (2002). State-of-the-art: software inspection after 25 years. *Software Testing Verification and Reliability, 12(3)*, 133-154.

Autili, M., & Pelliccione, P. (2006). Towards a Graphical Tool for Refining User to System Requirements. In: 5th GT-VMT'06 - ETAPS'06, to appear in ENTCS.

Autili, M., Inverardi, P., & Pelliccione, P.(2007). Graphical Scenarios for Specifying Temporal Properties: an Automated Approach, published in the Automated Software Engineering (ASE) journal. DOI - 10.1007/s10515-007-0012-6.

B. Nuseibeh. Weaving Together Requirements and Architectures. IEEE Computer, 34(3):115–117, March 2001.

B. Schmerl, D. Garlan. AcmeStudio: Supporting Style-Centered Architecture Development. Proc. International Conference on Software Engineering, ICSE'04, pages 704-705, Edinburgh, Scotland, May 2004.

Baar, T. (2003). The Definition of Transitive Closure with OCL – Limitations and Applications. In *Proceedings, Fifth Andrei Ershov International Conference, Perspectives of System Informatics*, Novosibirsk, Russia, volume 2890 of LNCS, Springer, pages 358–365.

Bach, K. The Semantics-Pragmatics Distinction: What It Is and Why It Matters, Retrieved in June 2005, from http://userwww.sfsu.edu/~kbach/semprag.html

Baker, P., Loh, S., & Well, F. (2005). *Model-Driven Engineering in a Large Industrial Context - Motorola Case Study.* Paper presented at the Model Driven Engineering Languages and Systems - MoDELS, Montego Bay, Jamaica.

Balsamo, S. , DiMarco, A., Inverardi, P. & Simeoni, M. (2004). Model-Based Performance Prediction in Software Development: A Survey. *IEEE Transactions on Software Engineering, 30*(5), 295-310.

Bansiya, J. (2000). Evaluating framework architecture structural stability. *ACM Comput. Surv.*, 32(1es):18.

Bansiya, J. and Davis, C. (2002). A hierarchical model for object-oriented design quality assessment. *IEEE Transactions on Software Engineering*, 28(1):4–17.

Barber, K. S., Graser, T. , & Holt, J. (2001). Providing early feedback in the development cycle through automated application of model checking to software architectures. In Proc. of 16th IEEE International Conference on Automated Software Engineering, (pp. 341–345).

Baresi, L., Heckel, R., Thöne, S. and Varro, D. (2004). Style-based refinement of dynamic software architectures. *Proc. 4ᵗʰ Working IEEE/IFIP Conference on Software Architecture WICSA* (pp. 155–164).

Baroni, A. L. (2005). Quantitative assessment of uml dynamic models. In *ESEC/FSE-13: Proceedings of the 10th European software engineering conference held jointly with 13th ACM SIGSOFT international symposium on Foundations of software engineering*, pages 366–369. ACM Press.

Baroni, A., Braz, S., and Abreu, F. (2002). Using OCL to formalize object-oriented design metrics definitions. In *ECOOP'02 Workshop on Quantitative Approaches in OO Software Engineering*.

Barrett, R., Patcas, L.M., Murphy, J. and Pahl, C. (2006). Model Driven Distribution Pattern Design for Dynamic Web Service Compositions. *International Conference on Web Engineering ICWE'06* (pp. 129-136).

Basili, V. & Rombach, H. (1988). The TAME project: towards improvement-oriented software environments. *IEEE Transactions on Software Engineering*, 14(6), 728-738.

Basili, V. R., Caldiera, G., & Rombach, H. D. (1994). *Goal Question Metric Paradigm.* Encyclopaedia of Software Engineering, pp.: 528-532. John Wiley&Sons.

Basili, V. R., Green, S., Laitenberger, O., Shull, F., Sorumgard, S., & Zelkowitz, M. V. (1996). The empirical investigation of perspective-based reading. *Empirical Software Engineering, 1*(2), 133-164.

Basili, V. R., Caldiera, G., and Rombach, H. D. (1994). The goal question metric approach. In *Encyclopedia of Software Engineering.* Wiley.

Basili, V., Caldiera, G., and Rombach, D. (1994). The Goal/Question/Metric approach. *Encyclopedia of Software Engineering*, Volume I, 528–532. Los Alamitos, CA: Wiley.

Basili, V.R., & Weiss, D.M. (1984). A methodology for collecting valid software engineering data. *IEEE Transactions on Software Engineering*, 10(6), 728-738.

Basili, V.R., Green, S., laitenberger, O., Lanubile,F., Shull, F., Sørumgård, S., et al. (1996). The empirical investigation of perspective-based reading, *Empirical Software Engineering, 1(2)*, 133-164.

Bass, L., Clements, P. and Kazman, R. (2003). *Software Architecture in Practice.* SEI Series in Software Engineering. Boston, MA: Addison-Wesley.

Baumeister, H., Hacklinger, F., Hennicker, R., Knapp, A., & Wirsing, A. (2006). A Component Model for Architectural Programming. Electronic Notes in Theoretical Computer Science (160), (pp. 75–96).

Baxter, I. D., Yahin, A., Moura, L., Sant'Anna, M., & Bier, L. (1998). Clone detection using abstract syntax trees. In *Proc. international conference on software maintenance (ICSM '98)* (p. 368). Washington, DC: IEEE Computer Society.

Beck, K., & Andres, C. (2005). Extreme Programming Explained: Embrace Change (Second Edition). Addison-Wesley.

Becker, S., Koziolek, H. & Reussner, R. (2007). Model-based Performance Prediction with the Palladio Component Model. In *Proceedings of the 6th Workshop on Software and Performance WOSP'07* (pp. 56-67). ACM Press

Becker, S.; Grunske, L.; Mirandola, R. & Overhage, S. (2005). Performance Prediction of Component-Based Systems: A Survey from an Engineering Perspective. In *Springer Lecture Notes in Computer Science Vol. 3938* (pp. 169-192).

Becker, Steffen & Brogi, Antonio & Gorton, Ian & Overhage, Sven & Romanowsky, Alexander & Tivoli, Massimo (2006). Towards an Engineering Approach to Component Adaptation. In Architecting Systems with Trustworthy Components, *Proceedings of Dagstuhl Seminar 04511.*

Beckers, J.B.C., & Heemels, W.P.M.H., & Bukkems, B.H.M. (2006). Effective industrial modeling: The example of Happy Flow. In Heemels, W.P.M.H., & Muller, G.J. (Eds.) *Model-based design of high-tech systems,* (pp. 77-88). Eindhoven: Embedded Systems Institute.

Beckert, B., Keller, U., and Schmitt, P. H. (2002). Translating the Object Constraint Language into First-order Predicate Logic. In *Proceedings of VERIFY, Workshop at Federated Logic Conferences (FLoC).*

Beine, M., Otterbach, R., & Jungmann, M. (2004). Development of safety-critical software using automatic code generation. In *Proc. SAE world congress.* Society of Automotive Engineers.

Bengtsson, J., Larsen, K. G., Larsson, F., Pettersson, P., & Yi, W.(1995). Uppaal - a Tool Suite for Automatic Verification of Real-Time Systems. In Proceedings of the 4th DIMACS Workshop on Verification and Control of Hybrid Systems, New Brunswick, New Jersey, (pp. 22-24).

Berenbach, B. and Borotto, G. (2006). Metrics for model driven requirements development. In *ICSE '06: Proceeding of the 28th international conference on Software engineering*, pages 445–451, New York, NY, USA. ACM Press.

Berenbach, B., & Borotto, G. (2006). Metrics for Model Driven Requirements Development. The Twenty Eighth International Conference on Software Engineering (ICSE 2006), Shanghai, China, May 20-28, 2006.

Bergin, J. (2000). Fourteen Pedagogical Patterns. The Fifth European Conference on Pattern Languages of Programs (EuroPLoP 2000), Irsee, Germany, July 5-9, 2000.

Bernardo, M., & Inverardi, P. (2003). Formal Methods for Software Architectures, Tutorial book on Software Architectures and Formal Methods. SFM-03:SA Lectures, LNCS 2804.

Berns, G. M. (1984). Assessing software maintainability. *Communications of the ACM*, 27 (1), 14-23.

Bertolino, A. & Mirandola, R. (2004). CB-SPE Tool: Putting Component-Based Performance Engineering into Practice. In Crnkovic, I., Stafford, J. A., Schmidt, H. W. & Wallnau, K. C. (Ed.), *Proceedings of the 7ᵗʰ International Symposium on Component-Based Software Engineering, CBSE2004* (pp. 233-248). Springer Lecture Notes in Computer Science, Vol. 3054

Bertolino, A., Marchetti, E., & Muccini, H. (2004) Introducing a Reasonably Complete and Coherent Approach for Model-based Testing. (In: Testing and Analysis of Component-Based Systems Workshop, Tacos).

Beus-Dukic, L., & Myers, C. (2005). Use and Abuse Cases. The First International Workshop on Requirements Engineering Education and Training (REET 2005), Paris, France, August 29-September 2, 2005.

Beydeda, S., Book, M., & Gruhn, V. (2005). Model-Driven Software Development. Springer.

Bézivin, J. (2005). On the unification power of models. *Software and Systems Modeling, 4*(3), 171-188.

Bézivin, J., Jouault, F., Rosenthal, P., & Valduriez, P. (2005). *Modeling in the Large and Modeling in the Small.* Paper presented at the European MDA Workshops: Foundations and Applications, MDAFA 2003 and MDAFA 2004.

Biddle, R., Noble, J., & Tempero, E. (2001). Patterns for Essential Use Cases. Technical Report CS-TR-01/02. School of Mathematics, Statistics and Computer Science, Victoria University of Wellington, Wellington,

New Zealand. May 20, 2001.

Biermann, E., Ehrig, K., Köhler, C., Taentzer, G., & Weiss, E. (2006). Graphical Definition of In-Place Transformations in the Eclipse Modeling Framework. In O. Nierstrasz (Ed.), *Proceedings of International Conference on Model Driven Engineering Languages and Systems* (pp. 425-439), Lecture Notes in Computer Science 4199, Heidelberg: Springer.

Bittner, K., & Spence, I. (2003). Use Case Modeling. Addison-Wesley.

Björnvig, G. (2003). Patterns for the Role of Use Cases. The Eighth European Conference on Pattern Languages of Programs (EuroPLoP 2003), Irsee, Germany, June 25-29, 2003.

Blackburn, M., Busser, R. Nauman, A. Knickerbocker, & Kasunder, R. (2002). Mars Polar Lander fault identification using model-based testing. In *26th NASA Goddard Software Engineering Workshop*, Greenbelt, MD (pp. 128-135) IEEE/NASA.

Blackwell, A.F. & Green, T.R.G. (2000) A Cognitive Dimensions questionnaire optimised for users. In: *Proceedings of the Twelth Annual Meeting of the Psychology of Programming Interest Group* (pp.137-152).

Blunden, B. (2003). Software Exorcism: A Handbook for Debugging and Optimizing Legacy Code. Apress.

Bobkowska, A.E. (2001) *Software Quality Prediction with UML*, Unpublished doctoral dissertation, Gdansk University of Technology.

Bobkowska, A.E. (2005) A methodology of Visual Modeling Language Evaluation, In: *Proceedings of SOFSEM 2005*, LNCS 3381 (pp. 72-81).

Boehm, B. (1989). *Software Risk Management*. Los Alamos: IEEE.

Boehm, B. W. (1981). *Software engineering economics*. Englewood Cliffs, NJ: Prentice-Hall.

Boehm, B. W., Abts, C., Brown, A. W., Chulani, S., Clark, B. K., Horowitz, E., Madachy, R., Reifer, D., & Steece, B. (2001). Software Cost Estimation with COCOMO II. Prentice Hall.

Boehm, B. W., Brown, J. R., Kaspar, H., Lipow, M., Macleod, G. J., & Merrit, M. J. (1978). *Characteristics of software quality*. New York, NY: North-Holland.

Boehm, B.W., Brown, J.R., & Lipow, M. (1976). Quantitative evaluation of software quality, *Proceedings of the 2nd international conference on Software Engineering*, 592-605.

Boger, M., Sturm, T., & Fragemann, P. (2002). Refactoring Browser for UML. In M. Marchesi, G. Succi (Eds.), *Proceedings 3rd International Conference on eXtreme Programming and Flexible Processes in Software Engineering* (pp. 77-81), Alghero, Italy.

Bois, B. D., Lange, C. F., Demeyer, S., and Chaudron, M. R. (2006). A Qualitative Investigation of UML Modeling Conventions. In (Kuzniarz et al., 2006), pages 79–94.

Bolloju, N., & Leung, F. S. K. (2006). Assisting Novice Analysts in Developing Quality Conceptual Models with UML. Communications of the ACM, 49(7), 108-112.

Bondarev, E., de With, P., Chaudron, M. & Musken, J. (2005). Modelling of Input-Parameter Dependency for Performance Predictions of Component-Based Embedded Systems. In *Proceedings of the 31th EUROMICRO Conference (EUROMICRO'05)*

Booch, G. (1994) *Object-Oriented Analysis and Design with Applications*. Benjamin/Cummings.

Booch, G., Jacobson, I., & Rumbaugh, J. (2005). The Unified Modeling Language Reference Manual (Second Edition). Addison-Wesley.

Boronat, A., Carsí J.A., & Ramos I. (2006). *Algebraic Specification of a Model Transformation Engine*. Proceedings of the Fundamental Approaches to Software Engineering (FASE'06). ETAPS'06. Vienna, Austria, 262–277.

Boronat, A., Carsí, J.Á., Ramos, I. (2005). *MOMENT: a formal MOdel manageMENT tool*. School on Generative and Transformational Techniques in SE. Braga, Portugal.

Bose, P.(1999). Automated translation of uml models of architectures for verification and simulation using spin. In Proc. of 14th IEEE International Conference on Automated Software Engineering, (pp. 102–109).

Botafogo, R. A., Rivlin, E., & Shneiderman, B. (1992). *Structural analysis of hypertexts: identifying hierarchies and useful metrics*. ACM Transactions on Information Systems, Vol. 10(2). pp.: 142-180.

Bottoni, P., Parisi-Presicce, F., Mason, G., & Taentzer, G. (2005). Specifying Coherent Refactoring of Software Artefacts with Distributed Graph Transformations. In P. van Bommel (Ed.), *Handbook on Transformation of Knowledge, Information, and Data: Theory and Applications* (pp. 95-125). Hershey, PA: Information Science Publishing.

Bouden, S. (2006). *Étude de la traçabilité entre refactorisations du modèle de classes et refactorisations du code*. Unpublished masters dissertation, Université de Montréal, Canada.

Bourque, P., Dupuis, R., Abran, A., Moore, J. W., Tripp, L., & Wolff, S. (2002). Fundamental Principles of Software Engineering - A Journey. Journal of Systems and Software, 62(1), 59-70.

Bowen, J.P., & Hinchey, M.G. (1995) Ten commandments of formal methods. *IEEE Computer, 28(4)*, 56-63.

Brand, Klaus-Peter & Buchholz, Bernd (2003). *Systemanforderungen an interoperable Geräte und Systeme der Stationsautomatisierung*. In (Schwarz, Karlheinz (Edt.): Offene Kommunikation nach IEC 61850 für die Schutz- und Stationsleittechnik.

Briand, L. C., Morasca, S., and Basili, V. R. (1996). Property-based software engineering measurement. *Software Engineering*, 22(1):68–86.

Briand, L.C., Daly, J., Porter, V., & Wüst, J. (1998). A comprehensive empirical validation of design measures for object oriented system. Proceedings of the 5th International Software Metrics Symposium, 246-257.

Briand, L.C., Labiche, Y., Penta, M.D., Yan-Bondoc, H.D. (2005). An experimental investigation of formality in UML-based development. *IEEE Transactions on Software Engineering, 31(10)*, 833-849

Briand, L.C., Wüst, J., Daly, J.W., & Porter, D.V. (2000). Exploring the relationships between design measures and software quality in object-oriented systems, *The Journal of Systems and Software, 51(3)*, 245-273.

Bril, R.J., Krikhaar, R.L., Postma, A. (2005). Architectural Support in Industry: a reflection using C-POSH. Journal of Software Maintenance and Evolution.

Brito, I. (2004). Aspect-Oriented Requirements Engineering. The Seventh International Conference on the Unified Modeling Language (<<UML 2004>>), Lisbon, Portugal, October 11-15, 2004.

Brooks, F. P. (1995). No Silver Bullet: Essence and accidents of software engineering. In *The Mythical Man-Month: Essays on Software Engineering, 20th Anniversary Edition*. Reading, MA: Addison-Wesley.

Brottier, E., Fleurey, F., & Le Traon, Y. (2006). Metamodel-based Test Generation for Model Transformations: an Algorithm and a Tool. In *Proceedings 17th International Symposium on Reliability Engineering* (pp. 85-94), IEEE Computer Society.

Broy, M., Deissenboeck, F., & Pizka, M. (2006). Demystifying maintainability. In *Proc. the 4th workshop on software quality*. New York, NY: ACM Press.

Brucker, A. D. and Wolff, B. (2006). *The HOL-OCL Book*. Technical Report 525, ETH Zurich, Switzerland.

Brucker, A. D., Doser, J., and Wolff, B. (2006). Semantic Issues of OCL: Past, Present, and Future. In *Proceedings of the 6th OCL Workshop at the UML/MoDELS Conference 2006*, pages 213-228.

Brykczynski, B. (1999, January) A survey of Software Inspection checklists. *ACM SIGSOFT Software Engineering Notes* 24(1), 82-89.

Büchi, J. (1960). On a decision method in restricted second order arithmetic. In: International Congress on Logic, Method and Philosophical Sciences.

Budinsky, F. , Steinberg, D., Merks, E., Ellersick, R., & Grose, T.J. (2003). Eclipse Modeling Framework. Addison Wesley.

Buhr, R. J. A. (1998). Use Case Maps as Architectural Entities for Complex Systems. IEEE Transactions on Software Engineering, 24(12), 1131-1155.

Bundesministerium für Wirtschaft (2004). *Gesetz für den Vorrang Erneuerbarer Energien* (EEG) in der Fassung vom 21.7.2004, BGBL, I:1918

Buschmann, F., Meunier, R., Rohnert, H., Sommerlad, P., and Stal, M. (1996). *Pattern-oriented Software Architecture: a System of Patterns*. John Wiley & Sons, Inc. New York, NY, USA.

Cabot, J. (2006). Ambiguity Issues in OCL Postconditions. In *Proceedings of the 6th OCL Workshop at the UML/MoDELS Conference 2006*, pages 194–204.

Cabot, J. and Teniente, E. (2006). A metric for measuring the complexity of ocl expressions. In *Model Size Metrics Workshop co-located with MODELS'06*.

Caporuscio, M., DiMarco, A. & Inverardi, P. (2007), Model-based system reconfiguration for dynamic performance management. *Journal of Systems and Software, 80*(4), (pp. 455-473). Elsevier

Cengarle, M. V. and Knapp, A. (2004). OCL 1.4/5 vs. 2.0 Expressions Formal Semantics and Expressiveness. *Software and Systems Modeling*, 3(1):9–30.

Chen, S.-K., Lei, H., Wahler, M., Chang, H., Bhaskaran, K., and Frank, J. (2006). A Model Driven XML Transformation Framework for Business Performance Management Model Creation. In *International Journal of Electronic Business*, volume 4, pages 281–301. Inderscience.

Cheng, Betty H.C, & Konrad, S.(2006). Automated Analysis of Natural Language Properties for UML Models. Jean-Michel Bruel, editor, Satellite Events at the MoDELS 2005, n. 3844 in LNCS, (pp. 48-57). Springer Verlag.

Chidamber, S.R., & Kemerer, C.F. (1994). A metrics suite for object oriented design. *IEEE Transaction on Software Engineering, 20(6)*, 476-493. .

Chiorean, D., Bortes, M., and Corutiu, D. (2005). Proposals for a Widespread Use of OCL. In Baar, T., editor, *Proceedings of the MoDELS'05 Conference Workshop on Tool Support for OCL and Related Formalisms - Needs and Trends*, Montego Bay, Jamaica, October 4, 2005, Technical Report LGL-REPORT-2005-001, pages 68–82. EPFL, Lausanne, Switzerland.

Chretienne, P., Jean-Marie, A., Le Lann, G., Stefani, J., Atos Origin, and Dassault Aviation (2004). Programme d'Étude Amont Mesure de la compléxité (marché n°00-34-007). Technical report, DGA.

Chrissis, M., Konrad, M., and Shrum, S. (2003). *CMMI: Guidelines for Process Integration and Product Improvement*. Addison-Wesley Professional.

Chung, L., & Nixon, B.A., & Yu, E. (2000). *Non-functional requirements in software engineering*. Boston: Kluwer.

Clarke, E. M., Grumberg, O., & Peled, D. A. (2000). Model Checking. The MIT Press, Cambridge, second edition.

Clarke, E.M., & Wing, J.M. (1996). Formal methods: State of the art and future directions, *ACM Computing Survey, 28(4)*, 626-643.

Clavel, M., Durán, F., Eker, S., Lincoln, P., Martí-Oliet, N., Meseguer, J., & Talcott, C. (2005). Maude 2.2 manual and examples, from http://maude.cs.uiuc.edu/maude2-manual

Clemen, R. T. (1996). Making Hard Decisions: An Introduction to Decision Analysis (Second Edition). Duxbury Press.

Cockburn, A. (2001). Writing Effective Use Cases. Addison-Wesley.

Cockburn, A. (2005). Crystal Clear: A Human-Powered Methodology for Small Teams. Addison-Wesley.

Coleman, D., Ash, D., Lowther, B., & Oman, P. W. (1994). Using metrics to evaluate software system maintainability. *Computer*, 27 (8), 44-49.

Conradi, R., Mohagheghi, P., Arif, T., Hegde, L. C., Bunde, G. A., & Pedersen, A. (2003). Inspection of UML Diagrams using OORT - An Industrial Experiment. European Conference for Object-Oriented Programming (ECOOP 2003), Darmstadt, Germany, July 21-25, 2003.

Cook, S. (2000). The UML Family: Profiles, Prefaces and Packages. In Evans, A., Kent, S., and Selic, B., editors, *UML 2000 - The Unified Modeling Language, Advancing the Standard, Third International Conference*, York, UK, October 2-6, 2000, Proceedings, volume 1939 of LNCS, pages 255–264. Springer.

Corporaal, H. (2006a). Embedded System Design. In *Progress White Papers 2006* (pp. 7-25). Utrecht: STW Progress.

Corporaal, H. (2006b), Embedded System Design. STW Progress presentation, May 10, 2006. Retrieved 4 March 2007, from: www.ics.ele.nl/~heco.

Correa, A., & Werner, C. (2004). Applying Refactoring Techniques to UML/OCL Models. In *Proceedings International Conference UML 2004* (pp. 173-187), Lecture Notes in Computer Science 3273, Heidelberg: Springer.

Cortellessa, V., Di Marco, A. and Inverardi, P. (2006). Software performance model-driven architecture. *Proc. ACM Symposium on Applied Computing SAC'06* (pp. 1218–1223).

Costal, D., Gómez, C., Queralt, A., Raventós, R., and Teniente, E. (2006). Facilitating the Definition of General Constraints in UML. In Nierstrasz, O., Whittle, J., Harel, D., and Reggio, G., editors, *MoDELS 2006*, volume 4199 in LNCS, pages 260–274. Springer-Verlag.

Costello, R. J. and Liu, D.-B. (1995). Metrics for requirements engineering. *J. Syst. Softw.*, 29(1):39–63.

Cowling, A. J. (2005). The Role of Modelling in the Software Engineering Curriculum. Journal of Systems and Software, 75(1-2), 41-53.

Cox, K. (2000) Cognitive Dimensions of use cases: feedback from a student questionnaire. In: *Proceedings of the Twelth Annual Meeting of the Psychology of Programming Interest Group*.

Cox, K. (2000). Cognitive Dimensions of Use Cases: Feedback from a Student Questionnaire. The Twelfth Annual Meeting of the Psychology of Programming Interest Group, Corigliano Calabro, Italy, April 10-13, 2000.

Cox, K., & Phalp, K. (2000). Replicating the CREWS Use Case Authoring Guidelines Experiment. Empirical Software Engineering Journal, 5(3), 245-267.

Cox, K., Phalp, K., & Shepperd, M. (2001). Comparing Use Case Writing Guidelines. The Seventh International Workshop on Requirements Engineering: Foundation for Software Quality, Interlaken, Switzerland, June 4-5, 2001.

Crosby, P. B. (1979). *Quality is Free. The Art of Making Quality Certain*. McGraw-Hill Book Company.

Cruz-Lemus, J. A., Genero, M., Manso, M. E., & Piattini, M. (2005). Evaluating the effect of composite states on the understandability of UML statechart diagrams. In *Proc. 8th int. conf. on model driven engineering languages and systems*. Berlin, Heidelberg: Springer-Verlag.

Cuesta, C. E., del Pilar Romay, M., de la Fuente, P. and Barrio-Solorzano, M. (2005). Architectural Aspects of Architectural Aspects. *Proc. 2nd European Workshop on Software Architecture EWSA 2005*. Springer LNCS 3047.

Czarnecki, K., & Eisenecker, E. (2000). Generative programming. Addison-Wesley Professional.

Czarnecki, K., & Helsen, S. (2006). Feature-based survey of model transformation approaches. *IBM Systems Journal*, 45(3), 621–645.

Czarnecki, Krzysztof & Eisenecker, Ulrich (2000). *Generative Programming - Methods, Tools, and Applications*. Addison-Wesley.

D'Souza, D., "Model-Driven Architecture and Integration: Opportunities and Challenges", Version 1.1. http://www.catalysis.org/publications/papers/2001mda-reqs-desmond-6.pdf

Dag, Hasan & Urkan, Ulmut (2004). *An XML Based Data Exchange Model for Power System Studies*. ARI - The Bulletin of the Istanbul Technical University, 2.

Dashofy, E. M., van der Hoek, A., & Taylor, R. N. (2002). An infrastructure for the rapid development of xml-based architecture description languages. In ICSE '02: Proceedings of the 24th Int. Conf. on Software Eng., (pp. 266–276), New York, NY, USA, ACM Press.

David, A., Möller, M.O., & Yi, W. (2002). Formal verification of UML statecharts with real-Time extensions, *Lecture Notes in Computer Science, 2306*, 208-241.

Davies, I., Green, P., Rosemann, M., Indulska, M., & Gallo, S. (2006). How do Practitioners Use Conceptual Modeling in Practice? Data and Knowledge Engineering, 58(3), 358-380.

Davis, A., Overmyer, S., Jordan, K., Caruso, J., Dandashi, F., Dinh, A., Kincaid, G., Ledeboer, G., Reynolds, P., Sitaram, P., Ta, A., and Theofanos, M. (1993). Identifying and measuring quality in a software requirements specification. In *Proceedings of the First International Software Metrics Symposium.*

Davis, P. K. and Bigelow, J. H. (2002). Motivated Metamodels. In *Proceedings of the 2002 PerMIS Workshop.*

De Champeaux, D.& Faure, P. (1992) A comparative study of object-oriented analysis methods. In: Journal of Object-Oriented Programming, 1(5) 21-33.

de Lara, J., & Vangheluwe, H. (2002). *AToM³: A tool for multi-formalism modelling and meta-modelling.* In Proceedings of ETAPS/FASE'02. Lecture Notes in Computer Science, Vol. 2306, pp.: 174-188. Springer-Verlag. See the AToM³ home page: http://atom3.cs.mcgill.ca, and http://astreo.ii.uam.es/~jlara/doctorado.2006/ATOM3_deploy.zip for the version described in this chapter.

De Miguel, M., Jourdan, J., & Salicki, S. (2002). *Practical Experiences in the Application of MDA.* Paper presented at the The 6th International Conference on The Unified Modeling Language - «UML» 2002.

De Miguel, M., Jourdan, J., Salicki, S.:(2002) *Practical Experiences in the Application of MDA.* In: Stevens, P., Whittle, J., Booch, G. (eds.): The 6th Int. Conf. on UML, Vol. 2460, Springer-Verlag (2002) 128-139.

Dean, M., & Schreiber, G. (2004). OWL Web Ontology Language Reference. W3C Recommendation. World Wide Web Consortium (W3C). February 10, 2004.

Debusmann, M. and Geihs, K. (2003). Efficient and Transparent Instrumentation of Application Components using an Aspect-oriented Approach. *Proc. IFIP/IEEE Workshop on Distributed Systems: Operations and Management DSOM 2003* (pp. 209–220). Springer LNCS 2867.

Debusmann, M., Schmid, M. and Kroeger, R. (2002). Measuring End-to-End Performance of CORBA Applications using a Generic Instrumentation Approach. *Proc. 7th Int. Symp. on Computers and Communications ISCC '02* (pp. 181–186).

Deissenboeck, F., Pizka, M., & Seifert, T. (2005). Tool support for continuous quality assessment. In *Proc. 13th IEEE international workshop on software technology and engineering practice (STEP '05)* (p. 127-136). Los Alamitos, CA: IEEE Computer Society.

Deissenboeck, F., Wagner, S., Pizka, M., Teuchert, S., & Girard, J.-F. (2007). An activity-based quality model for maintainability. In *Proc. 23rd international conference on software maintenance (ICSM '07)*. Washington, DC: IEEE Computer Society.

Demeyer, S., Ducasse, S., & Nierstrasz, O. (2000). Finding Refactorings Via Change Metrics. In *Proceedings International Conference OOPSLA 2000* (pp. 166-177). ACM SIGPLAN Notices 35(10), ACM Press.

deVos & Rowbotham (2001). *Knowledge Representation for Power System Modeling*, In (IEEE Publishing Edt.): Proceedings of the PICA 2001 (The 22nd International Conference on Power Industry Computer Applications), IEEE Power Engineering Society.

deVos & Widergren & Zhu (2001). *XML for CIM Model Exchange.* In (IEEE Publishing Edt.): Proceedings of the PICA 2001 (The 22nd International Conference on Power Industry Computer Applications), IEEE Power Engineering Society.

deVos, Arnold (2000). *Simplified RDF Syntax for Power System Model Exchange.* Longdale Consultants, 2000, available at http://www.langdale.com.au/CIMXML/.

Di Battista, G., Eades, P., Tamassia, R., & Tollis, I. G. (1999). Graph Drawing: Algorithms for the Visualization of Graphs. Prentice-Hall.

Diaconescu, A., Mos, A. and Murphy, J. (2004). Automatic Performance Management in Component Based Systems. *Proc. 1st Int. Conf. on Autonomous Computing ICAC'04* (pp. 214–221).

Díaz, P., Aedo, I., & Panetsos, F. (2001). *Modeling the dynamic behavior of hypermedia applications.* IEEE Transactions on Software Engineering, 27 (6), pp.: 550-572.

Díaz, P., Montero, S., & Aedo, I. (2005). *Modeling hypermedia and web applications: the Ariadne Development Method.* Information Systems, Vol. 30(8), pp.: 649-673.

Dijkstra, E. W. (1968). Goto statement considered harmful. *Communications of the ACM*, 11 (3), 147-148.

Doan & Madhavan & Domingos, & Halevy (2002). Learning to map between ontologies on the semantic web. In: Proceedings of the Eleventh International WWW Conference, Hawaii, US.

Dobrica, L., & Niemela, E. A Survey on Software Architecture Analysis Methods. IEEE Transactions on Software Engineering, VOL. 28, NO. 7.

Dobrzanski, L., & Kuzniarz, L. (2006). An approach to refactoring of executable UML models. In Proc. *2006 ACM symposium on applied computing (SAC '06)* (pp. 1273-1279). New York, NY: ACM Press.

Dromey, R. G. (1995). A model for software product quality. *IEEE Transactions on Software Engineering*, 21 (2), 146-162.

Dromey, R. G. (2003). Software Quality - Prevention Versus Cure? Software Quality Journal, 11(3), 197-210.

DSLTools from Microsoft, 2007: http://msdn.microsoft.com/vstudio/DSLTools/

dSpace. (2006). *Modeling guidelines for MATLAB/ Simulink/ Stateflow and TargetLink.*

Du Bois, B. (2006). *Quality-Oriented Refactoring.* Unpublished doctoral dissertation, Universiteit Antwepen, Belgium.

Dunsmore, A., Roper, M., & Wood, M. (2001).. Systematic object-oriented inspection—an empirical study. *Proceedings of the 23rd International Conference on Software Engineering*, 135-144.

Dwyer, M. B., Avrunin, G. S., & Corbett, J. C. (1999). Patterns in property specifications for finite-state verification. In ICSE, (pp. 411–420).

Dwyer, M. B., Avrunin, G. S., and Corbett, J. C. (1998). Property Specification Patterns for Finite-state Verification. In *FMSP '98: Proceedings of the second workshop on Formal methods in software practice*, pages 7–15, New York, NY, USA. ACM Press.

Edmonds, B. (1999). *Syntactic Measures of Complexity.* PhD thesis, University of Manchester.

Egyed, A. (2006). Instant consistency checking for the UML. In *Proc. International Conference on Software Engineering* (pp. 31-390), ACM.

Ehrig & Sure (2004). Ontology Mapping - An Integrated Approach. Proceedings of the First European Semantic

Web Symposium. Lecture Notes in Computer Science, Vol. 3053, Springer Verlag, Heraklion, Greece, May 2004, S. 76-91.

Ehrig, H, Ehrig, K. Prange, U. & Taentzer, G. (2006). *Fundamental Approach to Graph Transformation.* EATCS Monographs, Heidelberg: Springer.

Ehrig, H., Ehrig, K., Prange, U., & Taentzer, G. (2006). *Fundamentals of algebraic graph transformation.* Monographs in Theoretical Computer Science. Springer.

Ehrig, H., Tsioalikis, A. (2000). Consistency analysis of UML class and sequence diagrams using attributed graph grammars. In *ETAPS 2000 workshop on graph transformation systems* (pp. 77-86).

Eick, S. G., Graves, T. L., Karr, A. F., Marron, J. S., & Mockus, A. (2001). Does code decay? assessing the evidence from change management data. *IEEE Transactions on Software Engineering*, 27 (1), 1-12.

El Wakil, M., El Bastawissi, A., Boshra, M., and Fahmy, A. (2005). A novel approach to formalize and collect object-oriented design-metrics. In *Proceedings of the 9th International Conference on Empirical Assessment in Software Engineering.*

El-Attar, M., & Miller, J. (2006). Matching Antipatterns to Improve the Quality of Use Case Models. The Fourteenth International Requirements Engineering Conference (RE 2006), Minneapolis-St. Paul, USA. September 11-15, 2006.

El-Emam, K., Melo, W., & Machado, J.C. (2001). The prediction of faulty classes using object-oriented design metrics. *Journal of Systems and Software, 56(1),* 63-75.

Elvesæter, Brian & Hahn, Axel & Berre, Arne-Jørgen & Neple, Tor (2005). Towards an Interoperability Framework for Model-Driven Development of Software Systems, Proceedings of the 2005 International Conference on Interoperability for Enterprise Software and Applications (I-ESA 2005).

Engels, G., Heckel, R., & Küster, J.M. (2003). The consistency workbench: A tool for consistency management in UML-based development. *Lecture Notes in Computer Sciences, 2893,* 356-359.

Engels, G., Küster, J.M, Heckel, R., & Groenewegen, L. (2001). A methodology for specifying and analyzing consistency of object-oriented behavioral models. *ACM SIGSOFT Software Engineering Notes, 26(5)*, 186-195.

Eppler, M. J. (2001). The Concept of Information Quality: An Interdisciplinary Evaluation of Recent Information Quality Frameworks. Studies in Communication Sciences, 1(2), 167-182.

Eriksson, H.-E., Penker, M., Lyons, B., & Fado D. (2004). UML 2 Toolkit, chapter Ch. 7, Representing Architecture, (pp. 251–279). John Wiley and Sons..

Erlikh, L. (2000). Leveraging legacy system dollars for e-business. *IT Professional*, 2 (3), 17-23.

Eskenazi, E., Fioukov, A. & Hammer, D. (2004). Performance Prediction for Component Compositions. In Crnkovic, I., Stafford, J. A., Schmidt, H. W. & Wallnau, K. C. (Ed.), *Proceedings of the 7th International Symposium on Component-Based Software Engineering, CBSE2004.* Springer Lecture Notes in Computer Science, Vol. 3054 Grassi, V., Mirandola, R. & Sabetta, A. (2005). From design to analysis models: a kernel language for performance and reliability analysis of component-based systems. In *Proceedings of the 5th international workshop on Software and performance, WOSP '05* (pp. 25-36). ACM Press

EStdIT - Entwicklungsstandard für IT-Systeme des Bundes (1997): *V-Modell - Vorgehensmodell Kurzbeschreibung.* Retrieved from URL: http://www.v-modell. iabg.de

Esterel Technologies, Inc. (2007): *SCADE Product Suite.* URL: http://www.esterel-technologies.com/products/scade-suite

ETAS GmbH (2007): ASCET Product Family, ASCET-MD (Modeling & Design). URL: http://en.etasgroup. com /products/ascet

European Parlament (2003). Richtlinie 2003/54/EG des Europäischen Parlaments und des Rates vom 26.Juli 2003 über die gemeinsamen Vorschriften für den Elektrizitätsbinnenmarkt und zur Aufhebung der Richtlinie 96/92/EG.

Evans, A., Maskeri, G., Sammut, P., & Willians, J. S. (2003). *Building Families of Languages for Model-Driven System Development.* Paper presented at the Workshop in Software Model Engineering, San Francisco, CA.

Evans, Eric (2004). *Domain-Driven Design – Tackling Complexity in the Heart Of Software.* Addison-Wesley.

Fagan, M. (1976). Design and code inspection to reduce errors in program development. *IBM Systems Journal, 15(3)*, 182-211.

Fagan, M. (1986). Advances in software inspections. *IEEE Transactions on Software Engineering, 12(7)*, 744-751.

Fagan, M. E. (1976). Design and code inspections to reduce errors in program development. *IBM Systems Journal, 15*(3), 182-211.

Fagan, M.E. (1976) Design and Code Inspections to Reduce Errors in Program Development. *IBM Systems Journal*, 15(3), 182-211.

Fantechi, A., Gnesi, S., Lami, G., & Maccari, A. (2003). Applications of Linguistic Techniques for Use Case Analysis. Requirements Engineering, 8(3), 161-170.

Fantechi, A., Gnesi, S., Lami, G., and Maccari, A. (2002). Application of linguistic techniques for use case analysis. In *RE '02: Proceedings of the 10th Anniversary IEEE Joint International Conference on Requirements Engineering*, pages 157–164, Washington, DC, USA. IEEE Computer Society.

Farkas, T. & Röbig H. (2007): *Automatisierte, werkzeugübergreifende Richtlinienprüfung zur Unterstützung des Automotive-Entwicklungsprozesses.* M. Conrad, H. Giese, B. Rumpe, B. Schätz (Ed.): Proceedings of the Dagstuhl-Workshop MBEES: Modellbasierte Entwicklung eingebetteter Systeme III., Informatics-Report 2007-01, Technical University Braunschweig, January 2007, Dagstuhl, Germany.

Farkas, T., Hein, C. & Ritter, T. (2006): *Automatic Evaluation of Modeling Rules and Design Guidelines.* European Conference on Model Driven Architecture - Foundations and Applications (ECMDA2006), Lecture Notes in Computer Science, ISBN-10: 3540359095, Springer-Verlag, July 2006, Bilbao, Spain.

Farkas, T., Leicher, A. & Röbig H., et al. (2006): *Werkzeugübergreifende Konsistenzsicherung von Artefakten bei der Entwicklung softwarebasierter Systeme im*

Automobil. 4th Workshop on Automotive Software Engineering, Informatik 2006, Jahrestagung der Gesellschaft für Informatik, October 2006, Dresden, Germany.

Favre, J.-M. (2004). *Towards a basic theory to model driven engineering.* Workshop on Software Model Engineering, WISME 2004, joint event with UML'2004, Lisbon.

Fenton, N. E. (1996). *Software metrics: A rigorous and practical approach (2nd edition).* International Thomson Computer Press.

Fenton, N. E., & Pfleeger, S. L. (1997). Software Metrics: A Rigorous & Practical Approach. International Thomson Computer Press.

Fenton, N. E. (1991). *Software Metrics: A Rigorous Approach.* Chapman & Hall.

Fenton, N., & Pfleeger, S. L. (1997). *Software Metrics: A Rigorous and Practical Approach* (2nd edition). London, UK: International Thomson Computer Press.

Fenton, N.E. (1999). *Software metrics, a rigorous approach.* London: Chapman & Hall.

Fenton, N.E., & Neil, M. (1999). Software metrics: Successes, failures, and new directions. *Journal of Systems and Software, 47(2-3),* 149-157.

Filman, R, Elrad, T., Clarke, S., & Mehmet, A. (2005). Aspect-Oriented Software Development. Addison-Wesley.

Firesmith, D., Henderson-Sellers, B., Graham, I.& Page-Jones, M. (1996) OPEN Modeling Language (OML). Reference Manual.

Fogg, B. J., & Tseng, S. (1999). The Elements of Computer Credibility. The ACM CHI 99 Conference on Human Factors in Computing Systems, Pittsburgh, USA, May 15-20, 1999.

Form, T. (2006): *Systems Engineering im Spannungsfeld von Architekturen und Prozesse.* 10. EUROFORUM-Jahrestagung Elektronik-Systeme im Automobil, Technical University Braunschweig, Munich, Germany.

Fowler, M. (1999) *Refactoring: Improving the Design of Existing Code.* Addison-Wesley.

Fowler, M. (2003). UML Distilled: A Brief Guide to the Standard Object Modeling Language (Third Edition). Addison-Wesley.

Fowler, M., Beck, K., Brant, J., Opdyke, W., & Roberts, D.(1999). Refactoring: Improving the Design of Existing Code. Addison-Wesley.

Fowler, Martin (2005). Language Workbenches: The Killer-App For Domain-Specific Languages? Retrieved 2007/05/30, from http://www.martinfowler.com/articles/languageWorkbench.html

France, R., & Rumpe, B. (2007). *Model-Driven Development of Complex Software: A Research Roadmap.* Paper presented at the 29th International Conference on Software Engineering, Minneapolis, MN, USA.

France, R., Evans, A., Lano, K., & Rumpe, B. (1998). The UML as a formal modeling notation. *Computer Standards & Interfaces, 19(7),* 325-334.

Frankel, D.S, *Model Driven Architecture. Applying MDA to Enterprise Computing.* Indianapolis, Indiana. Wiley. 2003.

Fraunhofer Institute FOKUS (2007): *OSLO – Open Source Library for the Object Constraint Language (OCL).* Retrieved from URL: http://oslo-project. berlios.de

Gamma, E., Helm, R., Johnson, R. and Vlissides, J. (1995). *Design Patterns: Elements of Reusable Design.* Boston, MA: Addison Wesley.

Object-Oriented Software. Addison-Wesley Longman Publishing Co., Inc., Boston, MA, USA.

García, F., Bertoa, M. F., Calero, C., Vallecillo, A., Ruiz, F., Piattini, M., & Genero, M. (2006). *Towards a consistent terminology for software measurement.* Information and Software Technology 48, pp.: 631-644. Elsevier.

Garlan, D. and Schmerl, B. (2006). Architecture-driven modelling and analysis. *Proc. 11th Australian Workshop on Safety Related Programmable Systems SCS'06,* volume 69 of Conferences in Research and Practice in Information Technology.

Garvin, D. A. (1984). What does product quality really mean? *MIT Sloan Management Review,* 26 (1), 25-43.

General German Automobile Association (ADAC) (2007): *The ADAC-Breakdown statistic 2006*. ADAC Paper Manual Nr. 5, May 2007. Retrieved from URL: http://www.adac.de

Genero, M., Manso, M., Visaggio, A., Canfora, G. & Piattini, M. (2007) Building measure-based prediction models for UML class diagram maintainability. *Empirical Software Engineering* (to appear).

Genero, M., Miranda, D., and Piattini, M. (2002). Defining and validating metrics for uml statechart diagrams. In *Proceedings of QAOOSE'2002*.

Genero, M., Moody, D., & Piattini, M. (2005). Assessing the capability of internal metrics as early indicators of maintenance effort through experimentation. *Journal of Software Maintenance and Evolution: Research and Practice*, 17, 225-246.

Genero, M., Piattini, M., and Calero, C. (2000). Early measures for UML class diagrams. *L'Objet*, 6(4):489–505.

Genero, M., Piattini, M., and Caleron, C. (2005). A survey of metrics for UML class diagrams. *Journal of Object Technology*, 4:59–92.

Genero, M., Piattini, M., Manso, E., & Cantone, G. (2003). Building UML class diagram maintainability prediction models based on early metrics. In *Proc. 9th international symposium on software metrics (Metrics '03)* (pp. 263-275). Washington, DC, USA: IEEE Computer Society.

Genova, G., Valiente, M. C., & Nubiola, J. (2005). A Semiotic Approach to UML Models. The First Workshop on Philosophical Foundations of Information Systems Engineering (PHISE 2005), Porto, Portugal, June 13, 2005.

Genuchten, M. van. (1991). Why is Software Late? An Empirical Study of Reasons for Delay in Software Development. *IEEE Transactions on Software Engineering*, 17 (6), 582-590.

Genuchten, M. van. (2007), The Impact of Software Growth on the Electronics Industry. *IEEE Computer*, 40(1), 106-108.

Gheyi, R., Massoni, T., & Borba, P. (2005). A Rigorous Approach for Proving Model Refactorings. In *Proceedings 20th IEEE/ACM International Conference*

Automated Software Engineering (pp. 372-375). IEEE Computer Society.

Gheyi, R., Massoni, T., & Borba, P. (2005). Type-safe Refactorings for Alloy. In *Proceedings 8th Brazilian Symposium on Formal Methods* (pp. 174-190). Porto Alegre, Brazil.

Ghezzi, C., Jazayeri, M., & Mandrioli, D. (2003). Fundamentals of Software Engineering (Second Edition). Prentice-Hall.

Giesecke, S. (2006). A Method for Integrating Enterprise Information Systems based on Middleware Styles. *Proc. International Conference on Enterprise Information Systems ICEIS'06*, Doctoral Symposium (pp. 24–37).

Gîrba, T., Lanza, M., and Ducasse, S. (2005). Characterizing the evolution of class hierarchies. In *Proceedings of 9th European Conference on Software Maintenance and Reengineering (CSMR'05)*, pages 2–11. IEEE Computer Society.

Gitzel, R. and Hildenbrand, T. (2005). *A Taxonomy of Metamodel Hierarchies*. Working Paper 2/2005.

Glass, R. L. (1989). Software maintenance is a solution, not a problem. *System Development*, 9 (1), 8-9.

Glinz, M. (2000). Problems and Deficiencies of UML as a Requirements Specification Language. The Tenth International Workshop on Software Specification and Design (IWSSD-10), San Diego, USA, November 5-7, 2000.

GMF, 2007: The Eclipse Graphical Modeling Framework home page: http://www.eclipse.org/gmf

Goedicke, M., Meyer, T., & Taentzer, G. (1999). Viewpoint-oriented software development by distributed graph transformation: Towards a basis for living with inconsistencies. In *Proceedings International Conference Requirements Engineering* (pp. 92-99). IEEE Computer Society.

Gogolla, M., & Henderson-Sellers, B. (2002). *Analysis of UML Stereotypes in the UML Metamodel*. Paper presented at the UML 2002, Dresden.

Gomaa, H., & Wijesekera, D. (2001). The Role of UML, OCL and ADLs in Software Architecture. In Proc. of the Workshop on Describing Software Architecture with UML, in ICSE 2001, Toronto, Canada.

Gool, L. van, & Punter, T., & Hamilton, M. (2006). Compositional MDA. In O. Nierstrasz et al (Ed.), *Proceedings of Models 2006 LNCS 4199*, (pp. 126-139). Berlin: Springer.

Goulo, M., & Abreu, F.(2003). Bridging the gap between Acme and UML for CBD. In Specification and Verification of Component-Based Systems.

Graaf, B., & Weber, S., & Deursen, A. van. (2006), Migrating Supervisory Control Architectures Using Model Transformations. In *Proceedings of 10th European Conference on Software Maintenance and Reengineering CSMR 2006* (pp.153-164). Los Alamos: IEEE Computer Society.

Grassi, V., Mirandola, R. & Sabetta, A. (2007). A Model-Driven Approach to Performability Analysis of Dynamically Reconfigurable Component-Based Systems. In *Proceedings of the 6th international workshop on Software and performance, WOSP '07* (pp. 142-153). ACM Press

Gray, J., Rossi, M., & Tolvanen, J.-P. (2004). Special issue on Domain-Specific Modeling with Visual Languages of the Journal of Visual Languages & Computing, Vol. 15 (3-4). Elsevier.

Green, T. R. G. (1989). Cognitive Dimensions of Notations. In: Sutcliffe, V. A., & Macaulay, L. (Eds.). People and Computers. Cambridge University Press, 443-460.

Greenfield, J., Short, K., Cook, S., Kent, S., & Crupi, J. (2004). *Software factories: assembling applications with patterns, models, frameworks, and tools*. Wiley.

Grotehen, T. & Dittrich, K.R. *The MeTHOOD Approach: Measures, Transformation Rules, and Heuristics for Object-Oriented Design*, Technical Report., retrieved in October 2003 from http://www.ifi.unizh.ch/groups/dbtg/MeTHOOD/index.html

Gruber, T. R. (1993). Toward Principles for the Design of Ontologies Used for Knowledge Sharing. In: Formal Ontology in Conceptual Analysis and Knowledge Representation. Kluwer Academic Publishers.

Grünbacher, P., Egyed, A., & Medvidovic, N. (2003). Reconciling Software Requirements and Architectures with Intermediate Models. Springer Journal of Software and System Modeling. Accepted for publication. Published online on SpringerLink.

Grundy, J. C., Hosking, J.G., & Mugridge W. B. (1998). Inconsistency Management for Multiple-View Software Development Environments, IEEE *Transactions on Software Engineering*, 24(11), 960-981.

Grunske, L., Geiger, L., Zündorf, A., Van Eetvelde, N., Van Gorp, P., & Varro, D. (2005). Using Graph Transformation for Practical Model Driven Software Engineering. In S. Beydeda, M. Book, & V. Gruhn (Eds.), *Model-driven Software Development* (pp. 91-118). Heidelberg: Springer.

Gu A., Henderson-Sellers B.& Lowe D. (2002) Web Modeling Languages: The Gap Between Requirements And Current Exemplars. In *Proceedings Of The Eighth Australian World Wide Web Conference.*

Guelfi, N., Hammouche, D., Sterges, P., & Biberstein, O. (2001). FIDJI Project Annual Activities Report, Applied Computer Science Department technical report n° TR-DIA-02-01, Luxembourg University of Applied Sciences, Luxembourg-Kirchberg, Luxembourg.

Guerra, E., & de Lara, J. (2006). *Model View Management with Triple Graph Transformation Systems*. Proc. ICGT'2006. Lecture Notes in Computer Science, Vol. 4178, pp.: 351-366. Springer.

Guerra, E., & de Lara, J. (2007). *Meta-modelling and graph transformation for the definition of multi-view visual languages*. Chapter of the book "Visual Languages for Interactive Computing: Definitions and Formalization", Idea Group Publishers, edited by Fernando Ferri.

Guerra, E., Díaz, P., & de Lara, J. (2006). *Visual specification of metrics for domain specific visual languages*. In Proceedings of Graph-Transformation Visual Modelling Techniques.

Guerra, E., Diaz, P., and de Lara, J. (2006). Visual specification of metrics for domain specific visual languages. In *Graph Transformation and Visual Modeling Techniques (GT-VMT 2006)*.

Guerra, E., Sanz, D., Díaz, P., & Aedo, I. (2007). *A transformation-driven approach to the verification of security policies web designs*. In Procedings of the 7th International Conference on Web Engineering. L. Baresi, P. Fraternali, and G. J. Houben, Eds. Lecture Notes in Computer Science, Vol. 4607. Springer. pp.: 269-284.

Gurp, J. van, & Bosch, J. (2002). Design erosion: problems and causes. *The Journal of Systems and Software, 61* (2), 105-119.

Hacklinger, F. (2004). Java/A – Taking Components into Java. IASSE 2004, (pp. 163-168).

Halpin, T. A., & Bloesch, A. (1998). A Comparison of UML and ORM for Data Modeling. Third International Workshop on Evaluation of Modeling Methods in Systems Analysis and Design (EMMSAD 1998), Pisa, Italy, June 8-9, 1998.

Halstead, M. (1977). *Elements of software science.* New York, NY: Elsevier Science Inc.

Hamlet, D., Mason, D. & Woit, D. (2004). Properties of Software Systems Synthesized from Components. In Lau, K. (Ed.), *Component-Based Software Development: Case Studies* (pp. 129-159). World Scientific Publishing Company

Happe, J., Koziolek, H., & Reussner, R. H. (2007). Parametric Performance Contracts for Software Components with Concurrent Behaviour. In *Electronical Notes of Theoretical Computer Science,* Vol. 182 (pp. 91-106), Elsevier.

Harmer, T. J. and Wilkie, F. G. (2002). An extensible metrics extraction environment for object-oriented programming languages. In *Proceedings of the International Conference on Software Maintenance.*

Harrison, R., Counsell, S., & Nithi, R. (2000). Experimental assessment of the effect of inheritance on the maintainability of object-oriented systems. *Journal of Systems and Software, 2(3),* 173-179.

Hasselbring, Wilhelm & Reussner, Ralf & Jaekel, Holger & Schlegelmilch, Jürgen & Teschke, Thorsten & Krieghoff, Stefan (2004). The Dublo Architecture Pattern for Smooth Migration of Business Information Systems: An Experience Report. *Proceedings of the 26th International Conference on Software Engineering* (pp. 117-126). IEEE Computer Society Press.

Heemels, W.P.M.H., & Muller, G.J. (Eds.) (2006). *Model-based design of high-tech systems,* Eindhoven, Embedded Systems Institute.

Heitmeyer, C. L. (1998). On the need for practical formal methods. In *FTRTFT '98: Proceedings of the 5th International Symposium on Formal Techniques in Real-Time and Fault-Tolerant Systems,* pages 18–26, London, UK. Springer-Verlag.

Henderson-Sellers, B. (1996). *Object-Oriented Metrics, measures of complexity.* Prentice Hall.

Hess, Andreas & Humm, Bernhard & Voss, Markus (2006). Regeln für serviceorientierte Architekturen hoher Qualität. *Informatik-Spektrum, 29*(6), 395-411.

Highsmith, J. (2002). Agile Software Development Ecosystems. Addison-Wesley.

Hissam, S. A., Moreno, G. A., Stafford, J. A. & Wallnau, K. C. (2002). Packaging Predictable Assembly. In *CD'02: Proceedings of the IFIP/ACM Working Conference on Component Deployment* (pp. 108-124). Springer-Verlag

Hofmeister, C., Kruchten, P., Nord, R.L., Obbink, H., Ran, A., & America, P. (2007). A general model of software architecture design derived from five industrial approaches. J. Syst. Softw., 80(1), (pp.106-126).

Holzmann, G. J. (2002). The logic of bugs. In Proc. of Foundations of Software Engineering (SIGSOFT 2002/FSE-10).

Holzmann, G.J. (2003).The SPIN Model Checker: Primer and Reference Manual. Addison-Wesley.

Hommes, B.J.& van Reijswoud, V. (2000) Assessing the Quality of Business Process Modeling Techniques, In *Proceedings of the 33rd Hawaii International Conference on System Sciences.*

Hong, S. & Goor, G. (1993) A Formal Approach to the Comparison of Object-Oriented Analysis and Design Methodologies. In *Proceedings of the 26th International Hawaii International Conference on System Sciences.*

Hooman, J. & Mulyar, N., & Posta, L. (2004). Coupling Simulink and UML models. In Schnieder, B., & Tarnai, G. (Eds), *Proceedings Symposium FORMS/FORMATS 2004, 304-311.* Retrieved 29 October 2007, from http://www.ita.cs.ru.nl/publications/papers/ hooman/ FORMS04.pdf.

Hörmann, K., Dittmann, L., Hindel, B. & Müller, M. (2006): *SPiCE in der Praxis - Interpretationshilfe für Anwender und Assessoren,* dPunkt Verlag, ISBN-13 978-3898643412, Heidelberg, Germany.

Huang J., & Voeten J.P.M., & Groothuis M., (2007a). A Model Driven Approach for Mechatronic Systems. In *Proceedings of IEEE International Conference on Application of Concurrency to System Design (ACSD)* (pp.127-136). Los Alamos: IEEE Computer Society.

Huang, J. (2005). *Predictability in real-time software design* (PhD thesis). Eindhoven: Eindhoven University of the Technology.

Huang, J., & Voeten J.P.M., & Ventevogel, A. (2004). Predictability in Real-Time System Development - (1) Semantics Support for Development Languages. In Vachoux, A. (Ed.), *The Forum on Specification and Design Languages (FDL'04)*, (pp. 123-140). Gières: ECSI.

Huang, J., & Voeten, J.P.M., & Corporaal, H. (2007b). Predictable real-time software synthesis. *Journal of Real-time Systems*, 36 (3), 159-198.

Huang, J., & Voeten, J.P.M., & Putten, P. van der (2002). Performance Evaluation of Complex Real-time Systems: A Case Study. In *Proceedings of PROGRESS 2002*, (pp. 77-82). Utrecht: STW Progress.

Huang, S.-J., & Lai, R. (2003). Measuring the maintainability of a communication protocol based on its formal specification. *IEEE Transactions on Software Engineering*, 29 (4), 327-344.

Hylands, C., & Lee, E., & Liu, J. (2003). *Overview of the Ptolemy project*, Technical Memorandum UCB/ERL M03/05. Retrieved 21 November 2006, from http://ptolemy.eecs.berkeley.edu/.

IBM (2007). Rational Software Architect. http://www-306.ibm.com/software/awdtools/architect/swarchitect/index.html.

IEC (2003). IEC - International Electrotechnical Commission: IEC 61970-301: *Energy management system application program interface (EMS-API) – Part 301: Common Information Model (CIM) Base*. International Electrotechnical Commission.

IEC (2004). IEC - International Electrotechnical Commission: IEC 61970-501: *Energy management system application program interface (EMS-API) – Part 501: CIM RDF Schema – Revision 4*. International Electrotechnical Commission.

IEC (2004)b. IEC - International Electrotechnical Commission: Draft IEC 61970: *Energy Management System Application Program Interface (EMS-API) – Part 503: CIM XML Model Exchange Format - Draft 3b*. International Electrotechnical Commission.

IEEE (1990). Institute of Electrical and Electronics Engineers: IEEE Standard Computer Dictionary: A Compilation of IEEE Standard Computer Glossaries.

IEEE Learning Technology Standards Committee LTSC (2001). *IEEE P1484.1/D8. Draft Standard for Learning Technology - Learning Technology Systems Architecture LTSA*. IEEE Computer Society.

IEEE. (1998). 1219 Software maintenance (Standard).

IEEE-CS/ACM. (2004). Software Engineering 2004: Curriculum Guidelines for Undergraduate Degree Programs in Software Engineering (SE 2004). Institute of Electrical and Electronics Engineers Computer Society (IEEE-CS)/Association for Computing Machinery (ACM) Steering Committee. August 23, 2004.

Insfran, E. (2003). *A Requirements Engineering Approach for Object-Oriented Conceptual Modeling*, PhD Thesis, DSIC, Valencia University of Technology, Spain.

Insfran, E., Pastor, O. & Wieringa, R. (2002). Requirements Engineering-Based Conceptual Modelling. *Journal of Requirements Engineering*, 7 (2), 61–72, Springer-Verlag.

International Organisation for Standardisation (2007): *ISO/IEC 9126, Software engineering—Product quality. Part 1-4*, URL: http://www.iso.org

International Standard Organization, & Commission, I. E. (2001). *Software engineering – Product quality Part: 1 Quality model*. Genevao. Document Number)

Inverardi, P., Muccini, H., Pelliccione, P. (2005). CHARMY: an extensible tool for architectural analysis. In: ESEC/FSE-13: Proceedings of the 10th European software engineering conference, New York, NY, USA, ACM Press (pp.111–114).

ISO 9126 (2001). Information technology - *Software product evaluation, Quality characteristics and guidelines for their use*. Geneve: ISO/IEC.

ISO 9126-1 Software engineering - Product quality - Part 1: Quality model (International Standard). (2003). ISO.

ISO International Organisation for Standardisation (2004): *ISO 9000 family of Quality management system. ISO 9001:2004.*

ISO International Organization for Standardization & IEC International Electrotechnical Commission (1998): *ISO/IEC TR 15504 - Information technology: Process assessment and the Assessment Requirements for CMMI.*

ISO International Organization for Standardization & IEC International Electrotechnical Commission (2002): *ISO/TS 16949:2002 Automotive Quality Standard.*

ISO International Organization for Standardization & IEC International Electrotechnical Commission (1998): *IEC-61508 Functional safety of electrical/electronic/programmable electronic safety-related system.*

ISO, ISO/IEC 9126-1, (2001). Software Engineering – Product quality – Part 1: Quality model.

ISO/IEC (2001). *ISO/IEC 9126. Software engineering – Product quality.* ISO/IEC.

ISO/IEC 15939 (2002). Software Engineering – Software Measurement Process.

ISO/IEC 9126 (1991). Software Engineering – Product Quality.

ISO/IEC. *ISO 9126 Software Engineering – Product Quality – Part 1: Quality Model.* Published Standard.

Ivers, J. , Clements, P., Garlan, D., Nord, R., Schmerl, D., & Silva, J. R. O. (2004). Documenting Component and Connector Views with UML 2.0. Technical Report CMU/SEI-2004-TR-008, Carnegie Mellon University, Software Engineering Institute.

Ivkovic, I., & Kontogiannis, K. A. (2006). *Framework for Software Architecture Refactoring using Model Transformations and Semantic Annotations,* Proc. of the Conference on Software Maintenance and Reengineering (CSMR'06), 135–144.

Jackman, B. & Sanyanga, S. (2005): *A Software Component Architecture for Improving Vehicle Software Quality and Integration.* Society of Automotive Engineers (SAE) Centenary World Congress, Detroit, USA.

Jackson, D. (2002). Alloy: A Lightweight Object Modelling Notation. ACM *Transactions on Software Engineering and Methodology,* 11(2):256–290.

Jacobson, I. (2003). Use Cases: Yesterday, Today, and Tomorrow. IBM developerWorks, November 20, 2003.

Jacobson, I., & Ng, P.-W. (2005). Aspect-Oriented Software Development with Use Cases. Addison-Wesley.

Jacobson, I., Booch, G., & Rumbaugh, J. (1999). The Unified Software Development Process. Addison-Wesley.

Jacobson, I., Christerson, M., Jonsson, P., & Övergaard, G. (1992). Object-Oriented Software Engineering: A Use Case Driven Approach. Addison-Wesley.

Jacobson, I., Griss, M., & Jonsson, P. (1997). *Software reuse: architecture, process and organization for business success.* New York, NY: ACM Press and Addison-Wesley.

Jerad, C., & Barkaoui, K. (2005). On the use of rewriting logic for verification of distributed software architecture description based lfp. In Proc. Of 16th IEEE International Workshop on Rapid System Prototyping (pp. 202-208).

Jeusfeld, Manfred A. & Backlund, Per & Ralyté, Jolita (2007). Classifying Interoperability Problems for a Method Chunk Repository, Proceedings of the 3rd International Conference on Interoperability for Enterprise Software and Applications (I-ESA 2007).

Johannisson, K. (2005). Formal and Informal Software Specifications. PhD thesis, C. Technology and Göteborg Univ., SE-412 96 Göteborg, Sweden.

Jouault, F., Bézivin, J., Consel, C., Kurtev, I., & Latry, F. (2006). *Building DSLs with AMMA/ATL, a Case Study on SPL and CPL Telephony Languages.* Paper presented at the 1st ECOOP Workshop on Domain-Specific Program Development (DSPD).

Jurista, N. & Moreno, A. M. (2001). *Basics of Software Engineering Experimentation.* Kluwer Academic Publishers.

Kalmbach, R. & Dannenberg, J. (2001): *Automobiltechnologie 2010. Technologische Veränderungen im Automobil und ihre Konsequenzen für Hersteller, Zulieferer und Ausrüster*. Study of the HypoVereinsbank and Mercer Management Consulting, Munich, Germany.

Kamthan, P. (2004). A Framework for Addressing the Quality of UML Artifacts. *Studies in Communication Sciences*, 4(2), 85-114.

Kamthan, P. (2004). A Framework for Addressing the Quality of UML Artifacts. Studies in Communication Sciences, 4(2), 85-114.

Kamthan, P. (2005). Pair Modeling. The 2005 Canadian University Software Engineering Conference (CUSEC 2005), Ottawa, Canada, January 14-16, 2005.

Kamthan, P. (2006). How Useful are Your UML Models? The 2006 Canadian University Software Engineering Conference (CUSEC 2006), Montreal, Canada, January 19-21, 2006.

Kan, S. H. (2002). *Metrics and Models in Software Quality Engineering*. Addison-Wesley.

Kan, S. H. (1995). *Metrics and Models in Software Quality Engineering*. Addison Wesley, Reading, MA.

Kan, S.,(2002) *Metrics and Models in Software Quality Engineering*. 2nd Edition; Addison Wesley.

Kande', M. M. , Crettaz, V. , Strohmeier, A. & Sendall, S. (2002). Bridging the gap between IEEE 1471, Architecture Description Languages and UML. Software and System Modeling, 2 (pp. 98–112)

Kandula, G. and Sathrasala, V. K. (2005). Product and Management Metrics for Requirements. Master thesis. Umea University.

Kaner, C. (1995). Liability for Defective Documentation. Software QA Quarterly, 2(3).

Karlsson, E-A. (1995). *Software Reuse: A Holistic Approach*. Wiley.

Kazman, R., Carriere, S.J. and Woods, S.G. (2000). Toward a Discipline of Scenario-based Architectural Evolution. *Annals of Software Engineering*, 9(1-4), 5–33.

Keller, D. (1990). A Guide to Natural Naming. ACM SIGPLAN Notices, 25(5), 95-102.

Kelly, J.C., Sherif, J.S., & Hops, J. (1992, February). An Analysis of Defect Densities Found During Software Inspections. *Journal of Systems and Software*. 17(2), 150-166.

Kent, S. (2002). *Model Driven Engineering*. In Proceedings of the 3rd International Conference on Integrated Formal Methods. M. J. Butler, L. Petre, and K. Sere, Eds. Lecture Notes in Computer Science, Vol. 2335. Springer-Verlag. pp.: 286-298.

Kerhervé, B., Nguyen, K. K., Gerbé, O., & Jaumard, B. A. (2006). Framework for Quality-Driven Delivery in Distributed Multimedia Systems, Proc. of the Advanced International Conference on Telecommunications and International Conference on Internet and Web Applications and Services (AICT/ICIW 2006), 195–205.

Kerievsky, J. (2004). *Refactoring to Patterns*. Addison-Wesley.

Kiewkanya, M., Jindasawat, N., & Muenchaisri, P. (2004). A methodology for constructing maintainability model of object-oriented design. In *Proc. fourth international conference on quality software (QSIC '04)* (pp. 206-213). Washington, DC, USA: IEEE Computer Society Press.

Kim, H., & Boldyreff, C. (2002). Developing Software Metrics Applicable to UML Models. Sixth ECOOP Workshop on Quantitative Approaches in Object-Oriented Software Engineering (QAOOSE 2002), Malaga, Spain, June 11, 2002.

Kitchenham, B. A., Pickard, L. M., and Linkman, S. J. (1990). An evaluation of some design metrics. *Softw. Eng. J.*, 5(1):50–58.

Kitchenham, B., & Pfleeger, S. L. (1996). Software quality: The elusive target. *IEEE Software*, 13 (1), 12-21.

Kitchenham, B., Linkman, S., Pasquini, A., & Nanni, V. (1997, September). The SQUID approach to defining a quality model. *Software Quality Journal*, 6 (3), 211-233.

Kitchenham, B., Pfleeger, S. L., & Fenton, N. (1995). Towards a framework for software measurement validation. *IEEE Transactions on Software Engineering*, 21 (12), 929-944.

Klar, V., Quick, A. and Soetz, F. (1991). Tools for a Model–driven Instrumentation for Monitoring. *Proc. 5th Int. Conf. on Modelling Techniques and Tools for Computer Performance Evaluation* (pp. 165–180).

Kleppe, A. and Warmer, J. (2003). *The Object Constraint Language. Second Edition*. Addison-Wesley.

Kleppe, A., Warmer, J., & W. Bast (2003), *MDA Explained. The Practice and Promise of the Model Driven Architecture*. Addison-Wesley, 2003.

Kneuper, R. (2006): *CMMI: Verbesserung von Softwareprozessen mit Capability Maturity Model Integration*. dPunkt Verlag, ISBN-10: 3898643735, Heidelberg, Germany.

Königs, A. & Schürr, A. (2006). Tool Integration with Triple Graph Grammars - A Survey . In R. Heckel (Ed.), *Proceedings of the SegraVis School on Foundations of Visual Modelling Techniques* (pp. 113-150). Electronic Notes in Theoretical Computer Science 148, Amsterdam: Elsevier.

Koziolek, H. & Firus, V. (2007). Parametric Performance Contracts: Non-Markovian Loop Modelling and an Experimental Evaluation. In *Electronical Notes of Theoretical Computer Science*, Vol. 176 (pp. 69-87), Elsevier

Koziolek, H., Happe, J. & Becker, S. (2006). Parameter Dependent Performance Specifications of Software Components. In Hofmeister, C., Crnkovic, I., Reussner, R. & Becker, S. (Ed.) *Proceedings of the 2nd International Conference on the Quality of Software Architecture, QoSA2006* (pp. 163-179). Springer Lecture Notes in Computer Science, Vol. 4214

Koziolek, H., Happe, J. & Becker, S. (2007). Predicting the Performance of Component-based Software Architectures with different Usage Profiles. In Szyperski, C. & Overhage, S. (Ed.) *Proceedings of the 3rd International Conference on the Quality of Software Architecture, QoSA2007*. Springer Lecture Notes in Computer Science, To Appear

Kruchten, P. (1995). Architectural Blueprints - The "4+1" View Model of Software Architecture. IEEE Software, 12(6) (pp. 42–50).

Kruchten, P. (2000). The rational Unified Process An Introduction, second edition, Addison-Wesley.

Kruchten, P. B. (1995). The 4+1 View Model of Architecture. IEEE Software, 12(6), 42-50.

Kuehne, T. (2006). Matters of (meta-) modeling. *Software and System Modeling*, 5(4):369–385.

Kurtev, I. (2005). *Adaptability of Model Transformations*. PhD Thesis, University of Twente, The Nederlands.

Kutar, M., Britton, C.& Barker, T. A. (2002) Comparison of Empirical Study and Cognitive Dimensions Analysis in the Evaluation of UML Diagrams. In *Proceedings of the Fourteenth Annual Meeting of the Psychology of Programming Interest Group*.

Kuzniarz, L., & Staron, M. (2002). *On Practical Usage of Stereotypes in UML-Based Software Development*. Paper presented at the Forum on Design and Specification Languages, Marseille.

Kuzniarz, L., Sourrouille, J. L., Straeten, R. V. D., Staron, M., Chaudron, M., Förster, A., and Reggio, G., editors (2006). *Proceedings of the 1st Workshop on Quality in Modeling. Co-located with the ACM/IEEE 9th International Conference on Model Driven Engineering Languages and Systems (MoDELS 2006)*, Genova, Italy.

Kuzniarz, L., Staron, M., & Wohlin, C. (2004). *An Empirical Study on Using Stereotypes to Improve Understanding of UML Models*. Paper presented at the The 12th International Workshop on Program Comprehension, Bari, Italy.

Lague, B., Proulx, D., Mayrand, J., Merlo, E. M., & Hudepohl, J. (1997). Assessing the benefits of incorporating function clone detection in a development process. In *Proc. International conference on software maintenance (ICSM '97)*. Washington, DC: IEEE Computer Society.

Laitenberger, O. (2002). *A survey of software inspection technologies*. In Handbook on Software Engineering and Knowledge Engineering. World Scientific Publishing.

Laitenberger, O., Atkinson, C., Schlich, M., & Emam, K. E. (2000). An experimental comparison of reading techniques for defect detection in UML design documents. *The Journal of Systems and Software, 53*(2), 183-204.

Laitenberger, O., Beil, T., & Schwinn, T. (2002). An industrial case study to examine a non traditional inspection implementation for requirements specifications. *Empirical Software Engineering, 7(4)*, 345-374.

Lämmel, R. (2002). *Towards generic refactoring*. In Proceedings of the 2002 ACM SIGPLAN Workshop on Rule-Based Programming. ACM Press. pp.: 15-28.

Lange, C. F. J. (2006). Improving the Quality of UML Models in Practice. The Twenty Eighth International Conference on Software Engineering (ICSE 2006), Shanghai, China, May 20-28, 2006.

Lange, C. F. J. and Chaudron, M. R. V. (2006). Effects of Defects in UML Models: an Experimental Investigation. In *ICSE '06: Proceeding of the 28th international conference on Software engineering*, pages 401–411, New York, NY, USA. ACM Press.

Lange, C. F. J., & Chaudron, M. R. V. (2006). Effects of Defects in UML Models: An Experimental Investigation. The Twenty Eighth International Conference on Software Engineering (ICSE 2006), Shanghai, China, May 20-28, 2006.

Lange, C. F. J., & Chaudron, R. V., Michel. (2005). Managing model quality in UML-based software development. In *Proc. 13th IEEE international workshop on software technology and engineering practice* (pp. 7-16). Washington, DC: IEEE Computer Society.

Lange, C.F. J., DuBois, B., & Chaudron, M.R.V. (2005). Experimentally investigating the effectiveness and effort of modeling conventions for the UML. *Lecture Notes in Computer Science*, 4364, 91-100.

Lange, C.F.J., & Chaudron, M.R.V. (2005). Managing model quality in UML-based software development, *Proceedings of IEEE Conference on Software Technology and Engineering Practice 2005 (STEP)*, 7-16.

Lange, C.F.J., & Chaudron, M.R.V., & Muskens, J. (2006b). UML Software Architecture and Design Description. *IEEE Software*, 23(2), 40-46.

Lange, C.F.J., & DuBois, B., & Chaudron, M.R.V. (2006a). An Experimental Investigation of UML Modeling Conventions. In O. Nierstrasz et al (Ed), *Proceedings of Models 2006 LNCS 4199*, (pp. 27-41). Berlin: Springer.

Lanza, M., & Ducasse, S. (2002). *Beyond language independent object-oriented metrics: Model independent metrics*. In Proceedings of QAOOSE'02, pp.: 77-84.

Lédczi, A., Bakay, A., Marói, M., Vögyesi, P., Nordstrom, G., Sprinkle, J., & Karsai, G. (2001). *Composing domain-specific design environments*. IEEE Computer, pp.: 44-51.

Leffingwell, D., & Widrig, D. (2003). Managing Software Requirements: A Use Case Approach (Second Edition). Addison-Wesley.

Lehman, M. M., Ramil, J. F., Wernick, P. D., Perry D. E., & Turski, W. M. (1997). Metrics and laws of software evolution: The nineties view. In *Proceedings of International Symposium on Software Metrics* (pp. 20-32). IEEE Computer Society Press.

Lehmann, E. & Wegener, J. (2000): *Test Case Design by Means of the CTE XL*. Proc. 8. Europ. Int. Conf. on Software Testing, Analysis & Review (EuroSTAR 2000), Copenhagen, Denmark.

Leung, F., & Bolloju, N. (2005). Analyzing the quality of domain models developed by novice systems analysts. *Proceedings of the 38th Hawaii International Conference on System Sciences*, 188b-188b.

Leveson, N. G. (1986). Software safety: why, what, and how. *ACM Computing Surveys*, 18 (2), 125-163.

Lientz, B. P., Bennet, P., Swanson, E. B., & Burton, E. (1980). *Software maintenance management: A study of the maintenance of computer application software in 487 data processing organizations*. Reading: Addison Wesley.

Liggesmeyer, P., & Rothfelder, M, & Rettelbach, M. (1998). Quality assurance of software-based systems (in German). *Informatik-Spektrum*, 21(5), 249-258.

Liggesmeyer, R. & Rombach, D. (2005): *Software Engineering eingebetteter Systeme*. Spektrum Akademischer Verlag, 1st Edition, ISBN-10: 3827415330, Munich, Germany.

Lilja, D. J. (2000). *Measuring Computer Performance: A Practitioner's Guide*. Cambridge, UK: Cambridge University Press.

Lindland, O. I., Sindre G., & Sølvberg A. (1994). Understanding quality in conceptual modeling. *IEEE Software*, 11(2), 42–49.

Liu, W., Easterbrook, S., & Mylopoulos, J. (2002). Rule-based detection of inconsistency in UML models. In *Proceedings UML Workshop on Consistency Problems in UML-based Software Development* (pp. 106-123). Blekinge Insitute of Technology.

Lorenz, M. & Kidd, J. (1994) *Object-oriented Software Metrics. A Practical Guide.,* Prentice Hall.

Ma, H., Ji, Z., Shao, W., and Zhang, L. (2005). Towards the uml evaluation using taxonomic patterns on meta-classes. In *Proceedings of the Fifth International Conference on Quality Software (QSIC'05)*, volume 0, pages 37–44.

Ma, H., Shao, W., L.Zhang, Z.Ma, and Y.Jiang (2004). Applying OO metrics to assess UML meta-models. In *Proceedings of MODELS/UML'2004*. UML 2004.

MAAB. (2001). Controller style guidelines for production intent using Matlab, Simulink and Stateflow.

Magee, J., Kramer, J., & Giannakopoulou, D. (1999). Behaviour Analysis of Software Architectures. In I Working IFIP Conf. Sw Architecture, WICSA.

Mahmood, S. and Lai, R. (2005). Measuring the complexity of a uml component specification. In *QSIC '05: Proceedings of the Fifth International Conference on Quality Software*, pages 150–160, Washington, DC, USA. IEEE Computer Society.

Mahrenholz, D., Spinczyk, O. and Schroeder-Preikschat, W. (2002). Program Instrumentation for Debugging and Monitoring with AspectC++. *Proc. 5th Int. Symp. on Object-Oriented Real-Time Distributed Computing ISORC'02* (pp. 249–256).

Manna, Z., & Pnueli, A. (1992). The temporal logic of reactive and concurrent systems. Springer-Verlag New York, Inc.

Mannion, M. & Keepence, B. (1995). SMART Requirements. *ACM SIGSOFT Software Engineering Notes*, 20(2), 42-47.

Marinescu, R., & Ratiu, D. (2004). Quantifying the quality of object-oriented design: The factor-strategy model. In *Proc. 11th working conference on reverse engineering (WCRE '04)*. Washington, DC: IEEE Computer Society.

Markovic, S., & Baar, T. (2005). Refactoring OCL Annotated UML Class Diagrams. In L. Briand, C. Williams (Eds.), *Proceedings International Conference Model Driven Engineering Languages and Systems* (pp. 280-294). Lecture Notes in Computer Science 3713, Heidelberg: Springer

Markovic, S., & Baar, T. (2005). *Refactoring OCL annotated UML class diagrams*. In Proc. of the 8th Int. Conference on Model Driven Engineering Languages and Systems, 280–294.

Martin, J. (1993) *Principles of object-oriented analysis and design*, Prentice Hall

Martín, M. A. & Olsina, L. (2003). *Towards an ontology for software metrics and indicators as the foundation for a cataloging Web system*. In Proceedings of LA-WEB. IEEE Computer Society.

Martin, R. C. (1998). Java and C++: A Critical Comparison. In *Java Gems: Jewels from Java Report*, pages 51–68.

Marx Gómez & Brehm (2007). *KMU-Software-Umfrage 2006 zur Nutzung betrieblicher Standardsoftware kleiner und mittelständischer Unternehmen in Deutschland*, Dep. of Business Information Systems, University of Oldenburg, Study.

MathWorks. (2006). Simulink reference.

Mattsson, M. and Bosch, J. (1999). Characterizing stability in evolving frameworks. In *TOOLS '99: Proceedings of the Technology of Object-Oriented Languages and Systems*, page 118, Washington, DC, USA. IEEE Computer Society.

McCabe, T. (1976). A complexity measure. *IEEE Transactions on Software Engineering*, SE-2 (4), 308-320.

McCall, J., & Walters, G. (1977). *Factors in software quality*. Springfield, VA: The National Technical Information Service (NTIS).

McCall, J.A., Richards, P.K., & Walters, G.F. (1977). *Factors in software quality*, vol. 1-3 of AD/A-049-015/055. Springfield.

McCoy, J. (2003). Use Case Quality Attributes. The Third Annual NASA Office of Safety and Mission Assurance Software Assurance Symposium (OSMA SAS 2003), Morgantown, USA, July 30-August 1, 2003.

McGregor, J.D. (1998), The fifty-foot look at the analysis and design models, *Journal of Object-Oriented Programming* 11(4) 10-15.

McQuillan, J. A., & Power, J. F. (2006). Some Observations on the Application of Software Metrics to UML Models. The First Workshop on Model Size Metrics, Genoa, Italy, October 3, 2006.

McQuillan, J. A. and Power, J. F. (2006). Experiences of using the dagstuhl middle metamodel for defining software metrics. In *Proceedings of the 4th International Conference on Principles and Practices of Programming in Java.*

McUmber, W.E., & Cheng, B. (2001). A general framework for formalizing UML with formal languages. *Proceedings of the 23rd International Conference on Software Engineering (ICSE '01)*, 433-442.

Medina Mora, M. and Denger, C. (2003). Requirements metrics. an initial literature survey on measurement approaches for requirements specifications. Technical report, Fraunhofer IESE.

Medvidovic, N. & Taylor, R. N. (2000). A Classification and Comparison Framework for Software Architecture Description Languages. IEEE Transactions on Software Engineering, 26(1).

Medvidovic, N. , Grünbacher, P. , Egyed, A., & Boehm, B. (2003). Bridging Models across the Software Life-Cycle. Journal for Software Systems (JSS), 68(3) (pp. 199–215).

Medvidovic, N. and Taylor, R.N. (2000). A Classification and Comparison Framework for Software Architecture Description Languages. *IEEE Transactions on Software Engineering, 26*(1), 70-93.

Medvidovic, N. , Rosenblum, D. S. , Redmiles, D. F., & Robbins, J. E. (2002). Modeling Software Architectures in the Unified Modeling Language. *ACM Transactions on Software Engineering and Methodology (TOSEM)*, 11(1).

Mellor, S. J., & Balcer, M. J. (2002). *Executable UML : a foundation for model-driven architecture.* Boston ; San Francisco ; New York: Addison-Wesley.

Mellor, S. J., Kendall, S., Uhl, A., & Weise, D. (2002). *Model-Driven Architecture.* Paper presented at the Object-Oriented Information Systems, Montpellier.

Mellor, S.J., Clark, A.N., & Futagami, T. (2003). Model-driven development – Guest editor's introduction. *IEEE Software, 20(5)*, 14-18.

Melton, A. C., Baker, A. L., Bieman, J. M., and Gustafson, D. M. (1990). A mathematical perspective for software measures research. *Software Engineering Journal*, 5:246–254.

Mendes, O., & Abran, A. (2004). Software Engineering Ontology: A Development Methodology. Metrics News, 9(1), 64-71.

Mens, T. & Lanza, M. (2002). *A Graph-Based Metamodel for Object-Oriented Software Metrics.* Electronic Notes in Theoretical Computer Science, Vol. 72(2)

Mens, T. (2006). *On the use of graph transformations for model refactoring.* In Proceedings of Generative and Transformational Techniques in Software Engineering, pp.: 219-257

Mens, T. (2006). On the use of graph transformations for model refactoring. In *Generative and Transformational Techniques in Software Engineering* (pp. 219-257). Lecture Notes in Computer Science 4143, Heidelberg: Springer.

Mens, T. and Lanza, M. (2002). A graph-based metamodel for object-oriented software metrics. *Electronic Notes in Theoretical Computer Science*, 72:57–68.

Mens, T., & Tourwé, T. (2004). A Survey of Software Refactoring. IEEE *Transactions on Software Engineering*, 30(2), 126-162.

Mens, T., Taentzer, G., & Runge, O. (2007). Analyzing Refactoring Dependencies Using Graph Transformation. *Journal on Software and Systems Modeling*, 6(3), 269-285.

Mens, T., Van Der Straeten, R., & D'Hondt, M. (2006). Detecting and resolving model inconsistencies using transformation dependency analysis, In O. Nierstrasz

(Ed.), *Proceedings International Conference on Model-Driven Engineering Languages and Systems* (pp. 200-214). Lecture Notes in Computer Science 4199, Heidelberg: Springer.

Mens, T., Van Eetvelde, N., Demeyer, S., & Janssens, D. (2005). Formalizing refactorings with graph transformations. *Journal on Software Maintenance and Evolution*, 17(4), 247-276.

Merilinna, J. (2005). *A Tool for Quality-Driven Architecture Model Transformation.* Espoo, VTT Electronics, VTT Publications.

Miliauskaitė, E. and Nemuraitė, L. (2005). Representation of Integrity Constraints in Conceptual Models. *Information Technology and Control*, 34(4):355–365.

Miller, J., & Mukerji, J (January 2007), *Model Driven Architecture (MDA)*, http://www.omg.org/docs/ormsc/01-07-01.pdf

Miller, J., & Mukerji, J. (2003). MDA Guide. 1.0.1. Retrieved 2004-01-10, 2004, from http://www.omg.org/mda/

Misic, V. B. & Moser, S. (1997). *From Formal Metamodels to Metrics: An Object-Oriented Approach.* In Proceedings of 24th International Conference on Technology of Object-Oriented Languages and Systems, pp.: 330-339.

Misic, V. B. and Moser, S. (1997). From formal metamodels to metrics: An object-oriented approach. In *TOOLS '97: Proceedings of the Technology of Object-Oriented Languages and Systems-Tools - 24*, page 330, Washington, DC, USA. IEEE Computer Society.

MISRA Consortium, The Motor Industry Software Reliability Association (1998): *MISRA-C - Guidelines for the Use of the C Language in Vehicle Based Systems*, ISBN-10: 0952415690. URL: http://www.misra.org.uk

Modelware Project (2006a). D2.2 MDD Engineering Metrics Definition. Technical report, Framework Programme Information Society Technologies.

Moody, D. L. (2005). Theoretical and Practical Issues in Evaluating the Quality of Conceptual Models: Current State and Future Directions. Data and Knowledge Engineering, 55(3), 243-276.

Mottu, J.-M., Baudry, B., & Le Traon, Y. (2006). Mutation Analysis Testing for Model Transformations. In *Proceedings 2nd European Conference on Model Driven Architecture – Foundations and Applications* (pp. 376-390). Lecture Notes in Computer Science 4066, Heidelberg: Springer.

Muccini, H. & Hierons, R. Editors (2006). ROSATEA 2006: The Role Of Software Architecture in Testing and Analysis. ACM Digital Library.

Muller, G.J. (2004). *CAFCR: A Multi-view Method for Embedded Systems Architecting; Balancing Genericity and Specificity* (PhD-Thesis). Delft: Delft University of Technology.

Muller, P. A., Fleurey, F., and Jézéquel, J. M. (2005). Weaving executability into object-oriented meta-languages. In *Proceedings of MODELS/UML 2005*.

MultiSpeak (2003). *MultiSpeak Version 2.2* Specification (10/07/03), NRECA, Virginia, available online at http://www.multispeak.org.

Munro, M., J. (2005). *Product metrics for automatic identification of "bad smell" design problems in Java source-code.* In Proceedings of 11th International Software Metrics Symposium, IEEE Computer Society.

Murphy, G.C., Notkin, D., & Sullivan, K.J. (2001). Software reflexion models: Bridging the gap between design and implementation. *IEEE Transactions on Software Engineering, 27(4)*, 364-380.

Mustapic, G., Wall, A., Norstrom, C., Crnkovic, I., Sandstrom, K., & Andersson, J. (2004). Real world influences on software architecture - interviews with industrial system experts. In: Fourth Working IEEE/IFIP Conference on Software Architecture, WICSA (pp. 101–111).

NASA. (1998). *Formal Methods Specification and Verification Guidebook for Software and Computer Systems, Volume I: Planning and Technology Insertion.* NASA/TP-98-208193 http://eis.jpl.nasa.gov/quality/Formal_Methods/document/NASAgb1.doc

Nechypurenko, A., Tao lu., Gan deng. , Douglas,C & Anirudha Gokhule (2003) Applying MDA and Component Middleware to Large Scale Distributed Systems, Vanderbilt University, Nashville,TN,USA

Nelson, H. J., & Monarchi, D. E. (2007). Ensuring the Quality of Conceptual Representations. Software Quality Journal, 15(2), 213-233.

Neumann (2003). *Comparison of IEC CIM and NRECA MultiSpeak*, UISOL.

Newman, M. H. A. (1942). On Theories with a Combinatorial Definition of "Equivalence". *The Annals of Mathematics*, 43(2):223–243.

Nieuwelaar, B. van den (2004), *Supervisory Machine Control by Predictive-Reactive Scheduling* (PhD thesis). Eindhoven: Eindhoven University of Technology.

Nipkow, T., Paulson, L. C., and Wenzel, M. (2002). *Isabelle/HOL - A Proof Assistant for Higher-Order Logic*. Number 2283 in LNCS. Springer-Verlag Berlin Heidelberg New York.

Nosek, J. T., & Palvia, P. (1990). Software maintenance management: changes in the last decade. *Journal of Software Maintenance*, 2 (3), 157-174.

Nöth, W. (1990). Handbook of Semiotics. Indiana University Press.

Object Management Group (2003). *MDA Model-Driven Architecture Guide V1.0.1*. OMG.

Object Management Group (2004). *MOF 2.0, OMG document ptc/04-10-15*. web: http://www.omg.org/cgi-bin/apps/doc?ptc/04-10-14.pdf.

Object Management Group (OMG) (2003). *UML 2.0 OCL Final Adopted Specification*. http://www.omg.org/cgi-bin/apps/doc?ptc/03-10-14.pdf.

Object Management Group, OMG (2003). MDA Guide Version 1.0.1.

Object Management Group. (2003). Unified Modeling Language Specification v. 1.5. Retrieved 2003-10-01, 2003, from www.omg.org

Object Management Group. (2004, December 2003). Unified Modeling Language Specification: Infrastructure version 2.0. Retrieved 2004-02-20, 2004, from www.omg.org

Oman, P. W., & Cook, C. R. (1990). Typographic style is more than cosmetic. *ACM Communications*, 33 (5), 506-520.

Oman, P., & Hagemeister, J. (1992). Metrics for assessing a software system's maintainability. In *Proc. international conference on software maintenance (ICSM '92)*. Washington, DC: IEEE Computer Society.

OMG (2004a). MOF 2.0 specification. Technical report, Object Management Group.

OMG (2004b). UML 2.0 superstructure. Technical report, Object Management Group.

OMG (2006a). *Meta Object Facility (MOF) Core Specification*. Version 2.0. http://www.omg.org/cgi-bin/doc?formal/2006-01-01.

OMG (2006b). *Unified Modeling Language: Superstructure. Version 2.1*. OMG document ptc/06-04-02. http://www.omg.org/cgibin/doc?ptc/2006-04-02.

OMG Object Management Group (2003): *Meta Object Facility 2.0 Specification*, Retrieved from URL: http://www.omg.org/cgi-bin/doc?ptc/03-10-04.pdf

OMG Object Management Group (2003): *Model Driven Architecture. MDA Guide Version 1.0.1*, Retrieved from http://www.omg.org/docs/omg/03-06-01.pdf

OMG Object Management Group (2003): *UML 2.0 OCL Specification*, Retrieved from URL: http://www.omg.org/docs/ptc/03-10-14.pdf

OMG, (2003). MDA Guide, from http://www.omg.org/docs/omg/03-06-01.pdf. Version 1.0.1.

OMG, (2004). Meta Object Facility (MOF) 2.0 Core Specification, ptc/04-10-15.

OMG, (2005). OMG, MOF 2.0 Query/Views/Transformations Final Adopted Specification, Object Management Group, from http://www.omg.org/cgibin/apps/doc?ad/05-11-01.pdf

OMG, (2006). OMG, UML 2.1 Unified Modeling Language™

OMG: Object Management Group (2005). UML Profile for Schedulability, Performance and Time. *http://www.omg.org/cgi-bin/doc?formal/2005-01-02*

Opdahl, A.L.& Henderson-Sellers, B. (2002) Ontological Evaluation of the UML Using the Bunge–Wand–Weber Model. *Journal of Software and System Modeling*, 1.

Opzeeland, D.J.A. (2005). *Automated techniques for reconstructing and assessing correspondence between UML designs and implementations.* Unpublished master thesis, Technische Universiteit Eindhoven, Eindhoven, The Netherlands.

Oquendo, F., Warboys, B.C., Morrison, R., Dindeleux, R., Gallo, F., Garavel, H. and Occhipinti, C. (2005). ArchWARE: Architecting Evolvable Software. *Proc. 2nd European Workshop on Software Architecture EWSA 2005.* Springer LNCS 3047.

Otero, M. C., & Dolado, J. J. (2004). Evaluation of the Comprehension of the Dynamic Modeling in UML. *Information and Software Technology,* 46(1), 35-53.

Övergaard, G., & Palmkvist, K. (2005). Use Cases: Patterns and Blueprints. Addison-Wesley.

P. R. Crossley & J. A. Cook (1991): *Control 91.* Conference Publication 332, IEEE International Conference, March 1991, Edinburgh, U.K.

Pahl, C., Barrett, R. and Kenny, C. (2004). Supporting Active Database Learning and Training through Interactive Multimedia. *Proc. Intl. Conf. on Innovation and Technology in Computer Science Education ITiCSE'04.*

Pap, Z. Majzik, I., Pataricza A., & Szegi, A. (2001 April). Completeness and Consistency Analysis of UML Statechart Specifications, *Proceedings of the DDECS 2001 Workshop,* Győr, Hungary (pp. 83-90).

Park, D. and Kang, S. (2004). Design phase analysis of software performance using aspect-oriented programming. *Proc. 5th Aspect-Oriented Modeling Workshop,* UML'2004.

Park, R, & Goethert, W., & Florac, W. (1996). *Goal-driven software measurement - a guidebook* (SEI report CMU/SEI-96-HB-002). Pittsburg: Carnegie Mellon University/Software Engineering Institute.

Parnas, D. L. (1994). Software aging. In *Proc. 16th international conference on software engineering (ICSE '94)* (pp. 279-287). Washington, DC: IEEE Computer Society.

Parnas, D.L., & Weiss, D.M. (1985). Active design review: Principles and practices. *Proceedings of the 8th international conference on Software engineering,* 132-136.

Paulk, M. C., Weber, C. V., Curtis, B., & Chrissis, M. B. (1995). The Capability Maturity Model: Guidelines for Improving the Software Process. Addison-Wesley.

Pawlak, R., Noguera, C., and Petitprez, N. (2006). Spoon: Program analysis and transformation in java. Technical Report 5901, INRIA.

Pelliccione, P. (2005). CHARMY: A framework for Software Architecture Specification and Analysis. PhD thesis, Computer Science Dept., U. L'Aquila.

Pender, T. (2003). UML Bible, chapter Part V: Modeling the Application Architecture, page 940. Wiley Pub.

Perez-Martinez, J. E., & Sierra-Alonso, A. (2004). UML 1.4 versus UML 2.0 as languages to describe Software Architectures. In Proc. EWSA 2004. LNCS n. 3047.

Perry, D. E., & Wolf, A. L. (1992). Foundations for the Study of Software Architecture. ACM SIGSOFT Softw. Eng. Notes, 17(4), (pp. 40–52).

Petre, M. (1995). Why Looking Isn't Always Seeing: Readership Skills and Graphical Programming. Communications of the ACM, 38(6), 33-44.

Petriu, D. B. & Woodside, M. (2005). An intermediate metamodel with scenarios and resources for generating performance models from UML designs. *Springer Journal on Software and Systems Modeling*

Pfleeger, S.L., & Hatton, L. (1997). Investigating the influence of formal methods. *IEEE Computer, 30(2),* 33-43.

Phalp, K. T., Vincent, J., & Cox, K. (2007). Assessing the Quality in Use Case Descriptions. Software Quality Journal, 15(1), 69-97.

Pilskalns, O., Andrews, A., Knight, A., Ghosh, S., and France, R. (2007). Testing uml designs. *Information and Software Technology,* 49(8):892–912.

Plasil, F. and Visnovsky, S. (2002). Behavior Protocols for Software Components. *ACM Transactions on Software Engineering,* 28(11), 1056-1075.

Ploeger, S.C.W., & Somers, L. (2006), *Analysis and Verification of an Automatic Document Feeder* (CS-Report 06-25). Eindhoven: University of Technology.

Podmore, Robin et al. (1999). *Common Information Model - a Developer's Perspective.* In (Sprague, R. Edt.): Proceedings of the 32nd Hawaii International Conference on System Sciences, IEEE Publishing.

Pohjonen, R., & Tolvanen, J-P. (2002). *Automated production of family members: Lessons learned.* In Proceedings of International Workshop on Product Line Engineering The Early Steps: Planning, Modeling, and Managing, pp.: 49-57.

Porres, I. (2003). Model refactorings as rule-based update transformations. In: P. Stevens, J. Whittle, G. Booch (Eds.), In *Proceedings of 6th International Conference UML 2003 - The Unified Modeling Language. Model Languages and Applications* (pp. 159-174). Lecture Notes in Computer Science 2863, Heidelberg: Springer.

Porter, A. A., Votta, L. G., Jr., & Basili, V. R. (1995). Comparing detection methods for software requirements inspections: a replicated experiment. *Software Engineering, IEEE Transactions on, 21*(6), 563-575.

Porter, A.A., Siy, H.P., Toman, C.A., Votta, L.G. (1997). An Experiment to assess the cost-benefits of code inspections in large scale software development. *IEEE Transactions on Software Engineering, 23(6)*, 329-346.

Pretschner, A., & Prenninger, A. (2007). Computing Refactorings of State Machines, *Journal on Software and Systems Modeling.* To appear.

Pretschner, A., Prenninger, W., Wagner, S., Kühnel, C., Baumgartner, M., Sostawa, B., et al. (2005). One evaluation of model-based testing and its automation. In *Proc. 27th international conference on software engineering (ICSE '05).* New York, NY: ACM Press.

PRISMA: Official Web Site: http://prisma.dsic.upv.es/.

Ptolemy (2007). Ptolemy project site, University of California at Berkely. Retrieved October 22, 2007, from http://ptolemy.eecs.berkeley.edu/.

Punter, T. (2001). *Goal-oriented evaluation of software* (in Dutch) (PhD-Thesis). Eindhoven: Eindhoven University of Technology.

Punter, T., & Hamilton, M., & Gurzhiy, T. (2007). Modeling the coordination idiom. In: Voeten, J.P.M. & Engelen, R. van, (Ed), IDEALS: evolvability in high-tech systems (pp.69-79). Eindhoven: Embedded Systems Institute.

Punter, T., & Kusters, R., & Trienekens. J.J.M. (2004). The W-Process for Software Product Evaluation: A method for goal-oriented implementation of the ISO 14598 standard. *Software Quality Journal*, 12(2), 137-158.

Punter, T., & Trendowicz, A., & Kaiser, P. (2002). Evaluating Evolutionary Software Systems. In M. Oivu, & S. Komi Sirviö (Eds), *Proceedings of the 4th International Conference PROFES 2002 LCNS 2559.* Berlin: Springer.

Rahm & Bernstein (2001). A survey of approaches to automatic schema matching, The VLDB Journal, 10, 2001.

Rational Unified Process (RUP) is a trademark of IBM

Reinhartz-Berger, H. & Dori, D. (2005). OPM vs. UML—Experimenting with Comprehension and Construction of Web Application Models. *Empirical Software Engineering*, 10, 57–79.

Reissing, R. (2001). Towards a model for object-oriented design measurement. In *ECOOP'01 Workshop QAOOSE.*

Reiter, R. and Criscuolo, G. (1981). On Interacting Defaults. *Proceedings of the Seventh International Joint Conference on Artificial Intelligence (IJCAI'81)*, pages 94–100.

Reussner, Ralf (2005). *MINT – Modellgetriebene Integration von Informationssystemen*, Description of Work, Forschungsoffensive „Software Engineering 2006".

Reussner. R. H., Becker, S., Happe, J., Koziolek, H., Krogmann, K. & Kuperberg. M. (2007). *The Palladio Component Model.* Internal Report Universität Karlsruhe (TH)

Reynoso, L., Genero, M., and Piattini, M. (2003). Measuring ocl expressions: a "tracing"-based approach. In *Proceedings of QAOOSE'2003.*

Ricardo UK (2007): *Mint — Style checker for Simulink and Stateflow.* Retrieved from URL: http://www.ricardo.com

Robbins, J. E. , Medvidovic, N. , Redmiles, D. F., & Rosenblum, D. (1998). Integrating architecture description languages with a standard design method. In Proc. 20th Int. Conf. on Software Engineering.

Roberts, D., Brant, J., & Johnson, R. (1997). *A refactoring tool for Smalltalk*. Theory and Practice of Object Systems, Vol. 3, pp.: 253-263.

Robillard, P. N., D'Astous, P., & Kruchten, P. (2003). Software Engineering Process with the UPEDU. Addison-Wesley.

Robinson, Greg (2002)a. *Key Standards for Utility Enterprise Application Integration* (EAI), Proceedings of the Distributech 2002, Miami, Pennwell, 2002.

Robinson, Greg (2002)b. *Model Driven Integration (MDI) for Electric Utilities*, Proceedings of the Distributech 2002 Miami, Pennwell, 2002.

Roh, S., Kim, K., & Jeon, T. (2004). Architecture Modeling Language based on UML2.0. In Proocedings of the 11th Asia-Pacific Software Engineering Conference (APSEC).

Roos, N. (2006), No to requirements (in Dutch). In *Bits & Chips magazine*, Vol. 9. (pp. 24-26). Nijmegen: Techwatch.

Rosenberg, D., & Scott, K. (1999). Use Case Driven Object Modeling with UML: A Practical Approach. Addison-Wesley.

Rosenberg, D., Stephens, M. & Collins-Cope, M. (2005). Agile Development with ICONIX Process. Apress.

Rottger S., & Zschaler, S. (2004). Model-Driven Development for Non-functional Properties: Refinement through Model Transformation, In LNCS Volume 3273, The Unified Modelling Language (UML) Conference, pp. 275–289.

Rui, K., & Butler, G. (2003). Refactoring Use Case Models: A Metamodel. The Twenty Sixth Australasian Computer Science Conference (ACSC 2003), February 4-7, 2003, Adelaide, Australia.

Rumbaugh, J. (1999) Notation Notes: Principles for choosing notation, In *Journal of Object-Oriented Programming*, 12, 4,.

Runeson, P., & Isacsson, P. (1998). Software quality assurance – concept and misconception. *Proceedings of the 24th. EUROMICRO Conference (EUROMICRO'98)*, 2, 853-859.

Saeki, M. (1999). Reusing Use Case Descriptions for Requirements Specification: Towards Use Case Patterns. Sixth Asia-Pacific Software Engineering Conference (APSEC 1999), Takamatsu, Japan, December 7-10, 1999.

Saeki, M. and Kaiya, H. (2006). Model metrics and metrics of model transformation. In *Proc. of 1st Workshop on Quality in Modeling*, pages 31–45.

Sandee, J.H., & Heemels, W.P.M.H., & Muller, G.J. (2006). Threads of reasoning. In: Heemels, W.P.M.H., & Muller, G.J. (Eds.), *Model-based design of high-tech systems*, (pp. 43-57). Eindhoven: Embedded Systems Institute.

Sangiorgi, D. and Walker, D. (2001). *The π-calculus – A Theory of Mobile Processes*. Cambridge, UK: Cambridge University Press.

Sarda, N. (1990). Extensions to SQL for Historical Databases. *IEEE Transactions on Knowledge and Data Engineering*, 2(2), 220–230.

Schmidt, D. (2006). Cover feature – Model Driven Engineering. *IEEE Computer*, 39(2), 25-31.

Schneidewind, N. F. (1992). Methodology for validating software metrics. *IEEE Trans. Software Eng.*, 18(5):410–422.

Schulmeyer, G. and Mcmanus, J. (1999). *The Handbook of Software Quality Assurance*. Prentice Hall.

Schürr, A. (1994). *Specification of graph translators with Triple Graph Grammars*. In Lecture Notes in Computer Science, Vol. 903, pp.: 151-163. Springer.

Schürr, A. (1994). Specification of Graph Translators with Triple Graph Grammars. In: G. Tinhofer (Ed.), *WG94 20th International Workshop on Graph-Theoretic Concepts in Computer Science* (pp. 151-163). Lecture Notes in Computer Science 903, Heidelberg: Springer.

SDMetric home page: http://www.sdmetrics.com

Seffah, A., Donyaee, M., Kline, R. B., & Padda, H. K. (2006). Usability measurement and metrics: A consolidated model. *Software Quality Control*, 14 (2), 159-178.

Sefika, M., Sane, A., & Campbell, R. H. (1996). Monitoring compliance of a software system with its high-level design models. *Proceedings of the 18ᵗʰ International Conference on Software Engineering*, 387–396.

SEI (2007), Software Engineering Institute, Carnegie Mellon University, CMMi site. Retrieved October 22, 2007, from: http://www.sei.cmu.edu/cmmi/.

SEI Software Engineering Institute (2006): *CMMI - Capability Maturity Model Integration. CMMI for Development*. Standard Version 1.2, August 2006. URL: http://www.sei.cmu.edu/cmmi

Seidewitz, E. (2003). What Models Mean. IEEE Software, 20(5), 26-32.

Seifert, T., Beneken, G., & Baehr, N. (2004). Engineering long-lived applications using MDA. In *Proc. IASTED international conference on software engineering and applications* (pp. 241-246). Calgary: IASTED/ACTA Press.

Selic, B. (2003) The Pragmatics of Model-Driven Development, *IEEE Software 9*, 19-25.

Selic, B., & J. Rumbaugh, J. (1998). *Using UML for Modeling Complex Real-Time Systems*

Shahidehpour, Mohammad & Wang, Yaoyu (2003). *Communication and Control in Electric Power Systems: Applications of Parallel and Distributed Processing*, IEEE Press Series on Power Engineering, 2003.

Shanks, G. (1999). Semiotic Approach to Understanding Representation in Information Systems. Information Systems Foundations Workshop, Sydney, Australia, September 29, 1999.

Shaw, M. (2000). *Software engineering education: a roadmap*. Paper presented at the International Conference on Software Engineering, Limerick, Ireland.

Shull, F.; Basili, V.; Boehm, B.; Brown, A.W.; Costa, P.; Lindvall, M.; Port, D.; Rus, I.; Tesoriero, R.; Zelkowitz, M. (2002 June). What we have learned about fighting defects"; *Proceedings. Eighth IEEE Symposium on Software Metrics* (pp. 249 – 258).

Simon, F., Löffler, S., & Lewerentz, C. (1999). *Distance based cohesion measuring*. In Proceedings of 2ⁿᵈ European Software Measurement Conference, pp.: 69-83.

Simon, H. (1996). The Sciences of the Artificial (Third Edition). The MIT Press.

Sitaraman, M., Kuczycki, G., Krone, J., Ogden, W.F. & Reddy, A. (2001). Performance Specifications of Software Components. In *Proceedings of the Symposium on Software Reusability 2001* (pp. 3-10).

Skogan, D., Grønmo, R. and Solheim I. (2004). Web Service Composition in UML. *Proc. 8th International IEEE Enterprise Distributed Object Computing Conference EDOC'2004* (pp. 47-57).

Smith, R. L., Avrunin, G. S., Clarke, L. A., & Osterweil, L. J. (2002). PROPEL: An Approach Supporting Property Elucidation. In Proc. of 24th International Conference on Software Engineering (ICSE), (pp 11–21).

Snodgrass, R. (1987). The temporal query language tquel. *ACM Trans. Database Syst., 12*(2), 247–298.

Snodgrass, R. (1988). A Relational Approach to Monitoring Complex Systems. *ACM Transactions on Computer Systems, 6*(2), 157–196.

Sommerville, I.: Software engineering (7th ed.). Addison-Wesley Longman Publishing Co., Inc., Boston, MA, USA (2004).

Sottet, J. S., Calvary, G., & Favre, J. M. (2006). Mapping Model: A First Step to Ensure Usability for sustaining User Interface Plasticity, In: Proc. of the MODELS 2006 Workshop on Model Driven Development of Advanced User Interfaces.

Sowmya, K.,(2005) *Reflections on MDA Case studies, MDA Research Initiative (MRI), Chennai, India*

Sowmya, K.,(2007) Improving Air traffic control management system by adopting the MDA strategy, MDA Research Initiative, Chennai, India

Spanoudakis, G., & Zisman, A. (2001). Inconsistency management in software engineering: Survey and open research issues. In *Handbook of Software Engineering and Knowledge Engineering* (pp. 329-80). World Scientific

Spitznagel, B. and Garlan, D. (1998). Architecture-based performance analysis. *Proc. Conference on Software Engineering and Knowledge Engineering SEKE'98*.

SPQR/20. (1995). *User Manual*. Software Productivity Research Inc.

SPSS, SPSS 11.5, Syntax Reference Guide. 2002, SPSS Inc.: Chicago, USA.

Stahl, T., & Völter, M. (2006). *Model-driven software development.* Wiley.

Staron, M. (2006). *Adopting MDD in Industry - A Case Study at Two Companies.* Paper presented at the ACM/IEEE 9th International Conference on Model Driven Engineering Languages and Systems, Genova, Italy.

Staron, M., & Wohlin, C. (2006). An Industrial Case Study on the Choice Between Language Customization Mechanisms. In Münch, J., & Vierima, M. (Eds.), *Proceedings of 7th International Conference on Product-Focused Software Process Improvement (PROFES 2006) LNCS 4034,* (pp. 177-191). Berlin: Springer.

Staron, M., & Wohlin, C. (2006, June 12-14, 2006.). *An Industrial Case Study on the Choice between Language Customization Mechanisms.* Paper presented at the 7th International Conference, PROFES 2006, Amsterdam, The Netherlands.

Staron, M., Kuzniarz, L., & Thurn, C. (2005). *An Empirical Assessment of Using Stereotypes to Improve Reading Techniques in Software Inspections.* Paper presented at the Third Workshop on Software Quality, St. Louis, MO.

Staron, M., Kuzniarz, L., & Wallin, L. (2004a). A Case Study on Industrial MDA Realization - Determinants of Effectiveness. *Nordic Journal of Computing, 11*(3), 254-278.

Staron, M., Kuzniarz, L., & Wallin, L. (2004b). *Factors Determining Effective Realization of MDA in Industry.* Paper presented at the 2nd Nordic Workshop on the Unified Modeling Language, Turku, Finland.

Staron, M., Kuzniarz, L., & Wohlin, C. (2004). *An Industrial Replication of an Empirical Study on Using Stereotypes To Improve Understanding of UML Models.* Paper presented at the Software Engineering Research and Practice in Sweden, Linköping, Sweden.

Staron, M., Kuzniarz, L., & Wohlin, C. (2006). Empirical assessment of using stereotypes to improve comprehension of UML models: A set of experiments. *Journal of Systems and Software, 79*(5), 727-742.

Starr, L. (2002). *Executable UML: how to build class models.* Upper Saddle River, NJ: Prentice Hall.

STRAW '03: Second Int. Workshop From Software Requirements to Architectures, May 09, 2003, Portland, Oregon, USA.

Stürmer, I., Kreuz, I., Schäfer, W. & Schürr, A. (2007): *The MATE Approach: Enhanced Simulink and Statfelow Model Transformation.* Proc. of MathWorks Automotive Conference, Jun. 19-20, Dearborn (MI), USA.

Sunyé, G., Pollet, D., Le Traon, Y., & Jézéquel, J.-M. (2001). Refactoring UML models, In *Proceedings International Conference Unified Modeling Language* (pp. 134-138). Lecture Notes in Computer Science 2185, Heidelberg: Springer.

Süß, J. G. (2006). Sugar for OCL. *In Proceedings of the 6th OCL Workshop at the UML/MoDELS Conference 2006*, pages 240–251.

Szyperski, C., Gruntz, D. & Murer, S. (2002). *Component Software: Beyond Object-Oriented Programming.* Addison-Wesley

Tahvildari, L., & Kontogiannis, K. (2004). Improving Design Quality Using Meta-Pattern Transformations: A Metric-Based Approach, *Journal of Software Maintenance and Evolution,* 16(4-5), 331-361.

Telelogic, *DOORS Release 8.0,* URL: http://www.telelogic.com /products/doors

The MathWorks Inc. (2007): *Automotive Applications - Examples in Documentation, Simulink Demos,* MATLAB/Simulink/Stateflow, Part of the MATLAB Product, Release 2007a.

The MathWorks Inc. (2007): *MATLAB/Simulink/Stateflow,* Products in the Release 2007a. URL: http://www.mathworks.com

The MathWorks Inc. (2007): *The MathWorks Automotive Advisory Board (MAAB),* URL: http://www.mathworks.com/industries/ auto/maab.html

The Systems Modeling Language (SysML) open source specification project. http://www.sysml.org/

Thelin, T., Runeson, P., & Wohlin, C. (2003). An Experimental Comparison of Usage-Based and Checklist-Based

Reading. IEEE Transactions on Software Engineering, 29(8), 687-704.

Thöne, S., Depke, R. and Engels, G. (2002). Process-Oriented, Flexible Composition of Web Services with UML. *Proc. Joint Workshop on Conceptual Modeling Approaches for e-Business eCOMO 2002.*

Tian, J. (2004). Quality-evaluation models and measurements. *IEEE Software*, 21 (3), 84-91.

Together Technologies home page: http://www.borland.com/us/products/together

Tolbert, D., *CWM: A Model-Based Architecture for Data Warehouse Interchange*, Workshop on Evaluating Software Architectural Solutions 2000, University of California at Irvine, May, 2000. http://www.cwmforum.org/uciwesas2000.htm

Topaloglu, N.Y. and Capilla, R. (2004). Modeling the Variability of Web Services from a Pattern Point of View. *Proc. European Conf. on Web Services ECOWS'04* (pp. 128–138). Springer LNCS 3250.

Törner, F., Ivarsson, M, Pettersson, F., & Öhman. P. (2006). An Empirical Quality Assessment of Automotive Use Cases. The Fourteenth International Requirements Engineering Conference (RE 2006), Minneapolis-St. Paul, USA. September 11-15, 2006.

Tourwé, T., & Mens, T. (2003). *Identifying refactoring opportunities using logic meta programming.* In Proceedings of 7th European Conference on Software Maintenance and Reengineering, pp.: 91-100.

Traore, L., & Aredo, D.B. (2004). Enhancing structured review with model-based verification. *IEEE Transactions on Software Engineering, 30(11)*, 736-753.

Tsalidis, C., Christodoulakis, D., & Maritsas, D. (1992). ATHENA: a software measurement and metrics environment. *Journal of Software Maintenance* 4, 2. pp.: 61-81.

Tvedt, R.T., Costa, P., & Lindvall, M. (2002). Does the code match the design? *Proceedings of the International Conference on Software Maintenance (ICSM)*, 393-401.

Uhl, A., & Lichter, H. (2002). *A UML Variant for Modeling System Searchability.* Paper presented at the Object Oriented Information Systems, Monpellier.

UML 2.0 specification at the OMG home page (2006). http://www.omg.org/UML

Unhelkar, B. (2005). Verification and Validation for Quality of UML 2.0 Models. John Wiley and Sons.

Unified Modeling Language (UML) and Business Process Modeling Notation (BPMN) are registered marks of OMG

Uslar, Mathias et al (2005): *Interaction of EMS related Systems by Using the CIM Standard,* In: Walter Leal Filho, Jorge Marx Gómez, Claus Rautenstrauch (Hrsg.): ITEE 2005: Second International ICSC Symposium on Information Technologies in Environmental Engineering: Proceedings, Otto-von-Guericke Universität Magdeburg, Shaker Verlag, 2005.

Vaandrager, F. (2006), Does it pay-off? Model-based verification and validation of embedded systems! In *Progress White Papers 2006* (pp. 43-66). Utrecht: STW Progress.

Van Belle, J. (2002). Towards a syntactic signature for domain models: Proposed descriptive metrics for visualizing the entity fan-out frequency distribution. In *Proceedings of SAICSIT 2002.*

Van den Heuvel, Willem-Jan & Hasselbring, Wilhelm & Papazoglou, Mike (2000). Top-Down Enterprise Application Integration with Reference Models. *Australian Journal of Information Systems, 8*(1), 126-136.

van der Aalst, W., ter Hofstede, A., Kiepuszewski, B., and Barros, A. (2003). Workflow patterns. *In Distributed and Parallel Databases*, Springer, 2003, 14, 5-51

van der Aalst, W.M.P., Kiepuszewski, B., ter Hofstede, A.H.M. and Barros, A.P. (2003). Workflow Patterns. *Distributed and Parallel Databases, 14*, 5–51.

Van Der Straeten, R. (2005). *Inconsistency Management in Model-driven Engineering: An Approach using Description Logics.* Unpublished doctoral dissertation, Vrije Universiteit Brussel, Belgium.

Van Der Straeten, R., & D'Hondt, M. (2006). Model refactorings through rule-based inconsistency resolution. In *Proceedings Symposium on Applied computing* (pp. 1210-1217). New York: ACM Press

Van Der Straeten, R., Jonckers, V., & Mens, T. (2004). Supporting Model Refactorings through Behaviour

Inheritance Consistencies. In T. Baar, A. Strohmeier, & A. Moreira (Eds.), *Proceedings of International Conference on The Unified Modeling Language* (pp. 305-319). Lecture Notes in Computer Science 3273, Heidelberg: Springer.

Van Der Straeten, R., Mens, T., Simmonds, J., & Jonckers, V. (2003). Using description logics to maintain consistency between UML models. In *Proceedings International Conference on The Unified Modeling Language* (pp. 326-340). Lecture Notes in Computer Science 2863, Heidelberg: Springer.

van Deursen, A., & Moonen, L. (2002). The Video Store Revisited: Thoughts on Refactoring and Testing, In M. Marchesi, G. Succi (Eds.), *Proceedings 3rd International Conference on Extreme Programming and Flexible Processes in Software Engineering* (pp. 71-76). Alghero, Italy.

van Deursen, A., Moonen, L., van den Bergh, A., & Kok, G. (2002). Refactoring Test Code, In G. Succi, M. Marchesi, D. Wells, & L. Williams (Eds.), *Extreme Programming Perspectives* (pp. 141-152). Addison-Wesley.

Van Gorp, P., Stenten, H., Mens, T., & Demeyer, S. (2003). Towards automating source-consistent UML refactorings. In P. Stevens & J. Whittle & G. Booch (Eds.), *Proceedings International Conference on The Unified Modeling Language* (pp. 144-158). Lecture Notes in Computer Science 2863, Heidelberg: Springer.

Van Kempen, M., Chaudron, M., Koudrie, D., & Boake, A. (2005). Towards Proving Preservation of Behaviour of Refactoring of UML Models. In *Proceedings SAICSIT 2005* (pp. 111-118).

Vasko, M. and Duskar, S. (2004). An Analysis of Web Services Flow Patterns in Collaxa. *Proc. European Conf. on Web Services ECOWS'04* (pp. 1–14). Springer LNCS 3250.

VDI — Society for Automotive and Traffic Systems Technology (2005): *Electronic Systems for Vehicles*. 12th International Conference, Baden-Baden, Germany.

Verhoef, M.H.G., & Hooman, J.J.M. (2006). Evaluating embedded system architectures. In Heemels, W.P.M.H., & Muller, G.J. (Eds.) *Model-based design of high-tech systems*, (pp. 151-159). Eindhoven: Embedded Systems Institute.

Vokac, M., & Glattetre, J. M. (2005). *Using a Domain-Specific Language and Custom Tools to Model a Multi-tier Service Oriented Application - Experiences and Challenges*. Paper presented at the Model Driven Engineering Languages and Systems, Montego Bay, Jamaica.

Völter, M. & Stahl, M. (2006). *Model-driven Software Development*. Wiley & Sons

Völter, M., Stahl, T., Bettin, J., Haase, A., & Helsen, S. (2006). Model-Driven Software Development: Technology, Engineering, Management. John Wiley and Sons.

Vranken, H. (1998). *Design for test and debug in hardware/software systems* (PhD thesis). Eindhoven: Eindhoven University of Technology.

Wagner, S., & Deissenboeck, F. (2007). An integrated approach to quality modelling. In *Proc. 5th workshop on software quality (5-WoSQ)*. Washington, DC: IEEE Computer Society.

Wahler, M., Koehler, J., and Brucker, A. D. (2007). Model-Driven Constraint Engineering. *Electronic Communications of the EASST*, 5.

Warmer, J., & Kleppe, A. (2003). *The object constraint language: Getting your models ready for MDA*, 2nd Edition. Pearson Education. Boston, MA.

Warmer, J., & Kleppe, A. (2003). The Object Constraint Language: Precise Modeling with UML (Second Edition). Addison-Wesley.

Weber, H. (2005). From Programme Engineering to Software Engineering . *Proc. Theory and Practice of Software Development TAPSOFT'2005*. (invited talk).

Weinberg, G. M. (1998). The Psychology of Computer Programming (Silver Anniversary Edition). Dorset House.

Whitmire, S. A. (1997). *Object oriented design measurement*. John Wiley & Sons, Inc.

Wiegers, K. (2002). Peer Reviews in Software: A Practical Guide. Addison-Wesley.

Wilson, W. M., Rosenberg, L. H., and Hyatt, L. E. (1996). Automated quality analysis of natural language requirement specifications. In *Proceeding of the PNSQC Conference*.

Wing, J.M. (1990). A specifier's introduction to formal methods. *IEEE Computer, 23(9),* 8-24.

Winter, Andreas & Ziemann, Jörg (2006). *Model-based Migration to Service-Oriented Architectures.* In U. Kaiser, P. Kroha, A. Winter (Eds.), *3. Workshop Reengineering Prozesse (RePro 2006) Software Migration* (pp. 16-17). Mainz: Johannes Gutenberg University Mainz.

Winters, G. (2005). Use Case Terminology. IEEE Software, 22(2), 67.

Wirfs-Brock, R. (1993). Stereotyping: a technique for characterizing objects and their interactions. *Object Magazine, 3*(4), 50-53.

Wirfs-Brock, R., Wilkerson, B., & Wiener, L. (1994). Responsibility-driven design: Adding to your conceptual toolkit. *ROAD, 2*(1), 27-34.

Wohlin C., Runeson P., Höst M., Ohlson M., Regnell B. and Wesslén A. (2000). *Experimentation in Software Engineering: An Introduction.* Kluwer Academic Publishers.

Wohlin, C., Runeson, P., Höst, M., Ohlsson, M. C., Regnell, B., & Wesslèn, A. (2000). *Experimentation in Software Engineering: An Introduction.* Boston MA: Kluwer Academic Publisher.

Wolf, W. (2003). A decade of hardware / software co-design. *IEEE Computer,* 36 (4), 38 – 43.

Wong, B. (2006). Different Views of Software Quality. In: Measuring Information Systems Delivery Quality. E. Duggan & J. Reichgelt (Eds.). Idea Group, 55-88.

Woodside, M., Franks, G. & Petriu D. C. (2007). The Future of Software Performance Engineering. In *Proceedings of 29th International. Conference on Software Engineering, ICSE'07.* Track: Future of Software Engineering.

Wu, X. & Woodside, M. (2004). Performance modeling from software components. In *Proceedings of the 4th International Workshop on Software Performance, WOSP2004* (pp. 290-301). ACM SIGSOFT Software Engineering Notes

www.metamodel.com (2007). *How do I tell a good metamodel from a bad one?* Online article. http://www.metamodel.com/staticpages/index.php?page=20021010225607569. Visited April 2007.

Xenos, M., Stavrinoudis, D., Zikouli, K., and Christodoulakis, D. (2000). Object-oriented metrics - a survey. In *Proceedings of the FESMA Conference (FESMA'2000).*

Yeung, K., Kelly, P.H.J. and Bennett, S. (2004). Dynamic Instrumentation for Java Using a Virtual JVM. *Performance Analysis and Grid Computing,* 175–187.

Yilmaz, C., Krishna, A. S., Memon, A., Porter, A., Schmidt, D. C., Gokhale, A., et al. (2005). Main effects screening: a distributed continuous quality assurance process for monitoring performance degradation in evolving software systems. In *Proc. 27th international conference on software engineering (ICSE '05)* (pp. 293-302). New York, NY: ACM Press.

Zander-Nowicka, J., Schieferdecker, I. & Farkas, T. (2006): *Derivation of Executable Test Models From Embedded System Models using Model Driven Architecture Artifacts - Automotive Domain.* Proceedings of the Dagstuhl-Workshop MBEES: Modellbasierte Entwicklung eingebetteter Systeme III., Informatics-Report 2006-01, Technical University Braunschweig, January 2006, Dagstuhl, Germany.

Zaniolo,C., Ceri, S., Faloutsos, C., Snodgrass, Subrahmanian, V. S. and Zicari, R. (1997). *Advanced Database Systems.* San Fransisco, CA: Morgan Kaufmann Publishers.

Zhang, J., Lin, Y., & Gray, J. (2005). Generic and Domain-Specific Model Refactoring using a Model Transformation Engine. In *Model-driven Software Development - Research and Practice in Software Engineering.* Springer.

Zhang, P. C., Muccini, H. , & Li, B. X. (2007). A comparative study of model checking methods on software architecture. Technical Report, Chair of Software Testing and Verification, Southeast University. http://cse.seu.edu.cn/people/bx.li/en/cstv.htm

Zhou, E.Z. (2000). *XML and data exchange for power system analysis.* In (IEEE Edt.): IEEE Power Engineering Review, 20, 66-68.

Zhu, X., Maiden, N., & Pavan, P. (2003). Scenarios: Bringing requirements and architectures together. In 2nd International Workshop on Scenarios and State Machines: Models, Algorithms, and Tools.

Ziemann, Jörg & Leyking, Katrina & Kahl, Timo & Werth, Dirk (2006). Enterprise Model driven Migration from Legacy to SOA. In R. Gimnich, A. Winter (Eds.), *Workshop Software-Reengineering und Services* (pp. 18-27). Koblenz: University of Koblenz-Landau.

Zimmermann, Olaf & Doubrovski, Vadim & Grundler, Jonas & Hogg, Kerard (2005). *Service-oriented architecture and business process choreography in an order management scenario: rationale, concepts, lessons learned.* In OOPSLA Companion (301-312).

Zimmermann, Olaf & Köhler, Jana & Leymann, Frank (2006). *The Role of Architectural Decisions in Model-Driven Service-Oriented Architecture Construction.* In L.A. Skar, A.A. Bjerkestrand, *Best Practices and Methodologies in Service-Oriented Architectures, OOPSLA 2006 Workshop.*

Zou, Y., Kontogiannis, K. (2003). Quality Driven Transformation Framework for OO Migration. In. *Proc. 2nd ASERC Workshop on Software Architecture*, Banff, Canada, pp. 18–24.

About the Contributors

Jörg Rech is a senior scientist and project manager at the Fraunhofer Institute for Experimental Software Engineering (IESE). He worked on different German and European research projects as in the areas software engineering and knowledge management. In several industrial projects he helped on analyzing, evaluating, and improving the software development process and product for the diagnosis of defects and the indications of improvements. His research mainly concerns software patterns & antipatterns, software diagnostics (quality assurance), refactoring (software evolution), intelligent assistance, semantic technologies, experience-based resp. pattern-oriented software development, esp., in the area of model-driven software engineering. Dr. Rech authored over 35 international journal articles, book chapters, and refereed conference papers, mainly on software engineering and knowledge management. Additionally, he is a member of the German Computer Society (Gesellschaft für Informatik, GI) and served as a PC member for different workshops and conferences as well as an editor for several books in the domain of software engineering and the Semantic Web. Currently, he is also the speaker of the GI working group on architectural and design patterns.

Christian Bunse is an associate professor for software engineering at the International University, Germany. He received a PhD in computer science from the University of Kaiserslautern, Germany and a BS (Vordiplom) and MS (Diplom) in computer science with a minor in medicine from the University of Dortmund, Germany. His research interests concern model-based software development with a specific focus on components, adaptive service engineering, and resource awareness. Bunse authored several international journal articles, books (author and editor), book chapters, and refereed conference papers that mainly focus on software engineering, model-based development, and quality assurance. In addition, he served as a reviewer for several international journals, as well as a PC member and/or organizer of international workshops and conferences. He is a member of the German Computer Society (Gesellschaft für Informatik, GI).

* * *

Sven Abels is a member of the research and development group at TIE Nederland B.V. He started working as a freelancer about 12 years ago by founding his own software company, "Abelssoft". Within those activities he conceptualized and implemented software products for end users and also offered IT-consulting for small and mid-sized enterprises. Abels received a bachelor's degree (BSc), a master's degree (Dipl.-Inform) and a PhD (Dr) from the University of Oldenburg (Germany). He also organized several academic workshops and has over 40 publications in journals, proceedings and books. Abels joined TIE Nederland B.V. in 2006 and works in the research and development group providing concepts and solutions for modern e-Business. He also runs his own Web site for research issues at http://www.svenabels.org.

Silvia Abrahão is a tenure-track assistant professor at the Department of Computer Science and Computation, Valencia University of Technology (Spain), where she teaches Web quality and databases. She received a PhD in computer science from this same university in 2004. Currently, she is a member of the Software Engineering and Information Systems Research Group and the management committee of the COST Action 294 "Towards the Maturity of IT Usability Evaluation". She regularly serves as an editorial board member of the *Journal of Software Measurement, International Journal of Software Engineering* and *Its Application*, and in the PC of several international conferences (ESEM, PROFES, ISESE, RCIS, CADUI, ICSOFT, LA-Web, Mensura, SMEF, etc.). Her current research focuses on quality assurance in model-driven development, usability engineering, Web quality, functional size measurement and empirical software engineering.

Ronan Barrett is a postgraduate research student at Dublin City University. Barrett's research focuses on service engineering and model-driven development. In his forthcoming PhD thesis, he investigates the role of distribution patterns in the model-driven development of high-quality service based software systems. He has also investigated performance aspects of distributed systems and has been involved in the design and implementation of Web- and service-based learning technology systems. Barrett has published his work across a range of highly reputable conferences and has been a reviewer for conferences on Web service technologies.

Steffen Becker is a PhD student from DFG-project group Palladio at the University of Karlsruhe, Germany. In 2003, he graduated from the Technical University of Darmstadt with honors in information management. Becker is speaker of the working group on model-driven software development of the German Gesellschaft für Informatik. He is member of the steering committee of the International Conferences on the Quality of Software Architectures (QoSA). His PhD thesis introduces the concept of coupled model transformations from high-level models into code and extra-functional models.

Anna E. Bobkowska graduated from Gdansk University of Technology, Faculty of Electronics, Telecommunication and Informatics in 1996. She took part in the research on 'A methodology of quality evaluation of information systems' supported by National Research Council, she designed innovative group project methods within Tempus programme and she was developing a generic model of telecontrol protocols in the industrial research project COMSOFT for ABB Transmit, Finland. She defended her PhD thesis, "Software quality prediction with UML models" in 2001. She received young researcher grant from EU SegraVis project (Syntactic and Semantic Integration of Visual Modeling Techniques) and was visiting University of Kent, UK. She works in the Department of Software Engineering at Gdansk University of Technology, Poland.

Marko Bošković is a graduate student at the TrustSoft Research Training Group, University of Oldenburg, Germany. His research interests are instrumentation, measurements and empirical performance evaluation of software systems. In his PhD thesis he investigates performance measurements and metrics, possibility of temporal databases application in the empirical evaluation, and integration of it in the process of model driven development.

Antonio Bucchiarone received his first master's degree in computer science from the University of L'Aquila (2003) and the second in information technologies from University of Pisa (2005). He is a PhD student at IMT of Lucca since 2005 and he is a collaborator of ISTI-CNR of Pisa. Bucchiaron's research interests are in dynamic software architecture-based development and analysis of global computing systems, requirements engineering and service-oriented architecture. From April 2007 he is working at Nokia Siemens Networks of Lisbon, involved in a Research Project on Software Architecture for Embedded System.

José Ángel Carsí received a PhD in computer science from the Valencia University of Technology in 1999. He is currently an associate professor at the same university, where he teaches software engineering. His research interests are: model management, model compilers, software evolution, component models, software architectures and aspect-oriented software development.

Joel Champeau has a PhD in computer science on FPGA synthesis with dedicated language. He is teacher-researcher at the ENSIETA since 1995 in the DTN Laboratory (New Technologies Development). He is involved in the modelling domain for embedded systems. He applies MDE methodology and techniques on a system modelling framework based on executable metamodels and on platform modelling for software and hardware code generation. This work is related to industrial concerns particularly with Thales AS, Thales Air Sys.

Michel Chaudron is an associate professor in computer science at the Technische Universiteit Eindhoven and at Leiden Universties's Institute for Advanced Computer Science (LIACS). During his MSc and PhD he was a visitor at the Programming Research Lab at Oxford University and the Formal Methods Group at Imperial College, London. After completing his PhD he worked for two years for an IT company in the area of traffic and transport telematics. His research interests are in software architecting and component-based software development, esp. in supporting of design-trade-offs in the architecting of complex systems. He has been performing empirical studies into the use of UML in professional software development since 1999. Chaudron has published about his research in international and professional journals and conferences. He serves on the program committee of conferences in the area of component-based software engineering, software processes and distributed systems.

Florian Deissenboeck is a research assistant in the Software & Systems Engineering Group of Prof. M. Broy at the Technische Universität München. Currently he works on his PhD thesis about software quality controlling. His academic interests lie in software maintenance, software product quality and program comprehension. He studied computer science at the Technische Universität München and the Asian Institute of Technology, Bangkok.

Paloma Díaz received a degree and a doctorate both in computer science from the Polytechnic University of Madrid. Since 1992, she has been working in the Universidad Carlos III of Madrid, where she is currently a full professor in the Computer Science Department and is the head of the DEI research group. She has been mainly researching in hypermedia/Web engineering, access control modelling, e-learning and emergency information systems. She is co-author of several articles and books, member of the ACM and senior member of the IEEE.

Tibor Farkas was born 1974 in Berlin, Germany. Since 1999 he is certified as "Microsoft professional" (MCP) and "Microsoft certified systems engineer" (MCSE) and has been Microsoft partner and chief executive director of QuadConsult GmbH in 2000-2004. In 2005 he obtained his Diploma in Technical Informatics from the Technical University Berlin with the thesis "Model-based systems engineering of embedded automotive systems". Since 2005 he works as research assistant at the Fraunhofer Institute FOKUS in the Competence Center Modeling and Testing for Systems and Service Solutions (MOTION), where since 2006 he is head of working area embedded systems engineering.

Martin S. Feather is a principal in the Software Assurance Technology & Reliability Group at the Jet Propulsion Laboratory, California Institute of Technology. He works on developing research ideas and maturing them into practice, with current activities in the areas of software validation (specification, analysis, test automation, V&V techniques), early phase requirements engineering and risk management, and infusion of software engineering research results into practical application. For more details, see http://eis.jpl.nasa.gov/~mfeather. He obtained bachelor's and master's degrees in mathematics and computer science from Cambridge University, England, and a PhD in artificial intelligence from the University of Edinburgh, Scotland.

Marcela Genero is an associate professor at the Department of Information Systems and Technologies at the University of Castilla-La Mancha, Ciudad Real, Spain. She received her MSc in computer science in the Department of Computer Science, University of South, Argentine in 1989, and her PhD at the University of Castilla-La Mancha, Ciudad Real, Spain in 2002. Her research interests are: empirical software engineering, software metrics, conceptual models quality, database quality, quality in product lines, quality in model-driven development, etc. Genero has published in prestigious journals (*Information and Software Technology, Journal of Software Maintenance and Evolution, Research and Practice, L'Objet, Data and Knowledge Engineering, Empirical Software Engineering, Journal of Object Technology, Journal of Research and Practice in Information Technology*, etc.), and conferences (CAiSE, ER, MODELS/UML, ISESE, METRICS, ESEM, SEKE, etc). She edited with Mario Piattini and Coral Calero the books titled *Data and Information Quality* (Kluwer, 2001), and *Metrics for Software Conceptual Models* (Imperial College, 2005). She is member of the International Software Engineering Research Network (ISERN).

Jean-François Girard received a bachelor's and master's degree in computer science from McGill University and a PhD from the Technical University Kaiserslautern. Between 1996 and 2004 he worked at the Fraunhofer Institute for Experimental Software Engineering, where he was responsible for reverse engineering. Since 2005, he works for MAN Nutzfahrzeuge AG in the software development and technology department, where he is responsible for the project management and the change management systems used in software development. Dr. Girard represents MAN in the ASAM-AE-ISSUE workgroup and in the AUTOSAR work package "Methodology, Configuration and Templates". He is author of multiple publications.

Esther Guerra is an assistant professor at the Computer Science Department of the Universidad Carlos III, Madrid. Her research interests include meta-modelling, graph transformation, and their application to the generation of environments for domain specific visual languages including advanced features, such as consistency of multi-view languages, metrics specification and analysis mechanisms. He has been a doctoral researcher at the Institute of Theoretical Computer Science (TU Berlin) and the Department of Computer Science, University of Rome "Sapienza".

Jens Happe is a PhD student from the Graduate School "TrustSoft", University of Oldenburg, Germany. He wrote his master's thesis about reliability prediction for component-based software systems at Monash University in Melbourne, Australia. In his PhD thesis, he analyses concurrency aspects of component-based software systems to improve quality-of-service predictions.

Since 2000, **Wilhelm Hasselbring** is professor at the Department of Computing Science, University of Oldenburg, Germany. His previous work included assistant professorship at the University of Tilburg, The Netherlands and work as an assistant at the software technology group at the University of Dortmund, Germany. He is currently the head of the software engineering group. His main research interests include software engineering processes, patterns languages, grid technology, trustworthy computer systems and model driven software development. Hasselbring is also chair of the graduate school on trustworthy software systems TrustSoft at the University of Oldenburg and has been director of the Department of Computer Science.

Brigitte Hoeltzener received her PhD in automatic option robotic from the University Paul Sabatier, Toulouse France, on December 1984. She has participated as French expert to NATO Research Group (RSG9 AC243 Panel 3) in the fields of target detection, data fusion and recognition chain evaluation. Then she has integrated the department of system engineering of complex system, DSP; Délégation Générale de l'Armement . Actually, she works in ENSIETA in the research laboratory: E3I2 EA 3678 . Her research deals with the design of information system dedicated to radar and sonar applications and also, with the complexity of very large system including Human in the loop (Individual or collective integration).

Jinfeng Huang received his BEng in computer science from China University of Mining and Technology, China (1997), and his MSc in computer science from Xi'an Jiaotong University, China (2000, respectively). In 2005, he received his PhD from Eindhoven University of Technology, The Netherlands, for his work on predictable real-time software design. Since April 2005, he works as a postdoc researcher at Electrical Engineering Department, Eindhoven University of Technology. His research interests include formal methods on concurrent, real-time and distributed systems and software synthesis.

Emilio Insfrán is an associate professor at the Department of Information Systems and Computation (DISC) of the Valencia University of Technology, Spain and member of the Software Engineering and Information Systems Research Group in the DSIC. He received an MS in computer science from the Cantabria University, Spain in 1994 and a PhD from the Valencia University of Technology in 2003. He was a visiting research scientist at the Department of Computer Science, University of Twente, The Netherlands (1999) and at the Department of Information Systems at the Brigham Young University,

Utah, USA (2001). His research interests are requirements engineering, model-driven software development, and software quality. He has published more than 40 journal and conference papers and he has been involved in a number of national and international projects.

Jean-Marc Jezequel received an engineering degree in telecommunications from the ENSTB in 1986, and a PhD in computer science from the University of Rennes, France, in 1989. He first worked in telecom industry (at Transpac) before joining the CNRS (Centre National de la Recherche Scientifique) in 1991. Since October 2000, he is a professor at the University of Rennes, leading an INRIA research team called Triskell. His interests include model driven software engineering based on object oriented technologies for telecommunications and distributed systems. He is the author of the books *Object-Oriented Software Engineering with Eiffel* and *Design Patterns and Contracts* (Addison-Wesley, 1996 and 1999), and of more than 90 publications in international journals and conferences. He is a member of the steering committee of the MODELS/UML conference series. He also served on the editorial boards of *IEEE Transactions on Software Engineering* and *Journal on Software and System Modeling: SoSyM* and *Journal of Object Technology.*

Pankaj Kamthan has been teaching in academia and industry for several years. He has also been a technical editor, participated in standards development, served on program committees of international conferences, and is on the editorial board of the *International Journal of Technology Enhanced Learning* and the *International Journal of Teaching and Case Studies.* His professional interests and experience include knowledge representation, requirements engineering, and software quality.

Sowmya Karunakaran is a research engineer, who started the MDA research initiative (MRI) at Chennai in May 2004. She has been doing MDA related research since 2004. Her areas of interest include model transformations, domain patterns, code generators, MDA tools, standards, UML and object constraint language. She has published several IEEE papers and whitepapers on MDA. Her whitepaper on "Reflections on MDA Case Studies" sought the attention and compliments of many MDA researchers. She has conducted experiments on piloting MDA for software projects and analyzing the benefits and best practices. Her other research interests include human machine interface computing and virtual reality. She has also suggested MDA style of development for some Fortune 500 companies. She is currently involved in pioneering MDA for projects and also conducting various training programs on MDA concepts.

Mori Khorrami is a principal in software engineering (embedded systems) at the Jet Propulsion Laboratory, California Institute of Technology. He is currently a project element manger on a flight software task in addition to being the technical group supervisor for Instrument Flight Software Development. He has over 27 years of experience in the Software and firmware design and development. His current interests are in the common architectures, H/W interface modeling and simulation, object-oriented architectures and design, modeling tools, and field programmable gate arrays. He obtained his bachelor's degrees in electrical engineering from Tehran University and two master's degrees in electrical engineering and computer science from California State University Northridge.

Heiko Koziolek is a PhD student from the Graduate School "TrustSoft", University of Oldenburg, Germany. He completed his master's degree in computer science at the University of Oldenburg in 2005 and has worked for IBM and the Germany software company sd&m. His research focuses on modeling parameter dependencies for performance specification of software components.

Juan de Lara is an associate professor at the Computer Science Department, Universidad Autónoma in Madrid, where he teaches software engineering, model-driven development, and automata theory. He holds a PhD degree in computer science, and works in areas such as modelling and simulation, meta-modelling, visual languages and graph transformation. He has been a post-doctoral researcher at the MSDL Lab (McGill University), the Institute of Theoretical Computer Science (TU Berlin) and the Department of Computer Science of the University of Rome "Sapienza".

Tom Mens obtained the degrees of Licentiate in Mathematics and Advanced Master in Computer Science at the Vrije Universiteit Brussel. He was a teaching and research assistant and obtained his PhD at the Vrije Universiteit Brussel in September 1999. After occupying a postdoctoral fellowship of the Fund for Scientific Research, Flanders, he became a lecturer at the University ode Mons-Hainaut in October 2003. He carries out research on formal foundations and tool support for evolving software. He published numerous international research articles on this topic, and took part in the organisation of numerous international conferences and workshops. He has been involved in several interuniversity research projects and networks, and is director of the ERCIM Working Group on Software Evolution.

Martin Monperus is a PhD student in computer science in the University of Rennes. He received an engineering degree and a MSc from the Compiegne University of Technology in 2004. His research interests include machine learning and software engineering. He currently focuses on measurement in the context of model driven software engineering.

Henry Muccini received his PhD in computer science from the University of Rome – La Sapienza (2002). He is currently an assistant professor at the University of L'Aquila since 2002 and he has been visiting professor at Information & Computer Science, University of California, Irvine in 2001 and 2006. Muccini's research interests are on software architecture verification and validation, model-based analysis, testing and model-checking. He has published over 50 conference and journal articles on these topics, and co-organized events on software testing, analysis, and fault tolerance. He teaches courses on web design, computer architecture lab, and analysis and testing of component-based systems. He is the coordinator of the GSEEM, the Global Software Engineering European Master degree. He collaborates with many industries and universities in Europe and in the U.S.

Dirk Müller is a research associate at the Philipps-Universität Marburg. He obtained his diploma degree in computer science from the University of Leipzig in 2002 and his doctoral degree in engineering from the University of Kassel in 2006. His field of work combines model-driven engineering and refactoring with an interdisciplinary project—together with biology and philosophy—on the driving role of metaphors in the information sciences. He also teaches model-driven engineering at Fulda University of Applied Sciences.

Ariadi Nugroho is a PhD student at Leiden Institute of Advanced Computer Science (LIACS), Leiden Unversity, The Netherlands. He completed his master degree in ICT in business from the same institute in 2006. His research interest has been in the area of software modeling: he graduated with a thesis titled "Modeling Web Service Orchestration with Paradigm" (paradigm is a coordination language developed at LIACS). After finishing his master's study, Ariadi immediately continued with his PhD research, which focuses on empirical research in quality of UML modeling and software fault prediction. As part of his research Ariadi also works regularly in an IT company to keep his research approaches and findings applicable to the industry.

Jane Oh is the group supervisor of the Software Assurance Technology and Reliability Group at JPL. She is the principal investigator of Research and Technology Development projects, "Software assurance for the emerging discipline of model-based design" and "FPGA based verification simulation accelerator and assurance for FPGA/Firmware model-based design". Apropos to this study, she lead a team to adopt model-based requirements and design analysis that enables systems reliability of safety-critical functions that run in real-time. Her PhD is from the University of Michigan, Ann Arbor.

Patrizio Pelliccione is an assistant professor at the University of L'Aquila, Computer Science Department and he got its PhD in the same university. From April 2005 to April 2006 Patrizio was senior researcher at the Faculty of Sciences, Technologies and Communications of the University of Luxembourg. Patrizio is author of more than 30 publications in international journals and conferences. The research topics are mainly in software architectures, component-based systems, fault-tolerance, model checking, and formal methods. Patrizio is chair of the international workshop on Engineering Fault Tolerant Systems (EFTS), is editor of the book *Software Engineering of Fault Tolerant Systems*, and is reviewer of several workshops, conferences, and journals.

Claus Pahl is a senior lecturer and the leader of the Software and Systems Engineering research group at Dublin City University, which focuses on Web technologies and Web service engineering in particular. His specific interests include model-driven software development, software composition, semantic Web service technologies, and applications of software and service engineering in Web-based software systems, such as learning technology systems. Claus has published more than 150 papers including a wide range of journal articles, book chapters, and conference contributions on service engineering and model-driven development. He is on the editorial board of several journals and is a regular reviewer for journals in the area of software engineering, Web technologies, and e-learning.

Mario Piattini is a full professor at the University of Castilla-La Mancha (UCLM), Spain. His research interests include software quality, metrics and maintenance. He gained his PhD in Computer Science at the Polytechnic University of Madrid, and he leads the Alarcos Research Group. He is CISA and CISM by ISACA. He is a member of ACM and the IEEE Computer Society.

Teade Punter received his master's degree from Twente University in 1991. He was course team leader at the Open University, The Netherlands from 1992-1996. Punter earned his PhD from Eindhoven University of Technology in 2001 for his work on software product certification. He worked from 2000 till 2004 as groupleader at Fraunhofer IESE. After that he worked as consultant at the Laboratory for Software Quality at Eindhoven University of Technology. Since January 2007, he works as Knowledge Manager at the Embedded Systems Institute. Teade's research interests are in model driven development of systems, testing and technology transfer.

Isidro Ramos is a full professor since 1976. He has been teaching during 36 years in several universities. Currently, he is a teacher at the Valencia University of Technology and the leader of the Software Engineering and Information Systems research group of the same university. He has been a key researcher in 21 Research Projects, member and president of different Programme Committees of relevant conferences. He has also been the international coordinator of the VII CYTED Subprogram on Applied Electronics and Computing, and the rector of the University of Castilla la Mancha. He has recently received the Spanish Computer Science National Award 2006. He is currently working in the model-driven engineering and software architectures fields.

Ralf Reussner is a professor for computer science at the University of Karlsruhe and heads the chair "Software Design & Quality" since 2006. He is also director at the technology transfer center FZI, Karlsruhe. He got his master's degree in 1997 and his PhD in 2001 from the University of Karlsruhe. Reussner is editor of the German *Handbook on Software Architecture* and member of the steering committee of the International Conference on the Quality of Software Architectures (QoSA). His research interests lie in component-based software engineering and prediction of extra-functional properties.

Davide Di Ruscio received his PhD in computer science from the University of L'Aquila (Italy) in 2007 with a thesis titled "Specification of Model Transformation and Weaving in Model Driven Engineering". Currently, he is research fellow at the Computer Science Department of the University of L'Aquila and his main research interests include UML, MDA, EMF, code generation, and methodologies for Web development. During his PhD program, he has been involved in the study of formal and pragmatic characteristics of model transformations in model driven engineering. In particular, a formal approach based on Abstract State Machines for supporting the implementation independent specification of model transformations has been defined and validated in different applicative domains (data-intensive Web applications, software architecture, middleware based systems). Recently, he started the investigation of more complex model operations like model evolution, synchronization and difference. Currently, Di Ruscio is involved in the European project PLASTIC (Providing Lightweight & Adaptable Service Technology for pervasive Information & Communication) of the Sixth Framework Programme.

Miroslaw Staron obtained a PhD in software engineering from Blekinge Institute of Technology in Ronneby, Sweden in 2005. He has obtained his MSc from Wroclaw University of Technology in Wroclaw, Poland in 2001. His research interests include model driven software development and software measurements. His main focus is on using empirical software engineering methods in the above areas and close cooperation with industry – Ericsson and Volvo IT. Miroslaw is involved in organizing the series of consistency and quality workshops at the MODELS conference as well as the series of Nordic Workshops on UML and MDE.

Niels Streekmann graduated form University of Oldenburg in 2005 with a major in computer science. He is currently with OFFIS, Oldenburg where he is working in the department business information systems. His main research focuses on the public-private project MINT dealing with the model-driven integration of systems in the utility domain. Streekmann is member of the GI, bringing in his expertise within the working group for model-driven architectures.

Gabriele Taentzer is professor for software engineering at the Faculty of Mathematics and Computer Science of the Philipps-Universität Marburg in Germany. She achieved the habilitation in computer science at the Technische UniversitŠt Berlin in 2003. Her research interests include model-driven software development, especially domain-specific visual languages, model transformation, and graph transformation. Since 2002, she is a member of the steering committee for conferences and workshops on graph transformation and has been program committee member of many international workshops and conferences in the area of software engineering. She has been involved in various research projects on graph transformation, visual languages and model-based software development.

Stefan Teuchert received an electrical engineering degree, with specialization in the area of measurement and control systems from the Technical University Hamburg. At MAN Nutzfahrzeuge AG, he was first development engineer in the central division Electric/Electronic/Control and ECU systems (TSE). Since 2005, Mr. Teuchert leads the software development and technology department.

Mathias Uslar graduated from Oldenburg University in 2004 with a major in computer science and a minor in legal informatics. Currently, he is with the OFFIS in Oldenburg, a third-party funded institute affiliated with the university. His major work deals with interoperability and enterprise application integration in the utilities domain using the Common Information Model CIM (IEC 61970). He furthermore focuses on knowledge management and electronic democracy. Mathias is member of the GI, ACM and IEEE.

Jeroen Voeten received his master's degree in mathematics and computing science in 1991 and his PhD in electrical engineering in 1997 from the Eindhoven University of Technology, The Netherlands. Since 1997 he is working as an assistant professor in the Electronic Systems Group, Faculty of Electrical Engineering. As from January 2005 he is also working as a senior research fellow at the Embedded Systems Institute in Eindhoven. His research interests include system-level design methodology and performance modeling for embedded systems.

Stefan Wagner received a diploma in computer science from the University of Applied Sciences Augsburg, an MSc in distributed and multimedia information systems with distinction from Heriot-Watt University, Edinburgh, and a PhD in computer science from the Technische Universität München. He works as a post-doctoral researcher at the Software & Systems Engineering Group at TU München. His main interests include quality modelling, analysis and especially the connection to economics. He is member of the IEEE computer society, the ACM SIGSOFT, and the German informatics society (GI).

Michael Wahler is a doctoral student in the Business Integration Technologies Group at the IBM Zurich Research Laboratory. He received a diploma in computer science from the Technical University of Munich, Germany, in 2003 and plans to complete a PhD in computer science at the Swiss Federal Institute of Technology Zurich, Switzerland, in 2008. Michael's research focuses on engineering approaches for developing reliable software, particularly involving model-driven software development. He is currently working in the area of data modeling, for which he is developing a pattern approach for concise and consistency-preserving refinement of class models.

Index